THE ENCYCLOPEDIA OF
GREAT FILMMAKERS

JOHN C. TIBBETTS AND JAMES M. WELSH

Series Editors

Gene Phillips, Tony Williams, Ron Wilson

Foreword by
Kevin Brownlow

Checkmark Books®

An imprint of Facts On File, Inc.

The Encyclopedia of Great Filmmakers

Checkmark Books
An imprint of Facts On File, Inc.
132 West 31st Street
New York NY 10001

Library of Congress Cataloging-in-Publication Data

Tibbetts, John C.
The encyclopedia of great filmmakers / John C. Tibbetts and James M. Welsh ;
contributing editors, Gene Phillips, Tony Williams, Ron Wilson; foreword by Kevin Brownlow
p. cm.
Includes bibliographical references and index.
ISBN 0-8160-4385-X
1. Motion picture producers and directors—Biography—Dictionaries.
I. Welsh, James Michael. II. Title.
PN1998.2 .T54 2002
791.43'0233'0922—dc21   2002067357

Text design by Erika K. Arroyo
Cover design by Nora Wertz
Illustrations by John C. Tibbetts

Printed in the United States of America

VB FOF 10 9 8 7 6 5 4 3 2 1

This book is printed on acid-free paper.

CONTENTS

▯▯▯

FOREWORD

□ □ □

CHASING THE PARADE

By Kevin Brownlow

I have always had a soft spot for film directors. The job is the hardest I have ever tackled, and to succeed (which I didn't) you need qualities of determination, patience, and creativity that very few human beings are born with. Politicians who circle the globe failing to end conflicts should be replaced by film directors, for they are the ideal people to charm both sides, to organize spectacular withdrawals, and then, so as not to disappoint anyone, to stage the battles—harmlessly—to show what might have been. The best of them are miracle workers.

Imagine what it is like, setting up a film, particularly nowadays when so many productions are made for so little. You have to work on the script, find the money (this can take years), track down the locations, supervise the sets, select the crew, persuade the cast, shoot tests, all the time worrying yourself sick about the inadequacies of the budget. Then, when you are near exhaustion, you are ready to go on the floor to make the picture. Critics should be barred from their job until they have done this at least once. Ideally, directors should be trained not in film schools but in the Marine Corps. Making a film is a lot like going to war (business class).

Historically, many directors were treated shabbily by Hollywood. They were well paid, admittedly, but having created the language of cinema, they became mere cogs in the machine. At the height of the studio system, in the 1930s and '40s, scripts were tossed to them along with the morning paper; they were assigned cast and crew and they didn't have the right even to edit their own picture. A few prominent directors kept a degree of creative control, but the fate of the majority was dependent on the feudal power of the producers.

Today, with stars commanding higher salaries than the budget for *Billy Elliott,* directors are often hired hands again. When a new poster goes up, I always look for the name of the director in the batch of credits contractually provided like the small print on the back of a medicine bottle. If you can read the director's name, the chances are it will mean nothing. What happens to all those poor fellows who make one feature and are never heard of again?

The good old days really were exceptional. In the 1920s the director was the whole show; he chose the story, and sometimes wrote it, selected the cast, staged every scene, and often edited the result himself. Producers in those happy days were content to run the studio. Only with the insidious rise of the so-called supervisor was the director's autonomy threatened. The producer put up the money and he wanted to be part of the creative process—at least he wanted people to think he was. I used to wonder what the producer actually did, because he always employed men to do his work for him—the supervisor, the associate producer, the production manager. If you look at the credits of a modern film you will often see as many as seven producers. The job of director has become more difficult than ever. It is tough enough to make a film under perfect conditions. To have to argue with seven producers, not to mention their battalions of yes men, must take all the pleasure out of filmmaking. It would drive me to drink.

Drink is a touchy subject in this context. It is astounding how many directors were alcoholics. Alcohol has always been the curse of the Irish, and most early film directors were Irish, or of Irish descent. Traditionally, Jews didn't drink, so it made sense for Jews to run the business and let the Irish make the pictures. The Irish had a sense of poetry and of theatre, a warmth in dealing with people and a colorful personality. That was, all too often, a euphemism for a drunk. But what drunks they were! Foremost among the great names of early cinema was the incorrigible Marshall (Mickey) Neilan, who made many of Mary Pickford's best pictures. His assistant was an important man, because Mickey would often be overcome by thirst and would leave the set in his charge. John Ford was more disciplined, and drank (to excess) only between pictures. Eddie Sutherland, a delightful fellow who directed many memorable comedies, was known as the Iron Man because he could go out all night and yet be able to direct in the morning. There ought to be a book devoted to the Alcoholic Film Director.

For if directing is hard, directing with a hangover must have been excruciating. George Fitz-maurice used to start the day with something undemanding—like a closeup of a door handle—so he could recover his momentum. To be able to produce so many magnificent pictures under those conditions is indeed astonishing and a tribute to the luck of the Irish. (There were a few Italians who liked the bottle as well, like the brilliant Gregory la Cava.) But there were plenty of sober directors, like King Vidor or Henry King, who made outstanding pictures from a deep love of the medium.

I became aware of these remarkable personalities when I began reading the old fan magazine *Photoplay,* which, under the editorship of James Quirk (Irish), was a fine periodical that took films—and their directors—seriously. It was in these pages that I first read about Rex Ingram, the handsome Dublin-born artist who made Valentino a star in *The Four Horsemen of the Apocalypse* (1921). When Valentino left, he made a star of another young Latin—Ramon Novarro. Deeply disappointed when MGM would not give him *Ben-Hur,* he went to the south of France and set up his own studio. It became a meeting point for artists—George Bernard Shaw, Isadora Duncan, Somerset Maugham. The stills photographer and sometime actor was Michael Powell. He and David Lean, who was profoundly impressed by Ingram's work, expressed their gratitude to Rex Ingram throughout their lives, just as subsequent directors proclaimed their debt to Powell and Lean.

The silent directors seemed to me of exceptional importance because they began it all. There was a generation before Ingram and Neilan and La Cava, however, which consisted mostly of middle-aged men from the theatre, who often took up movies as a last resort. The work was not considered respectable. These little-known names—Otis Turner, William Humphreys, Oscar Apfel—directed the one- and two-reelers that formed the nickelodeon programs. Their names seldom appeared on the films, which were close duplicates of the theatrical experience, filmed in master shot without any use of what we would call "cinema." And yet they could surprise you; Oscar Apfel's *The Passer-By* (1912) opened and closed with a scene of an old man recalling his youth. The camera tracked smoothly in, dissolved from the old to the young man, and reversed the procedure at the end. These early directors were superseded so quickly that many of them ended up as actors in the 1920s, playing bits in films by more talented and ambitious men.

As I watched the silent films I bought from junk shops and other collectors, I acquired a deep admiration for the men who made them. My friend, Bill Everson, a fellow collector and historian, was so impressed with the work of William K. Howard that he altered the order of his first names from Keith William to William K. Everson. I would happily have changed my name, too, but "Clarence," after my idol Clarence Brown—would not have sounded quite right.

It was the acquisition of a Clarence Brown film, *The Goose Woman* (1925), that persuaded me once and for all that the American silent era contained buried treasure. Here was a little-known film so brilliantly thought out and beautifully directed that it was a far more satisfying experience than many of the "classics" promoted by organizations like the British Film Institute. In 1958, when I acquired it, it was superior both in content and technique to most of the films being shown commercially. Yet Universal had destroyed all 35-mm prints of this and their other silent films. (Had the same thing happened to Old Master paintings, the perpetrators would have gone to jail.)

The Goose Woman had been made only about 40 years earlier. It struck me that Clarence Brown, indeed many of the filmmakers of the silent era, might still be alive if one could but know. It was like being fascinated by literature with Scott Fitzgerald still available for interviews! It seemed crazy that pages of critical theory were devoted to a director's intentions, and not one of these writers had the wit to contact the director and find out

what *he* thought. I was an assistant editor, earning £6 10s. a week, living in a bed-sit in Hampstead; I had no hope of traveling to Hollywood. But I felt that someone should do it.

I was pushed into it by a series of extraordinary events. One of the first films I acquired, when I was 11, was a 9.5-mm abridgment of an early Douglas Fairbanks film. It had the title *The First Man*. I went to the local library to see if they had any film books that might mention it—they had one, Bardeche and Brasillach's *History of the Film*. As I took it off the shelf, it fell open at a picture of Fairbanks in a scene from the very film I had just acquired. It was more than a coincidence; it was the start of my career as a film historian. The caption gave the correct title, *American Aristocracy*, produced by Triangle in 1916. When I became a member of the British Film Institute at 13, I discovered their library held an index to the films of Triangle. It listed the cast for *American Aristocracy*, and I can remember it to this day: Jewel Carmen, Albert S. Parker, Charles de Lima, Charles Stevens. . . . When I was 19 and working at a documentary film company, I heard of an actors' agency called Al Parker, Ltd. With my one-track mind, I assumed this referred to *my* Albert Parker, and one day plucked up the courage to ring Mr. Parker up. "Did you ever act with Douglas Fairbanks senior?" I asked. "Act with him?" replied Parker. "I directed him!" Parker invited me to his Park Lane office, and I found myself staring in astonishment at the framed photographs from *The Black Pirate* (1926) lining the walls. Parker loved to talk about Hollywood, although he tended to claim that he discovered Valentino, because he had directed one of his early films (admittedly the one that June Mathis saw and that led to her casting him in *The Four Horsemen*). He was so proud of this film, *The Eyes of Youth* (1919), which starred Clara Kimball Young, that one evening he invited all his top clients—Trevor Howard, Hardy Kruger, James Mason—to his apartment in Mount Street, Mayfair, and I projected it for them.

Parker gave me the untarnished atmosphere of the early days. He was an easterner, had been a stage actor and fellow-roisterer with John Barrymore, whom he directed in *Sherlock Holmes* (1922). I think he based elements of his own persona on that of Barrymore. He was a tough old bird, with an impressive Roman nose (have you noticed how many directors have impressive noses?) and a manner half-aggressive, half-humorous. He terrified the people who worked for him, and he wouldn't have lasted an hour in the politically correct climate of today. He spoke in the vernacular of the time—I was surprised how rude they could be in the age of innocence—and he came up with many silent era jokes. "As Marshall Neilan used to say, There are more horses' asses in the world than there are horses." He and his wife, the actress Margaret Johnston, were very generous to me; they introduced me to Douglas Fairbanks, Jr., who then lived in London, to Clive Brook, another client, and to anyone they thought might be helpful. Curiously, the one thing Parker would not permit was tape recording. I suppose it was the innate suspicion of an agent. So I missed a lot of what he had to say, either because I forgot, or because I was furiously scribbling notes. He relaxed this rule only when it was too late, and his memory had drifted back to his childhood, to the New York of the 1890s—fascinating but frustrating, for all recollection of Hollywood had gone.

I went to America as soon as I could afford it. I had finished work on my first feature (*It Happened Here*) in 1964 and decided to take advantage of TWA's cheap three-week trip to New York. The fact that I had fallen for an American actress provided the impetus. She was busy with rehearsals, so I had plenty of free time. I began to track down veterans who lived in Manhattan. Most were hospitable and helpful, but they were surprised that someone in his twenties should be so fascinated by the past. "Silent pictures look pretty silly today, don't they?" The first part of the encounter was invariably spent restoring their confidence in their work, explaining that silent films were not jerky,

flickery and technically incompetent, despite the damage television might have done. It amazed and saddened me to find that these popular misconceptions had spread even to those who worked in silent pictures. I used to carry a strip of 35-mm film shot in 1915 and a strip shot in 1963; comparing these under the light provided proof of the superb quality of orthochromatic film.

Even when interviewing actors and actresses, I concentrated on my favorite subject: directors. Lillian Gish, as fragile and beautiful as if seen through gauze, talked of her days with the man then regarded as the greatest of all, D. W. Griffith.

"Dedicated? I suppose I was. I knew the financial burden he was carrying. The others didn't. But it was a dedicated life then. You had no social life. You had to have lunch or dinner, but it was always spent talking over work—talking over stories, or cutting or titles. I don't see how any human worked the way he did. Never less than 18 hours a day, seven days a week. They say he saw other people's pictures. He never had the time. If you insisted, he'd borrow a print of *The Last Laugh* and run it at the studio, but that was very rare. He didn't have time to see pictures; he was too busy making them."

Griffith was the subject of universal adulation in those days. *The Birth of a Nation* was regarded as the greatest film of the era. No one seemed aware of the violence of its politics. Said one veteran, "To me, the Klan chasing the Negroes was the same as cowboys chasing Indians." He would have been staggered had he been told that 40 years on, the D. W. Griffith Award would be stripped of its name by the Directors Guild because of that very film.

That December, I managed another trip and flew on to Los Angeles. I stayed in a house high in the Hollywood hills, and remember sitting by the telephone with a sense of omnipotence. I could meet practically anyone I wanted—Buster Keaton, Harold Lloyd, or Josef von Sternberg. It was an incredible feeling, marred only by a crippling sense of shyness and the fact that no celebrity worth his salt would have put his name in the phone book.

The Screen Directors Guild—"We're sorry, no addresses"—agreed to pass my inquiry to their members by mail. Since I was there for so short a time, this was no help.

One night, I was in the Masquers Club, where I was told several silent stars would be present. In the lobby were photographs of past presidents of the club, and sitting on a couch nearby was an intriguing looking woman in her sixties. I was convinced that she had been in silent pictures, so I began a conversation with a mention of Fred Niblo, whose picture was just above her head.

"Oh yes, he was married to—"

"Enid Bennett."

"Oh yes—but you don't remember. . . ."

"No, but I'm very interested in this period. Particularly in directors."

"Well, my husband was a director."

"Really? What is his name?"

"Oh, you wouldn't have heard of him. Joseph Henabery."

"Joseph Henabery!" I sat down heavily on the arm of a chair. Henabery played Abraham Lincoln in *The Birth of a Nation* and became a director of Douglas Fairbanks and Valentino.

"I've not only heard of him. I have a print of one of his pictures."

We arranged to drive out to the Henaberys' Tarzana home at the weekend. California was having its worst flooding for 10 years; torrents of water cascaded down the side streets and cars sent up bow waves. We were late, but Joseph Henabery was warm and welcoming. He was a fervent admirer of D. W. Griffith, whom he somewhat resembled—tall, a striking face dominated by a long nose, with a deep, melodious voice. He had an amazing recall for events that had taken place 50 years before, and he talked solidly and grippingly for four hours, while Mrs. Henabery fed us coffee and toasted cheese sandwiches. This encounter astonished me. We in England all thought that the Feast of Belshazzar scene in *Intol-*

erance, with the camera apparently moving down from the clouds, had been shot from a captive balloon. Henabery told me it was achieved with a massive tower built on mining rails. It was this that determined me to put all these reminiscences into a book, which became *The Parade's Gone By* (1968) and which is still in print from the University of California Press.

The next director I located was Sidney Franklin, who made *The Good Earth* and *The Barretts of Wimpole Street* in the 1930s. With his brother, Chester, he had also made some remarkably imaginative pictures in the '10s, and become a major director in the '20s with films like *Smilin' Thru* with Norma Talmadge and *Quality Street* with Marion Davies.

When I called him, a deep, dignified, almost English voice answered. "I'm not very keen to do this . . . so many times what is written is inaccurate. I never give interviews or anything like that." When I told him I had been collecting Sidney Franklin pictures since the age of 14, his attitude began to change. Reluctantly, he arranged a date. This reluctance was still noticeable as we began the interview. He was a slightly built, gray-haired man with a moustache; a dark blue jacket and white trousers made him resemble a cricket blue. Franklin had been in love with everything English—many of his pictures, from *The Safety Curtain* (1918), which he directed, to *Mrs. Miniver* (1942), which he produced, had been set in England. But this affection had taken a beating when he finally came to work in London, in 1949, at the height of postwar austerity.

At first he talked with his eyebrows raised, as though full of disdain, but he would unexpectedly break into a mischievous grin. He would begin a tantalizing story, then stop, and say confidingly, "That's for my book." I would try another question. A short pause and he would begin to provide an answer. But just as it became interesting he would break off, "Now, tell me about yourself." I eroded his resistance a little by describing his films to him. "I didn't know I was that darn good," he said. The atmosphere gradually became warmer and the reminiscences livelier. Inevitably, his memory returned to D. W. Griffith.

"On *Intolerance,* there were a thousand idiots on top of the walls of Babylon, throwing down burning oil and big rocks made of plaster of Paris. Well, if one of them hit you, it could kill you. They were dropping so many things that no one could get the extras up to the walls. I was in charge of a group of 500, and Christy Cabanne had a group of another 500. And since I was out in front, I made a speech—'Come on, boys, don't be afraid to approach the walls; follow me!' I charged towards the walls, thinking and hoping they'd all follow. It took a lot of courage. 'Follow me!'—and I'd no sooner got the words out of my mouth than a rock came hurtling from 50 feet up and struck my shield. The shield knocked me cold and my 500 extras went the other way. My mother came across to the studio and said 'Is my son in there?' 'Yes,' they told her. 'His brains are all over the lot.'"

The Franklins became close friends. A few years later, when I was working for the short-lived Oral History department of the American Film Institute, I persuaded him to write his memoirs—I realized that the only way he was ever going to do it was if I sat there, prompting him, letting him drift off into funny stories, making it fun. So this is what we did, and although the result, *We Laughed and We Cried,* was never published, it contained fascinating historical information, which has been used for several books. When he retired, Franklin had brought home all his files from MGM, and in the folder for *Madame Curie* I discovered memos from Scott Fitzgerald in his own handwriting. Franklin told me that he played a lot of golf, and at his favorite course in Palm Desert lived his close friend Clarence Brown.

Oddly enough, this contact did not make it any easier to meet Brown, who was even more suspicious of authors than Franklin. When I returned to London, I dropped him a line mentioning that I had a print of his *The Goose Woman,* and he was intrigued enough to want to

see it again. He came to the Motor Show in Paris every year. He had a friend there, a correspondent for the *New York Herald-Tribune,* Thomas Quinn Curtiss, who frequently came to London. One day, Curtiss telephoned me from the Savoy Hotel, and asked me to come round with my projector and show him *The Goose Woman.* I thought this a pretty blatant way of vetting me, but I had no objection . . . so long as eventually I met my idol. Curtiss, very impressed by the film, gave me the okay and I traveled to Paris to the Hôtel Georges V.

Brown was unlike the other directors I had met. He was of Northern Irish Protestant stock, and he was burly, tough, and remote. He and I differed on everything; he had been on the side of the House Un-American Activities Committee during the McCarthy era, and made no secret of his extreme right-wing views. He was reluctant to be recorded, so I had to hold the microphone under the dinner table, for I was determined not to miss a word of what he said. Once he began talking about films, all the toughness fell away and he exposed a deeply sensitive side—the side that appears so strongly in his pictures. When he spoke of the director he first worked for—Maurice Tourneur—he was near to tears. The hard-bitten exterior was a shell to protect a shy and delicate personality. But it didn't make it any easier to converse. He had no small talk. He was primarily interested in cars, airplanes, and real estate. He had made money out of pictures, but he was infinitely richer than his fellow directors, and that was due to real estate. I remember telling him that Lake Arrowhead, location for Murnau's *Sunrise* (1927) as well as for several of his own films, now had houses around the edge. "I know," he said. "I built most of them." When I protested, he snapped: "They've got to live somewhere."

I had the privilege of showing Brown several of his silent pictures, and hearing at first hand the problems he had in making them. At the Cinemathèque in Paris, I arranged with curator Henri Langlois to show him Maurice Tourneur's *Last of the Mohicans* (1920)—and it turned out he had directed most of it after Tourneur was injured. Despite Brown's hard-bitten personality, I became very fond of him, and felt I should write his biography. I hesitated, because I knew all I wanted to know, and I left it to someone else less involved with the man to do a proper job. I am relieved to say that Gwenda Young, a lecturer from University College Cork, is now working on a book about his life and his career.

In the 1960s, I regretted that I was able to record these memories only on audio tape rather than film. One seldom has a second chance in life, but 10 years later I returned for Thames Television, with David Gill, to film no less than 85 interviews for the *Hollywood* series, which was transmitted in 1980, was released on video and laser disc, and continues to be shown in America to this day. Among the directors who appeared in that documentary were King Vidor, Clarence Brown, Henry King, Al Rogell, Raoul Walsh, William Wellman, Allan Dwan, Henry Hathaway, Lewis Milestone, George Cukor, Frank Capra, and William Wyler. (The British Film Institute will soon release an uncut version on DVD.)

However elusive, however reluctant to talk, most of these great names of Hollywood displayed astonishing friendliness and cooperation once the barriers were overcome. And they all proved to be remarkable people. Some were in their seventies, some well over 80, yet none were senile—none were even old, in the sense that they had retired from life. They were nearly all active, either in the industry, like William Wyler, or in writing or painting. And the sense of exhilaration they communicated made me realize why the '20s was such an astonishing era—when they were young and making pictures.

—Kevin Brownlow
London, November 2001

INTRODUCTION

*I'm master in the darkroom, stirring my prints in the magic developing bath.
I shuffle like cards the lives that I deal with. Their faces stare out at me.*

—Billy Kwan in Peter Weir's *The Year of Living Dangerously*

"Author! Author!"—Will the Real *Auteur* Please Stand Up?

Second only to the popularity and prestige of today's movie stars is the recognition by critics and public of the presence and stylistic traits of a handful of directors. These days a film like *Erin Brockovich* is not just a vehicle for Julia Roberts but also a work crafted by Stephen Soderbergh. And occasionally, recent films like *Pi* and *The Winslow Boy* are noted not for their casts so much as for, respectively, the emergence of an exciting new directorial talent (Darren Aronofsky) and the ongoing work of a prominent playwright/director (David Mamet). To be sure, remarking the work of specific film directors is nothing new; it has been the special passion of critics and filmgoers since the inception of the commercial cinema at the turn of the 20th century. Indeed, the names of filmmakers were publicly known years before the names of cast members were acknowledged.

In the first two decades of the cinema, Edwin S. Porter, Mack Sennett, Sidney Olcott, Thomas Ince, Oscar Micheaux, and D. W. Griffith in America; Georges Méliès and Louis Feuillade in France; Cecil Hepworth and George Pearson in England; Victor Sjöstrom and Mauritz Striller in Sweden; Giovanni Pastrone and Enrico Guazzoni in Italy; Benjamin Christiansen in Denmark—all were singled out for notice in the pages of the trade journals and in the press, and their names were used in the promotion of their pictures. None of them had any prior training in filmmaking or precedents to draw upon; whether they were stage actors or directors, machinists, itinerant salesmen, cowboys, or even explorers (like Robert Flaherty and Ernest Schoedsack), they had to make it up as they went along. If they were not all great, to paraphrase Shakespeare, greatness was at least thrust upon them. In any event, the cult of the director has always been with us, and now that independent cinema is flourishing in so many different directions, and the very apparatus of filmmaking is so accessible and ubiquitous, that fascination and that recognition will continue unabated.

Just as a poet is a maker of poems, a cinema director is a maker of films. Whereas one gives shape, structure, and meaning to verbal images, the director gives shape, structure, and meaning to visual images. This analogy is not new. It was first articulated by the French novelist, critic, and filmmaker Alexandre Astruc in 1948, who claimed that cinema could become "a means of writing just as flexible and subtle as written language." If the cinema was to become a language, the "camera-stylo"—or *camera pen,* as he called it—was the instrument for "writing" it. "By language," Astruc explained, "I mean a form in which and by which an artist can express his thoughts, however abstract they may be, or translate his obsessions exactly as he does in a contemporary essay or novel. That is why I would like to call this new age of cinema the age of the camera-stylo."

Astruc's formulation constituted a major shift in emphasis in accepted theories of film authorship. As John Caughie notes in his *Theories of Authorship,* "traditionally, the reference to the *auteur* in French film criticism had identified either the author who wrote the script, or, in the general sense of the term, the artist who created the film. [Now] the latter sense came to replace the former, and the *auteur* was the artist whose personality was 'written' in the film." Moreover, a film, though produced collectively, "is most likely to be valuable when it is essentially the product of its director . . . and that this personality can be traced in a thematic and/or stylistic consistency over all (or almost all) the director's films." Thus was the so-called *auteur theory* born, to which we will return presently.

The roads to the director's chair have been many. Sometimes forgotten is the fact that many of the silent film directors were formerly actors, chief among them, of course, D. W. Griffith. Charles Chaplin, one of the original "United Artists," quickly emerged from the supervision of Mack Sennett to assume complete charge of every aspect of his films, as Kevin Brownlow's estimable documentary, *The Unknown Chaplin,* amply testifies. And although Chaplin's chief artistic rival, Buster Keaton, credited himself as the nominal director in only a handful of his films, there is no question that his was the presiding genius and controlling force of everything he did (at least in the silent years). The same is true of those other actor-auteurs of the silent period, whose names are con-

spicuously absent from the credits of their films, Mary Pickford, Douglas Fairbanks, and Harold Lloyd.

Although a few actors have essayed the role of director only once—Charles Laughton's *The Night of the Hunter* (1957) remains the best example, an imaginative contribution to the genre of allegorical film; while Marlon Brando's postmodernist western, *One-Eyed Jacks* (1961), wallows in self-indulgence—so numerous are the actresses and actors who have seriously turned to directing that a brief survey will have to suffice. Among the first actresses-turned-director was Lois Weber, who co-starred in films with her husband before assuming the director's chair in 1913, becoming the highest salaried woman director in the world. After Ida Lupino assessed her own actor status as "a poor man's Bette Davis," she turned to directing in the 1950s (she was virtually the only female director working at that time), with *Hard, Fast and Beautiful* (1951) and *The Hitch-Hiker* (1953). More recent examples include Barbra Streisand's sporadic efforts as both actress and director, as the "Yeshiva boy" in an adaptation of I. B. Singer's *Yentl* (1983) and as an English professor futilely trying to conduct a platonic relationship in *The Mirror Has Two Faces* (1996); Swedish actress Liv Ullmann's first directorial efforts after leaving the acting ensemble of Ingmar Bergman, in *Sofie* (1993) and an adaptation of Sigrid Undset's epic *Kristin Lavransdatter* (1995); television actress (*Laverne and Shirley*) Penny Marshall's box-office hits *Big* (1988) and *A League of Their Own* (1992); and Anjelica Huston's *Bastard out of Carolina* (1996) and *Agnes Browne* (1999), in which she cast herself as the widow Browne, a Dubliner with no inheritance and seven children to support after the death of her husband.

A brief overview of the numerous male actors-turned-director can likewise provide no more than a hint of a roll call that is vast and varied. Vittorio De Sica's Italian neorealist classics like *The Bicycle Thief* (1948) have overshadowed his early fame as a suave leading man in prewar Italian cinema. Similarly, Ernst Lubitsch's celebrated and sophisticated American satires like *Ninotchka* (1939) made him more of a celebrity than his initial stage and screen career as a Jewish comedian. John Cassavetes's experience in improvisational acting helped revolutionize the independent cinema in his first film, *Shadows* (1959). Ron Howard's television acting and apprenticeship under Roger Corman led him to a prestigious movie career that began with his breakthrough film, *Night Shift* (1982). Clint Eastwood's tutelage under Sergio Leone and Don Siegel influenced his signature deliberate pacing and stylized, choreographed violence, particularly evident in *Pale Rider* (1985) and *Unforgiven* (1992). Robert Redford has also exploited his experience as an actor in his character-driven pictures, most notably *Ordinary People* (1980) and *Quiz Show* (1994). More recently, several younger-generation actors have shown promise in their budding directorial careers. Stanley Tucci's directorial debut was the box-office smash, *Big Night* (1996), which was followed by the critically acclaimed *Joe Gould's Secret* (2000). Tim Robbins's *Bob Roberts* (1992), the Oscar-nominated *Dead Man Walking* (1996), and *The Cradle Will Rock* (2000) reveal a thoughtful, probing talent. And Sean Penn's *The Indian Runner* (1991), *The Crossing Guard* (1995), and *The Pledge* (2000) are corrosive dissections of the dark side of human nature.

However, most actors-turned-director have not risen to the artistic level and/or prestige of De Sica, Lubitsch, Eastwood, Redford, and Howard. John Wayne, for example, directed *The Alamo* in 1960 and co-directed *The Green Berets* in 1969, but the results did nothing to dispel his primary credentials as an actor. Fresh from his stint in the *M★A★S★H* television series, Alan Alda has had only moderate success in writing and directing *The Seduction of Joe Tynan* (1979) and *Four Seasons* (1981). Billy Crystal left his *Soap* television series and began his directorial career with the largely forgettable *Mr. Saturday Night* in 1992.

Some of the most important directors had their formative experience as theater playwrights, directors, and producers. Soviet film genius Sergei Eisenstein (*Strike* [1924] and *Potemkin* [1926]) gained his early training from the circus theatres and constructivist techniques of Vsevelod Meyerhold. Before directing his first film, *Ingeborg Holm,* in 1913, the Swedish master Victor Sjöstrom enjoyed a formidable reputation as an actor-director in the theater. In Hollywood, many directors came from Broadway. The first great migration of Broadway directors came on the heels of the coming of sound in 1929. These luminaries included Rouben Mamoulian (*Applause* [1929]) and George Cukor (*The Philadelphia Story* [1940]). The 1940s saw another notable exodus. Orson Welles was not only an actor but also a gifted theater director, whose success with numerous stage and radio dramas for the Federal Theatre and the Mercury Players (*Macbeth, Five Kings, War of the Worlds*) paved the way to a significant but checkered career in Hollywood and abroad with masterpieces (*Citizen Kane* [1941]) and near misses (*The Lady from Shanghai* [1948] and *Mr. Arkadin* [1955]). Elia Kazan left the Group Theatre in 1945 to launch a series of classic dramatic and literary adaptations, like *Streetcar Named Desire* (1951). Vincente Minnelli quit designing sumptuous Broadway revues to inaugurate a series of groundbreaking musicals with *Meet Me in St. Louis* (1944) and *An American in Paris* (1951). Another musical theater maestro, Stanley Donen, teamed up with Broadway dancer Gene Kelly to make movies like *On the Town* (1949) and *Singin' in the Rain* (1952). In the last half-century the list has continued, numbering dance choreographer Bob Fosse (*Cabaret* [1972]), director Josh Logan (*Picnic* [1956]), and playwrights David Mamet (*The Winslow Boy* [1999]) and Tom Stoppard (*Rosencrantz and Guildenstern Are Dead* [1990]).

Preeminent in this galaxy of theatrical notables are Laurence Olivier and Kenneth Branagh. Olivier's early experience in the Birmingham Repertory Theatre and later in the Old Vic fueled his series of Shakespearean classics, *Henry V* (1944), *Hamlet* (1948), *Richard III* (1955), and *Othello*

(1965). Branagh's background in the Royal Shakespeare Company and his Renaissance Theatre Company has led to his own Shakespearean adaptations, beginning with *Henry V* (1989) and continuing through *Much Ado about Nothing* (1993) and *Hamlet* (1996). His *Midwinter's Tale* (1995), a backstage look at a production of *Hamlet* in a rural region of England, remains one of the canniest and wittiest of the screen's meditations on the Bard and the theater in general.

From the ranks of photographers and cameramen have come Stanley Kubrick and Gordon Parks, who worked as photographers for *Look* and *Life* magazines before making their first films, *Killer's Kiss* (1953) and *The Learning Tree* (1967), respectively; Haskell Wexler and Ricky Leacock, with *Medium Cool* (1969) and the *vérité* classic, *Primary* (1960), respectively; Zhang Yimou with *Red Sorghum* (1987); Nicholas Roeg with *Walkabout* (1971); and Jan De Bont (*Speed*).

Indeed, it seems every conceivable background has lent itself in some way to directing. From the editing bench have come such luminaries as Robert Wise (*The Sound of Music* [1965]) and Peter Watkins (*The War Game* [1964]). Beginning in the late 1950s a host of young film critics turned to filmmaking—François Truffaut and Jean-Luc Godard in France (*The 400 Blows* [1959] and *Breathless* [1959]), Tony Richardson (*Look Back in Anger* [1959]) and Lindsay Anderson in England (*This Sporting Life* [1963]), and Peter Bogdanovich in America (*The Last Picture Show* [1964]). Documentary filmmaker Frederick Wiseman was a lawyer before documenting American institutions (*High School* [1962]); and another documentarist, Michael Moore, was a crusading journalist before turning to *Roger and Me* (1985).

Those with backgrounds in drawing and painting include Alfred Hitchcock, whose talents as a graphic artist preceded his first directorial efforts, *The Lodger* (1926) and *Blackmail* (1929); Satyajit Ray, who studied painting and art history at Shintiniketan University before making his breakthrough film, *Pather Panchali* (1955); Kenji Mizoguchi, who left art school and advertising design to make some of the greatest masterpieces in the Japanese cinema (*Life of Oharu* [1951] and *Ugetsu* [1953]); David Lynch, who was trained at the Pennsylvania Academy of Fine Art in Philadphia before turning to cinema classics like *Eraserhead* (1976) and *The Elephant Man* (1980); Tim Burton, who, before making *Pee-Wee's Big Adventure* (1985), had won a Disney fellowship to study animation at the California Institute of the Arts; Peter Greenaway, who first studied painting at the Walthamstow Art College before turning to film editing and, later, film directing with *The Draughtsman's Contract* (1983); Derek Jarman, whose education at the Slade School of Fine Arts and work as a set designer for the Royal Ballet and the English National Opera enhanced his *Caravaggio* (1986), an idiosyncratic bio-pic of the great Italian baroque painter.

Recently, directors have learned their craft by working in television and by directing commercials and music videos.

Many of these directors were able, by sheer force of personality or controlling vision, to stamp their distinctive personalities and their signatures, as it were, onto their films. Some of them have even been regarded as "auteurs," or authors, by today's critics and moviegoers. However, to what degree they are auteurs constitutes an ongoing debate. Quarrels over such designations came to a head in the 1940s and 1950s when French critics and screenwriters began debating and discussing the issue at length. Critic André Bazin, writing in *Revue du cinéma* in 1946–49, cited the celebrated 1948 essay, "Le camera-stylo," by Alexandre Astruc as a proposition that artists could use the film medium to express their ideas and feelings "as a writer writes with his pen." When Jacques Doniol-Valcroze founded the monthly *Cahiers du cinéma,* Bazin became its chief critic and began referring to particular films as a "Billy Wilder film," or a "Robert Bresson film," or a "Roberto Rossellini film" in the same breath. To paraphrase a popular catchphrase, "It's the *director,* stupid!"

In the January 1954 issue of *Cahiers* an essay entitled "A Certain Tendency in the French Cinema" called for the overthrow of the prestige cinema of literary adaptations that was dominating postwar French cinema. The author, 21-year-old François Truffaut, advocated replacing this "Tradition of Quality" with a cinema that was ruled by the director and not the writer. The "true men of the cinema," Truffaut declared, those deserving the appellation of auteur, included Jean Renoir, Robert Bresson, Jean Cocteau, Jacques Tati, Max Ophuls, and others who wrote their own stories and dialogue. Three years later in *Cahiers,* Bazin defended "the personal factor in artistic creation as a standard of reference," assuming that "it continues and even progresses from one film to the next." As Hilliers writes, Bazin prophetically warned that this attitude could easily degenerate into a "cult of personality" that ignored the contextual realities behind any filmmaker's work: "So there can be no definitive criticism of genius or talent which does not first take into consideration the social determination, the historical combination of circumstances, and the technical background which to a large extent determine it." Bazin's cautionary views would be echoed soon by American critics like Pauline Kael.

From the auteurist position, it was but a short trip to a more extreme view, i.e., that prominent directors in Hollywood deserved auteur status—not just producer-directors like Howard Hawks but also contract directors like Frank Tashlin. In spite of the system in which they worked, or within the burden of their assignment, they were nonetheless able to impose their own stamp or signature upon the finished product. The extent to which a director's "signature" overcame, or peeked through, the cage of the assignment, as it were, determined the degree to which he or she earned favor as an auteur. This view came to be called the *politique des auteurs.*

An indignant response from French screenwriters was immediate, and *Cahiers* was chastised for abandoning the serenity of film studies for the heat of polemic. Other objections came from England in the autumn 1960 issue of *Sight and Sound,* when Richard Roud and Penelope Houston deplored this "cult of America," which too often placed sensationalist action pictures by Sam Fuller and tawdry melodramas by Douglas Sirk on the same level as more contemplative films by venerated Asian and Indian masters like Satyajit Ray and Yasujiro Ozu. There was no justification, they argued, in taking the bargain-basement brand of American cinema and its directorial auteurs seriously.

Meanwhile, in a shift to American shores, Andrew Sarris began promoting what he called the "auteur theory" as a useful mechanism to understand film criticism and history. Sarris's groundbreaking "Notes on the Auteur Theory in 1962" took up the battle cry of Giraudoux's epigram, "There are no works; there are only authors." A criterion of value in a given director is his "distinguishable personality" and "certain recurring characteristics of style, which serve as his signature." Using Bazin's 1957 article as his springboard, Sarris argued that the auteur theory finds its "decisive battleground" in American cinema; that "film for film, director for director, the American cinema has been consistently superior to that of the rest of the world from 1915 through 1962," as quoted in Harrington. In Hollywood, "because so much of the American cinema is commissioned, a director is forced to express his personality through the *visual* [italics added] treatment of material rather than through the literary content of the material." Directors could be identified and evaluated through three criteria of value, three "concentric circles," as Sarris put it: the outer circle refers to a director's "technical competence"; the middle circle to a director's "signature," i.e., repetitions of certain techniques and themes; and the inner circle to the "interior meaning" that may be derived from the discernible tension between a director's personality and his material. In Sarris's "pantheon" of auteurs were Max Ophüls, Jean Renoir, Kenji Mizoguchi, Alfred Hitchcock,

Charles Chaplin, John Ford, Orson Welles, Carl Dreyer, Rossellini, F. W. Murnau, D. W. Griffith, Josef von Sternberg, Sergei Eisenstein, von Stroheim, Luis Buñuel, Robert Bresson, Howard Hawks, Fritz Lang, Robert Flaherty, and Jean Vigo.

This manifesto was later expanded in the Introductions to Sarris's *Interviews with Film Directors* (1967) and the book-length *The American Cinema,* published a year later, two of the most influential film books ever published. Again, the personally expressive qualities of a director, particularly the Hollywood director, were applauded. Indeed, he declared in 1968, "A film history could reasonably limit itself to a history of film directors." It was especially important to rescue from oblivion those directors and those films that had been overshadowed by the unquestioned prestige of the "art" directors of Europe: "Quite often, Hollywood directors have labored in obscurity to evolve an extraordinary economy of expression that escapes so-called highbrow critics in search of the obvious stylistic flourish. Consequently, there has been a tendency to overrate the European directors because of their relative articulateness about their artistic *angst,* and now a reaction has set in against some of the disproportionate pomposity that has ensued." It is possible now, he continued in *Interviews with Film Directors,* "to speak of Alfred Hitchcock and Michelangelo Antonioni in the same breath and with the same critical terminology. Amid the conflicting critical camps, both Rays, Nicholas and Satyajit, have gained a respectful hearing." Sarris then proceeds to rank and categorize hundreds of auteurs, including "Pantheon Directors" (Chaplin, Ford, Renoir, etc.), "The Far Side of Paradise" (Frank Capra, Vincente Minnelli, Nicholas Ray, etc.), "Expressive Esoterica" (Stanley Donen, Allan Dwan, Frank Tashlin, etc.), and "Less than Meets the Eye" (John Huston, Elia Kazan, Billy Wilder, etc.).

In 1970 appeared Sarris's "Notes on the Auteur Theory in 1970." And seven years later came yet another article, "The Auteur Theory Revisited," which reiterated that auteurist writings from the very beginning had performed a valuable function, if only in that they rescued the film medium and film studies from a frankly exclusionary agenda: "The cinema was no longer a holy temple to which only certain sanctified works were admitted," he wrote. "Cinema was to be found on every movie screen in the world, and Hollywood movies were no less cinematic than anything else." Sarris defended auteurist agendas as more a tendency than a theory, more a mystique than a methodology, "more a critical instrument than a creative inspiration." He also defended it against the structuralists by noting that instead of knowing all the answers before formulating the questions, auteurism knows all the questions before finding the answers.

A rebuke to Sarris's writings was not long in coming. In her famous "Circles and Squares" article in the Spring 1963 issue of *Film Quarterly,* critic Pauline Kael attacked the proposition that a director's distinguishable personality is the prime criterion of value: "Traditionally, in any art, the personalities of all those involved in a production have been a factor in judgment," she wrote, "but that the distinguishability of personality should in itself be a criterion of value completely confuses normal judgment. The smell of a skunk is more distinguishable than the perfume of a rose; does that make it better?" The mere repetition of styles and subjects is hardly anything new, she continues, "In every art form critics traditionally notice and point out the way the artists borrow from themselves (as well as from others) and how the same devices, techniques, and themes reappear in their work." She agreed that the director should have "creative control" of a picture, but not *absolute* power. Moreover, she rejected Sarris's "three circles" of meaning, one by one: The first, "technical competence," was of no value, she said, when it became more important than thematic concerns. Besides, mere technical competence is the province of hacks, not of artists who sometimes must violate it in the service of art. The second, a director's "signature," can only make us more conscious of the director's personality than of the subject. Lastly, "interior meaning" extrapolated from the tension between a director's personality and his material, is nothing more than a thinly veiled affirmation of the studio system, where a director "directs any script that's handed to him, and expresses himself by shoving bits of style up the crevasses of the plots."

The impact of this debate on academic film studies in America has been profound. Ironically, an approach to film studies and criticism that began as a rejection of what Truffaut called the "Tradition of Quality" has catapulted film straight into the groves of academe. As Bordwell and Thompson contend, "the premise of individual artistic expression proved congenial to scholars trained in art, literature, and theater. Moreover, auteurism's emphasis on the interpretation of a film called on skills already cultivated by literary education." Due to the great proliferation in the 1950s of 16-mm film distribution and the subsequent boom in the accessibility of titles on videotape and now DVD, scholars suddenly had a formidable corpus of films and directors to study, not just the "great directors" and the "great films" formerly sanctioned by the establishment. In this way it was possible to trace and analyze the evolution of recurring themes, images, stylistic choices (modes of editing, lighting, camera placement, mise-en-scène arrangements), and plot situations over the course of a director's entire career. Meanwhile, publishers continue to issue a steady stream of individual monographs and biographies of directors as needed to feed the numerous film societies and college classes springing up all over America.

Meanwhile, the auteur theory itself has been subject to reexamination and revision. Beginning in the late 1960s a new generation of critics questioned it as naïve because, in the assessment of Tom Gunning, "it lacked a true understanding of the Hollywood mode of production and the constraints placed on a director's self-expression; suspect because it staked a meaningful interpretation

on a 'theological' account of the author-as-creator." In America, historians David Bordwell, Janet Staiger, and Kristin Thompson argued that the impersonal, standardized "group style" of the Hollywood "classical" studio period necessarily subordinated any individual directorial style to only sporadic expression. "[O]vert narration, the presence of a self-conscious 'author' not motivated by realism or genre or story causality, can only be intermittent and fluctuating in the classical film," they wrote in *The Classical Hollywood Cinema.* Otherwise, "for social and economic reasons, no Hollywood film can provide a distinct and coherent alternative to the classical model." In England, a group of writers associated with the British Film Institute attempted to invest the auteurist approach with insights from structuralist linguistics and anthropology, as explicated in Peter Wollen's *Signs and Meaning in the Cinema.*

Meanwhile, thinkers like Michel Foucault and Roland Barthes have reviewed, even questioned, an "author" presence in a given work. In "What Is an Author?" Foucault contends that an author never simply speaks in his own voice; rather, between the actual writer and the reader a series of speakers intervene. Putting it another way, authorship is a process by which "a voluntary obliteration of the self" occurs, where the work murders its author. Putting it in a slightly different way, in "The Death of the Author," Barthes contends that as soon as a fact is narrated, a "disconnection occurs, the voice loses its origin, and the author enters into his own death, writing begins."

No matter how learned or how exotic are these variants and revisions of the auteurist theme, the question—if not the possibility—of directorial authorship has remained central to most film scholarship. In his important new study of Fritz Lang's authorship, *The Films of Fritz Lang: Allegories of Vision and Modernity,* Tom Gunning returns to fundamental issues in the auteur discourse. After acknowledging that a director must struggle to assert authorship over the "authorless discourse" of the film medium, Gunning argues that the author ultimately becomes a "construction" in those films, a creation as much as any of his films are: "His hand beckons to us to enter his texts and find him, but entices us into a maze rather than setting up a direct encounter. . . . The search for the author takes place in a labyrinth in which at times even the film director himself may have lost his way." In sum, the authorial presence remains "precisely poised on the threshold of the work, evident in the film itself, but also standing outside it, absent except in the imprint left behind."

For a full account of the auteur debates, see John Caughie's anthology, *Theories of Authorship.*

This book, which is a condensed edition of our two-volume *Encyclopedia of Filmmakers*, by its very nature makes its own presumptions that certain of the many directors examined herein exercised a degree of influence over their finished works. The directors discussed in this book are as various as their accomplishments. Some pioneered film form (Edwin S. Porter and Cecil Hepworth), benefited from established artistic traditions (Ingmar Bergman and Elia Kazan), worked within a studio system (Vincente Minnelli and Henry King), belonged to the various "New Wave" movements of the 1960s and 1970s (Tony Richardson in England, François Truffaut in France, Peter Weir in Australia, and Robert Altman in America), conducted cinematic experiments (Norman McLaren and Stan Brakhage), existed on the margins of the industry (John Sayles and Orson Welles), or worked wholly independently (Frederick Wiseman and Oscar Micheaux). Certainly our task here is not to categorize directors in any particular order or rank. That sort of evaluation and categorization has already been attempted, with mixed success, as has been outlined earlier. Rather, it is our purpose merely to present a representative cross-section of biographical and critical commentary on each director in the hopes that readers may use this information to pursue further investigations of their own pertaining to the particular individuality and merit of a given director.

Some readers may scoff at our presumptive title. We are calling this book an encyclopedia, but in limiting its roster to no more than 150 names, it is hardly a comprehensive one. We invited learned scholars to write entries on directors they considered "significant," college professors to write about those filmmakers pertinent to their classroom studies, and buffs anxious that their favorite directors (no matter how little known) should not escape public notice. We asked only that our contributors make a case for the directors' place and/or status within their particular professional and cultural contexts. We also insisted that our contributors, whatever their background, ignore the jargon of the specialist and write in a common idiom understandable to the general reader.

—John C. Tibbetts, University of Kansas,
Lawrence, Kansas
—James M. Welsh, Salisbury University,
Salisbury, Maryland

REFERENCES

Astruc, Alexandre, "The Birth of a New Avant-Garde: La Camera-stylo," in *The New Wave,* ed. Peter Graham (Garden City, N.Y.: Doubleday, 1968), pp. 17–23. It originally appeared in the weekly *L'Écran français* in 1948.

Barthes, Roland, "The Death of the Author," in *Image-Music-Text,* Roland Barthes (New York: Hill and Wang, 1978), pp. 142–148.

Bazin, André, "On the *politique des auteurs,*" in *Cahiers du cinéma: The 1950s: Neo-Realism, Hollywood, New Wave,* ed. Jim Hilliers (Cambridge, Mass.: Harvard University Press, 1985), pp. 248–258. It originally appeared in *Cahiers du cinéma,* no. 70 (April 1957).

Bordwell, David, *Making Meaning* (Cambridge, Mass.: Harvard University Press, 1991).

Bordwell, David, and Kristin Thompson. *Film History: An Introduction* (New York: McGraw-Hill, 1994).

Bordwell, David, Janet Staiger, and Kristin Thompson, *The Classical Hollywood Cinema: Film Style & Mode of Production to 1960* (New York: Columbia University Press, 1985).

Caughie, John, *Theories of Authorship* (London: Routledge and Kegan Paul, 1981).

Eberwein, Robert T., *A Viewer's Guide to Film Theory and Criticism* (Metuchen, N.J.: Scarecrow Press, 1979).

Foucault, Michel, "What Is an Author?" in *Language, Counter-Memory, Practice: Selected Essays and Interviews,* ed. Donald F. Bouchard (Ithaca, N.Y.: Cornell University Press, 1977).

Gunning, Tom, *The Films of Fritz Lang: Allegories of Vision and Modernity* (London: British Film Institute, 2000).

Kael, Pauline, "Circles and Squares: Joys and Sarris," in *I Lost It at the Movies* (New York: Bantam Books), pp. 264–288. Originally in *Film Quarterly* 16, no. 3 (Spring 1963).

Murray, Edward, *Nine American Film Critics: A Study of Theory and Practice* (New York: Frederick Ungar, 1975).

Sarris, Andrew, *Interviews with Film Directors* (New York: Avon Books, 1967).

———, *The American Cinema: Directors and Directions, 1929–1968* (New York: E. P. Dutton, 1968).

———, *Confessions of a Cultist: On the Cinema, 1955–1969* (New York: Simon and Schuster, 1970).

———, "Notes on the Auteur Theory in 1962," in *Film and/as Literature,* ed. John Harrington (Englewood Cliffs, N.J.: Prentice-Hall, 1977), pp. 240–253. Originally in *Film Culture* 27 (Winter 1962–1963): 1–8.

———, "The American Cinema," *Film Culture* 28 (Spring): 1–51.

———, "The Auteur Theory Revisited," *American Film,* July–August 1977: 49–53.

Stam Robert, *Film Theory: An Introduction* (Malden, Mass.: Blackwell Publishers, 2000).

Truffaut, François, "A Certain Tendency of the French Cinema," *Cahiers du cinéma* 31 (January 1954).

Wollen, Peter, *Signs and Meaning in the Cinema* (Bloomington: Indiana University Press, 1972).

ENTRIES A to Z

Allen, Woody (1935–) Allan Stewart Konigsberg was born on December 1, 1935, in Brooklyn, New York, to Martin and Nettie Konigsberg. A contentious couple, Allen's parents and their relationship would figure prominently in much of his later work. Marty Konigsberg moved from job to job during Allen's childhood as the family (which included sister Letty) moved from home to home before settling down in the Midwood section of Brooklyn. Allen despised school and later claimed that he learned nothing in his years of New York public schooling or his short stints at New York University and the City College of New York. By the age of 20, he had dropped out of both colleges, gotten engaged to a neighborhood girl named Harlene Rosen (their marriage would last six years, until 1962), and begun writing one-liners and getting them published by local columnists. At around this same time, the young gagwriter adopted "Woody Allen" first as his nom-de-plume and eventually as his permanent name.

Allen's comedy writing career blossomed in the late 1950s, first as a staff writer for NBC's *Colgate Comedy Hour,* then as a writer for Sid Caesar and Garry Moore. He jumped into stand-up comedy as a performer in his own right in the early 1960s, and established a reputation as one of the country's brightest young comics, with Las Vegas bookings and regular guest spots on Johnny Carson's *Tonight Show* and *The Ed Sullivan Show.*

By the mid-1960s, Allen was expanding his comic repertoire with essays in *Playboy* and the *New Yorker* magazines and acting roles in movies such as *What's New, Pussycat?* (1965) and *Casino Royale* (1967). Although he had written a new dialogue track for an old Japanese action picture that became *What's Up, Tiger Lily?* (1966), Allen's true film directorial debut was with *Take the Money and Run* (1969), the story of an inept bank robber played by Allen himself, a practice that set the stage for many future acting/directorial efforts.

In the 1970s, Allen turned almost exclusively to feature film directing and acting, leaving behind the television work he despised but continuing to write essays and comic monologues. The early-1970s films directed by Allen are characterized by broad, oftentimes physical, comedy. Included in this period are *Bananas* (1971); *Everything You Wanted to Know About Sex . . .* (1972), a series of vignettes dealing with sexual mores and customs; *Sleeper* (1973), Allen's comic science fiction vision of the future; and *Love and Death* (1975), a spoof on Russian historical romance novels. Throughout this period he continued to play roles in other

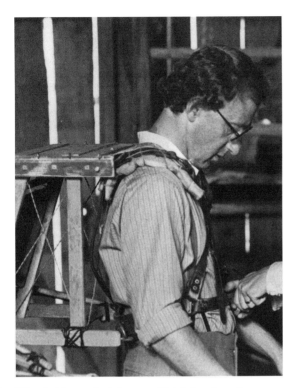

Woody Allen in *A Midsummer Night's Sex Comedy* (Orion)

people's films, including *Play It Again, Sam* (1972) and a rare dramatic role in *The Front* (1976). Allen's two late-1970s masterpieces, *Annie Hall* (1977) and *Manhattan* (1979), represent the peak of his financial and artistic success, with *Annie Hall* garnering the best picture Oscar and a best director Oscar for Allen. These films cemented a new screen persona for Allen, less the frantic slapstick comic of the early 1970s and more the image of the sophisticated if somewhat neurotic New Yorker that he has maintained in the years since.

Through the 1980s and 1990s, Allen has delivered about a film a year in a wide variety of genres and styles. *Stardust Memories* (1980) portrayed Allen as a film director in a Fellini-esque mode; *Zelig* (1983) was a mock documentary about a chameleon-like historical figure; *Broadway Danny Rose* (1984) portrayed Allen as a nightclub comic

mixed up with the Mafia; and *The Purple Rose of Cairo* (1985) was a movie fantasy in which a matinee idol comes to life from the screen. Allen hit another artistic high point in 1986 with *Hannah and Her Sisters* (1986), which garnered another best picture nomination.

For much of his career, Allen has been identified with two actresses, both of whom were also his lovers: Diane Keaton, who starred in *Sleeper, Love and Death,* and *Annie Hall* (for which she won the best actress Oscar); and Mia Farrow, who starred in almost all of Allen's 1980s films, including *Broadway Danny Rose, The Purple Rose of Cairo, Hannah and Her Sisters, Radio Days* (1987), and *Alice* (1990). His relationship with Farrow ended, and a scandal exploded onto the front pages of tabloids in 1991 when it was revealed that Allen was in a relationship with Farrow's adopted daughter, Soon-Yi Previn, who was more than 20 years his junior. He and Previn married in 1997.

The scandal resonated in Allen's first film to be released in its wake, the aptly titled *Husbands and Wives* (1992). Allen's other 1990s films include *Manhattan Murder Mystery* (1993), in which Allen reteamed with Keaton; *Bullets Over Broadway* (1994), a lush period piece about a Broadway playwright; *Everyone Says I Love You* (1996), a comic musical; and *Deconstructing Harry* (1997). Allen ended the decade with the mock jazz bio-pic *Sweet and Lowdown* (1999).

Other Films *Interiors* (1978); *A Midsummer Night's Sex Comedy* (1982); *September* (1987); *Another Woman* (1988); *New York Stories* (1989), "Oedipus Wrecks" segment; *Crimes and Misdemeanors* (1989); *Shadows and Fog* (1992); *Mighty Aphrodite* (1995); *Celebrity* (1998); *Small Time Crooks* (2000).

References Meade, Marion, *The Unruly Life of Woody Allen: A Biography* (New York: Scribner, 2000); Nichols, Mary P., *Reconstructing Woody* (Lanham, Md.: Rowman & Littlefield, 1998).

—C.M.

Altman, Robert (1925–) Robert Altman was born on February 20, 1925, in Kansas City,

Missouri, the son of B. C. and Helen Altman. Altman's father (the B. C. stood for Bernard Clement) was something of a legend in the insurance sales business in Kansas City, while his mother concentrated on homemaking, hobbies, and family (which included two younger sisters, Joan and Barbara). After stints in Catholic school and military school, Altman enlisted in the Army Air Force at the tail end of World War II, becoming the copilot of a B-24.

From the late 1940s to the mid-1950s, Altman worked at the Calvin Film Company, a local industrial, educational, and commercial filmmaker in Kansas City, an employment punctuated by several failed attempts to break into the Hollywood film industry. *The Delinquents* (1957), an independent feature in the teen exploitation picture mold and written, directed, and produced by Altman in Kansas City, served as his overdue entree into Hollywood; ALFRED HITCHCOCK, reportedly impressed by the film, invited Altman to direct episodes of his television program, *Alfred Hitchcock Presents.*

For the remainder of the 1950s and the first half of the 1960s, Altman worked as a journeyman TV director, logging dozens of credits on such programs as the Hitchcock show, *Bonanza, Combat! The Millionaire,* and *The Roaring Twenties.* In this period, Altman gained a reputation as a maverick that hindered his career in the mid-1960s when he had grown frustrated with TV but had no other viable career options. Finally, Warner Bros. hired him to direct the science-fiction feature *Countdown* (1968). Altman next directed the independent feature *That Cold Day in the Park* (1969) before landing the plum job of helming the 20th Century-Fox adaptation of *M★A★S★H* (1970). *M★A★S★H* was an overwhelming artistic and financial success that allowed Altman to pick and finance his projects for much of the 1970s.

The next few years saw a flurry of projects that represent Altman's artistic apex: *Brewster McCloud* (1970); *McCabe and Mrs. Miller* (1971), with Warren Beatty and Julie Christie; *Images* (1972); *The Long Goodbye* (1973), with Elliott Gould as a latter-day

Philip Marlowe; *California Split* (1974); and *Thieves Like Us* (1974). During the first half of the 1970s, Altman's reputation improved as he became an astute stylist specializing in genre revision (e.g., the detective film with *The Long Goodbye,* the gangster film with *Thieves Like Us*), and he attracted a "repertory company" of sorts composed of actors who would appear in several of his films (including Shelley Duvall, Michael Murphy, Keith Carradine, Bert Remsen, Elliott Gould, Bud Cort, and Henry Gibson). *Nashville* (1975) is arguably Altman's single greatest film, with its incisive examination of the country music industry and of American culture and politics circa the Bicentennial, as well as its innovative techniques of interweaving several storylines and two dozen major characters.

In the late 1970s, Altman's career would falter with some disastrous pictures that included the Paul Newman science fiction film *Quintet* (1979) and the intriguing but financially unsuccessful *3*

Robert Altman

Women (1977). After the legendary failure of *Pop-eye* (1980), Altman retreated almost completely from mainstream filmmaking and spent all of the 1980s making modest filmic adaptations of stage plays. This retreat was physical as well as artistic, as Altman and his creative associates relocated to Paris for much of the decade. *Come Back to the Five and Dime, Jimmy Dean, Jimmy Dean* (1982) and *Secret Honor* (1984) are the high points of this period, while *Beyond Therapy* (1987) is almost certainly the nadir. In the late 1980s, Altman returned to television with projects such as a remake of *The Caine Mutiny Court-Martial* and the multi-part HBO series *Tanner '88* (both 1988).

Altman resumed his position in the Hollywood "mainstream" with the critically acclaimed *The Player* (1992), a biting satire of film industry practices and stereotypes. This was followed by *Short Cuts* (1993), a multi-character, multi-story film similar to *Nashville,* this time focused on the lives and tribulations of a group of Los Angeles residents. Another attempt at the multi-character form, *Ready to Wear* (1994), was less successful in its examination of the Paris fashion industry. Altman's remaining 1990s films have included an homage to his hometown with *Kansas City* (1996), the neo-noir thriller *The Gingerbread Man* (1998), and the tragicomic multi-character *Cookie's Fortune* (1999). Altman's first film of the new century was another multi-character story, *Dr. T and the Women* (2000).

Other Films *The James Dean Story* (1957); *Buffalo Bill and the Indians* (1976); *A Wedding* (1978); *A Perfect Couple* (1979); *H.E.A.L.T.H.* (1979); *Streamers* (1983); *Fool for Love* (1985); *O.C. and Stiggs* (1987); *Aria* (1988), "Les Boreades" segment; *Vincent and Theo* (1990).

References McGilligan, Patrick, *Robert Altman: Jumping Off the Cliff* (New York: St. Martin's Press, 1989); O'Brien, Daniel, *Robert Altman: Hollywood Survivor* (New York: Continuum, 1995).

—C.M.

Anderson, Lindsay (1923–1994) Lindsay

Anderson was born in Bangalore, India (April 17, 1923), where his father was stationed with the Royal Engineers. He was educated in England at Cheltenham College and later at Oxford University, where he, along with Gavin Lambert, founded the magazine *Sequence,* which he continued to edit for five years (1947–52), beyond the granting of his M.A. degree in 1948. Between 1948 and 1954 he learned filmmaking by making four industrial documentaries for Richard Sutcliffe, Ltd. In 1953 he made two short personal documentaries. *Saturday's Children,* concerning children at the Royal School for the Deaf in Margate, won an Academy Award in 1955 for best short subject, and *O Dreamland* was a "rather satirical" 12-minute film about an amusement park in Margate. A 40-minute short, *Every Day Except Christmas,* followed in 1957 documenting the workers at London's Covent Garden market, and won the Grand Prix at the Venice Film Festival of 1957. During this period Anderson also made several government-sponsored short films.

In 1957 Anderson directed his first play at the Royal Court Theatre and was appointed artistic director of the Royal Court in 1959. He directed several stage plays for the next five years before returning to work in cinema. When he resumed making pictures, Anderson's first professional feature film, *This Sporting Life* (1963), adapted by David Storey from his own novel of the same title, was one of the defining pictures of the Angry Young Man movement, transferring from stage to screen the story of a coal miner, Frank Machin (Richard Harris), whose brutal strength makes him an excellent rugby player. Though successful as a professional rugby player, he is unable to adjust successfully to his altered station in life. He is exploited for his athletic ability and becomes a pawn in a power struggle between two businessmen who want to control the club. Anderson won widespread praise for his realistic treatment of this angry, inarticulate, working-class character.

The theme of economic and social exploitation was to become central to Anderson's later films, especially the allegorical features he scripted with

David Sherwin. These can be viewed as filmed essays in social criticism, excoriating institutions and attempting to show the possible consequences of social privilege and the exploitation of the common man. Anderson took a surreal turn with *If . . .* (1968), the first of a trilogy he made with David Sherwin as scriptwriter, a blistering attack upon the educational system in Britain, exposed as being not only trivial, but also perverse and corrupt. If the circumstances become too extreme and the system is not reformed, Anderson's film suggests, the natural response is likely to be first rebellion, then revolution. The film attacks not only a particular institution but also the very fabric of privileged British society. Although released during the year of student protests and demonstrations in Europe and America, the script, entitled "Crusaders," was completed as early as 1960. Anderson described the film to Elizabeth Sussex as being "deeply anarchistic," involving "a social and political philosophy which puts the highest possible value on responsibility."

If . . . made Malcolm McDowell, who played student rebel Mick Travis, a star. McDowell would later play Alex, the central thug-protagonist of STANLEY KUBRICK's *A Clockwork Orange* (1971), but McDowell would also go on to play Mick Travis, Anderson's allegorical, contemporary Everyman, in *O Lucky Man!* (1973) and in *Britannia Hospital* (1982), with each Travis feature becoming increasingly satirical and bitter. The story line of *O Lucky Man!*—loosely based upon the life of Malcolm McDowell—traces the progress of an innocent young man who sets forth optimistically as a coffee salesman in the north of England, is buffeted by the cynical and corrupt world he encounters, but is rescued by a stroke of good fortune at the end when a film director, played by Lindsay Anderson himself, "discovers" him and makes him famous, lifting him out of poverty and depression. Though he encounters a mad scientist and an evil, unscrupulous capitalist who betrays him, Mick is protected by his innocence and good nature, aided by a little bit of luck.

After perfecting an outrageous satiric style with *O Lucky Man!* Anderson tested its outer limits with *Britannia Hospital* (1982), the eponymous hospital run by the lunatic Dr. Millar (Graham Croden), the same mad scientist who experimented on human beings in *O Lucky Man!* Mick Travis now appears as an investigative journalist out to expose the bizarre goings-on at the hospital, which becomes an emblem for Britain in social, political, and economic disarray, a nation crossing over into madness and anarchy, a diseased nation that is incurably ill. It's a nasty situation, and a nasty—though often humorous—film. "The film took a terrible beating at the time," as Gavin Lambert has written, "partly because its release coincided with the Falklands War, and failed to march to the beat of Thatcher's patriotic drum."

In 1987 Anderson made his first American film, *The Whales of August,* adapted by David Berry from his stage play and starring two movie legends, Lillian Gish and Bette Davis, as two sisters spending their 50th summer together in their coastal Maine cottage. In 1990 Anderson returned to satire with *Glory! Glory!* a blistering attack on hypocritical TV evangelism. In the words of Derek Elley, who reviewed Anderson's last film, *Is That All There Is?* for *Variety* (November 29, 1993), "Lindsay Anderson's typically eclectic contribution to 'The Director's Place,' the BBC Scotland's series of self-portraits, shows the septuagenarian helmer alive and well and feisty," surrounded by friends such as the designer Jocelyn Herbert, writers David Sherwin and David Storey, and composer Alan Price, with whom he had worked on the Mick Travis trilogy. The film proved to be valedictory, however, since Anderson died on August 30, 1994, within a year of its conclusion.

Though he made only a handful of feature films, all of them were distinctive, groundbreaking efforts, informed with political agendas and frequently satirical. His influence was enormous. He organized the first "Free Cinema" program at London's National Film Theatre in 1956, for example, and wrote extensively about directors he admired, such as JOHN FORD, and those he did not, criticizing the Grierson school of documentary filmmaking, for example. He felt that responsible artists should deal with the realities of 20th-century life. His last film, *Is That All There Is?* began with a quotation from his 1956 Free Cinema manifesto: "Perfection is not an aim"—ironic words to live by. His friend Gavin Lambert eulogized Anderson as "the Great Outsider of British films," basically "a romantic at war with reality as he perceived it." He was a great satirist, and like all great satirists, often misunderstood: "His satire is a defence against pain," Lambert explained, "and he scolds because he loves."

References Armes, Roy, *A Critical History of British Cinema* (New York: Oxford University Press, 1978); Graham, Allison, *Lindsay Anderson* (Boston: Twayne, 1981); Lambert, Gavin, "Lindsay Anderson, Unrequited Lover," *Sight and Sound* 4, no. 10 (October 1994): 18–21; Lambert, Gavin, *Mainly About Lindsay Anderson* (New York: Knopf, 2000); Silet, Charles P., *Lindsay Anderson: A Guide to References and Resources* (Boston: G. K. Hall, 1979); Sussex, Elizabeth, *Lindsay Anderson* (New York: Praeger, 1969).

—J.M.W.

Angelopoulos, Theo (1935–   )   Greece's most important filmmaker actively contributed to a renaissance in Greek literature, music, and art in the 1970s and 1980s. Theodoros Angelopoulos was born in Athens on April 27, 1935, one of four children of Spyros and Katerina Angelopoulos. Although his upper-middle-class family had deep roots in the countryside, it had moved to the city, like many other families at the time. During the Second World War and the subsequent civil war in Greece (1944–49), the Angelopoulos family survived many hardships, including hunger and the political persecution of their father, Spyros. From 1953 to 1957, Theo studied law. After his military service (1959–60) he moved to Paris, France, where he studied film and anthropology. He returned to Greece in 1963, worked for a left-

wing newspaper, the *Dimokratiki Allaghi,* and three years later made his first short film, *The Broadcast (I ekpombi).*

At a time when the Greek cinema consisted mostly of melodramas and low comedies, Angelopoulos's first feature-length film, *Reconstruction (Anaparastasis* [1970]), was a revelation. Its subject was taken from a newspaper article about a village woman who murdered her husband after his return from Germany, where he had been a guest worker for several years. The story is retold and restaged several times, so that the motives and even the identity of the killer are thrown into doubt. As the director has remarked, the choice of the title was based on Dostoyevsky's *Crime and Punishment:* "It is rather that her environment is the real murderer, that has murdered her spirit. It's very important that she says, 'I will have no one judge me. I will have no one judge me.' I respect her. She is an amazing person." The movie was filmed in black and white on a tight budget and utilized nonprofessional actors. By preferring to film on location, near the Greek-Albanian border, Angelopoulos set a precedent that he would follow for the remainder of his career. As he has explained, "I believe something special happens on location, in the real place, and I do not mean just the ability to photograph the decor, the landscape. But it is more that when I am in the place I have set the film, all five of my senses are working. I become more completely aware. I therefore feel I am living the experiences I want to film." *Reconstruction* won a major award in Berlin and it was the centerpiece of the Thessaloniki Film Festival.

After his first film, Angelopoulos embarked on a historical tetralogy about Greece in the 1930–70 time period, consisting of *Days of 36 (Meres tou '36* [1972]), *The Travelling Players (O thiasos* [1975]), *The Hunters (I kinigi* [1977]), and *Alexander the Great (O megalexandros* [1980]). *Days of 36* was Angelopoulos's first film in color. It was made in the last days of the military junta that had governed Greece since 1967, and the rising director felt that he could then challenge it more directly by exposing the cultural climate and historical circumstances from which it had emerged. He submitted a cleansed script to the censors and started shooting. By the time production was completed, observes historian Dan Georgakas, "the junta was out of power but the new government was nearly as hostile to its political perspective as the junta would have been." The second film in the tetralogy is probably the most celebrated by critics. *The Travelling Players* centers on an itinerant theater troupe that performs sentimental melodramas during the years 1939–52, that is, throughout the Second World War and the ensuing civil war. The fates of the actors serve as mirrors of the broader events in the tumultuous history of the country. Moreover, they also parallel the Greek tragedy of the House of Atreus. The interplay between performance, history, and myth is carried out through a dexterous manipulation of time, as in the long take when a man begins a walk in the year 1952 but arrives in 1939. "This shifting in time within one long take is not meant to be cynical, but economically and unequivocally to nail down the political linkage of a pre-war military regime with a postwar military regime." In a similar scene, a group of Fascists marches away from a 1946 New Year's dance in full-throated song to arrive at their destination in the year 1952. Police start to beat strikers in one time period and finish the task in another. Angelopoulos's manipulations of time are only one of the devices he utilizes with the intent to offer an alternative to the conventional Hollywood narrative paradigm. He prefers the use of the long take to the standard American montage techniques; and in a departure from Hollywood's emphasis on a "star system," he frames his players in long shots, thus diminishing their centrality and imparting more importance to groups than to individuals. Moreover, he breaks the "fourth wall" by having the actors tell their stories directly to the camera; and he stages the action laterally in horizontal compositional configurations, emulating, in effect, the flat, mural-like effect of a frieze. All these strategies form part of what David Bordwell calls the "political modernism" of Angelopoulos, a tendency whose origins Bordwell locates in the work of his predecessors, such as JEAN-LUC GODARD, Jean Marie Straub and Danielle Huillet, Miklos Jancso, and MICHELANGELO ANTONIONI.

With *The Hunters,* Angelopoulos continued his examination of the conflict between left and right, between populists and monarchists in Greek history. In this film, the action transpires on New Year, 1977, when a bourgeois hunting party stumbles upon the corpse of a guerrilla fighter from the civil war of 30 years earlier. The mystery lies in the fact that the body is still warm! Angelopoulos continued this historical exploration in *Alexander the Great,* whose action is set at the beginning of the 20th century. But this time, much of his attention centered on the internecine fights within the left, and this fact caused many who had cheered his earlier films to turn against him. The majority of the critics did applaud the film's courage, however, especially when seen in the context of the earlier work by Angelopoulos.

During the 1980s, the director's films took yet another turn from social drama to an emphasis on more individual characters, though always framing them in the context of broader societal events. In *Voyage to Cythera,* the protagonist, named Spyros, like Angelopoulos's own father, is an old Greek communist who has lived in exile in Tashkent (then part of the USSR) after the civil war, and who returns to his country after an amnesty only to be finally rejected by modern Greece. In 1983, came *The Beekeeper (O melissokomos),* another film about a teacher, also named Spyros, who leaves his wife and daughter to return to the profession of his father and grandfather, beekeeping. In the course of his travel back to the countryside, he finds a young and promiscuous hitchhiker who accompanies him and leaves him at different points in his trip.

Angelopoulos's most accessible film, *Landscape in the Mist* (which won the European "Felix" as best film of 1989), could be subtitled *Children in a Documentary Fairy Tale.* It forms the third part of what Angelopoulos has called a "trilogy of silence," together with *Voyage* and *The Beekeeper.* History (and for that matter, the world of adults) is left behind in this tale, Angelopoulos's only film centered on children. In this film, two children, Voula and her younger brother Alexander, start a journey through Greece in search of their father, a man they don't remember and who might even not exist. This primary focus of the film is myth and fairy tale. As Horton points out, when we see Alexander and Voula walking on a northern Greece highway, "we are left to consider these two figures as simply a young girl and young boy walking in a vast, dark landscape. The minimalism involved—no speech, little action—leads us to dwell upon the scene in our own minds, to open it up to interpretation, meditation, exploration, and thus to consider the mythic dimensions of these to character's lives."

After the resounding success of *Landscape in the Mist,* and throughout the decade of the 1990s, Angelopoulos expanded his scope from Greece to the surrounding Balkan region, with stories that increasingly focused on the plight of this turbulent area of the world, then engulfed in successive conflicts over national borders and identities in Slovenia, Bosnia-Herzegovina, and, lately, Kosovo. In *The Suspended Step of the Stork* (*To meteoro vima to pelargou* [1991]), he revisits the myth of Telemachus and Odysseus, with the former embodied by a young television journalist (Gregory Karr) who is looking for a famous Greek politician (Marcello Mastroianni) who went off on a journey and has never been seen again. Instead of a conqueror or adventurer, this modern Odysseus has decided to live with the unfortunate refugees of the Balkan wars.

Angelopoulos's next film, *Ulysses' Gaze* (*To vlemma tou odyssea* [1995]), takes another step out of Greece to explore the disintegration of Yugoslavia in the Republic of Macedonia (called "Skopje" by the Greeks). This time the protagonist is a Greek-American filmmaker (Harvey Keitel) who travels from Greece throughout the Balkans, crossing into Bulgaria, Romania, Serbia, and finally Bosnia, where his journey takes him to war-torn Sarajevo. The film, again taking on the Homeric tradition, also alludes to the Platonic idea that is synthesized in the philosopher's utterance, "And thus, the soul too, if it wishes to know itself, will have to look into the soul." Angelopoulos's first film to be made outside of Greece, predominantly in English and with an international cast, it deepened the concerns he had explored in *Suspended Step,* and it succeeded brilliantly with critics and audiences in Europe, where it won the Grand Prix at the Cannes Film Festival in 1995. Angelopoulos's latest film, *Eternity and a Day* (*Mia aiwniothta kai mia mera* [1998]), has an aging Bruno Ganz playing an exiled writer called Alexandre, dying from an unspecified illness, when he has a fateful encounter with an eight-year-old Albanian refugee (Achilleas Skevis). As he had done in the past, Angelopoulos glides between past and present in conflating the end of Alexandre's life with his happier years with his wife and daughter in the 1960s.

References   Horton, Andrew, ed., *The Last Modernist, The Films of Theo Angelopoulos* (Westport, Conn.: Greenwood Press, 1997); Horton, Andrew, ed., *The Films of Theo Angelopoulos: A Cinema of Contemplation* (Princeton, N.J.: Princeton University Press, 1997).

—F.A.

Antonioni, Michelangelo   (1912–)

Michelangelo Antonioni was born September 29, 1912, in Ferrara, Italy. He studied economics at the University of Bologna from 1931 to 1935 and was employed as a bank clerk and journalist from 1935 to 1939. In 1939 he moved to Rome and began to contribute articles to film journals including *Il Corriere Padano.* In 1940 he served as the editorial secretary of *Cinema,* published by the Fascist Entertainment Guild. From 1940 to 1941 he studied at the Centro Sperimentale di Cinematografia in Rome. Like several other students who attended the school founded by the Fascist government, Antonioni would go on to make films whose themes often opposed institutional values. He married Letizia Balboni in 1942 (he has been married to his second wife Enrica since 1986). He collaborated on the script of *Un pilota ritorna,* directed by Rossellini in 1942, and was assigned by the Italian production company to work with Marcel Carné on *Les visiteurs du soir* (1942). Following the end of the war, he continued to collaborate with screenwriters and directors.

In 1943 Antonioni filmed his first documentary short titled *Gente del Po (People of the Po),* which was not released until 1947. He directed six more documentaries between 1943 and 1950. An adulterous love affair was the subject of his first feature: *Cronaca di un amore (Story of a Love Affair* [1950]). This was followed by *La signora senza camelie (Camille without Camelias* [1953]), an account of a young actress and her film producer husband. North Italy would be the setting for the next two features: *Le amiche (The Girlfriends* [1955]), set among the upper class of Turin and *Il grido (The Cry* [1957]), where Antonioni returns to his native Po valley for a tale of a forlorn artisan named Aldo. Many critics describe Antonioni's work of the 1960s as the Italian version of the French *nouvelle vague.* Although older than his counterparts of the New Wave, his films are marked by the same auteur qualities.

L'avventura (The Adventure [1960]), for which he wrote the story and collaborated on the script, appeared in the same year as *La dolce vita.* Both in their own way would transform Italian cinema. Antonioni's film won the Special Jury Prize at Cannes, although the audience booed and hissed during the screening. Such viewer response prompted strident critical support that guaranteed international release and a chance to attract wider attention. Early audiences may not have known what to think of the film, but by the end of the century *L'avventura* would appear on nearly every list of the most important films ever made. The story involves characters thrust into an unfamiliar landscape who, although arriving at a level of self-knowledge not previously attained, are still bound by the consequences of previous actions. Monica Vitti, the actress who plays Claudia, gave a remarkable, understated performance and Antonioni would rely on her presence for other major projects of the 1960s. She came to define the Antonioni heroine: enigmatic, aloof, and fashionably attired.

La notte (The Night [1961]) starred Jeanne Moreau, Marcello Mastroianni, and Vitti in a story that led to the end of a marriage. The film asked viewers to consider the moral standards they accept or deny as factors in making choices. As in many of Antonioni's films, it is the shift of emotion rather than action that propels the unresolved narrative. The third film in what some have labeled a "trilogy" is *L'eclisse (The Eclipse* [1962]), a tale with Vitti and Alain Delon as lovers whose affair contrasts their individual searches for meaning in the relationships they form. This film also won the Special Jury Prize at Cannes, but by 1962, audiences were more receptive to both the themes and aesthetic of Antonioni's work.

Il deserto rosso (Red Desert [1964]) was Antonioni's first color film. Set in the northern industrial town of Ravenna, this work would prove the importance of color as a formal element but also its role in describing the psychological drama of individuals who become increasingly estranged from their environment. The bleak world of factories and technology does not control the action, yet characters are defined by their responses to this environment. Vitti appears as Giuliana and viewers recognize she is an individual at an impasse: Will she choose life in this austere world? The power of the director's vision is that he neither reviles nor celebrates this industrial world. As a modernist, his worldview is not one of nostalgia for the past and he does not bemoan the loss of a traditional culture but does suggest that the waste technology generates is both industrial by-product and human alienation.

Blow-Up (1966) marked the first international project Antonioni filmed outside Italy and in English. It won the best director award from the National Society of Film Critics and the Palme d'Or at Cannes. David Hemmings plays a photographer in "swinging London" who, as a maker of images, comes to question his perception of the images he captures on film. Antonioni traveled to the United States to film *Zabriskie Point* (1969). The film about the American counterculture was the director's examination of a generation foreign in both age and values. Critics in the United States reviled the film. The director witnessed a similar response from Chinese authorities to *Chung-Kuo Cina* (1972). Antonioni documented the China of the Cultural Revolution at the invitation of government leaders. His view of life in the final cut was not the one authorities wished to project to the world, and the film was never shown in China.

The director returned to feature films with *Professione: Reporter* (*The Passenger* [1975]). The story is that of a reporter (Jack Nicholson) who acts impulsively and assumes the identity of a dead gunrunner, only to face a similar violent end. The extraordinary final shot is one frequently examined by film students. Antonioni's films of the 1980s include *Il Mistero di Oberwald* (*The Oberwald Mystery* [1980]) and *Identificazione di una donna* (*Identification of a Woman* [1982]). Antonioni experiments with new video technology but retains familiar themes of individuals searching for identity in their relationships with others and their world.

In the mid-1980s, a stroke and failing health slowed the director's output. With the collaboration of WIM WENDERS, plus a screenplay of his own short stories, Antonioni directed *Par delà les nuages* (*Beyond the clouds*) in 1995. His most recent films are: *Destinazione Verna* (2000) and *Tanto per stare insieme* (*Just to Be Together* [2001]). As a director, Antonioni continues to defy easy labeling. Sometime minimalist, auteur, and neorealist, he can perhaps be understood as adhering to many features of the latter category if the label is used to define what he reacted against rather than what he shared with other directors (beyond the tendency to employ indeterminate endings). Antonioni never limits the reading of his films to a single tradition. He certainly remains the leader among directors of

what some term as European "art cinema," an artist with a sophisticated sense of abstract values and a fascination for human emotion, providing viewers with memorable, wordless sequences and indelible images. He has received numerous awards for lifetime achievement in film (Cannes 1982, Venice 1983, and an Oscar in 1995).

Other Films *I vinti* (*The Vanquished* [1952]); *L'amore in città* (*Love in the City* [1953]); *Kumbha Mela* (1989); *Roma '90* (1989).

References Brunette, Peter, *The Films of Michelangelo Antonioni* (Cambridge, U.K.: Cambridge University Press, 1998); Chatman, Seymour, *Antonioni; or, The Surface of the World* (Berkeley: University of California Press, 1985); Perry, Ted, and René Prieto, *Michelangelo Antonioni: A Guide to References and Resources* (Boston: G. K. Hall, 1986); Rohdie, Sam, *Antonioni* (London: BFI, 1990); Wenders, Wim, *My Time with Antonioni: The Diary of an Extraordinary Experience* (London: Faber, 2000).

—J.A.D.

Armstrong, Gillian (1950–) With her strong feminist bent, Gillian Armstrong brought her own distinctive flair to the so-called Australian Renaissance of the 1960s and 1970s. She was born in Melbourne on December 18, 1950, and educated at Swinburne College. After studying filmmaking at the Melbourne and Australian Film and Television School, Sydney, she worked as a production assistant and editor before making a series of documentary films tracking the lives of their female subjects, *Smokes and Lollies* (1975), *14's Good, 18's Better* (1980), and *Bingo, Bridesmaids and Braces* (1988). Feminist historian Gwendolyn Audrey Foster reports that Armstrong tried to capture the everyday paths of average young females, in which "the sorting out process begins—sexual attraction—stereotypes—you start working out what you are considered to be in society. I'm the pretty one; I'm ugly; If only I had this. . . ." Indeed, continues Foster, "The gap between confining socially imposed gender identities and the wish to define ourselves as women is a consistent theme through Armstrong's films."

Gillian Armstrong (right) on the set of *Oscar and Lucinda* (Twentieth Century Fox)

After directing her first feature, *The Singer and the Dancer* in 1976, the 27-year-old Armstrong went on to direct her "breakthrough" film, *My Brilliant Career* (1979), the first feature film directed by a woman in Australia in more than 45 years. It garnered international acclaim, especially from feminists who regarded it as a celebration of female rebellion against societal codes. Adapted from an autobiographical 1901 novel by the precocious Miles Franklin (a pseudonym for the 19-year-old novelist Stella Maria Miles Franklin), the film depicted the efforts of rebellious young Sybylla Melvyn (Judy Davis), a Bush woman, to escape the life of wife and mother in order to become a writer. As Brian McFarlane has noted, "it uses its narrative set in the 1890s to explore and comment on late 1970s feminist issues. . . . The

parallels with Australian women in the 1970s working out the terms of their own lives are as apparent as they are unforced." Critic Molly Haskell reports that some feminists resisted the film's ending: "However vehemently they had argued for new, anti-romantic endings in which women would go off into the sunset alone, would stand tall and strong and solitary without needing men to complete them, when push came to shove they didn't understand why Judy Davis couldn't have a writing career and Sam Neill, too." Indeed, Haskell continues, audiences in general had difficulty accepting the idea that "nuptial bliss might dull the budding writer's acuteness, that companionability might take the edge off the urge to create—particularly for a young woman in that era with the kind of social responsibilities she might anticipate." Three years later Armstrong's *Starstruck* again told the story of an ambitious heroine, only this time it was formatted as a contemporary rock musical.

Her first American film was *Mrs. Soffel* (1984), starring Mel Gibson and Diane Keaton as ill-fated lovers escaping the Allegheny County Prison in Pennsylvania at the turn of the century. Since then, her career has criss-crossed the ocean, making more films in Australia (*High Tide,* 1987) and America (*Little Women,* 1994). In the former, arguably Armstrong's most beautiful film, a trio of women—Judy Davis as Lilli, a drifter; Claudia Karvan as Aly, the daughter Lilli left behind; and Jan Adele as Bet, Aly's mother-in-law—live out their mundane lives in a poor coastal town in New South Wales. "The transient lifestyles of these women are painted against a backdrop of a society that looks for easily read 'family values,'" writes Foster. "Nothing is obvious or easily read in *High Tide,* most especially the motivations of Lilli, who rejects suitors, family, success, and everything else she is expected to embrace." In the latter a superb cast, including Wynona Ryder as Jo March and Susan Sarandon as "Marmee" March, is wedded to a script containing more than a liberal dose of feminist rhetoric. The character of Sybylla Mervyn has returned in the incarnation of Jo, who in the end triumphs in the establishment of her own school.

Her most recent film, *Oscar and Lucinda* (1997), is her most ambitious. Adapted from the 1988 book by the Australian novelist Peter Carey, the story begins in 1847 and traces the intersecting lives of Oscar, a boy brought up in the remote countryside of Devon under the stern discipline of his father, a fanatical cleric; and Lucinda, a wayward child in New South Wales. Oscar grows up to be an Anglican cleric, and Lucinda becomes the manager of a glass-works factory. When they meet, these two disparate characters discover their common passion—gambling. Together, they launch the most colossal gamble of their lives, the transportation to a remote village in the outback

of a church made entirely of iron and glass. *Oscar and Lucinda* is a miracle of a movie, a luminous, lyric, lovingly detailed sprawl of a story. If at times Ralph Fiennes tends to make his terminally timid character of Oscar seem like a kind of benevolent Uriah Heep, and if the story itself betrays its novelistic origins with some lumpy continuity and shortcomings in the delineation of the secondary characters, this unlikely blend of romance, historical epic, and adventure story is held together by its blazing affirmation of faith and love between the two principals and by the spectacular landscape photography.

"One thing I'm very sensitive about—and have been since film school—is this preconception about women film directors," says Armstrong. "We're always seen as having to be the little mother on the set, which is the last thing I ever was.... But it's very hard for any working mother. One advantage female directors have is at least you're not working full time, all the time.... Actually, I have wonderful people on my production crew who mother and look after me, and many of them are men."

Other Films   *Having a Go* (1983); *Hard to Handle: Bob Dylan with Tom Petty and the Heartbreakers* (1986); *Fires Within* (1991); *The Last Days of Chez Nous* (1992).

References   Foster, Gwendolyn Audrey, *Women Film Directors: An International Bio-Critical Dictionary* (Westport, Conn.: Greenwood Press, 1995); Hardesty, Mary, "The Brilliant Career of Gillian Armstrong," *DGA Magazine* 20, no. 4 (September–October 1995): 21–24; Haskell, Molly, "Wildflowers," *Film Comment* 29, no. 2 (March–April 1993): 35–37; McFarlane, Brian, *Australian Cinema, 1970–1985* (London: Secker and Warburg, 1987); Warrick, Steve, "High Tide," *Film Quarterly* 42, no. 4 (Summer 1989): 21–26; Wolf, Jamie, "A Hard Woman Is Good to Find," *American Film,* January–February 1985, pp. 20–26.

—J.C.T.

Arzner, Dorothy (1900–1979)   "There should be more of us directing," said Dorothy Arzner in 1932. "Try as any man may, he will never be able to get the woman's viewpoint in directing certain stories. . . . A great percent of our audience is women. That too is something to think about."

Dorothy Arzner was the only woman director to develop a body of work during the Hollywood studio years from the mid-1920s to the early 1940s. She was the only woman director to make the transition from silent to sound film, and her work includes four silent films and 13 sound pictures from 1927 to 1943. The next woman to direct in Hollywood was IDA LUPINO, whose first film was released in 1949. Unlike other women directors, Arzner had a strong belief in feminism. She was a lesbian and consistently wore masculine attire on the sets of her films as if to make a stand for feminism and lesbianism. If the studio bosses minded, she never heard about it.

Arzner began her film career at the bottom and worked her way up the production ladder. Her first job in the film industry was typing scripts for Famous Players-Lasky, and in 1920 she began editing in addition to her typing chores. She was assigned to the Famous Players-Lasky subsidiary, Realart, where she worked as both script girl and editor. She claimed to have learned more about films in the cutting room than anywhere else. As she became known as a first-rate editor, well-known directors such as Fred Niblo and James Cruze began asking specifically for her to edit their films. Meanwhile she was continuing to write scripts for other directors at other studios, including Columbia.

When she told Columbia she would like to direct her next script and they agreed, Paramount made her a better offer and her first film was *Fashions for Women* (1927) with Esther Ralston. It was a commercial success, thanks in part to the star, a proven box-office draw; but it also served to get Arzner a long-term contract as a director at Paramount, where she remained until it was reorganized in 1932. She made Paramount's first "talkie," *The Wild Party,* with Clara Bow in 1929 (her second film with Bow). After leaving Paramount she worked freelance and worked with all the major stars of the period, including Katharine Hepburn, Lucille Ball, Clara Bow, Claudette Colbert, Sylvia Sidney, Joan Crawford, and Merle Oberon, at the studios of RKO, Columbia, and MGM. Her best films from a stylistic and popular standpoint include *Merrily We Go To Hell* (1932), *Christopher Strong* (1933), *Craig's Wife* (1936), *The Bride Wore Red* (1937), and *Dance Girl, Dance* (1940).

She stopped making films in 1943, retiring with her domestic partner of 13 years, Marion Morgan, to their home in Santa Monica. Arzner taught film for four years at UCLA in the 1960s where one of her pupils was Francis Ford Coppola. After Morgan died in 1971 Arzner moved to Palm Springs where she died in 1979. She once said of her success, relative to her male cohorts, "I made one box office hit after another, so they knew they could gamble a banker's money on me. If I had a failure in the middle I would have been finished."

Other Films *Manhattan Cocktail* (1928); *Sarah and Son* (1930); *Working Girls* (1931); *First Comes Courage* (1943).

References Acker, Ally, *Reel Women: Pioneers of the Cinema, 1896–Present* (New York: Continuum Press, 1991); Flately, Guy, "At the Movies," *New York Times,* August 20, 1976, p. C-5; Kuhn, Annette, and Susannah Radstone, eds., *The Woman's Companion to International Film* (Berkeley: University of California Press, 1994); *New York Herald-Tribune,* June 26, 1932, sec. vii, p. 6; Slide, Anthony, *The Silent Feminists* (Lanham, Md.: Scarecrow Press, 1996); Smith, Sharon, *Women Who Make Movies* (New York: Hopkinson and Blake, 1975).

—C.L.P.

Attenborough, [Lord] Richard [Samuel]

(1923–) British actor, producer, and director Richard Attenborough was born in Cambridge on August 29, 1923. Frederick L. Attenborough, his father, affectionately known in family circles as the "Governor," was an academic administrator who retired as principal of Leicester University College. The Governor started as a schoolmaster in Liverpool, won a scholarship to Immanuel

College, Cambridge, where he taught as a don when Richard was born until 1925, when he was appointed principal of the Borough Road Training College in Isleworth, now known as the West London Institute of Higher Education. The Attenboroughs were social activists who sheltered Basque children from Spain during the Spanish Civil War and Jewish children from Germany during World War II. Richard was educated at Wyggeston Grammar School in Leicester and later earned the highly competitive Leverhulme scholarship to the Royal Academy of Dramatic Art, London, where, in 1942, he was awarded the Bancroft Medal. His stage debut was at the Intimate Theatre, Palmers Green, during the summer of 1941. In June 1943 he joined the Royal Air Force Volunteer Reserve, going into the RAF Film Unit in February 1944, where he served until 1946.

Attenborough's first film role was in DAVID LEAN's *In Which We Serve* (1942), in which he played a sailor suffering from war nerves. He was featured in more than 60 films, continuing to act

Director Richard Attenborough on the set of *In Love and War* (New Line)

even after he launched his directing career. Of special notice was his portrayal of Pinkie, the teenaged killer in the film adaptation of Graham Greene's *Brighton Rock* (1947). Other memorable movie roles included two with Steve McQueen, *The Great Escape* (1962) and *The Sand Pebbles* (1966). He worked with director Robert Aldrich in *Flight of the Phoenix* (1965) and with SATYAJIT RAY in *The Chess Players* (1977). He would return to acting later in his career to play John Hammond, the eccentric founder of Jurassic Park, in the eponymous film by STEVEN SPIELBERG, in 1993, and the English Ambassador in KENNETH BRANAGH's *Hamlet* (1995).

Attenborough formed his own production company, Beaver Films, in 1959, and, with director Bryan Forbes, produced a series of seminal films that helped to launch the British New Wave, notably *The Angry Silence* (1960), *The L-Shaped Room* (1962), and *Séance on a Wet Afternoon* (1964). He later described his first film, *The Angry Silence,* as an attack "on subversion and on the lunatic far left fringe of the trade union and the Labour movements." His breakthrough film as director was *Gandhi* (1984), first suggested to him by Motilal Kothari, a civil servant with the Indian High Commission in London. His casting of a relatively unknown actor, Ben Kingsley, as Gandhi, helped to make this three-hour spectacle, made on location in India, a hit. *Gandhi* won eight Academy Awards, including best film, best director, best screenplay, and best actor (for Kingsley), out of 11 nominations.

Before the tremendous success of *Gandhi,* Attenborough, whose debut picture as director was an adaptation of Joan Littlewood's antiwar musical *Oh! What a Lovely War* (1969), perfected his craft with several pictures: *Young Winston* (1972), starring Simon Ward as Churchill, made for producer Carl Forman, was adapted from Sir Winston Churchill's autobiography *My Early Life: A Roving Commission;* two films written by William Goldman would follow. *A Bridge Too Far* (1977) featured Robert Redford, and *Magic* (1978), an odd but effective picture, starred Anthony Hopkins as a ventriloquist whose personality is being taken over by his evil dummy.

His next film came as something of a surprise, an adaptation of the hit musical *A Chorus Line* (1985), which got three Oscar nominations, followed by *Cry Freedom* (1987) with Denzel Washington playing the antiapartheid activist Steve Biko and Kevin Kline playing journalist Donald Woods, who had written a book about Biko. The film was adapted from Woods's book about Biko, described by Attenborough as "one of the brightest, most charismatic, intelligent and fascinating men ever born in South Africa," murdered "whilst in police custody," and Woods's own autobiography, *Asking for Trouble*. Attenborough had long wanted to make a film about South Africa and had earlier optioned failed projects, one entitled *God Is a Bad Policeman*. He told Frank Price, the head of Columbia Pictures who became head of Universal, "I've got a subject which is bound to be as difficult as *Gandhi*. It's based on two books written by the exiled newspaper editor Donald Woods." Price replied, "I know them well," and offered to make the film at Universal. The director then contacted screenwriter John Briley, who had written the screenplay for *Gandhi,* and the project was in motion.

Other biographical features were to follow. *Chaplin* (1992) starred Robert Downey, Jr., who wanted the role so badly that he worked for a year with mime expert Dan Kamin so that he could play Chaplin convincingly. Downey went on to earn an Oscar nomination for his work and perseverance and won the British Academy Award for best actor. Next was *Shadowlands* (1994), adapted by William Nicholson from his play about the improbable romance between the English writer C. S. Lewis (Anthony Hopkins) and Joy Gresham (Deborah Winger), a much younger divorcée from New York. Debra Winger was nominated for an Oscar, as was William Nicholson for best adapted screenplay. *Shadowlands* won a British Academy Award for best film. In 1996 Attenborough directed *In Love and War,* starring Chris O'Donnell and Sandra Bullock, adapted from the book *Hemingway in Love and War: The Lost Diary of Agnes von Kurowsky,* by Henry S. Villard and James Nagel, published in 1989. Producer Dimitri Villard was the son of Henry Villard, Ernest Hemingway's wartime friend, who, after graduating from Harvard, volunteered as an ambulance driver for the Red Cross in Italy in 1918. Aside from the odd musical, then, Attenborough concentrated on biographical films during his later career. Attenborough later described *A Chorus Line* as "an experience I would not have missed," however. "It was a terrific challenge and technically is probably the best film I've ever made."

Attenborough's record of service was also impressive. For years he served as chairman of Channel Four and of the Royal Academy Dramatic Art (where he was trained as an actor), vice president of British Academy of Film and Television Arts, and Governor of the National Film School; he also served on the British Screen Advisory Council. During the 1990s he became pro-chancellor of Sussex University. In 1976 Attenborough was knighted (CBE), then elevated to a life peerage in 1993 in recognition of his achievements and service, becoming Lord Attenborough of Richmond-on-Thames. He summarized his career for the London *Sunday Times* by saying "I'm not a genius, I'm not an auteur, I'm a craftsman—but not a bad one."

References Attenborough, Richard, *In Search of Gandhi* (Piscataway, N.J.: New Century, 1982); *Richard Attenborough's Cry Freedom* (London: Bodley Head, 1987).

—J.M.W.

Beresford, Bruce (1940–) With fellow Australians PETER WEIR and FRED SCHEPISI, Bruce Beresford appeared in the vanguard of the renaissance in Australian filmmaking in the 1970s. One of the most eclectic artists working today, his subjects and style vary greatly from picture to picture. He was born on August 16, 1940, in Sydney, Australia. After graduating from Sydney University, he worked in advertising and television for the Australian Broadcasting Company. In 1961 he relocated to London, where he secured a series of odd jobs, including teaching at a girls' school at Williesden. Ever peripatetic, from 1964 to 1966 he landed a position with the East Nigerian Film Unit in Africa. Back in London he was hired as film officer of the production board of the British Film Institute and as film adviser to the Arts Council of Great Britain, positions he held until 1970. After the passage in Australia of governmental decrees assisting film production, Beresford returned to begin his career in feature films. The time was propitious. The Australian Film Development Corporation (AFDC), the Experimental Film and Television Fund, and a national Film and Television School assisted the financing of feature films and television programs. The AFDC's first major investment was

Beresford's *The Adventures of Barry McKenzie* (1972)—based on the satirical comic strip by Barry Humphries—the first of what historian Brian McFarlane refers to as his "ocker" films. It and *Don's Party* (1976), *Barry McKenzie Holds His Own* (1974), and *Money Movers* (1978) presented the cliched image of Australian men as "boorish but good humored, sexually and nationally chauvinistic."

This agenda would change with *The Getting of Wisdom* (1977) and *Breaker Morant* (1979). The first picture was based on an autobiographical 1910 novel by Henry Handel (née Ethel Lindsay) Richardson about the struggles of the free-spirited Laura Ramsbotham (Susannah Fowle), the daughter of an impoverished country postmistress, to survive a moribund educational system and become a writer. Like GILLIAN ARMSTRONG's *My Brilliant Career,* which it slightly resembles, it depicts something of the marginalized position of women in Australian society at the turn of the century. *Breaker Morant* was a fact-based historical drama about Australian guerrilla troops in the Boer War. Three officers of the Bushveldt Carabineers (Edward Woodward, Bryan Brown, Lewis FitzGerald) are court-martialed by a British court on trumped-up charges of atrocities against the Boers, despite their pleas that they were following the British commander's orders as relayed through their commanding officer. The court trial is interrupted by flashbacks reflecting the testimony of various witnesses. Historian McFarlane defends the film against charges of its being a simpleminded anti-British tirade: "Certainly, it deplores imperialism and the brutalities practiced in its name; but more complexly it offers a subtle and absorbing examination of a hierarchy of loyalties and orders. . . . If [Lord] Kitchener is discharging responsibilities, as he sees them, to the British government, Morant, Handcock, and Witton justifiably claim loyalty to . . . their commanding officer, through whom, in turn, they receive Kitchener's orders." Not only does the film reflect contemporary issues raised by atrocities in Vietnam, but also, as McFarlane notes, "it reflects that questioning of blind allegiance to a British cause which surfaced tentatively in Australian parliamentary debates of the time." It received international acclaim and was nominated for an Academy Award for best screenplay.

An invitation to come to Hollywood led to his next film, *Tender Mercies* (1983), a Horton Foote script about an alcoholic country singer (Robert Duvall), whose relationship with a young woman and her daughter rejuvenates him spiritually and professionally. Beresford was nominated for an Oscar for best director, and the film went on to receive two Oscars, for best actor and screenplay. His next film, *King David* (1985), thankfully broke from the DeMille tradition of biblical epics, but was less successful with critics and the public, as was *Crimes of the Heart* (1986), based on a play by Beth Henley about a reunion of three sisters—Diane Keaton, Jessica Lange, Sissy Spacek—after the youngest has casually shot her husband. Beresford bounced back with his most successful film to date, *Driving Miss Daisy* (1989), another theatrical adaptation, starring Jessica Tandy and Morgan Freeman as an elderly Southern aristocrat and her black chauffeur.

Bruce Beresford directing *Tender Mercies* (Universal)

It won four Oscars, including best actress and best picture.

In his recent films Beresford has tackled a wildly varied roster of subjects. *Her Alibi* (1990) was a slapstick adventure starring Tom Selleck as a mystery writer deriving inspiration from a relationship with a wrongfully accused young woman; *Mister Johnson* (1991) was based on a Joyce Cary novel about an English engineer in West Africa during the 1920s; *Black Robe* (1992) was a harrowing depiction of the grim realities awaiting French Jesuit missionaries among the Indian tribes of Canada; and *Paradise Road* (1997) told the fact-based story of the imprisonment and brutalization of female prisoners in a Japanese internment camp in the jungles of Sumatra during World War II.

Black Robe is a remarkable achievement and unlike anything else Beresford has directed. It chronicles the encounters in the early 17th century between French Jesuit missionaries and the

Huron, Algonquin, and Iroquois Indian tribes, resulting in privations and death for the former, and the spiritual and physical corruption of the latter. After surviving the hazards of the 1,500-mile trip from New France to Quebec, Father Laforgue (Lothaire Bluteau) finds himself a captive of the fierce Iroquois. No sooner does he escape than he comes across a Catholic mission manned by a dying priest. He learns that the Huron village has been ravaged by fever and the handful of survivors are threatening the mission. Laforgue takes over and mollifies the Indians, who dutifully submit to communion. A concluding title ironically notes that after accepting Christianity, the now-peaceful Hurons were decimated by neighboring tribes. Neither before nor since has Beresford (or anyone else, for that matter) made a picture with such grim and unrelenting realism. The surface textures are absolutely convincing. It was shot on location in Quebec on the banks of the Saguenay River, and near Tadoussac, one of the earliest settlements in North America. All the dialogue with the Indians is in authentic Cree and Mohawk dialects (the Huron language is now extinct). And the savagery of the Huron torture sequences is not for the faint-hearted viewer.

The work of few directors has been as unpredictable—and as uneven—as that of Bruce Beresford. One watches with curiosity, mixed with a certain wary speculation, for each new project.

Other Films *Side by Side* (1975); *The Club* (1980); *Puberty Blues* (1981); *The Fringe Dwellers* (1984); *Rich in Love* (1993); *Double Jeopardy* (1999).

Reference McFarlane, Brian, *Australian Cinema, 1970–1985* (London: Secker & Warburg, 1987).

—J.C.T.

Bergman, Ingmar (1918–) The great themes of this Swedish master are Big Issues of identity and society—birth, death, the psychology of relationships, dreams, legends and superstitions, frauds and miracles, and the breakdown of faith in modern society.

Ingmar Bergman was born on July 14, 1918, in Uppsala, Sweden, the son of a Lutheran pastor who was chaplain to the king in Stockholm. A sensitive child, he developed an early predilection for the performing arts, presenting shows in his own puppet theater and making short films of his own. At age 19, he rebelled against his parents' stringent discipline and left home determined to become a stage director. In 1944 he became director of the Helsingborg City Theatre, relocating later to Malmo, Gothenburg, and Stockholm, and indeed, stage work remained a major part of his artistic life, even after he became a celebrated filmmaker (he continued to direct at the Malmo Theater from 1953 to 1960 and at the Royal Dramatic Theater in Stockholm from 1960 to 1976). His productions of Strindberg, Ibsen, Anouilh, Chekhov, Moliere, and a number of operas have all been reflected in his choice of subjects and attitudes in his films. He once remarked that theatre "is like a loyal wife; film is the great adventure, the costly and demanding mistress."

Signing on with Svenskfilmindustrie as a screenwriter, he debuted with his script for Alf Sjöberg's film, *Torment* (1944), the story of an obsessive relationship between a student and a teacher. After making nine films, including *The Devil's Wanton* (1949), he found his voice with *Summer Interlude* (1951), an account of a doomed teenage love affair against the backdrop of a lyrical summer landscape. Actress Harriet Andersson, one of many performers whose career he would foster, first appeared in *Summer with Monika* (1953). A circus setting dominates the tawdry relationships in *The Naked Night* (1953).

Smiles of a Summer Night (1955) brought Bergman to international attention. Its story of awakening sensuality takes place in Sweden during the belle epoque. A potion with allegedly magical properties triggers an assortment of chance meetings, fervent declamations of love, betrayals, suicide attempts, and a duel of Russian roulette. Amusing, brittle, and bittersweet by turns, it is one of the few Bergman films that harks back directly to the sex comedies of his great Swedish predecessor, MAURITZ STILLER. "[It is] a joy for the moment," Bergman said, "a romantic story, playing with all the cliches of the comedy of errors—the old castle, the young lovers, the elopement."

The three films that followed consolidated his reputation, *The Seventh Seal* (1957), *Wild Strawberries* (1957), and the Oscar-winning *The Virgin Spring* (1960). In *The Seventh Seal,* set in medieval times, Max von Sydow portrays Antonius Block, a knight returned from a crusade to the Holy Land. A plague is ravaging Sweden and people are mortifying themselves in a mass panic. Block encounters the figure of Death, who has come to claim him. To forestall him, Block talks him into a game of chess, a battle of wits where life and death are the stakes. As a result, although Block loses the game, he does manage to save a family of itinerant jugglers, which symbolizes the survival of universal innocence and good. *Wild Strawberries* was intensely autobiographical, a drama about a man trying to resolve the emotional failures and estrangements of his life. Swedish film master Victor Sjöström portrayed Professor Isak Borg, who is on his way to receive an honorary degree in Stockholm. His journey is one of revelation into the sterility of Borg's relationships with his family. Time, reality, and fantasy commingle in a seamless flow as flashbacks and dreams intrude upon his waking hours. At the end, after the doctoral ceremony, Borg goes to sleep, finally at peace with himself and his past.

Bergman's "chamber trilogy" of *Through a Glass Darkly* (1961), *Winter Light* (1963), and *The Silence* (1963) burrows inward to the darker recesses of his characters, to a place where God and understanding are absent. *Persona* (1966), however, marked a turning point in Bergman's work. Metaphysics are abandoned in favor of a psychological study of the symbiotic relationship between a traumatized actress and her nurse. *Cries and Whispers* (1973) continues this examination of mutually lacerating female relationships.

Charges that Bergman's "Nordic gloom"—an early film of his was once described as a story that "moves in a cruel and voluptuous arc from birth to death"—was all encompassing are not entirely accurate. Several of his films ridicule those very pretensions. *The Magician* (1958) is a witty look at the boundaries separating stage illusion from genuine magic in the confrontation between a scientist and an itinerant charlatan. *The Devil's Eye* (1960) is subtitled "a rondo capriccioso with music by Scarlatti." Because Satan is afflicted by a sore eye—a condition that can be cured only by the despoiling of a virgin—he sends Don Juan to seduce the 20-year-old daughter of a pastor. But Satan's plans misfire when Don Juan falls genuinely in love with his intended victim. The stye is cured, however, when the girl's virginity is vanquished on her wedding night. *All These Women* (1964), his first color film, is set in the 1920s and gaily chronicles the affairs of a brilliant cello virtuoso.

Bergman's close-knit "family" of cast and crew unravelled in the 1970s as he lost his home base and was bedeviled with tax problems. He relocated to West Germany, where he was engaged as director at the Residenz Theater in Munich until 1982. The autobiographical *Fanny and Alexander* (1982) marked a return to form, although it is avowedly his last directed film.

All of Bergman's films, in essence, are preoccupied with some aspect of theatrical illusion. As biographer Peter Cowie writes, "The moment of truth is the moment when the mask is torn aside and the real face uncovered. Every Bergman film turns on this process. The mask is shown, examined, and then removed." Thus, the theater, for all its shabby illusions and pasteboard characters, can satisfy our deepest hunger and aspiration to move the commonplace toward the miraculous. It is a process that is like the dream of the juggler Jof, in *The Seventh Seal,* i.e., that his baby son Mikael will one day be a great juggler and perform an impossible trick—make a ball stand still in the air.

Nowhere in Bergman's film output is the interface of theater and film, and the issues of life and death, reality and illusion, experience and innocence, more lucidly and compactly examined than in *The Magic Flute,* his cinematic interpretation of Mozart's last opera. It was made for Swedish television in 1975, and was filmed on the same kind of simple wooden stage on which the opera had been born. Bergman initially wanted to shoot it inside the celebrated Drottningholm Palace, located in a royal park outside Stockholm, but the structure proved to be too fragile to accommodate the performers and crew, so it was reconstructed in the studios of the Swedish Film Institute as it was in Mozart's time. Resisting the temptation to "open out" its stage-bound allegory into a more cinematic realism, Bergman used his camera instead to "expose," even celebrate, the artifice of the crude stage machinery. In this, as in all his films, the great truth is that, like Pamina and Tamino, we are all marionettes dangling from strings plucked by inscrutable gods, surrounded by the illusions of painted backdrops and wind machines.

The film's formal strategy resembles LAURENCE OLIVIER's *Henry V* (1944). It is a perfect arch, beginning on a small stage surrounded by an audience—a typage of huge closeups of shining faces welling out of the darkness—with a curtain rising on a sparely appointed stage. Periodically we hear the creaking of the stage machinery and get glimpses of the backstage activities of the stagehands. After a series of widening dramatic and scenic arcs—in Act Two there is a more cinematic handling of the hallucinations and temptations visited upon the hapless lovers by Sarastro and the Queen—we return at the end to the stark simplicity of the proscenium frame as the Queen's dark forces are banished and love is restored. Close-ups of watchful eyes dominate the film—the gaze of Sarastro, the recurring eyes of the little girl in the audience, the enormous close-ups of the players as they gaze out as *us.* Like Sarastro and the Queen, we, too, are gods for whom these players strut and fret. Who could blame us if, at the end, we glance upward—to see who is up there watching *us.*

Arguably, no other film director has ever dominated a national cinema to the extent that Bergman has. And few have left behind a more personal record of the many demons he has fought throughout his life—disastrous relationships with women, breakdowns, and threats of madness and suicide. "Whether I make a comedy or a farce," he says, "a melodrama or a drama, every film—except for those films made to order—are taken from my private life." In his autobiography, *Images* (1994), he delivers an enlightening comment on the nature of faith and religion in his world: "As long as there was a God in my world, I couldn't even get close to my goals. My humility was not humble enough. My love remained nonetheless far less than the love of Christ or of the saints or even my own mother's love. And my piety was forever poisoned by grave doubts. Now that God is gone, I feel that *all this* is mine; *piety* toward life, *humility* before my meaningless fate and *love* for the other children who are afraid, who are ill, who are cruel."

Other Films *A Lesson in Love* (1954); *The Virgin Spring* (1960); *Hour of the Wolf* (1968); *Shame* (1968); *The Passion of Anna* (1969); *Scenes from a Marriage* (1973); *The Serpent's Egg* (1977); *Autumn Sonata* (1978); *From the Life of the Marionettes* (1980).

References Bergman, Ingmar, "My Three Powerfully Effective Commandments," *Film Comment* 6, no. 2 (Summer 1970): 9–12; Bergman, Ingmar, *Images: My Life in Film* (New York: Arcade, 1994); Cowie, Peter, *Ingmar Bergman: A Critical Biography* (New York: Scribner, 1982); McLean, Theodore, "Knocking on Heaven's Door," *American Film,* June 1983, pp. 55–61.

—J.C.T.

Bertolucci, Bernardo (1940–) Bernardo Bertolucci was born on March 16, 1940. Influenced by his father, the poet and film critic Attilio Bertolucci, he began writing poetry from a very early age and published it in journals before he reached the age of 12. Eight years later, while attending Rome University, Bertolucci won a poetry prize for his collection *In Search of Mystery*.

Like many formative talents, Bertolucci had shown an interest in cinema by making several nonprofessional 16-mm films. But when his father introduced him to PIER PAOLO PASOLINI (who was also a famous literary talent and critic) in 1961, Bertolucci dropped out of college to become assistant director on Pasolini's first film *Accatone!* Pasolini became impressed with Bertolucci's abilities, leading him to pass on to the young filmmaker the direction and screenwriting of his next project *La Commare Secca* (1962), based on Pasolini's own story. This early film revealed significant traces of the sophisticated visual style and complex narrative techniques Bertolucci would develop in his later films. Focusing on the murder

of a prostitute and the ensuing police investigation, the film amalgamated film noir, sophisticated flashback devices, and neorealism.

Bertolucci's next film, *Before the Revolution* (1964), was a visually accomplished adaptation of Stendahl's *The Charterhouse of Parma*. Indebted to French New Wave visual techniques, especially the early style of JEAN-LUC GODARD, *Before the Revolution* began the first exploration of elements Bertolucci would investigate in his later films, such as the relationship between politics and sexuality, freedom and conformity, and the individual's relationship to the contemporary forces of Freud and Marx. These last two elements were featured as competing influences in Bertolucci's films of the 1960s and 1970s. Although they became dormant in his later work, they are not entirely absent from

Bernardo Bertolucci on location during the filming of *The Last Emperor* (Columbia)

the spiritual dilemmas his protagonists face in the director's more recent films.

Like his mentor, Pasolini, Bertolucci chose to explore the humanistic aspect of personal relationships in his own particular manner. *Before the Revolution* was widely acclaimed in America and France, earning Bertolucci the MAX OPHULS prize in France. After working on a documentary series, contributing to one of the many cinematic compilations peculiar to the sixties, and collaborating on the screenplay of SERGIO LEONE's *Once Upon A Time in the West* (1967), Bertolucci decided to explore his fascination with Godard's political cinema by making an adaptation of Dostoyevsky's *The Double*. Retitled *Partner* (1968), the adaptation gave Bertolucci the opportunity to explore cinema in his own manner.

After directing *The Spider's Stratagem* (1970) for Italian television, Bertolucci delved further into his fascination with the connection between Freud's Oedipal trajectory and politics in *The Conformist* (1970). Shot in a beautifully colored surrealistic style with elaborate camera movements, the film represented his first collaboration with director of photography Vittorio Storaro, who would work on most of his subsequent films. Based on a novel by Alberto Moravia, *The Conformist* represented both Bertolucci's movement toward a more opulent Italian style represented by Luchino Visconti and another contribution to his cinematic philosophy regarding the medium as "the true poetic language."

The acclaim of *The Conformist* led to Bertolucci's most controversial film, *Last Tango in Paris* (1972). Featuring Marlon Brando, newcomer Maria Schneider, and Truffaut actor Jean-Pierre Leaud as a naive, satirical representation of the French New Wave, the film explored the violent conjunction of sexual energy and social constraints. Although these themes occurred in his earlier films, *Last Tango in Paris* developed them in an implosive manner resulting in alienation and death at the climax. As well as representing an older son's rage (Brando's performance is clearly reminiscent of a middle-aged Stanley Kowalski) against patriarchal institutions, the film also represents another Bertolucci movement away from his cinematic legacy, if we see Schneider representing the non-actor approach of Italian neorealism and Leaud as the now burnt-out legacy of the French New Wave. Storaro's cinematography and Gatto Barbieri's musical soundtrack also contributed to the film's stylistic intensity.

Bertolucci then gained the financial resources to make his cherished operatic, Marxist-Freudian epic, *1900* (1976). Shown in two three-hour parts in Europe but edited to three hours for American distribution, *1900* employed American and European stars such as Robert De Niro, Gerard Depardieu, Donald Sutherland, Alida Valli and Stephania Sandrelli (both of whom had worked with Bertolucci before), and Burt Lancaster in a project that also represented Bertolucci's goals of synthesizing American and European cinematic styles as well as exploring historical issues against the framework of the then-prevailing contemporary discourses of Marx and Freud. This ambitious work explored many of Bertolucci's key themes, such as the relationship of politics and sexuality, which returned to a state of curious stasis between two opposing political and sexual forces after the Italian partisan victory of 1945. On the other hand, the film was strongly emblematic of the post-1968 stagnation affecting once-dominant historical and political forces.

After finishing this ambitious epic work, Bertolucci directed *La Luna* in 1979. Starring Jill Clayburgh, the film was an intimate chamber drama focusing upon an American opera singer's relationship to her young son and their eventual reunion with his father (Tomas Milian). The film heralded Bertolucci's movement toward exploring a more intimate world of personal relationships affected by the conflicting worlds of different cultures. After directing *The Tragedy of A Ridiculous Man* (1981), Bertolucci returned to a wider historical canvas by exploring the evolution of a human subject moving from "darkness to light" and continued by depicting the transformation from "a dragon to a butterfly" in *The Last Emperor* (1987), the first film ever shot in Beijing's Forbidden City. Bertolucci then adapted Paul Bowles's novel *The Sheltering Sky* (1990), with John Malkovich and Debra Winger, a box-office failure followed by *Little Buddha* (1994). Emphasizing the spiritual dimensions of human existence linking both East and West, the film contained an outstanding painterly style of camerawork by Vittorio Storaro, especially in the scenes of Siddhartha's transformation. In 1998, Bertolucci decided to return to his low-budget roots with *Besieged,* a subtle chamber drama dealing with the romantic interaction between the worlds of the West (David Thewlis) and Africa (Thandie Newton).

References Bertolucci, Bernardo, *Bertolucci by Bertolucci* (London: Plexus, 1987); Kolker, Robert Phillip, *Bernardo Bertolucci* (Oxford: Oxford University Press, 1985).

—T.W.

Branagh, Kenneth (1960–)

Branagh, Kenneth (1960–) Kenneth Charles Branagh was born on December 10, 1960, in Belfast, Northern Ireland, the son of Francis Harper Branagh and William Branagh, who were married in 1954 at St. Anne's Cathedral, Belfast. His father, a joiner by trade, was forced to find work in England in 1967, visiting his family in Belfast every third Friday for three years, until the lot of them moved from Northern Ireland to Reading. Kenneth became interested in school dramatic productions and eventually joined the Progress Youth Theatre. Eventually, he auditioned for the Central School of Speech and Drama and the Royal Academy of Dramatic Art in 1979 and was offered a place at the latter, where he did well, eventually earning the Bancroft Gold Medal.

Leaving RADA in 1982, he made his professional West End debut in Julian Mitchell's *Another Country,* earning two awards as most promising newcomer of 1982. In 1984 he joined the Royal Shakespeare Company and played the lead role in *Henry V.* In 1985 he wrote and directed *Tell Me Honestly,* produced at the Donmar Warehouse in London. In 1986 he directed and starred in the Lyric Theatre, Hammersmith, production of *Romeo and Juliet.* In 1987 he founded the Renaissance Theatre Company with fellow actor David Parfitt and wrote and starred in *Public Enemy,* about a Jimmy Cagney impersonator who imagines himself taking over Belfast as a Chicago-style gangster, produced during the company's first season. In later productions he played the title role of *Hamlet,* directed by Derek Jacobi, and starred with Emma Thompson in a West End production of John Osborne's *Look Back in Anger,* directed by Judi Dench.

Branagh was therefore already a celebrated actor when he directed and starred in the film version of *Henry V* in 1988, which earned him Academy Award nominations for best actor and best director and the Evening Standard Award for best film of 1989. As King Henry he wooed Emma Thompson, a gifted comedienne he also married, until they broke up in 1994. Branagh was soon invited to Hollywood to direct *Dead Again,* in which he also starred in a dual role with Thompson. This was followed by *Peter's Friends* in 1992 and *Much Ado About Nothing,* screened in competition at the 1993 Cannes Film Festival, which was a popular hit as well as a critical success. He directed and starred in *Mary Shelley's Frankenstein* in 1994, a financial success that earned over $100 million worldwide.

The next year he wrote and directed *A Midwinter's Tale,* an amusing comedy about a troupe of actors trying to mount a production of *Hamlet* in a dilapidated church in rural England. The film, which opened the 1996 Sundance Film Festival, was followed by his spectacular four-hour production of *Hamlet,* which had its world premiere on January 21, 1997, at Waterfront Hall in Branagh's native Belfast. It was a remarkable screen adaptation because Branagh was determined to retain the whole combined Folio and Quarto versions of the text, a feat never before attempted. His next Shakespeare film, *Love's Labours Lost* (2000), did not fare as well and was panned by reviewers who did not approve of his updating the play as a postmodern musical that incorporated the music of Cole Porter, Irving Berlin, Jerome Kern, and others.

Regardless of this temporary setback, Branagh has surely become the successor of Laurence Olivier in his ambition to film Shakespeare's plays, but he has also established himself as a viable Hollywood talent, and has had remarkable successes as actor, director, writer, and playwright, all before the age of 40.

Other Film   *The Flight of the Navigator* (1999).

References   Branagh, Kenneth, *Beginning* (London: Chatto & Windus, 1989); Shuttleworth, Ian, *Ken & Em: A Biography of Kenneth Branagh and Emma Thompson* (New York: St. Martin's Press, 1994).

—J.M.W.

Bresson, Robert (1907–1999)   Robert Bresson, one of France's most distinguished filmmakers, has been both praised and condemned for the apparent austerity of his subject matter and style, which makes few concessions to commercial cinema and popular tastes. Although all of his mature works—he directed only 13 films—were made within the parameters of the New Wave and Second Wave of filmmaking in France, he stands apart from his noisier and more radically expressive brethren. He was always his own man, as it were, on a pilgrimage to create a body of work as insistently personalized as any in the history of cinema.

He was born on September 25, 1907, in the mountainous Auvergne region of France. When he was eight years old his family moved to Paris, where in his teen years he studied to be a painter at the Lycé Lakanal in Sceaux. He worked in the 1930s as a painter and apprentice filmmaker. His first film, a short, *Les Affaires publiques* (1934), was presumed lost until it resurfaced in 1989. It is unlike anything he subsequently made, reports critic Jonathan Rosenbaum in his assessment of the film, a *comique fou* revealing a surreal series of scenes in a slapstick style reminiscent of the Marx Brothers.

After an incarceration by the Germans as a prisoner of war between June 1940 and April 1941, he was released and returned to occupied France in 1943, where he made his feature film debut with *Les Anges du péché* (*Angels of the Streets*). Winner of the Grand Prix du Cinéma Français, it is an astonishing film displaying Bresson's central thematic concerns—the search for spiritual grace and the transformative powers of love. The story involves the strange relationship between Anne-Marie, a novice about to take holy orders and Thérèse, a hardened murderess seeking shelter in Anne-Marie's convent. Near death and too weak to speak as a result of her sacrifices to save Thérèse's soul, Anne-Marie expires as Thérèse speaks her vows for her. Compared to the spareness of Bresson's later work, *Les Anges du péché* has a more flamboyant style, including a "background" musical score, chiaroscuro lighting, and the use of professional actors. Nonetheless, it is a striking debut film and one fully prophetic of the mature style to come.

From the mid-1940s on, Bresson made a succession of noteworthy films, all of which have become acknowledged classics in world cinema: *Les Dames du Bois de Boulogne* (*The Ladies of the Bois de Boulogne* [1945]) depicts the struggle of a young man to find spiritual love with a prostitute; *Le Journal d'un curé de campagne* (*Diary of a Country Priest* [1951]) is based on Georges Bernanos's novel about a young priest who achieves grace through a process of sacrifice and self-starvation; *Un condamné à mort s'est échappé* (*A Man Escaped* [1956]) documents a true story of a prison break; *Pickpocket* (1959) depicts a young thief's willful attempts to be caught and imprisoned; *Procés de Jeanne d'Arc* (*The Trial of Joan of Arc* [1962]) uses transcripts of Joan's trial to chronicle her last days; *Au hasard Balthazar* (1966) is a Christian parable about a series of encounters between a donkey and situations representing the deadly sins of humanity; *Mouchette* (1967) is based on Bernanos's novel about the isolation and hardships endured by a 14-year-old servant girl; *Une femme douce* (*A Gentle Creature* [1969]) derives from a Dostoevsky story about a young woman's fatal inability to be a "faithful wife"; *Quatre nuits d'un rêveur* (*Four Nights of a Dreamer* [1971]), is adapted from another Dostoevsky story, "White Nights," about a young man's doomed love for a suicidal woman; and *Lancelot du Lac* (1974) is an interpretation of the Grail myth. His last two films, *Le Diable, probablement* (*The Devil, Probably* [1977]), and *L'Argent* (*Money* [1982]) mark a shift from dramas of individual regeneration and redemption to chronicles of, in the words of commentator Kent Jones, "the feelings of defeat and lethargy in the young people around him." They are like nothing else in modern cinema, continues Jones, "as horrifying as they are lucid, as sure of the inherent beauty of the world as they are insistent on the recognition of its manmade horror."

Bresson may be regarded as one of the cinema's true auteurs. His 13 films display a subject and style that are instantly and uniquely his own. As critic Molly Haskell writes, "Bresson has virtually declared himself on a holy mission to turn back the clock, wrest movies from layers of artifice and convention, free our eyes and ears from the glaze of habit and allow us to see and hear with newborn curiosity." His basic theme, says Susan Sontag, is "the meaning of confinement and liberty," wherein the disparity between the spiritual and the immanent is ongoing, and the sense of a release is impending. States of austerity and transcendence—problematic terms that are frequently applied to his work—are approached, not just by the characters in his films, but in the narrative modes of the films themselves.

On the face of it, approaching transcendence on film might seem an impossibility, a "laughable presumption," in Carl Jung's words. Man, avers Jung, can only say something about the "knowable" but nothing about the "unknowable" ("of the latter, nothing can be determined"). Yet, says Bresson, "I would like in my films to be able to render perceptible to an audience a feeling of a man's soul and also the presence of something superior to man which can be called God."

Bresson's method has been examined in detail in the past by such distinguished commentators as Raymond Durgnat, Charles Barr, André Bazin, and Paul Schrader (Schrader's book, *Transcendental Style in Film,* presents a particularly lucid and accessible discussion of four films from Bresson's middle period) and most recently in two symposia of commentators in the May–June 1999 and July–August issues of *Film Comment.* Paradoxically, Bresson begins with the knowable, with the everyday. He has precedents in Byzantine and Chinese art, where a fanatical attention to minute detail renders the surfaces of reality so precisely—without resorting to signifying or connotative suggestions—that a sense of the supernatural is achieved (rather like the hyper-clarity of some surrealistic paintings). Whenever possible he films on location—at Fort Montluc for *A Man Escaped,* at the Gare de Lyon for *Pickpocket.* He concentrates on and celebrates the trivial, the small sounds, a creaking door, a chirping bird, static views, blank faces. "He works painstakingly so that his films appear to register and acknowledge all things equally," declares Kent Jones, "—a bouquet of daisies thrown on an asphalt road becomes just as moving as the face of a man behind bars at long last acknowledging his love for the woman on the other side." About the rigorous depiction of the prisoner's cell in *A Man Escaped,* for example, Bresson said, "I was hoping to make a film about objects which would at the same time have a soul. That is to say, to reach the latter through the former." He ruthlessly strips action of its significance and regards a scene in terms of its fewest possibilities. He achieves this in several ways:

1. *Plot.* Bresson dislikes plot. He wants to suppress it. For him, plot establishes a too simple and facile relationship between the viewer and the event. He wants the viewer to have no intercourse with the story. The real drama is an internal one, not an external machination. "Dramatic stories should be thrown out," he has said. "They have nothing whatsoever to do with cinema."

2. *Acting.* Just as the plot is too simple a reduction of life, so does the professional actor traditionally simplify too much his own or his "character's" complexities. He modifies his character's "unfathomable complexities into relatively simple, demonstrable characteristics," resulting in "too simple an image of a human being, and therefore a false image." Rather, Bresson wants his actors—usually nonprofessionals—to convey a reality that is not limited to any one character. He forces the actor to sublimate his personality and to "act" in an automatic matter. Bresson refuses to give actors interpretive advice on the set; rather, he gives only precise, physical instructions—what angle to hold the head, when and how far to turn the wrist, etc. André Bazin argues that this hieratic tempo of acting, the slow gestures, the "obstinate recurrence of certain behavioral patterns," the dreamlike slow motion confirms that "nothing purely accidental" could ever happen to these people, that each is inexorably committed to his or her own way of life.

3. *Camerawork.* Camera movements and vantage points, particularly the stylization of the track, the high angle, the pan, the close-up, inevitably convey attitudes toward the character and story. Bresson wishes to avoid this. He restricts himself to the relatively shallow depth-of-field of the 50-mm lens and one basic vantage point (usually a medium shot from chest level). He calls the results a "flat" image: "If you take a steam iron to your image," he explains, "flattening it out . . . and you put that image next to an image of the same kind, all of a sudden that image may have a violent effect on another one and both take on another appearance."

4. *Editing.* Bresson prefers the straight, unostentatious cut. Scenes are usually cut short, the shots merely set end to end.

5. *Soundtrack.* Bresson uses asynchronous sound sometimes, but not for editorial purposes. Sound can only reinforce the cold reality. His soundtracks consist mostly of natural sounds, "close-up" sounds that help confirm for us a great concern for the minutiae of life. He avoids using "background" music, reserving bursts of music only for the climactic moments of his films. When the prisoner in *A Man Escaped* breaks free, when Joan is burned, the pickpocket imprisoned, the priest dies, then music on the soundtrack assists in this sense of transformation. At these points, the contrast between the elegantly profound music of Mozart and Monteverdi presents an almost unbearable contrast with the blunt coldness of the images.

6. *Doubling.* Through the use of repeated action and pleonastic dialogue, Bresson makes single events happen several times in different ways. The audiovisual redundancy of Michel's diary entries in *Pickpocket* is an example. Usually an interior narration exactly duplicates the action visible on the screen. Narration does not give the viewer any new information, but only reiterates and emphasizes what he already knows.

7. *Disjunction.* Bresson emphasizes the disparity between characters and environment. Examples include the priest's alienation from his surroundings in *Diary,* the self-incriminating testimony of Joan of Arc, and the inexorable thievery of the eponymous pickpocket. These characters do things quite at odds with their surroundings. The priest renounces the world at the cost of his life; Joan's testimony leads to her immolation at the stake; and the thief steals not through the need for money, but because he must follow the Will to Pickpocket. This disparity grows as the characters behave as if in the grip of something apart from the physical world, an "Other," as he calls it. Nothing on earth can placate their inner passion, says Schrader, "because their passion does not come from earth. . . . They do not respond to their environment, but instead to that sense of the Other which seems much more immediate."

8. *The metaphor of confinement.* The prison cell is the dominant metaphor of Bresson's films, most

obviously in *A Condemned Man,* but it needs to be understood in two ways. His characters are both escaping from a prison of one sort and surrendering to a prison of another. The human body is usually regarded as the most confining prison of all. Suicide frequently occurs in his films. (Indeed, Bresson "killed off" his actors, in the sense that he refused to use an actor in more than one film.)

9. *The human face.* If the prison cell is the dominant metaphor, then the human face is the dominating sign, both iconic and indexical. Bresson used the interrogations of Joan of Arc, not to provide historical information, but, as he explains, "to provoke on Joan's face her profound impressions, to imprint on the film the movements of her soul." Critic André Bazin applauds this technique: "Naturally Bresson, like [CARL THEODOR] DREYER, is only concerned with the countenance as flesh, which, when not involved in playing a role, is a man's true imprint, the most visible mark of his soul. It is then that the countenance takes on the dignity of a sign. He would have us be concerned here not with the psychology but with the physiology of existence."

As a result of the foregoing, Bresson is not so much making the viewer see everyday life in a certain way, but rather preventing him from seeing it in the manner to which he has become accustomed. The everyday is something intractable, and it will not allow the viewer to apply his or her natural interpretive devices. As Paul Schrader says, in Bresson's films "the viewer becomes aware that his feelings are being spurned; he is not called upon, as in most films, to make either intellectual or emotional judgments on what he sees. His feelings have neither place nor purpose in the scheme of the everyday."

In all of Bresson's films there is a final moment, a decisive action that demands commitment from the viewer. Bresson calls this the moment of "transformation." The viewer must, in that moment, face the dilemma of the protagonist, confront "an explicably spiritual act within a cold environment, an act which now requests his participation and approval. Irony can no longer postpone his decision. It is a 'miracle' which must be accepted or rejected."

To be sure, these final moments do not resolve the disparity of man and environment. Rather, a stasis is achieved, a paradox wherein the spiritual coexists with the physical in a way that no earthly logic can explain. Precedents for this condition may be found in the portrait iconography of Byzantine art—especially the frontal, isolated views of saints. In stasis, says Schrader, "The viewer is able to cross interpret between what seemed to be contradictions: he can read deep emotion into the inexpressive faces and cold environment, and he can read factuality into the inexplicable spiritual actions." However, his characters must remain ultimately inexplicable. They never reveal anything but their mystery—like God.

Characteristically, Bresson always refused to indulge in such metaphysical speculation about his films. Indeed, in a number of interviews he resisted being labeled as a "transcendental" filmmaker. He insisted simply that his films are not *spiritual* experiences so much as *emotional* ones. In a 1962 interview, he tersely noted what he expects viewers to bring to his films: "Not their brains but their capacity for feeling."

Robert Bresson died on December 22, 1999.

References *The Films of Robert Bresson* [essays by Amédée Ayfre, Charles Barr, André Bazin, Raymond Durgnat, Phil Hardy, Daniel Millar, and Leo Murray] (New York: Praeger Books, 1969); Cameron, Ian, "Robert Bresson," in *Interviews with Film Directors,* ed. Andrew Sarris (New York: Avon Books, 1967); Schrader, Paul, *Transcendental Style in Film* (University of California Press, 1972). Two issues of *Film Comment* have been devoted to symposia on Bresson and his work: 35, no. 3 (May/June 1999): 36–62; 35, no. 4 (July/August 1999): 36–54.

—J.C.T.

Buñuel, Luis (1900–1983) Luis Buñuel was the most distinctive Spanish filmmaker of the 20th century, even though, paradoxically, he made most of his best-known films while living in self-imposed exile from his native land, in Mexico and in France. A master of surreal satire who was as charming as he was controversial, Buñuel was also an astute social critic and documentarian. His unique, frequently playful tone gave his films an additional aura of baffling mystery.

Luis Buñuel was born on February 22, 1900, in Calanda, Spain. He was educated from an early age in Jesuit schools, and this strict, dogmatic religious training profoundly influenced his life and art. Though Buñuel claimed that "at sixteen I lost my religious belief" and became a self-proclaimed atheist, religious images would always dominate his films, although portrayed in satiric and surreal ways. According to Buñuel, what his Jesuit education taught him was "a profound eroticism, at first sublimated in a great religious faith, and in permanent consciousness of death." Both eroticism and the ubiquity of death permeate many aspects of his films. A childhood fascination with music, theatre, and animals would also later appear in his films.

Buñuel was educated at the University of Madrid and after graduation went to Paris in 1925. Buñuel began to associate with surrealist writers and artists in Paris who would influence his later work. Their ideas helped to shape Buñuel's awareness of the cinema and its potential and suggested how he might incorporate dreams and fantasy to portray the ills of society. His first feature, *Un chien andalou* (1929), done in collaboration with the artist Salvador Dalí, became a touchstone of surrealist cinema. His famous image of an eyeball being sliced by a razor is recognized as quintessentially surreal, an "eye-opener" that continues to shock and discomfit audiences. Although the film has been scrutinized—to no avail—by puzzled critics in search of meaning, its haunting images are not easily forgotten. Asked to explain this enigmatic film, Buñuel simply called it

"an incitement to murder." *L'Âge d'or* (1930), Buñuel's next surreal film, blasphemously fused religion with eroticism and was even more controversial. Its release provoked widespread riots and condemnation, which pleased Buñuel because, he explained, the point was *not* to like it.

Las Hurdes (*Land Without Bread* [1932]), an ironic travelogue on the surface, made a political statement concerning a poverty-stricken region of Spain that showed such devastating and desolate people, the Spanish government was eventually forced to establish aid programs. The film was eventually banned by Franco's government. Buñuel's dreamlike, surreal images in this film were all the more disturbing for being reality-based. Critic Anthony Lane was impressed by Buñuel's "tough link between a refined artistic movement and the rawness of political protest."

After *Land Without Bread,* Buñuel would not direct another film for 15 years. During this time, Buñuel worked in the United States in Hollywood as a dubber for Spanish films, and later at the Museum of Modern Art as a film archivist and editor. It was remarkable that a director who made such an auspicious and controversial film debut with *Un chien andalou* could not direct for so many years, but the Second World War disrupted many film careers. Nonetheless, Buñuel seemed content working in the United States during this period, but he eventually wanted and perhaps needed to make more films.

Consequently, Buñuel settled in Mexico, which began a second fertile period in his enigmatic and illustrious creative career. Mexico City would become Buñuel's adopted home city. *Los olvidados* (1950) brought Buñuel nearly as much attention as his earlier trio of films. The film is an ostensible portrait of Mexico City's lost children—delinquents living on the streets and in the slums. Buñuel accurately depicts the nightmarish world of violence and degradation that plagues the young victims of Mexico's bourgeois capitalist system. The film garnered international attention from critics. Buñuel then filmed surreal adaptations of the novels *Robinson Crusoe* (1952) and *Wuthering Heights* (1953), followed by *El* (1952), also known as *This Strange Passion,* Buñuel's savage attack on the church and the bourgeois class.

Eventually, Buñuel returned to Spain and made *Viridiana* (1961), another antireligious, surrealist parable that Buñuel managed to get by the censors and went on to win the Palme d'Or at the Cannes Film Festival. Viridiana, a novitiate nun, is tricked into marriage and becomes the heiress of a large estate after the uncle who claims to have defiled her dies. Driven by religious motivation, she invites a group of thieves and beggars into her country estate, which they take over. The film became famous for its visual parody of Da Vinci's *Last Supper,* with drunkards and beggars arranged around the table in the positions of Christ and his disciples. As one critic noted, Buñuel was not mocking Christ himself but the "manner in which Christ's image is worshipped." The film was so powerful in its satiric depiction of religion that the Vatican denounced it as "an insult to Christianity." Although the Spanish government tried to destroy the film, it nevertheless was shown at Cannes, where it won the Palme d'Or.

The Exterminating Angel (*El angel exterminador* [1962]) represents a sort of descent into hell and has been compared to Jean-Paul Sartre's play about metaphysical alienation, *No Exit.* In both, the characters are isolated, cut off from the world at large, trapped in a salon where, over time, they are forced to reveal themselves. But the alienation of Buñuel's film is different in that his characters are the helpless victims of a social and religious system. Buñuel's son, Juan, described this as "essentially a comic film, but with a very strong corrosive interior." He claimed there were no "symbolic interpretations" at issue, though the design seems most certainly allegorical.

The Diary of a Chambermaid (Le Journal d'une femme de chambre [1964]) has been considered Buñuel's most political film. According to David Cook, "Buñuel's equation of fascism, decadence,

and sexual perversion is perfectly made." The film was shot in France, a country that embraced Buñuel until the end of his career, where he would make his final—often considered his best—films. *Belle de Jour* (1967), for example, a tale of erotic obsession secured Buñuel's reputation as provocateur. In the film, a bored housewife, played by Catherine Deneuve, decides to work afternoons in a brothel. Reality and fantasy mesh as the film progresses until it is not easy to distinguish one from the other. Critic Andrew Sarris called the film Buñuel's "most surrealistic."

In *The Milky Way* (*La Voie lactée* [1969]) Buñuel presented a symbolic, surreal history of the Roman Catholic Church, told in an episodic narrative about two tramps traveling from Paris to Spain. This attack on religion was only moderately received by critics. Buñuel described the film as "a journey through fanaticism, where each person obstinately clings to his own particle of truth." Among other themes of sex, food, and nature, the film also presents a relaxed, almost giddy portrait of Jesus Christ. This film might be considered a companion piece to *Simón del desierto (Simon of the Desert)* (1965), a 42-minute parable concerning a saintly medieval anchorite who is tempted by the devil and finally loses his faith when the devil transports him into the hopelessly hedonistic future of the 20th century.

Tristana (1970), set in Spain, tells the story of a virginal girl seduced by her guardian, whom she eventually murders by neglecting to call a doctor after he suffers a heart attack, even though he has nursed her through an illness that brought about the amputation of one of her legs. Joan Mellen interprets the film as a political allegory, with Tristana representing "the generation to be maimed by the [Spanish] Civil War."

The Discreet Charm of the Bourgeoisie (1973), Buñuel's most popular film, satirizes the trivialities of the privileged class; it won an Oscar for best foreign film and was also a critical favorite. It is structured as an extended dream, wherein six friends who try to have an elegant, sophisticated dinner party are continuously interrupted before they can begin. David Cook sees the film as "one long pattern of interrupted episodes, and in this sense Buñuel has created a delightful parody of the mechanisms of narrative cinema." The film is as funny as it is serious about the follies of the privileged class, whose appetites are not entirely dulled by immediate threats of random assassins.

The Phantom of Liberty (*Le Fantôme de la liberté* [1974]) has no discernible trace of a clear narrative plot, or even a fixed set of characters, and has thus been called Buñuel's most surreal film since *Un chien andalou*. Vincent Canby claimed "there is no single correct way to read" the film. Joan Mellen identifies one of the film's major points: "The betrayal of revolutions and the growth of 'revolutionary' societies more repressive than those they replaced have made a mockery of revolution as a quest for liberty." David Cook describes the film as "an authentically surrealist essay on the political violence, necrophilia, and sadism that underlie bourgeois cultural conventions and make an elusive phantom of personal freedom." Through its combination of flashback, dream sequence, and allusion, *The Phantom of Liberty* is a challenging film that breaks the usual conventions of narrative logic and demands repeated viewings to parse out its multiple meanings.

Buñuel's final film, *That Obscure Object of Desire* (1977), is an ironic parable about a young girl who dupes a middle-aged Frenchman out of his money and even his identity. Buñuel cast two actresses with clearly different physical appearances as the lead—the "object" of the title—thus adding to the irony of the film. The film ends with a loud explosion, prompting critic Lane to suggest "Buñuel was back where he had begun," a reference to the immediacy and shock—the explosion—of his first feature, *Un chien andalou*. This final film is a culmination of the themes that have surfaced in many Buñuel films: "In addition to the theme of the impossibility of ever truly possessing a woman's body," Buñuel noted, "the film insists upon maintaining that climate of insecurity and imminent disaster—an atmosphere we all recognize, because it is our own."

Luis Buñuel died in his adopted home of Mexico City in 1983. Throughout his long and distinguished career, Buñuel managed to create a body of work that makes him the definitive auteur and, in the words of David Cook, "the most experimental and anarchistic filmmaker in the history of narrative cinema."

Other Films *Gran Casino* (1947); *El gran calavera* (1949); *Susana* (1951); *La hija del engaño* (1951); *Una mujer sin amor* (1951); *Subida al cielo* (1951); *El bruto* (1952); *La ilusión viaja en tranvía* (1953); *Cumbres borrascosas* (1953); *El río y la muerte* (1954); *Cela s'appelle l'aurore* (1955); *Ensayo de un crimen / The Criminal Life of Archibald de la Cruz* (1955); *La Mort en ce jardin* (1956); *Nazarín* (1958).

References Buñuel, Luis, *My Last Sigh* (New York: Knopf, 1983); Cook, David, *A History of Narrative Film* (New York: Norton, 1996); Lane, Anthony, "In Your Dreams," *New Yorker* (Dec. 18, 2000); Mellen, Joan, ed., *The World of Luis Buñuel: Essays in Criticism* (New York: Oxford University Press, 1978).

—W.V. and J.M.W.

Capra, Frank (1897–1991) A Sicilian immigrant whose tributes to and critiques of the American way of life established him as one of cinema's most influential directors, Frank Capra was born on May 18, 1897, in Palermo, Sicily, to a peasant family. With his parents and three of his six siblings, he came to Los Angeles, California, when he was six years old. Often experiencing the widespread prejudice toward Italians in Anglo-dominated America, Capra would always be conscious of his status as an immigrant and "outsider," a feeling reflected in much of his work. In California, Capra's father found work as a fruit picker while his mother and siblings also held various jobs to support the family. Frank himself sold newspapers on the streets, "stuffed" papers at the *Los Angeles Times,* and played the guitar in a downtown brothel to help pay for his education at Manual Arts High School. Burning with youthful ambition, he later toiled in a steel plant to earn enough to enter the California Institute of Technology in 1916, where his interest in the sciences shifted to literature. Capra was building a distinguished academic record when his father, having just bought a lemon grove with his savings, died in a farm accident, a tragedy that would resonate in several of the director's future films. With his family now in a precarious financial situation, Capra was loaned a tuition fee by Caltech officials to complete his education. After graduating in 1918 with a degree in chemical engineering and after completing a short hitch in the army during the closing days of World War I, Capra began a three-year period of drifting. He performed manual labor, sold books and stocks, worked as a poker player, and had his first jobs in the film industry in 1919–20 as an extra in Hollywood.

His permanent involvement in motion pictures began in San Francisco in 1921 when he was hired by a local producer to direct a one-reel adaptation of a Rudyard Kipling poem, *Fultah Fisher's Boarding House.* For the next two years, Capra worked as an assistant at a San Francisco film lab and the editor of the locally produced two-reel Center Comedies. In the fall of 1923, Capra, newly married to actress Helen Howell, moved to Hollywood where he worked briefly for the Hal Roach studio as a writer before being hired by Mack Sennett. There, he became part of a writing team collaborating on a series of two-reel comedies featuring Harry Langdon. Langdon soon became Sennett's biggest star and in the fall of 1925, the comedian left the studio to start his own company, taking Capra with him. After assisting Langdon and director Harry Edwards on their first feature, *Tramp, Tramp, Tramp* (1926), Capra directed Langdon in *The Strong Man,* a major critical and popular success upon its release in 1926. Capra's touch was already apparent in the comic story of a Belgian war veteran, a wide-eyed innocent who goes to America in search of a girl, his pen pal during the war, and ends up defeating a corrupt gang of bootleggers that have taken over her small town. Capra's immigrant background clearly found expression in his feature debut, while Langdon's encounter with city slickers and his battle with the forces of corruption foreshadow similar situations in subsequent Capra films.

The production history of *Long Pants* (1927), the second film in which Capra directed Langdon, was much more troubled. Beset with problems in his marriage and creative differences with Langdon on the set, Capra was fired by the star after the completion of the film. Capra next went to New York to direct Claudette Colbert in her film debut, *For the Love of Mike* (1927). But the film proved such a flop that Capra briefly returned to his writing job for Sennett before being hired as a director by producer Harry Cohn for his up-and-coming studio, Columbia.

With the release of his first features for the studio in 1928, Capra soon became its preeminent director. The success of *Submarine* (1928), a large-scale action adventure film about navy fliers, inspired two more epics, *Flight* (1929), depicting the actions of Marines in Nicaragua, and *Dirigible* (1931), the story of an expedition to the South Pole. Columbia, however, was still ranked as a Poverty Row company, so most of Capra's films were made quickly, with smaller budgets. Yet it was in these more modest pictures that he began to express his distinctive personal vision. His third Columbia film, *The Matinee Idol* (1928), starring Bessie Love as the manager of a traveling stage troupe, reveals Capra's appreciation for strong women characters as well as his ability to combine hilarious comedy with poignant drama. When the

heroine acts in a hammy Civil War melodrama her father wrote, the sophisticated New York audience bursts into laughter, convulsed by its amateurishness. Her father flees in humiliation while she berates the audience, reminding them that it is not a comedy. This situation of small-town folk being derided by urban pseudo-sophisticates would recur in later Capra works like *Mr. Deeds Goes to Town* and *Mr. Smith Goes to Washington.* Capra's consuming interest in the newspaper world, reflecting his early experiences working at the *Los Angeles Times,* is first evident in his final Columbia silent, *The Power of the Press* (1929), about a reporter (Douglas Fairbanks, Jr.) who discovers that a criminal gang is guilty of the murder for which his fiancee (Jobyna Ralston) has been unfairly accused.

Capra's first experiment with sound, *The Younger Generation* (1929), shifts between silent and talking sequences to depict the experiences of a Jewish immigrant family in New York. The film is a powerful indictment of materialism, relating how a young, upwardly mobile Jew (played by Ricardo Cortez), in his quest for money and status, rejects his own Lower East Side family as obstacles to his social advancement. Too late he discovers the value of human relationships. By then, his father has died and his family has abandoned him. All he has left as the film ends is his lavish but empty and cold mansion.

Capra eagerly met the challenge of sound and was in the forefront of those seeking to liberate early talkies from the confines of the then-prevalent "canned photoplays." A sterling example of his fluid technique in his first film of the '30s, *Ladies of Leisure* (1930), is a scene in an apartment intercutting between the working-class heroine (Barbara Stanwyck) and the well-to-do artist (Ralph Graves) painting her portrait. There is no music or dialogue, just the sound of rain pouring down, an effect that intensifies the eroticism of the scene. Capra's sensitivity in directing players is apparent in Barbara Stanwyck's remarkable performance, a role that made her a major star in only her fourth film and inaugurated her fruitful collaboration with Capra. *Ladies of Leisure* is yet another example of the director's social critique of the upper classes, with the artist rebelling against his father's snobbish values by falling in love with Stanwyck. Capra's scorn for the artificial is underscored when the hero insists that the girl remove her makeup so she can appear more natural when modeling for the painting.

Capra became well known for his close association with the screenwriters working on his films, especially Robert Riskin, a New York playwright brought out to Hollywood by Columbia in 1931. While the director had been developing his personal vision on film since his debut in 1926, Riskin's long partnership with Capra proved essential to the filmmaker's career. Having the theatrical experience Capra lacked, Riskin effectively used his ability to draw character on paper. This, together with his flair for witty dialogue, including his uncanny ear for the rhythms of contemporary speech, helped Capra realize a remarkable series of films. Some critics contend that Riskin was Capra's conscience or the source of his vision. While Capra undoubtedly deepened his perspective when exchanging ideas with Riskin, who had a strong, articulate social conscience of his own, the Capraesque social vision was apparent in the very first films that the director made. Also, to assert as some critics have that Capra did not acknowledge the screenwriter's contributions belies the facts. Capra made many statements over the years, including in his autobiography, expressing his admiration for and gratitude to Riskin. At the same time, Capra believed strongly that the director was the auteur of the picture, what he called the "one man, one film" concept. Riskin and other Capra screenwriters collaborated with the director on the scripts from their inception. It was usually Capra who selected the story he wanted to adapt to the screen. During the course of scripting, he was constantly in contact with the writer, often adding or rewriting scenes himself. So from the beginning to the final editing that the director supervised, the films were ultimately Capra's creations and bore his personal stylistic imprint.

Frank Capra (Author's collection)

Riskin first collaborated with Capra by writing dialogue for the 1931 comedy *Platinum Blonde.* A delightful social comedy featuring an engaging cast headed by Robert Williams, Jean Harlow, and Loretta Young, the film concerns a newspaper reporter (Williams) who, while working on a story, meets and falls in love with a beautiful rich girl (Harlow). But after they are married, his easy-going, natural manner fails to adjust to the artificiality of her wealthy family's lifestyle. In the end, he returns to his roots by moving into an ordinary apartment where he begins working on a play with the help of his true love, fellow reporter Loretta Young. Capra's vision in those years also embraced a darker take on the human condition. *Rain or Shine* (1930), a broad comedy set in a circus, concludes with an amazing sequence in which the circus audience, incited by villains trying to steal the enterprise, becomes a raging mob, destroying the circus. In the 1931 drama *The Miracle Woman,* based on a play coauthored by Riskin, Capra indicts phony evangelism. A young minister's daughter (Barbara Stanwyck), embittered by societal hypocrisy, enters into partnership with an unscrupulous promoter to become a charismatic evangelist, offering hope and redemption to the suckers in exchange for their money. In the 1932 drama *Forbidden,* from an original story by Capra himself, an editor (Ralph Bellamy) is obsessed with trying to unmask the private life of a powerful politician (Adolphe Menjou). Menjou is a married man who has for years hidden his illicit affair and the fact that his adopted daughter is actually his own, the result of his liaison with the other woman (Barbara Stanwyck). Far from being a heroic crusader exposing corruption in high places, the editor is portrayed as a vicious pitbull, emblematic of a hypocritical society that insists people deny their true feelings in order to conform to a "respectable" public image.

American Madness (1932), a joint project of Capra and Riskin, was the director's first depiction of the social conflicts of the depression era. In this cinematic masterwork Capra capitalized on the economic unrest and bank failures of the early 1930s by depicting an idealistic bank president (Walter Huston) whose faith in people is in conflict with the bank's conservative board of directors. When mass panic over a robbery leads to a run on the bank, Huston's intervention proves a calming influence and prevents the crowd from degenerating into a violent mob. Capra's next film, *The Bitter Tea of General Yen* (1933), is one of the most unusual films of its time. The story concerns an American missionary (Barbara Stanwyck) trapped in a civil war in China and then rescued by a warlord, General Yen (Nils Asther), whose personality is an extraordinary combination of ruthlessness and tenderness. Finding herself falling in love with the general in spite of herself, her efforts to "reform" him by inducing him to spare the life of his former mistress results only in his betrayal and death. Rich in psychological insight and moral complexity, *The Bitter Tea of General Yen* was a brave attempt to confront controversial subject matter.

Capra's next two films, *Lady for a Day* (1933) and *It Happened One Night* (1934), brought him closer to the formula for which he is best known today. The first was a sentimental comedy, a heartwarming modern fairy tale in which a woman (May Robson) has been reduced to poverty as an apple vendor in order to provide for her daughter's upbringing abroad. When the girl and her aristocratic European fiancé visit New York, the elderly lady, aided by her underworld friends as well as the governor and the mayor, masquerades as a wealthy dowager. Capra remade it in 1962 under the title, *A Pocketful of Miracles. It Happened One Night* had its origins in Samuel Hopkins Adams's "Night Bus," a magazine story that Capra and Riskin refashioned into an exhilarating, witty comedy. Its stars, Clark Gable as the newspaperman pursuing a story about a runaway heiress, and Claudette Colbert as the rich girl, were loaned to Columbia by their studios and gave performances with such brilliance and élan that they helped launch the so-called screwball cycle of the 1930s. Capra insisted on shooting much of the film on location to convey the spirit of America in the depression years, the look and feel of highways, the rural regions, the buses and motels. Again, Capra's critique of materialism emerges when reporter Gable rejects the phony lifestyle of the idle rich and ultimately wins Colbert over to his romantic celebration of a life freed from artificial social constraints. (This perspective reappeared in Capra's second film of 1934, *Broadway Bill,* starring Warner Baxter and Myrna Loy, a tale of a man who rejects the acquisitive monopoly capitalism of his father-in-law to enjoy the simpler pleasure of training a race horse.)

When *It Happened One Night* swept all the major awards at the Motion Picture Academy ceremony in 1935, Capra, who for some years had set his sights on an Oscar, reached the pinnacle of his career. He had triumphed in film beyond his wildest expectations while helping to raise Columbia to the status of a major studio. In his personal life, too, he was now happily married (since 1932) to Lucille Warner and the proud father of a growing family. Yet having to all intents achieved the American dream, Capra was suddenly wracked with self-doubt and a feeling he was somehow unworthy of all this success. These inner torments brought on a severe illness from which he emerged determined to make films that would champion the cause of the common man.

The first film to result from his renewed commitment was the classic comedy-drama, *Mr. Deeds Goes to Town* (1936), starring Gary Cooper and Jean Arthur. A variant on the country hick besting the city slickers, the story concerns Longfellow Deeds (Cooper), an eccentric, tuba-playing idealist in a small town who suddenly inherits a fortune and migrates to New York where he comes up against the corruption, jaded impersonality, and pseudo-sophistication of the big city. After he is mocked and caricatured by the press, he eventually faces an insanity charge when he attempts to give away his millions to the poor. Ultimately, Deeds's innate goodness wins over his detractors, including the cynical newspaperwoman (Arthur) who, after writing damaging stories about him, finds herself falling in love with him. Cooper's innate sanity and good sense win out, of course, underscoring Capra's belief in individuality resisting the mass conformity of modern life.

With *Lost Horizon* (1937) Capra turned to the vein of exotic romance he had tapped in *General Yen*. This spectacular dramatization of James Hilton's novel about the mythical country of Shangri-La, a land hidden in the Himalayas and governed by a High Lama according to the principles of peace and love, featured Ronald Colman as Conway, a visionary Englishman. Made at a time when the world was rapidly moving toward a global conflict, *Lost Horizon* skillfully captures the yearning of the era for a resolution to the problems that were tearing humanity apart. By contrast, *You Can't Take It With You* (1938), based on the George S. Kaufman–Moss Hart play, is a work of optimistic Americana, about a family of endear-ingly eccentric Americans who do as they please in defiance of the Great Depression.

Capra's work in the 1930s culminated with *Mr. Smith Goes to Washington* (1939), often cited as his greatest film. With a cast headed by James Stewart and Jean Arthur, the film deals with an idealistic, newly appointed junior senator, Jefferson Smith (Stewart), who discovers that a corrupt political machine is running his state. When he learns that his state's senior senator (Claude Rains), whom he had admired all his life as a man of principle, has long since sold out to a corrupt boss (Edward Arnold) with near-dictatorial control over the state, his ideals are shaken. The machine musters all its power to destroy Smith when he tries to expose the level of corruption in his state. He makes a ringing defense of democracy in a speech on the Senate floor—but it is only the confession of the now-penitent senator who had earlier denounced him that finally saves the day. Capra's depiction of high-level corruption and the cynical Washington press corps aroused considerable controversy at the time. But *Mr. Smith Goes to Washington* has long since been recognized as one of the most incisive studies of American political processes ever captured on film.

As the 1940s began and with the rest of the world embroiled in war, Capra, now the president of the Director's Guild, was becoming more and more vocal about social inequities and the threat posed to democracy by fascism. Along with scores of other liberal-minded Hollywood luminaries, Capra's name appeared in ads in the *New York Times* supporting President Roosevelt's 1940 reelection bid and rallying to the defense of the Soviet Union when it was invaded by the Nazis in 1941. Professionally, Capra ended his long, sometimes contentious association with Harry Cohn and Columbia to form a partnership with Riskin to produce independent pictures. The film they created, *Meet John Doe* (1941), reflected Capra's apprehensions about fascism. Gary Cooper plays a drifter, an unemployed bush-league baseball player turned into a headline story by newspaper reporter Barbara Stanwyck, who represents him as a critic of the world's injustices. Newspaper owner Edward Arnold decides to use Cooper's image to create an idealistic movement, the John Doe Clubs, a front for his drive to become an American dictator. When Cooper discovers the media mogul's real agenda, he is prevented from going public by an outraged mob arrayed against their former idol. Because of Capra's indecision about the ending, the film concludes with a draw between the tycoon and those citizens in the clubs who have come to their senses about Cooper and rallied to his defense. Harking back to *The Miracle Woman, Meet John Doe* traces a far greater conspiracy, an attempted final coup d'état by the wealthy to impose a fascistic, militarist regime in the United States. It remains one of American cinema's most powerful and prophetic works, an extraordinarily bleak vision of idealism masking a totalitarian, reactionary agenda.

With the increasing likelihood that the United States would soon enter World War II, Capra volunteered his services to the Army Signal Corps. Before leaving Hollywood, he directed a madcap film version of the Broadway hit *Arsenic and Old Lace* (1944) for Warner Bros. an assignment he took on in order to keep his family solvent while he went to work for the military. He completed shooting just after the Pearl Harbor attack. In Washington, D.C., the government assigned him to supervise a series of army training films intended to explain to the troops the history of the war and the reasons why the United States had entered the fray. By skillfully editing film clips, including footage shot by the enemy, and interweaving them with stirring music and narration, Capra and his team of writers and technicians created the *Why We Fight* series, some of the most effective propaganda documentaries ever made. Although he was committed heart and soul to the Allied cause, he was appalled to realize that his own side, the champion of freedom and democracy, was bombing civilians in the enemy countries, atrocities akin to the terrors of the Ger-

man air raids that he experienced in London. Sickened by the slaughter on both sides, Capra recorded his dismay in his diaries at the time. He emerged from this inner conflict with a strong commitment to pacifism and a fresh determination to restate on film his belief in a more just and equitable world based on the value of the individual.

Capra returned to Hollywood and civilian life determined to maintain his creative independence. In partnership with fellow directors WILLIAM WYLER and GEORGE STEVENS, he formed a new organization, Liberty Films, to produce their own films. It was for Liberty that Capra created the film which, in a very real sense, distilled all his own life experiences and two decades of filmmaking into a masterpiece that has touched innumerable people over the decades, *It's a Wonderful Life,* first shown during the 1946 Christmas season. The story concerns George Bailey (James Stewart), his life in the New England town of Bedford Falls, the thwarting of his youthful dreams and aspirations by the realities of having to keep the family savings and loan association afloat, his courtship and marriage to Mary (Donna Reed), and the thwarting of his attempts to help the people in his community by the grasping town banker, Mr. Potter (Lionel Barrymore). Pushed over the edge to suicide, George is rescued by an angel named Clarence (Henry Travers), who provides him with a vision of what the town might be like had he never existed. Capra's most extraordinary variation on the immigrant motif, George becomes a stranger in his own community as the townspeople, even his own mother, fail to recognize him. The town, now known as Pottersville, is a dark, corrupt city dominated by the banker, Capra's grim vision of man's existence filled with all the angst of what might yet be the American future. Finally, after one desperate encounter after another and his realization that his life had indeed touched many others for the better, George is released from this nightmarish state. The film ends on a note of affirmation as he is reunited with his family and friends and saved by their financial generosity. But while they have escaped Potter's clutches, as in *Meet John Doe*, the capitalist villain goes unpunished. Critical and popular reaction to *It's a Wonderful Life* was mixed in 1946–47, but in the 1970s, it reemerged as a television staple and became Capra's most beloved and oft-seen film, enlisting widely varying interpretations but clearly recognized by most as one of the great works of American cinema.

Capra's second film for Liberty, *State of the Union* (1948), starred Spencer Tracy as a liberal Republican candidate for the presidency and Katharine Hepburn as his wife. Tracy sees the White House as a chance to realize his progressive beliefs; however, caught up in the corruption of power politics, he sells out in order to win votes. Chastened by his wife's criticism as well as his own conscience, he publicly renounces his quest in a televised address reproaching his own failings and decrying the state of American politics. With Capra poised to surrender his independence to join the industry as a contract director, the film has obvious autobiographical overtones. It would also be the last of his classic political films. Significantly, the visionary ideals of a world government aroused opposition from the increasingly powerful right wing in an America and Hollywood now being intimidated by the House Un-American Activities Committee.

Capra directed only four more films after the dissolution of Liberty: two Bing Crosby vehicles for Paramount, *Riding High* (1950) (a musical remake of *Broadway Bill*), and *Here Comes the Groom* (1951); *A Hole in the Head* (1957), a comedy starring Frank Sinatra; and his last film, *A Pocketful of Miracles* (1961), a remake of *Lady for a Day*. Between the Crosby and Sinatra films, he returned to his first love, science, directing four informative and entertaining television programs on the subject, a series so skillfully put together that it was shown in classrooms across the country for years.

Unlike contemporaries of his such as ALFRED HITCHCOCK, JOHN FORD, HOWARD HAWKS, and Wyler who did some of their most notable work in the 1950s and 1960s, Capra disappeared from the Hollywood film industry for much of this period. But in a sense, Capra, like Griffith before him, had always stood apart from the industry. At Columbia, he attained an autonomy denied most directors of the time since, once the budget was agreed upon, he was able, with Cohn's blessing, to make whatever film he chose without interference. His most impressive post-Columbia films, *Meet John Doe, It's a Wonderful Life,* and *State of the Union,* were all independently produced. Along with Capra's inability to adapt to the structure of the industry, the changing political and social climate in the post-war years was a further factor in his eclipse in the 1950s. The height of his popularity in the 1930s and early 1940s coincided with the era of Populism and the Popular Front, uniting people of progressive faith to fight the Great Depression. This coalition quickly fell apart after the war. The now-ascendant rightists viewed Capra's films as particularly suspect. Indeed, a 1947 internal report by J. Edgar Hoover's FBI cited *It's a Wonderful Life* and *Mr. Smith Goes to Washington* as subversive, left-wing attacks on capitalism. Moreover, to the beleaguered liberals of the 1950s, Capra's idealism now seemed fuzzy and naively out of touch with postwar realities.

Capra, however, was never a man to fade quietly into obscurity. In 1971, he reemerged with *The Name Above the Title*, a vastly entertaining if not always accurate autobiography recording his struggles and triumphs. To the rebellious college youth of the '70s disillusioned by the Vietnam War and the contemporary power structure, Capra's films with their combination of idealistic faith in the individual and distrust of institutions were highly relevant. As a result, the director became a popular featured speaker at college campuses.

In 1982 Capra received the American Film Institute's Lifetime Achievement Award. Following the death of his wife, Lucille, with whom he had shared an exceptionally close relationship for over half a century, he suffered a stroke in 1985 and withdrew from the public eye. He died on September 3, 1991, at the age of 94 in his home in La Quinta, California. Survivors included a daughter and two sons, one of whom, Frank Capra, Jr., had become a prominent film producer in his own right.

Frank Capra remains one of the cinema's most provocative and intellectually stimulating directors. His work has been the subject of countless analyses including those by Jeanine Basinger, Leland Poague, and Raymond Carney, whose brilliant study of the filmmaker links him to American transcendentalism and romantic painting. His work has been a continual source of inspiration to later U.S. directors such as Oliver Stone, Ron Howard, and John Cassavetes and Japan's Akira Kurosawa and Nagisa Oshima. He has received universal praise for his exceptional cinematic skills and his unusual gift for directing actors. It was Capra who made Barbara Stanwyck and Jean Arthur stars and helped shape the screen images of Gary Cooper, James Stewart, Clark Gable, and Claudette Colbert. And from the standpoint of his thematics, the Sicilian immigrant, along with John Ford, was the director who was most responsible for expressing the American national consciousness on screen in the 1930s and 1940s. However, Capra still has fierce detractors like Joseph McBride, whose biography of the director depicts him as an opportunist more interested in self-promotion than the ideals expressed in his films. McBride's interpretation, deriving from his highly selective approach to research, was embraced by critics who had long disparaged the filmmaker as the sweetly sentimental purveyor of "Capracorn." Ironically, this view of Capra as a complacent manipulator of mass emotions has also been promulgated by his latter-day conservative admirers who have sought to recast him as the "family values" director in contrast to contemporary Hollywood's supposed ultraliberalism. Even among the critics who most appreciate him as a subtle and powerful artist, there are sharp divisions between those who revere him as an idealist with an affirmative vision of humankind and those who see his point of view as darker and much more despairing. In truth, Capra resists any attempt at simple categorization because his work is multilayered. Much like his literary antecedents Charles Dickens and Mark Twain, Capra was both a popular, humorous entertainer and a complex visionary artist. Also like Dickens and Twain, Capra was simultaneously radical and conservative in his outlook, a romantic and a realist in his aesthetics, a man of both tremendous faith and immense doubt. The force and enthusiasm with which he developed and transmitted his vision galvanized his gifted collaborators who responded with equal conviction to his magnetism. The architect of his films from start to finish, Frank Capra was one of the film's premier geniuses who helped realize the art's full potential through a body of work that continues to challenge and appeal to the mind and heart.

Other Films *For the Love of Mike* (1927); *That Certain Thing* (1928); *So This Is Love* (1928); *The Way of the Strong* (1928); *Say It with Sables* (1928); *The Donovan Affair* (1929).

References Capra, Frank, *The Name Above the Title* (New York: Macmillan, 1971); Drew, William M., "Frank Capra: A Lighthouse in a Foggy World" (interview), *American Classic Screen* 3, no. 6 (July–August 1979): 14–16; Maland, Charles J., *Frank Capra* (Boston: Twayne, 1980); McBride, Joseph, *Frank Capra: The Catastrophe of Success* (New York: Simon and Schuster, 1992); Phelps, Glenn Alan, "The 'Populist' Films of Frank Capra," *Journal of American Studies* 13, no. 3 (December 1979): 377–392; Tibbetts, John C., "The Wisdom of the Serpent: Frauds and Miracles in Frank Capra's *The Miracle Woman*," *The Journal of Popular Culture* 7, no. 3 (1979), 293–309; Willis, Donald C., *The Films of Frank Capra* (Metuchen, N.J.: Scarecrow Press, 1974).

—W.M.D.

Carné, Marcel (1906–1996) Although not as prolific as his French contemporaries JEAN

RENOIR and RENÉ CLAIR, Marcel Carné stands in the front rank of directors working in the 1930s and 1940s. He was born in Batignolles, in Paris, on August 18, 1906, the son of a cabinetmaker. In the mid-1920s he worked as an insurance clerk before moving on to a more desirable profession, cinematographer and director. He began as an assistant with René Clair on his landmark sound film, *Under the Roofs of Paris (Sous les toits de Paris)* in 1929 and, after gaining more experience with the support of another veteran director, Jacques Feyder, directed his first theatrical feature in 1936, *Jenny.* In the meantime, he wrote film criticism for *Cinémagazine* and *Cinémonde* under the pseudonym "Albert Cranche."

His 10-year, fruitful collaboration with the esteemed poet-playwright-scenarist Jacques Prevert produced four of the undisputed masterpieces of the French cinema of the 1930s and early 1940s: *Port of Shadows (Quai des brumes* [1938]), *Daybreak (Le Jour se lève* [1939]), *The Devil's Envoys (Les Visiteurs du soir* [1942]), and *Children of Paradise (Les Enfants du paradis* [1945]). The first two films were exemplars of what has come to be known as "poetic realism," a species of fatalistic romantic melodrama wreathed in a noirish atmosphere of shadows and fog. Actor Jean Gabin starred in both as a doomed figure on the run from a troubled past. *Daybreak* was particularly noted for its intricately realized flashback structure. (It was remade in the 1940s by Anatole Litvak under the title of *The Long Night*.) Critic André Bazin looked back upon these two classics with affection: "Everything came together to make of these two films the most perfect expression of a rather characteristic tendency of French cinema between 1934 and 1939: the *film noir*."

With the German occupation during the war, Carné—who, unlike Renoir and Clair, remained in France—and Prévert abandoned the urban gloom in favor of a more highly theatricalized spectacle for the latter two films. *The Devil's Envoys* was a medieval fable about two agents of the devil (Alain Cuny and Arletty) who attend a baronial banquet and disrupt everyone's lives. When one of the envoys falls in love for real, the devil himself (Jules Berry) intervenes and transforms the lovers into statues. *Children of Paradise,* Carné's masterpiece, was an ambitious, three-hour tribute to the French theater and a thinly disguised evocation of the enduring French spirit that transcends war.

Only 36 years of age at the conclusion of the war, Carné's bright future prospects somehow failed to materialize. His first postwar film, *Gates of the Night (Les Portes de la nuit* [1946]), a story about collaborators and black marketeers in postwar Paris, flopped at the box office; and the ill-fated *Fleur de l'age* marked the end of his relationship with Prévert. A dozen more films followed, but Carné never regained the influence and prestige he had hitherto enjoyed. Despite his generosity toward a younger generation of filmmakers, he was dismayed to find he had fallen out of favor with the emerging "New Wave" artists. It was only in 1980 that his foremost detractor, FRANÇOIS TRUFFAUT, had occasion to revise his opinion. "I have made 23 pictures," Truffaut said. "I would swap them all for the chance to have made *Les Enfants du paradis.*"

Children of Paradise deserves special mention. It was designated in 1979 by the French Academy of Cinema Arts and Techniques as "the best film in the history of talking pictures in France." It is, more to the point, Carné's masterpiece and the one picture in which he most perfectly fused the styles and tone of poetic realism with the artifice of the theater. What Carné himself described as "a tribute to the theater" relies on the conventions of pantomime, farce, melodrama, and Shakespearean tragedy to underscore its story of love's triumphs and frustrations. The setting is Paris during the monarchy of Louis-Philippe in the 1840s, at Carnival time. The action is framed by the rise and fall of a theater curtain, and the story transpires in the Boulevard du Temple, Paris's theater district, which teems with acrobats, clowns, mimes, barkers, peepshows, and animal acts. Two of the story's principal characters are actors based on real-life figures—the elegant mime Jean-Gaspard Deburau (played by Jean-Louis Barrault as "Baptiste Deburau") and the flamboyant Shakespearean actor Frederick Lemaître (Pierre Brasseur). Each performs in his own theater, Baptiste at the Théâtre du Funambules and Lemaître at the Grand Théâtre. What unites them—and links them with the more peripheral characters, the villainous Lacenaire (Marcel Herrand) and the slimy aristocrat Edward de Monteray (Louis Salou)—is their fatal attraction to the enigmatic beauty, Garance (Arletty).

"Jealousy belongs to everyone," observes Lemaître, "even if women belong to no one!" Baptiste and Lemaître must turn to their art to survive. The theater offers them not only solace but also a kind of creative whetstone. As Lemaître says, "When I act, I am desperately in love, desperately, do you understand? But when the curtain falls, the audience goes away, and takes 'my love' with it. You see, I make the audience a present of my love. The audience is very happy, and so am I. And I become wise and free and calm and sensible again, like Baptiste!" Made during the last months of the German occupation of France—it was one of the first films to be released after the liberation—*Children of Paradise* is also about the enduring French spirit during the German occupation. It has been demonstrated that theatrical activities, not political actions, were France's chief bulwark against the Nazi oppression. In the words of Edward Baron Turk, France's theaters were "the 'safe houses' of those collective dreams that take the form of plays and movies [and which] provided a public site for relief from political oppression." Moreover, continues Turk, the film pointed toward the imminent resurgence of the French spirit: "All those who had experienced the outrage, humiliation, and despair of the occupation could perceive in it the infallible sign of assurance that French civilization would reestablish its position of prestige and leadership in the world."

Carné was an officer of the Légion d'honneur and received the Prix Louis Delluc. He resided in an apartment on the rue de l'Abbaye in Paris. In 1977 he completed *La Bible,* a 90-minute documentary on the mosaics of the Monreale Basilica in Sicily, and he continued to experiment with what he called the "spectacle audiovisuel," the multimedia projection of images on a large screen accompanied by a quadrophonic sound system. He was one of the screen's supreme poets of loneliness, writes biographer Turk: "It is perhaps inevitable that a film director who portrays life's essential loneliness will fail to command universal assent. But to overlook Carné's cinema of sadness is to misrepresent the past in conformity with a wish for only positive images of human possibility. Carné's films bear out the Baudelairean view of sorrow and melancholy as fundamental components of art."

Other Films *Bizarre Bizaar* (*Drole de drame* [1937]); *La Marie du port* (1949); *Thérèse Raquin* (1953); *The Cheaters* (*Les Tricheurs* [1958]); *The Young Wolves* (*Les Jeunes loups* [1967]); *The Wonderful Visit* (*La Merveilleuse visite* [1974]).

References Bazin, André, "The Disincarnation of Carné," in *Rediscovering French Film,* ed. Mary Lea Bandy (New York: Museum of Modern Art, 1983), pp. 131–135; Turk, Edward Baron, *Child of Paradise: Marcel Carné and the Golden Age of French Cinema* (Cambridge, Mass.: Harvard University Press, 1989); Turk, Edward Baron, "The Birth of *Children of Paradise,"* *American Film,* July–August 1979, pp. 42–49.

—J.C.T.

Cassavetes, John (1929–1989) John Cassavetes's reputation as a director has spanned the spectrum from vilification to glorification, depending upon the willingness of the viewer to learn the language Cassavetes is speaking. His work has been labeled clumsy, poorly and sloppily edited, suffering from bad acting and weakness of plot, as well as bad lighting and atrocious sound. These very same characteristics, however, have been applauded by others as indicators of innova-

tive genius. He was nominated for Oscars as a director, writer, and actor.

John Cassavetes was born December 9, 1929, in New York City. He studied at the Actor's Studio and undoubtedly brought to his directing some of the lessons learned from being trained as a "method" actor. His television acting career started in the early 1950s on well-respected shows such as *Omnibus, Playhouse 90, Studio One,* and *Kraft Theatre.* Beginning in 1953 he appeared in the feature films *Taxi, The Night Holds Terror, Crime in the Streets, Saddle the Wind,* and *Edge of the City.* He made his directorial debut with *Shadows* in 1959, which won five awards at the Venice Film Festival and the Jean George Oriol Award (the French equivalent of the Pulitzer Prize). The success of this film led to his being offered work on two studio films, *Too Late Blues,* starring Bobby Darin and Stella Stevens, and *A Child Is Waiting,* starring Gena Rowlands, Burt Lancaster, and Judy Garland. The ultimate disagreements and arguments over editing of the second film led producer STANLEY KRAMER (whom Cassavetes expert Ray Carney refers to as one of the most powerful men on the West Coast at that time) to label Cassavetes "difficult" and resulted in his virtual blacklisting in Hollywood for nearly a decade.

Cassavetes spent his time in exile furiously writing several scripts for stage plays. One of those scripts was converted into a screenplay for *Faces,* in part reflecting Cassavetes's response to the "casual brutality" of West Coast/Los Angeles shallowness, hypocrisy, and deal making. *Faces* began filming on New Year's Day of 1965, shooting around the cast and crew's "real" jobs, continuing on weekends and evenings until June of that year. The film was shot with primitive equipment (16 mm) and little money. He asked his actors to work for deferred salaries. The principle shooting locations were Cassavetes's own residence and that of his mother-in-law, and the editing and sound mixing was done in the Cassavetes garage. It took three years and five acting jobs by Cassavetes to scrape together the money to complete

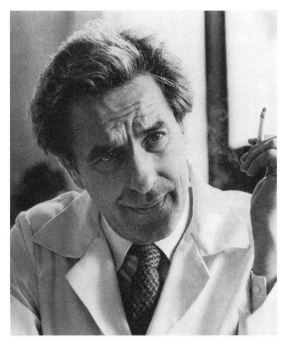

John Cassavetes starring in *Whose Life Is It, Anyway?* (Metro-Goldwyn-Mayer Film Co.)

work for the 1968 debut of what Carney calls "one of the supreme works of genius in all of American film."

Husbands, filmed in 1969 and released in 1970, and *Minnie and Moskowitz,* filmed and released in 1971, followed. *A Woman Under the Influence,* filmed in 1972 and released in 1974, found director Cassavetes, wife and star Gena Rowlands, friends, and other cast members traveling coast to coast to promote and book the film themselves. His next film, *The Killing of a Chinese Bookie,* was filmed and released in 1976 and rereleased in 1978 in a completely reedited print. *Opening Night,* filmed in 1977 and released in 1978, was withdrawn and rereleased in 1991. *Gloria* was filmed and released 1980. His last film, *Love Streams,* was filmed in 1983 and released in 1984. His name appears on *Big Trouble,* but since he was neither the first director nor the editor, he has disavowed this work as his. His son, Nick Cassavetes, shared direction credit with him on *She's So Lovely,* but John Cassavetes's only contribution was the screenplay.

Cassavetes's philosophy of filmmaking was stubbornly individual, and his unwillingness to make things easy for critics and viewers hurt his commercial prospects. His harshest critics said his films went nowhere and took a long time doing it. Narrative and storytelling, however, cannot be said to be the true goals of a Cassavetes film. He felt that plot was confining to his characters. "Don't worry about the words," he would tell his players, "if you get the character right, the plot will take care of itself." He believed in shooting in sequence to help the actors stay in touch with the emotional development of their character. In order to avoid disrupting the flow of the shoot, he relied heavily on medium-distance camera setups and eschewed complicated lighting schemes. As his biographer has stated, "For him, direction was not about control, but responsiveness." Cassavetes felt he learned about these characters from his actors, and said he tackled some of the projects he did to learn more about them. For example, his feelings changed about the characters in *Husbands* from contempt to pity after gaining a deeper understanding of them by making the film. Cassavetes wanted his audience to participate in this act of discovery as well. He wanted to keep the process open and moving. Repeated viewing of his films only enriches the perceptions, since there is no one "right" way of seeing them. He kept his characters liquid and flowing. For example, as Carney described Mabel's costuming in *A Woman Under the Influence.*

> It is significant that in the rare scenes in which props or costumes do figure prominently as conveyors of meaning in *A Woman Under the Influence*—as Mabel's wacky, mismatched clothing does in the school-bus scene—it is not sociologically possible to stereotype her, but to indicate how she eludes categorization. Far from defining her as a representative of a group, the weirdness of her appearance suggest energies that defy economic, ethnic, religious, or ideological categories of understanding. . . . Mabel creates her own identity; it is not created for her by her clothing or ethnic background. If we want to understand her, we must look at her performance, not the furniture of her life.

Actor Peter Falk, who frequently appeared in his films, labeled Cassavetes a man obsessed with making films. His relentless pursuit of getting the shots he was after resulted in his shooting as much as a million feet of film per picture, with retakes running from 10 to 30 or more. He wanted to keep his films fluid and uncongealed, and felt that abstract concepts were a dead end. Any preplanned schema was considered cliché. His films had an improvised feel that he worked hard to achieve, although after *Shadows,* all his films were fully scripted. He has been quoted as saying the *process* was what was important to him, and that after the films were complete, he had little interest in them. The process could take years, however, and Cassavetes sometimes confounded even his supporters. After *Shadows* had won awards, he rewrote, reshot, and reedited much of it.

Cassavetes used film as other artists used clay or paint, or as jazz musicians explore a piece of music: to investigate, analyze, and discover a subject. His was not an art of didacticism in the normal Hollywood sense, and this is what confused his critics and audiences. He wanted to explore the "realness" of language, human emotion, and interaction. He was interested in the bumpiness and raw edges that other filmmakers tried to eliminate from their work. Cassavetes's habit of reshooting and reediting was intended precisely to capture the unguarded moment of body language, the flickering of emotion across a face, or the stumbling, stammering cadence of real language.

He was interested in exploring relationships and the nature of love, but he kept his characters moving in venues that ran the gamut from screwball comedy (*Minnie and Moskowitz*) to film noir (*Killing of a Chinese Bookie*) to tragedy (*A Woman*

Under the Influence) to playing with the illusion of reality via a play within a play (*Opening Night*). Even with this diverse body of work to pick through, however, a primary theme emerges: people's inability to express themselves. Characters are inclined to either give too much of themselves away and be defined by the people around them, or they are so uncomfortable in their own skin that they create an artificial persona they can hide behind. The former is best illustrated by Mabel Longhetti in *A Woman Under the Influence*. This character is vulnerable, in pain, and searching for her identity. The other end of this spectrum is illustrated by Cosmo Vitelli, who veils himself in style over substance. This character first emerged as Ben in *Shadows* and repeatedly appears all the way through Cassavetes's work, finally becoming Robert in *Love Streams*. We see people who are disappearing by either turning themselves over to others, or hiding behind illusion and affectation and getting lost behind all the smoke and mirrors.

If one compares film to a mirror reflecting life, Cassavetes would throw that mirror to the ground, retrieve the shards, and glue them together with the sharp edges not quite fitting together. The danger of getting cut and the resulting pain would also be a part of that mosaic. Cassavetes felt that we as a culture were abstracted from reality to such a degree that we were no longer in touch with ways of expressing ourselves. He devoted his life to finding a way through that barrier.

John Cassavetes died on February 3, 1989, from complications of cirrhosis of the liver.

References Carney, R., *The Films of John Cassavetes* (Cambridge, U.K.: Cambridge University Press, 1994); Carney, R., *John Cassavetes: The Adventure of Insecurity* (Boston: Boston University Press, 2000).

—G.M.

Chabrol, Claude (1930–)

The director of over 50 feature films was born June 24, 1930, in Paris, France. The son of a pharmacist, he himself studied pharmacy before turning his energies to the arts. After completing his studies at the University of Paris and the Politiques Ecole Libre des Sciences he worked as a press agent for Fox Studios in Paris. He also wrote film criticism for *Cahiers du cinéma* where, along with FRANÇOIS TRUFFAUT and ERIC ROHMER, he defended film as an art form equal to literature. He helped promote the auteur theory that a film should be marked by the artistry of its "author" or director. He contributed two articles in the 1954 issue of the *Cahiers* devoted to the films of ALFRED HITCHCOCK and collaborated with Rohmer on the 1957 book *Hitchcock*. He played bit parts in some of his own films and those of his contemporaries. He worked as technical adviser on JEAN-LUC GODARD's *À Bout de souffle/Breathless* (1959).

Like several of the *Cahiers* critics, Chabrol soon moved into directing and began a prolific career that was initially supported by government funding for low-budget films. With the inheritance of his first wife Agnes Goule, Chabrol was able to finance his first film. Following the success of his second film he established his own production company that produced films by Rivette, Rohmer, and de Broca. Chabrol and the other directors in his circle would come to be known as the *nouvelle vague* in French cinema. They favored a neorealist style that promoted location shooting, use of available light, and panning/tracking shots.

Chabrol, working as both screenwriter and director, employed open-ended plots and nontraditional narrative. His first feature was *Le Beau Serge* (*Bitter Reunion*) of 1958, followed by *Les Cousins* (*The Cousins* [1959]). *Les Bonnes femmes* (1960), although not well received by audiences and critics at its debut, is now counted among the major films of the French New Wave. This story of four Parisian shop girls is told with the same neutral irony of his earlier films. In the early 1960s he directed *Les Godelureaux* (1960), *L'Oeil du Malin* (*The Third Lover* [1962]), *Ophélia* (1962), and *Landru* (*Bluebeard* [1963]). The latter, a Hitchcock homage, stars Charles Denner in the title role of a mass-murderer.

The mid-1960s period of his career is marked by commercial spy thrillers. Themes such as murder, obsession, and bourgeois criminality appear in his films of the late 1960s, of which *La Femme infidèle* (*Unfaithful Wife* [1968]), *Le Boucher* (*The Butcher* [1969]), and *Les Biches* (*The Does / Girlfriends / Bad Girls* [1968]) were highlights. The latter, starring his second wife Stéphane Audran (Chabrol is currently married to his third wife, Aurore Pajot), was written in collaboration with Paul Gégauff who also worked with Chabrol on a number of projects including *Les Bonnes femmes.* Chabrol writes or collaborates on the writing of most of the scripts for his films.

Marriage and infidelity are subjects that Chabrol regularly addressed in his films including those of the 1970s: *Juste avant la nuit* (*Just Before Nightfall* [1971]), *Le Noces rouge* (*Wedding in Blood* [1973]), *Folies bourgeoises* (*The Twist* [1976]). There is a triad of recurring character names—Hélène, Charles, and Paul—that appear in at least six of Chabrol's films about relationships and infidelity. He employed a similar triad of actors, including Audran, Michel Bouquet, and Jean Yanne.

Chabrol made a number of suspense films in the 1980s: *Poulet au vinaigre* (*Coq au Vin* [1984]), *Inspector Lavardin* (1986), *Masques* (1987). Chabrol ignores conventional thriller plots in favor of emphasizing what he has described as the confrontation between character and story. It is often psychological inquiry that motivates his direction and many of his films are based on factual events, including *Violette Noziere* (1978), which was Chabrol's first film to star Isabelle Huppert as a daughter who poisons her parents. The duo would go on to make *Une affaire des femmes* (*The Story of Women* [1988]), which won the New York Film Critics Circle Award for best foreign film. The grim account of an abortionist in Vichy France, who becomes the last woman to be executed by guillotine, contains an outstanding performance by Huppert as the not entirely sympathetic protagonist. The collaboration continued with *Madame Bovary* (1991), *La Cérémonie* (*A Judgment in Stone* [1995]), *Rien ne va plus* (*The Swindle* [1997]), and *Merci pour le chocolat* (*Nightcap* [2000]).

Chabrol is now often described as a "woman's director" for his later films that focus on a female perspective yet incorporate the recurring themes of class conflict and crime. While his prolific output is often criticized as being of uneven quality, Chabrol's films continually offer a range of ideas, narrative structures, and styles that none of the other New Wave directors equalled.

Other Films *A Double Tour* (*Web of Passion* [1959]); *Le Tigre aime le chair fraîche* (*The Tiger Likes Fresh Blood* [1964]); *Marie-Chantal contre le Docteur Kha* (1965); *La Ligne de demarcation* (*Line of Demarcation* [1966]); *La Rupture* (*The Breakup* [1970]); *Que la bête meure* (*This Man Must Die* [1970]); *La Décade prodigieuse* (*Ten Days' Wonder* [1972]); *Une Partie de plaisir* (*Pleasure Party* [1975]); *The Proud Ones* (1980); *Les Liens de sang* (*Blood Relative* [1983]); *Betty* (1993); *L'Oeil de Vichy* (*The Eye of Vichy* [1993]); *L'Enfer* (*Hell* [1994]); *Au coeur du mensonge* (*Color of Lies* [1999]).

References Austin, Guy, *Claude Chabrol* (New York: St. Martins, 1999); Blanchet, Christian, *Claude Chabrol* (Paris: Rivages, 1989); Magny, Joël, *Claude Chabrol* (Paris: Cahiers du cinéma, 1987); Wood, Robin, et al., *Claude Chabrol* (New York: Praeger, 1970).

—J.A.D.

Chaplin, Charles (1889–1977)

Charles Chaplin was born in London on April 16, 1889. Both of his parents were moderately successful music hall entertainers. When he was still a youngster, his father died of alcoholism, and his mother retired from the stage because of poor physical health and mental illness. Consequently, Chaplin was forced to earn his living in vaudeville before he reached his teens. Mack Sennett, the creator of the Keystone comedies, saw Chaplin perform while the comedian was touring the United States with Fred Karno's vaudeville company and invited Chaplin to go into pictures in 1913. Chaplin left the stage for a career in movies the following year.

Chaplin created the character of Charlie the Tramp and made his first short comedies shortly after joining Sennett. He explained that the Tramp was his conception of the average man. The Tramp is everyman, with whom we can all identify: the well-meaning but inept little fellow whose reach forever exceeds his grasp, but who is always ready to pick himself up, dust himself off, and continue down the road of life, twirling his cane with disarming bravado. Chaplin left Sennett's Keystone studio in 1915 after a year, and transferred first to Essanay, and then to Mutual in 1916–17. With each new contract Chaplin negotiated at each new studio, he received still greater artistic independence. He was now able to make his short films with more care and to explore further the possibilities of integrating a serious dimension into his comedy material. The Tramp character began to be more clearly defined as the pathetic outsider, longing for an acceptance from others that he will never achieve. Perhaps the greatest of his Mutual shorts is *The Immigrant* (1917), which dealt with a subject close to Chaplin's heart, since he had come to America himself as an immigrant in 1913. Moreover, because the immigrant is perhaps the quintessential example of a lonely outsider striving for acceptance in an alien milieu, the role fit the personality of Charlie the Tramp perfectly. When Chaplin left Mutual for First National in 1918, he took yet another step toward total artistic control of his films. Chaplin now became his own producer, as well as writer, director, and star. Moreover, most of the First National comedies were longer than the one- and two-reelers that he had made for other studios, since they averaged three reels apiece; as such, they were to become the prototypes of his later features.

The Kid (1921), running to six reels, was Chaplin's first feature. Prior to his First National films, Chaplin portrayed the Tramp as a rambunctious ragamuffin who felt that he had to cheat to survive in a cold and brutal world. In the First National films, particularly *The Kid,* Charlie emerges as a gentler kind of person, one who receives the kicks that life administers to him with more resignation and less of a will for retaliation than he had exhibited in his earlier comedies. In *The Kid* the Tramp finds an abandoned child (Jackie Coogan) and cares for him until his mother is discovered. The story takes place in an authentically grimy slum setting, reminiscent of the circumstances in which Chaplin himself grew up. In fact, more than any film that Chaplin ever made, *The Kid* is deeply rooted in Chaplin's wretched childhood.

The weaving together of comic and serious elements into a seamless fabric, foreshadowed in earlier films such as *The Immigrant* and *The Kid,* was for the first time fully accomplished in *The Gold Rush* (1925), which he made for United Artists, a production company that he formed

Charlie Chaplin (Author's collection)

in partnership with DAVID WARK GRIFFITH, Douglas Fairbanks, and Mary Pickford, to distribute the feature films each of them made. *The Gold Rush* has scenes that are almost straight drama, in which Chaplin becomes more of an actor and less of a clown, and hence the film is appropriately subtitled *A Dramatic Comedy.* In *The Gold Rush* Charlie the Tramp is called the Lone Prospector, again emphasizing his status as an outsider. He hopes to gain society's acceptance by discovering gold in the Klondike. The ongoing theme in Chaplin's films clearly surfaces in *The Gold Rush:* man's struggle for survival in a tough world, as evidenced in the Lone Prospector's resourcefulness in coping with whatever obstacles life puts in his way. That struggle was never more concretely visualized than in the first appearance of the Tramp in the film: overloaded with gear and shambling along a snowy mountainside, blithely unaware that he is being pursued by a huge bear.

As Chaplin was preparing *City Lights* (1931), talking pictures took Hollywood by storm. Given the faulty sound quality of early talkies, Chaplin decided to make *City Lights* as a silent picture. The only concession that the picture made to the advent of sound was the addition of a musical score, which he composed himself. The film itself, in which the Tramp falls in love with a blind flower girl, combines comedy and drama after the manner of *The Gold Rush.* The film ends with the Tramp meeting the girl after her sight has been restored. While she was blind, Charlie had led her to believe that he was wealthy; and she is surprised to see him for the pathetic Tramp he really is. The final close-up of Charlie that ends the picture is one of the most poignant in cinema history. The Tramp's face reflects several conflicting emotions all at once: he is glad that she recognizes him, but ashamed that he is not the rich man she imagined him to be; he hopes that she will accept him but is afraid that she will not. On this note of uncertainty the movie ends.

The Great Dictator (1940) was his first sound picture to employ spoken dialogue. Made on the eve of World War II, it starred Chaplin in a dual role as a Jewish barber very much akin to the Tramp and as Adenoid Hynkel, the dictator of Tomania—an obvious parody of Adolf Hitler. *Monsieur Verdoux* (1947) had Chaplin playing the title role of a former bank clerk down on his luck who supports his wife and son by marrying and murdering a series of rich widows for their fortunes. When *Verdoux* first appeared, moviegoers were not prepared to see Chaplin in the role of the dapper murderer Verdoux; the Tramp had always wanted to be a lady killer, but this is literally what Verdoux has become. In essence, audiences were not equipped to appreciate black comedy, the genre that finds humor in situations usually reserved for serious treatment. *Verdoux* actually proved that Chaplin was ahead of his time, for only in the wake of later black comedies like Kubrick's *Dr. Strangelove* could audiences appreciate in retrospect the artistry of *Verdoux.* Chaplin's next film was *Limelight* (1952), in which he played Calvero, a has-been music hall performer whose day has long passed.

When Chaplin set sail for Europe in September 1952 for the European premieres of *Limelight,* he was informed in mid-ocean by cable from the U.S. attorney general that he would not be permitted to reenter the country without facing an investigation into his personal character and political beliefs. Chaplin settled down in Switzerland. This incident occurred during the Cold War years that followed the Second World War, in which Senator Joseph McCarthy was conducting his anticommunist witch-hunt. Chaplin was accordingly accused of being a communist sympathizer because he had urged the United States to help Russia in warding off the Nazi invasion. He was further criticized for never becoming an American citizen, although, as he had often said, his patriotism "rests with the whole world, the pity of the whole world and the common people." Chaplin's last film was *A Countess from Hong Kong* (1967), which he wrote, directed, and scored, but in which he did not star.

Chaplin's achievements did not go unrewarded during his lifetime. When the first Academy Awards were presented in 1928, a special award went to Charles Chaplin for "his genius and versatility in writing, acting, directing and producing his films." At the 1972 award ceremonies Chaplin was on hand to be honored again, this time for "the incalculable effect he has had in making motion pictures the art form of this century." In addition, he was knighted in 1975, in recognition of his supreme importance in shaping the motion picture medium as an art form. In the course of *Limelight,* Calvero the clown muses that entertainers are "amateurs—that's all any of us are—amateurs. We don't live long enough to be anything else." Chaplin lived long enough.

Other Films *A Woman of Paris* (1925); *The Circus* (1928); *Modern Times* (1936).

References Chaplin, Charles, *My Autobiography* (New York: Penguin, 1992); Phillips, Gene D., *Major Film Directors of the American and British Cinema* (Cranbury, N.J.: Associated University Presses, 1999).

—G.D.P.

Clair, René (1898–1981) Although indisputably among France's greatest film masters, René Clair shared the curious fate of other great directors like DAVID WARK GRIFFITH, ABEL GANCE, and ORSON GEORGE WELLES, to name just a few, whose greatest successes came early, overshadowing the work of late maturity. He was born René Chomette in Paris on November 11, 1898, to prosperous parents in the grocery store business. After completing his education at the Lycée Montaigne and the Lycée Louis-le-Grand, he served in the Ambulance Corps during World War I. In 1920 under the name René Clair he began acting at the Gaumont Studios. This was a time when the young, ever-restless Clair was in turmoil, smoking opium and secluding himself for a while in a Dominican cloister.

Two years later he directed his first film, *The Crazy Ray,* a fantasy about an invention that suspends all motion. During the shooting he was so poor that he lived in a garret and cut the film with scissors and straight pins. Sometimes he didn't even have enough money to buy tickets to his main location site, the Eiffel Tower. Contemptuous of outworn plot formulas, he chose as his aesthetic model the slapstick of Mack Sennett. "[Sennett] created fantasy-poems in which clowns, bathing beauties, a car, a little dog, a bottle of milk, the sky, the sea, and a firecracker are the interchangeable elements whose every combination creates laughter and astonishment," noted Clair. "Sennett's rapid and fresh lyricism reveals to us a light world in which the law of gravity seems to be replaced by the joy of movement." These precepts are more dazzlingly apparent in the numerous Dadaist visual and editing effects of his next film, a freewheeling experimental short called *Entr'acte.* This landmark in the history of French avant-garde cinema was originally intended as an "intermission" feature for the Francis Picabia–Eric Satie ballet, *Relache.* The first half of the film consists of seemingly disconnected shots in keeping with the anarchic Dadaist spirit. The second takes the viewer to a funeral ceremony led by a camel-driven hearse. A wild chase ensues. Everywhere are bizarre image juxtapositions—a chessboard that contains the Place de la Concorde, an egg that contains a pigeon, a paper boat floating freely over the rooftops, a ballet dancer with the legs of a girl and the face of a bearded man. Finally, a magician springs out of a coffin and, with a wave of his wand, vanishes himself (and, presumably, the theater audience). Less overtly experimental, but just as visually inventive was Clair's classic 1927 farce comedy, *The Italian Straw Hat,* adapted from a stage work by Labiche. But the best was yet to come.

Clair's finest hour came with the advent of synchronized sound. *Sous les toits de Paris* (Under the roofs of paris), *A nous la liberté* (roughly, We are free), and *Le Million* (The millionaire)—all scripted by Clair, designed by Lazare Meerson, and photographed by Georges Perinal—appeared in rapid succession from 1929 to 1932, and they took ample opportunity to exploit the potentials of the asynchronous union of image and sound. Clair had initially been dubious about the coming of sound. "We were being asked to change our tools and our language in a few months," he recalled in his autobiography, *Cinema Yesterday and Today.* "Hence our hesitation, trouble of mind, and regrets." Contrary to the standard practices of "canned drama" so prevalent at the time, Clair sought to manipulate sound and image independently of one another, creating a kind of counterpoint between the two (he even said that musicians would make better film editors than professional filmmakers). As historian Lucy Fischer has said of this trilogy of films, "The uses of sound had not yet been codified, and the works reflect an aural conception that is far more open and explorative than it would come to be in later years. . . . His explorations were all involved with subverting the illusion of realistic sound in order to liberate the medium and restore to it its poetic powers." *Le Million* is arguably his masterpiece. The whimsical story about a lottery winner and his pursuit of the elusive ticket employs all manner of visual-aural combinations—scenes played out silently with only musical accompaniment, voices declaiming words in rhythmic articulation, lip movements matched to the sounds of musical instruments, song renditions replacing dialogue, choral music that represents a character's internal thoughts, sounds and music that are nonspecific and disconnected from the specific circumstances of a scene, and the "punning" use of sounds, as when a chase for the jacket is accompanied by the sounds of a cheering crowd at a football game. Thus, as Fischer notes, "The film continually alternates between evoking operetta, musical comedy, ballet, and silent scored film."

In response to charges that his pictures lacked social relevance, Clair made *The Last Millionaire* in 1934, but it was such a flop that Clair went into a 14-year exile, traveling to England and America for six English-language features. *The Ghost Goes West* (1936), *I Married a Witch* (1943), and *And Then There Were None* (1945) all had their virtues, chief among them the signature Clair whimsy underscored by darker implications. His return to France and his subsequent postwar films rarely recapture this delicate blend, but their maturity and emotional depth deserve a second look. *Beauty and the Devil* (1950) is a Faustian allegory that contains a vision of atomic holocaust; *Beauties of the Night* (1952) blends eroticism with intimations of suicide; and *Gates of Paris* (1957) ends with a homicide. By the end of the 1950s Clair found himself under attack by New Wave filmmaker FRANÇOIS TRUFFAUT for his alleged emotionless, studio-bound artifice. He was regarded, notes biographer R. C. Dale, as "a marionette master whose strings were showing." His reputation never fully recovered from this onslaught, and his last films received only a lukewarm reception. He reserved his last years for directing for the theater and for his 1970 autobiographical commentary on his films, *Cinema Yesterday and Today.* Biographer R. C. Dale sums up his essential greatness: "His has been a career with little waste and excess to it, and is thus all the more substantial. Clair's technical contributions to the cinema are many, still in use today. But it is something else, an elusive quality of grace that animates his characters, and thus his films. . . ."

Other Films *Two Timid Souls* (1928); *July 4th, 1933* (1933); *Break the News* (1937); *The Flame of New Orleans* (1940); *It Happened Tomorrow* (1943); *The Grand Maneuvers* (1945); *Silence Is Golden* (1947); *The Gallant Festivities* (1965).

References Dale, R. C., *The Films of René Clair,* vol. 1, *Exposition and Analysis,* and vol. 2, *Documentation* (Metuchen, N.J.: Scarecrow Press, 1986); Fischer, Lucy, "René Clair, *Le Million,* and the Coming of Sound," *Cinema Journal* 16, no. 2 (spring 1977): 33–50; McGerr, Celia, *Rene Clair* (Boston: Twayne, 1980).

—J.C.T.

Clouzot, Henri-Georges (1907–1977)

Acclaimed for his postwar melodramas, Henri-Georges Clouzot was born in Niort, France, on

November 20, 1907. He received his education at the École Navale in Brest and worked for a while as a reporter for *Paris-Midi*. He was offered a job in the film industry while he was interviewing Adolphe Osso in 1930, and between 1930 and 1934 he worked as an assistant to Carmine Gallone, Anatole Litvak, E. A. Dupont, and others. At this same time he contributed dialogue to several films, including: *Le Roi des palaces* (1932), *Caprice de princesse* (1933), and *Tout pour l'amour* (1933). In 1931 Clouzot coscripted and directed the short film, *Le Terreur des Batignolles.* From 1934 to 1938 Clouzot suffered from an extended bout of pleurisy and was confined to several sanitoriums. He returned to the film industry in 1938 and worked as a writer providing dialogue and lyrics to such films as *Le Revolte* (1938), *Le Duel* (1939), *Le Monde tremblera* (*La Revolte des vivants*), *Le Dernier des six* (1941), and *Les Inconnus dans la maison* (1941).

During the Occupation, Clouzot was able (because of the paucity of directors) to move from screenwriting to film directing. His premiere effort, *L'Assassin habite au 21* (The murderer lives at number 21) was a routine police drama. Clouzot's next film, *Le Corbeau* (*The Raven* [1943]), was a suspense thriller concerning poison pen letters being sent to numerous inhabitants of a small village. The film was produced by a German-owned company, Continentale. Although it was deemed "anti-French" at the time, and after the war Clouzot was briefly suspended from the film industry, it is now considered by many critics and historians as being more anti-German in its critique of small-town mores and people under the tyranny of hearsay and scandal.

Clouzot was barred from the film industry for two years by the "purification committee" for having made films during the Occupation that allegedly maligned the French character and demoralized the country. He resumed filmmaking in 1947 with *Quai des Orfèvres* (English title: *Jenny Lamour*) with Louis Jouvet. This film and his next, *Manon* (1948), evoked the film noir style and mood with their lowlife settings and atmosphere. During the fifties Clouzot was able to reach his widest audience and popularity with two films that are considered classic suspense thrillers: *Le Salaire de la peure* (*The Wages of Fear* [1952]) and *Les Diaboliques* (1954). *Le Salaire de la peure* was one of the first postwar French films to obtain wide distribution in English-speaking countries. It concerned the efforts of a group of down-and-out European expatriates in South America to deliver a truck load of nitroglycerin to a burning oil field. It received the Grandes Prix International at the 1953 Cannes Film Festival. *Les Diaboliques* was adapted from a novel by Pierre Boileau and Thomas Narcejac. The film is a brilliant exercise in horror involving a complicated murder plot set in a small boarding school. This particular film helped garner Clouzot a reputation as a master of suspense in the tradition of Hitchcock.

In 1956 the director made an ingenious documentary film about the nature of art. Pablo Picasso is filmed as he paints 15 new works of art before Clouzot's camera. All of these art pieces are destroyed at the end of the film, so that they exist only as part of the film itself. Clouzot shot the film in desaturated color and in CinemaScope. In 1984 the French government declared *Le Mystère Picasso (The Mystery of Picasso)* a national treasure. Ill health plagued many of Clouzot's subsequent film projects. Only three films were completed after *Le Mystère Picasso—Les Espions* (1957), *La Vérité* (1960), and *La Prisonnière* (1968). Henri-Georges Clouzot died in Paris, France, on January 12, 1977. Film historian Roy Armes said of Clouzot's ouevre: "The world of Clouzot's films is one where beauty and tenderness have no place and even love and friendship are rare. It is not at all an unemotional world, but the passions it contains are of the kind which involve dominance and degradation. . . . His natural source material is the thriller and he is at his best in depicting this genre's conventional setting . . . his world is very much a timeless one of human vices."

Other Films *Retour à la vie* (1949); *Miquette et sa mère* (1950); *Karajan: Early Images, Vol. 2* (1965–66) (for French television).

References Armes, Roy, *French Cinema* (London: Secker & Warburg, 1985); Crisp, Colin, *The Classic French Cinema, 1930–1960* (Bloomington: Indiana University Press, 1993); Pilard, Philippe, *H-G. Clouzot* (Paris: Editions Seghers, 1969).

—R.W.

Cocteau, Jean (1889–1963) A versatile and prolific poet, novelist, playwright, painter, and filmmaker, Jean Cocteau found in the film medium his most personalized expression of mortality and magic. He was born to a middle-class family in Maisons-Laffitte, near Paris, on July 5, 1889. He attended the Lycée Condorcet and was promptly expelled in 1904. As a teenager and protégé of the homosexual actor Edouard de Max, he found his first audiences while declaiming his poems at the Théâtre Femina. During the war years, he began writing for the Ballets Russes (his *Parade* was the "succes de scandale" of 1917), and he volunteered for service at the front with an ambulance unit. He vaulted into public notoriety in the decade of the 1920s with the pantomine ballet *Boeuf sur le toit,* modernistic stage adaptations of Sophocles and Shakespeare, his own play, *Orphée* (1925), volumes of poetry, and numerous paintings and designs.

Blood of the Poet (*Le Sang d'un poète* [1930]) was his first film, "a realistic documentation of unreal events," as he described it. It brought all his diverse talents in poetry and image-making to bear upon an intensely autobiographical document. Cocteau found in the film medium a highly personalized mode of expression. As commentator Arthur B. Evans has observed, "Cocteau was a stubborn independent who learned the science of film on his own—trial and error. A playwright and poet, Cocteau applied his literary talents to the screen, and many of his films are directly identifiable, in terms of technique, to his poetic works. The balance between his use of word and image on the screen is unmistakable." *Blood of a Poet* begins when a young poet walks through a mirror into a mysterious hotel corridor. After traversing the passage and witnessing a succession of scenes through the keyholes of the rooms, he is forced to commit ritual suicide. Crowned now in laurel leaves, the resurrected poet emerges from the mirror and is transformed into a statue. The cinematic devices include slow motion, skewed camera angles, and non-diegetic aural effects. The imagery is highly personal—the snowball fight is reminiscent of a painful childhood memory (repeated later in *The Terrible Children*), the opium smoker reflects his own drug abuse, the gunshots are a reference to his own father's suicide, and the sexual stigmata suggest his own sexual ambivalence. Bracketing the story are shots of a factory chimney collapsing— its fall interrupted at the beginning and then completed at the end. In other words, the entire film is to be regarded as taking place in but an instant.

For the next 15 years, Cocteau directed no more films but wrote scenarios and adaptations for other directors, the most important of which were the scenario for *The Eternal Return* (*L'Éternel retour* [1943]), directed by Jean Delannoy, and the dialogue for *The Ladies of the Bois de Boulogne* (*Les Dames du Bois de Boulogne* [1945]). His second film as director came in 1946 with *Beauty and the Beast (Belle et le bête).* Perhaps the finest fairy tale ever translated to film, it benefits from the elaborate scenic décor of the Beast's castle and from some gorgeous cinematic trickery, including the sparing but effective use of slow motion. As commentator Michael Popkin observes, in the original tale, the central character is Beauty, but in Cocteau's film, the Beast (Jean Marais) occupies center stage. Like the poet, he must die in one form in order to be reborn in another (echoing Cocteau's dictum, "To live you must die").

Four years later came *Orpheus,* a loose adaptation of his 1925 stage play, *Orphée*—as well as an elaboration of his earlier *Blood of a Poet*—that won the first prize at the International Film Festival in Venice and has come to be regarded as one of the masterworks of the French cinema. The figure of Orpheus is not a great priest, as in the Greek myth, but a famous contemporary poet whose celebrity has annoyed the avant-garde (who stand in for the Bacchantes of the fable). Departures from the original include replacing the horse's sinister oracular messages with radio broadcasts, transforming the glazier Heurtebise into the chauffeur of a fatal Rolls-Royce, and adding the characters of a rival young poet Cegeste and a squad of black-clad motorcyclists as agents of Death (Maria Casares). Like *Blood*, there is a passage through a mirror (the effect accomplished through the use of a vat of mercury), a slow-motion journey through a "Zone," or Underworld of magical visions and encounters, and a confrontation with a black-gowned female representing Death (Casares). Upon reviving the dead Eurydice and bringing her back to the upper world, Orpheus inadvertently breaks his promise never to look at her by inadvertently glimpsing her in the rear-view mirror of the fatal Rolls-Royce. Orpheus is subsequently shot dead and two of Death's motorcyclists bear his body away. Death, meanwhile, who has fallen in love with Orpheus, "kills" him and sends him back to life. For her transgression of the natural laws, she is consigned to a punishment "unimaginable to man." Orpheus and Eurydice, meanwhile, will live happily ever after. Despite the obvious elements of fantasy, Cocteau strove to keep its surface elements relatively commonplace: "The closer one approaches to mystery, the more important it becomes to remain a realist. Automobile radios, code messages, short-wave broadcasts, power failures—such elements, familiar to all, make it possible for me to keep things down to earth."

Cocteau wrote the screenplay and assisted JEAN-PIERRE MELVILLE in a 1952 adaptation of his 1929 novel, *The Terrible Children (Les Enfants terribles)*. It begins with a student named Paul (Edouard Dermit) being wounded during a snowball fight. Invalided at home, Paul is nursed by his sister, Elisabeth (Nicole Stéphane). When their

Jean Cocteau

mother dies, brother and sister embark on their respective love affairs, Paul with a model who resembles his sister, and Elisabeth with a wealthy American. They nonetheless remain bonded together in a virtually incestuous embrace. After a series of confused identities and mismatches, Paul dies from poison and Elisabeth is left to mourn. The film is a claustrophobic fable of sibling love, rivalry, and mutual destruction.

The Testament of Orpheus (Le Testament d'Orphée [1960]) was Cocteau's last film. Commentator Evans suggests that it must be regarded as "a lasting epitaph of his entire life, works, and self-examinations as a poet." It is the 70-year-old Cocteau himself who at last portrays on screen the role he has assumed all along in his life and work, that of a modern-day Orpheus. Despite its baffling subtitle, "Don't Ask Me Why," he has volunteered the explanation that this film tampers with time and abolishes its narrow limitations; moreover, cinema in general is "the only language suitable for bringing my night into the daylight and putting it on a table in the full sun." Events experienced by the poet within the film seem to transpire with the illogic of a dream, rather in the manner of the earlier *Blood of a Poet.* It begins with a portrait of the poet in 18th-century garb, lost in space-time, who seeks orientation from a professor of science by means of a small box of magical bullets that travel faster than light. After being shot by one of the bullets, the poet falls to the ground and bounces back to his feet in the modern day and wearing a new suit. Thus ensues a series of incidents and encounters with a man wearing a horse's mask, the resurrected figure of Cegeste (late of the earlier *Orpheus*), a dead hibiscus flower, which the poet is enjoined to bring back to life, a tribunal where the characters Heurtebise and Death (also from the earlier *Orpheus*) condemn him to a "life" sentence as a poet, his own "double" (who ignores him), a strange statuelike oracle that spews forth pages of literary works, and, finally, the goddess Minerva, who slays him with the point of her spear. Cocteau expires amid the rubble, his eyes wide open and smoke curling from his mouth. "Pretend that you are crying, my friends," he says, "since poets only pretend they are dead." At which point, the poet rises to his feet and leaves the temple and disappears into the rocky cliffs outside. It is the last of the many deaths and rebirths that have afflicted the poet.

Cocteau's preoccupation with the mythic, particularly the Orpheus story of art, death, and rebirth, was of primary importance to his work. Orphic allusions surface everywhere, particularly in *The Blood of a Poet,* a seminal document in the surrealistic cinema, and thereafter in *Orpheus* and *The Testament of Orpheus.* Moreover, the concomitant metaphors of mirrors, angels, and acrobats were crucial in exploring that myth. The mirror reflected back to man his own mortality. The figure of the angel shuttled back and forth between the polar states of life and death. Death was not a terminal condition of mortality for Cocteau, but a condition, a speculation, a dream that conveyed him to conditions beyond mere exterior surfaces. Poised precariously between these binary conditions of reality and magic was the third metaphor, the figure of the highwire acrobat, balanced between the circus ring below and the tent roof above. Cocteau himself—and, indeed, the Artist in general—was that angel and that acrobat, either commuting, as it were, between instinct and calculation, between the mundane and the marvelous; or hovering between them. His personal "death journey," as he called it, was frequently achieved by means of opium. In his art—in this case, the film medium—it was gained by the manipulation of plastic materials for the sake of marvelous effects and unlikely juxtapositions of shots that provoked unexpected meanings in the minds of his "enchanted" viewers.

Early in his career Cocteau had received two injunctions, or incantations, that influenced the rest of his life: The ballet impresario Diaghilev had once enjoined him to "astonish me"; and his friend and lover Raymond Radiguet had observed that "elegance consists in *not* astonishing." Perhaps the film medium, which he referred to as a "machine of dreams" and as "the Tenth Muse," was Cocteau's ideal engine in pursuing those dual but contradictory prerogatives. "I search for only the relief and the detail of the images that came forth from the great night of the human body," he said. "I then immediately adopt them as the documentary scenes of another realm."

Jean Cocteau died of an attack of pulmonary edema at Milly-la-Forêt on October 11, 1963. So vivid had been his presence in life that few at the funeral seemed to realize he was dead at all. "Indeed," writes his biographer Frederick Brown, "there were those who half expected him to leap out of the wings and bark stage directions with that resonant, nasal voice of his, persuading the celebrants to do his bidding." The writer François Mauriac noted at the time: "I'm amazed that he could do something as natural, as simple, as undevised as dying."

Other Films *The Two-Headed Eagle* (*L'Aigle à deux têtes* [1947]); *The Terrible Parents* (*Les Parents terribles* [1948]); *La Villa Santo-Sospir* (1952).

References Brown, Frederick, *An Impersonation of Angels: A Biography of Jean Cocteau* (New York: Viking Press, 1968); Evans, Arthur B., *Jean Cocteau and His Films of Orphic Identity* (Philadelphia: Arts Alliance Press, 1977); Popkin, Michael, "Cocteau's *Beauty and the Beast:* the Poet as Monster," *Literature/Film Quarterly* 10, no. 2 (1982): 100–109.

—J.C.T.

Coppola, Francis Ford (1939–) Francis Ford Coppola was born on April 7, 1939, in Detroit, Michigan, to Carmine and Italia Coppola. Coppola's middle name was a tribute to Henry Ford, as Carmine Coppola served as the musical arranger for the *Ford Sunday Evening Hour* on CBS radio. Carmine Coppola worked as a musician throughout Coppola's childhood, while Coppola's mother served as the family's Italian matriarch and raised Francis, older brother August, and younger sister Talia (who later became an actress not only in Coppola's films but also in Sylvester Stallone's *Rocky* series). Coppola's New York youth was steeped in Italian-American culture, music, new technologies such as television, and a bout of polio suffered at the age of 10. With his parents' support, Coppola

Francis Ford Coppola (left) on the set of *Gardens of Stone* (Tri-Star)

developed an interest in drama, which he studied as an undergraduate at Hofstra University, receiving his degree in 1959. The following year, he enrolled in the UCLA film school, where he made a number of short films and made a contact that would prove crucial to establishing his directing career: Roger Corman.

Coppola became a jack-of-all-trades for Corman in the early 1960s, working on several films and eventually persuading Corman to let him direct his first feature, *Dementia 13* (1963). After working as a screenwriter-for-hire in the mid-1960s, Coppola got another chance to direct when Warner Bros. allowed him to direct a script he wrote while under their employ. The resulting film, *You're a Big Boy Now* (1966), showed the influence of not only the French New Wave but also British cinema of the mid-1960s. The favorable notices for this first Warner Bros. effort led the studio to hire Coppola for a more ambitious directorial project: the big-budget musical *Finian's Rainbow* (1968). When this film ended up as a critical and commercial disaster, Coppola retreated to the maverick, independent type of production he was more used to and directed *The Rain People* (1969), another picture reminiscent of the French New Wave. With this film, Coppola inaugurated American Zoetrope, which would become one of his obsessions throughout the 1970s, as he attempted to turn the vanity label into a full-fledged studio (with little lasting success).

The failures of *Finian's Rainbow* and the first incarnation of American Zoetrope lowered Coppola's stock as a director but did not stop Paramount's Robert Evans from enlisting him for the film adaptation of Mario Puzo's novel *The Godfather* (1972). Coppola directed the picture not as a gangster film but as a family saga, and the film became perhaps the biggest artistic and financial success of Coppola's career, winning the Academy Award for best picture and helping to launch the blockbuster trend of the 1970s. The sequel, *The Godfather, Part II* (1974), nearly matched its success,

again winning best picture and establishing Coppola as one of the premier directors of the 1970s. In between the two *Godfather* pictures, Coppola wrote and directed *The Conversation* (1974), which was a critical success but failed to make an impact at the box office. Coppola spent the remainder of the 1970s engaged in the production of his Vietnam epic *Apocalypse Now* (1979), a film that was an astonishing artistic success but had a checkered and infamous production that included several false stops, health problems for various members of the cast and crew, and a number of problems with the Filipino government, in whose country the filming took place.

In the 1980s, Coppola focused mostly on less-ambitious projects such as the adaptations of the S. E. Hinton novels *The Outsiders* and *Rumble Fish* (both 1983), *Peggy Sue Got Married* (1986), and *Tucker: The Man and His Dreams* (1988). An exception to this was *The Cotton Club* (1984), a film about the 1930s Harlem club scene that had a production almost as storied as that of *Apocalypse Now*. After a delay of many years, Coppola next returned to the *Godfather* saga with *The Godfather, Part III* (1990), in which he concluded the story of the Corleone family. Although he has in recent years resurfaced as a director-for-hire, Coppola's most significant 1990s project was *Bram Stoker's Dracula* (1992), an ornate, baroque version of the classic vampire story.

Other Films   *One from the Heart* (1982); *Gardens of Stone* (1987); *New York Stories* ("Life Without Zoe" segment [1989]); *Jack* (1996); *The Rainmaker* (1997).

References   Bergan, Ronald, *Francis Ford Coppola Close Up: The Making of His Movies* (New York: Thunder's Mouth Press, 1997); Cowie, Peter, *Coppola* (New York: Scribner, 1990); Goodwin, Michael, and Naomi Wise, *On the Edge: The Life and Times of Francis Coppola* (New York: William Morrow, 1989).

—C.M.

Costa-Gavras, Constantin (1933–   )   With the release of his picture *Z* (1969), for which he won the Jury Prize at the Cannes Film Festival in

1970, Costa-Gavras became Europe's foremost political filmmaker by revisioning the events of the Lambrakis affair, involving a right-wing assassination in 1963 in Greece, but structuring those events in the manner of detective fiction. Reality-based politics would dominate much of his subsequent work, from *L'Aveu* (*The Confession* [1970]), based on Artur London's autobiography, to *État de siège* (*State of Siege* [1973]), scripted by Franco Solinas and concerning an American "adviser," kidnapped, tried, and executed by the Tupamaros guerrillas in Uruguay, to *Missing* (1982), which won an Academy Award for best screenplay and the Palme d'Or at the 1982 Cannes Film Festival. But the film was controversial, as was its director, as controversial in his way as Oliver Stone was later to become in America.

Konstantinos (Costa) Gavras was born in Kilvia in the Peloponnesus, the son of a Russian father and a Greek mother, in 1933. Because his father was a suspected communist, he was denied entry to Greek universities and unable to get a visa to study in the United States. He was educated in Paris, however, at the Sorbonne and the I.D. Hautes Études Cinématographiques, and in 1956 he became a naturalized French citizen. Before directing his first film, *Compartiment tueurs* (*The Sleeping Car Murders*) in 1966, he had been working since 1958 as an assistant to Yves Allegret, René Clair, René Clément, Henri Verneuil, and Jacques Demy.

Z began as a novel by the Greek writer Vassilis Vassilikos, published in 1966 and described by Stanley Kauffmann as a "thinly disguised account of the murder of Gregorios Lambrakis, a leftist deputy and professor of medicine at the University of Athens. After Lambrakis had protested the deployment of Polaris missiles in Greece in 1963 at a political meeting in Salonika, he was struck by a truck and killed, but this was no mere accident." As Kauffmann explained, in Greek "the initial *Z* stands for *zei*—he lives." In the film the murdered deputy was played by Yves Montand, and Jean-Louis Trintignant is the magistrate investigating

the death. His quest for justice is the mechanism that drives the film.

Like *Z, State of Siege* derives from and was patterned after an actual political event. In August 1970 a number of political kidnappings took place in the republic of Uruguay, instigated by a terrorist group, the Tupamaros. Among the kidnapped were Daniel Mitrione, a 50-year-old ex-police chief from Richmond, Indiana, and Claude Fly, an agronomist employed by a private firm. Mitrione, once an instructor at the International Police Academy in Washington, D.C., was serving as a "technical adviser" (called an "expert in communications" in the film) to the Uruguayan police, and was believed by the Tupamaros to be an American spy. The Tupamaros demanded the release of some 150 political prisoners, but the government refused to capitulate and ordered some 12,000 soldiers to seek out the terrorists and also round up some 20 suspected urban guerrillas, including former Socialist Party leader Raúl Sendic.

Consequently, the Tupamaros made good their threat: the body of Daniel Mitrione was eventually found in a parked and stolen 1948 Buick convertible. The American Department of State was apparently in agreement and sympathy with the course of action President Jorge Pacheco Areco had followed: "If we pressure governments to accede to such extreme demands," the State Department declared, "it would serve, in our view, only to encourage other terrorist groups to kidnap Americans." The Tupamaros were then placed in the position of having to take the political (and moral) consequences of following through with their threat—either to commit murder or to lose their credibility as a viable political force. This dilemma is at the heart of the film.

State of Siege made its controversial American premiere in April 1973 not at the Kennedy Center's American Film Institute Theatre, as originally scheduled, but at the Outer Circle Theatre in the city because George Stevens, Jr., national director

Constantin Costa-Gavras directing a scene in *Music Box* (Tri-Star)

of the AFI, decided that the film was "an inappropriate choice" for screening at the Kennedy Center because it allegedly "rationalizes an act of political assassination." The Nixon administration was notoriously sensitive to criticism in general, and the Kennedy administration had links to the International Police Academy. According to screenwriter Franco Solinas, the story "was based on an actual chronicle which took place in Latin America a few years ago, a story that tries to explain some of the ways used by imperialism to penetrate, dominate, and, when it succeeds, alter the reality of Latin America today." Nearly 10 years later, Costa-Gavras would take on another controversial film touching on the State Department's activities in Latin America.

Costa-Gavras crossed over to mainstream Hollywood filmmaking with the film *Missing* (1982), another true story, involving the frustrated attempt of Ed Horman (played by Jack Lemmon in one of his best roles) to locate his son, Charles, who turns up "missing" as a political prisoner in Latin America. The father joins his daughter-in-law, Joyce (Sissy Spacek), in Chile, where he runs into a bureaucratic brick wall, and gets absolutely no help or real cooperation from the United States Embassy. Following a script adapted from Thomas Hauser's book, *The Execution of Charles Horman* (1978), the director's methods in *Missing* are very similar to *Z*, with a comparable level of incremental outrage and disbelief over governmental abuses. The issue was political: "The horror is of a family which hopes the missing person is alive, but does not know. It is a kind of game between hope and death," Costa-Gavras explained to an interviewer. "You go on with hope, which every day becomes bigger—and thinner. It's a permanent torture, and some governments use this as a message of repression. When one man disappears, ten people around him are scared."

Initially, Costa-Gavras was reluctant to offer this project to an American studio "because the subject was too inflammatory, too violently political." But this was an American story, and finally he was convinced to let Universal Studios handle the film. The film proved to be controversial: the State Department issued denials and the battle was joined in the op-ed pages of the *Washington Post,* the *New York Times,* and other papers. Two main contenders were Flora Lewis, foreign affairs correspondent of the *New York Times,* and Alan Berger of the *Boston Globe,* who wrote that Lewis "was no doubt right to suggest that the film *Missing* is not an exact replica of reality. But if she had consulted the facts she accused Costa-Gavras of distorting, she would have found a reality far more disquieting than any cinematic recreation."

Not all of Costa-Gavras's films have been political thrillers. *The Minor Apocalypse* (1995), for example, in the words of *New York Times* reporter Stephen Holden, was a "comedy satirizing the fall of Communism, aging 1960s radicals, capitalist opportunism and the omnivorous media," starring Czech director Jiri Menzel as an unemployed Polish émigré writer, down and out in Paris. In 1997 Costa-Gavras launched another attack and exposé of media madness and mob psychology in *Mad City,* starring Dustin Hoffman as a hotshot television reporter caught in a museum with a desperate, armed museum guard (John Travolta), who has been laid off and threatens to bomb the museum if he is not given his job back. He takes a group of children hostage and accidentally shoots another guard. The situation escalates from there into an out-of-control media circus. Costa-Gavras, a prime architect of the political thriller as well as a social critic with his camera, was still in excellent form.

Other Films *Un homme de trop* (*Shock Troops* [1968]); *Section spéciale* (*Special Section* [1975]); *Clair de femme* (*A Woman's Glow* [1979]); *Hanna K.* (1983); *Family Business* (1985); *Betrayed* (*Summer Lightning* [1988]); *Betrayed* (1988); *Music Box* (1990); *Raspoutine* (1995).

References Armes, Roy, *French Cinema* (New York: Oxford University Press, 1985); Kauffmann, Stanley, "On Films: *Z,*" *New Republic,* December 13, 1969, pp. 22, 32; Michalczyk, John J., *Costa-Gavras: The Political Fiction Film* (Philadelphia: Art Alliance Press, 1984); Ray, Michele, "Interview with Franco Solinas and Costa-Gavras," in *State of Siege,* trans. Raymond Rosenthal (New York: Ballantine Books, 1973); Monaco, James, "The Costa-Gavras Syndrome," *Cineaste* 7, no. 2 (Spring 1976): 18–21; Welsh, J. M., "Beyond Melodrama: Art, Politics, and *State of Siege,*" *Film Criticism* 2, no. 1 (Fall 1977): 24–31.

—J.M.W.

Cukor, George (1899–1983) George Cukor, who was born in New York City in 1899, began his professional career as a stage manager in Chicago in 1919, and went to New York thereafter to direct for the Broadway theater during the 1920s. When the movies learned to talk, Cukor, like other stage directors, was summoned to Hollywood in the early 1930s. He became a dialogue director, a position usually filled by someone with theatrical experience who was hired to help silent-film directors make the transition to talking pictures more smoothly. One of the films he worked on in that capacity was *All Quiet on the Western Front* (1930); later, producers finally decided that he was ready to direct on his own and assigned him to *Tarnished Lady* (1931), starring Tallulah Bankhead.

From the beginning of his career as a director, he always sought to be faithful to his films' literary sources, most of which were novels and plays. He felt that a director can modify the source story to some extent, but he really should not change it in any major fashion; he should rather follow the original work as closely as possible. His films range from classics with Greta Garbo in *Camille* (1937), through his films with Spencer Tracy and Katharine Hepburn such as *Pat and Mike* (1952), to the Judy Garland musical *A Star*

George Cukor

identified with the roles he plays that, while enacting Othello, he develops a murderous streak of jealousy that eventually destroys him. The attempt of individuals to reconcile their cherished dreams with the sober realities of their lives can likewise be found in movies as superficially different as *Holiday* (1938), *Gaslight* (1944), and *Dinner at Eight* (1933). His films also suggest that everyone must seek to sort out fantasy from fact if they are to cope realistically with their problems—something Cukor's characters frequently fail to do, as is the case with the central character in *A Double Life.*

In sum, his movies remain firmly rooted in, and committed to, the workaday world of reality. In film after film, Cukor sought to prod the mass audience to reconsider their cherished illusions in order to gain fresh insights into the problems that confront everyone. Film critics have therefore pointed out that his films are both entertaining and thought provoking. It could be said that Cukor was the prototype of the ideal Hollywood director, for he was a skilled craftsman who recognized that a good film is the product of many talents. He was, therefore, able to work successfully within the Hollywood system and at the same time add a personal touch to the motion pictures he directed. Cukor directed his last film, *Rich and Famous,* in 1981, thus earning the distinction of being one of the oldest directors ever to direct a major motion picture. He was likewise marked as enjoying one of the longest continuous careers of any director working in films and television. Cukor received his share of accolades, including the prestigious Life Achievement Award from the Directors Guild of America in 1981. He also won an Academy Award as best director (after five nominations) for *My Fair Lady* (1964), and an Emmy for directing his first television film, *Love Among the Ruins* (1975). Yet some of the satisfaction he derived from his long career, he told this writer, was grounded in the fact that he brought so much enjoyment to so many people. As one critic put it, Cukor's films can be appreciated—or rather, liked—at one level or another by just about everyone.

is Born (1954). Although many of his pictures are derived from literary works, the sum total of his movies nevertheless reflects the personal vision of the man who made them all, because he always chose material that was consistent with his personal view of reality.

Most often he explored the conflict between illusion and reality in people's lives. The chief characters of his pictures are frequently actors and actresses, for they, more than the rest of us, run the risk of allowing the world of illusion, with which they are constantly involved, to become their reality. This theme is obvious in many of Cukor's best films, including *A Double Life* (1947). Ronald Colman earned an Academy Award for his performance in the film as an actor who becomes so

George Cukor (Author's collection)

Other Films *The Philadelphia Story* (1940); *Adam's Rib* (1949).

References Phillips, Gene D., *Major Film Directors of the American and British Cinema* (Cranbury, N.J.: Associated University Presses, 1999); Long, Robert Emmett, ed. *George Cukor: Interviews* (Jackson: University Press of Mississippi, 2001).

—G.D.P.

Curtiz, Michael (1888–1962) As "Michael Curtiz," Hungarian-born Mihaly Kertesz became one of Hollywood's most versatile and prolific directors. He was born on December 24, 1888, in Budapest and educated at Markoszy University and the Royal Academy of Theatre and Art. He first entered show business at the age of 14 when he became an extra for a Viennese theater company. His first film was also Hungary's first feature film, *The Last Bohemian* (1912). After two years service in the Hungarian Infantry during World War I, he left Hungary and worked for brief periods in Sweden, France, and Germany. Little is known about this period in his career, and too many historians have written off his pre-Hollywood years. A reassessment is badly needed.

Producer Jack Warner brought him to Hollywood in 1926 where he made a hundred films, culminating in *The Comancheros* in the year of his death, 1962. From the outset, Curtiz established himself as one of Warner Bros.'s top directors. He directed two of their biggest part-talkies, *Tenderloin* and *Noah's Ark* (both 1928), and in 1930 he made no less than six features. Few directors can match Curtiz for his longevity and the diversity of his film output. He was the ultimate Hollywood contract director, comfortably in charge, a consummate craftsman, ready to take on any project, and never fussy about innovative or experimental techniques. "I put all the art in my pictures I think the audience can stand," he said wryly. Nonetheless, most of his films are distinguished by crisp photography, a mobile camera, and a fine eye for detail.

He was notorious for on-set antics—he was nothing short of a tireless and demanding autocrat—and his fractured English ("What are they trying to make from me, a jingle bells?" he once asked a writer). He is best remembered today for his Warner Bros. films from the 1930s and 1940s, including the classic adventure swashbucklers and westerns with Errol Flynn, *Captain Blood* (1935), *Charge of the Light Brigade* (1937), *The Adventures of Robin Hood* (1938), *Dodge City* (1939), *The Sea Hawk* (1940); melodramas with Bette Davis and Joan Crawford, *Private Lives of Elizabeth and Essex* (1939), *Mildred Pierce* (1945); biopics, *Yankee Doodle Dandy* (1942), about George M. Cohan, *Night and Day* (1946), about George Gershwin, *Young Man with a Horn* (1950), about Bix Beiderbecke, *Jim Thorpe—All American* (1951); musicals, *Romance on the High Seas* (1948), *The Jazz Singer* (1953); gangster films, *20,000 Years in Sing Sing* (1933),

Angels with Dirty Faces (1938); and horror classics, *Doctor X* (1932), *Mystery of the Wax Museum* (1933). He even directed one of Elvis Presley's first (and best) pictures, *King Creole* (1958).

Undoubtedly his best known film is *Casablanca* (1943), the only film for which he received an Oscar for best director. Humphrey Bogart's breakout performance as Rick, the proprietor of the Café Americaine, symbolized the dilemma of America and its citizens while on the sidelines of the European war, poised between an apolitical, neutral stance and the patriotic call to arms in time of crisis. Its distinguished cast—in addition to Bogart, there was Ingrid Bergman, Claude Rains, Conrad Veidt, and Paul Henried—clever script by Julius and Philip Epstein and Howard Koch, music score by Max Steiner, and, of course, Dooley Wilson's memorable rendition of "As Time Goes By," all blended into one of the most perfect entertainments ever to come out of Hollywood. Scenarist Howard Koch notes that it was perhaps because of the disagreements he and Curtiz had over the story's tone—Koch wanted to emphasize political intrigue and characterization and Curtiz preferred to underscore the romantic elements of the story—that the film achieved a magical balance between the two.

Everywhere in Curtiz's output there are special pleasures—the monumental size and scale of the flood scenes in *Noah's Ark*; the stunning beauty of the two-color Technicolor process in *The Mystery of the Wax Museum*; the loving recreation of the "Give My Regards to Broadway" number in *Yankee Doodle Dandy*; the sea battle between Captain Geoffrey Thorpe's (Errol Flynn) ship and a Spanish galleon in *The Sea Hawk*; the "Begin the Beguine" sequence in *Night and Day*; and the startling execution scene at the end of *Angels with Dirty Faces*. In 1953 Curtiz left Warner Bros. after making 80 pictures. The remainder of his career was spent at other studios, where he continued to make a variety of subjects. He died on April 11, 1962. Curtiz himself summed up his special brand of unpretentious artistry: "To make the best pictures I can that will give audiences their money's worth; to please myself as much as I can without forgetting that the pleasure of my audiences comes first. Thus only do I think I can make any substantial contribution to the art of motion pictures."

Other Films   *Sodom and Gomorrah* (1923); *Moon of Israel* (1924); *The Kennel Murder Case* (1933); *Black Fury* (1935); *Virginia City* (1939); *Santa Fe Trail* (1940); *Passage to Marseille* (1944); *Life with Father* (1947); *White Christmas* (1954); *The Adventures of Huckleberry Finn* (1960).

References   Kinnard, Roy, and R. J. Vitone, *The American Films of Michael Curtiz* (Metuchen, N.J.: Scarecrow, Press, 1986); Koch, Howard, *Casablanca: Script and Legend* (New York: Overlook Press, 1992).

—J.C.T.

DeMille, Cecil B[lount] (1881–1959)

The pioneering American director and producer, Cecil B. DeMille, was born on August 12, 1881, in Ashfield, Massachusetts, to Henry Churchill de Mille and the former Mathilda Beatrice Samuel. Both of his parents had theatrical interests. His mother had been an actress before her marriage, and his father, a lay Episcopal preacher and schoolmaster, wrote plays in his spare time. A friend and eventual partner of David Belasco, one of the best-known American playwrights and directors of the late 19th century, Henry de Mille was eventually successful enough in his writing to change his career. When Cecil was 12, his father suddenly died of typhus. The young DeMille, who later changed the structure of his last name, would continue to idolize his father throughout his life.

In 1896 Cecil was sent to the Pennsylvania Military College in Chester, Pennsylvania, and in 1898 he enrolled in the American Academy of Dramatic Arts in New York City to study acting. From 1900 to 1910, DeMille acted in several Broadway plays and for numerous touring road shows. He began writing plays with his brother William in 1906. After Beatrice de Mille founded a theatrical agency, the De Mille Play Company in 1910, DeMille met Jesse Lasky and Samuel

Goldfish (later Goldwyn) through his mother's contacts, and with them formed the Jesse L. Lasky Feature Play Company in 1912. Their first film was *The Squaw Man* (1914), directed by DeMille and adapted from an old Broadway play. This six-reel film was the first feature-length motion picture made in the United States. Shot largely around Los Angeles, this enormously successful film helped to establish the city as the center for American motion picture production, and DeMille has therefore often been credited for having "founded" Hollywood.

DeMille directed seven more features in 1914, including *Brewster's Millions* and *The Virginian,* based on Owen Wister's classic western novel. By the end of that year DeMille had established himself as one of the leading film directors in the nation. In his early film career, DeMille preferred shooting stories based on traditional stage melodramas. Over the next two years he directed 22 feature-length films, often writing the screenplays and editing the films himself. The best known of these films was *The Cheat* (1915), a film much admired in France and a film that many critics consider his finest work. *The Cheat* was an audacious melodrama that featured Fannie Ward as an upper-class woman married to a stockbroker who foolishly invests charity funds in a risky stock, loses all, and then turns for help to a nefarious Asian jade dealer (Sessue Hayakawa), who exploits her economically and sexually. The film used experimental lighting, and DeMille developed an editing and visual style that enhanced the psychology of his characters.

DeMille also directed the operatic diva Geraldine Farrar in *Carmen* in 1915, lending motion pictures a new air of respectability. Farrar starred in several other DeMille films, including *Temptation* (1916), *Maria Rosa* (1916), and *Joan the Woman* (1917), DeMille's take on Joan of Arc. *Joan the Woman* was an especially significant film in

DeMille's body of work in that it began the long tradition of grand historical epics in which DeMille later specialized. In 1916 the Lasky Company merged with Adolph Zukor's Famous Players to form Paramount Pictures. DeMille was made responsible for all of the films that the studio released.

Later in the decade DeMille's pictures took a new direction, anticipating the changes in public mood that would result from the experience of World War I, and the transforming mores in American society. DeMille's target audience was always the middle class, and his socio-sexual films of the later 1910s and early 1920s reflected a new morality that was overtaking America. *Old Wives for New* (1918), *We Can't Have Everything* (1918), *Don't Change Your Husband* (1919), *Male and Female* (1919), and *Why Change Your Wife?* (1920) all featured wealthy couples who often changed their partners, only to reunite with their original husbands or wives. The films reflected a staple of DeMille's later films—his combination of sexual titillation and overt moral sermonizing. Several of the films starred Gloria Swanson, who became a major star under DeMille's direction. As his forays into sophisticated salaciousness and amoral decadence progressed in such films as *Saturday Night* (1922) and *Manslaughter* (1922), the once highly respected director found himself under attack by cultural critics. Some historians have argued that DeMille did as much to shape the sexual morality of the 1920s as he did to reflect it.

In 1923 DeMille's career took another sharp turn with *The Ten Commandments*. One of the first of his great biblical epics, the film proved to be one of the greatest moneymakers of the silent era. The biblical story was only half of the film, the latter half being a modern-day Cain and Abel parable. One of the first films with production costs over $1 million, the motion picture recouped its costs several times over. This biblical epic was to be followed by DeMille's $2.5-million production *King of Kings* in 1927, another of his most successful films, and one that played well

Cecil B. DeMille (Author's collection)

into the 1950s as a special exhibition. This lavish, reverential, and spectacular film was DeMille's personal favorite.

DeMille remained an eclectic filmmaker throughout the 1920s, although his moralizing became more focused and mindful in the creation of his films. In 1925 DeMille was forced out of Paramount due to various mergers and takeovers and because of his inability to contain the costs of his productions. With the help of bankers, he formed the Cinema Corporation of America and became his own producer. His last film with CCA as an independent producer was *The Godless Girl* (1929), an "exposé" of atheists attempting to take over the public school system. In 1928 CCA came into the hands of Joseph Kennedy, and DeMille's unit was transplanted to MGM. His first sound film was *Dynamite* (1929), but DeMille's initial sound films (which included a third version of *The Squaw Man* [1931]) were commercially unsuccessful, and there was talk that DeMille would simply be another victim of the transition to talking pictures.

In 1931 DeMille returned to Paramount for a mere fraction of his previous salary. The director rebounded, however, with *Sign of the Cross* (1932), which returned to his tried-and-true formula of overt sexuality and debauchery (during Nero's reign, this time), with ample sermonizing over the sinner's eventual downfall. The film, which starred Charles Laughton, Fredric March, and Claudette Colbert, was financially successful but was criticized severely by many in the religious community for DeMille's lascivious scenes, which included Colbert bathing in milk, implied lesbianism, and barbarous torture.

DeMille followed up *Sign of the Cross* with two more historical epics—*Cleopatra* (1934) and *The Crusades* (1935). After the latter film lost over $700,000, DeMille switched to the western genre, filming *The Plainsman* (1937), *The Buccaneer* (1938), *Union Pacific* (1939), and *North West Mounted Police* (1940). All of these films were financially successful.

Meanwhile, in 1936 DeMille entered into radio programming, presenting the *Lux Radio Theatre of the Air,* which recreated shortened versions of Hollywood movies dramatized for radio. As a member of the American Federation of Radio Artists, DeMille was asked in August of 1944 for a one dollar contribution to defeat a proposed California state amendment to end the closed shop. DeMille not only publicly refused to donate to this cause, but also resigned from the radio show and established the DeMille Foundation for Political Freedom. Thereafter, he became one of the most visible and vocal conservatives in postwar Hollywood, and his organization became a rallying point for the later communist witch-hunts.

After several lackluster films, DeMille rebounded again with *Samson and Delilah* (1949), a biblical epic that earned more than $12 million and began a Hollywood trend to cash in on Bible stories. Still another DeMille box-office winner, *The Greatest Show on Earth* (1952), went on to earn an Oscar for best picture (perhaps reflecting the extent of McCarthyism's influence on Hollywood). DeMille's last film, *The Ten Commandments* (1956), was a remake of the 1923 film and was even more epic in scope than the earlier version. A tremendous blockbuster, the film is still telecast annually. DeMille was scheduled to remake *The Buccaneer,* but was prevented from doing so when he suffered a heart attack while filming *The Ten Commandments.* He let his son-in-law Anthony Quinn have his first directing job on that film, while he served as producer. While on a publicity tour for the film, DeMille suffered another heart attack and died in his home a month later. His autobiography was published posthumously in 1959. DeMille was considered a consummate showman and an expert in self-promotion. He became the symbol of the tyrannical director, wearing a costume that included riding boots and breeches, the figure he portrayed in the Hollywood classic *Sunset Boulevard* (1950), which also featured the star he had created, Gloria Swanson.

References Essoe, Gabe, and Raymond Lee, *DeMille: The Man and His Pictures* (New York: Castle Books, 1970); Higashi, Sumiko, *Cecil B. DeMille and American Culture: The Silent Era* (Berkeley: University of California Press, 1994); Higashi, Sumiko, *Cecil B. DeMille: A Guide to References and Resources* (Boston: G. K. Hall, 1985).

—G.B.

Demme, Jonathan (1944–) Perhaps no contemporary American director has succeeded in such a wide range of film genres as Jonathan Demme. Born February 22, 1944, in Baldwin, New York, Demme's family moved to Florida when he was young. He attended the University of Florida, where he wrote movie reviews, and then, after some time in the air force, worked for producer Joseph E. Levine. He had other jobs on the fringes of show business, including doing publicity work for movie companies and writing for *Film Daily,* before finding himself under the tutelage of ROGER CORMAN. When he struck out on his own, he created a body of work that captured many idiosyncrasies and quirks of the American character. From offbeat comedies to the most highly acclaimed rock concert film to the only horror film to be awarded the Academy Award for best picture, Demme is fearless in tackling varied subject matter and eliciting often career-defining performances from his actors.

Melvin and Howard (1980) was Demme's breakthrough film—the uniquely American tale of common man Melvin Dummar, whose fabled meeting with Howard Hughes almost makes him rich. Mary Steenburgen, as Dummar's wife, received an Oscar for best supporting actress, the first of four Oscar-winning performances Demme has directed. The film is a bittersweet take on the seeming unattainability of the American Dream, its obsession with success and fame, and a consumer culture full of kitsch. However, like much of Demme's later work, the film maintains a sympathy and generosity of spirit for the lovable losers at the heart of this quintessentially American tale.

Demme embraces the eccentricities of his characters and never condescends to them. Melvin is constantly trying to change himself, to become something better, but always seems to fail. Later Demme heroes like Charlie and Audrey in *Something Wild* (1986), Angela in *Married to the Mob* (1988), and Clarice in *The Silence of the Lambs* (1991) will have greater success fulfilling the American notion of self-transformation.

Demme is known for his eclectic taste in music throughout his films, so it is no wonder that he directed the Talking Heads concert film, *Stop Making Sense* (1984), commonly regarded as the greatest concert movie ever made. Employing footage from three nights at a 1983 concert at the Hollywood Pantages Theater, Demme fashioned one of the great musical celebrations on film. A true collaboration with Talking Heads front man, David Byrne, Demme's film captures the energy and urgency of the group's music and the concert experience itself through expert editing and a variety of camera angles. Byrne in his big suit flopping about onstage is one of the most joyous images in a Demme film.

While Demme is one of the most talented filmmakers of his generation, his films have not gained the wide audiences they deserve. Two such films are *Something Wild* and *Married to the Mob,* comedies that play with genre expectations. *Something Wild,* possibly Demme's greatest achievement, is a kind of updated 1930s screwball comedy with the sexy free spirit (Melanie Griffith in her best performance ever) liberating the repressed yuppie (Jeff Daniels) from his constraining middle-class existence and hitting the road with him. *Something Wild* is funny, sexy, and, best of all, unpredictable—an energized journey into the heart of Americana that is at once familiar and new all at the same time. When Ray Liotta, as Griffith's estranged husband, shows up in the last act, the film takes an unexpected turn and goes in a whole new direction—one that is both dangerous and thrilling.

Married to the Mob is a gangster comedy with a twist—it focuses on a woman, a mob widow trying to rebuild her life away from the family. Michelle Pfeiffer has never been funnier or more appealing (Demme seems to have a way with female performers), and Dean Stockwell and Mercedes Ruehl are wonderful in support. The details of gangster kitsch, from the way the wives style their hair to the goofy restaurants where the mob guys eat, make the film a wacky delight and yet another underappreciated gem of the 1980s.

Demme's commercial breakthrough came with *The Silence of the Lambs,* which garnered the top five Academy Awards (picture, director, actor [Anthony Hopkins], actress [Jodie Foster], and adapted screenplay). Based on Thomas Harris's novel about an FBI trainee who enlists the help of a brilliant serial killer to help track down another killer, *Silence* is a masterpiece of the horror genre and something completely unexpected from Demme, who before had flirted with the darker elements of American culture but here flings himself headfirst into new territory. The performances are excellent, the confrontations between Hopkins and Foster are tense, and the pacing and editing maintain a level of suspense throughout the film right up to the nerve-racking climax. *Silence* exemplifies a filmmaker commanding all the elements of his craft in service of a taut, thrilling story.

Philadelphia (1993) represents yet another change of pace for Demme. The first mainstream Hollywood movie to deal with AIDS, *Philadelphia* revolves around the struggles of a lawyer (Tom Hanks in an Oscar-winning role) who is fired from his firm because of his disease. Some critics claimed that the film was simplistic and that it played down the homosexuality of the lead character and his lover and gave the hero an unbelievably supportive family to make the project more palatable to a wide audience. And yet *Philadelphia,* while not a radical work, is a worthy entry in the tradition of socially conscious filmmaking. It puts a human face on the AIDS crisis and delivers on an emotional level.

Demme's most recent film, *Beloved* (1998), based on Toni Morrison's novel, is arguably a major misstep in his career. A shapeless, confusing mess about the aftermath of slavery, it features a muted performance by Oprah Winfrey in the pivotal role of a former slave haunted by the daughter she killed to free her from life as a slave. *Beloved* trades the clarity of Demme's best work for an attempt at something grand and epic, but the film is never emotionally moving and often downright puzzling. It is also tedious—one adjective that could never before have applied to Demme's work. Demme ultimately is the one director who can touch the pulse of contemporary America in all its beautiful and frightening oddity, from the wistful dreamers of *Melvin and Howard* to the free-wheeling romantics of *Something Wild* to the serial killers of *The Silence of the Lambs*. A portentous stream-of-consciousness period piece about slavery's horrible legacy does not fit the unique sensibility of one of America's greatest living filmmakers.

Other Films *Caged Heat* (1974); *Crazy Mama* (1975); *Fighting Mad* (1976); *Citizens Band/Handle with Care* (1977); *Last Embrace* (1979); *Swing Shift* (1984); *Swimming to Cambodia* (1987); *Cousin Bobby* (1991).

References Bliss, Michael, and Christina Banks, *What Goes Around Comes Around: The Films of Jonathan Demme* (Carbondale: Southern Illinois University Press, 1996); Conlon, James, "Silencing Lambs and Educating Women," *Post Script* 12, no. 1 (Fall 1992): 3–12; Fawell, John, "The Musicality of the Filmscript," *Literature/Film Quarterly* 17, no. 1 (1989): 44–49; Fischer, Lucy, "Mr. Dummar Goes to Town: An Analysis of *Melvin and Howard*," *Film Quarterly* 36, no. 1 (Fall 1982): 32–40; Murphy, Kathleen, "Communion," *Film Comment* 27, 1 (January–February 1991): 31–32; Negra, Diane, "Coveting the Feminine: Victor Frankenstein, Norman Bates, and Buffalo Bill," *Literature/Film Quarterly* 24, no. 2 (1996): 193–200; Smith, Gavin, "Identity Check," *Film Comment* 27, no. 1 (January–February 1991): 28–30; Sundelson, David, "The Demon Therapist and Other Dangers: Jonathan Demme's *The Silence of the Lambs*," *Journal of Popular Film and Television* 21, no. 1 (Spring

1993): 12–17; Tibbetts, John C., "Oprah's Belabored *Beloved,*" *Literature/Film Quarterly* 27, no. 1 (1999): 74–76.

—P.N.C.

De Palma, Brian (1940–) Brian De Palma has sustained a career in Hollywood despite numerous setbacks, including outraged protest groups, major flops, and scathing reviews. Yet just when many critics are ready to write him off as a director whose films have never lived up to the promise of his early work, he returns to the limelight with a commercially successful film. Often too easily dismissed as a pale ALFRED HITCHCOCK imitation, De Palma should be judged by the depth and breadth of his work, not simply by his most obvious cinematic fixations.

Born on September 11, 1940, in Newark, New Jersey, De Palma seemed to be transfixed by the technology of the cinema at an early age. There is a story linking his voyeuristic style to a particular childhood trauma. As a young child, his parents split up, his mother accusing his father of infidelity. The young De Palma apparently spent several days stalking his dad with recording equipment, hoping to find evidence to confirm his mother's suspicions. Whether this story is based on hard facts or myth-building fiction, the story reaffirms De Palma's signature approach: the camera as ultimate voyeur, constantly peering at his characters' most personal, intimate moments. His earliest films, largely unseen by American audiences, are considered by many contemporary critics to be ahead of their time. Dark comedy and social satire were not trademarks of early 1960s cinema, yet these films stand up today due largely to De Palma's insightful, humorous social observations.

His first feature-length films, including *Greetings* (1968), *Hi, Mom!* (1970), and *Get to Know Your Rabbit* (1970), were very much in the 1960s counterculture vein, but they received limited distribution. De Palma achieved widespread acclaim in 1973 with *Sisters,* a disturbing thriller dealing with Siamese twins, one aggressive and the other pas-

sive. The film, while only a modest box-office success, alerted critics to De Palma's abilities as a talented director of psychological horror stories. His next job, as director of *The Phantom of the Paradise* (1974), allowed De Palma to update the classic *Phantom of the Opera* tale as a Faustian rock opera. Deftly satirizing the music business while using split screens and video technology to great effect, many consider *Phantom* to be one of De Palma's strongest movies. While many critics dismissed his next film, 1976's *Obsession,* as more of a Hitchcock rip-off than the *hommage* he intended, he finally achieved breakthrough commercial success with his cinematic version of Stephen King's novel, *Carrie* (1976). Sissy Spacek's portrayal of the film's sympathetic lead character struck a note with the horror crowd, elevating the film above most of the derivative exploitation films of the day.

Perhaps feeling the invincible power that came with success, De Palma followed *Carrie* with *The Fury* (1978), another psychological horror story that exploited his previous film's mental telepathy storyline to excess. The film, though featuring some excellent set pieces, was a commercial failure, due largely to the weak script. De Palma, in turn, retreated from big-budget filmmaking to make *Home Movies* (1979), a flaky farce reminiscent of his first films, which starred his then wife, actress Nancy Allen. *Dressed to Kill* (1980) followed, reviving calls of Hitchcockian plagiarism and offending many women's groups at the same time. While the film's plot at times recalled *Psycho,* the graphic sexuality and violence ensured controversy and led to numerous protests by newly empowered feminist organizations. *Dressed to Kill* does ape some Hitchcock techniques, but the film's stylistic content rarely outweighs De Palma's power to chill the audience. While not a hit in its initial box-office run, De Palma's next film, *Blow Out* (1981), has aged nicely. The story revolves around a Hollywood soundman who may have inadvertently recorded a political assassination while combing a city park for sound effects. Though needlessly violent at its climax, *Blow Out* captures De Palma's strengths as a master of suspenseful action sequences, certainly in debt to Hitchcock, but with a voice and vision of his own. In 1983, *Scarface* brought renewed charges of racial insensitivity and excessive, graphic violence, and was savaged by critics at the time of its release. Like several other De Palma films, however, *Scarface* found life on the then-emerging technology of home video, spawning legions of dialogue-quoting devotees.

By the time of *Body Double* (1984), his critics were accusing him of needless repetition, perhaps accounting for De Palma's turn away from Hitchcockian-style suspense vehicles. However, his films since that point have turned more workmanlike, and it is more difficult to discern the auteur imprint so prevalent in his earlier films. *Wiseguys* (1986), a misguided attempt at broad genre comedy, led to *The Untouchables* (1987), a commercial success without the trademark flourishes of stylistic suspense he had become known for. A laughable, though technically proficient, reworking of the "Odessa Steps sequence" from SERGEI EISENSTEIN's *Battleship Potemkin* led many critics to wonder if De Palma had grown bored with the filmmaking process. *Casualties of War* (1989) is an honest, highly personalized attempt to critique the futility of the Vietnam war. However, perhaps due to the ham-fisted histrionics of Sean Penn as an angry young soldier, *Casualties* feels at times as though De Palma, belonging to the "film school generation" of the 1960s and early 1970s, is making the film out of some sort of obligation to the liberal values supposedly championed by filmmakers his age.

The year 1990 brought *The Bonfire of the Vanities,* an ill-fated adaptation of Tom Wolfe's popular novel. Wildly inconsistent style, miscast actors, and attempts to soften the book's sarcastic tone are all cited as reasons for the film's failure, one of Hollywood's biggest of recent years. (An excellent account of the film's making can be read in Julie Salamon's book *The Devil's Candy.*) Both *Raising Cain* (1992) and *Carlito's Way* (1993) received modest critical praise, returning De Palma

Brian De Palma (Filmways Pictures)

to more familiar ground in the horror and criminal/gangster genres, respectively. The success of 1996's *Mission: Impossible,* from the 1960s television series and starring Tom Cruise as Ethan Hunt, seemed to garner attention for everyone involved, save director De Palma. The film was rescued from a dense, convoluted script by virtuoso action sequences, though De Palma's signature style had seemingly been left out. His latest films, *Snake Eyes* (1998) and *Mission to Mars* (2000), were major critical and commercial disappointments. However, one should not take this as an indication of De Palma's potential future performance, as he has shown a knack for perseverance in such an unforgiving profession as directing.

Other Films *Icarus* (1960); *660124: The Story of an IBM Card* (1961); *Wotan's Wake* (1962); *Jennifer* (1964); *Bridge That Gap* (1965); *Show Me a Strong Town and I'll Show You a Strong Bank* (1966); *The Responsive Eye* (1966); *Murder a la Mod* (1968); *The Wedding Party* (1969); *Dionysus* (1970); *Mr. Hughes* (2000).

References Bliss, Michael, *Brian De Palma* (Metuchen, N.J.: Scarecrow Press, 1983); Bouzereau, Laurent, *The De Palma Cut: The Films of America's Most Controversial Director* (New York: Dembner, dist. by Norton, 1988); Dworkin, Susan, *Double De Palma: A Film Study With Brian De Palma* (New York: Newmarket Press, 1984); MacKinnon, Kenneth, *Misogyny in the Movies: The De Palma Question* (Newark: University of Delaware Press, 1990); Salamon, Julie, *The Devil's Candy: The Bonfire of the Vanities Goes to Hollywood* (Boston: Houghton Mifflin, 1991).

—J.A.

De Sica, Vittorio (1901–1974)

Best known for his contributions to the movement known as "Italian neorealism," Vittorio De Sica was also known in his own country as a fine stage and screen actor. Born in Sora, Italy, on July 7, 1901, he was the son of an Italian businessman. Throughout his childhood Vittorio was on the move, first to Naples (1904–06), then Florence (1907), and finally to Rome (1912). During his adolescence De Sica became involved in theatrical activity—primarily amateur groups. When Vittorio was 21 he fulfilled his military obligation by serving in the Grenadier's Regiment. A few years later he began his professional career as an actor with the theater company of Tatiana Pavlova, a Russian director who was presenting plays in Rome. Between 1923 and 1924 De Sica performed as *secondo brillante* (supporting comic roles) in Pavlova's company. Soon De Sica was playing romantic leads in musical comedies and light and serious dramas. By 1930 De Sica was a full-fledged "star" on the Italian stage, having performed with such companies as the Compagnia Artiste Associati. From 1930 to 1940 De Sica further pursued his acting career in various companies and various successes, and it was during this period that De Sica became known as the "Italian Chevalier." It wasn't until after 1949 that his stage appearances began to decrease, due to his successes as a screen actor and film director.

De Sica appeared in films as early as 1918, when he had a small part as the young Clemenceau in Eduardo Bencivenga's *Il processo Clemenceau*. His first speaking role was in one of Italy's first "talking pictures," Amleto Palermi's *La vecchia signora* (1931). Throughout the thirties De Sica appeared in numerous Italian films, continuing his stage appearances as well. Overall De Sica appeared in 160 films between 1918 and 1974. In 1940, while he was acting in two films and was in between stage appearances, De Sica began his career as a film director. De Sica's first choice was a 1936 stage play, *Twenty Four Red Roses*, which he had performed and was familiar with. The comedy-romance was a success and De Sica followed it with another light comedy, *Maddalena, Zero for Conduct* (1941). De Sica's fifth film, *The Children Are Watching* (*I bambini ci guardano* [1942]) marked a distinct shift in style. This story of the impact of adult folly on a child's mind was the beginning of his collaboration with screenwriter Cesare Zavattini, which would stretch over 23 of his 31 films. Particularly noteworthy are two of the most notable films representative of what came to be called the Italian neorealist movement, *Shoeshine* (*Sciuscia* [1946]) and *The Bicycle Thief* (*Ladri di biciclette* [1948]). With little money available to him, De Sica initiated the use of real locations and nonprofessional actors. Both films bared the truth about conditions in postwar Italy. *Shoeshine* received a Special Academy Award in 1947 and was instrumental in establishing the category of best foreign film.

The Bicycle Thief remains De Sica's most famous film, as well as the most famous of his neorealist pictures. Upon the slim plot, derived from a novel by Luigi Bartolini—the search for a stolen bicycle, which is the sole source of a father's livelihood—hangs a searching examination of postwar conditions in Italy. Among the characters and situations that the bicyclist, Ricci (played by a nonprofessional actor, Lamberto Maggiorani, a factory worker), meets in the course of his search are: striking workers, black marketeers, a drowned child, a gang of toughs, sanitation workers, and poor people praying in a church. After his fruitless search, Ricci is forced to try to steal a bicycle. Apprehended and released, he is as poor as ever, but now aware of the shame he now must bear as a would-be thief. "Its social message is not detached," wrote André Bazin, "it remains immanent in the event, but it is so clear that nobody can overlook it. . . . The thesis implied is wondrously and outrageously simple: in the world where this workman lives, the poor must steal from each other in order to survive." According to John Darretta, De Sica and Zavattini "sought to examine the social and economic problems of postwar Italy and their effects on the ordinary individual. They searched for 'real' characters and filmed them in their everyday landscapes with a camera and editing style that would capture the verisimilitude of a documentary. They had reached the zenith of the neorealistic period."

Miracle in Milan (*Miracolo a Milano* [1951]) and *Umberto D* (1952) confirmed De Sica's international reputation. The former was a break from the severity of the *Bicycle Thief*, a whimsical fantasy about the odyssey of Toto the Good (Francesco Golisano), an orphan who struggles to become an apostle for the beggars of Milan. When they are threatened with violence by a wicked landowner, Toto provides his band of beggars with brooms, with which they fly away to a land "where there is only peace, love, and good." De Sica's use of the fanciful does not obscure the social commentary about the exploitation and dispossession of the innocent by industrial forces. Attacked as being communistic by the Italian right, it was warmly received in the United States, where it was named best foreign film by the New York Film Critics.

Umberto D is considered in some quarters to be De Sica's purest neorealist document. Told in real time, the story of an old man's poverty, loneliness, and alienation from society was called by André Bazin "a truly realist cinema of the time." Further, "It is a matter of making 'life time'—the continuing to be a person to whom nothing in particular happens—that takes on the quality of spectacle. . . ." Umberto D (a nonprofessional actor named Carlo Battisti) is a retired civil servant who is about to be dispossessed of his lodgings and whose only companion is his little dog. Failing to commit suicide, he returns to his hopeless and bleak existence. Although attacked by Italian commentators as an accusation against conditions in contemporary Italy, Bazin predicted rightly that *Umberto D* would prove "a masterpiece to which film history is certainly going to grant a place of honour. . . ."

In the early 1950s De Sica visited the United States where a project with RKO studios was abandoned. De Sica did make an arrangement with producer David O. Selznick to make a film to be shot on location in Italy. The resulting film, *Stazione Termini* (1954), released in the United States as *Indiscretion of an American Wife,* starring Jennifer Jones and Montgomery Clift, was a box-office bomb. De Sica's next project was an omnibus film based on several Neapolitan stories by Giuseppe Marotta. *The Gold of Naples* (*L'oro di Napoli* [1954]) was shot on location with a mix of professional and nonprofessional actors. De Sica then made *The Roof* (*Il tetto* [1954]), shot in Rome, also with a cast of non professionals, which is considered by many to be the last neorealist film. In 1959 the director made *Two Women (La ciociara)* with Sophia Loren. The film won an Academy Award for best actress, the first time that award had been given to a foreign language film. Many critics lambasted the film as a "sellout" to commercialism. During the 1960s De Sica did indeed make his most commercial films, such as *Boccacio '70* (Act III, "The Raffle" [1962]), *The Condemned of Altona* (1962), *Yesterday, Today, and Tomorrow* (*Ieri, oggi, domani* [1963]), *Marriage Italian Style* (1963), and *After the Fox* (1966). In 1970 De Sica once again won the admiration of the critics with *The Garden of the Finzi-Continis (Il giardino dei Finzi-Contini).* The film concerned the effects of the war on a family of wealthy Italian Jews. It received the Academy Award for best foreign film at the 1971 Oscars.

Meanwhile, it should be noted that De Sica returned to acting on the screen in 1959 when he appeared in the title role of ROBERTO ROSSELLINI's wartime drama, *General della Rovere.* As Bertone, a con man with a gift for impersonation who is forced by the Germans to masquerade as General della Rovere, an important Italian Resistance figure, De Sica lent the role a credibility with audiences already familiar with his acting talents.

In August of 1973, De Sica entered a hospital in Geneva for an operation on a lung cyst. The ailment was to prove fatal, though the severity of it was kept from the director. De Sica's final film, *The Voyage* (1974), starred Sophia Loren and Richard Burton. The evening of its premiere in Paris, November 13, 1974, Vittorio De Sica died at the age of 72. John Darretta states that, "Despite the prevailing attitudes that the director of *Shoeshine, The Bicycle Thief,* and *Umberto D* had betrayed the ideals of his 'movement' and sold out to commercialism, both *The Garden of the Finzi-Continis* and *A Brief Vacation*—when placed next to *Red Roses* and *Maddalena, Zero for Conduct*—reveal De Sica's long journey from apprentice to expert craftsman."

Other Films *A Garibaldian in the Convent* (1941); *Gate of Heaven* (1946); *Anna of Brooklyn* (1960); *The Witches* (1966); *A New World* (1966); *Woman Times Seven* (1967); *A Place for Lovers* (1969); *Sunflower* (1970); *A Brief Vacation* (1973).

References Bondanella, Peter, *Italian Cinema: From Neorealism to the Present* (New York: Continuum Publishing, 1999); Darretta, John, *Vittorio De Sica: A Guide to References and Resources* (Boston: G. K. Hall, 1983); Bazin, André, "De Sica: Metteur en Scene," in *André Bazin, What Is Cinema?,* ed. Hugh Gray, vol. 2 (Berkeley: University of California Press, 1972), pp. 61–78.

—R.W.

Diegues, Carlos (1940–)

The most controversial and intensely personal of the Cinema Novo directors, Carlos Diegues was born on May 19, 1940, in Maceio, Brazil, the capital of the northeastern state of Alagoas. After moving with his family to Rio de Janeiro, he completed a law degree at the Catholic University, then worked as a journalist before he became active in the film society at the Rio de Janeiro Museum of Modern Art, where he met other participants of the emerging Cinema Novo. His first professional film was *Samba School, Joy of Living* (*Escola de samba, alegria de viver* [1962]), followed a year later by his first feature, *Ganga Zumba,* the first significant work of Cinema Novo to treat Afro-Brazilian history from an insider's perspective. That year Diegues stated his goal for the movement, i.e., "to study in depth the social relations of each city and region as a way of critically exposing, as if in miniature, the socio-cultural structure of the country as a whole."

Diegues's *Xica da Silva* (1976), his most successful film to that date, was based on the life of a legendary slave woman in 18th-century Minas Gerais. Xica (Zeze Motta) is a house slave who seduces an aristocrat and quickly dominates the white society of Arraial do Tijuco. Her outrageous dress and scandalous behavior arouse the anger of the Portuguese authorities, who destroy her palace. She escapes and reunites with her lover, Jose (Stepan Nercessian), and they conspire to continue their subversion of the king and his followers. As historian Peter Rist points out, the film has been the center of controversy due to its focus on the myth of the Afro-Brazilian as a predominantly sexual being.

Bye Bye Brazil (1980) was his eighth feature film and an international success, grossing over $1.3 million in America (making it the third most successful Brazilian film of all time in that country). It is dedicated to Brazilians of the 21st century. As historian Randal Johnson notes, it is "a vast mural of Brazil which is as varied as the country itself." It reveals the country in a process of rapid transformation as an agro-pastoral economy yields to rapid industrialization and the inhabitants of the Amazon jungles retreat before the occupation of multinational corporations. Each of the characters in the Caravana Rolidei, a small-time carioca and circus troupe—a magician/clairvoyant Lord Cigano (Jose Wilker), exotic dancer Salome (Betty Faria), the strongman Andorinha (Principe Nabor), accordionist Cico (Fabio, Jr.) and his pregnant wife Dasdo (Zaira Zambelli)—represents a different aspect of contemporary Brazilian culture. The troupe travels from the sea to the Trans-Amazonian highway to Altamira, presenting their show to small towns not yet "contaminated" by the dreaded television antenna. After a brief separation, the members reunite in Brasilia. The character of Lord Cigano, says Johnson, may be construed as Diegues himself, "an urban artist who has travelled the long roads of Brazil in search of the perfect audience and the optimum form of spectacle." Moreover, continues Johnson, the film's narrative and formal trajectory recall the history of Cinema Novo itself, from its documentary-style opening to the euphoria of the developmentalist period to the disillusionment with the mounting bureaucracy of the government. Just as the troupe has difficulty competing with television and American movies for its audiences and subsequently has to rely on the largess of local mayors, the Cinema Novo movement likewise was forced to turn to state subsidies to survive. The ubiquity of television antennas suggests, notes Johnson, that television is responsible for the destruction of Brazilian indigenous and folk cultures as well as the homogenization of Brazilian cultural expression. Yet, Johnson qualifies this presumption by noting that television "is only part of a larger process of the gradual extinction of indigenous cultures," merely one component of the larger process by which "advanced technology has brought isolated and feudal regions of Brazil into the space age."

The concern of "Caca" Diegues (as he is popularly known) with different forms of cultural communication has led him to experiment with different cinematic styles and genres. As Johnson demonstrates, *Ganga Zumba* contains a sequence wherein slaves act out master/slave relationships. *The Big City* (*A grande cidade* [1965]) is a mixture of western, documentary, melodrama, and thriller genres. *The Heirs* (*Os herdeiros* [1970]) focuses on the role of the National Radio as a consciousness-forming medium in Brazilian history

beginning in the 1930s. *When Carnival Comes* (*Quando of carnaval chegar* [1972]) depicts the adventures of a musical troupe in its tribute to the style of the *chanchada* ("light musical comedy"). He has continued to make films, like *Quilombo* (1984) and *Rio's Love Songs* (1994), despite the disarray and virtual collapse of Brazil's film industry in the 1980s.

Other Films *Joanna Francesca* (1973); *Summer Showers* (*Chuvas de verao* [1977]); *Un tren para las estrellas* (1987); *Dias melhores virao* (1994).

References Barnard, Timothy, and Peter Rist, *South American Cinema: A Critical Filmography, 1915–1994* (Austin: University of Texas Press, 1996); Johnson, Randal, "Film Television and Traditional Folk Culture in *Bye Bye Brasil*," *Journal of Popular Culture* 18, no. 1 (Summer 1984): 121–131; Johnson, Randal, *Cinema Novo x 5: Masters of Contemporary Brazilian Film* (Austin: University of Texas Press, 1994).

—J.C.T.

Dovzhenko, Alexander Petrovich

(1894–1956) Considered a cinematic poet, Dovzhenko was part of the triad of great Soviet filmmakers, along with SERGEI EISENSTEIN and VSEVELOD ILLARIONOVICH PUDOVKIN, but his vision, linked to his native Ukraine, was decidedly different. His loyalty to Ukraine is obvious in the way his films poetically evoke the landscape and folkways, but his films, made in the service of the state, could not be evocative of Ukrainian nationalism, especially during the Stalinist regime, and he had to walk a tightrope politically, lest he fall out of favor.

Alexander Dovzhenko was born of peasant stock in Sosnitsa, in the province of Chernigov in the northeast of Ukraine on September 12, 1894, and he trained to be a primary schoolteacher. He served in the Red Army during the civil war. After the Revolution, he joined the Communist Party and worked as a civil servant for the Ukrainian Commissariat of Education. He then became a career diplomat assigned first to the Soviet Embassy in Warsaw, later becoming secretary of the Berlin consulate. While in Berlin he studied art under Erik Heckel.

In 1923 Dovzhenko returned to the Soviet Union and worked for a while as a book illustrator and political cartoonist, whose work was published in the Ukrainian film magazine, *Kino*. At the age of 32 he decided to take up filmmaking and went to Odessa, where he submitted a film script and was then permitted to direct *Vasya, the Reformer,* a short comedy, for Odessa Studios in 1926. Another comedy, *The Little Fruits of Love,* followed in 1926, then an espionage thriller, *The Diplomatic Pouch* (1927), another popular success that enabled him to take on more ambitious projects.

Zvenigora (1928) was the first film that would define Dovzhenko's poetic and lyrical style, but studio heads in Odessa were puzzled by its metaphorical profusion and would not approve its release until after it had been endorsed by Eisenstein and Pudovkin, both of whom were impressed. "Pudovkin and I had a wonderful task," Eisenstein would later write, "to answer the questioning eyes of the auditorium with a joyful welcome of our new colleague. And to be the first to greet him."

The scope of the film was immense, a symbolic and free-flowing survey of Ukrainian history and folklore spanning centuries, from the Viking invasions to the Revolution. The film offered a symbolic anthology of Ukrainian folk myths, centered upon a grandfather figure who stands for the spirit of the Ukraine. The grandfather tells his grandson, Pavlo, stories about treasures hidden in the mountains of Zvenigora, which proves to be an allegory concerning the true treasures of the Ukrainian people, their intelligence and initiative in harnessing the land's mineral wealth. Dovzhenko later described *Zvenigora* as "a catalog of all my creative capabilities."

Arsenal (1929) was less symbolic and more in keeping with the goals of "socialist realism." It offered a sweeping account of the Ukraine from the World War through the February and October Revolutions, to the suppression of a workers' rebellion in 1918. The style was again symbolic. To demonstrate the brutality of the czarist regime, Dovzhenko filmed Czar Nicholas writing in his diary, "Today I shot a crow," juxtaposed with a shot of an old peasant collapsing in a field from exhaustion. Jay Leyda wrote that this was "the first masterpiece of the Ukrainian cinema [which] broke entirely with traditional film structure and subject, depending solely on a flow of ideas and emotions rather than upon conflicts between individual characters."

Earth (*Zemlya* [1930]) has also been considered a masterpiece of the Soviet silent cinema, but the film was denounced as being "counterrevolutionary," as the Soviet leadership was changing and even Eisenstein was falling out of official favor because of his formalist tendencies. It told the story of young peasants of a Ukrainian village wanting to set up collective farms, in conflict with the *kulaks* (rich landowners), who are attempting to protect their land. The collective farmers are celebrating the arrival of a tractor. One of them, Vasili, walking home down a moonlit path, begins to dance and is murdered by a jealous *kulak* assassin, not because he is an official of the collective farm, but because "he was dancing!" Hope resides in the soil and the regenerative power of the life cycle; apples, seen at both the beginning and the end of the film, are symbolic of the fertility of the land. In the film's final sequence, Vasili's body is carried past apple trees to his burial in the soil. As he is buried, Dovzhenko cuts to shots of a peasant woman giving birth.

Dovzhenko married Yulia Solntseva (1901–89), who was his assistant director on *Earth* and on his first sound film, *Ivan* (1932), about the industrialization of Ukraine, which was not considered a success. She became his most loyal supporter and collaborator, and, after her husband's death, was to become a successful filmmaker on her own, named People's Artist of the USSR in 1981.

In 1935 Dovzhenko directed *Aerograd* (*Air City,* aka *Frontier*), remarkable for its images of the Siberian landscape and its promise of a hopeful future in opening and developing the Soviet Far Eastern frontier. The party was pleased and Dovzhenko was awarded the prestigious Order of Lenin. Stalin then encouraged Dovzhenko to make "a Ukrainian *Chapayev,*" after the model of the civil-war film made by the Vassiliev brothers, under Stalin's scrutiny. What resulted, after three years and at least one false start, was *Shors* (*Shchors* [1939]), a highly personal work, telling the story of Nikolai Shors, the Red commander of the Ukraine from 1917 to 1919. The film eventually won the State Prize in 1941, but it was also admired abroad. Scenes such as "the silver blaze of ripe wheat and sunflowers full of struggling men, crazed horses and black explosions are still able to make any perceptive U.S. filmgoer," *Time* critic James Agee wrote, "wonder, seriously, whether he has ever seen a real moving picture before."

In 1940 Dovzhenko was pressed into service again to make *Liberation* (1940) to celebrate the reunification of Ukraine after the Nazi-Soviet pact, putting a Soviet spin on the reannexation of the Western Ukraine into the USSR. Just after taking over as artistic head of the Kiev Studios in 1941, war broke out, and Dovzhenko spent the next two years in Moscow, where he wrote a novel entitled *Victory* and supervised three documentary features—*Battle for the Ukraine* (1943), *The Kharkov Trial* (1945), and *Victory in the Ukraine* (1945)—that, according to Alexander Birkos, were in fact directed by his wife, Yulia Solntseva.

Back in Kiev after the war, Dovzhenko wrote a stage play about the Russian horticulturalist Ivan Michurin that was then adapted to a film entitled *Love in Bloom,* which was started in 1946 but not completed until 1949 and finally released under the title *Michurin.* The film was made, then remade so as to reflect the theories of T. D. Lysenko, a botanist admired by Stalin. During the final years of Stalinism, creative conditions were not favorable in the Soviet Union. Dovzhenko continued to write screenplays and was about to start filming *Poem of an Inland Sea* when he died of heart fail-

ure on November 26, 1956. His wife later made *Poem of an Inland Sea* in 1958, a film about the creation of the Kakhosk hydroelectric station. She also made *The Flaming Years* (1960) from a Dovzhenko screenplay set during the war, and *Ukraine on Fire* (1967), based on Dovzhenko's wartime stories, carrying forward the legacy of her husband's vision.

References Birkos, Alexander S., *Soviet Cinema: Directors & Films* (Hamden, Conn.: Archon Books, 1976); Kepley, Vance, Jr., *In the Service of the State: The Cinema of Alexander Dovzhenko* (Madison: University of Wisconsin Press, 1986); Leyda, Jay, *Kino: A History of the Russian and Soviet Film* (New York: Collier Books, 1973); Youngblood, Denise J., *Soviet Cinema in the Silent Era, 1918–1935* (Austin: University of Texas Press, 1991).

—J.M.W.

Dreyer, Carl Theodor (1889–1968) In a 50-year career Carl Dreyer made only 14 feature films, yet he is unquestionably the greatest filmmaker in the Danish cinema and, according to biographer Tom Milne, an artist whose work constitutes "the greatest and most loving voyage of exploration of the human soul the cinema has yet witnessed." He was born in Copenhagen, Denmark, in February 1889. Orphaned as a child, he was adopted and brought up by a strict Lutheran family. He took piano lessons and worked on his first job as a pianist in a Copenhagen café. After a stint as a journalist in Copenhagen from 1909 to 1913, where he covered trials, sports, and the theater, he joined Nordisk Films Kompagni in 1913 as a title writer.

His first film was *The President* (1919), which established the precedent he followed all his life, i.e, adapting his films from either novels or plays. Based on Karl Emil Franzos's novel, it is a melodrama about the past sins of a respected judge coming back to haunt him. *Leaves from Satan's Book* (1920) is a four-part allegory of Satan's incarnations as a Pharisee who tempts Judas to betray Christ, as a Grand Inquisitor in 16th-century Spain, as a revolutionary in 1793 Paris who persuades a young man to betray his lover and the Cause; and as an unfrocked Red monk during the Russo-Finnish war of 1918 trying to entice a young Finnish girl to betray her country. This was followed by an early masterpiece, *The Parson's Widow* (1920), which Dreyer made for the Swedish company, Svensk Filmindustri. A thoroughly enchanting fable rooted in a detailed and picturesque 17th-century village setting, it was about a young parson who upon inheriting his first parish must agree to marry the previous incumbent's widow. He does so only on the condition that his girl friend (introduced to the old lady as his sister) be hired as a maid in the parsonage. The penultimate scene in which the old woman takes leave of her beloved farm before lying down to die is among the most moving scenes in all of cinema.

The Master of the House (1925), drawn from a play by Svend Rindom, was a quiet and sophisticated dissection of a troubled marriage. After his wife leaves him, an overbearing husband comes to realize how cruelly he has exploited her; and the two eventually reconcile. Its detailed examination of everyday life, photographed with a canny sense of the three-dimensionality of the house interior, justifies claims that the film is a precursor to Italian neorealism.

Under the auspices in France of the Société Générale de Films, Dreyer made his last silent film, *The Passion of Joan of Arc* (1928), a landmark in the silent-film era. Despite the exhaustive research into period detail, costume, and ritual—the scenario was drawn from transcripts of Joan's trial—the film consists almost entirely of tight closeups that fragment and limit our vision of the total mise-en-scène of the Palais de Justice at Rouen. Falconetti's performance is likewise a concatenation of facial closeups seen from every conceivable angle. Joan's 29 examinations, lasting 18 months, are telescoped into one trial that lasts just 24 hours.

After a four-year hiatus during which Dreyer returned to journalism, he directed a classic horror film, *Vampyr* (1932), derived from J. Sheridan Le Fanu's vampire story, "Carmilla." Instead of the expected dark chiaroscuro of a standard horror thriller, punctuated with a series of noisy shocks and featuring a vampire with cloak and teeth, *Vampyr* is a "white" film that proceeds deliberately and (mostly) silently, featuring a vampire who is ultimately suffocated by a fall of snowy plaster in a mill. Phantom shadows crawl across the white walls and undulate in the reflections in a lake. The burial sequence, seen from the perspective of the entombed man about to be interred alive, is one of the horror genre's most celebrated sequences. And the vampires are a beautiful young woman and a birdlike little old doctor.

Over the remaining span of years until his death on March 20, 1968, Dreyer completed only a handful of film projects. *Day of Wrath* (1943), based on a play by Hans Wiers-Jenssen, was filmed during the German occupation of Denmark. Despite his protests that it was nonpolitical in nature, it was seized upon by the beleaguered Danes as a symbol of resistance and as a critique of the Jewish persecution by German invaders. It depicts the trial and condemnation to death by burning of two women accused of being witches. The eldest is a relatively harmless soul; her daughter, by contrast, uses her sexual wiles to exact a revenge on her mother's persecutors. Both women are ultimately consigned to the flames. "I am afraid neither of Heaven nor Hell, I'm only afraid to die," moans the old woman under pain of torture. The pacing is deliberately slow, the action muted, the terror and the torture muffled as the persecutors move quietly about their purpose. *Ordet* (1955) was based on a play by Kaj Munk about a young woman who dies in childbirth but is brought back to life by an act of faith. Naturalistic surface textures blend with quietly miraculous events. Again, the film is marked by restrained acting, simple sets, long uncut sequences, and a deliberately slow pace.

Gertrude (1964), based on a play by Hjalmar Soderberg, was his last film. The title character is an atheist who believes in her freedom to do what she wants with her life; and as a result she rejects

all men and retires into solitude out of her conviction that a perfect love is not possible. "The
man with whom I live must belong to me
entirely," she declares. "I must come first. I don't
want to be an object to be played with from time
to time." Its technique pares down Dreyer's already
notoriously ascetic style. The film's stark indifference to commercial tastes and its garnering of
poor reviews guaranteed its disastrous reception at
the box office. One critic said it was a film wholly
of "photographed sofa conversations."

A project that remained incomplete at Dreyer's
death was a proposed script for a life of Christ.
Begun during a trip to America in 1949–50, it was
to be filmed at last in 1967, but when Dreyer
insisted that the film should be made on location
in Israel, it was aborted. A year later Dreyer's negotiations with Italian television were abruptly cut
short by his death. As Tom Milne points out, ideas,
themes, and images recur so persistently throughout Dreyer's work that it is possible to define a
typical Dreyer film: "The period is almost invariably the past. The subject is a small, self-enclosed
group—a family, a village, a victim and her
judges—with the action rarely moving outside an
extremely restricted area, and rarely stretching over
more than a few hours or days; and within the
group, a lonely figure gradually detaches itself, the
object of either deliberate or unconscious cruelty."
Stylistically, Dreyer has a penchant for close-ups
or, at least, closely observed characters, detailed
décor, soft-toned lighting, protracted camera takes,
the use of inexperienced actors, and a stately
tempo moving toward the final catharsis of
tragedy. The mystic powers of good and evil are
very real in Dreyer, and his characters, especially
his women, relentlessly but unsuccessfully pursue
their quest for perfect love. Meanwhile, all forms
of cruelty, prejudice, superstition, hypocrisy, and
rigid religious dogma are denounced.

Notoriously reticent about his private life,
fiercely protective of his own artistic integrity, elusive in interviews, rather other-worldly in his attitude, Dreyer has yet to gain the popular
acceptance that he deserves. "What I look for in
my films," he said, "what I want to do, is to penetrate, by way of their most subtle expressions, to
the deepest thoughts of my actors. For it is these
expressions which reveal the personality of a character, his unconscious feelings, the secrets hidden
deep within his soul." Perhaps an insight into his
character and sensibility may be derived from the
opening title card of *Vampyr:* "There exist certain
predestined beings whose very lives seem bound
by invisible threads to the supernatural world.
They crave solitude . . . they dream . . . their imagination is so developed that their vision reaches far
beyond that of most men."

Other Films   *Love One Another* (1921); *Once Upon
a Time* (1922); *Michael* (1924); *Two People* (1944); *Thor-
waldsen* (1949).

References   Bordwell, David, *The Films of Carl-
Theodor Dreyer* (Berkeley: University of California Press,
1981); Milne, Tom, *The Cinema of Carl Dreyer* (New
York: A. S. Barnes, 1981).

—J.C.T.

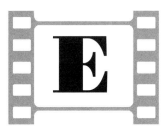

Eastwood, Clint (1930–)   Clint Eastwood became a movie star of the first magnitude, but his reputation as a director has grown over the years to make him more than simply an actor who has also directed films. His films have ranged from the merely silly to the nearly sublime. After spending years on the sets of other directors, notably SERGIO LEONE and DON SIEGEL, he gradually learned the tricks of the trade. His later films go well beyond merely competent craftsmanship. Not all of them have been blockbusters, by any means, but some have. His post-western *Unforgiven* (1992), for example, resurrected an apparently dead genre, reminding viewers of what the western was and what it could accomplish. His adaptation of *The Bridges of Madison County* (1995), based on a wretchedly pretentious and maudlin, sentimental novel, showed viewers what the novel might have become, had it been written by someone more talented than Robert James Waller. Eastwood desentimentalized the character of Waller's sappy photographer, Robert Kincaid, providing him with a sense of dignity, clarity, and muscle, where there had been only flab. Toning up the character and tuning up the novel, Eastwood fixed and rebuilt *The Bridges of Madison County.*

Clinton Eastwood, Jr., was born in San Francisco, California, on May 31, 1930. After graduat-ing from high school, he served with the Army Special Services from 1950 to 1954 before starting his career as an actor in the television series *Rawhide.* He then migrated to Italy to star in Sergio Leone's so-called spaghetti westerns, starting with *A Fistful of Dollars* in 1964. Finally, he translated his laconic western persona into an urban cowboy when he played Harry Callahan for Don Siegel in *Dirty Harry* (1971), a role that made him a superstar and put him in the position of calling his own shots.

Eastwood's first film as director was *Play Misty for Me* (1971), followed by *High Plains Drifter* and *Breezy* (both 1973). *Play Misty for Me,* the story of a jazz disk jockey (Eastwood) who gets involved with a psychotic young woman, has been compared to *Psycho* and the later *Fatal Attraction.* Eastwood claims the critics said "We're not ready for him as an actor, much less a director," but the film was a modest success. Although Eastwood continued to act in films directed by others, his own directing credits continued to build. He directed comedies, mysteries, thrillers, and action-adventures, such as *The Eiger Sanction* (1975), *Firefox* and *Honkytonk Man* (both 1982), *Sudden Impact* (1983), *Tightrope* (1984), credited to Richard Tuggle, but actually directed by Eastwood, *Heartbreak Ridge* (1986), *The Rookie* (1990), *Absolute Power* and *Mid-*

night in the Garden of Good and Evil (both 1997), *True Crime* (1999), and *Space Cowboys* (2000), a decidedly mixed bag overall, including some critical misfires, but many of them made popular by Eastwood's presence.

The pictures just named do not represent Eastwood's best work, however. Eastwood was at his best when driven by his enthusiasms and his interest in obsessive and self-destructive characters. *White Hunter Black Heart* (1990) was a tribute to the director JOHN HUSTON. *Bird* (1988), a neglected film but one of Eastwood's very best, was a tribute to the jazz musician out of Kansas City, Charlie "Bird" Parker. Eastwood's enthusiasm for jazz also prompted him to make the documentary *Thelonius Monk: Straight, No Chaser* (1989). Eastwood also continued to make westerns. *Pale Rider* (1985) was essentially a remake of the classic *Shane* (1953), with Eastwood himself playing a far more intimidating gunman than Alan Ladd had played for GEORGE STEVENS's classic western, refigured as a story about a big mining operation trying to drive away independent miners panning for gold and staking claims, instead of a big rancher trying to drive away homesteaders.

Pale Rider was an interesting imitation and a distinctive Eastwood western, but *Unforgiven* was wholly original, with Eastwood playing a truly retired gunfighter, Will Munny, who becomes a bounty hunter in order to save the failing family farm. *Unforgiven* was Eastwood's greatest success, winning multiple Academy Awards, including best picture and best director, a masterpiece of genre filmmaking, but also a character-driven picture that went considerably beyond stereotypes. At the age of 62, Eastwood pursued roles of older characters who had seen the world and responded on the basis of their experience. Will Munny, no longer a hard-living hothead, for example, had to relearn his gunfighting skills in order to extract justice from Gene Hackman's lawman, Little Bill Daggett.

Always willing to take chances with risky projects, Eastwood followed the tremendous success of

Clint Eastwood (right) directed and starred in *The Rookie* (Warner Bros.)

Unforgiven with *A Perfect World* (1993), an odd coming-of-age movie about a seven-year-old boy kidnapped by an escaped convict, Butch Haines (Kevin Costner), on the run from a manhunt led by a world-weary Texas Ranger (Clint Eastwood). This film was set in 1963 in Texas, just before the Kennedy assassination, just as the country was "on the brink of a great turning towards the void that will take hold of America," as Eastwood remembered the project.

Eastwood's star power made him a latter-day John Wayne, but Wayne made his best films with the director JOHN FORD and steered clear of directing himself, with two exceptions, *The Alamo* (1960) and his patriotic folly, *The Green Berets* (1969), which he apparently codirected with Ray Kellogg. Eastwood, in contrast, combined the talents of both John Wayne and John Ford, directing his best pictures himself. Major retrospectives of Eastwood's work were mounted in New York at the Museum of Modern Art in 1980 and in Paris at the Cinémathéque Française in 1985, culminating in the French government's naming him Chevalier des Arts et Lettres. Back in California in 1986, this archetypal American was elected mayor of Carmel and served in office until 1988.

"My career in directing started strictly by accident," Eastwood told interviewer Iain Blair in 1997. "The only way I could get to direct was to act in the picture and the only way I could get the picture made was to act in it. So in 1970 I got the job to do both in *Play Misty for Me,* and back then very few actors also directed. Then I'd find a story like *High Plains Drifter,* where I liked the story and also liked the character, so I interspersed them with films where someone else would direct." That flexibility freed him from his two main acting roles—the Man with No Name in the Leone films, and "Dirty Harry" Callahan in the Don Siegel films. Eastwood was able to take control of his image and his career. As Robert E. Kapsis has written, "No other contemporary dramatic star has directed himself so often."

References Gallafent, Edward, *Clint Eastwood: Filmmaker and Star* (New York: Continuum, 1994); Kapsis, Robert E., and Kathie Coblentz, *Clint Eastwood: Interviews* (Jackson: University Press of Mississippi, 1999); Schickel, Richard, *Clint Eastwood: A Biography* (New York: Knopf, 1996).

—J.M.W.

Edwards, Blake (1922–) One of Hollywood's most enduring, versatile, and productive filmmakers, Blake Edwards has become known primarily for his screen comedies. He was born in Tulsa, Oklahoma, July 26, 1922, to a show-business family. His father was one of the top assistant directors and production managers during Hollywood's heyday, and his grandfather, J. Jordon Edwards, had been a leading director during the silent-film era (he directed several Theda Bara vehicles). Blake began his own show-business career in 1942 as an actor in the film *Ten Gentlemen from West Point.* His debut as a writer came six years later with *Panhan-*

dle. He turned to radio drama in 1949 when he created the enormously popular radio serial, *Yours Truly, Johnny Dollar.* For television, his many writing credits included *Hey, Mulligan* and *Richard Diamond* (1957–59), *Peter Gunn* (1958–61), and *Mr. Lucky* (1961–62). His first movie scripts were *My Sister Eileen* (1955), *Operation Mad Ball* (1957), and *The Notorious Landlady* (1962).

Early directorial efforts embraced a variety of genres, like the comedies *This Happy Feeling* (1958) and *Operation Petticoat* (1959); the bittersweet romance, *Breakfast at Tiffany's* (1961); the social-problem film, *The Days of Wine and Roses* (1962); and the thriller, *Experiment in Terror* (1962). His best-known comedies, the slapstick "Pink Panther" series starring Peter Sellers, began with *The Pink Panther* in 1963, starring Peter Sellers as the inimitable, bumbling Inspector Clouseau, and continued with *A Shot in the Dark* (1964), *The Return of the Pink Panther* (1975), *The Pink Panther Strikes Again* (1976), *Revenge of the Pink Panther* (1978), *Trail of the Pink Panther* (1982), and *Curse of the Pink Panther* (1982). Clouseau is one of the most enduring characters in all of screen comedy. "Clouseau is in largest measure funny because of his sustained faith in himself," comments Myron Meisel in his study of Edwards, "even in the face of the most outrageous challenges to his inner placidity. . . . Clouseau belongs to the tradition of the charmed fool, and his considerable virtues and minor flaws as a comic creation essentially derive from that benighted tradition."

After the failure of the big-budget *The Great Race* (1964), Edwards determined to venture into different directions. "I decided at one point in my career that I would not go on being a director unless I had creative freedom," he recalls. "I was lucky enough to have directed a series of films that made a lot of money, which is what the Hollywood Establishment understands, and I took advantage of it." Subsequent independent efforts included *The Tamarind Seed* (1974), *What Did You Do in the War, Daddy?* (1966), *10* (1979)—his biggest success, *S.O.B.* (1980), *The Man Who Loved*

Producer-director-writer Blake Edwards (left) on the set of *Victor/Victoria* (Ladbroke Entertainments Limited/MGM)

Women (1983), *Victor/Victoria* (1982), *A Fine Mess* (1986), and *Blind Date* (1986). Seven of his films featured Julie Andrews, whom he married in 1969. *That's Life,* released in 1986, about the late mid-life crisis of an architect, was semiautobiographical. Edwards scripted the picture, and Andrews and Jack Lemmon portrayed the Fairchilds, based vaguely on the Edwards clan (Edwards's daughter, Jennifer, and Andrews's daughter, Emma Walton, appeared in the cast). "A lot of the situations that occur in the story have happened in our lives," says Andrews. "All the actors were able to fall back on real-life situations for this improvisational film."

In his study of Edwards, Myron Meisel declares, "Blake Edwards, the most important comic stylist (along with Richard Lester) of the 1960s, and without peer today, parlayed deadpan farce and intricate gag construction into a profound comic metaphysic devoted to whatever possibilities remain for wit and romance in the postwar age."

Other Films   *Gunn* (1968); *The Party* (1970); *Wild Rovers* (1971); *The Carey Treatment* (1972); *Micki & Maude* (1984); *Skin Deep* (1989); *Switch* (1991); *Son of the Pink Panther* (1993).

References   Meisel, Myron, "Blake Edwards," in Jean-Pierre Cloursodon, *American Directors,* vol. 2 (New York: McGraw-Hill, 1983), pp. 117–132.

—J.C.T.

Eisenstein, Sergei (1898–1948)   Leading architect of a revolution in Soviet cinema in the 1920s, Sergei Eisenstein was an important theorist as well as a celebrated filmmaker. Sergei Mikhailovich Eisenstein was born on January 23, 1898, to assimilated and baptized Jewish parents in Riga, Latvia, in czarist Russia. His father was an architect and civil engineer for the city of Riga. When his parents separated in 1905, Eisenstein divided his boyhood years between Riga and St. Petersburg. Fluent in French, German, and English, he bowed to pressure from his father to study civil engineering. However, his real interests lay with the theater and the cinema, and his first cinematic encounter was a viewing in Paris of the films of GEORGES MÉLIÈS.

Even the Bolshevik Revolution couldn't deter Eisenstein from his love of the arts. After serving in the civil war in the Red Army as a civil engineer, he abandoned his career in engineering and attached himself to the swirl of theatrical activity surrounding the great Russian theater visionary, Vsevelod Meyerhold. This radical experimentalist had broken from the traditional "naturalist" theater and pursued in his classes and productions the modernist movements of "constructivism" and "biomechanics." Like every other student, Eisenstein participated in every aspect of production, including writing and acting. Indeed, in some measure the October Revolution not only broke down the old social, economic, and political order, as historian Richard Taylor suggests, "it also overthrew the traditional notions of art and of the arts. If one thing characterizes the revolutionary Soviet artists of the 1920s it is the relative ease with which they moved from one art form to another, from literature to scriptwriting, from painting to set design—in Eisenstein's case from sketching through set design and stage direction to film-making—and this in turn helps to explain the ease with which they drew upon the techniques of those various art forms to enhance the effectiveness of their own activity in one particular form." And one finds in Eisenstein's first published article, "The Eighth Art" (1922), a wildly eclectic discussion of the techniques of the circus, the detective story, and the films of Charlie Chaplin. Later writings would pinwheel out into the realms of Charles Dickens, Kabuki theater, and the Japanese ideogram.

In 1924, the Proletkult Theater offered him the job of directing the first of eight episodes of the film series, *Towards the Dictatorship.* He completed only one episode, but it was enough to alter the course of Soviet cinema. *Strike* (1925), which premiered on April 28, 1925, depicted the brutal czarist crushing of a worker's strike. Its episodes depicted the working conditions of the workers, the preparations for a strike, the infiltration of the workers by capitalist-hired spies and provocateurs, the daily activities of the workers during the strike, and the slaughter of the strikers by mounted troops. With *Strike* Eisenstein found in the concepts of montage, which he had first studied in the legendary workshops of his mentor, Lev Kuleshov, the formal artistic equivalent to the Marxist revolution and Hegelian evolutionary theory. Moreover, he adopted the concept of the multiple protagonist, or collective hero, as an ideological and structural element.

Eisenstein's theories of montage—which he called the "cinema of attractions"—have often compared the juxtapositions, or "collisions," of shots to the explosions in an internal combustion engine that drive an automobile forward. The result is the creation of a synthesis in the mind of the viewer, a third element that is greater than the sum of the two shots. Nowhere is this strategy more fully worked out than in his next film *Battleship Potemkin,* made in 1925 to celebrate the anniversary of the 1905 Revolution. The 28-year-old Eisenstein had left the Proletkult Theatre after abandoning plans to make the remaining films in the planned prerevolutionary cycle. Coscripted by Nina Agadzhanova, it again is a story of revolution, in this case the mutiny of sailors against ship's officers in June and July of 1905 aboard the *Battleship Potemkin.* When the sympathetic people of Odessa are crushed by mounted czarist troops, the mutineers turn their ship's guns on the town. The sequence depicting the Cossacks' slaughter of the townspeople, the celebrated "Odessa Steps" sequence, is a veritable catalogue of Eisenstein's methods, including flash frames, extreme close-ups, jarring jump cuts, skewed angles, dynamic compositions, and the compression and expansion of time. Crowds surge, boots stomp, rifle barrels level toward targets, sabers pierce flesh, and a baby carriage trundles down the steps. After more than 75 years, the cumulative impact of this sequence is still overwhelming. Ironically, this scene was not included in the original script. Eisenstein himself related the inspiration for the scene: "No scene of shooting on the Odessa Steps appeared in any of the preliminary versions or in any of the montage lists that were prepared [before filming began]. It was born in the instant of immediate contact." The film's reception alone deserves an extended volume. Its international career began with its enthusiastic reception in Berlin (thanks to the entrepreneurship of Russian intellectual Vladimir Mayakovsky) and quickly extended to the United States and beyond. Interestingly, it was Douglas Fairbanks, Sr., who saw the film in July 1926 during his tour of Russia, and whose favorable pronouncements hastened the film's release in New York, where it premiered on December 5, 1926 (in a version reedited for the American market by none other than John Grierson).

Battleship Potemkin was the last film over which Eisenstein would exercise total control. In 1927 he was called upon by the Soviet film agency, Sovkino, to make a film commemorating the 10th anniversary of the Bolshevik Revolution of October 1917. This was mostly in response to the assignment by the film trust, Mezhrapom, that Eisenstein's colleague and rival, VSEVELOD ILLARI-ONOVICH PUDOVKIN, would chronicle similar events in his *The End of St. Petersburg* (1927). Both directors worked simultaneously on their respective projects. *October* (released internationally as *Ten Days that Shook the World,* a title borrowed from the book by John Reed), coscripted by his assistant, Alexandrov, was originally intended to be shot in two parts. The first part would cover events from February to October 1917; and the second, the subsequent civil war. Only the first part was realized. It featured extensive use of what Eisenstein called "intellectual montage," i.e., the selection of juxtaposed images to create metaphors in the service of political ideology. In his article, "Beyond the Shot" (1929), he declared, "Each [shot] taken separately corresponds to an object but their combination corresponds to a *concept.*

The combination of two 'representable' objects achieves the representation of something that cannot be graphically represented." Because the film was made at a peak in the fight against leftist opposition, before its release Eisenstein was instructed to edit out nearly one-third of the film, including scenes of many of the leading participants in the revolution, notably Leon Trotsky. It was premiered to the general public on March 14, 1928. Composer Edmund Meisel, who had written the music score for *Potemkin,* came aboard to write the score. What survives, notably the recreation of the storming of the Winter Palace in Leningrad and Kerensky's assumption of power, reveals Eisenstein at the height of his powers.

In August 1929, Eisenstein set off for a trip to Europe and North America. After lecturing and attending film congresses throughout Europe, he arrived in the United States in 1930 to work and to study modern film techniques. He was already armed with a contract signed by Jesse Lasky, production head of Paramount, when he arrived in Hollywood. Among the numerous projects Eisenstein suggested, but which were aborted in various stages of conception and/or production, was a screen dramatization of *An American Tragedy.* Historian Marie Seton reports that Eisenstein's script ran afoul of the Paramount brass: "They wished to be rid of him, and his refusal to compromise over *An American Tragedy* opened the way."

In December 1930 Eisenstein left Hollywood after signing a contract with Upton Sinclair, a muckraking novelist and socialist reformer who wanted to produce a film about Mexico. Immediately charmed and fascinated by Mexico, its people, and its folkways, he determined to make *¡Que viva México!,* a six-episode chronicle of a large portion of Mexican history. However, due to conflicts with Sinclair—Eisenstein had been pursuing a perfectionist course that overran Sinclair's budget—the collaboration deteriorated and Eisenstein was forced to halt shooting in January 1932. When he tried to return to Hollywood to edit his footage, he was refused entrance into the United

States. Sinclair, moreover, reneged in an agreement to ship the film to the Soviet Union. Although a version of *¡Que Viva México!* was eventually edited by Eisenstein's biographer and friend, Marie Seton, it proved to be but a poor shadow of what the film could have been.

After returning to the Soviet Union in 1933 he retreated to the Caucasus in extreme depression. He led a reclusive life, devoting himself to his theoretical work, eventually deciding to return to Moscow to teach at the Film Institute. Moscow had changed since his trip to America. Under Stalin, the left opposition had been exiled, imprisoned, or killed, and any opposition to the bureaucracy in the party had been stifled. The bureaucracy had declared war upon dialectical materialism, and this could be seen in the realm not only of politics but also of the sciences and arts. Eisenstein's contemporaries and colleagues, LEV VLADIMIROVICH KULESHOV, DZIGA (DENIS KAUFMAN) VERTOV, Pudovkin, and others had all fallen under the shadow of accusations of being "formalists" who had betrayed the Soviet ideology. Only one filmmaker, Lev Kuleshov, came to his defense. Under this pressure, Eisenstein, who had long carried on a fight against the conventions of plot and story, changed his technique to the new aesthetic, socialist realism.

In the middle of 1935, he began work on his first film in over three years, *Bezhin Meadow.* This story of the martyrdom of young peasants to the Soviet cause was commissioned by the Communist Youth League to commemorate the contribution of the Young Pioneers to collective farm work. Several problems conspired to abort the project, including Eisenstein's own succumbing to smallpox and, later, influenza.

In 1937, after the installation of a new film administration more favorable to him, Eisenstein was given the task of making a film that would not only provoke the patriotic spirit of Russian citizens against the perceived German threat but would also serve as a warning to the Germans that war against the Soviet Union would be fatal. To do this he would reach back to the 13th century to retell the saga of Prince Alexander Nevsky, who raised up an army from the Russian peasantry to beat back the Teutonic knights. *Alexander Nevsky,* coscripted by Pyotr Pavlenko, was completed in 1938 and earned Eisenstein the Order of Lenin as well as the title of Doctor of the Science of Art Studies. It was his first sound film, and it benefited from an effective music score by Sergei Prokofiev. The spectacular Battle on the Ice, its most famous sequence, was, amazingly, not shot on ice at all, but during a summer heat wave in a field that had been leveled and covered with a solution of sodium silicate to "duplicate" the appearance of ice. So closely did Eisenstein work with composer Prokofiev, that, as Jay Leyda reports, "the music was to determine the filming or cutting as often as the filming was to determine the music." *Alexander Nevsky* premiered on December 1, 1938. In the meantime, the finished film revealed that Eisenstein's formalistic insistence on strategies of montage had been replaced by the more politically approved camera and editing techniques—extended takes and composition-in-depth shots—that were closer to the mise-en-scène school of the French.

Eisenstein's next film was projected to be a three-part historical spectacle about Ivan the Terrible, the Russian czar who unified the country into one nation in the 16th century. Ivan had resorted to the most ruthless measures to destroy the rule of the boyar nobility, thus earning him the "terrible" sobriquet. The film was to be another epic about a great national hero that would win Eisenstein favor from the party. Reuniting with composer Prokofiev and the actor Nikolai Cherkassov (who had played Nevsky), Eisenstein commenced shooting in 1942. Every facility was placed at his disposal. Its spectacle, pacing, and mise-en-scène resembled more a grand opera than a motion picture. When *Ivan the Terrible, Part One,* was released in 1945, it won the Stalin Prize, first class, for Eisenstein, Cherkassov, Prokofiev, and several others who worked on the film. In 1946, *Ivan the Terrible, Part Two,* was completed. It had the same cast and production crew as Part One, and it continued the story of the fight for Russian nationhood. The character of Ivan by this time had undergone a major change. In a paranoid rage, he relied increasingly on his handpicked band of fanatical young security guards, the *Oprichniki,* to carry out his vendettas against the boyars. Before the film could be released, however, Eisenstein was stricken with a heart attack at a dinner celebrating the completion of the editing of Part Two. Moreover, and unfortunately for Eisenstein, the film was considered by many to be a thinly disguised attack on Stalin, and it was later condemned by the Central Committee of the Communist Party. In February 1946 Stalin declared he would approve its release only after extensive reshooting and reediting. Eisenstein's health by then had deteriorated to the point that further work on the film was impossible, and he spent his last months at his flat in Potylika, happy in the knowledge that colleague and friend Jay Leyda had arranged for the publication of his aesthetic writings, *The Film Form* and *The Film Sense,* and putting in order his voluminous collection of notes, correspondence, and scenarios. He died on February 9, 1948.

Not long before his death he published a statement concerning his long struggles with his art and with the Soviet state, touching specifically upon the controversies surrounding his *Ivan.* "Some of us forgot the incessant struggle against our Soviet ideals and ideology which goes on in the whole world," he wrote in a generally conciliatory tone. "We lost for the time comprehension of the honourable, militant educational task which lies on our art during the years of hard work to construct the Communist Society in which all people are involved. The Central Committee justly pointed out to us that the Soviet artist cannot treat his duties in a light-minded and irresponsible way. Workers of the cinema should study deeply whatever they undertake. Our chief mistake is that we did not fulfil these demands in our creative work."

It is impossible to overestimate Eisenstein's significance to the history of cinema. In his invaluable volume of collected writings by Eisenstein, Richard Taylor declares: "If there was one person who could properly lay claim to the title of 'cinema Shakespeare' it would have to be Eisenstein. His position in the development of cinema as an art form was in many ways similar to that of Shakespeare in the development of modern drama and it was certainly as seminal. But, unlike Shakespeare, Eisenstein was more than the leading practitioner of his art: he was also its principal theorist. He was therefore not only cinema's Shakespeare: he was also in some sense its Stanislavsky, its Brecht—or perhaps most appropriately, its Meyerhold."

References Eisenstein, Sergei, *Film Form* (Meridian Books, 1957), p. 37; Bergen, Ronald, *Sergei Eisenstein: A Life in Conflict* (New York: Overlook Press, 1997); Bordwell, David, *The Cinema of Eisenstein* (Cambridge, Mass.: Harvard University Press, 1993); Marshall, Herbert, *Sergei Eisenstein: Nonindifferent Nature* (Cambridge, U.K.: Cambridge University Press, 1987); Seton, Marie, *Sergei M. Eisenstein* (New York: A. A. Wyn, n.d.); Taylor, Richard, ed., *Eisenstein: Writings 1922–1934* (Bloomington: Indiana University Press, 1988).

—B.M. and J.C.T.

Fassbinder, Rainer Werner (1945–1982)
The leading figure and guiding spirit of the "New German Cinema," Rainer Werner Fassbinder is often considered the most original and important European filmmaker of the 1970s. When the scowling wunderkind of German cinema died at the age of 36 after a night of ingesting an excessive amount of alcohol, valium, and cocaine, he left the world 41 feature films made in a period of 13 years. Many of Fassbinder's films are now considered landmarks in world cinema, leading Vincent Canby to call Fassbinder "the most dazzling, talented, provocative, original, puzzling, prolific and exhilarating filmmaker of his generation."

Rainer Werner Fassbinder was born on May 31, 1946, in the Bavarian town of Bad Wörishofen. His family was financially secure and they were highly respected members of the community, his father being a doctor and his mother a translator. The young Fassbinder rebelled early on, shocking his parents when he declared his homosexuality at age 15. While still a teenager he made himself at home in the gay bars, where he took up the profession of pimp for the local drag queens, including Udo Kier, who would act in a number of his later films. During this period, Fassbinder became obsessed with both the aura of American movie stars and the melodramatic excesses of Hollywood films, particularly the work of Douglas Sirk and Samuel Fuller. Fassbinder claimed that as a teenager, he would watch as many as 15 movies a week.

Even though Fassbinder hated school, he was so determined to become a filmmaker that he applied to the Berlin School of Film. When his application was rejected, he moved to Munich and started a theater company he named the "Anti-Theater." He not only wrote original scripts for the company, but also staged the productions and performed on stage. Many of the actors employed in the Anti-Theater would stay a part of Fassbinder's extended family, becoming principal players in his films, including Hanna Schygulla, Ulli Lommel, Kurt Raab, and Harry Baer.

The fame of the Anti-Theater gave Fassbinder the opportunity to make a series of films for German television. In 1969, he made his first theatrical film, *Love Is Colder than Death (Liebe ist kälter als der Tod),* a gritty gangster film indebted to the American B-films of Samuel Fuller. Hanna Schygulla played the femme fatale, with Fassbinder himself taking on the role of the film's anti-hero, an ex-con and pimp. It was hardly a success and was booed when it was shown at the Berlin Film Festival. Fassbinder's next film fared better with both critics and festival audiences. *Katzelmacher* (1969), an attack on bourgeois fascism and German xenophobia, won numerous awards including one from the German Academy for outstanding artistic achievement. His early films, including *Why Does Herr R. Run Amok?* (*Warum läuft Herr R. Amok?* [1970]) and *Beware a Holy Whore* (*Warnung vor einer heiligen Nutte* [1970]), followed in the tracks of *Love Is Colder than Death* and *Katzelmacher,* a mixture of Hollywood film noir and European neorealism, depending largely on improvisational acting.

With *The Bitter Tears of Petra von Kant* (*Die bitteren tränen der Petra von Kant* [1972]) a new impulse begins to emerge, one indebted more to the over-the-top melodramas of Douglas Sirk than the gritty work of Samuel Fuller. *The Bitter Tears of Petra von Kant* is a lurid, highly stylized view of the jealousies and sadomasochistic passions that engulf three lesbians. The film is set in the opulent apartment of high-fashion designer Petra von Kant (Margit Carsensen) where she and the object of her desire, a fashion model played by Hanna Schygulla, engage in an increasingly destructive rondelet of mind games.

Ali: Fear Eats the Soul (*Angst essen Seele auf* [1974]) is even more indebted to the Hollywood melodramas of Douglas Sirk. A radical revisioning of Sirk's *All that Heaven Allows* (1955), it's a bittersweet, melodramatic love story between a lonely 60-year-old German cleaning lady and an attractive 30-year-old Moroccan auto mechanic. As they seek to find comfort in each other's arms, family objections, social rejection, and racial prejudice increasingly invade the private world they have tried to create. The theme of class difference is also at the center of *Fox and His Friends* (*Faustrecht der Freiheit* [1975]), Fassbinder's first film to explore gay male relationships. Fox, a subproletarian carnival worker (played by Fassbinder), wins a lottery worth 500,000 DM. His new wealth leads him into a romance with a bourgeois lover who tries to turn Fox into a model of middle-class respectability while swindling him out of his money and his self-respect. The film won praise for its nonstereotypical, if not always flattering, portrayal of its gay characters. The *New York Times* declared it "the first serious, explicit but non-sensational movie about homosexuality to be shown in this country."

The Marriage of Maria Braun (1978) proved to be Fassbinder's greatest international success and is often considered to be his masterpiece. In the ribald comedy, Hanna Schygulla plays Maria Braun, an ambition-driven woman who manages to use the marriage vow to raise herself from the ashes of post–World War II Germany to become a titan of industry.

Fassbinder returned to the world of gay culture for *In a Year of Thirteen Moons* (*In einem Jahr mit 13 Monden* [1979]), a sad depiction of the last days of a transsexual who impulsively undergoes a sex change operation only to please a rich lover, who then rejects her. Broke and alone, Elvira turns to her family and friends, only to experience further rejection and betrayal. In the *New York Times,* Vincent Canby declared the film to be "grotesque, arbitrary, sentimental and cold as ice. It's only redeeming feature is genius."

In 1980, Fassbinder produced one of his most audacious projects, *Berlin Alexanderplatz,* a 15-hour epic made for German television that follows a dim-witted transit worker, living in Berlin between the wars, who becomes involved with the criminal underworld as the country falls increasingly under the spell of Nazism. The next year, Fassbinder turned again toward Hollywood to make *Veronika Voss* (1981), a hypnotic, quite mad tribute to Billy Wilder's *Sunset Boulevard* (1950). The film's ceaseless camera movements chronicle a faded movie star's descent into morphine addiction and emotional collapse.

By the completion of *Veronika Voss,* Fassbinder's own life, never stable, seemed to be imitating Veronika's descent into addiction and increasingly obsessive-compulsive behavior. As his fame grew, his personal life, always self-publicized, became increasingly complicated by gossip and public scandal. Actors in his films recounted to an ever-eager press his violent outbursts. Some, like Irm Hermann, claimed physical abuse. Two of his lovers committed suicide, one hanging himself after a murderous rampage, another found dead in Fassbinder's apartment.

By the time Fassbinder made his last film, *Querelle,* the enfant terrible of German cinema seemed increasingly out of control. In *Querelle,* based on the novel by Jean Genet, American actor Brad Davis plays the title role of a cocky, amoral sailor, a stud who flaunts his sensuality in any and all directions. After killing a fellow sailor, Querelle takes refuge in a brothel, where he begins to come to terms with the depths of his homosexual lusts. Franco Nero is the officer who succumbs to Querelle's advances and Jeanne Moreau is the chanteuse who likewise comes under his sway.

Beyond the already sensational nature of the story, Fassbinder played out the drama on a stylized, purposefully artificial set depicting the French port of Brest as a landscape of kitschy phallus-shaped towers complete with archetypal gay iconography, from leather men to barechested Tom of Finland–like sailors, to a tortured Jeanne Moreau, all shot against a backdrop, described by Gary Morris as "a kind of permanent orange sunset, as if the world were at its end."

Those connected with the production of *Querelle* report that it was a tortured period for the director, and indeed the filmmaker seemed to be working at the end of his own world. Shortly after completion of *Querelle,* Fassbinder was found dead, apparently from an overdose of whiskey, valium, and cocaine. As Morris notes, "Fassbinder left this world in the same way as many of his cinematic creations: overworked, overwrought, and finally overdosed on life." Even so, "This prodigiously inventive artist distilled the best elements of his sources, Brechtian theatrics, Artaud, the Hollywood studio look, classical narrative, and a gay sensibility . . . into a body of work that continues to enlighten and disturb."

Other Films *Gods of the Plague* (*Götter der Pest* [1969]); *The American Soldier* (*Der Amerikanische Soldat* [1970]); *The Merchant of Four Seasons* (*Händler der vier Jahreszeiten* [1971]); *Effi Briest* (*Fontane Effie Briest* [1974]); *Mother Küster's Journey to Heaven* (*Mutter Küsters Fahrt zum Himmel* [1975]); *Satan's Brew* (*Satansbraten* [1976]); *Lili Marleen* (1980); *Lola* (1981).

References Elsaesser, Thomas, *New German Cinema: A History* (New Brunswick, N.J.: Rutgers University Press, 1989); Hayman, Ronald, *Fassbinder: Filmmaker* (New York: Simon and Schuster, 1985); Morris, Gary, "Profile: Fassbinder," *Bright Lights Film Journal* 12 (May 1998).

—T.P.

Fellini, Federico (1920–1993)

Federico Fellini is one of the most celebrated directors in the history of cinema, whose oeuvre spans the years from Italian neorealism to his own maturity as one of cinema's most idiosyncratic and visually extravagant directors. He was born on January 20, 1920, at the viale Dardanelli 10, in the resort city of Rimini, on the Adriatic coast of northeastern Italy. Although he rarely returned to his native city in later life, its social milieu and its geographical location would influence his work, surfacing, for example, in his fascination with itinerant entertainers and the cinema, his erotic preoccupation with women, his ambivalence toward the Catholic religion, and his tendency to use the sea as a symbolic setting in many of his pictures. Of his childhood, Fellini said, "As a child, I was very timid, solitary, vulnerable to the point of fainting. . . . I liked to be pitied, to appear unreadable, mysterious. I liked to be misunderstood, to feel myself a victim, unknowable." A particular form of escape and pleasure for the young man were the carnivals and circuses that passed through Rimini each year. Because of his use of these character types—often outcasts—his later films are often considered grotesque theatrical spectacles. "The cinema is also circus," he has said, "carnival, fun-fair, a game for acrobats."

Fellini's father was a wholesaler in groceries who traveled frequently while his mother remained at home. Federico was educated in Catholic schools in Rimini until 1938 when he left for Florence, where his early aptitude for drawing, especially in caricature and cartoon, was put to work for local comics and newspapers. Commentator Edward Murray has noted that Fellini's training in drawing and writing for the comics "not only supplied him with part of his future subject matter but may have also taught him some valuable lessons in cinematic form." Fellini himself remarked regarding his storyboards, "Any ideas I have immediately become concrete in sketches and drawings." Meanwhile, his writing skills eventually led to assignments for papers in Rome, a city that became for Fellini a new home and place of protection and creative freedom. It was there in 1943 that he met and married the actress Giulietta Masina, who would appear in seven of Fellini's films.

It was his work with director ROBERTO ROSSELLINI that essentially led him to directing his own films. Fellini coscripted Rossellini's *Open City* (1945); *Paisan* (1946), for which he also served as assistant director; and the controversial *The Miracle* (1948), in which he also acted the part of a wandering shepherd who seduces a peasant woman (Anna Magnani). *Variety Lights* (*Luci del varieta* [1950]) and *The White Sheik* (*Lo Sceicco bianco* [1952]), Fellini's first directorial efforts, both reveal vestiges of neorealism in their gritty surface details, although they deal with theatrical performers and the treacherous fantasy of illusions. In *Variety Lights,* codirected by Alberto Lattuada, the leader of a fading vaudeville troupe abandons his lover and troupe for another girl. *The White Sheik* alludes to the world of the *fumetti,* those popular Italian comic strips whose illustrations were composed of photographs, not drawings. The story is about a young bride who is lured away from her commonplace life by the charms of the comic strip character, "The White Sheik," her romantic dream hero (Alberto Sordi). *I Vitelloni* (*The Young*

Ones [1953]), Fellini's first masterpiece, is a semi-autobiographical tale about five adolescents in Rimini caught up in the transition from carefree youth to responsible adulthood. Through the course of the picture, as commentator Peter Bondanella has observed, "Each of the *vitelloni* experiences a crisis as his illusions collide with reality." One of them, Moraldo, suffers a moment of truth that impels him to leave the provinces. "Moraldo realizes that childhood illusions," continues Bondanella, "such as the ones his fellow *vitelloni* never abandon, are unworthy of a mature individual in the adult world. And so, Moraldo sets out, as Fellini did years earlier."

Fellini's next two films, *La Strada* (*The Road* [1954]) and *Nights of Cabiria* (*Le notti di Cabiria* [1958]), constituted his "breakthrough" into international renown. The first is a variant of the Beauty and the Beast fable, a tale of a pair of itinerant performers, the waif-like Gelsomina (Giulietta Masina) and the brutish strongman Zampano (Anthony Quinn), that is heartbreaking in its poignancy and pathos. The abuse of the woman and the tragedy of the strongman demonstrate the power of redemption through suffering. *La Strada* won the Oscar for best foreign film in 1954. *Nights of Cabiria* also won best foreign film Oscar, and again reiterates the theme of spiritual redemption. In the film, a young prostitute (Masina in the title role) survives the hazards of a cruel world and opportunistic men by clinging to her romantic ideals of love and innocence. It remains one of Fellini's most sensitive and compassionate pictures and later inspired the Bob Fosse musical, *Sweet Charity.* These two films, notes biographer John Baxter, present a characteristically Felliniesque image of the female: "Equally common in his early work is a beaming androgyne, clown-like and sexless, famously embodied by Giulietta Masina in *La Strada* and *Le notti di Cabiria.* Just as much as the fertility figures of the later films, Gelsomina and Cabiria are a child's vision of sexuality: half playmate, half puppet, sexually neutral."

On the other hand, there is a lack of spiritual redemption and purity evident in Fellini's most well-known and popular film, *La Dolce Vita* (1960), which also won an Oscar for best foreign film, as well as the Palme D'Or at Cannes. The film depicts an almost infernal journey through the high life of Rome, a soulless, empty universe where the paparazzi and spoiled bourgeois aristocrats play out the endless round of their sterile lives. This decadent world of the upper class is regarded through the eyes of a journalist, played by Marcello Mastroianni (who would become Fellini's onscreen alter ego), who, despite loathing the degradation around him, is himself caught up in it. At the same time, it is also a love letter to the city of Rome. Fellini said, "The star of my film is Rome, the Babylon of my dreams." He also commented on the tragedy of spiritual collapse, suggesting, "There is a vertical line in spirituality that goes from the beast to the angel, and on which we oscillate. Every day, every minute, carries the possibility of losing ground, of falling down again toward the beast." Commentator David Cook says of the film, "Its superficially realistic milieu is corruption and decadence, and its visual extravagance borders on the fantastic." *La Dolce Vita* solidified Fellini's international reputation as an auteur.

His next picture, *8 1/2* (1963), also a best foreign film winner, is often regarded by critics as Fellini's masterpiece. Though not as popular among general audiences as *La Dolce Vita, 8 1/2* is an astonishing achievement, not just for its story and theme, but also for its distinctive style and seamless blend of reality and dream, life and art. The film is a self-reflective meditation on the cinema itself, on filmmaking and illusion. It is both autobiographical and allegorical, depicting conflicting feelings of art and reality, of spectacle and normalcy. The film is also an existential examination about the meaning—and meaninglessness—of life. Fellini said, "*8 1/2* is meant to be an attempt to reach an agreement with life ... an attempt and not a completed result. I think for now it might indicate a solution: to make friends with yourself completely, without

hesitations, without false modesty, without fears and without hopes." *8 1/2* is ultimately about its own making—the central character is a film director (Mastroianni)—and about the wellsprings of the creative urge. It remains, for most critics, Fellini's crowning achievement.

Juliet of the Spirits (*Giulietta degli spiriti* [1965]) was Fellini's first foray into color, and in some ways it was a feminine counterpart to *8 1/2*. It also uses dream sequences and surreal settings to depict the nature of the female psyche. The female mystique has always been important to Fellini's films. He believed that women represent to man his darker impulses, the mysterious side of him that he cannot comprehend. The female characters often dominate the men and show how they (the men) remain helpless and confused.

Fellini Satyricon (1969) is another vision of decadent Roman society transplanted to the time of Petronius. Perhaps because its bizarre, extravagant visuals—Fellini's obsessive fascination with the ugly, the misshapen, the crippled is nowhere more in evidence than here—swamped the thin storyline, it was attacked by critics and ignored at the box office. Somewhat more moderate in tone, *The Clowns* (1970) is a made-for-television documentary about the history of the circus clown and his role in art and society. The film is also a nostalgic look at the clownish pleasures Fellini enjoyed as a boy. Clowns are representative of society, he said: "Clowns are the first and most ancient antiestablishment figures and it's a pity that they are destined to disappear under the feet of technological progress. It's not just a fascinating human microcosm that is vanishing, but also a view of life and the world."

After *Fellini's Roma* (1972), an examination of his adopted city, Fellini made *Amarcord* (1973), another best foreign film Oscar winner (the title is relatively meaningless, a mere cipher). The film is one of Fellini's testaments, a semiautobiographical story of provincial Italian life in Rimini. Because the town no longer existed as he remembered, he seized the opportunity to remake the place and its people according to his own memory and imagination. "My cinema has always been about the provinces," Fellini said, "therefore childhood, and a whole lifetime that one dreams one is seeing again." Biographer Baxter notes that the picture also brought out Fellini's attitudes about the fascist politics of his youth: "Fascism dominated Fellini's public pronouncements about *Amarcord*. The Fascists, he said, conspired with the Church to keep his generation in a sort of moral and emotional slavery. 'Fascism is always waiting within us,' he warned, taking a high moral tone at odds with his usual indifference to politics. 'There is always the danger of an upbringing, a Catholic upbringing, that knows only one goal: to place a person in a situation of intellectual dependence, to limit his integrity, to take from him any sense of responsibility in order to keep him in a never-ending state of immaturity.'" For most critics, *Amarcord* marks the end of Fellini's most creative output.

The last 20 years of Fellini's film career produced only intermittent moments of brilliance. Still, Fellini made several more features that are as engaging and interesting as his earlier, more successful work, though he never regained the notoriety he once held. *City of Women* (*La Città delle donne* [1980]), as Baxter notes, is "a parade of sexually charged images from childhood" and from the brothels of Rome. At the same time, continues Baxter, "Women in Fellini's films . . . are infantile symbols of idealized motherhood." The protagonist's (Mastroianni again) lack of understanding of women is ultimately tested when he finds himself trapped at a large feminist convention. He is forced to relive his childhood sexual confusions, a subsequent unhappy marriage, and his many later conquests. *Ginger and Fred* (1985) is a satire on the intrusion and ubiquity of television and the media. It is also an elegy to a time when art and extravagance could flourish, as contrasted with a modern world where style and beauty no longer have a place. *Intervista* (1988) is a homage to Cinecitta, the studio where Fellini made almost all of his films. It is also an excellent documentary on film-making and Fellini himself, who makes it clear that the only reality he knows is that which he can create on screen. Fellini's final film, *The Voice of the Moon* (*La Voce della luna* [1990]), marks a last return to the provincial countryside. It is a comic attempt to show how true communication can be achieved without the aid or influence of multifaceted communication vessels such as television.

Fellini died on October 31, 1993. As David Cook suggests, "Fellini was first and foremost a great ringmaster whose circus was the human comedy as it existed both inside and outside himself; his theme was the mystery of identity."

Other Films *The Swindle* (*Il bidone* [1955]); *Spirits of the Dead,* third episode (1967); *Fellini's Casanova* (1976); *Orchestra Rehearsal* (1978); *And the Ship Sails On* (1983).

References Baxter, John, *Fellini: The Biography* (New York: St. Martin's Press, 1993); Burke, Frank, *Federico Fellini: "Variety Lights" to "La Dolce Vita"* (Boston: Twayne Publishers, 1984); Cook, David, *A History of Narrative Film* (New York: Norton, 1996); Murray, Edward, *Fellini The Artist* (New York: Frederick Ungar, 1985); Costantini, Costanzo, *Conversations with Fellini* (New York: Harcourt Brace, 1995).

—W.V. and J.C.T.

Ford, John (1894–1973)

Once, when he was asked which film directors he most admired, ORSON GEORGE WELLES is said to have replied, "The old masters, by which I mean John Ford, John Ford, and John Ford." Similarly, the great Japanese director AKIRA KUROSAWA habitually wore sunglasses on the set of his films, not because he was bothered by sunlight, but because he had once seen a photograph of his idol, John Ford, wearing the same dark glasses. Over the course of his near-59-year career as a filmmaker, Ford would win four Academy Awards for direction, and was the first recipient of the AFI's lifetime achievement award. Yet, for all of this, the man himself remained deceptively simple and self-effacing, often introducing himself by saying "My name's John Ford. I make westerns."

Born John Martin Feeney on February 1, 1894, the eventual John Ford was the 10th child of John A. Feeney and Barbara Curran, Irish immigrants. As a boy, Ford spent a great deal of time at the local nickelodeon. But Ford first felt the pull of a career in the movies through the influence of his older brother, Frank T. Feeney, who was over 12 years Ford's senior. Frank, who had literally run away to join the circus, had not been heard from in 10 years before young John saw him in a western at the local nickelodeon.

John soon joined his brother in California in 1914, where he entered into a kind of apprenticeship under his elder brother, who was now called Francis Ford and was a highly successful director/actor. Young John, then called Jack, quickly adopted the new surname as well. For the next three years he worked as an actor, stuntman, extra, assistant director, and any number of other jobs under Francis and others. Ford even made his way into DAVID WARK GRIFFITH's *Birth of a Nation* (1915) as one of the heroic Klansmen. Then, in 1917, he was given a chance to direct his first picture, *The Tornado,* in which he also starred. Two more two-reel action pictures followed, and Ford's reputation began to grow. The year 1917 also introduced John Ford to one of the most important figures of his life: actor and western star Harry Carey. Carey and Ford would collaborate on 25 silent films over the next four years. Ford's relationship with Carey would be echoed throughout the rest of Ford's career through his relationships with such performers as Victor McLaglen, Will Rogers, Henry Fonda, James Stewart, Ward Bond, and John Wayne.

Between 1917 and 1927 (and the coming of sound) Ford directed over 60 films, many of them westerns, including such titles as *Straight Shooting* (1917), *The Outcasts of Poker Flat* (1919), *The Iron Horse* (1924), and *3 Bad Men* (1926). Prior to his 1939 landmark, *Stagecoach,* however, Ford's early sound career was relatively free of cowpokes and gunfights. Instead he produced a string of action pictures (*Seas Beneath* [1931]), war films (*The Lost Patrol* [1934]), prestige period dramas (*Mary of Scotland* [1936]), a Shirley Temple adventure (*Wee Willie Winkie* [1937]), and three Will Rogers comedies (*Doctor Bull* [1933], *Judge Priest* [1934], and *Steamboat 'Round the Bend* [1935]). His most important pre-1939 film, however, was 1935's *The Informer,* a moody, atmospheric drama about an IRA soldier (Victor McLaglen) tortured by guilt after he becomes an informant. The film's black and white photography showed the influence of German expressionism, and the Irish setting was one to which Ford would return in subsequent films, most importantly in 1952's *The Quiet Man.* Indeed, characters and motifs from Ford's ancestral homeland would become one of the strongest thematic threads linking nearly all of Ford's films.

The year 1939 was seminal in Ford's career. Over the course of those 12 months he released

John Ford

three films that would, along with a number of other 1939 releases, come to symbolize the Hollywood studio system at its best. The first of these was *Stagecoach,* an exciting western whose box-office success is credited with rescuing the career of John Wayne, a dear friend of Ford, from B-movie doldrums and restoring the prominence of the western genre. *Young Mr. Lincoln,* which features Henry Fonda in the title role, was similarly successful at the box office. The film is a moving and amusing depiction of the future president as a young, idealistic lawyer. Ford's final 1939 film, *Drums Along the Mohawk,* a Revolutionary War adventure also starring Fonda, is remarkable primarily because it was Ford's first color film. The next two years saw Ford produce such classics as *The Grapes of Wrath* (1940); *The Long Voyage Home* (1940), an adaptation of several Eugene O'Neill plays and reportedly the author's favorite of all the film adaptations of his work; and *How Green Was My Valley* (1941), the film that took home the best picture Oscar over *Citizen Kane. Valley* would also prove to be Ford's last feature film for four years.

The onset of World War II brought Ford into active duty as a lieutenant commander in the U.S. Navy. Ford went to work for the Office of War Information and began producing a series of short docudramas on the U.S. war effort. The most notable of these is probably 1942's *The Battle of Midway,* which featured some of the most incredible combat footage of the war. Ford took up the camera himself on a number of sequences, including one in which several U.S. sailors risk their lives to raise the American flag while under heavy Japanese bombardment. Ford was wounded in the eye during the battle and was awarded the Purple Heart and took to wearing those dark glasses so admired by Kurosawa.

Near the end of the war Ford returned to feature filmmaking to produce *They Were Expendable* (1945), a substantially true story about the men who piloted the U.S. Navy's PT Boats in the Philippines at the beginning of World War II. The year 1946 saw Ford return to the western with *My Darling Clementine,* a mythic retelling of the legend of Wyatt Earp, whom Ford had actually met during the silent era. In 1948 Ford directed *Fort Apache,* the first in his so-called cavalry trilogy, which has often been viewed as lionizing the U.S. Cavalry while demonizing the Native American combatants. However, a close viewing of *Fort Apache* reveals a more evenhanded approach to both subjects. The cavalry is depicted as being riddled with class warfare, drunkards, and ineffectual commanding officers while the Apache are briefly seen as an honorable people at the end of their rope—victimized by unfair treaties and corrupt government officials. *Apache* is also notable as Ford's only screen pairing of his two favorite leading men, John Wayne and Henry Fonda. The other films in the trilogy, 1949's *She Wore a Yellow Ribbon* and 1950's *Rio Grande,* are both exciting and entertaining, though somewhat less interesting than *Fort Apache.* In 1955 Ford again teamed with Fonda for what would prove to be the final film in their long collaboration, *Mister Roberts.* Fonda, who had played the title role on Broadway for a number of years, disagreed with some of the choices Ford made, and the two eventually came to blows over the film. Not long after, Ford took ill and was replaced by Mervin Leroy.

In 1956 Ford released what was arguably his last epic masterpiece, *The Searchers.* A morality tale in the guise of a western, the film used its Monument Valley locations, seen in many earlier Ford films, as a kind of stage upon which unfolded a near-Shakespearean drama of hatred, murder, and vengeance. Ethan Edwards (Wayne in perhaps his best role) is a Southern Civil War vet and virulent racist, who spends years questing after revenge for the murder of his brother's family and the kidnapping and probable rape of his nieces by a band of Comanche. Stark, violent, and centered around a thoroughly unsympathetic protagonist, *The Searchers* is perhaps the strongest film of Ford's long career. Its imprint can be seen in such disparate films as Kurosawa's *Hidden Fortress* (1958), Scorsese's *Taxi Driver* (1976), and Spielberg's *Saving Private Ryan* (1998).

The 1960s would prove to be Ford's last productive decade, and one in which he seemed to try to redress some of the "sins" of his past. *Sergeant Rutledge* (1960) is a well-meaning but flawed depiction of the African-American "Buffalo Soldiers" of the U.S. Cavalry. Woody Strode played the title character, a brave soldier accused of the rape and murder of a white woman. Though the courtroom sequences are stilted and too on-the-nose, the film's action sequences are quite good, and one of them, in which Rutledge rescues his pursuers from attacking Indians and then makes his escape across a river, can be seen as historic. As Strode himself said, "You never seen a Negro come off a mountain like John Wayne before. I had the greatest Glory Hallelujah ride across the Pecos River that any black man ever had on the screen. And I did it myself. I carried the whole black race across that river." In 1963 Ford bid farewell to Wayne when the two teamed a final time for *Donovan's Reef,* an amusing but forgettable comedy set in Hawaii. *Cheyenne Autumn* (1964) would prove to be Ford's farewell to both the western and Monument Valley. The film was an attempt to redress the negative image of Native Americans in earlier Ford works like *Stagecoach.* In 1966 Ford released what would prove to be his final feature film, *7 Women.* Ironically, a filmmaker who had built his career on tough films about macho soldiers, cowboys, and boxers, bowed out with a film about a group of women missionaries fighting off a horde of Mongolian bandits. Though Ford continued to plan projects over the remaining seven years of his life, none of them ever came together. On August 31, 1973, Ford died of cancer, ending a film career that had stretched from the silent era through the fall of the studio system.

Ford was, by anyone's estimation, a central figure in the history of American cinema. Stories about him quickly attained the status of legend, such as the time a studio executive once complained to him that he was four pages behind schedule on his latest film. Without a word, Ford picked up the script, ripped out four pages at random and said, "Now we're back on schedule." He was also a man of contradictions. A political conservative who once declared, "God bless Richard Nixon," Ford was instrumental in heading off CECIL B[LOUNT] DEMILLE's attempted right-wing takeover of the Director's Guild during the height of 1950s McCarthyism. Though he could often be cruel and insulting on the set, he nevertheless was deeply loyal to actors he liked and always made sure they had work, thus giving rise to his famous "stock company." A happily married man for over 50 years, to the former Barbara Smith, he was occasionally thought to have affairs (most notably with Katharine Hepburn during the production of *Mary of Scotland*). And finally, though often in the employ of the major studios, Ford was able to create a body of personal, artistic work that has been compared to that of such foreign film artists as Jean Renoir and Kurosawa. He may have modestly said, "I make westerns," but he clearly did much more than that.

Other Films *The Fugitive* (1947); *3 Godfathers* (1948); *Wagonmaster* (1950); *The Last Hurrah* (1958); *The Man Who Shot Liberty Valance* (1962).

References Doherty, Thomas, *Projections of War* (New York: Columbia University Press, 1993); Gallagher, Tag, *John Ford: The Man and His Films* (Berkeley: University of California Press, 1986); Hardy, Phil, ed., *The Overlook Film Encyclopedia: The Western* (Woodstock, N.Y.: Overlook Press, 1991); Place, J. A., *The Western Films of John Ford* (Secaucus, N.J.: Citadel Press, 1974).

—F.H.

Forman, Miloš (1932–)

"I was born in the town of Čáslav in central Bohemia," Miloš Forman wrote in his memoir, *Turnaround* (1994), "a town of about ten thousand people, whose history went back to the thirteenth century." The year was 1932, on February 18. His father, Rudolf Formanova, was a professor at the Teachers' Institute in Čáslav. His parents built a summer hotel in 1927 on a lake in northern Bohemia, which his mother, Anna, managed. In 1940, after the Germans arrived in Čáslav, Forman's father was arrested by the Gestapo because he belonged to Pribina, an underground resistance group. Then, in 1942, his mother was also arrested and sent to Auschwitz, where she died in March of 1943. Her son was left in the care of his grandfather.

In 1945 Forman attended a school for war orphans in the town of Poděbrady, where he first met Ivan Passer, with whom he would much later collaborate on Czech films. Another classmate was Václav Havel from Prague, later destined to become a dissident writer and, finally, president of the Czech Republic. Thereafter, Forman was accepted into the screenwriting program at the Prague Film Academy, where he studied with the poet and writer Milan Kundera. After graduating from the Film Academy in 1954, Forman moved quickly into a career in television and film.

In 1958 Forman collaborated with Alfred Radok on two projects: *Grandpa Automobile* (*Dědeček automobil*) and *Laterna magika* (*Magic Lantern*), shown at the Brussels Exposition of 1958. *Latern magika II* followed in 1960. In 1963 he made two short films in collaboration with his friends Ivan Passer and cinematographer Miroslav Ondříček, *Audition/Talent Competition* and *If There Were No Music* (*Kdyby ty muziky nebyly*), that were combined to make a feature entitled *Konkurs* (Talent competition). This documentary, "hitherto unequalled in Czechoslovakian cinema," was criticized by Josef Škvorecký as "a cruel record of female self-love, conceit and dreams of fame," but Forman replied, "The cruelty which glares at you from the screen is present in the very nature of the audition," and to "deprive it of that cruelty would mean depriving it of its essence."

Forman's next film, *Black Peter* (*Černý Petr* [1964]), was adapted from a short story by Jaroslav Papoušek, set in 1947 and transformed into a study of teen apathy that escaped government notice because, as Forman calculated, "People don't take comedies seriously." The film won first prize at the Locarno Film Festival, and Forman continued his analysis of Czech family life in *Loves of a Blonde* (*Lásky jedné plavovlásky* [1965]). According to Peter Hames, both films not only focused upon "the impermanence of young love, the confusion and despair of middle age, and the gulf between the generations," but were also critical of "some of the obvious absurdities" within Czech society. Forman's last Czech film, *The Fireman's Ball* (*Hoří, má panenko* [1967]) pushed the envelope of satire too far in its criticism of governmental bureaucracy. "The Czech ideology was that film had to reflect life as it should be. We wanted to show life as it is. That required some fancy strutting around the censors, and subjects which on the surface were innocent. But between the lines, the audiences could read something more." After the Soviet invasion of Prague in 1968, a tougher government banned the film for 20 years after Forman's escape from communism. When the Soviets invaded, Forman was in Paris, and he did not return home.

Taking Off (1971), Forman's first American film, was a continuation of themes Forman had first explored in Czechoslovakia. Nothing much seems to happen. A girl (Linnea Heacock) runs away from home, auditions for a singing lead (she literally can't sing), meets and presumably falls in love with a young rock musician, and returns home. (One of the auditioning singers is Carly Simon.) The young lovers are not the well-scrubbed models of youthful perfection found in Erich Segal's *Love Story* (1970), but the focus of the film falls not on the youngsters, but on their parents (Buck Henry and Lynn Carlin). The father blunders into a situation of his own making: Thinking that his daughter has run off, he overreacts, gets roaring drunk, then brutalizes the girl when he returns home to find her there. Consequently, she *does* run off. Desperate to find her, the parents join a group called SPFC (Society for the Parents of Fugitive Children), which turns out to be simply a group of pot-smoking ninnies. Significantly, the daughter

Miloš Forman (Dino De Laurentiis Corporation/
Paramount)

seems not at all interested in dope, whereas the parents, in an idiotic attempt to "understand" her, get presumably stoned, shedding their inhibitions—ultimately to their own chagrin. Though *Taking Off* won the Special Jury Prize at the Cannes Film Festival of 1971, it was not a commercial success.

Taking Off was a less than brilliant debut effort, but respectable enough, and certainly typical of Forman's concerns at the time. Forman's next project was the decathlon episode of the Munich Olympics film, *Visions of Eight* (1972), another respectable effort, but his next film, *One Flew Over the Cuckoo's Nest* (1975), adapted from Ken Kesey's novel (1962) and Dale Wasserman's play adaptation (1971), was to establish Forman as one of Hollywood's major talents. The casting was brilliant, with Jack Nicholson playing troublemaker Randle Patrick McMurphy, a patient at the Oregon State Hospital in Salem, and Louise Fletcher as his nemesis at the mental hospital, Nurse Ratched, a control freak. A strong support-

ing cast included Danny DeVito, Christopher Lloyd, and Will Samson as Chief Bromden. The film won five Academy Awards, including best picture and best director. In 1977 Forman became an American citizen.

Forman's Academy Award sweep was followed by a film adaptation of a defining musical of the protest generation, *Hair* (1979), but the problem was that by the time Forman had arranged funding and organized the project, the Age of Aquarius had long since passed. Working with choreographer Twyla Tharp and playwright Michael Weller, Forman opened up the play to location shooting in New York's Central Park and the Lincoln Memorial in Washington, D.C., and developed a new story line that Forman claimed "was hidden in the original one," but the film, involving a tribe of hippies protesting conscription in the Vietnam War, did not appear until four years after the evacuation of Saigon. The approach was highly imaginative and visionary, but the subject was dated.

Two more outstanding adaptations were to follow, both of which would earn critical acclaim, keeping Forman at the top of his game. The first was *Ragtime* (1981), beautifully adapted by Michael Weller from the 1975 novel by E. L. Doctorow, involving more plots and characters (historical and fictional) from the turn of the century than any film could possibly digest. The central plot concerns a ragtime piano player named Coalhouse Walker (Howard E. Rollins, Jr.), whose automobile, a prized possession, is trashed by some racist volunteer firemen in New Rochelle, New York, where his wife, Sarah, works for a prosperous middle-class family; in the aftermath, Sarah is killed, and Coalhouse becomes the leader of a group of black terrorists who take over the J. P. Morgan library. The film featured a fine cast that included Mandy Patinkin, novelist Norman Mailer (as the architect Stanford White), and Jimmy Cagney, in his last film appearance, as the New York police commissioner.

Forman told Doctorow that the story was "too sprawling. It must be focused. I decided we will concentrate on three characters, Coalhouse Walker, Younger Brother and Evelyn Nesbit. We will build them up, strengthen their mutual relationship, make it into a *story.*" The final cut came in at just under three hours. Producer Dino De Laurentiis pressured Forman into cutting an additional 20 minutes, the Emma Goldman subplot, which caused the director to consider the film "an amputee." Even so, the film got eight Oscar nominations.

His next film, *Amadeus* (1984), not only adapted but also rewritten and restructured by Peter Shaffer from his hit play, would fare far better. It grossed nearly $55 million and swept seven Academy Awards, including best picture and Forman's second best director award. With F. Murray Abraham in the lead as the poisonous Antonio Salieri leading another brilliant cast, Forman was able to make the film in Prague, with its picturesque streets that made the picture wonderfully atmospheric, but the miracle of this adaptation was the way in which Shaffer restructured the play so that the music of Mozart could be perfectly incorporated, in ways not possible on the stage.

Forman's next film, *Valmont* (1989), was a superior adaptation of the novel *Les Liaisons dangereuses,* but it was overlooked and neglected because it had been eclipsed by the tremendous success of the Stephen Frears adaptation of Christopher Hampton's play version. *Dangerous Liaisons,* made the year before and involving the same characters. Forman's next film, *The People vs. Larry Flint* (1996), earned Forman another Oscar nomination for best director and Woody Harrelson for best actor, but this film was attacked by some feminists and excoriated because it dealt sympathetically with the smut merchant who built an empire publishing *Hustler* magazine. "The film just died," Forman told *Entertainment Weekly* in 1999. "That pains me because I think it was very unjust. The film never committed the crimes for which it was accused. In general, I believe in the arguments supporting what Flynt does. But I've never bought a *Hustler* magazine, and I'm not

planning to." Forman's following film was another biopic, *Man on the Moon* (1999), starring Jim Carrey as the eccentric comedian Andy Kaufman. The film got much media attention but was not a box-office success. Forman's main talent has been for satire and, especially, for his extraordinary ability to adapt literary and dramatic works successfully to the screen, not for biography.

Other Films *Dob e placená procházka* (*A Well-Paid Stroll,* TV [1966]); *The Little Black Book* (1999).

References Buckley, Tom, "The Forman Formula," *New York Times Magazine,* March 1, 1981, pp. 28–31, 42–44, 50; Forman, Miloš, and Jan Novak, *Turnaround: A Memoir* (New York: Villard Books, 1994); Hames, Peter, *The Czechoslovak New Wave* (Berkeley: University of California Press, 1985); Jensen, Jeff, "Moon Landing," *Entertainment Weekly,* December 10, 1999, pp. 51–54; McCreadie, Marsha, "*One Flew Over the Cuckoo's Nest:* Some Reasons for One Happy Adaptation," *Literature/Film Quarterly* 2 (Spring 1977): 125–131; Safer, Elaine B., "'It's the Truth Even If It Didn't Happen': Ken Kesey's *One Flew Over the Cuckoo's Nest,*" *Literature/Film Quarterly* 2 (Spring 1977): 132–141.

—J.M.W.

Frankenheimer, John (1930–) John Frankenheimer is an illustrious member of that cadre of American film directors—including Arthur Penn, Sidney Lumet, and Delbert Mann—who gained their apprenticeship in the Golden Age of "live" television. He was born in Malba, New York, on February 19, 1930, and grew up in the borough of Queens. He attended La Salle Military Academy during his high school years. His first experience in making movies came in the U.S. Air Force's Film Squadron unit, when he directed documentaries while stationed in Burbank, California. After military service, he went to CBS in the early 1950s to pursue a career in television. Quick, versatile, and technically adept in the new medium, his first projects were varied, to say the least—a religious series, *Lamp Unto My Feet;* an interview show with Edward

R. Murrow, *Person to Person;* a variety show, *The Garry Moore Show;* and 152 "live" dramatic presentations for anthology programs, like *Climax!* and *Playhouse 90,* between 1954 and 1960. Examples of the highly literate nature of many of these programs are *The Turn of the Screw,* based on Henry James's novella and starring Ingrid Bergman, and *The Last Tycoon,* adapted from F. Scott Fitzgerald's novel.

Moving into theatrical features, his first film was *The Young Stranger* (1956). His best-known films include the political assassination thriller, *The Manchurian Candidate* (1962); a fable about the military takeover of the American government, *Seven Days in May* (1963); and *Grand Prix,* a Cinerama racing epic. Less familiar, but no less full of quirky surprises, are *The Train* (1965), a World War II thriller about Nazi theft of art masterpieces; *French Connection II* (1975), an offbeat sequel to the William Friedkin original, and *The Fourth War* (1990), one of the first spy melodramas to reflect the thaw in cold-war tensions between East and West. Arguably his masterpiece is *Seconds* (1966), a lamentably undervalued modernization of the Faust allegory, starring Rock Hudson in his finest role. As an exercise in Kafkaesque horror, it occupies a special niche in the American horror cinema.

Director John Frankenheimer on the set of *The Island of Dr. Moreau* (New Line Productions)

Frankenheimer's television experience has contributed to his visual style. He is known for glaring closeups and staging in depth, rather than width, which necessitates working with a preproduction storyboard artist; and he consistently employs hard lighting, wide-angle lenses, and hand-held cameras to impart a restless, edgy quality to his dramas. Thematically speaking, he is preoccupied with the conflicts between individuals and society. In *The Train,* the "enemy" is the Nazi regime; in *Birdman of Alcatraz,* the prison government; in *52 Pick-Up,* the corruption of ruthless people; in *Manchurian Candidate,* political greed.

In recent years, aside from a few theatrical releases, like *Ronin* (1997) and *Reindeer Games* (2000), he has returned to television, directing a series of films for Turner and HBO Television, including *Against the Wall,* about the Attica prison revolt; *The Burning Season,* the story of Chico Mendes; and *Andersonville,* about the Civil War prison camp. Because they are not mainstream subjects, Frankenheimer is convinced they could not have been financed as theatrical feature films. "There shouldn't be any stigma attached to a director who says he wants to do a cable movie, or a movie of the week. Why not do a wonderful subject for TV that will be seen by millions of people rather than the nonsense they're doing now and have it do no business." Frankenheimer was honored in 1996 by a double retrospective at the Museum of Modern Art and the Museum of Television and Radio.

Other Films *The Young Savages* (1961); *The Fixer* (1968); *The Gypsy Moths* (1969); *Black Sunday* (1976); *The Island of Dr. Moreau* (1996).

References "Dialogue on Film: John Frankenheimer," *American Film,* March 1989, pp. 20–24; Pratley, Gerald, *The Cinema of John Frankenheimer* (New York: 1969).

—J.C.T.

Friedkin, William (1935–) William "Hurricane Billy" Friedkin was born on August 29, 1935, in Chicago, Illinois, the son of Raechael

(Rae) Friedkin and Louis Friedkin. His mother was an operating room nurse, his father a semiprofessional softball player, a merchant seaman, and a discount clothing salesman. Friedkin's parents were unable to send him to college, so he began working in the mailroom of WGN-TV in Chicago, a position he sought after reading an ad promising "opportunities for young men to succeed in television." He started in 1953 and was in the mailroom for six months before being promoted to floor manager, then to director, in short order. He was barely 18 years old.

From 1953 to 1961 Friedkin directed some 2,000 television programs, ranging from classic drama to baseball games. Eventually he became interested in documentary film, an interest that led to his production *The People versus Paul Crump,* which won the Golden Gate Award at the San Francisco Film Festival in 1962 and was also cited for several other international awards. This success enabled him to work on his first feature film, *Good Times* (1967), starring Sonny and Cher, a production Friedkin now considers "not viewable." In 1968, *The Night They Raided Minsky's* was released, starring Jason Robards, Britt Eklund, and several other talented actors, an enjoyable and promising film, although flawed. In the same year *The Birthday Party* was released starring Robert Shaw, an adaptation of the play by Harold Pinter, and a production Friedkin is still proud of. *The Boys in the Band,* adapted from Mart Crowley's play and released in 1970, was reputed to be the first mainstream film about gay life in the United States. After completing these projects, Friedkin later claimed that no one should film a play. Even so, in 1998, Friedkin successfully took on another adaptation, *12 Angry Men,* structured like a stageplay but originally written as a teleplay by Reginald Rose and made into a feature film by Sidney Lumet in 1957. Friedkin's television remake was nominated for the Director's Guild of America award.

In 1971, Friedkin's first great success, *The French Connection,* was released and gained him

international acclaim. It is a brilliant, gritty film starring Gene Hackman, Fernando Rey, Roy Scheider, and Tony Lo Bianco. The plot involves two New York policemen who assist in breaking up a heroin ring in the late 1960s. It featured one of the most famous and exciting car chase sequences ever filmed and won an Academy Award for Friedkin as best director. His brilliant directing continued with *The Exorcist,* released in 1973, which earned another Oscar nomination for best director. Friedkin has said that "*The Exorcist* is the 'only' film I've ever made that I think is pretty good." *The Exorcist* starred Ellen Burstyn, Max von Sydow, and, in her film debut, Linda Blair.

In 1977 *Sorcerer* was released, a remake of the 1953 Henri-Georges Clouzot film *The Wages of Fear.* Friedkin still believes *Sorcerer* is very watchable, but, unfortunately, it flopped at the box office, as did *Cruising* (1980), starring Al Pacino, Paul Sorvino, and Karen Allen. *To Live and Die in L.A.* (1985), starring William L. Peterson and Willem Dafoe, was a moderately successful film about the drug trade from the point of view of secret service agents. Nine years later, *Blue Chips* was released, in 1994. The director was drawn to this script because as a high-school student he was a smallish (5 feet 11 inches) but talented basketball player. The film starred Nick Nolte, Mary McDonnell, and J. T. Walsh, and also included Bob Cousy and Shaquille O'Neal in smaller roles. This film was a moderate success because of its game sequence realism. *Jade* followed in 1995, starring David Caruso, Linda Fiorentino, and Chazz Palminteri, scripted by Joe Ezsterhas. Again, this film flopped.

Rules of Engagement, released in 2000, fared better, though reviews were mixed. The film starred Samuel L. Jackson as Col. Terry Childers, a highly decorated Marine who leads a rescue mission to the American Embassy in Yemen and orders his men to fire upon an angry group of armed street demonstrators. The cowardly ambassador who was rescued refuses to support Childers's account of

William Friedkin (left) on the set of *Rules of Engagement* (Paramount)

the incident when Childers finds himself the target of an investigation and trial for murder. Tommy Lee Jones played Col. Hays Hodges, whom Childers asks to serve as his defense attorney, who convinces the jury that the Marines fired upon the crowd out of self-defense. Civilian and military prosecutors alike are all cardboard martinets, while Childers and Hodges are the grizzled patriots who know better than anybody else what the proper "rules of engagement" are. The film's right-wing, militaristic spin alienated some reviewers. His next project, *Night Train,* starring Ving Rhames, was still in production in 2000. New projects under consideration in 2000 were *The Diary of Jack The Ripper* and *The Sonny Liston Story.*

Friedkin has enjoyed a long but checkered directing career in film and television. Many of his best sequences derive from the handheld camera, especially in *The French Connection.* His definition of the director's job is to keep in his head the shape of the entire film, from setup to completed shots. He has yet to equal the early successes of *The French Connection* or *The Exorcist.* His first and best Hollywood lesson was "success has many fathers, but failure is an orphan."

Other Films   *Deal of the Century* (1983); *The Twilight Zone,* TV series (1985); *Cat Squad,* TV (1986).

References   Biskind, Peter, *Easy Riders, Raging Bulls* (New York: Simon and Schuster, 1998); Emery, Robert J., "William Friedkin," in *The Directors/Take Two* (New York: TV Books, 2000); Segaloff, Nat, *Hurricane Billy: The Stormy Life and Times of William Friedkin* (New York: Morrow, 1990).

—J.B.

Gance, Abel (1889–1981)   One of the most important figures in the development of cinema as an art, Abel Gance was born on October 25, 1889, in Paris, France. Until his death in Paris on November 10, 1981, at the age of 92, the director's account of his background as a child of the well-to-do French bourgeoisie was accepted as accurate. Subsequent research revealed that Gance was the illegitimate son of Abel Flamant, a prosperous Jewish physician, and Françoise Pèrethon, who was of the working class. The stigma of being both Jewish and illegitimate in a France where anti-Semitic and class prejudices still persisted, despite a revolutionary heritage, may help explain the rebellious, anti-aristocratic sentiments that would color much of his film work. Abel was raised by his maternal grandparents in the village of Commentry until he was eight. When his mother married Adolphe Gance, a chauffeur and mechanic who later became a taxi driver, Abel moved to Paris to live with them. Although he adopted his stepfather's surname, his natural father continued to provide for him and gave him the benefit of an excellent education. Given this stimulus, the youth began reading omnivorously and developed literary and theatrical ambitions at odds with his father's desire that he should take up the law.

Although he worked for a time in a law office, by the time he was 19, Gance had become an actor on the stage and in 1909 began working in the new medium of cinema as an actor and scriptwriter. In 1911, with the help of friends, Gance formed a production company and directed his first film, *La Digue (ou Pour sauver la Hollande),* a one-reel costume drama. He followed this with several other successful short narrative films noted for their rich lighting and décor. As with all of his silent features and a majority of his sound films, Gance also wrote the scripts. Yet he had not lost sight of his theatrical ambitions and authored *Victoire de Samothrace,* a play intended to star Sarah Bernhardt. But the outbreak of the First World War prevented its production, and Gance returned to filmmaking with the startling short, *La Folie du Docteur Tube* (1915). Working for the first time with cameraman Léonce-Henry Burel, Gance employed mirrors for the distorted effects in this avant-garde comedy about a mad doctor who is able to transform people's appearances through a special powder he has invented. In embryonic form, the film, however playfully, marks Gance's first excursion into the conception of a visionary able to transform reality and can also be read as an allegory of the cinema's special, magical properties.

Gance's next films were feature-length thrillers for Film d'Art in 1916, in which he introduced into French cinema the kind of editing style that had been developed in America by DAVID WARK GRIFFITH. And in some of them, like *Barberousse* (1916), he began devising his own technical innovations, including huge close-ups, low-angled close-ups, tracking shots, wipes, and the triptych effect.

In 1917, inspired by the French success of CECIL B[LOUNT] DEMILLE's *The Cheat,* Gance turned to society dramas in which the narrative centered on human emotions and psychological conflicts. The first of these was *Le Droit à la vie,* followed by *Mater Dolorosa,* the story of a woman's troubled marriage to a doctor. With its striking chiaroscuro photography, *Mater Dolorosa* scored a major box-office success, both in France and in other countries, including the United States. The series of society dramas culminated with a masterpiece, *La Dixième Symphonie* (1918), in which a composer's marital problems inspire him to write a symphony expressing his sufferings. Establishing the director as the new artistic leader of the French cinema, the narrative enabled him to comment on the nature of genius. The shots of enraptured listeners during the first performance of the composer's new symphony illustrate Gance's belief in the transformative power of art.

Gance's next work, *J'accuse* (1919), was his first epic film, a massive, deeply moving indictment of war. Profoundly affected by the horrors of the First World War, which had devastated France and taken the lives of many of his friends, Gance created a film that, upon its release soon after the Armistice, became the screen's first cry of revolt against the organized slaughter that had ravaged modern civilization from 1914 to 1918. In the film's famous climax, the hero, a poet, develops the mystic power to call back the ghosts of the war dead (played by real soldiers from the front, many of whom died in battle shortly after appearing in the sequence) to accuse the living and demand to know the reason for their sacrifice. Gance's use of rapid cutting, superimposition, masking, and a wildly tracking camera accentuates the intensely emotional blending of camera actuality and poetic drama. The film was a spectacular hit throughout Europe, and Gance, hoping for an American success, took it across the Atlantic, where he presented it at a special screening in New York in 1921 for an appreciative audience that included D. W. Griffith and the Gish sisters. But the U. S. distributors mutilated *J'accuse* for its subsequent general release, even distorting its antiwar message into an endorsement of conventional militaristic attitudes.

Gance's American journey was sandwiched in between his work on his second epic, *La Roue,* which he filmed during 1919–20 and completed final editing in preparation for its 1922 release upon his return from the United States. A monumental production 32 reels long and requiring three evenings for its original presentation, *La Roue* is a powerful drama of life among railroad workers, rich in psychological characterization and symbolic imagery. To dramatize his story of a railroad mechanic's tortured love for his adopted daughter, Gance elaborated his use of masking and superimposition and perfected his fast cutting into the rapid montage that would soon be adopted by Russian and Japanese silent filmmakers for whom *La Roue* was a seminal influence. Complex in its thematics, the film's images animate machines and the forces of nature with a life and spirit of their own while the wheel (*roue*) of the film's title becomes a metaphor for life itself. Gance's extraordinary symbolism is exemplified in the film's conclusion: as the old railway mechanic dies quietly and painlessly in his mountain chalet, his daughter joins the local villagers outside in the snow in a circular farandole dance, a dance in which nature itself, in the form of clouds, participates. Shot entirely on location at the railroad yards in Nice and in the Alps, *La Roue* remains a work of extraordinary beauty and depth. JEAN COCTEAU said of the film, "There is the cinema before and after *La Roue* as there is painting before and after Picasso," while AKIRA KUROSAWA stated, "The first film that really impressed me was *La Roue.*"

Gance climaxed his work in the silent era with *Napoléon,* an epic historical re-creation of Napoleon Bonaparte's early career during the French Revolution. A superspectacle, the film advanced the technique of cinematic language far beyond any single production of the decade. The definitive version originally ran over six hours in length, and its amazing innovations accomplished Gance's intent of making the spectator part of the action. To create this effect, Gance utilizes rapid montage and the handheld camera extensively. An example of his technique is the "double tempest" sequence in which shots of Bonaparte—on a small boat tossing in a stormy sea as huge waves splash across the screen—are intercut with a stormy session of the revolutionary Convention, at which the camera, attached to a pendulum, swings back and forth across the seething crowd. For the climax, Gance devised a special wide-screen process employing three screens and three projectors. He called this invention Polyvision, using the greatly expanded screen for both vast panoramas and parallel triptych images. As with *La Roue,* the film's unusual length enables Gance to develop his narrative fully, peopled with numerous characters, both historical and fictional, who bring to life the epoch of the late 1700s. The director began filming *Napoléon* in 1925 and finally unveiled his masterpiece to the world at a gala premiere at the Paris Opera in 1927. Although many of those who saw Gance's original cuts (both the six-hour version and a shorter one he supervised) recognized *Napoléon* as an unequaled artistic triumph, the film ultimately proved too technically advanced for the industry of its period. MGM, which bought international distribution rights, presented the film in Europe in various mangled and mutilated versions. Their American release, shown as sound was sweeping the industry in 1929, ran only 72 minutes and eliminated all of Gance's pyrotechnics. Although film historian KEVIN BROWNLOW's later restoration would eventually establish for many *Napoléon*'s artistic preeminence, the film remains one of the cinema's controversial masterworks—

due not only to a technique and scope that broke all the rules of filmmaking but also to Gance's admiring depiction of the young Bonaparte.

Gance portrayed Bonaparte as an idealistic, visionary leader championing the French Revolution, an interpretation characterized by some critics as "fascistic," but a conception that belies an informed consideration of Gance's personal history and beliefs, and one that ignores the fact that his 1927 film was only the first of a planned series of films on Napoleon's life. In the succeeding films, he had intended to depict Napoleon drifting more and more away from his revolutionary beginnings as he became an emperor. The heroic portrayal of the young Bonaparte in the film he did make is very much in the democratic Romantic tradition of great writers like Byron, Hugo, and Heine, who had exalted the Man of Destiny as the very embodiment of revolutionary energy. That Gance should view with sympathy a leader who did much to liberate European society from aristocratic and feudal privileges should come as no surprise, given the director's own "outsider" background. Gance's radical technique is thus wedded to a radical vision of history at odds with the classical restraint that had long held both social organization and aesthetics in check. Further underscoring the director's philosophy is his own memorable performance in the film as the "Archangel of the Revolution," the left-wing Jacobin leader, St. Just.

Gance pioneered the coming of sound in France in 1930 with another ambitious epic, *La Fin du monde,* an imaginative science fiction film with pacifist overtones in which a conflict-ridden world narrowly escapes destruction by an oncoming comet, with Gance himself playing the lead role of a scientist who foresees the catastrophe. After the film was slashed and reedited by the producers for its 1931 release, a discouraged Gance had to settle for directing and supervising less-ambitious projects over the next few years. In 1934, he attempted to bring back past glories by dubbing dialogue onto a revamped version of his silent *Napoléon,* adding another innovation, stereophonic sound. Within a year, his cinematic fortunes began to turn around and he directed a series of films that demonstrated once again his mastery of cinema. Although Gance's work in the sound era spanned over three decades, his talkies have often been dismissed as a long decline from the heights of his career in the silent era. While it is true he never again created works as ambitious as *La Roue* or *Napoléon,* it is clear, as FRANÇOIS TRUFFAUT pointed out, that he continued to explore characteristic themes in highly accomplished works revealing him to be as great a master of film form as he had been in the 1920s.

The first of his major sound films, *Lucrèce Borgia* (1935), is an astonishing drama of the political intrigues of the Borgia family in Renaissance Italy, with scenes of full-frontal female nudity that were a striking departure from the prevailing cinematic codes of the time. In his depiction of Cesare Borgia's brutal rule, Gance created a historical film whose figures stand in striking contrast to those in *Napoléon.* Whereas Bonaparte and the other French Revolutionary leaders pursue power in order to realize ideals, Cesare Borgia's ruthless drive for domination reflects no more exalted idea than the satisfaction of his own lust and self-aggrandizement. The people's aspirations for freedom, voiced by another farsighted leader, Savonarola, are also thwarted by the dictatorship of Cesare's corrupt father, Pope Alexander VI. In reflecting Gance's deeply rooted aversion to aristocratic rule, this portrayal of the Borgias' intrigues may represent a cinematic response to the French rightists of the 1930s who still yearned for a restoration of monarchy and aristocracy.

The following year, Gance directed one of his two greatest sound films, *Un grande amour de Beethoven,* a fictionalized biography of the composer (memorably portrayed by Harry Bauer), in which Gance returned to his theme of creative genius and his conviction that artists are forever misunderstood by their contemporaries. By far his most technically innovative film since *Napoléon,*

Gance blended rapid montage with sound, creating striking effects new to the medium. In the scenes culminating in Beethoven's composition of the *Pastoral* Symphony during a stormy night, Gance conveys the sense of Beethoven's oncoming deafness when the sound track is suddenly completely silent. Gance manifests his antipathy to aristocracy once again, contrasting Beethoven's artistic dedication and purity of spirit amidst poverty and neglect with the unworthy dilettante nobleman, Count Gallenberg, who marries the woman the composer loves. Released in 1937 to widespread international critical acclaim, *Beethoven* established Gance as just as great a leader in the creation of sound films as he had been in the silents.

Gance's next film, a new version of *J'accuse,* was his other monumental artistic triumph of the sound era. Although he included some battle-scene footage from the 1919 silent version and based several of the characters on those in the earlier production, the new *J'accuse* was essentially a different film, a reworking with new plot elements, rather than simply a remake. Released in 1938, the film's hero is yet another seer, a World War I veteran who develops an invention intended to prevent war. His plans are sabotaged by an unscrupulous politician and manufacturer, allied with the corrupt ruling establishment, who steals his invention and uses it not for peace but to foment war instead. In the awe-inspiring climax, Gance passionately denounces the coming Second World War, with his hero once again summoning forth the spirits of the war dead (played this time by mutilated veterans of the first conflagration) to indict the living at a time of renewed war hysteria.

In striking contrast, Gance's two 1939 films, *Louise* and *Le Paradis perdu,* mark a nostalgic return to the pre–World War I Paris of the director's youth. *Louise,* adapted from Gustave Charpentier's opera, with Grace Moore in the lead, allowed the director to incorporate cinematic techniques during the operatic sequences, such as images of a singing working class superimposed over awakening Paris streets, or the subtle play of light and shadow when Louise's father, gently swaying her back and forth, sings his aria. *Le Paradis perdu* includes both romantic lyricism and high comedy as it chronicles several generations. The story of a man whose happiness is destroyed by the First World War is especially poignant in its resemblance to Gance's own life and career and that of his country, both soon to be affected by yet another war.

Gance directed two films during the war, *La Vénus aveugle* (1941), a drama with feminist overtones, and *Le Capitaine Fracasse* (1942), an exhilarating swashbuckler, before the unsettled climate of a France menaced by the Germans forced him into a temporary sojourn in Spain, then ostensibly neutral. But there he encountered further difficulties, failing in his efforts to direct a film. Beset with hardships in postwar France, Gance struggled in vain to direct an epic film about the life of Christ, to be entitled *La Divine Tragédie.* After over a decade of absence from directing, he made *La Tour de Nesle,* a costume film released in 1954. He followed this with *Magirama,* a 1956 program featuring several shorts in which he revived his three-screen technique of Polyvision. For these experiments, he worked for the first time with Nelly Kaplan, a young admirer of his from Argentina, who later became a prominent director in her own right. Kaplan also assisted Gance on his last two theatrical features, *Austerlitz* (1960) and *Cyrano et d'Artagnan* (1963). Although a return to the Napoleonic saga, *Austerlitz* fell victim to studio interference so that, despite characteristic Gance touches, the finished product was far below his expectations. But the visually striking *Cyrano et d'Artagnan* proved to be an outstanding late work. This stylish swashbuckler with dialogue in Alexandrine verse, philosophical and psychological insights, and another heroic dreamer in the person of the poet and inventor Cyrano de Bergerac, was by far the best of Gance's postwar films.

In the years immediately succeeding *Cyrano et d'Artagnan,* Gance directed two films for French television, *Marie Tudor* (1965) and *Valmy* (1967),

and in 1971 released a final revision of *Napoléon* retitled *Bonaparte and the Revolution,* for which he shot new footage to be added to the original silent work, creating a film less coherent than the original. Even so, his opportunities in his old age were sharply diminished. While his period of greatest productivity had ended in the early 1940s, all through the lean years he continued to be caught up in plans for new cinematic innovations and dreams for fresh epic projects. The unrealized *Le Divine Tragédie* had itself derived from a series of films on the founders of the world's great religions, *Les Grands Initiés,* which he had conceived decades before as a means to promote peace and brotherhood. In 1939 he did extensive research for an epic film about Christopher Columbus, but the outbreak of World War II scuttled his immediate plans for the film. Nevertheless, he returned to the idea, writing an elaborate screenplay for the Columbus film. Indeed, in his last years, his attempts to raise funds to direct the film became his consuming passion. These later years of unfulfilled dreams were marked by persistent poverty. He continued to share his life with his third wife, Odette (Sylvie?) Vérité, whom he married in 1933 and who died in 1978. His first marriage was to Mathilde Thizeau in the 1910s, and his second, in the 1920s, to Marguerite Danis, who also acted in films, including *Napoléon* and Jean Epstein's *The Fall of the House of Usher* (1928).

The adversities of his last years were somewhat alleviated by the work of film historians, especially Kevin Brownlow, who brought him to the attention of a new generation with his documentary on the director, *The Charm of Dynamite,* and his history of the silent film, *The Parade's Gone By* (1968). In a final twist of irony worthy of his films, Gance received his greatest recognition at the very end of his life, when Brownlow's restoration of the silent *Napoléon* was theatrically revived around the world with live orchestras in 1980–81. The *Napoléon* revival of the early 1980s, besides heralding a newfound interest in silent films as a whole, seemed to augur a full though belated critical and popular recognition of Gance, particularly in the United States, where the mutilation of his work by commercial interests in earlier decades had hindered his reputation.

Yet, despite initial rhapsodic reviews of *Napoléon* in the popular press, some critics, instead of expressing regret that Gance had not received his due during his lifetime, sought to justify his treatment at the hands of the industry and earlier critics. They recycled the argument that his techniques were overblown self-indulgence, that he had little of real importance to say, and this his long career in the sound era was an unmitigated decline. Perhaps worst of all, these critics soon turned to the kind of ideological axe-grinding that had also damaged Griffith's reputation. Although Gance was far from being a highly political artist and, as Steven Kramer maintained, was "only consistent within his own semi-mystical framework," the director's critics began inferring that his admiration for visionary heroes like Bonaparte reflected some sort of protofascist agenda. The line of attack apparently succeeded in dampening enthusiasm for any sustained revival of Gance's work in the United States. Although more of his films are now available on video, there has been no full retrospective of Gance's work outside France in the two decades since his death and the *Napoléon* revival. The restored versions of his three silent epics—*J'accuse, La Roue,* and the even more complete *Napoléon* (expanded beyond the shortened Coppola version)—never became accessible to American film devotees. Despite this comparative neglect, Gance remains one of the greatest directors in film history, a genius whose artistic courage and romantic, humanist vision created major works of cinema while inspiring many other directors, from his silent-film contemporaries to the French *nouvelle vague* of the 1950s and later. This pioneer invented Polyvision, a precursor of Cinerama (*Écran panoramique triple de l'écran ordinaire, polyvision et écran variable,* patented in 1926), Perspective Sound (*Perspective sonore,* patented in 1929, improved in 1932), and the *Pictographe*

(1938). The failure of the critical establishment to recognize or fully appreciate Gance's artistry has been a shameful oversight that succeeding generations will surely rectify.

Other Films   *Mater Dolorosa/Le Serment* (1934); *Le Maître de forges* (1933); *Poliche* (1934); *La Dame aux Camélias* (1934); *Le Roman d'un jeune homme pauvre* (1935); *Jérôme Perreau, héro des barricades* (1936); *Le Voleur de femmes* (1936); *Quatorze Juillet* (1953).

References   Brownlow, Kevin, *The Parade's Gone By* (New York: Alfred A. Knopf, 1968); Brownlow, Kevin, *Napoleon: Abel Gance's Classic Film* (New York: Alfred A. Knopf, 1983); Welsh, James M., and Steven Philip Kramer, *Abel Gance* (Boston: Twayne, 1978).

—W.M.D.

Godard, Jean-Luc (1930–)   Jean-Luc

Godard, the guiding spirit of the French *nouvelle vague* of the 1960s, is the cinema's most famous revolutionary. The international impact of Godard's *Breathless* (aka *A Bout de souffle* [1960]) offered a challenge to the tenets of the "classic Hollywood film" that had a lasting impact on the history of world cinema. As critic, theorist, and filmmaker, Godard's personal project, spanning four decades, has been nothing less than to redefine the very nature of the cinema's content and form.

Jean-Luc Godard was born in Paris into an upper-middle-class Protestant family on December 3, 1930. While a student at the Sorbonne, he attended the *Ciné-Club du Quartier Latin* more regularly than his university classes. While attending film programs at the *Ciné-Club,* the young Godard met Jacques Rivette and ERIC ROHMER. In 1950, the three would found *La Gazette du Cinéma,* a monthly film journal that lasted five issues. Two years later Godard started writing film criticism for *Cahiers du cinéma* and *Amis du Cinéma.* In addition to film criticism, he wrote also theoretical essays on the nature of the cinema, one titled "Towards a Political Cinema" extolling the political engagement of the Soviet cinema in which he declared, "No doubt only Russia feels at this moment that the images moving across its screens are those of its own destiny." In another essay, Godard decries that, in the modern world, "we have forgotten how to see." The quest for a cinema that will allow us to see again will inform all of Godard's own films.

Between October 1952 and August 1956, Godard took a respite from his writing to travel and, for a while, labor as a construction worker in Switzerland. Meanwhile, he used the money he made as a worker to make his first short, 20-minute film, *Operation Beton*. In 1957, he returned to Paris and became a regular contributor to both *Arts* magazine and *Cahiers du cinéma*. As Godard later said, "All of us at *Cahiers* thought of ourselves as future directors." Between August 17 and September 15, 1959, Godard took leave of his writing to shoot his first feature film, from a screenplay by fellow *Cahiers* critic FRANÇOIS TRUFFAUT, *Breathless*.

In making *Breathless,* Godard said, "what I wanted was to take a conventional story and remake, but differently, everything the cinema had done. I also wanted to give the feeling that the techniques of film-making had just been discovered or experienced for the first time." The "conventional" story involves a petty thief become cop killer, Michel Poiccard (Jean-Paul Belmondo), who fancies himself a Bogart-like romantic hero. Michel has a brief affair with an American expatriate (Jean Seberg). They talk; they make love; they talk some more; she betrays him to the police. But Godard tells his "conventional" story "differently" as a fragmented and elliptical narrative, with an iconoclastic camera and editing style employing a handheld camera, jump-cutting, flash-shots, and a disregard for continuity.

Godard's second film, *The Little Soldier* (*Le Petit soldat* [1960]), generated political controversy due to its criticism of the French-Algerian war. The film was scheduled for release in the fall of 1960, but was banned for two years by the French Censorship Board. In 1961, Godard made his third film, *A Woman Is a Woman* (*Une Femme est une femme*), starring Jean-Paul Belmondo and Anna

Karina (whom Godard married that year). The wife wants to have a baby; the husband does not. When the husband accuses his wife of using trickery to get her way, accusing her of being "dishonorable," she counters, "No, I am a woman." During the period of Godard's marriage to Karina, a number of his films would explore the difficulties of married love and the impossibility of men and women communicating with each other, as in *The Little Soldier, My Life to Live* (*Vivre sa vie* [1962]), *Band of Outsiders* (*Bande à part* [1964]), *Pierrot le fou* (1965), and *Alphaville* (1965). After a tempestuous marriage, Godard and Karina were divorced in 1965. Two years later, he married actress Anne Wiazemsky.

Masculin féminin (1966) continued to meld charming moments with hard-edged cultural analyses of the new generation coming to age in the 1960s, the children of "Marx and Coca-Cola." As Godard's work progressed through the second half of the 1960s, his films became less narrative and increasingly took on the form of filmed philosophical and political essays. In *Made in USA* (1966), *La Chinoise* (1967), and *Weekend* (1967), traditional narrative takes second place to lengthy monologues on a wide range of political subjects. *Made in USA* (1966) employs a fictional story of a woman's attempt to discover the identity of her lover's murderer as a pretext for an exploration of the Ben Barka murder and the assassination of John F. Kennedy. In *La Chinoise,* Godard declares his sole allegiance to an "agit-prop" aesthetic. The film depicts five middle-class Parisian Maoists as they plot their first terrorist attack. At one point, the hero, Guillaume (Jean-Pierre Léaud), stands at a blackboard that lists the names of influential writers and artists, which he erases one at a time until only the name "Brecht" is left.

As the political crisis in France intensified during the spring of 1968, Godard all but abolished narrative altogether in an attempt to reinvent a revolutionary cinema capable of inciting revolutionary action. In *Joyful Wisdom* (*Le Gai savoir* [1968]), two filmmakers, played by Jean-Pierre

Leaud and Juliet Berto, sit in a television studio and try to reinvent a language of images and sound. As the film director played by Yves Montand says in *Tout va bien* (1972), the cinema must search for "new forms for new contents."

In the midst of the May Uprising, Godard left France for London to begin filming *One Plus One,* also titled *Sympathy for the Devil* (1969). In the film, the Rolling Stones are shown recording their album *Beggar's Banquet;* a figure representing liberal democracy, named Eve Democracy (Anne Wiazemsky), wanders through the streets of London writing political slogans on walls. These scenes are intercut with the revolutionary activities of a Black Power group juxtaposed with a bookseller who publishes pornography and reads *Mein Kampf* while inciting his customers to harass Jews.

In 1971, Godard was involved in a serious motorcycle accident, which marked a turning point in his life and work. During his rehabilitation, Godard divorced Wiazemsky and married the woman who had been his working partner for the past 30 years, Anne-Marie Miéville. He also grew disillusioned by his earlier hortatory embrace of Maoism. *Tout va bien* (1972) was seen as something of an apology for the Marxist reductionism of his earlier films. The film concerns a disillusioned film director (Yves Montand) who stops making films after the Paris Uprising of 1968 only to end up making TV commercials for a living.

Between 1974 and 1978, Godard and Miéville moved to Rolle, Switzerland, and worked together on three experimental films and two video series. In the late 1970s, Miéville urged Godard to return to more mainstream filmmaking. *Every Man for Himself* (*Sauve qui peut la vie* [1980]) continued Godard's experimentation with cinematic form; however, it once again relied on characters and story. Much of the film is autobiographical. A filmmaker named Paul Godard follows his girlfriend, also a filmmaker, to a new life in the Swiss country. Godard has referred to it as his "second first film." It was also his most commercially successful film besides *Breathless.*

During the 1980s, Godard reestablished his reputation as a director of innovative feature-length films. *First Name: Carmen* (*Prénom: Carmen* [1983]) won the Golden Lion at the Venice Film Festival, and Godard's 1985 *Hail, Mary* (*Je vous salue, Marie*) generated controversy (and publicity) when religious groups protested the filmmaker's modern retelling of the Immaculate Conception. Mary is a basketball-playing teenager who pumps gas at her father's filling station, Joseph is a cab driver, and the archangel Gabriel is an unshaven bum. As critic Jack Ellis observed, "To many it was 'shocking and profoundly blasphemous'; to others it was a continuation of Godard's recurrent meditations on the alluring mystery of woman and her ultimate strangeness, which he began with *Breathless* and *A Woman Is a Woman* twenty-five years earlier."

In 1985 Godard began a film collaboration with novelist Norman Mailer for a film based on *King Lear.* A character named William Shakespeare, Jr. (Burgess Meredith), seeks to recover the works of his ancestor, which have been lost in the technological holocaust of Chernobyl. Writing in the *New Yorker,* Richard Brody noted that "True to Godard's later style, the film's real story is precisely how to tell the story, or whether it is in fact possible to do so."

Godard continues to seek new ways to tell a story and, if "it is in fact possible to do so," releasing three films in 2001—*After the Reconciliation, The Old Place,* and *In Praise of Love*—as well as five hours of an eight-part series of meditations on filmmaking titled *Histoire(s) du Cinéma.*

Other Films *The Riflemen* (*Les Carabiniers* [1963]); *Contempt* (*Le Mépris* [1963]); *Letter to Jane* (1972); *Passion* (1982).

References Brody, Richard, "Profiles: An Exile in Paradise," *New Yorker,* November 20, 2000, pp. 62–76; MacCabe, Colin, *Godard: Images, Sounds, Politics* (Bloomington: Indiana University Press, 1980); Narboni, Jean, and Tom Milne, eds., *Godard on Godard* (New York: Viking Press, 1972); Sterritt, David, *The Films of Jean-luc Godard* (Cambridge, U.K.: Cambridge University Press, 1999).

—T.P.

Greenaway, Peter (1942–) One of cinema's most relentlessly formalistic directors, Peter Greenaway reduces sex, violence, and politics to the grids of numbers, letters, and patterns. "I want to regard my public as infinitely intelligent," he has said, "as understanding notions of the suspension of disbelief and as realizing all the time that this is not a slice of life, this is openly a film." For the films of Peter Greenaway, this statement may be of assistance in understanding this highly artistic director whose list of films includes *A Walk Through H* (1978), *The Draughtsman's Contract* (1982), *The Belly of an Architect* (1987), and *The Cook, the Thief, His Wife, and Her Lover* (1989).

Born in 1942 in Newport, Wales, Greenaway informed his parents at the age of 12 that he intended to be a painter. He bypassed a university education and went to the Walthamstow College of Art, which considerably disappointed his family who believed his artistic endeavors were worthless. In 1965, he began work as a film editor for the Central Office of Information, where he spent 11 years cutting films that were designed to portray the intricacies of the British way of life through numbers and statistics. It has been argued that this was Greenaway's greatest stylistic influence, though Greenaway himself states that one of his primary influences is his desire to "dump" narrative considerations. According to Greenaway, if you want to tell a story, you should be a writer; the vocabulary of the cinema should no longer be used for the sole purpose of telling stories. In sum, the cinema has much to offer *outside* the slavery of the narrative. However, Greenaway has also stated that he wants to make mainstream movies: "I don't want to be an underground filmmaker; I want to make movies for the largest possible audience, but arrogantly, I want to make them on my terms."

Listing, organizing, counting, and tabling are primary themes in many of Peter Greenaway's films. The director feels that when you name a thing, you possess it. He is fascinated by the lists present in 19th-century science and 20th-century literature and the seriousness with which they were created. Greenaway acknowledges that such list-making is ephemeral, in that it is an attempt at an ownership and a comprehension that cannot be obtained. Moreover, his films are often rife with full frontal nudity, referencing painterly traditions of the nude in art history. Greenaway states that the loss of physicality would preface the loss of perspective over all the other senses.

Peter Greenaway has been significantly influenced by television and has described his film approach as influenced by the language of television. He often employs the use of the smaller frame within the larger frame along with the shifting of color schemes, as evident in some of his best-known films, like *Prospero's Books* (1991—an astonishing attempt to adapt Shakespeare's *The Tempest* to the screen, word for word, and to visualize the text itself in boxlike inserts—and *The Draughtsman's Contract,* wherein the world is viewed through the device of the artist's optical grid. Indeed, *Prospero's Books* is one of his most densely layered visual experiences. In his article about the film, "Anatomy of a Wizard," Howard A. Rodman takes inventory: "Actors vie for screen space with superimposed calligraphy, Muybridge-like animatics and all manner of body parts. Greenaway's trademark long lateral tracking shots—now a seminaked woman skipping rope, now a tableau from Hals or Vermeer, now a very young boy urinating with gleeful (artificially enhanced?) abandon into a swimming pool where Sir John [Gielgud] is bathing—compete for attention with cadenced drops of water, rhythmically pulsing balls of fire and, above all, the lovingly rendered scrape of pen against parchment." As with many Greenaway films, reaction to each of these supposedly accessible films was mixed upon their release.

His most commercially successful film, *The Cook, the Thief, His Wife, and Her Lover,* centers around the lives of the Thief (played by Michael Gambon), an abusive, violent, and perverse man whose Wife (Helen Mirren) endures the brunt of his abuses until she happens upon a quiet and unassuming man (her Lover) and begins an affair with him in a restaurant with the aid of the Cook, the owner of the restaurant and a perfectionist, forever seeking a new culinary challenge. The film is visually stunning, to the point of extravagance, as costume, set, and character are lit with the lush color of each room: red for the dining room, white for the bathroom, and green for the kitchen. According to Greenaway, the restaurant is a microcosm of our modern, consumerist society. People like the Thief and the Wife go to restaurants to see and be seen as much as to eat. The setting and characters underline the gluttony and excess of this consumerist society. This theme of consumption is the focal point of the film—firstly as the Thief gorges like a pig at the table, secondly as he force-feeds the Lover to his death, and finally, as the Thief himself is forced to consume his own evil doings. As empathetic a character as the Wife is, she is not the passive and victimized character the viewer assumes, for by the conclusion of the film, it is she who takes action to put an end to all the torment by providing the crucial solution to her own suffering.

The Pillow Book (1996) is a story of a fetish and the hold it maintains on a young woman. Nagiko, the female protagonist in this film, is presented each birthday with a passage from the Pillow Book, the diary of Sei Sho-Nagon, lady in waiting to the imperial court during the Heian Dynasty. The characters of the text are painted on her face and neck by her father, a calligrapher. The smell of the ink and the act of the painting are intertwined, for Nagiko, with the blackmailing of her father, who is forced by his publisher to be the man's sexual slave. Eventually, Nagiko is forced to marry the publisher's son, who burns her books and diaries, resulting in Nagiko's move to Hong Kong. There, she becomes a model and is obsessed with inscribing calligraphy on her body, first executed by herself and then by a series of lovers. Finally she meets the young Englishman, Jerome (Ewan McGregor), with whom she falls in love. He opens a new world for Nagiko by asking that she decorate him, in effect making the woman who would be paper into a pen. In a tragic twist, Jerome is also the lover of a man, the same publisher of her father now operating out of Hong Kong. Nagiko sends her explicit poetry to the publisher by way of Jerome's skin, and the poetry is rejected. Jerome dies in what was to be a suicide attempt, his body exhumed by the publisher, and the poems published in an elegant book. The stated purpose of the film, in Greenaway's ever-artistic and experimental style, is to mesh flesh with text, sex with literature. Style and story are fused expertly in the film as Japanese characters scroll down the movie screen and frames beget frames, within which human skin becomes paper and flesh becomes literature.

The intersections of looking and seeing, observation and comprehension stand at the core of Greenaway's wickedly melodramatic *The Draughtsman's Contract* (1982). The action is set in the 17th century in an English manor where sex, betrayal, and murder run rampant. Dissatisfied with his marriage, a landowner (Dave Hill) leaves his estate to take a two-week vacation alone. In an attempt to save the relationship, his wife asks a draughtsman (Anthony Higgins) to paint 12 pictures of their estate from 12 different vantage points as a surprise gift. The draughtsman consents but only if the wife agrees to another contract, i.e., to provide him with daily sexual favors. The daughter of the family becomes sexually involved with the draughtsman as well, and the debauchery carries on until one day the lord of the manor is found dead in the moat. The draughtsman is suspected, and he tries to defend himself by noting that the clues to the real murderer's identity may be found in his paintings (executed by Greenaway himself). The draughtsman has scrupulously painted everything within the frame of his optical grid during his daily sittings, including tell-tale details of a murderous conspiracy, i.e., a ladder balanced against a window, a garment flung over a hedge, etc. But he records only what is *seen* and not what is *known* (the difference between observation and knowledge). He perishes at the hands of assassins. "The draughtsman comes to grief," notes commentator Alan Woods, "because, well aware of the relations between property and image, he remains satisfied with drawings in which objects are represented as if in an inventory. . . . Within the spaces which he records, are, however, objects as symbols, clues regarding murder or adultery. He is drawing stage sets, filled not with property, but with properties, but he will not or cannot recognize this. . . ." This offbeat film is a witty and baroque exercise in color, décor, and costume. The film was praised not only for its mesmerizing photography and costume but also for the elegantly rambunctious musical score by Michael Nyman.

The less-accessible films of Greenaway are said to require a doctorate in semiotics to be understood. Of these, perhaps the most widely known is the early film, *A Walk Through H* (1978), financed by the British Film Institute. It details, in a nonlinear manner, the deciphering of the connection between various books, birds, and objets d'art. The film journeys through a series of 92 maps and 1,418 species of birds presented by Tulse Luper (Greenaway's alter ego appearing or referenced in numerous films), who states that the time to decide what H stands for is at the end of the journey, at which time its meaning will scarcely matter. Order and chaos are held in an equipoise. "Order, in Greenaway's work," writes Alan Woods, "—his films, his writings, his pictures, his exhibitions—is always linked to absurdity and human vanity." However, continues Woods, "Order, in the world, is mocked by disorder and decay, counting is helpless in the face of the countless things to count; this is what we are reminded of by Greenaway's organizing principles and counting games, because their arbitrary and whimsical nature is foregrounded." Less adulatory is critic Julian Bell's assessment that much of Greenaway's work is much ado about nothing, that beneath his fascinating and intricate surfaces are the "banal" propositions that humans are "bodies driven by biology" and that "any representation (by men, maps, films, etc.) always traduces or is inadequate to the reality (of women, nature, the body, etc.)." Thus, his "intricate conceits" are hollow; "the hollowness lies in his wishing to push them forward as if they were urgent, unacknowledged truths."

Greenaway's latest film, *8½ Women* (1999), details the experiences of a father, distraught over the recent death of his wife, whose son encourages him to rediscover his sexual being by opening a bordello. The idea is taken directly from Fellini's 1963 film, *8½*. Among the members of the "harem" are Kito, the strong but repressed business woman; Palmira, the spiritual woman who is more attracted to the aging widower than his young son; and Giulietta, the simple but mysterious woman with amputated legs, which factor into the title along with the homage to Fellini and the significance that this is Greenaway's eighth-and-a-half feature film. The themes of *8½ Women* include sexual power, miscommunication between men and women, the inevitability of chance, and art as a metaphor for both human form and human existence.

Greenaway is about to embark on the most ambitious project of his life, *The Tulse Luper Suitcase,* in which the director will use the full battery of techniques that can be brought to the screen. This alter ego was created by Greenaway himself years ago—Tulse to rhyme with pulse and Luper, the Latin word for wolf, meaning the wolf on your pulse. This life work is an 18-hour-long project that starts by discussing American fascism in 1933 Utah and finishes at the end of the Cultural Revolution in China. It is also a project about the history of the 92nd element, uranium, which Greenaway calls the ultimate American treasure, and which is being buried again now, at the end of the cold war. There are 92 suitcases that have to be packed and unpacked in the film, and a great many games are played with the letter "U" in USA and the "u" in uranium. *The Tulse Luper Suitcase* project has involved the production of a film a year over a span of four years, a 52-part television series, two back-to-back CD-ROMs, a book, and possibly an exhibition at the Guggenheim Museum. Another aspect involves the rewriting of the *Arabian Nights.*

The 1,001 tales will be posted on the internet, one every night, just as Scheherezade related them to the Sultan.

Greenaway has long been merging art with the cinema, cinema with technology, technology with ritual and obsession. His works move beyond cinema into the other arts with his various painting exhibitions and, recently, the production of an opera. According to the director himself, "Creation to me, is to try to orchestrate the universe to understand what surrounds us. Even if, to accomplish that, we use all sorts of stratagems which in the end prove completely incapable of staving off chaos."

Other Films *Train* (1966); *Tree* (1966); *5 Postcards from Capital Cities* (1967); *Revolution* (1967); *Love Love Love* (1968); *Intervals* (1969); *Erosion* (1971); *Coastline* (1971); *H Is for House* (1973); *Windows* (1974); *Water* (1975); *Water Wrackets* (1975); *Dear Phone* (1976); *Goole by Numbers* (1976); *One to One Hundred* (1978); *Eddie Kid* (1978); *Vertical Features Remake* (1978); *Zandra Rhoades* (1979); *The Falls* (1980); *Terrence Conran* (1981); *A Zed and Two Noughts* (1985); *The Belly of an Architect* (1987); *Drowning by Numbers* (1988); *Fear of Drowning* (1988); *Hubert Bals Handshake* (1988); *A Walk Through Prospero's Library* (1991); *Rosa* (1992); *The Baby of Macon* (1993); *Death of a Composer* (1999).

References Bell, Julian, "Lights, action, Darwin," *Times Literary Supplement,* February 27, 1998, p. 36; Corliss, Richard, "I Paint the Body Erotic, Peter Greenaway's Latest Film Transforms Creative Writing into a Living Art," *Time International,* March 10, 1997, p. 46; Howe, Desson, "The Greenaway Effect," *Washington Post,* May 26, 2000, p. 52; Rodman, Howard, A., "Anatomy of a Wizard," *American Film,* November–December 1991, pp. 35–39; Simon, John, "Movie Reviews," *National Review* 49 (July 14, 1997): 53; Woods, Alan, *Being Naked and Playing Dead: The Art of Peter Greenaway* (New York: St. Martin's Press, 1997), pp. 35–42.

—K.L.R.

Griffith, David Wark (1875–1948) Recognized throughout the world as the single most important individual in the development of film as

an art, D. W. Griffith was born on January 22, 1875, in Crestwood, Kentucky, to a middle-aged couple, Jacob Wark Griffith and Mary Perkins Oglesby, whose fortunes had suffered in the aftermath of the South's defeat. The elder Griffith was a Confederate Civil War veteran and Kentucky legislator, but he died when David was 10 years old, leaving a legacy of debt and poverty. By the time Griffith was 14 years old, his family was forced to abandon their unproductive farm for a new life in Louisville, where his mother opened a boarding house, an undertaking that soon failed. Griffith left high school to help provide for the family, taking a job in a dry-goods store, and, later, in a bookstore, which became his "university," exposing him to the world of ideas.

Fired with an ambition to become a playwright, Griffith began working on the stage in Louisville at the age of 20 and was soon touring in stock companies. For a decade he alternated work on the stage with manual labor, holding a variety of jobs as he continued to write. Griffith and his young actress wife, whom he had married in 1906, then turned to the new motion picture industry for their livelihood. Griffith began his work in motion pictures near the end of 1907 by playing the lead in *Rescued from an Eagle's Nest,* directed by EDWIN S. PORTER for the Edison Company and released in early 1908. Griffith soon moved to the Biograph Company in New York City, where he both acted in films and provided stories.

When Biograph's chief director became ill, Griffith was hired as a replacement. With the release of his first film, *The Adventures of Dollie,* in the summer of 1908, a new, decisive chapter in cinema history began. For the next five years, Griffith, working in anonymity as the studio refused to publicize the names of its talents, directed hundreds of mostly one-reel films for Biograph that reshaped the very language of film. In film after film, Griffith broke with the stagy, unimaginative approach to screen narrative still prevailing in the industry. Working in partnership with his brilliant cameraman, G. W. "Billy" Bitzer, Griffith demonstrated a singular genius in developing camera effects and movement, lighting, close-ups, and editing into a coordinated cinematic technique that gave motion pictures their basic grammar and transformed film into an art form. But Griffith's genius went far beyond technical tricks. His use of close-ups and medium shots enabled the spectator to empathize with the emotions expressed by the characters; his rhythmic editing style intensified the drama; his panoramic long shots created an impression of epic grandeur; and his innovations in lighting, with the help of Bitzer, added mood and aesthetic quality to the images. Placing great value on the use of locations for the realism he sought to heighten the drama, Griffith was one of the first filmmakers to work in Hollywood, when in 1910 he began annually taking his company from New York to California for seasonal filming.

Griffith built a stock company of young actors and actresses that included Mary Pickford, Blanche Sweet, Mae Marsh, Lillian and Dorothy Gish, Robert Harron, Henry B. Walthall, and Lionel Barrymore. Griffith drew from his players a new, more restrained acting style wholly different from that of the stage. In many of his films his actresses, for example, projected more assertive heroines, in keeping with the aspirations of the suffragette era.

His rhythmic editing style in chase films like *The Lonely Villa* (1909) and *The Lonedale Operator* (1911) created a sense of excitement by intercutting action between the chaser and the pursued, employing shorter and shorter shots to add to the suspense. Again, in *A Beast at Bay* (1912), he used the technique to film a race between the heroine's car and a train commandeered by her rescuing boyfriend. Extending this technique to such films as *The Battle at Elderbush Gulch* (1913), Griffith played a pivotal role in the development of the western genre.

Griffith also was dealing with many subjects in his films, reflective of his progressive social vision. In such films as *The Redman's View* (1909) and

D. W. Griffith (Author's collection)

Ramona (1910), he denounced the white man's oppression of the American Indian. He excoriated capitalism's injustice toward the poor in such films as *A Corner in Wheat* (1909) and focused his camera on scenes of urban poverty in *The Musketeers of Pig Alley* (1912) and many other works. Griffith climaxed his years at Biograph with his first feature-length film, *Judith of Bethulia* (1913), an epic dramatization of the apocryphal story of the ancient Jewish heroine who saved her community from invading Assyrians. Like many of his subsequent works, *Judith of Bethulia* demonstrated his abhorrence of imperialism through its depiction of the ravages of war and its effect on civilians.

Confronted with a Biograph still unwilling to tackle longer, more ambitious features, Griffith left the studio in 1914 and entered into a partnership with Harry Aitken of Mutual to set up his own independent company in Hollywood.

He took Billy Bitzer and many of his players with him, including Lillian and Dorothy Gish, Blanche Sweet, Mae Marsh, Henry B. Walthall, and Robert Harron. That same year he directed several feature films of which the most noted was *The Avenging Conscience,* a psychological thriller adapted from Edgar Allan Poe's "The Tell-Tale Heart." This was followed by the film that would make Griffith's name a household word and establish the motion picture as the dominant narrative medium in 20th-century America. At the same time, this film would create a controversy that has clouded Griffith's reputation over time. With the assistance of Frank E. Woods, he adapted *The Clansman,* a best-selling melodrama about the Reconstruction era by Thomas Dixon, expanding the story and its staged dramatization into a large-scale depiction of the Civil War and its aftermath, alternating spectacular scenes with poignant, intimate scenes of families caught up in the vortex of events. The director perfected techniques that he had been adapting and improving over a six-year period.

Released early in 1915, *The Birth of a Nation,* with an unprecedented running-time of three hours, electrified audiences across the country and became the American cinema's biggest box-office hit before the 1920s. It premiered in Los Angeles on February 8, in New York on March 3, and after a special White House screening, President Woodrow Wilson purportedly said it was like "writing history with lightning." Praised by many reviewers as the first great achievement of a new art, its presentation in legitimate theaters with orchestral accompaniment finally signaled that the motion picture had come of age.

But along with the plaudits came controversy, which has only increased over the decades. Griffith's portrayal of a Reconstruction era in which Southern whites were rescued by the Ku Klux Klan from vengeful carpetbaggers and unruly blacks reflected the prevailing historical view of Reconstruction put forth by the Dunning School. Led by the National Association for the

Advancement of Colored People, pressure groups repeatedly tried to ban the film as racist propaganda and an incitement to violence, claiming that *The Birth of a Nation* was the principal source of American racial violence from 1915 on and that its continued distribution was the leading factor in the Klan's revival during the 1920s. Records, in fact, do not support these claims and show, instead, that early 20th-century lynchings and race riots were unrelated to the film and part of a long pattern of racist practices and economic balances.

While the NAACP failed in its efforts to have the film banned outright, its strategy did serve to diminish appreciation of Griffith's overall achievement. Forgotten amidst all the emotional invective was the film's passionate indictment of the horrors of war and its effect on ordinary individuals, a point of view that added to its initial popularity at a time when public opinion was strongly opposed to U.S. involvement in World War I. Griffith himself believed he had presented an antiwar film and an accurate picture of the Civil War and Reconstruction and was shocked at the charges of racism and angered by attempts to suppress his film.

Griffith's next endeavor surpassed *The Birth of a Nation* in its scale and sweep. Intended in part as a response to the attacks on *Birth* (he published a broadside defending free speech in America), *Intolerance* (1916) introduced a revolutionary new narrative structure that broke with preceding conventions while further perfecting his use of dramatic close-ups, camera movement, and parallel editing to create what is perhaps the cinema's foremost masterpiece and surely the most ambitious film produced before the 1920s. In 1914, prior to the release of *The Birth of a Nation,* he had begun making what would become the "Modern Story" of *Intolerance,* a dramatic indictment of societal injustice toward the poor in the United States. With the working title of *The Mother and the Law,* this film included a powerful depiction of capitalism's brutal suppression of labor, an attack on capital punishment, and a forecast of the evils resulting from Prohibition. But seeking to outdo both *The Birth of a Nation* and spectacular European imports such as *Cabiria,* as well as responding to critics of his earlier film, Griffith decided to expand this narrative to encompass four stories from different periods in history, illustrating the persistence of intolerance and inhumanity throughout the ages.

Instead of telling these stories sequentially, Griffith intercut his "Modern Story" with the Judean Story portraying the events leading to the crucifixion of Christ, the French Story dramatizing the massacre of the Huguenots, and, most spectacular of all, the Babylonian Story depicting, with massive sets and thousands of extras, the destruction of ancient Babylon and its civilization by the imperialist forces of Cyrus of Persia in league with the city's reactionary clergy opposed to the reforms introduced by Prince Belshazzar. In the climax, "History itself," in the words of archivist Iris Barry, "seems to pour like a cataract across the screen" during the rapid intercutting between the four parallel stories. In scope, ambition, film form, and thematic complexity, *Intolerance* was a towering achievement.

The pacifist message of *Intolerance* was consistent with America's antiwar mood in 1915 and 1916. The film was quite popular upon its release, but as the United States moved toward full-scale war with Germany in 1917, attendance began to fall off, and, ultimately, *Intolerance* failed at the box office. Overseas, however, *Intolerance* enjoyed a far more sustained success. The film ran for 10 years in the USSR and became the single most important influence on the emerging Soviet filmmakers of the 1920s. In France, Germany, and Scandinavia, Griffith's epic also paved the way for a generation of filmmakers, while at home it was to influence such directors as CECIL B[LOUNT] DEMILLE, REX INGRAM, ERICH OSWALD (VON) STROHEIM, and KING VIDOR. Called by film historian Theodore Huff "the only film fugue," Griffith's masterpiece remains a timeless landmark of cinematic art.

Griffith followed *Intolerance* with *Hearts of the World* (1918), the most notable of several films he directed on behalf of the Allied cause in World War I. Though he later regretted the film's heavy propaganda as incompatible with his antiwar sentiments, Griffith provided another poignant portrayal of the devastating effects of war on ordinary citizens as a French village is overrun by Imperial German forces. After the war Griffith returned to the more tranquil world of his rural past through a series of films that included *True Heart Susie* (1919), an idyll starring Lillian Gish, acclaimed decades later as one of the world's greatest films by French New Wave directors Jacques Rivette and Eric Rohmer. Even more impressive was *Broken Blossoms* (1919), a poetic masterwork and the most influential of his intimate films. The story concerns a Chinese Buddhist (Richard Barthelmess) transplanted to London and the tragic outcome of his love for an innocent young white girl (Lillian Gish) whom he vainly attempts to shelter from her abusive, pugilist father. In this attack upon racism, Griffith's narrative fusing of realism and romanticism is accomplished through strikingly new and innovative soft-focus photography, bold close-ups, and an atmosphere created entirely through sets replicated at his studio. The film was an immediate critical and popular success. Griffith's ability to reproduce and transcend reality foreshadowed the German *Kammerspiel* films, while his sensitive direction of Lillian Gish and Richard Barthelmess in the leads set new standards for cinematic performances.

Meanwhile, Griffith had sought to maintain his independence and creative control in the Hollywood-based film industry. Initially releasing his features through Mutual, he had left that organization in 1915 to form Triangle in partnership with Mack Sennett and THOMAS HARPER INCE. He then left Triangle in 1917 and released his films, first through Paramount-Artcraft, and then through First National. In 1919 he joined with Mary Pickford, Douglas Fairbanks, Sr., and CHARLES CHAPLIN to form United Artists, and, in a further effort to remain free of industry control, moved his production company from Hollywood to a new studio in Mamaroneck, New York. He scored his greatest popular triumph since *The Birth of a Nation* with *Way Down East* (1920), the most acclaimed of his bucolic pictures. To intensify the drama, Griffith filmed on location in New England, including the famous climax on the ice floes in which Lillian Gish is rescued by Richard Barthelmess. Adapting a venerable turn-of-the-century melodrama about a country maiden betrayed by a callous playboy, Griffith transformed the story into a potent attack on Puritanism and the sexual double standard toward adultery. Although the film evoked nostalgia for agrarian America, its simultaneous indictment of provincial bigotry and sexism was very compatible with the emerging 1920s, which would grant women the right to vote, promising a new era of greater gender equality.

Griffith's next great film, *Orphans of the Storm* (1921), was a spectacular recreation of the French Revolution. As in his previous epics, Griffith presented events in human terms, showing his feminine protagonists, two sisters played by Lillian and Dorothy Gish, as separated by the *ancien régime* and caught up in the storm of revolution. Griffith's political hero is Danton, who leads the people in their struggle to overthrow the regime. The film's historical villain, Robespierre, is portrayed as a puritan who uses the license of the frenzied mob as a means to construct a new tyranny on the ruins of the old, an incipient moralistic orthodoxy that simply perpetuates despotism in a new guise. Once again, Griffith's narrative underscores his belief in the individual and his opposition to the historical oppression of women by the ruling elite.

Contrary to legend, most of Griffith's Mamaroneck films made money, but because of the debts incurred by the director in managing his studio and his ineptitude in business matters, he failed to realize the profits from the films made after *Way Down East*. The Hollywood establishment grew increasingly resentful of Griffith's Eastern-based defiance of the West Coast industry.

Moreover, it was claimed that Griffith was wedded to an old-fashioned, Victorian outlook and out of touch with the times. Nevertheless, he continued to produce solid achievements like the last of his rural films, *The White Rose* (1923), shot on location in the South, with Mae Marsh in the role of an unwed mother deceived by a minister, and *America* (1924), another large-scale epic, this time depicting the American Revolution. In between was *Dream Street* (1922), an impressionistic melodrama that featured some synchronized-sound sequences. Griffith's work at Mamaroneck climaxed with *Isn't Life Wonderful?* (1924), his most extraordinary experiment since *Broken Blossoms*. Distinguished for its social commentary, the film was made largely on location in Germany and depicted the harrowing conditions of postwar Europe. Centering his narrative upon the experiences of a refugee family struggling to survive in the chaos and deprivation that followed the German defeat, Griffith conveyed, with relative restraint, the poverty of the time in his scenes of listless, undernourished people with their meager savings crowding in line for meat as they watch the prices steadily climb (recalling similar scenes in his early one-reeler, *A Corner in Wheat*). An artistic triumph that anticipated Italian neorealism and influenced directors from King Vidor and FRANK BORZAGE to AKIRA KUROSAWA, whose *Wonderful Sunday* (1947) was a remake of Griffith's film, *Isn't Life Wonderful?* proved a risky commercial gamble. In the age of Coolidge prosperity, American audiences were less interested in films of social commentary that expected them to empathize with problems experienced by people abroad. Therefore, *Isn't Life Wonderful?* failed at the box office and Griffith was forced to become a contract director for Paramount.

Griffith's later films of the 1920s, made for Paramount on the East Coast and for producer Joseph Schenck at United Artists in Hollywood, have been dismissed as largely commercial imitations of other Hollywood productions of the time, but they do not necessarily represent a creative decline. The last of his Mamaroneck films, *Sally of the Sawdust* (1925) was intended for Paramount distribution but was released by United Artists. With W. C. Fields reprising his stage hit *Poppy, Sally of the Sawdust* combined Fields's comic genius with Griffith's own vision, as he drew on his youthful memories of working in the theater when actors were still shunned by respectable people. *The Sorrows of Satan* (1926), adapted from Marie Corelli's gothic romance about a critic who sacrifices his integrity in pursuit of the worldly success offered him by Satan, recalled the director's early years with Linda Arvidson, when he was attempting to establish himself as a writer. *The Battle of the Sexes* (1928), in its wryly comic depiction of a middle-aged businessman who allows himself to be seduced by an attractive gold-digger, arguably reflected the director's own mid-life crisis.

Griffith successfully met the challenge posed by the coming of sound with his 1930 biopic *Abraham Lincoln*. Walter Huston was memorable as the 16th president in a film that chronicled Lincoln's birth in a log cabin to his assassination at Ford's Theatre. The scenes of Lincoln's courtship of Ann Rutledge against a pastoral backdrop are in the classic vein of Griffith's rural films, while the Civil War scenes serve as another of the director's compelling commentaries on the suffering engendered by war, though Griffith's political sympathies are fully with Lincoln in his efforts to preserve the Union and abolish slavery. The film's box-office appeal did not match its critical success, however, and Griffith, unhappy with changes made in the final-release print requested by his producers, sundered his ties with Schenck to make one more try for independence.

His next film, *The Struggle,* made on the East Coast in 1931, would prove to be his last. Having suffered for several years from a drinking problem, Griffith conceived a film that reflected his own torments while opposing Prohibition. *The Struggle* relates the story of a good-natured but weak-willed working man who succumbs to the allure of the speakeasy, causing a personal decline that nearly destroys his family. Griffith took his cameras out into the streets of the Bronx to record the unvarnished reality of tenement life, an approach consistent with his earlier films but at odds with Hollywood's preference for studio work. The combination of Griffith's unpolished realism and an unheroic leading man in the throes of alcoholism (Broadway star Hal Skelly in an outstanding performance) held no appeal for depression-era audiences of 1931. The film was a commercial and critical disaster that ended Griffith's directorial career, although later critics would recognize it as one of his finest works.

Griffith's remaining years were marked by unfulfilled attempts to realize his literary ambitions and intermittent efforts to resume directing. He assisted Hal Roach on *One Million B.C.* (1940), for example, a project with which Griffith became quickly dissatisfied. Although frustrated by intermittent bouts of alcoholism, Griffith did make a belated effort to adjust to domestic life. Separated from Linda Arvidson for 25 years, he finally divorced her in 1936 and married Evelyn Baldwin, a young woman who had played a supporting role in *The Struggle,* but that marriage also ended in divorce. There were no children from either marriage. Although toward the end Griffith was not destitute, he was far from wealthy. The highlights of his later years were a special Oscar presented to him by the Academy of Motion Picture Arts and Sciences in 1936 for his contributions to film art, and a 1940 retrospective of his work by the Museum of Modern Art, which had begun the task of preserving and disseminating his films. On July 23, 1948, at the age of 73, Griffith died in Hollywood of a cerebral hemorrhage and was buried in Kentucky, near his birthplace.

After his death, Griffith's reputation rose, then fell. The high point came during the 1960s and 1970s, as the cinema-studies movement grew, culminating in a commemorative postage stamp issued in 1975, his centenary year. The ultimate decline of his reputation in his own country was

Hawks, Howard Winchester (1896–1977)
According to critic Andrew Sarris, Howard Hawks
has been one of the least known and least appreciated giants in American cinema. Reluctant to discuss his films as anything other than practical
working assignments, and remaining within the
Hollywood establishment throughout his life, he
seems on the face of it a poor candidate for true
auteur status. Historian Gerald Mast has referred to
him as an "invisible" man who made films less
idiosyncratic and stylized than his peers, like
FRANK CAPRA, JOHN FORD, and ALFRED HITCH-
COCK: "The seeming artlessness and ordinariness
[of his films] not only tends to make their creator
invisible but also makes it exceedingly difficult to
evaluate them according to the existing standards,
terms, and values for discussing films." Yet, in the
eight silent and 32 sound features he directed
between 1923 and 1970, there are consistent stylistic and thematic elements that demand close consideration.

He was born on May 30, 1896, into a prosperous business family in Goshen, Indiana. The eldest
of three sons, he was something of a daredevil and
preferred racing cars to studying in school. After a
stint at Cornell, where he majored in mechanical
engineering (but where he really studied gambling

and drinking), he went to work as a prop man at
Paramount in 1916. He flew in the Army Air
Corps during World War I and returned to Hollywood, to direct his first feature, *The Road to Glory,*
in 1926. Fiercely independent from the very
beginning, Hawks refused to attach himself to any
studio or type of film for very long and managed
to produce many of his own pictures.

In his 40-year career, his best films were made
for those companies that gave him the greatest
freedom and control. He wrote, or supervised the
writing of, every one of his films. His mania for
control and his slow shooting pace were maddening to one and all. In his personal life he had three
unsuccessful marriages, to Athole Shearer, Nancy
Raye ("Slim") Gross, and Dee Hartford; and few
lasting friends, excepting fellow director Victor
Fleming and cameraman Gregg Toland. His true
identity seems to have always been linked to his
work, to his passion for films. His versatility and
range were legendary. *Scarface* (1932), financed by
Howard Hughes and starring Paul Muni as an Italian gangster modeled after Al Capone, stands out
as the grittiest and bloodiest of the early 1930s
crime cycle. Hawks would top it later with *The
Big Sleep* (1946), a classic crime noir with a plot so
convoluted even the screenwriter, William

Howard Hawks (right) (Author's collection)

Faulkner, could not figure it out. *Twentieth Century* (1934), *Bringing Up Baby* (1938), and *His Girl Friday* (1940) are keystone films in the genre of the screwball comedy. Here, Hawks's penchant for nonstop verbal pyrotechnics, overlapping dialogue, and sexually suggestive banter reaches its apotheosis. Indeed, the sexual politics of *His Girl Friday*'s subtext—a female "Hildy Johnson" (Rosalind Russell) replaced the male role that had been in the original Broadway stage play and thus became a sexual and professional foil for Cary Grant's "Walter Burns"—hilarious as they are, in actuality function as a clever and probing examination and revision of conventional gender identity. Conversely, in *I Was A Male War Bride* transsexuality

works in the opposite direction, when Cary Grant spends much of the film in drag as a WAC.

Indeed, Hawks's treatment of women particularly and gender issues in general is a key element in his films. Paradoxically enough—for Hawks has been rightly accused of being a notorious sexist in his private life—Hawks frequently portrayed women positively in nontraditional roles: "He is one of the few classic Hollywood directors," notes historian Jean-Pierre Coursodon, "whose films are not based on the assumption that a woman's place is in the home and her happiness lies in caring for a family." However, this sometimes meant that his heroines had to be caricatured in order to claim center stage, as was the case with the two heroines in *Gentlemen Prefer Blondes,* who, says Coursodon, "are an interesting example of hyperfemaleness breaking through the sex barrier and coming full circle, back to a kind of masculinity." In other words, the more women are accepted on men's terms, the more "manly" they seem to become, as was the case with the character played by Paula Prentiss in an underrated Hawksian comedy, *Man's Favorite Sport* (1963). So powerful are these women at times, that they have to assume dominant positions over their men, whose behavior has been more like that of little boys than of mature males. One thinks of Joanne Dru and Jean Arthur intervening in the squabbling between the male rivals in their lives in, respectively, *Red River* (1948) and *Only Angels Have Wings* (1939). Coursodon speculates that these themes point toward Hawks's denial of femininity itself, "to ultimately erase sex distinction in favor of a system in which the sexes are interchangeable." Hawks characteristically dismisses such speculations as mere twaddle. "I haven't thought too much about the [women's liberation] movement," he said in a 1971 interview, "mostly because the people who seem to be doing most of the talking are so unattractive that I don't think it's fun. The kind of women that I use are just honest. The men I like are not very talkative, so the woman has to do a little about the thing. . . . That happens to be the kind of woman that I like—I don't see why they have to sit around and wash dishes."

All of this notwithstanding, Hawks also delivered solid action pictures about men in physical and psychological crisis, particularly in his highly personal aviation pictures, including *The Dawn Patrol* (1930), *Ceiling Zero* (1936), *Only Angels Have Wings* (1939), and *Air Force* (1943). Whereas in his comedies the men are plagued by failure, humiliation, and frustration, they are virile and self-assured in the dramas. They are, moreover, obsessed with "getting the job done" in a professional manner, whether it is shark fishing, flying the mail, bagging wild animals, conducting a bombing run, driving the cattle, racing a race car, or putting out oil fires. For Hawks the highest human emotion is the camaraderie of the exclusive, self-sufficient, all-male group, and it is necessary to pass a test of ability and courage to win admittance. "Professionals are the only people I'm interested in," says Hawks. "Amateurs I'm not interested in. I'm interested in the guys who are good. I hate losers, and the ones who are not good are bound to be losers. So I just don't pay any attention to them." While this is a rather confining agenda, marginal characters, especially women, can always be counted on to provide a measure of moral and emotional reorientation. *Only Angels* gave Cary Grant one of his best roles, casting him against romantic type as a hard-boiled airmail pilot. *Air Force* chronicled the odyssey of a B-17 bomber crew as it struggles to get into the war after the bombing of Pearl Harbor. As effective as the cast members are, including John Garfield and Harry Carey, Sr., it is the airplane that emerges as the real "star" of the film.

Of all Hawks's genre pictures, however, the westerns, particularly the later ones, pose special problems for critics and viewers. Frequently they tend toward a stylization verging on caricature and self-parody. While the aforementioned *Red River* (1948) pits trail boss Dunson (John Wayne) against Matthew Garth (Montgomery Clift) during a drive to get cattle to market, its denouement depends more heavily on sorting out a Freudian love triangle than anything else. Late westerns like *Rio Bravo* (1959), *El Dorado* (1966), and *Rio Lobo* (1970) are relatively static and stagebound, their male and female characters acting out their roles on a chessboard of formulaic schemas. They seem, at once, both anti-westerns and meta-westerns. In all of these genres and in all of these films, Hawks's visual style is obscured by what critic Manny Farber describes as an "undemonstrative camera" and a pacing that is a "straight-ahead motion." He never uses flashbacks, pretentious crane shots, odd camera angles, or decorative cutting. The talking may at times be nonstop, but, as Farber notes, there is little attention to profound themes; rather, a "poetic sense of action" emerges from strutting braggarts, boyishly cynical dialogue, and melodramatic situations. "I don't analyze any of these things," said Hawks. "I've found that if I think a thing is funny, the audience thinks it's funny. If I think it's exciting, the audience thinks so. If I like a girl, the audience likes her. If I like a man, the audience likes him. So I don't worry. I just go ahead and make a movie." Howard Hawks died on December 26, 1977, of complications sustained from a head injury.

Other Films *A Girl in Every Port* (1928); *The Criminal Code* (1931); *Tiger Shark* (1933); *To Have and Have Not* (1944); *The Big Sky* (1952); *Monkey Business* (1952); *Hatari!* (1962).

References Coursodon, Jean-Pierre, *American Directors,* vol. 2 (New York: McGraw-Hill, 1983); Goodwin, Michael, and Naomi Wise, "An Interview with Howard Hawks," *Take One* 3, no. 8 (November–December 1971): 19–25; Mast, Gerald, *Howard Hawks, Storyteller* (New York: Oxford University Press, 1982).

—J.C.T.

Herzog, Werner (1942–)

Werner Herzog is one of the original auteurs of *Das neue Kino,* the German "New Wave" that emerged during the 1970s. His strange, disturbing, and enigmatic films are not easily categorized; and perhaps that is part of their appeal. The images that dominate his films are at once mesmerizing and "sublime" but also distorted and perverse. Fantastic locales, fanatical characters, and idiosyncratic stories and incidents find safe haven in the Herzog universe.

Herzog was born Werner Stipetic on September 5, 1942, and spent his childhood in Bavaria with his divorced mother. He began writing scripts as a teenager while attending the Classical Gymnasium in Munich and stole a 35-mm camera to shoot his early films. Educated at the University of Munich, Herzog worked for German television and, for a time, as a welder in a steel factory for the U.S. National Aeronautics and Space Administration.

In 1966 he founded his own production company, Werner Herzog Filmproduktion. Herzog's first feature film, *Signs of Life* (*Lebenszeichen* [1967]), details the detention in a Greek island fortress of a German soldier who gradually grows from alienated prisoner to aggressive fighter. An almost mystical identification with landscapes— both native and exotic in his later films—becomes prominent in images and themes in Herzog's work. *Signs of Life* received much acclaim, both for its themes of alienation and aggression and for its almost documentary style, with the camera objectively recording the events (a style that would permeate his subsequent work). *Signs of Life* won the *Bundesfilmpreis* and the Silver Bear Award at the Berlin Film Festival.

Aguirre, the Wrath of God (*Aguirre, der Zorn Göttes* [1972]), considered by some to be his best film, depicts the life of a 16th-century conquistador intent on conquering the mythical Incan kingdom of El Dorado. The natural images of the Amazonian jungle are at once majestic and intimidating, dwarfing the characters as they traverse the terrain. Nature, for Herzog, is both seductive and potentially destructive. In *Aguirre,* Herzog visualizes nature as an antagonistic force that eventually destroys the person who intrudes or invades—the colonizer. It is a stunning film visually, and the presence of Klaus Kinski (Herzog's most dependable actor) as the obsessed and finally insane Aguirre, makes the film's themes of possession, madness, and colonialization even starker.

Kinski did his best work for Herzog. His astonishing presence also dominates *Nosferatu—Phantom der Nacht* (aka *Nosferatu, the Vampire* [1979]), Herzog's meticulous remake of and tribute to the classic silent film that F. W. MURNAU loosely adapted from Bram Stoker's *Dracula* in 1922; *Woyzeck* (1980), adapted from the fragmented play Georg Büchner wrote in 1936 about a soldier driven insane by "scientific" experimentations forced upon him by the military; and *Fitzcarraldo* (1981), in which Kinski played a mad Irishman obsessed with the desire to bring grand opera (and an opera house) to the interior of Brazil and Peru. Kinski had a particular talent for portraying Herzog's obsessed and afflicted central characters. Several of Herzog's best films are built upon the actor's considerable and eccentric skills. Herzog would later pay tribute to Kinski and their volatile relationship in the documentary, *My Best Fiend: Klaus Kinski* (1999).

Herzog himself has been appropriately characterized as a monomaniacal, maddening autocrat. Still, it cannot be denied that his temperament and style drive films like *The Mystery of Kaspar Hauser* (aka *Jeder für sich und Gott gegen alle* [1974]) and *Stroszek* (1978), both of which demonstrate sympathy for displaced and alienated characters and a pessimistic view of modern civilization. This is especially evident in *Stroszek,* in which Herzog's mysterious actor, identified as "Bruno S.," transplanted from a brutal existence in Germany to a godforsaken American landscape in Wisconsin, falls into a depression and finally commits suicide on a ski lift. For the film *Heart of Glass* (*Herz aus Glas* [1976]), Herzog had the actors hypnotized in the hope of portraying "people on the screen as we have never seen them before." Herzog believes that "film is not the art of scholars, but of illiterates."

Herzog's films are full of disparate characters: misfits, fanatics, dwarfs, megalomaniacs, rebels, and heretics. His two favorite, most frequently used actors, Kinski and Bruno S., have been compared to the grotesque, expressionistic characters of German silent film. Bruno S. is like a blank slate: the viewer has to interpret the actor's ambiguous blankness. Klaus Kinski, on the other hand, goes to the other extreme, projecting a hyperkinetic energy that reflects the director's own craziness and obsessions. While using these actors to depict his own dreamlike, adventurous self-realization and ideas, Herzog's films reflect the director's exaggerated and distorted vision. They also show moments of the sublime, whether it be in the Andes Mountains (*Aguirre*) or in the Wisconsin wheatfields (*Stroszek*).

Herzog's presentation and style are both romantic and realistic, coupling a childlike wonder at life with the ugly, disturbed nature of humankind. A continual theme in Herzog's work is that of aggressive colonialization and exploitation, with *Aguirre, Fitzcarraldo,* and *Where the Green Ants Dream* (*Wo die grünen Ameisen träumen* [1984]), which depicts the destruction by mining engineers of the land of Australia's aborigines. Herzog's films challenge viewers into reorienting themselves away from traditional movie styles, just as his actors must do when they enter his world.

Over his career, Herzog has made numerous documentaries, features he considers just as important as his narrative films. These documentaries often deconstruct the genre by using innovative filmic techniques. Beginning as early as 1970 with *Fata Morgana,* and more recently with *Wodaabe: Shepherds of the Sun* (*Wodaabe–Die Hirten der Sonne* [1988]), Herzog has unobtrusively observed people in their normal surroundings, performing normal rituals and behavior. They are a far cry from the intense, emotionally scarred characters of his narrative films. Still, the powerful images carry the subject's message, without relying upon fictional characters. (Herzog himself proved a fascinating subject in Les Blank's *Burden of Dreams* [1982], a documentary about Herzog and the making of *Fitzcarraldo.*) His films are paradoxical: they are at once disarming in their pessimism, but one often feels immense pleasure and awe derived from Herzog's eccentric but passionate, hauntingly beautiful, astonishing, and astounding images. The worlds of his films are haunting and passionate and intensely personal: "You must understand I am not a philosopher," Herzog has said. "I am not an intellectual. I make films to rid myself of them, like ridding myself of a nightmare. There seem to be many broken people in my films, and much cruelty. But there is also a dignity which transcends the suffering."

Other Films *Even Dwarfs Started Small* (*Auch Zwerge haben klein angefangen* [1970]); *Handicapped Future* (*Behinderte Zukunft* [1970]); *Land of Silence and Darkness* (*Land des Schweigens und der Dunkelheit* [1971]); *The Great Ecstasy of the Sculptor Steiner* (*Die grosse Ekstase des*

Bildschnitzers Steiner [1974]); *How Much Wood Does a Woodchuck Chuck* (1976); *Ballad of the Little Soldier* (*Ballad vom kleinen Soldaten* [1984]); *Gasherbaum–The Dark Glow of the Mountains* (*Gasherbaum–Der leuchtende Berg* [1984]); *Cobra Verde* (1987); *It Isn't Easy Being God* (*Es ist nicht leicht ein Gott zu sein* [1989]); *Echoes from a Somber Kingdom* (*Echos aus einem dustern Reich* [1990]); *Scream of Stone* (*Schrie aus Stein* [1991]); *Jag Mandir* (aka *The Eccentric Private Theatre of the Maharajah of Udaipur* [1991]); *Lessons of Darkness* (*Lektionen in Finsternis* [1992]); *Bells from the Deep* (*Glodcken aus der Tiefe* [1993]); *The Transformation of the World into Music* (*Die Verwaandlung der Welt in Musik* [1994]).

References Atkinson, Michael, "The Wanderings of Werner Herzog," *Film Comment* 36 (2000): 16; Basoli, A. G., "The Wrath of Klaus Kinski: An Interview with Werner Herzog," *Cineaste* 24 (1999): 32; Corrigan, Timothy, ed., *The Films of Werner Herzog* (New York: Methuen, 1986); *Images at the Horizon: A Workshop with Werner Herzog Conducted by Roger Ebert* (Chicago: Facets Multimedia, 1979); Ott, Frederick W., *The Great German Films* (Secaucus, N.J.: Citadel Press, 1986); Overbey, David L., "Every Man for Himself," *Sight and Sound* 2 (1975): 73–75.

—W.V. and J.M.W.

Hitchcock, Alfred (1899–1980) Although he worked in a wide range of genres, from straight drama to musicals, Alfred Hitchcock is known above all else for the genre that practically bears his shape—with which, indeed, his very shape, in its famous silhouetted form, is identified—the Hitchcockian suspense thriller. The genre is typically characterized by inventive plotting rich with red herrings (Hitchcock has come to be identified with the "MacGuffin"); and by stories invoking the struggle of common men against greater forces (Cary Grant ducking beneath the swooping plane in *North by Northwest*), subversively witty dialogue (the delightful repartee between Robert Donat and Madeleine Carroll in *The 39 Steps*), distinctive and often tricky technical facility (the long takes in *Rope*), the experiment in 3-D filming (*Dial M for Murder*), hallucinatory imagery (the distorting

effects in *Spellbound* and *Vertigo*), the psychopathological case study (*Strangers on a Train* and *Psycho*), subtexts concerning the voyeuristic experience of cinema spectatorship (the explicit theme in *Rear Window*), and of course the cameo appearance of the director himself (first seen in the 1926 *The Lodger*). Over the course of his long career, Hitchcock successfully managed the transition from silent film to sound (his early part-talkie, *Blackmail* [1929]), exists in both silent and sound versions); and with equal success he adapted to the new medium of television with the run of *Alfred Hitchcock Presents* from 1955 to 1962.

Yet, it is almost accidental that Hitchcock came to filmmaking at all. Born on August 13, 1899, in East London, Hitchcock studied under the Jesuits at Saint Ignatius College. His engineering studies were short-lived, since after the death of his father in 1914, he was forced into wage labor at Henley's Telegraph and Cable Company in 1915. When hired by the newly established London branch of Lasky's Famous Players in 1920, his aptitude for art led to a job designing and lettering title-cards. The opportunities in the fluid early film industry were rapidly taken advantage of by Hitchcock, who served in any available capacity—designing titles, writing scripts, editing—before finally being offered his first directing job at Gainsborough Studios with *Number Thirteen* (1922). More significant was his next film, *The Lodger* (1926), an atmospheric thriller about the hunt for a Jack the Ripper–like figure, which featured the first complete explication of the Hitchcockian theme of misplaced guilt and suspicion. According to FRANÇOIS TRUFFAUT, it was "the first true Hitchcock." As commentator Thomas R. Tietze notes, "transference of another's guilt becomes a pervasive psychological concern in nearly all of his subsequent films." In his first sound feature, *Blackmail* (1929), one of the most sophisticated early talkies of the period, sound cues were employed as an integral part of the developing suspense. His first 17 features are, in the opinion of historian Maurice Yacowar in his invaluable *Hitchcock's*

British Films, "a remarkably fruitful area of study for anyone interested in Hitchcock, in British films, or in aesthetics in general. For Hitchcock was from the outset a brilliant experimenter in cinematic expression."

Although Hitchcock would continue to work in a wide range of film genres in the 1930s, ranging from an adaptation of Sean O'Casey's *Juno and the Paycock* (1930) to the musical bio-pic of Johann Strauss, Jr., *Waltzes from Vienna* (1933), his most memorable work in the decade came in the half-dozen suspense thrillers he developed. These included *Murder!* (1930), a rare instance of a straight whodunit from Hitchcock's hand; *The Man Who Knew Too Much* (1934), a classic study of a family that finds itself trapped in a densely layered plot of intrigue; *The 39 Steps* (1935), a delightful mix of romance comedy and suspense thriller, which employed the British music hall as its central locus of events and intrigue; the spy yarn *Secret Agent* (1936), based on Somerset Maugham's novel *Ashenden; Sabotage* (1936), based on Joseph Conrad's *Secret Agent,* about anarchist conspiracies in London; and *The Lady Vanishes* (1938), rightly regarded by historian Maurice Yacowar as "the high point in Hitchcock's British period." Over the course of this remarkable body of work, Hitchcock steadily improved in his mastery over the medium, evident above all else in the increased control of atmospherics, dialogue, and suspenseful turns of plot.

Hitchcock was lured to Hollywood by David Selznick in 1939 to direct the romantic thriller *Rebecca* (1940), beginning a fascinating, but troubled relationship between the two men. Excepting for a brief time span in Britain to produce war propaganda, *Bon Voyage* and *Aventure Malgache,* Hitchcock would henceforward be a Hollywood director. And, although Hitchcock was still not quite a one-genre director—*Mr. and Mrs. Smith* (1941) is straight comedy and *Lifeboat* (1943) amounts to a philosophical meditation on people under the stress of war and survival—he increasingly hewed to the suspense-thriller genre. During

Alfred Hitchcock

the early war years Hitchcock stoked the cause of anti-Nazism with suspense plots rooted in the European conflict, like *Foreign Correspondent* (1940) and *Saboteur* (1942). The use in the latter film of a climactic chase atop the Statue of Liberty prefigures the fantastic chases of the later films, like the pursuit atop Mount Rushmore in *North by Northwest.* Other works of the period, such as *Suspicion* (1941) and the classic proto-noir, *Shadow of a Doubt* (1943), are more concerned with pathological characters and situations involving imperiled women than with politics.

Perhaps the richest period of film production for Hitchcock came in the postwar years, beginning with *Spellbound* (1945) and concluding with *The Birds* (1963) and *Marnie* (1964). These 18 films include many of his most widely acknowledged masterworks. In *Notorious,* characterized by Donald Spoto as "the artistic rendition of an inner life that might have exploded if denied expression," Hitchcock transmuted his personal grief over his mother's death into romantic suspense. The relatively neglected *Rope* not only experiments with fashioning a film out of a seeming single long take, but also explores Nietzschean ideas of the superman's transcending of conventional morality. A remarkable experiment, the stagebound drama dispenses with traditional suspense entirely since the audience knows the identity of the killers from the story's opening dialogue. A similar preoccupation with criminal pathology—played out against a series of set-piece scenes in a train, a tennis court, and an amusement park—informs the Hitchcock classic *Strangers on a Train* (1951). After adapting the stage thriller *Dial M for Murder* to the screen in 1954, Hitchcock directed his quintessential statement about the essentially voyeuristic implications of spectatorship and the film medium, *Rear Window.* James Stewart portrayed a disabled photographer whose curious gaze, aided by his telephoto lenses, reveal the circumstances of a murder in the apartment across the court from his second-story window. Ever fascinated by technical challenges, *Rear Window* required most of the action to be seen from the fixed vantage point of Stewart's window, a frame that functioned, in effect, like a stage proscenium, or the boundaries of a camera's viewfinder.

The remake of *The Man Who Knew Too Much* (1955) may or may not be better than Hitchcock's own original, but it provides an interesting variation on the theme, casting Doris Day as the woman whose song, "Que sera, sera," proves to be a vital element in the solving of a kidnaping plot. *The Trouble with Harry* (1955) is a rather atypical black comedy with a distinctly macabre edge.

Vertigo (1958) and *Psycho* (1960) are justly considered Hitchcock's most complex masterpieces. *Vertigo* has been described by Robin Wood in his seminal book as the "nearest to perfection" of all his films, "a perfect organism, each character, each sequence, each image, illuminating every other." Its high drama operates first in the depth of its under-

standing of the characters' obsessions and in its manipulations of the viewer's own voyeuristic tendencies. Based on *D'Entre des morts* (1954), by Pierre Boileau and Thomas Narcejac, the story concerns a man's obsessive attempts to transform a young woman into the simulacrum of his dead girl friend. Its voyeurism ideally suited Hitchcock, and it may be regarded as the middle third of a voyeuristic "trilogy," bracketed by *North by Northwest* and *Psycho.* As commentators like Donald Spoto and John Russell Taylor darkly suggest, *Vertigo* is about Hitchcock himself who, like Roger in the novel and Scottie (James Stewart) in the film, continually "made over" his leading ladies—Madeleine Carroll, Grace Kelly, Vera Miles, Kim Novak, Tippi Hedren—into his archetype of the icy, ethereal blonde, dictating their hair color, their clothing style, their deportment. "*Vertigo* in that respect," writes Taylor, "is alarmingly close to allegorized autobiography, a record of Hitch's obsessive pursuit of an ideal quite as much as a literal tale of love lost and found again."

Psycho (1960), shot on a shoestring in chilling black-and-white, blended the Grand Guignol theatrics of the Robert Bloch novel with a stunning psychological probe into the criminally disordered mind of the psychotic Norman Bates (Anthony Perkins). Its horrors, notes Robin Wood, "belong to the age that has witnessed on the one hand the discoveries of Freudian psychology and on the other the Nazi concentration camps." Significantly, its most celebrated sequence, the shower murder of Janet Leigh, is played out in a sterile, aseptic environment rather than a dark and dank dungeon. "When murder is committed in a gleamingly sanitary motel bathroom during a cleansing shower," notes critic Andrew Sarris, "the incursion of evil into our well-laundered existence becomes intolerable. We may laugh nervously or snort disgustedly, but we shall never be quite so complacent again." At the same time, notes Carol J. Clover in her classic study of the modern horror film, *Men, Women, and Chainsaws, Psycho* is "the appointed ancestor of the slasher film," with the now-familiar elements of a psychotic killer who is the product of a sick family, a victim who is a beautiful, sexually active woman, and a slaying that is particularly brutal and is registered from the victim's point of view. The film's reception was little short of sensational. "No amount of optimism or carefully orchestrated hucksterism could have prepared anyone—least of all Alfred Hitchcock—for the firestorm the film was creating," writes commentator Stephen Rebello in his analysis of the film. "Certainly no one could have predicted how powerfully *Psycho* tapped into the American subconscious. Faintings. Walk outs. Repeat visits. Boycotts. Angry phone calls and letters. Talk of banning the film rang from church pulpits and psychiatrists' offices. Never before had any director so worked the emotions of the audience like stops on an organ console."

If, as *Psycho*'s promotion justly proclaimed, we can never feel safe in the shower again after seeing it, *The Birds* (1963) will make anyone think twice before getting a pet parrot. But seriously, the fact that the invasion by the birds has no rational explanation is the very point of the film and the very stuff of Hitchcock's universe, according to Robin Wood. "This seems to me the very function of the birds," writes Wood. "They are a concrete embodiment of the arbitrary and unpredictable, of whatever makes human life and human relationships precarious, a reminder of fragility and instability that cannot be ignored or evaded and, beyond that, of the possibility that life is meaningless and absurd." *North by Northwest* (1959), on the other hand, brings Hitchcock back to the familiar, by contrast cozy, territories of endangerment, chase, and intrigue.

Meanwhile, beginning on the night of November 13, 1955, Hitchcock began introducing what would become 365 segments of his weekly half-hour television series, 20 episodes of which he directed himself. "In selecting the stories for my television shows," he later recalled, "I tried to make them as meaty as the sponsor and the network would stand for, and to offset any tendency toward the macabre with humor." In his essay on Hitchcock's television work, Gene D. Phillips points out that Hitchcock "consistently elected to direct teleplays that closely paralleled the situations and themes associated with his theatrical films, and often cast actors in these short movies whom he also used in his features." Hence, continues Phillips, "these TV films deserve analysis as part of the Hitchcock canon, especially since the series remains in permanent syndication." For example, the episode entitled "One More Mile to Go" (1955), contends Phillips, prefigures in its situation of a corpse concealed in a car trunk incidents in the later *Psycho*. Indeed, as Phillips demonstrates, the stripped-down techniques of television production provided the model for the making of *Psycho*. "*Psycho* was an experiment in this sense," Hitchcock said; "I asked myself if I could make a feature film under the same conditions as a television show." Moreover, several of the best of these television episodes were derived from master storytellers of the grim and ghastly, like John Collier ("Back for Christmas") and Roald Dahl ("The Landlady" and "Lamb to the Slaughter").

Hitchcock's later years were less productive, and critical opinion on the late work more divided. The 1960s saw his return to the genre of political thriller he had deserted after World War II; but neither *Torn Curtain* (1966) nor *Topaz* (1969) works the territory quite as successfully as his earlier work had. And while *Frenzy* marks a return not only to strong form but also to earlier themes (with a Ripper-esque killer loose in the streets of London), Hitchcock's final film, *Family Plot* (1976), has found few advocates. Still, after a career of over 60 films, a final fall from form can be forgiven the master. That we still designate the best suspenseful thrillers that make their way to the screen as "Hitchcockian" is surely testimony to his enduring impact on the suspense film genre. In summing up his work, filmmakers ERIC ROHMER and CLAUDE CHABROL stated: "Hitchcock is one of the greatest *inventors of form* in the entire history of the cinema. Perhaps only [F.W.] MURNAU and

[SERGEI] EISENSTEIN can sustain comparison with him when it comes to form. . . . An entire moral universe has been elaborated on the basis of this form and by its very rigor. In Hitchcock's work form does not embellish content, it creates it."

Other Films *The Pleasure Garden* (1925); *The Mountain Eagle* (1926); *Downhill* (1927); *Easy Virtue* (1927); *The Ring* (1927); *The Farmer's Wife* (1928); *Champagne* (1928); *The Manxman* (1929); *Juno and the Paycock* (1930); *The Skin Game* (1931); *Rich and Strange* (1932); *Number Seventeen* (1932); *Jamaica Inn* (1939); *The Paradine Case* (1947); *I Confess* (1953); *The Wrong Man* (1956); *Marnie* (1964).

References Auiler, Dan, *"Vertigo," the Making of a Hitchcock Classic* (New York: St. Martin's Press, 1998); Clover, Carol J., *Men, Women and Chainsaws* (Princeton: Princeton University Press, 1992); Leff, Leonard J., *Hitchcock & Selznick* (New York: Weidenfeld and Nicolson, 1987); Phillips, Gene D., "Hitchcock's Forgotten Films: The Twenty Teleplays," *Journal of Popular Film and Television* 10, no. 2 (Summer 1982): 73–76; Rebello, Stephen, *Alfred Hitchcock and the Making of "Psycho"* (New York: Dembner Books, 1990); Rohmer, Eric, and Claude Chabrol, *Hitchcock: The First Forty-Four Films* (New York: Frederick Ungar, 1979); Spoto, Donald, *The Dark Side of Genius: The Life of Alfred Hitchcock* (Boston: Little, Brown, 1983); Truffaut, François, *Hitchcock* (New York: Simon and Schuster, 1966); Wood, Robin, *Hitchcock's Films* (New York: A. S. Barnes, 1965); Yacowar, Maurice, *Hitchcock's British Films* (Hamden, Conn.: Archon Books, 1977).

—T. Prasch and J.C.T.

Huston, John (1906–1987)

Born on August 5, 1906, in Nevada, Missouri, to Rhea Gore and Walter Huston, John Marcellus Huston began his show business career on stage in Dallas, Texas, as "Yankee Doodle Dandy" at the age of three. Huston attended Lincoln Heights High School in Los Angeles from 1921 to 1922 and dropped out to become an art student at the Smith School of Art and Art Student's League. In 1924 John Huston left Los Angeles for New York where he began a professional acting career at the Provincetown Playhouse Theatre. His debut as a professional actor was in a 1925 production of *The Triumph of the Egg*. In 1926 Huston went to Mexico following a mastoid operation. There he received an honorary commission in the Mexican cavalry. He married Dorothy Jeanne Harvey in 1926 and settled in Malibu, California, to pursue a career as a writer. After a brief publishing career in New York he received an offer to become a contract writer for Goldwyn Studios in 1930. This began Huston's screenwriting career in the commercial cinema.

After six months at Goldwyn, with no writing assignments, Huston was hired by Universal Studios where he was a contract writer from 1931 to 1933. Some of the films that Huston served on as a screenwriter include *A House Divided, Law and Order,* and *Murders in the Rue Morgue.* Following a stay in Great Britain where he was employed by Gaumont-British, Huston returned to the United States and appeared in the WPA Theatre production of *The Lonely Man* in Chicago. Huston became a contract writer for Warner Bros. from 1938 to 1941. Among the films Huston wrote at Warners were *Jezebel, The Amazing Dr. Clitterhouse, Juarez, Dr. Ehrlich's Magic Bullet,* and *High Sierra.* His scripts for both *Dr. Ehrlich's Magic Bullet* and *High Sierra* received Oscar nominations and provided Huston with the opportunity to direct a feature film as a result of a clause in his contract. The film Huston chose was Dashiell Hammett's *The Maltese Falcon,* which had been filmed twice before at Warner's. The film featured Humphrey Bogart, the star of *High Sierra* and a Warners contract actor of long standing. After another screenwriting assignment, *Sergeant York,* Huston directed *Across the Pacific* and *In This Our Life,* both 1942, before entering the military service following Pearl Harbor. John Huston was commissioned as a lieutenant in the Signal Corps, which enlisted a number of Hollywood directors to record the war's progress. Huston made three outstanding wartime documentaries: *Report from the Aleutians* (1943), *The Battle of San Pietro* (1942–43), and *Let There Be Light* (1946). The latter film concerned psychologically disabled veterans and their attempts to adjust to civilian life. The film was suppressed by the military and not shown publicly until 1980.

Following his military service, Huston contributed to the screen adaptation of Ernest Hemingway's *The Killers* (1946), produced by Mark Hellinger and directed by ROBERT SIODMAK. In November 1946, Huston directed a stage production of Jean-Paul Sartre's *No Exit,* translated by Paul Bowles, at the Biltmore Theatre in New York. Huston's next film, *The Treasure of the Sierra Madre* (1948), is considered by many to be one of his finest achievements as a director. The film featured Humphrey Bogart and Huston's father, Walter Huston, who received an Academy Award for best supporting actor. John Huston received an Oscar for best screenplay and best director, thus marking the first time a father and son were nominated—and won—for the same film. Huston's screenplay was adapted from the novel by B. Traven. Huston's next film, *Key Largo* (1948), based on the verse drama by Maxwell Anderson, was his last film for Warner Bros.

Huston and producer Sam Spiegel formed their own production company, Horizon Pictures, the first production of which was *We Were Strangers* (1949), with John Garfield and Jennifer Jones. In 1947, Huston with director WILLIAM WYLER and screenwriter Phillip Dunne formed the short-lived Committee for the First Amendment in protest of the treatment of the Hollywood Ten by the House Un-American Activities Committee (HUAC). In 1950 Huston directed *The Asphalt Jungle,* the progenitor of the heist film, and the end of his film-noir period. Huston received Oscar nominations for both direction and screenplay for the film. Huston's next film, *The Red Badge of Courage* (1951), was based on the story by Stephen Crane and starred Audie Murphy. The film received critical, if not box-office, success. The next and final film for the short-lived Horizons Pictures company was *The African Queen* (1951). The film was shot in the Congo under adverse conditions and starred Humphrey Bogart and Katharine Hepburn. The film's screenplay, an adaptation of the novel by C. S. Forester, was written by James Agee and John Huston. The film was both a box-office and critical success and gave Humphrey Bogart his only Academy Award as best actor. Throughout the 1950s Huston undertook projects that were filmed in various countries and based on literary source material—a staple of his screen work. These films include *Moby Dick* (1956), *The Roots of Heaven* (1958), and *The Misfits* (1961).

In the 1960s Huston supplemented his directorial duties by acting in a number of films. Beginning with *The Cardinal* (1963), for which he received an Academy Award nomination for best supporting actor, Huston's subsequent acting career included such films as *Candy* (1968), *Myra Breckenridge* (1970), *Battle for the Planet of the Apes* (1973), and most prominently, *Chinatown* (1974). Among Huston's most critically acclaimed films as a director in the 1960s and 1970s are: *Night of the Iguana* (1964), *Fat City* (1972), *The Man Who Would Be King* (1975), and *Wise Blood* (1979). After a fiasco film version of the Broadway musical *Annie* (1982), which earned Huston a nomination for Worst Director from the Razzie Awards, the director returned to critical acclaim with *Under the Volcano* (1984) and *Prizzi's Honor* (1985). Huston received an Academy Award nomination for best director for *Prizzi's Honor,* an adaptation of a Richard Condon crime novel. In 1983 Huston was awarded the American Film Institute's Lifetime Achievement award. And in 1985 the Director's Guild of America presented Huston with its most prestigious award, the David Wark Griffith Award for Career Achievement. In 1986 Huston, in ill health, began work on what was to be his final film, an adaptation of James Joyce's short story *The Dead.* The film was written by his son, Tony Huston, and starred Huston's daughter, Angelica. Huston entered Charlton Memorial Hospital in Fall River, Massachusetts, on July 28, 1987. Huston died on August 28, 1987, in Middletown, Rhode Island, at the age of 81.

Other Films   As screenwriter: *Dark Waters* (1944); *The Stranger* (1946); *Three Strangers* (1946). As director: *Beat the Devil* (1954); *Heaven Knows, Mr. Allison* (1957); *The Barbarian and the Geisha* (1958); *The Unforgiven* (1960); *Freud* (1962); *The List of Adrian Messenger* (1963); *Reflections in a Golden Eye* (1967); *Casino Royale* (1967); *Sinful Davey* (1969); *The Kremlin Letter* (1970); *The Life and Times of Judge Roy Bean* (1970); *The Mackintosh Man* (1973); *Independence* (1976); *Love and Bullets* (1979); *Victory* (1981).

References   Cohen, Allen, and Harry Lawton, *John Huston: A Guide to References and Resources* (New York: G. K. Hall, 1997); Grobel, Lawrence, *The Hustons* (New York: Scribner's, 1990); Huston, John, *An Open Book* (New York: Knopf, 1980); Studlar, Gaylyn, and David Desser, eds., *Reflections in a Male Eye: John Huston and the American Experience* (Washington, D.C.: Smithsonian Institution Press, 1992).

—R.W.

Ichikawa, Kon (1915–) Born in the city of Ise, in Mie Prefecture, on November 20, 1915, Japanese director Kon Ichikawa was educated at the Osaka Commercial School and began his career as a cartoonist in the animation department of the J. O. Studios in 1933. He also won first prize in a story-writing contest sponsored by a newspaper, *Asahi Weekly,* and went on to write a screenplay for a film that was to have been directed by Mikio Naruse. His first directing credit was a puppet film entitled *A Girl of Dojo Temple* (1946) that was banned by the American Occupation forces because Ichikawa had not obtained official permission to make the film. In 1948 Ichikawa was promoted to director and went on to make a series of melodramas, beginning with *A Flower Blooms.* Ichikawa worked for Shin Toho, Nikkatsu, and, after 1956, primarily for Daei. In 1948 he married screenwriter Natto Wada, who wrote many of his film scripts.

His breakthrough picture, set during what the Japanese call the Pacific War (World War II), was *The Harp of Burma* (1956), adapted from the novel by Michio Takeyama, surely one of the most effective antiwar films ever made, about Private Mizushima (Shoji Yasui), a gentle soldier who has mastered the harp, converts to Buddhism, and devotes his life to burying the Japanese war dead. The story is about defeat, isolation, and, ultimately, spiritual regeneration, as Private Mizushima leaves his unit to persuade an isolated garrison into surrendering. He fails in this attempt and is knocked unconscious by artillery fire. Rescued by a passing Buddhist monk, Mizushima disguises himself as a Burmese Buddhist monk, and then gradually assumes the monk's calling. At first he intends to rejoin his company, but he becomes obsessed by the need to bury the Japanese bodies he finds strewn across the countryside. His colleagues worry about what may have happened to him, but they sense that he may have survived when they hear the strains of his distinctive harp-playing at night. The film won the San Giorgio Prize at the 1956 Venice Film festival as a film that best demonstrates "men's capacity to live with one another."

A second antiwar film was to follow, *Fires on the Plain* (1959), a brutally graphic depiction of the horrors of war involving cannibalism. Set during the final days of the Japanese occupation of the Philippines, a Japanese army unit is surrounded and isolated, deprived of all food and supplies, but determined to resist as long as possible and to die with dignity for the Imperial cause. In desperation, they are finally forced to feed upon the bodies of their own fallen comrades. Informed by Ichikawa's antitraditional view of human corruption, this film was as ghastly and realistic in its portrayal as his earlier film was gentle and "poetic." "War is an extreme situation which can change the nature of man," Ichikawa told Joan Mellen. "For this reason, I consider it to be the greatest sin."

Considered an idiosyncratic filmmaker with a fine sense of visual texture and a taste for black humor and obsessed characters, Ichikawa was most often interested in spiritually abnormal behavior resulting from the social environment of his characters. This tendency is found in *Odd Obsession* (1959), Ichikawa's adaptation of Junichiro Tanizaki's novel, *Kagi* (The key [1959]), a cynical and perverse black comedy of family intrigue, sexual indulgence, and murder involving a man going through a midlife crisis and his awful wife and daughters. *Conflagration* (1958), adapted from Yukio Mishima's *Temple of the Golden Pavilion,* tells the story of a young fanatic who burns down a beautiful historic temple in Kyoto in a purification ritual because he is appalled by the corruption he perceives in the world in which he lives. Identifying Ichikawa's recurring themes as "the loss of value of the individual in our modern world and outsiders who struggle to escape—not to change or accept," critic John Allyn claimed, "It is for these subjects and the satirical black comedies that Ichikawa will be most remembered. But," he added, "even the darkest subject matter is relieved by humor and beauty."

Other Films *365 Nights* (1948); *Human Patterns* [and] *Endless Passion* (both 1949); *Sanshiro of Ginza, The Hot Marshland, Pursuit at Dawn* (all 1950); *Nightshade Flower, The Lover, The Man without Nationality, Stolen Love, Bungawan Solo, Wedding March* (all 1951); *Mr. Lucky, Young People, The Woman Who Touched Legs, This Way—That Way* (all 1952); *Mr. Pu, The Blue Revolution, The Youth of Heiji Senigata, The Lover* (all 1953); *All of Myself, A Billionaire, Twelve Chapters about Women* (all 1954); *Ghost Story of Youth* [and] *The Heart* (1955); *Punishment Room* [and] *Bridge of Japan* (1956); *The Crowded Train, The Pit, The*

Men of Tohoku (all 1957); *Money and Three Bad Men* (1958); *Goodbye—Good Day* [and] *Police and Small Gangsters* (1959); *A Ginza Veteran, Bonchi, A Woman's Testament, Her Brother* (all 1960); *Ten Dark Women* (1961); *The Outcast* [and] *Being Two Isn't Easy* (1962); *An Actor's Revenge* [and] *Alone on the Pacific* (1963); *Money Talks* (1964); *Tokyo Olympiad* (1965); *The Tale of Genji* (1966); *Topo Gigio e sei Ladri* (Italy [1967]); *Tournament* (documentary [1968]); *Kyoto* (documentary [1969]); *To Love Again* (1972); *The Wanderers* [and] *Visions of Eight* (both 1973); *I Am a Cat* (1975); *Between Women and Wives* [codirected, and] *The Inugami Family* (both 1976); *The Devil's Bouncing Ball Song* (1977); *Queen Bee* [and] *Island of Horrors* (both 1978); *The Phoenix* [and] *House of Hanging* (both 1979); *Koto* (aka *Ancient City* [1980]); *Kofuku* (aka *Lonely Hearts* [1982]); *Sasame Yuki* (aka *The Makioka Sisters* [1983]); *The Actress* [and] *Princess from the Moon* (1987); *Tenkawa Densetsu Dsydijin Jiken* (1991); *Fusa* (1993); *47 Ronin* (1994).

References Allyn, John, *Kon Ichikawa: A Guide to References and Resources* (Boston: G.K. Hall, 1985); Mellen, Joan, *Voices from the Japanese Cinema* (New York: Liveright, 1975); Svensson, Arne, *Japan* (New York: A. S. Barnes, 1971).

—J.M.W.

Ivory, James (1928–)   With his partners, producer Ismail Merchant and writer Ruth Prawer Jhabvala, James Ivory has directed a notable series of "prestige" historical dramas and literary adaptations. Ivory was born on June 7, 1928, in Berkeley, California, into an upper-middle-class Irish-American family. He majored in fine arts at the University of Oregon and furthered his study in France. His first taste of "show business" came in working for Special Services with the Second Armored Division in Germany during the Korean War. "I learned basic lessons in the Army which proved very useful later on in filmmaking," he writes, "like. . . . how essential good advertising is; and, most important, accepting useful suggestions from all sorts of unlikely people without letting one's ego come into it. A film director should have no ego, or perhaps I should say he must be above ego, or outside it." Back in America he enrolled in the Film Department at USC, where he made his first film, *Venice: Theme and Variations* (1957), a 28-minute color documentary.

In 1960 he met a young Indian student, Ismael Noormohamed Abdul Rehman Merchant—Ismail Merchant—with whom he made a film called *The Householder,* about the coming of age of an ingenuous Indian youth named Prem in a Bengali village. The picture was to prove highly significant to the team, because it was based on a novel by Ruth Prawer Jhabvala, a Polish–German writer educated in Britain and married to an Indian. Her work on the film adaptation led to her subsequent involvement in all the Merchant-Ivory pictures. Their second feature, *Shakespeare Wallah!* (1965)—the term "wallah" in Hindustani means a small-time operator—set the standard that was to prevail in their subsequent efforts, i.e., juxtaposing a romantic tale against the contexts of class upheaval and cultural change. It chronicled the adventures of a small Shakespearean troupe of English players touring post-independence India. This modern India, culturally speaking, is a changing world more interested in the current novelty of Hollywood-style musical films than in its own literary traditions. The disasters that befall the Buckingham Players thus exemplify the schisms opening up between worlds old and new, between classical and popular entertainment. "One is always conscious of [the Buckinghams] as being constrained by their theatrical calling," notes historian Patrice Sorace, "which has lost popularity to Indian films that represent the new, indigenous Indian culture." The eminent filmmaker, Satyajit Ray, composed the score.

Although *Shakespeare Wallah!* was warmly received, four more years passed before Ivory directed his next feature, *Bombay Talkie* (1970), about a Western journalist (Jennifer Kendal) who becomes infatuated with a young Indian movie star (Shashi Kapoor). A variety of films followed: *Roseland* (1977) consisted of three vignettes about the

denizens of the fabled Roseland dance hall in New York City. *The Europeans* (1979) was Ivory's first Henry James–based film, a delicate comedy of manners occasioned by the arrival of a brother and sister, reared abroad, in the rural precincts of Boston in the mid-1840s. Another Jamesian adaptation was *The Bostonians* (1984), a re-creation of the cultural and social milieu of Boston in the 1870s. *Quartet* was an adaptation of Jean Rhys's autobiographical novel, an evocation of 1920s Paris. *Heat and Dust,* from Jhabvala's 1975 novel, juxtaposed a modern and a flashback narrative in its depiction of life in colonial India. Another tale of India was *The Deceivers* (1988), an action-filled drama of the clash between English spies and the deadly Thugee cult in the early 19th century. Two E. M. Forster adaptations rounded out the 1980s. *Room with a View* (1986) was based on Forster's 1907 novel about a series of complications arising from the interactions between a well-brought-up English girl (Helena Bonham-Carter) and two free-thinking English gentlemen (Denholm Elliott and Julian Sands) she meets in Italy. Critic Richard Schickel wrote that the "formality of James Ivory's style suits [the book] admirably, counterpointing and controlling the theatrical overplaying he encourages." It won three Oscars, including screenplay, art direction, and costume design. The second Forster adaptation was his autobiographical *Maurice* (1987), a story of homosexual love. Scripted by Ivory himself, it was photographed in the authentic locations of Cambridge and Pendersleigh, and its depiction of the relationship between Maurice (James Wilby) and the gamekeeper Alec (Rupert Graves) was depicted with dignity and reserve. "One of the virtues of the film," writes Long, "is its precision—its quiet, steady revelation of the oppressive formality in Edwardian society that keeps people apart, and the step-by-step inevitability of Maurice and Alec's desperation."

The decade of the 1990s saw the flowering of Merchant-Ivory with some of their finest films, all drawn from respectable literary sources and offering finely observed social commentaries and richly textured period re-creations. *Mr. and Mrs. Bridge* (1990) brought the Merchant-Ivory-Jhabvala team to Kansas City, Missouri, to film Evan Connell's classic novels, *Mrs. Bridge* and *Mr. Bridge,* about a driven businessman and his repressed wife. The setting of the Midwest in the 1930s—the first time a Merchant-Ivory film was set in America's heartland—particularly appealed to Ivory, who declared that it was the only film he made "about my own childhood and adolescence." Paul Newman and Joanne Woodward played the eponymous couple.

Howard's End (1992) was another Forster adaptation, a tale chronicling the intersections among three families who represent very different aspects of English class and culture at the turn of the century—the Schlegels are artists and intellectuals; the Wilcoxes are grasping businessmen; and the Basts are lowly, downtrodden souls at the edge of society. At the heart of this richly textured film are exemplary performances by Emma Thompson as Margaret Schlegel, the rightful heir of Howard's End, and Anthony Hopkins as the cruel, insensitive Mr. Wilcox.

The Remains of the Day (1993) reunites Anthony Hopkins and Emma Thompson in a drama of near-misses and might-have-beens that transpires in two time frames, the 1950s and the 1930s. A bittersweet, frustrated romance between two people in service to the Darlington Estate in England (Hopkins and Thompson) frames the larger context of the debate between isolationists and interventionists concerning England's role in the oncoming war. In both personal and public contexts, the rigid conventions of class and tradition struggle against new sensibilities emerging after the war.

Jefferson in Paris (1995) transpires in Paris in the 1780s. Jefferson (Nick Nolte) and his daughter arrive in a Paris that is already seething with angry citizens threatening revolution against the monarchy of Louis XVI and Marie Antoinette. As the minister plenipotentiary to the French court, Jefferson is immediately challenged by the Marquis de Lafayette for representing America as a democracy while slavery still persists there. During his courtly duties, consigning his daughter to a convent, and dallying with the delectable Maria Cosway (Greta Scacchi), Jefferson faces revolt from within his own house when his black slave, James Hemmings, begins demanding his own freedom. Moreover, Jefferson finds himself in the grip of a powerfully erotic attraction to James's sister, Sally. The faults and virtues of the Merchant-Ivory style are everywhere in evidence: On the debit side is a pace that is maddeningly deliberate and a narrative structure—alternating between the words of Jefferson's letters and the latter-day testimony of an alleged descendent of a Jefferson-Hemmings union—that seems unnecessarily convoluted. Its controversial (at the time) take on the Jefferson-Hemmings affair is so discreetly muted that it ultimately effaces itself. However, the real glory of the film lies in its ravishing visuals, as if Pre-Raphaelite painter Edward Burne-Jones had gone back a century to record life in late-18th-century Paris. "Paris is every day enlarging and beautifying," wrote Jefferson in one of his letters; and the entire film seems to share the sentiment. In addition to dwelling lovingly on locations like the Palais de la Légion d'Honneur, the Tuilleries, Les Halles Park, and the gardens of the Forest of Marly, there is a visit to one of Marie Antoinette's courtly pageants, a peek over the shoulder of painter John Trumbull at his easel, and a reserved seat at a performance of Sacchini's opera, *Dardanus.*

Ivory and his colleagues Merchant and Jhabvala show no sign of slackening their pace. Recent films include *Surviving Picasso* (1996), with Anthony Hopkins portraying the famous artist in his middle years; *A Soldier's Daughter Never Cries* (1998), with Kris Kristofferson in the role of an alcoholic novelist patterned after James Jones; and *The Golden Bowl* (2000), adapted from Henry James's late novel about the complications that ensue after the marriage between an impoverished Italian prince (Jeremy Northam) and an American heiress (Kate Beckinsale).

Ivory's sensitivity and impeccable visual taste are everywhere in evidence in his films. "It is often said that Ivory's films have his personal stamp on them," writes biographer Robert Emmet Long, "—a way of speaking, perhaps, of personal qualities that enter into them: sophistication, tolerant affection, sharp wit, a feeling for place.... Reviewers sometimes grouse that . . . the pacing of his movies is too slow, but his way is to be careful and probing as he creates texture and verisimilitude. He can't be hurried."

Other Films *The Delhi Way* (1964); *The Guru* (1969); *Adventures of a Brown Man in Search of Civilization* (1971); *Savages* (1972); *Autobiography of a Princess* (1975); *Hullabaloo Over Georgie and Bonnie's Pictures* (1978); *Jane Austen in Manhattan* (1980).

Reference Long, Robert Emmet, *The Films of Merchant Ivory* (New York: Citadel Press, 1993).

—J.C.T.

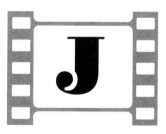

Jewison, Norman (1926–) Canadian filmmaker Norman Jewison was born on July 21, 1926, in Toronto, Ontario. Early on he studied piano and music theory at the Royal Conservatory. Jewison later staged and performed in dramas and musical comedies at the Malvern Collegiate Institute, and made his professional debut in a minstrel show, which he also directed and cowrote. His education was interrupted by service in World War II with the Royal Canadian Navy. Discharged in 1949, he enrolled at the University of Toronto, eventually earning a bachelor's degree in general arts. He spent his summers tending bar, waiting on tables, and producing shows at the Banff Springs Hotel.

After college Jewison took what acting assignments he could find on stage and in radio for the Canadian Broadcasting Corporation and eventually served a two-year work-study internship with the BBC, London. Returning to Canada, he wrote, directed, and produced for seven years before being lured to America in 1958 to direct for such CBS television shows as *Your Hit Parade* and *The Andy Williams Show.* He went on to earn three Emmy Awards after directing television specials with Judy Garland, Frank Sinatra, Danny Kaye, and Harry Belafonte.

Jewison's Hollywood career started modestly in 1962 with the Tony Curtis picture, *Forty Pounds of Trouble.* As a contract director for Universal, Jewison made *The Thrill of It All* (1963), *Send Me No Flowers* (1964), and *The Art of Love* (1965), the first two starring Doris Day. He then went to MGM as an independent filmmaker for *The Cincinnati Kid* (1965), which he also cowrote, a critical and box-office success with an all-star cast that included Steve McQueen, Edward G. Robinson, Ann-Margaret, Karl Malden, and Tuesday Weld. He would work again with Steve McQueen in *The Thomas Crown Affair* (1968), a signature film during his early career. Jewison directed successful pictures in several genres, including thrillers, political satire (*The Russians Are Coming! The Russians Are Coming!* [1966]), romantic comedy (*Moonstruck* [1988]), and, especially, such musicals as the rock opera *Jesus Christ Superstar* (1973) and *Fiddler on the Roof* (1971), a blockbuster hit that was especially praised by *New Yorker* critic Pauline Kael.

Though he knew how to entertain, Jewison will be best remembered for his more serious pictures that probed the legal system (*. . . And Justice for All* [1979]), the labor movement (*F.I.S.T.* [1978]), and, especially, race relations in the American South. *In the Heat of the Night,* for example, made at the peak of the Civil Rights movement in America, won five Academy Awards, including best picture of 1967. The film was later cloned into a popular television series. In 1984, moreover, Jewison worked with playwright Charles Fuller to direct *A Soldier's Story,* adapted from Fuller's 1982 Pulitzer Prize–winning drama, *A Soldier's Play,* a tragedy disguised as a murder mystery involving the death of an African-American sergeant on an army base in Louisiana in 1944. The cast was predominantly black and featured Howard E. Rollins, Jr., as the military lawyer, Captain Davenport, investigating the case, and talented actors from the original Negro Ensemble production, including Larry Riley, Denzel Washington in one of his very first movie roles, and Adolph Caesar, who played the murder victim. The film earned three Academy Award nominations, including best picture, but it was especially important for demonstrating that there was a possible "crossover" audience from the dominant white majority that would support what might once have been considered a "race" movie. Made on a budget of $6 million, the film earned $30 million for Columbia Pictures.

Another play adaptation, *Agnes of God* (1985), starring Jane Fonda, Meg Tilly, and Anne Bancroft, was less successful than *A Soldier's Story,* but John Pielmeier's 1979 play about a novitiate nun (Tilly) who becomes pregnant under mysterious circumstances was simply not as powerful as Charles Fuller's tragedy. Even so, Anne Bancroft, as the play's mother superior, and Meg Tilly, as the novitiate nun, both got best-supporting-actress Oscar nominations. *Other People's Money* (1991) was also adapted for Jewison by Alvin Sargent from Jerry Sterner's satirical play about corporate greed and a successful financial takeover, starring Danny DeVito as the caricatured, ruthless tycoon Lawrence Garfield, also known as "Larry the Liquidator."

One of Jewison's best films was adapted from Bobbie Ann Mason's novel *In Country* in 1989, featuring Emily Lloyd and Bruce Willis in one of his very best, serious movie roles as a traumatized Vietnam veteran. Despite this critical success with

Norman Jewison (Monarchy Enterprises B.V. and Regency Entertainment; photo by Suzanne Hanover)

Mason's novel, Jewison, who began his career as an actor, has been considered an actor's director who has often demonstrated a particular talent for adapting plays. *A Soldier's Story* was a marvel of cinematic construction, and *Agnes of God* also got Academy Award attention.

Jewison's career has also been sustained by well-made but less-serious entertainments as well. *Moonstruck,* for example, was an engaging romantic comedy, set in New York's Little Italy, scripted by Off-Broadway playwright John Patrick Shanley, and starring Cher and Nicolas Cage as an offbeat, eccentric couple. A box-office success, *Moonstruck* earned an Oscar nomination for best picture of 1988, while Cher and Olympia Dukakis won Oscars for best actress and best supporting actress, and Shanley won the Oscar for best original screenplay. In addition to the many

Oscar nominations his pictures have enjoyed, Jewison was also honored in Ottawa by being appointed an officer of the Order of Canada in 1982, Canada's highest civilian decoration. In 1986, Jewison founded the Canadian Center for Advanced Film Studies, following the model of the American Film Institute, to assist the career development of aspiring young filmmakers in his native country.

Other Films   *Gaily, Gaily* (1969); *Rollerball* (1975); *Best Friends* (1982); *Only You* (1994); *Bogus* (1996).

References   Singer, Michael, *A Cut Above: 50 Film Directors Talk about Their Craft* (Los Angeles: Lone Eagle, 1998); Welsh, Jim, "A Soldier's Story: A Paradigm for Justice," in *Columbia Pictures: Portrait of a Studio,* ed. Bernard F. Dick (Lexington: University Press of Kentucky, 1992).
—J.M.W.

Jordan, Neil (1950–)

Neil Jordan has become one of Ireland's most recognizable and respected filmmakers. His best films have a distinctive Irish feel to them, and encompass themes of alienation, freedom, politics, and love in various settings in Ireland and the United Kingdom. His work is highly stylized, often evoking strange or unusual images while maintaining sensitive, realistic character portraits.

Neil Jordan was born in Sligo, Ireland, on February 25, 1950, and grew up in Dublin, where he later studied history and literature at University College. Jordan began writing from an early age and, while working in fringe theater, published a collection of stories, *Night in Tunisia,* in 1976. He began writing for Irish television and the BBC and published a novel, *The Past,* in 1980 before directing his first film, *Angel* (1982). The film explores an individual who becomes inadvertently embroiled in violence.

Dealing with lost innocence and moral ambiguity, themes that recur in Jordan's work, *Angel* was one of the more auspicious film debuts sponsored by Channel 4 in Britain, a new media operation that also produced many other now-critically acclaimed filmmakers during the early 1980s. Jordan's foray into films was unexpected but surely welcomed. "The novel, as a form, seemed to me overloaded with history," Jordan has explained. "Narratively, there were more interesting things you could do in the cinema. And I also found that I was writing myself into a corner because my prose and fiction were so visual they were almost like blueprints for movies."

His next film, *The Company of Wolves* (1984), depicts a mixed nightmare world of fairy tale, horror, and psychoanalysis. Based on the Little Red Riding Hood story, the film has two distinct worlds of fantasy and reality that merge by the movie's end. It is a magical, stylistic film, embellished with nuanced terror and symbolic imagery. The movie won Jordan best film and best director awards from the London Critics Circle. Jordan's subsequent film, *Mona Lisa* (1986), garnered him international notice after it won best picture at Cannes. This was also a film about the loss of innocence, morality, and corruption, and deals with the social conflicts between the lower and upper classes. Of that film, Jordan said, "If I have a Point of View, it probably emerges more in [*Mona Lisa*] than in anything else I have done." It presents directly, often with biting humor, the unattractive world of prostitution and drug addiction, but also offers decent, emotional characters in search of understanding and redemption.

After making two American-financed films during the late 1980s, Jordan returned to Ireland to make *The Miracle* (1991), a darkly sensuous coming-of-age drama that takes an unexpected turn that surprises the audience. It was his next film, however, with its own unnerving and unsuspecting twist, that earned Jordan his most acclaim. *The Crying Game* (1992) won Jordan an Oscar for best screenplay. It is at once a tightly wound political drama, an action–thriller, and a love story. The plot twist became one of the most talked-about in recent screen history, which led the film to have both massive critical, media, and commercial success. It starts as a political drama, with an Irish Republican Army militant who kidnaps a British soldier and who later sets out to find the soldier's girlfriend, facing only obstacles and surprises once he does. All of the characters are unique and somewhat mysterious, imperfect yet impassioned.

Jordan's next project, an adaptation of Anne Rice's *Interview with the Vampire* (1994), was a glossy, expensive, Hollywood-backed film that was stereotyped and tedious, but still did marginally well because of the star power of Tom Cruise, Brad Pitt, and Antonio Banderas. A much better film was to follow, *Michael Collins* (1997), an historical portrait of the Easter Rebellion of 1916 and the establishment of the Irish Republic in 1922. Collins (Liam Neeson) and his Irish Free State forces battle De Valera (Alan Rickman), both of whom have different notions about how to gain freedom for Ireland during the civil war. It is a complex political history that, as the introductory titles suggest, conveys all the "triumph, terror, and tragedy of the period."

Another striking film was to follow, *The Butcher Boy* (1998), based on a 1993 novel by Patrick McCabe, one of the screen's most disturbing portraits of psychotic paranoia and mental disintegration. Set in 1962 during the Cuban missile crisis, what begins as a sort of Irish "Peck's Bad Boy" (Eammon Owens as "Francie Brady") lurches inexorably toward a darkly Gothic horror story, a sort of "Erin-go-boo!" The boy's descent into homicidal mania unleashes a slipstream of images, both real and fantastic, with the borderline in between growing ever more blurred. For example, when Francie plays cowboys, the idyllic green valley surrounding them erupts into a roiling atomic mushroom cloud (later Francie hallucinates that the entire village is littered with charred pigs' heads). And there's the terrifying moment when Francie, armed with butcher's tools, bursts into a woman's house and savagely slaughters her (later burying her body beneath a pile of garbage). A final confirmation of the boy's madness is his encounter with Sinead O'Connor, portrayed as the Madonna.

In Dreams (1998) is a horror film that is a cross between *Nightmare on Elm Street* and *Don't Look Now,* a triumph of dazzling visuals over trite subject matter. Annette Benning portrays Claire Cooper, whose violent nightmares—horrifying images of drowning children, red apples, and cryptic graffiti—are precognitions of the kidnapping of her child. These images, she claims, are telepathic transmissions from the kidnapper (Robert Downey, Jr.). The film's highlight is a performance by children of a fairy pageant. In a style that is pure Jordan, the boys and girls flit about in the twilight wood, wearing their fairy wings and intoning their rhymes. The disappearance of Claire's little girl is implied by the sight of her abandoned wings, caught on a bush, a poignant emblem of lost childhood and innocence.

Jordan's next film, an adaptation of Graham Greene's celebrated 1951 novel *The End of the Affair* (1999), is set during the London blitz. It was not only a subtle probe into the quirks of love and jealousy but also an existential examination of the enduring nature of love and the bewildering workings of God. Dominating the film is one of Jordan's most striking images, a bomb blast that becomes an epiphany for the character of Sara (Julianne Moore), an adulterous woman who is thereby transformed into a saintly presence who performs miracles. Because of its complex tangle of flashbacks and differing points of view, it might be considered the *Citizen Kane* of wartime melodramas.

Reflecting on his work, Jordan has said: "I like to choose characters who are surrounded by a life that seems understandable and who slowly find themselves in situations where everything has changed, where no rules exist and where emotions and realities are brought into play that they are not prepared for." Along with Peter Weir, Jordan is perhaps our finest poet of apocalypse.

Other Film *We're No Angels* (1989).

References Gould, Lois, "Neil Jordan Interview," *New York Times Magazine,* Jan. 9, 1944, p. 22; McSwiney, "Trying to Take the Gun Out of Irish Politics: an Interview with Neil Jordan." *Cineaste* 22 (1996): 20–24; Rogers, Lori, *Feminine Nation: Performance, Gender, and Resistance in the Works of John McGahern and Neil Jordan* (Lanham, Md.: University Press of America, 1998).

—-W.V. and J.C.T.

Kaufman, Philip (1936–) Writer-director Philip Kaufman was born in 1936, grew up on the North Side of Chicago, and was educated at the University of Chicago, where, as an aspiring novelist, he met Anaïs Nin in 1962, a meeting that eventually led to his film *Henry and June* (1990), nearly 30 years later. In 1963 he turned his unfinished novel into his first film, the comedy *Goldstein,* made on a shoestring budget and starring players from Chicago's "Second City" group. The picture won the Prix de la Nouvelle Critique at the 1964 Cannes Film Festival. In 1965 he wrote and directed *Fearless Frank,* a satire starring Jon Voight in his film debut, which led two years later to a contract with Universal Studios. Other early films included *The Great Northfield Minnesota Raid* (1971), a screwball western starring Robert Duvall and Cliff Robertson, and *The White Dawn* (1973). After moving to San Francisco in 1977, Kaufman made a striking remake of the Don Siegel classic *Invasion of the Body Snatchers* that carried that 1950s paranoia of the original to another level, and stood as a worthy remake in comparison to Siegel's adaptation of Jack Finney's novel. *The Wanderers,* his adaptation of Richard Price's gang novel, followed in 1979. His screenwriting credits include *The Out-*

law Josey Wales (1976) for Clint Eastwood and the original story for *Raiders of the Lost Ark* (1981) for George Lucas.

Kaufman's breakthrough picture was his brilliant and deviously satiric adaptation of Tom Wolfe's astronaut epic, *The Right Stuff* (1983), which received eight Academy Award nominations, including best picture, and won four Oscars. He earned Writers Guild and Directors Guild Award nominations for *The Right Stuff* and Writers Guild and Academy Award nominations for his adaptation of Czech writer Milan Kundera's novel, set during the turmoil of 1968s' Prague Spring, *The Unbearable Lightness of Being* (1988), which Kaufman directed and coscripted with Jean-Claude Carrière. Thereafter he won the international Orson Welles Award for best filmmaker of 1989.

Set in 1931–32, his film *Henry and June* (1990) was adapted from the diaries of Anaïs Nin and the autobiographical novels of Henry Miller (played by Fred Ward, with Uma Thurman as his wife June and Spanish actress Maria de Medeiros as Anaïs Nin). The director's wife, Rose Kaufman, cowrote the screenplay with him. Because of its sexual content, the film tested the limits of the MPAA rating system, and was originally rated X but eventually given the first NC-17 rating in motion pic-

Philip Kaufman (The Ladd Company/Warner Bros.)

ture history. Besides having met Anaïs Nin in Chicago, Kaufman had gone to Big Sur in 1960 to meet Henry Miller, the author of *Tropic of Cancer* and *Tropic of Capricorn,* two books that helped rewrite censorship laws in America, so it is appropriate that Kaufman's film treating Henry Miller's life managed to change the rating system of the Motion Picture Association of America. Regardless, the film was not a box-office success.

Kaufman had better success with his adaptation of Michael Crichton's Japan-bashing novel *Rising Sun* (1993), starring Sean Connery and Wesley Snipes, though Kaufman and Crichton were at odds about how the treatment should be handled. Kaufman's treatment made essential changes in the plot and characters, not the least of which was making the Wesley Snipes character an African American, and Crichton was outraged. Although this politically correct treatment changed the original story considerably, the damaged discourse did not seem to hurt the film's popularity.

Kaufman has always functioned best as a Hollywood maverick willing to push the envelope. His most recent film is *Quills* (2000), a picture made in England in which an Australian (Geoffrey Rush) plays the notorious Marquis de Sade, described by Kaufman's friend David Thomson as "wickedly funny, impious, [and] blasphemous," but also "mischievous, subversive, and liberating," arguably Kaufman's "best work yet." Thomson described this de Sade as "one more of Kaufman's outsider heroes, dangerous to themselves and alarming to society." In a *New York Times* piece written, perhaps, to hype the forthcoming film, Thomson referred to Kaufman as a "forgotten" filmmaker, but he has proved himself many times over as a gifted adaptor and an unquestionably talented director. He certainly caught the satiric tone of *The Right Stuff* far better than Brian De Palma was able to do in his later adaptation of Wolfe's *Bonfire of the Vanities* (1990). Though De Palma is the more famous director, Kaufman had "the right stuff."

References   Mitchell, Sean, "Strangers in a Strange Land," *Premiere* 6, no. 2 (August 1993), pp. 58–63, 111; Rafferty, Terrence, "Duplicity," *New Yorker,* October 8, 1990, pp. 98–101; Thomson, David, "A Filmmaker Both Promising and Forgotten at 64," *New York Times,* September 10, 2000, sec. II, pp. 63, 73.

—J.M.W.

Kazan, Elia (1909–) Elia Kazan successfully straddled the worlds of American theater and film in a career that brought many important playwrights and novelists to the screen. Born Elia Kazanjoglou (an Anatolian Greek) in Constantinople (now Istanbul), Turkey, on September 7, 1909, Kazan moved with his family to New York in 1913, where his father sold rugs for a living. Kazan attended the Mayfair School and New Rochelle High School in New York. Upon completion of an undergraduate education at Williams

College (1930) and drama study at Yale School of Drama (1930–32), Kazan became a member of the left-wing Group Theatre as both an actor and assistant manager. While a member of the Group Theatre, Kazan worked under such directors as Harold Clurman, Cheryl Crawford, and Lee Strasberg. Kazan began directing plays in 1938 and became one of the leading directors on Broadway throughout the 1940s. He directed the premiere productions of Thornton Wilder's *Skin of Our Teeth,* Tennessee Williams's *A Streetcar Named Desire* and *Cat on a Hot Tin Roof,* and Arthur Miller's *Death of a Salesman,* among others. Always the consummate actors' director, Kazan later recalled, "I worked like a maniac. . . . I took the Stanislavski training with utmost seriousness. . . . I thought of the roles mostly psychologically . . . [analyzing] the main drive of a character, and from the main drive there were stems, the 'beats' that would build up the whole part."

Such success caught the attention of Hollywood and producer Darryl F. Zanuck at 20th Century-Fox. Kazan had already had considerable experience in films. He had appeared in Ralph Steiner's documentary short, *Pie in the Sky* (1934), and had directed two documentary films, about Tennessee miners, *The People of the Cumberland* (1937), and food rationing, the U.S. Department of Agriculture's *It's Up to You* (1941). As an actor he had also gained favorable notices in two films directed by Anatole Litvak, *City for Conquest* (1940) and *Blues in the Night* (1941). But now he turned his energies toward directing theatrical feature films, debuting in 1945 with *A Tree Grows in Brooklyn,* adapted from Betty Smith's autobiographical novel about a poor girl growing up in New York. Subsequent critically and commercially successful films included another literary adaptation, *A Sea of Grass,* about the 19th-century struggle for possession of grasslands by farmers and cattle ranchers; *Gentleman's Agreement* (1947), an indictment of anti-Semitism in postwar America, which received eight Academy Award nominations (winning for best director, best picture,

and best supporting actress for Celeste Holm); *Boomerang!* (1947), a police procedural drama about a man wrongfully accused of murder; *Pinky* (1949), a light-skinned black woman who passes for white; and *Panic in the Streets* (1950), a documentary-style drama about a fugitive murderer infected with bubonic plague.

In 1951 Kazan brought his famous production of Tennessee Williams's *A Streetcar Named Desire* to the screen, with Marlon Brando recreating his stage role. In 1952, while filming *Viva Zapata!* based on a screenplay by John Steinbeck and also starring Brando, Kazan was called before HUAC (House Un-American Activities Committee) regarding his involvement with the Communist Party and the Group Theatre. Although Kazan had been a member of the Communist Party in the mid-1930s, he denied that the Group Theatre was a front for communist activity and refused to supply the committee with names of other communists. Later, when 20th Century-Fox president Spyros P. Skouras informed him that he faced the possibility of being blacklisted if he did not cooperate with HUAC, Kazan once again testified and this time supplied them with the names of friends and associates who were suspected communists. Among the names Kazan gave the committee were Clifford Odets, Lee and Paula Strasberg, Lillian Hellman, Joseph Bromberg, and John Garfield. Kazan was maligned by many in New York and Hollywood for "selling out" to save his Fox contract. Arthur Miller, who was one of Kazan's closest friends, spoke out against him in a letter to the *New York Post.* To this day Kazan continues to justify his belief that in postwar America the communists posed a real threat and in Russia repressed artistic activities.

In the 1950s and early 1960s Kazan directed a succession of some of his finest films. *On the Waterfront* was based on a script by Budd Schulberg, which in turn had drawn from a series of magazine articles by Malcolm Johnson about mob control of the New York area docks. It was filmed on location in Hoboken, New Jersey, and starred Marlon Brando and Eva Marie Saint. *On the Waterfront* won seven Oscars, including best picture, best director, best actor, and best cinematography (Boris Kaufman). Many consider the film as Kazan's justification of his HUAC testimony, citing the similarities between Terry Malloy's testimony before the crime committee with his own. Kazan's next film was *East of Eden,* starring James Dean and based on the last third of the novel by John Steinbeck. A retelling of the Cain and Abel story set in California's Salinas Valley at the turn of the century, it was a critical and commercial success, netting Kazan another Oscar nomination for best director. Working again from a Tennessee Williams play, Kazan directed *Baby Doll* in 1956, drawing heavily from the Actors Studio for his cast. The story of two men competing for the affections of "baby doll" Carroll Baker earned more censorial attacks than critical praise. In 1957 Kazan directed *A Face in the Crowd,* based on a script by Budd Schulberg, a scathing attack on the power of television and the cult of media celebrity, starring Andy Griffith as country yokel "Lonesome Rhodes," discovered by a reporter (Patricia Neal). Kazan's association with playwright William Inge resulted in *Splendor in the Grass,* based on Inge's Oscar-winning original screenplay about frustrated adolescent sex in a small midwestern town in the 1920s. *America, America* (1963) was based on Kazan's novel about the life of his Greek uncle and his immigration to the United States at the turn of the century.

Kazan's final film as a director was *The Last Tycoon* (1976), based on the unfinished novel by F. Scott Fitzgerald and adapted by playwright Harold Pinter. Kazan's autobiography, *A Life,* was published by Alfred Knopf in 1988. In 1998 Kazan was again in the spotlight and a center of controversy—aroused by his selection to receive the Academy of Motion Picture Arts and Sciences' Lifetime Achievement Award. Many continued to harbor resentment over Kazan's actions of 50 years earlier, claiming that the careers he ruined by naming names should deny him any further recog-

nition. Nonetheless, the televised ceremony prevailed. In assessing Kazan's career, historian Lloyd Michaels noted that "during a decade and a half [1950–1965] of anxiety, gimmickry, and entropy in Hollywood, Kazan remained one of the few American directors who continued to believe in the cinema as a medium for artistic expression and who brought forth films that consistently reflected his own creative vision."

Other Films   *Man on a Tightrope* (1953); *Wild River* (1960); *The Arrangement* (1969); *The Visitors* (1972).

References   Kazan, Elia, *A Life* (New York: Knopf, 1988); Michaels, Lloyd, *Elia Kazan: A Guide to References and Resources* (Boston: G. K. Hall, 1985); Pauly, Thomas H., *Elia Kazan and American Culture* (Philadelphia: Temple University Press, 1983); Smith, Wendy, *Real Life Drama: The Group Theatre and America, 1931–1940* (New York: Knopf, 1990); Young, Jeff, *Kazan: The Master Director Discusses His Films* (New York: Newmarket Press, 1999).

—R.W.

Keaton, Buster (1895–1966)   Comedian, acrobat, film director, and producer, Buster Keaton deserves a place in the pantheon of America's greatest comic geniuses. He was literally a child of storm. He claimed that Kansas tornadoes blew him into the world, christened him, and flung him onto the stage and screen. When his mother was eight months pregnant, a cyclone tore down the Keatons' medicine-show tent. A little later, on the night of his birth, October 4, 1895, in the tiny farming town of Piqua, Kansas, a twister almost leveled the town. Three years later, during another tour of the state, his parents left him in a boarding house during their performance—and a howling vortex sucked him out of a second-story window, sailed him over trees and houses, and deposited him safely in the middle of the street three blocks away. The toddler just blinked (the first of many deadpan reactions to life's catastrophes). Thereafter, his mother decided he would be safer on the stage with his family than left to the whims of the South Wind.

Buster Keaton (Author's collection)

But little Joseph Frank Keaton merely traded one disaster for another. As the newest member of the "Three Keatons," the roughest vaudeville act in show business, he found himself subjected to slapstick routines where he was kicked, pummeled, and hurled about the stage by his father, Joe Keaton. Aptly dubbed "Buster" by magician Harry Houdini, a member of the Keaton troupe—the story may be apocryphal—the rubber-limbed child grew up to become a vaudeville headliner, renowned for his hair-raising falls. By age 21, after a stint in the army, he was on his own in Hollywood, serving a kind of apprenticeship with another Kansan, the redoubtable Roscoe "Fatty" Arbuckle. By 1920 he had his own production company, and during the next decade made 30 shorts and features, most of them regarded today as classics of the American cinema.

His amazing acrobatics—falls from trains (*Sherlock, Jr.* [1924]), dives from waterfalls (*Our Hospi-*

tality [1923]), and tumbles down mountainsides (*The Paleface* [1922], *Seven Chances* [1925])—rival the stunts of the great Douglas Fairbanks, Sr. His impeccable period re-creations—the Old South in *Our Hospitality* (1923); the Civil War in *The General* (1926)—and his keen-edged social satires (*Seven Chances* [1925]) beat the more prestigious DAVID WARK GRIFFITH and ERNST LUBITSCH at their own game. His intricate, inventive gag trajectories (*Neighbors* [1920], *Cops* [1922], *The Navigator* [1924]) surpass anything by Harold Lloyd. And his penchant for bizarre, dreamlike situations (*The Playhouse* [1921], *Sherlock, Jr.*) are as peculiar as anything out of the contemporary French avant-garde.

While it is undeniably true Buster was funny, audiences during his peak years in the 1920s relegated him to third place as a box-office draw, well behind CHARLES CHAPLIN and Harold Lloyd. Even his masterpiece, *The General,* commonly cited in critics' polls as one of the 10 greatest films ever made, was originally dismissed by some critics as "a mild Civil War comedy" and rejected by audiences (it lost more money than any of his other films). Keaton's decline in the 1930s was as abrupt as one of his pratfalls. He lost his independent status when he left United Artists for MGM in 1928. Although his first MGM pictures made money (*The Cameraman* [1928], *Spite Marriage* [1929], *Parlor, Bedroom, and Bath* [1932]), his personal life was collapsing and he sank deep into alcoholism. By the mid-1930s he was down and out, estranged from the studio, and capable only of a string of cheap comedies that were but pale ghosts of his work a decade earlier.

The climb back was slow and painful. The upturn began with a successful marriage in 1940 to Eleanor Norris, a young dancer who would remain devoted to him during their 26 years of marriage. His alcoholism back under control, he returned to MGM as a writer and gag man for Red Skelton and Lucille Ball. Then, in rapid succession, came an adulatory tribute to him by the esteemed critic/writer James Agee for *Life* magazine in 1949; a successful stint in live television in the early 1950s; a movie biography, *The Buster Keaton Story* (1957); and memorable cameo roles in films like *Limelight* (1953) and *Around the World in 80 Days* (1956). A major revival of his films got under way in the early 1960s. And before his death from cancer on February 1, 1966, he was abashed but pleased to find himself the darling of the intelligentsia and the college crowd and secure in his status as a comic artist.

Like his screen personae, the real Buster had proven to be a tough and resilient fellow. "What I expected was hard knocks," he said in his autobiography, *My Wonderful World of Slapstick* (1957). "I always expected to have to work hard. Maybe harder than other people because of my lack of education. And when the knocks came, I felt it was no surprise. I had always known life was like that, full of uppercuts for the deserving and undeserving alike." Indeed, despite the hazards and exotic imagery, Buster remained ever the prairie pragmatist, the *bricoleur* (handyman) of the south forty. In every one of his films he took a moment to stand his ground and assess the situation. The pose is familiar: a small figure in flat porkpie hat and baggy pants leaning forward slightly against the wind, eyes shaded with the palm of his hand, his gaze mutely surveying the far horizon. Every crisis—a cattle stampede in *Go West* (1925), a runaway ocean liner in *The Navigator,* a stolen locomotive in *The General,* a deranged house in *The Haunted House* (1921), a cyclone in *Steamboat Bill, Jr.* (1928), a newsreel camera with a mind of its own in *The Cameraman*—was both a confrontation and a negotiation. "He is an explorer," wrote critic Walter Kerr in his indispensable *The Silent Clowns* (1975), one of the most insightful analyses on Keaton extant. "He explores the universe exactly as he explores film: with a view to measuring the immeasurable before he enters it, so that he will know how to behave when he is there." In 1995 the film preservationist David Shepard released through Kino International, of New York City, a generous package of all the surviving post-

Arbuckle shorts and silent features for the edification of a new and admiring generation of viewers. And finally, at this writing, Keaton and his world of silent comedy are the subject of annual "Keaton Festivals" in the town of Iola, Kansas, near his birthplace. Held during the last weekend of September, the festivals are a mix of humanities scholars, film historians, Hollywood celebrities, Keaton family members, and enthusiasts who attend screenings, symposia, discussions, dinners, and late-night parties. Keaton as a Kansan is always a prime topic. Is it not true that the flattest and most prosaic of landscapes may contain the wildest visions? And did not Keaton, the most silent of clowns—whose "deadly horizontal" hat (the term is Agee's) was such a perfect symbol for the level prairie—constantly confront the highest precipices, steepest descents, and most improbable of catastrophes? Keaton said it simply: "I used to daydream an awful lot in pictures; I could get carried away and visualize all the fairylands in the world."

Other Films *One Week* (1920); *The Saphead* (1920); *The Three Ages* (1923); *Battling Butler* (1926); *What, No Beer?* (1933); *Le Roi des Champs-Elysees* (1935).

References Keaton, Buster, *My Wonderful World of Slapstick* (Garden City: Doubleday, 1960); Kerr, Walter, *The Silent Clowns* (New York: Alfred A. Knopf, 1975); Tibbetts, John C., "The Whole Show: The Restored Films of Buster Keaton," *Literature/Film Quarterly* 23, no. 4 (1995): 230–242.

—J.C.T.

Kiarostami, Abbas (1940–)   In the words of commentator Godfrey Cheshire, Iranian filmmaker Abbas Kiarostami "is the most important filmmaker to appear on the world stage in the Nineties." His career parallels the time line of contemporary Iranian cinema—beginning with the New Wave of the late sixties, maturing in the seventies, and flowering with renewed brilliance in the nineties (when the film medium as an artistic enterprise was particularly venerated). A native of Iran's capital city, Tehran, Abbas Kiarostami was

born on June 22, 1940. In 1958 he won a painting competition and then left his home to study
graphic design at the Faculty of Fine Arts of
Tehran University. Throughout the 1960s, he
worked as a designer and illustrator, gaining a reputation especially for his poster designs and illustrations for children's books, but venturing also in
film and television through the design of commercials and credit sequences. He cites an early
viewing of FEDERICO FELLINI's *La Dolce Vita* as a
prime impetus in his interest in film.

The Iranian New Wave ignited in the late sixties after the spectacular success of a groundbreaking film, Dariush Mehrjui's *The Cow*. The
intellectual climate of the new movement was
defined by a rejection of the violence and spectacle that characterized older Iranian films, in imitation of Indian imports. Instead, filmmakers
returned to national culture and to the realities of
working-class Iranians, following the cinematic
path of Italian neorealism. Kiarostami took part in
this resurgence of his country's cinema, through
the creation of a film department at his place of
work, the Institute for the Intellectual Development of Children and Young Adults. He has
worked at this center ever since, and in his long
career has made more than 14 short and medium-
length films and six feature films.

Kiarostami's fame in the West came, however,
only in the early 1990s with the success in the
international festival circuit of his third feature-
length film, *Where Is My Friend's Home* (1987). It is
the story of a small child who finds out that he has
swapped with a classmate the notebook he needs to
do a homework assignment. Against his mother's
advice, he sets out to find his friend's house in a
neighboring town. The storyline of the movie was
suggested by an experience of Kiarostami's own
son, "within the allegorical structure of a mystical
tale," in Miriam Rosen's words.

His next film was *And Life Goes On* (1992),
inspired by a real event in the aftermath of the
1991 earthquake that devastated Iran. In it a fictional film director (who is supposed to have made

Where . . .) sets out in a quest to find whether the
child protagonist of his former film is still alive
after the earthquake. With his young son Puya, he
travels by car to the city of Rudbar, into the region
where the quake hit the worst. They have a series
of brief encounters with peasants around the town
of Koker, whom they help in different ways. The
director finds a baby alone in the woods and gives
it to his mother as she arrives. He helps a woman
load a gas cylinder and offers a ride to a man who
had worked in his previous film. Later, Puya goes
exploring and finds a woman who lost a son in the
disaster and who reproaches God for his death.
Puya reminds her that God did not allow Abraham
to sacrifice Isaac. As they continue driving, they
find a boy, Mohammed, who also had worked in
the film. They go with him to a place where some
survivors are trying to install an aerial antenna to
watch the Argentina-Brazil World Cup soccer
match. The father does not understand the villagers' frantic efforts to watch the game, while his
son sympathizes with them. As the film draws to
an end, the focus on finding the boy is gradually
lost, replaced by the images of life slowly resurging
amidst the ruins. As Kiarostami has said, "Finally, I
felt that perhaps it was more important to help the
survivors who bore no recognizable faces, but
were making every effort to start a new life for
themselves under very difficult conditions and in
the midst of an environment of natural beauty that
was going on with its old ways as if nothing had
happened. Such is life, it seemed to tell them, go
on, seize the day."

Just as *And Life Goes On* had been inspired in
the events surrounding the making of *Where Is My
Friend's Home,* Kiarostami's next film also sprang
up from the shooting of *And Life Goes On*. This
final entry in his "Koker trilogy" (so named after
the town where the three movies take place) is
entitled *Through the Olive Trees* (1994). This movie,
which film theorist Laura Mulvey cites as a proof
that cinema can "still be surprising, beautiful and
cerebral," concerns the efforts of a poor, illiterate
young man to marry a woman against the opposi-

tion of her family and the force of village tradition. By "sheer luck," they are cast opposite each other as actors in *And Life Goes On*. Throughout the movie, the viewers accompany the young man's persistent efforts to glean even a word from the woman, who does not even condescend to talk with him. As Mulvey writes, ". . . Kiarostami's film seemed to have more in common with the avant-garde than with art cinema, while his way of storytelling, shooting and dealing with cinematic reality touched on ideas familiar to film theory but defying any expected aesthetic and analytic framework. My sense of intellectual and aesthetic uncertainty was followed by a feeling of intense curiosity."

Kiarostami's next feature as a director was his most celebrated film, *A Taste of Cherry*. The story follows the attempts by a middle-aged man to recruit a helper among the unemployed day workers gathered in the outskirts of Tehran. He drives through the city, stopping here and there to approach the men, who clearly are appalled by his proposal. We soon learn that the man is under a terrible predicament and wants to commit suicide by taking sleeping pills. He needs a man who will go the next morning to the little tree that he has selected to mark his grave and bury him. Three men are the main targets of his effort: a young soldier, a student of Islamic theology, and an old man. Each of them tries to give him a reason not to kill himself. Kiarostami's strategy was to never show the actor playing the driver and to show the passengers in a two-shot, except in the case of the third passenger. In fact, for most of the film, Kiarostami himself occupied the driver's seat, with his camera and microphone ready to capture the interlocutor's thoughts on why life is worth living.

Critics in the West were enthusiastic. Richard Corliss in *Time* magazine proclaimed it simply "The Best Film of The Year." And Stephen Holden in the *New York Times* wrote that "Mr. Kiarostami, like no other filmmaker, has a vision of human scale that is simultaneously epic and precisely minuscule." Indeed, the celebrated Japanese

filmmaker AKIRA KUROSAWA praised Kiarostami as a rightful successor of SATYAJIT RAY, as a filmmaker with the ability to touch everyone, regardless of nationality, with stories about the human condition. "When Satyajit Ray died," said Kurosawa, "I became quite depressed, but after watching Kiarostami's films, I thought God had found the right person to take his place."

Identity is precisely the subject of another of Kiarostami's better-known films. *Close-up* (1989) started when Kiarostami saw a newspaper account of a real-life situation indirectly involving his fellow filmmaker Mohsen Makhmalbaf. A young man, Hossain Sabzian, had been accused of fraud and was going to trial. Earlier, Sabzian had impersonated Makhmalbaf and gotten some money from a family whom he persuaded to appear in a film he was supposedly making. Kiarostami took his cameras to the court and obtained the judge's approval to film all the involved parties, including the testimony of the accused, who explained, in pathetic tones, how Makhmalbaf was his hero and how he was tempted to initiate the charade when a woman confused him, a poor nobody, with the director while he was busy reading a film book on a bus. The woman was a member of the family who was accusing him of fraud. The movie, highly self-referential, was a dazzling example of Kiarostami's style and thematic concerns, mixing reality with fiction and providing a chance to reflect on the importance of cinephilia in Iran as well as on the role of filmmakers as bearers of an ethical as well as aesthetical mission.

The director's latest film to reach the West is *The Wind Will Carry Us*. In this film, Behzad, a television journalist, arrives at a remote village with the intention of filming the funeral of a 100-year-old woman, wherein the women of the town are supposed to scratch and scar their faces in mourning. As he arrives, however, it turns out that the woman is still ailing, and he has to wait in town for her imminent death. The city slicker, wielding a mobile phone and accompanied by a crew (which is unseen, but talked about throughout the picture), concocts a story about a buried treasure and enlists the help of a local boy to be his informer and main liaison with the villagers. Whenever he receives a phone call, he must drive to the top of a hill at the cemetery to be able to talk with the city. In one of these calls, he learns that by waiting for the woman's burial he is missing the funeral of one of his own relatives in the city. While he impatiently awaits the woman's death, Behzad also meets a worker who is digging a hole for some "telecommunications" purpose and the young fiancée of the man, whom he tries in vain to entice with flirtations. The title of the film is inspired by a line from an erotic poem by Foroogh Farrokhzaad (1935–67), a poet much revered in Iran.

For critic Jonathan Rosenbaum, "The particular ethics of *The Wind Will Carry Us* consist largely of Kiarostami reflecting on his own practice as a 'media person' exploiting poor people: Behzad may be the closest thing in Kiarostami's work to a critical self-portrait, at least since the hero in his highly uncharacteristic 1977 feature *Report*." As Rosenbaum also notes, the director here follows his concern of contrasting city to village and the power of the middle-class protagonists of his films in contrast with the working-class peasants who often become their employees, a theme that runs through the Koker trilogy as well as—in reverse—*Close-up* and finally *The Wind Will Carry Us.*

One of Kiarostami's most notable features is the complex blending of fiction and documentary. Casting nonprofessional actors, often children, Kiarostami departs from rigid distinctions between fact and fiction. His production strategies resemble those of postwar Italian films, but, as he explained to Pat Aufderheide, this is more due to circumstantial factors than to imitation: "Of course, I began watching movies by watching Italian neorealism, and I do feel a kinship with that work. But it's more a question of congruence of taste than it is a decision to follow their example." And he adds: "I think the most important and obvious reason

why there is a similarity is the similarity between the present situation of Iran and of postwar Italy. Italy then was under the pressure of the postwar situation, and we have similar circumstances. Another similarity that may provoke parallels is that I don't adapt from literature or mythology. I get my stories from daily life, like they did. I also don't have big, expensive sets and elaborate production values and special effects. My films are low budget."

The filmmaker's work has been subjected, however, to more overtly political readings. One of them is by Hamid Dabashi, an Iranian-born sociologist who works at Columbia University. He posits two historical paradigmatic discourses in Iranian literary culture, those of theocentricity and homocentricity. He situates Kiarostami within that dialectic on the side of homocentricity, following a long tradition of Persian poets, as opposed to prophets. For Dabashi, Kiarostami's cinema "puts forward a radically subversive reading of a culture of inhibition brutally institutionalized by a theocratic revolution." Furthermore, "If Kiarostami is successful in holding our attention constant for a while and thus teaching us to see differently—he has endured so far for some twenty-five years, through an imperial dictatorship, via a gut-wrenching revolution, in the thaws of an Islamic theocracy—he will map out the principal contours of a post-metaphysical mode of being in which no ideology, no absolutist claim to truth, no metanarrative of salvation, ever will monopolize the definition of our 'identity.'"

Lately, Kiarostami has adopted the latest technologies for his cinematic work. The filmmaker's latest film, still unreleased at the writing, is a documentary on AIDS in Africa. And he is planning to shoot his next project in digital video. In a review of French filmmaker AGNÈS VARDA's *The Gleaners and I,* Rosenbaum wrote: "One obvious thing that digital video does is place people on both sides of the camera on something that more nearly resembles an equal footing. A 35-millimeter camera creates something like apartheid between filmmakers and their typical subjects, fictional or nonfictional—because between them stand an entire industry, an ideology, and a great deal of money and equipment. This is the subject of many of Abbas Kiarostami's major features, including *Homework, Close-up, Life and Nothing More, Through the Olive Trees,* and *The Wind Will Carry Us;* he recently shifted to DV in part because he wanted to achieve something closer to equality with whom and what he shoots."

Other Films *Bread and Alley* (short film, 1970); *The Traveler* (Kiarostami's first feature, 1972); *The Report* (1977); *Case No. 1 Case No. 2* (1979).

References Afshari, Reza, "An Essay on Scholarship, Human Rights, and State Legitimacy: The Case of the Islamic Republic of Iran," *Human Rights Quarterly* 18, no. 3 (1996): 544–593; Aufderheide, Pat, "Real Life Is More Important Than Cinema, An Interview with Abbas Kiarostami," *Cineaste* 21, no. 3 (1995): 31–33; Cheshire, Geoffrey, "Abbas Kiarostami, A Cinema of Questions," *Film Comment* 32, no. 4 (July–August 1996): 34–42; Dabashi, Hamid, "Re-Reading Reality: Kiarostami's *Through the Olive Trees* and the Cultural Politics of a Post-Revolutionary Aesthetics," *Critical Studies: Iran and Middle East* 63, no. 79 (1995); Mulvey, Laura, "Kiarostami's Uncertainty Principle," *Sight and Sound* 8, no. 6 (June 1998): 24–27; Rosen, Miriam, "The Camera of Art: An Interview with Abbas Kiarostami," *Cineaste* 19, nos. 2–3 (1993): 38–40; Rosenbaum, Jonathan, "Precious Leftovers, *The Gleaners and I,*" *Chicago Reader,* May 11, 2001.

—F.A.

Kieślowski, Krzysztof (1941–1996) Krzysztof Kieślowski was one of the most distinguished directors to emerge from Poland during the late 1970s. Master of both documentary and narrative film, Kieślowski established himself as a master technician and storyteller, evoking unusual images and thoughtful character studies in his work. His reputation spread among film circles by virtue of his provocative, personal vision, though he was never a major commercial success. Yet, with his talent and drive, he produced over 20 documentaries

and 10 features, as well as shorts and films for television, which garnered him much critical praise.

Krzysztof Kieślowski was born on June 27, 1941, in Warsaw. He graduated from the prestigious Lódź Film School in 1969, where other noted Polish filmmakers—ANDRZEJ WAJDA, ROMAN POLANSKI, Skolimowski, Zanussi—also graduated. In his early documentaries he was, as Annette Insdorf suggests, "painfully aware of the discrepancies between screen images and the daily life of most Polish people; he turned his quietly inquisitive camera to a real—if bleak—world." Kieślowski emphasizes the reality of the society he documents: the working class, the economic structure of institutions, and the relationship between individuals and institutions. *From the City of Lodz* (1969), *I Was a Soldier* (1970), *Factory* (1970), and *Before the Rally* (1971) evince themes of workers at odds with the government and the general state of affairs in Polish life. For example, *From the City of Lodz* is a portrait of the town, and the town's unique eccentricities, shown in all of its deprivation—ruins, hovels, and foul sanitation practices. *Before the Rally* shows two Polish race car drivers as they prepare for the Monte Carlo rally. Their failure to finish the race may be construed as an allegory of Poland's economic and individual shortcomings. Other early documentaries include *Worker's '71* (1972), a film about a worker's strike, and *Hospital* (1976), which documents a group of surgeons on a 32-hour shift. Kieślowski mostly satirizes the bureaucracy in these films, shedding light on the injustices suffered by many individuals.

Kieślowski has said that shooting documentaries enabled him to film "a reality that is rich, magnificent, incommensurable, where nothing is repeated, where one cannot redo a take. Reality—and this is not a paradox—is the point of departure for the document. One merely has to believe totally in the dramaturgy of reality." According to Insdorf, Kieślowski "gradually [grew] into an artist by learning his craft, observing the world closely, and later developing a personal vision."

Indeed, Kieślowski's great subject, the plight of individuals in a constrictive society, is most clearly manifested in his narrative features. They retain the somber, if not pessimistic view of the world Kieślowski had clearly seen while making his documentaries. His first full-length feature, *The Scar* (1976), is a story about a man put in charge of the construction of a new chemical factory. Though his intentions are admirable, the townspeople are more concerned with their immediately tangible needs, and do not see the long-term benefits of a new factory. Growing more disillusioned, the man gives up the post. The film initiates themes that dominate Kieślowski's later work: disillusionment, conflict between individuals, and moral ambiguity. *Camera Buff* (1979) was a critical success and helped Kieślowski's reputation grow outside of Poland and Europe. It is an allegorical tale about a man who, after buying an 8-mm camera, begins to record his life and surroundings. Filming at work, the man faces censorship charges, which have extreme ramifications; as a result of his time spent filming, his wife, disillusioned with their marriage, leaves him. The complex images in the film are poignant, satiric commentaries on film sense and personal meaning in a cruel, harsh environment. Essentially, the protagonist loses his job, wife, and child because of his passion for the camera. The film is "about a character," Kieślowski said, where "humor is a manifestation of my sympathy, of sympathy for human miseries that can be funny." This idea—sympathy for human miseries—is found in *Blind Chance* (1981), where there are three different outcomes to the protagonist's life, stemming from a seemingly banal incident at the beginning of the film; and in *No End* (1984), where the daily lives of people are affected by a ghost.

Kieślowski's *Decalogue* (1988) is often recognized as his greatest achievement. The *Decalogue* is a series of 10 short films, made for television, based on the Ten Commandments. Two of these, *A Short Film about Killing* (1988) and *A Short Film about Love* (1988) were extended and released as features. *A Short Film about Killing* received the Grand Jury Prize at the Cannes Film Festival. The *Decalogue* brought Kieślowski international attention. "*Decalogue* is an attempt to narrate ten stories about ten or twenty individuals," he has said, "who—caught in a struggle precisely because of these and not other circumstances, circumstances which are fictitious but which could occur in every life—suddenly realize that they're going round and round in circles, that they're not achieving what they want." The universality of the themes presented in the *Decalogue* enabled viewers to locate their own beliefs and understandings of morality, law, religion, and politics. Insdorf notes, "Rather than asking us to be like-minded, the *Decalogue* provokes contemplation of how the spirit of the commandments might still be applicable to our daily lives."

The Double Life of Veronique (1991), a story about a young woman who has a double and thus leads a parallel life, brought Kieślowski more recognition as a world-class filmmaker. Lead actress Irene Jacob won the best actress award at the Cannes Film Festival. The film allows viewers to reflect on the ties that bind people to outside forces, forces we are unable to contain. Kieślowski's final three films form his *Three Colors* trilogy: *Blue* (1993), *White* (1993), and *Red* (1994). *Blue* won best film at the Venice Film Festival and lead actress Juliette Binoche won best actress. The films are loosely based on the concepts of liberty, equality, and fraternity, which are recurring themes in all three films. All three films are visually stunning, with bright, distinct colors juxtaposed with darker hues and shadows, and are characterized by individuals who seek meaning and existence in a world where things often seem futile and people distant or cruel. Kieślowski said, "All the three films are about people who have some sort of intuition or sensibility, who have gut feelings." In all three films, the characters, whether faced with tragedy or compassion, forge their own decisions and conclusions based on their needs or initial impulses. The protagonists, like so many in Kieślowski's work, struggle with the ambiguous relationship between reason and feeling. In the end, these films invoke similar feelings in audiences, which is why they are so compelling and appealing.

Kieślowski died of a heart attack in 1996. He was a self-admitted pessimist, and many of his films depict a decidedly somber picture of the world. However, his characters are also noble, inquisitive, and often admirable. Insdorf states that Kieślowski deals with "chance, faith, and self-delusion" in his films, and deals with them in a variety of ways and through an array of themes. Kieślowski's cinema is enriching, for his documentaries of real people and his complex characterizations in his features show true sides of human nature. In both documentary and narrative film, Kieślowski was a master, and his films provide rich, enjoyable, and arresting depictions of individuals very familiar to all audiences.

Other Films *The Calm* (1976); *I Don't Know* (1977); *A Short Working Day* (1981).

References Insdorf, Annette, *Double Lives, Second Chances* (New York: Miramax Books, 1999); Stok, Danusia, *Kieślowski on Kieślowski* (London: Faber and Faber, 1993).

—W.V.

Korda, Alexander (1893–1956)

Director of a handful of movie masterpieces, a producer/studio mogul responsible for many dozens more, and a true man of the world, Alexander Korda possessed an artistry that extended well past his more than a hundred films and into a colorful lifestyle that was his greatest achievement. He was outsized in many ways, in his private and public passions, in his extravagance, in his ambitions, in his failures as well as his achievements, and in his ability to win the undying loyalty of his associates. "He pressed a button and the greatest story tellers of the world went to work to turn out plots and scenarios," writes biographer Paul Tabori, "a man who lifted one finger and a herd of elephants or a pride of lions were caged for his pleasure. To his countless associates he was a charmer with a foreign accent and a wonderful command of invec-

tive; to his actors, directors, technicians he was something of a father-figure—as, indeed, he often called them 'my children.'"

He was born Sandor Laszlo Kellner on September 16, 1893, in the tiny Hungarian village of Pusztaturpaszto, the son of a farm bailiff. He was 13 years old when his father died and the family relocated to Budapest. Living in grinding poverty, he attended school and in his after hours wrote articles for a liberal daily newspaper. He adopted the surname Korda, from a journalistic term, "sursum corda" (meaning, "lift up your hearts"). He left school before graduating and, driven by the wanderlust that would afflict him for the rest of his life, departed for Paris to pursue a writing career. That did not work out, but he returned to Hungary aflame with a new enthusiasm, motion pictures.

He entered films working as a title writer for Pictograph Films, Budapest. His first directorial effort was *The Duped Journalist,* in 1915, followed by six more productions. Three years later he formed his own production unit, Corvin Films, in a northeastern suburb of Budapest. His first wife, Maria Corda, appeared in several of his films and would be featured in other subsequent productions. Although by this time he had become the leading film producer in Hungary, and had publicly declared his undying enthusiasm for the future of Hungarian film production, he had to flee the country after the Great War, when the Hungarian Soviet Republic was overthrown by Admiral Horthy's anti-Semitic and anti-liberal White Army.

He went to Vienna in 1919 and a few years later formed Korda-Films in Berlin. Ever on the move, he came to Hollywood and First National Pictures in 1927 to make *The Private Life of Helen of Troy,* starring his wife as Helen. Its sly wit and historical anachronisms would mark many of his later pictures; and its success earned him a series of features starring the actress Billie Dove. But the Hollywood personal and professional lifestyle irritated him. "I found working in Hollywood rather difficult," he said later. "They talk too much shop. Shop, shop, shop, from daybreak to sunset and on to daybreak again. There are very few people out there who are possessed of any general culture."

He left Hollywood in 1930, disgruntled at the experience, and, after directing three films in France, including the classic *Marius* (1931), went to London, where, as the founder of London Films and the builder of Denham Studios, he directed one of the most phenomenally popular British films of the day, *The Private Life of Henry VIII* (1932). While it is not true that it was the first British film to win international acclaim, it undeniably put Korda and his cast—including Charles Laughton, Merle Oberon (who would become his second wife), Binnie Barnes, and Robert Donat—on the cinematic map. The film was a highly romanticized version of the life of England's King Henry VIII that skipped over the political and religious ramifications of his reign and concentrated on his marital status, beginning on the day of Anne Boleyn's execution (the first wife, Catherine of Aragon, is not considered because, as an opening title explains, she was too respectable) and depicting the succession of wives thereafter. This was a king seen as a man rather than the other way around—history seen from bottom to top, as gossip, through the keyhole, as it were. Aside from the films he directed—*The Private Life of Don Juan* (1934), starring his old friend Douglas Fairbanks, Sr., in his last picture; *Rembrandt* (1936), with Charles Laughton in the title role; *That Hamilton Woman* (1941), pairing LAURENCE OLIVIER and Vivien Leigh as Admiral Nelson and his mistress Emma Hamilton—he supervised many others, including: *Catherine the Great* (1934); *The Scarlet Pimpernel* (1934), a story of the French Revolution with Leslie Howard; *The Drum* (1936), a justification of English imperialism in India; *The Four Feathers* (1938), a saga of English colonialism in the Sudan; *The Thief of Bagdad* (1940), an Oriental phantasmagoria starring Sabu; *The Fallen Idol* (1949), based on the short novel by Graham Greene; and *The Third Man* (1949), based on

another Greene script. After losing control of the Denham Studios in 1938, he relocated to Hollywood during the first two years of World War II to make *That Hamilton Woman* (for which he was knighted in 1942), occasionally returning to London on several projects.

That Hamilton Woman was not just a piece of patriotic puffery about the romance between Lord Nelson and Lady Emma Hamilton. Korda had been empowered by Winston Churchill himself to use this film to promote the British cause against Germany and to sway the isolationist American Congress and press toward an interventionist stance. Thus, the characters of Nelson and Napoleon, the antagonists of the film, would in actuality be "stand-ins" for Winston Churchill and Adolf Hitler. Indeed, the film's pro-British sentiments provoked the Foreign Relations Committee to order Korda to appear and justify his film. The bombing of Pearl Harbor, however, ended all that. Meanwhile, the film ran afoul of the Hollywood Production Code for other reasons, namely, it seemed to condone the adultery between Nelson and Hamilton. It was released only after Korda inserted some dialogue in which Nelson was made to admit the wrongness of his action.

After the war he reorganized London Films and founded the British Film Academy (now the British Academy of Film and Television Arts). Mention should be made that collaborating with him throughout his career were his two talented brothers, Zoltan, who also directed, and Vincent, who was an art director. Whether he directed or produced, all of his films are noteworthy for distinctive moments and affecting scenes—Laughton's card-playing banter with his prospective wife, Anne of Cleves (Elsa Lanchester), in *Private Life of Henry VIII;* Don Juan's (Douglas Fairbanks) confrontation on a theater stage with the actor impersonating him in *The Private Life of Don Juan;* Laughton again, as the aging Rembrandt surveying his wrinkled face in a cracked mirror, declaiming to himself, "Vanity, vanity; all is vanity. . . .";

Sabu's tussle with the giant spider in *The Thief of Bagdad;* Lady Hamilton's (Vivien Leigh) eager politicking with the queen of Naples on behalf of her lover, Admiral Nelson (Laurence Olivier); Orson Welles as Harry Lime emerging from the dark doorway in *The Third Man.*

Alexander Korda died of a heart attack in London on January 23, 1956. Reportedly, he was once asked who could be his successor after his death. "I don't know," he replied with a smile. "You see—I don't grow on trees." Biographer Tabori concludes that "films were his life and his obsession." Beneath his flamboyant lifestyle and undeniable artistry, moreover, was a solid understanding of the sheer *craft* of the medium: "He became one of the greatest technicians of the cinema and had every detail of its very complicated techniques at his fingertips; in set design or camera angles, problems of sound recording or make-up he could speak with equal authority."

Other Films *Man of Gold* (1918); *A Modern Dubarry* (1926); *The Stolen Bride* (1927); *Her Private Life* (1929); *Perfect Strangers* (1945); *An Ideal Husband* (1947).

References Kulik, Karol, *Korda: The Man Who Could Work Miracles* (New Rochelle, N.Y.: Arlington House Publishers, 1975); Slide, Anthony, *Fifty Classic British Films, 1932–1982* (New York: Dover, 1985); Tabori, Paul, *Alexander Korda: A Biography* (New York: Living Books, 1966).

—J.C.T.

Kozintsev, Grigori (1905–1973)

The career of Grigori Kozintsev was shaped by the artistic and theatrical experimentalism and turmoil of the Soviet Revolution, which took place as he was growing up. Consequently, his work has been overshadowed by the achievements of Sergei Eisenstein, Vsevolod Pudovkin, and the other great Soviet pioneers of the 1920s. Indeed, his most famous films, adaptations of Shakespeare and Cervantes, would not be made until after the death of Joseph Stalin in 1953. Not many of his films were easily available in the United States during the Cold War, when the cinema studies movement was just getting underway. A breakthrough for Kozintsev came in 1971 when his great adaptation of *King Lear* was featured at the World Shakespeare Congress held in Vancouver, Canada, with Kozintsev attending to introduce his film to other Shakespeareans.

A Ukrainian by nationality, Kozintsev was born in Kiev on March 22, 1905. By the time he was 12, the Bolsheviks had seized power. Before turning to theatre and film during the 1920s, Kozintsev studied art under the modernist painter Alexandra Exter. He found employment as a scene painter at the Lenin Theatre (formerly the Solutzovsky Theatre) in Kiev, where he formed a friendship with another artist, Sergei Yutkevitch, who would also go on to direct films, and with Leonid Trauberg, with whom he collaborated on his first several films, starting with *The Adventures of Oktyabrina* in 1924, and including their trilogy, which won the Stalin Prize in 1941: *The Youth of Maxim* (1935), *The Return of Maxim* (1937), and *The Vyborg Side* (1939). In 1921 they had founded the experimental Factory of the Eccentric Actor (FEKS), which carried over from theater to film and influenced the style of their later work. By 1947 their partnership ended, with Trauberg turning to screenwriting as Kozintsev continued to direct.

During the last phase of his career, Kozintsev created his most famous adaptations, starting with the classic Cervantes novel *Don Quixote* (1957), adapted by Yevgeni Schwartz, followed by Kozintsev's own adaptations of *Hamlet* (1963) and *King Lear* (1971), both films based on the Russian translations of Boris Pasternak. These latter are among the very best adaptations of Shakespeare ever filmed, a little old-fashioned, perhaps, in their interpretations of the plays, but beautifully realized and wonderfully acted by Innokenti Smoktunovski as Hamlet and Yuri Yarvet, whose native language was Estonian rather than Russian, as an unforgettable King Lear. Kozintsev died in Leningrad on May 11, 1973, finally recognized in the West as a major talent.

References Kozintsev, Grigori, *King Lear: The Space of Tragedy* (Berkeley: University of California Press, 1977); Kozintsev, G., *Shakespeare: Time and Conscience* (New York: Hill & Wang, 1966); Leaming, Barbara, *Grigori Kozintsev* (Boston: Twayne, 1980).

—J.M.W.

Kubrick, Stanley (1928–1999)

In a career that spanned 40 years—but included a mere baker's dozen of feature films, released in ever slower sequence as his tendencies toward reclusiveness and extended development of projects became more pronounced—Stanley Kubrick established a distinctive but divided reputation as a director, famous for controversy and unpredictability as much as for meticulous professionalism and technical innovation; and for producing works that have consistently divided critics as well as broader audiences. Kubrick famously got memorable performances from his best actors (think of Peter Sellers in *Dr. Strangelove* [1964] or Jack Nicholson in *The Shining* [1980]), but he also provoked actors with demanding and often lengthy shooting schedules and multiple retakes of even minor scenes. The Kubrick films *2001: A Space Odyssey* (1968) and *The Shining* essentially claimed for the big-budget cinematic mainstream the previously pulpish genres of science fiction and popular horror; but he was equally at home adapting relatively obscure literary works like William Makepeace Thackeray's *Barry Lyndon* (1975) or Arthur Schnitzler's *Traumnovelle* (the source for *Eyes Wide Shut* [1999]), working in established genres like the war film (*Paths of Glory* [1957] and *Full Metal Jacket* [1987]), or inventing entirely new categories of film (as he did most notably in the nuclear war comedy *Dr. Strangelove*).

The range of genres across which Kubrick worked makes his body of films difficult to categorize, although some basic common ground can be found. On a thematic level, all Kubrick's films feature a dark, sometimes even malevolent skepticism about human nature (but essentially male human nature; none of Kubrick's work shows much of an effort to understand women's psyches). In structural terms, many of his works involve highly divided plots (most obvious, perhaps, in *Full Metal Jacket,* but characteristic of other Kubrick films as well). On a technical level, they are marked by striking visual compositions (especially favoring a haunting symmetry), fluid camera movements (often employing newly developed technologies), and memorable use of musical scores.

Kubrick was born on July 26, 1928, in the Bronx, to a family of Romanian heritage. Critic Anthony Lane finds it highly significant that his father gave the young boy a still camera and taught him to play chess, "an inspired, if slightly ominous, combination." Kubrick, like Nabokov, continues Lane, "would later be hailed as the grand master of aesthetic strategy—or, if you prefer, as the Bobby Fischer of cinema, the hermit wonk who used his players like pawns and trapped his harried audiences in check." When Kubrick was 17, he got a job at *Look* magazine and continued in the position for four years before resuming his education. But in a very real sense, this *was* his education, as he noted to interviewer Alexander Walker: "Four and a half years of working for *Look* magazine, traveling all over America, seeing how things worked and the way people behaved, gave me some useful insights plus important experience in photography." He also cites MAX OPHULS's films, Stanislavsky's acting methods, and VSEVELOD ILLARIONOVICH PUDOVKIN's *Film Technique* as seminal influences on his camera strategies and directing and editing practices. After fashioning a trio of short documentaries, beginning with the self-financed *Day of the Fight* (1951), Kubrick plunged into feature films with *Fear and Desire* (1953), a war film about four soldiers lost behind enemy lines in an unnamed war. He followed this up with *Killer's Kiss* (1955), a boxing picture shot in New York City locations. He all but disowns the picture: "The only distinction I would claim for it is that, to the best of my belief, no one at the time had ever made a feature film in such amateur circumstances and then obtained world-wide distribution for it." More interesting was the noirish *The Killing* (1956), a racetrack heist tale enlivened by Sterling Hayden's portrayal of a just-paroled con man and the script assistance of novelist Jim Thompson. It was also the first film on which Kubrick was proud to have his name.

It is with *Paths of Glory* (1957), however, that Kubrick comes into his own. Again working with Thompson on the script, and with Kirk Douglas as his leading actor, Kubrick fashions a devastating critique of military hierarchies and class systems amid a brutal portrait of the trench warfare of World War I. *Paths* is divided between battle action, which re-creates much of the horror of the trenches, and a court-martial of three soldiers accused of refusing to follow orders, chosen to be made examples for the rest of the fighting forces. The battle sequences feature aggressively filmed dramatic action reinforced by the sounds of war, while the court-martial proceeds in relative silence, framed by the ironic elegance of a French chateau. If the horrors of war provide the story's background, its narrative focuses even more decisively on the French high command's class-based indifference to the plight of the common soldier.

Douglas would land Kubrick his next directing job, taking over the troubled shooting of *Spartacus* (1960) from director ANTHONY MANN. The epic account of a Roman gladiator who led a slave revolt remains a classic among the era's many historical reenactments of the Roman past, but Kubrick's inability to exert control over the studio's final cut cemented his disenchantment with the Hollywood studio system. After this, he moved to the semirural region of Hertfordshire, just outside London, and would for the rest of his career direct at an ocean and a continent's distance from Hollywood. It is true, declared British critic Alexander Walker in 1971, that Kubrick's seclusion in the English countryside assured him a quiet place "where time, energy, inspiration, confidence cannot be eroded by too much contact with the world"; however, continues Walker, it was also a

location where he "finds it easy and attractive to keep in contact with the international film scene, and, indeed, with the larger world, from wherever he happens to be."

His distrust of studio systems would be further reinforced by the difficulties surrounding his adaptation of Vladimir Nabokov's controversial novel *Lolita* (1962). Kubrick can be said, in response to the constraints of the time, to have found a way to substitute Humbert's ironic subjectivity (relying heavily on James Mason's insightful portrayal) for the more open sensuality the novel would seem to have demanded, but the resulting film was still controversial and suffered at the hands of the Hollywood censors. "I wasn't able to give any weight at all to the erotic aspect of Humbert's relationship with Lolita in the film," Kubrick told interviewer Gene D. Phillips, "and because I could only hint at the true nature of his attraction to Lolita, it was assumed too quickly by filmgoers that Humbert was in love with her. In the novel this comes as a discovery at the end, when Lolita is no longer a nymphet but a pregnant housewife; and it's this encounter, and the sudden realization of his love for her, that is one of the most poignant elements of the story." Still, many critics, including Pauline Kael, liked the results. "The surprise of *Lolita* is how enjoyable it is; it's the first new American comedy since those great days in the forties when Preston Sturges created comedy with verbal slapstick. *Lolita* is black slapstick and at times it's so far out that you gasp as you laugh."

If *Paths of Glory* established Kubrick as a director, his next project, *Dr. Strangelove, or How I Learned to Stop Worrying and Love the Bomb* (1964), loosely based on Peter George's novel, *Red Alert,* secured his independence. A wild, dark comedy about nuclear holocaust, the film employs a talented cast (most notably including Peter Sellers, in a range of roles, and George C. Scott) to create a menagerie of human grotesques responsible for carrying out the nightmare scenario of accidental nuclear destruction. Starkly outrageous in its portrait of out-of-control militarism, in its linkage of nuclear policy and Nazism, and in its celebratory rendition of the destruction of humanity, the film hardly seemed an obvious candidate for popular success in the duck-and-cover age of Cold War nuclear fears, but Kubrick's bleak slapstick hit a receptive nerve. "My idea of doing it as a nightmare comedy came in the early weeks of working on the screenplay," Kubrick told interviewer Phillips. "I found that in trying to put meat on the bones and to imagine the scenes fully, one had to keep leaving things out of it which were either absurd or paradoxical in order to keep it from being funny; and these things seem to be close to the heart of the scenes in question."

After four full years, *2001* appeared, based on Arthur C. Clarke's "The Sentinel," and marked a striking shift in tone, pace, and theme. About man's exploration of space, but also about intelligent life beyond Earth (and the possibility that that life has guided human development), with sideplots about violence as a principle underpinning human evolution, and the capabilities of artificial intelligence, and featuring the memorable psychedelic rollercoaster ride of its concluding segment, the film is a masterpiece of metaphysical mystery, working more through evocation than deliberate narrative. Regarding the celebrated opening sequence, where an ape discovers digital dexterity, Kubrick told interviewer Phillips: "Somebody said that man is the missing link between primitive apes and civilized human beings. You might say that the idea is inherent in the story of *2001* too. We are semicivilized, capable of cooperation and affection but needing some sort of transfiguration into a higher form of life." The film also involved Kubrick in extensive technical research, ensuring insofar as possible both the accuracy of his futurist vision and the technical means to bring it to the screen.

Kubrick followed *2001* with an adaptation of Anthony Burgess's 1962 novel, *Clockwork Orange.* Released in 1971, the film was a darkly dystopian nightmare vision of youth culture gone utterly awry, a portrait of an ultraviolent British future dominated by hedonist gangs inclined toward excess. Coming in the wake of a series of increasingly violent Hollywood releases (this was the era of SAM PECKINPAH's most active filmmaking, for example), its controversy was enhanced because the film's tone appeared deeply ambiguous, seemingly celebrating as much as condemning the dark violence of its vision, mixing brutality and slapstick, layering comic-book images into its most violent scenes, and offering a final "redemption" that plunged its hero back into the realm of gangster excess. Above all, the film was a kind of "dance of death." "It was necessary to find a way of stylizing the violence, just as Burgess does by his writing style," Kubrick explained to critic Andrew Bailey. "The ironic counterpoint of the music was certainly one of the ways of achieving this . . . and in a very broad sense, you could say that the violence is turned into dance, although, of course, it is in no way any kind of formal dance. But in cinematic terms, I should say that movement and music must inevitably be related to dance, just as the rotating space station and the docking Orion spaceship in *2001* moved to the 'Blue Danube.'" In 1974, disturbed about accounts of violent acts attributed to screenings of the film, he ordered it pulled from circulation in Britain, although it remained in release elsewhere.

In no subsequent film has Kubrick as successfully conveyed his vision or attained such solid commercial and critical acclaim. It is less a matter of lost control of craft—he continued to pioneer new film techniques, to bring actors to masterful exertions, and to produce films of elegant technical mastery, although continuity flaws, a mark of his method, became increasingly apparent—than of a faltering unity of vision, perhaps exacerbated by an increasing obsessiveness (evident in the slowing pace of releases and the multiplying tales of multiple takes). After *Clockwork Orange* (and several failed projects), Kubrick shifted gears again with *Barry Lyndon,* a slow-paced, narrative-heavy period piece set in the 18th century. The vision of humanity offered in its leisurely tour through battlefields and drawing rooms of the era is every bit as dark as that in his earlier work, although the restraint of the period style and the elegance of the settings somewhat ameliorate the pessimism of the tale. *The Shining* (1980) transforms Stephen King's pulp novel into a richly envisioned but distinctly interior meditation on insanity, spiced with the occultism and cathartic bursts of violence the genre demands. Kubrick contributed to the Vietnam genre of the later 1980s with *Full Metal Jacket* (1987), but the bitter antiwar drama suffers from a starkly split narrative, and its distanced detachment compares poorly with *Platoon*'s more vital grunt's-eye view of the war, which it had the misfortune to follow in release. Kubrick's last film, *Eyes Wide Shut* (1999), a dreamy, dark allegory about eroticism and human desire (and quite strikingly of desire rather than fulfillment), released shortly after the director's death, received a decidedly mixed reception, divided between those who celebrated its brilliance and those who found its allusive ambiguities merely irritating.

In a career highlighted by long development and work on multiple projects, Kubrick is almost as famous for films that were never made as for those he finished. Particularly noteworthy among these is *One-Eyed Jacks,* a project with Marlon Brando that had faltered by 1961, and an epic picture about Napoleon, envisioned by Kubrick in the late 1960s (and alluded to in both *Clockwork Orange*'s musical choices and *Barry Lyndon*'s emblematic final scene). Another long-term project, *A.I.* (for artificial intelligence), has been taken over by STEVEN SPIELBERG and is slated for release in summer 2001. Kubrick's undoubted genius tends to obscure an essential emptiness in his films, declares critic Anthony Lane: "He wanted to make everything new—the plushest costume drama ever, the most baroque science fiction, the war to end all wars—but, for all his erudition, he rarely paused to ponder what might lie in the bedrock of the old, or the ordinary, or the much loved." Kubrick died on March 7, 1999.

Other Films *Flying Padre* (1951); *The Seafarers* (1952).

References Kagan, Norman, *The Cinema of Stanley Kubrick* (New York: Holt, Rinehart and Winston, 1972); Lane, Anthony, "The Last Emperor: How Stanley Kubrick Called the World to Order," *The New Yorker,* March 22, 1999, pp. 120–123; LoBrutto, Vincent, *Stanley Kubrick: A Biography* (New York: Donald I. Fine, 1997); Nelson, Thomas Allen, *Kubrick: Inside a Film Artist's Maze* (Bloomington: Indiana University Press, 1982); Phillips, Gene D., *Stanley Kubrick: A Film Odyssey* (New York: Popular Library, 1975); Raphael, Frederick, *Eyes Wide Open: A Memoir of Stanley Kubrick* (New York: Ballantine Books, 1999).

—T. Prasch

Kurosawa, Akira (1910–1998) Long regarded as Japan's most famous film director, Akira Kurosawa has successfully breached the gulf between Western and Eastern cinema. He was born in Tokyo on March 23, 1910, the youngest of eight children, to Isamu and Shima Kurosawa, of the Samurai class. Displaying an early interest in art, he was allowed to attend a private art school while still a teenager. Aspiring to become a commercial artist, he studied at the Doshusha School of Western Painting in 1927 and attended the Tokyo Academy of Fine Arts. He worked as a painter and illustrator with the Japan Proletariat Artists' Group before deciding on a career in film, when, in 1936, he began working as an assistant director at Toho Film Studios and eventually met the actor Toshiro Mifune, who would play a prominent part in many subsequent Kurosawa films, during the shooting of *Drunken Angel* (1947). He directed his first film, *Sugata Sanshiro* (*Judo Saga* [1943]) at the age of 33.

Kurosawa directed 10 more films during the 1940s, but it was his film *Rashomon,* released in 1950, that gained international attention when it won the 1951 Golden Lion Award from the Venice Film Festival and later won the Oscar for best foreign film in 1952. Influenced by such foreign directors as JOHN FORD and WILLIAM WYLER, and inspired by Western literary classics and popular culture, Kurosawa made well-plotted, character-driven films that crossed over cultural divides and were easily accessible to foreign viewers.

A number of remarkably successful films followed throughout the late 1940s and beyond, confirming Kurosawa's status as a world-class filmmaker. Especially famous for his samurai films, Kurosawa also directed many literary adaptations, including *The Idiot* (*Hakuchi* [1951]), adapted from Dostoyevsky's novel; *The Lower Depths* (*Donzoko* [1957]), based on Maxim Gorky's play; his celebrated *Throne of Blood* (*Kumonosu-jo* [1957], aka *The Castle of the Spider's Web*), loosely adapted from Shakespeare's *Macbeth;* and contemporary dramas, such as the detective thrillers *Stray Dog* (*Nora inu* [1949]) and *High and Low* (*Tengoku to jigoku* [1963]); social-problem films, like *I Live in Fear* (*Ikimono no kiroku* [1955], aka *Record of a Living Being*), treating the post-Hiroshima "fear" of nuclear devastation, and *Red Beard* (*Akahige* [1965]), which treats problems in bringing modern medicine to tradition-bound Japan; and intensely moving character-driven dramas, particularly *To Live* (*Ikiru* [1952]), one of the screen's most poignant depictions of an elderly man facing death. It is worth noting here that in his last film, *Madadayo* (*No, Not Yet* [1993]), Kurosawa returned to the theme of a life well lived in telling the story of a retired professor. Quite apart from their subject matter and acting, these and other films display Kurosawa's genius for wide-screen formats, composition in depth, and the employment of deep-focus shots.

Of course, Kurosawa's fame for many viewers resides in his *jidai-geki* films, or period costume films, such as *Shichinin no samurai* (*The Seven Samurai* [1954]), *Yojimbo* (*The Bodyguard* [1960]), and *Sanjuro* (1962), described as "the thinking man's *Yojimbo,*" which attracted his largest following abroad. Audiences admired these films for their visual beauty and spectacular action scenes, which combined long tracking shots, slow-motion sequences, and fast-paced editing. For the monumental battle sequences of *The Seven Samurai,* which he knew would be impossible to match-cut

in the way he envisioned them, Kurosawa used three cameras running simultaneously: "I put the 'A' camera in the most orthodox positions, used the 'B' camera for quick, decisive shots, and the 'C' camera as a kind of guerrilla unit," Kurosawa explained. He would continue to make use of this shooting technique throughout his career: "With multiple moving cameras," Kurosawa pointed out, "the actor has no time to figure out which one is shooting him."

In all of his films, Kurosawa delighted in framing his characters against vast backdrops of sky—not merely for the beauty of the shot, but to contrast the scope of man's endeavors with the enormity of the world around him, a technique especially evident in *Ran* (*Chaos* [1985]), his wonderfully visual and colorful transformation of Shakespeare's *King Lear*. His films were particularly admired in the West for their humanistic values; they unfailingly emphasize the dignity of the individual, deeply rooted in the Japanese samurai code of behavior, which extols working for the good of others and the subordination of selfish desires.

Since Kurosawa's films possessed universal appeal, European and American filmmakers openly imitated them. *Shichinin no samurai* and *Yojimbo,* for example, inspired two popular and influential westerns: *The Magnificent Seven* (1960) and *Per un pugno di dollari* (1964), released as *A Fistful of Dollars* in America in 1967. Even the American science fiction classic *Star Wars* (1977) was, in part, an imitation of *Kakushi toride no san akunin* (*The Hidden Fortress* [1958]).

During the 1960s Kurosawa's reputation began a steady decline from the pinnacle of success he had achieved in the late 1950s. In Japan, he was criticized for being too "western" and his choice of such writers as Shakespeare, Dostoyevsky, and Dashiell Hammett was viewed with suspicion. Some critics began to regard his work as outdated and overly melodramatic. In 1971, Kurosawa attempted suicide.

It is a further tribute to Akira Kurosawa that his recovery from the depths of the depression that had led to his suicide attempt was to result in the achievement of a new level of success that surpassed even his previous one. In 1975, he found regained respect with *Dersu Urzala,* a film made in the USSR. *Kagemusha (The Shadow Warrior),* his tale of a man who serves as a "double" for a dead feudal lord, won the Golden Palm from Cannes in 1980. In 1985, his version of *King Lear,* titled *Ran,* was released and later received an Oscar nomination for best director in 1986. Kurosawa's other films of this period include *Akira Kurosawa's Dreams* (1990), *Hachigatsu no Kyoshikyoku (Rhapsody in August* [1991]), and *Madadayo (No, Not Yet* [1993]). The latter film, set in Tokyo during World War II and the postwar era, was a portrait not only of a teacher, Michael Wilmington wrote in the *Chicago Tribune* but "also of the culture of Kurosawa's youth and young manhood, a meditation, like the films of his longtime model, John Ford, on a vanished past."

More popular internationally than in his native Japan, Kurosawa was courted many times by the Hollywood establishment. And although he was contracted to codirect a binational production of *Tora! Tora! Tora!* (1970), he left the project over a controversy with the producers and never came to Hollywood. In 1990, the Motion Picture Academy presented Kurosawa with an Honorary Award for cinematic accomplishments that have inspired, delighted, enriched, and entertained worldwide audiences and influenced filmmakers throughout the world. Two years later Kurosawa received the D. W. Griffith Award from the Directors Guild of America.

On Sunday, the 6th of September, 1998, the director was felled by a stroke at the age of 88. The world mourned his loss, and the Japanese government awarded him the People's Honor Award, a national prize given for high cultural achievement.

Kurosawa's experimental *Rashomon* is demonstrative of that achievement and deserves special attention. Kurosawa combined two short stories by Akutagawa: "In a Grove," which provides the basis for the main story, and "Rashomon," which con-

Akira Kurosawa

stitutes the frame of the main narrative. The film's title refers to the Rajomon gate in Kyoto, a main gate to the outer precincts of an ancient capital. Essentially, the central action involves a murder and the presumed rape of a young princess, the details of which are continually contradicted by the differing accounts given by the participants and witnesses. It not only opened the floodgates of Japanese cinema to the West, but also its treatment of the theme of the subjective relativity of truth has never been surpassed, although director MARTIN RITT took a crack at it when he directed a loose adaptation, *The Outrage* (1964). "Human beings are unable to be honest with themselves about themselves," writes Kurosawa. "They cannot talk about themselves without embellishing. . . . Egoism is a sin the human being carries with him from birth; it is the most difficult to redeem." Interestingly, Joseph Anderson and Donald Richie point out that this theme "is essentially un-Japanese," running "contrary to the prevailing philosophy of Japanese" filmmakers. Thus, even within his own culture, Kurosawa was a completely original talent. He has left a legacy of over 30 films that future generations may continue to enjoy.

"I don't really like talking about my films," Kurosawa once said. "Everything I want to say is in the film itself; for me to say anything more is, as the proverb goes, like 'drawing legs on a picture of a snake.'" However, Kurosawa's autobiographical essay, *Something Like an Autobiography,* published in 1982, contains many interesting insights into the man and his work.

Other Films *Men Who Tread on the Tiger's Tail* (*Tora no o wo fumu otokotachi* [1945]); *No Regrets for Our Youth* (*Waga seishun ni kuinashi*) and *Those Who Make Tomorrow* (*Asu o tsukuru hitobito* [both 1946]); *Drunken Angel* (*Yoidore tenshi* [1948]); *The Bad Sleep Well* (*Warui yatsu hodo yoku nemuru* [1960]); *Dodes'ka-den* (1970).

References Anderson, Joseph L., and Donald Richie, *The Japanese Film: Art and Industry* (Princeton, N.J.: Princeton University Press, 1982); Ficarra, Carmen, "The Director's Heart: Akira Kurosawa, 1910–1998," *MovieMaker Magazine* 31 (December 1998); Kurosawa, Akira, *Something Like an Autobiography* (New York: Knopf, 1982); Prince, Stephen, *The Warrior's Camera: The Cinema of Akira Kurosawa* (Princeton, N.J.: Princeton University Press, 1991); Richie, Donald, *The Films of Akira Kurosawa* (Berkeley: University of California Press, 1969); Sato, Tadao, *Currents in Japanese Cinema* (Tokyo: Kodansha Intl., 1987).

—D.K.

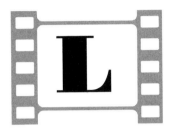

Lang, Fritz (1890–1976) In a career that spanned Germany, France, and America, the silent and sound film, and virtually every genre and category of storytelling, Fritz Lang belongs to that select group of filmmakers whose entire oeuvre bears the marks of a distinctive style and vision. Friedrich Christian Anton Lang was born in Vienna on December 5, 1890, and spent his formative years in Germany. Refusing his architect father's wishes that he pursue the same profession, he enrolled in the Vienna Academy of Graphic Arts in 1908 to study painting. After traveling across Europe and the Far East, collecting art pieces, he found himself embroiled in World War I, suffering a loss of sight in one eye that caused him to be released as unfit for service. In 1918 he signed a contract with Eric Pommer at Decla in Berlin, where, after acting and writing scripts, he began directing. His first two assignments, *The Half-Caste* and *The Master of Love* (both 1919), are lost, but they were successful enough that Lang was entrusted with an adventure serial, *The Spiders* (1919). It was at this time he married writer Thea von Harbou, with whom he collaborated throughout the 1920s and whom he would divorce after leaving Germany in 1933. After making a notable series of fantasies and thrillers in the 1920s, Lang left Germany as Hitler and Goebbels were assuming power. A brief stint in France was followed by immigration to America, where he remained for the rest of his life.

Tom Gunning's recent study of Lang proposes that Lang's oeuvre reveals a general direction from allegory to modernity. He divides the films into six basic groups: first, the richly textured silent German thrillers and allegorical films, like *The Spiders, Destiny* (1920), *Dr. Mabuse, the Gambler* (1922), *Siegfried* (1923), *Kriemhild's Revenge* (1923), and *Metropolis* (1927); second, the more contemporary cycle of German police thrillers, *Spies* (1928), *M* (1931), *The Testament of Dr. Mabuse* (1932); third, the American depression-oriented pictures, especially the social trilogy of *Fury* (1935), *You Only Live Once* (1937), *You and Me* (1938); fourth, the noirish psychological studies of the 1940s, like *The Woman in the Window* (1944), *Scarlet Street* (1945), and *The Secret Beyond the Door* (1948); fifth, the visually stark exposés of public corruption of the 1950s, like *The Big Heat* (1952), *While the City Sleeps* (1956), *Beyond a Reasonable Doubt* (1956); and sixth, Lang's return to the "master criminal" thriller in his last film, *The Thousand Eyes of Dr. Mabuse* (1960). Less easily categorized are the wartime melodramas *Manhunt* (1941) and *Hang-*

men Also Die (1943), the western *Rancho Notorious* (1952), the swashbuckler *Moonfleet* (1955), and the exotica of Lang's late work in India, *The Tiger of Eschnapur* (1959).

Throughout, Lang struggled to assert sole responsibility for his work. Unlike ALFRED HITCH-COCK, Lang's counterpart in so many aspects of theme and style, Lang lacked the major studio backing and security necessary to always assume such complete control. His own production company, Diana Films, was short-lived and a casualty of the turmoil in the American film industry in the late 1940s. Moreover, as biographer E. Ann Kaplan asserts, Lang remained essentially German and never became truly integrated into American life: "There was always a split between Lang's personal sense of alienation in America and his longing for what he had lost in Germany on the one hand, and his public stance of love for America and what it stood for, on the other." Probably no director has more consistently blended insights into criminal psychopathology, a taste for exotic and bizarre fantasy, and a paranoid fear of the dehumanization of the modern world. His two best-known films, *M* and *Metropolis,* are cases in point. *M* is a chilling, by turns stark and expressionistic, portrait of a child murderer delineated against a backdrop of blunting urban conformity. *Metropolis* fuses a gothic penchant for hallucinatory states, mad inventors, and virgins in peril with futurist visions of rampant, repressive technocracy and divisive labor-capital strife. This UFA-produced wonder picture—the most ambitious and expensive film ever produced in Germany at that time—was both an allegorical fable and a modernist critique.

Tom Gunning asserts, "Lang understood, more fully, I would claim, than any other director, that cinema would provide the image by which the twentieth century, the era of late modernity, would grasp itself. He understood how to use montage structure not only to portray the interlocking conditions of space and time, but to narrate breathtaking tales of suspense and danger, to make an audience both gasp and reflect upon this experience through a new form of story-telling." Despite Lang's avowed aim to carry the secrets of his personal life to the grave, recent research by McGilligan and Gunning has rebutted the hagiography of Lotte Eisner's biography (1976) and exposed the inaccuracies of Peter Bogdanovich's interview volume (1969), revealing that he invented the circumstances of his own life with the same ingenious, twisted flair that he devised his master films. Particularly interesting are accusations of pyromania, sadism, chronic mendacity, and even the suspicion of his murder of his first wife. There is new information concerning the circumstances of his departure from Nazi Germany—not as abrupt and not as politically motivated as he alleged—and his subsequent combative relations with the Hollywood establishment. His ego and his mania for control were his own worst enemies. He never received an Academy Award (he wasn't even nominated), although late in life he received numerous tributes from the international film community. After the onset of blindness and a long illness, he died in Beverly Hills on August 2, 1976.

Other Films *Liliom* (1934); *The Return of Frank James* (1940); *Western Union* (1941); *Moontide* (1942); *Ministry of Fear* (1944); *Cloak and Dagger* (1946); *House by the River* (1950); *Clash by Night* (1952); *The Blue Gardenia* (1953); *Human Desire* (1954); *The Indian Tomb* (1959).

References Appel, Alfred, Jr., "Fritz Lang's American Nightmare," *Film Comment* 10, no. 6 (November–December 1974): 12–17; Armour, Robert A., *Fritz Lang* (Boston: Twayne, 1977); Eisner, Lotte H., *Fritz Lang* (New York: Oxford University Press, 1977); Gunning, Tom, *The Films of Fritz Lang: Allegories of Vision and Modernity* (London: British Film Institute, 2000); Jensen, Paul, *The Cinema of Fritz Lang* (New York: A. S. Barnes, 1969); Kaplan, E. Ann, *Fritz Lang: A Guide to References and Resources* (Boston: G. K. Hall, 1981); McGilligan, Peter, *Fritz Lang: The Nature of the Beast* (New York: St. Martin's, 1997).

—J.C.T.

Lean, David (1908–1991) British director

David Lean was born in Croydon, England, in

1908 and got his first job in a film studio as a teenager serving tea to the cast and crew during breaks in the shooting. At the age of 20 he became an assistant cameraman. He eventually became an assistant director and then an assistant editor. After a term spent in editing *British Movietone News,* he graduated to editing feature films. Lean's first break as a director came when Noël Coward offered him the chance to codirect *In Which We Serve* (1942), for which Coward had written an original screenplay about the survivors of a destroyer torpedoed during World War II. Lean and Coward brought to bear the realistic techniques being used in wartime documentaries to give their film an urgent sense of authenticity, to which Lean's experience as a newsreel editor contributed a great deal.

The trend toward greater realism in British cinema, which developed during the war years because of morale-building movies like *In Which We Serve,* continued to grow after the war. Then, when realism gained the ascendancy in postwar British cinema, Lean turned to Coward's bittersweet one-act drama of middle-aged romance, *Still Life,* which became Lean's first important international success, *Brief Encounter* (1945). This tale of how the casual relationship of a housewife and a local doctor slowly develops into romance marked Lean as a very promising filmmaker.

Great Expectations (1946) was the first of Lean's two adaptations of Dickens. Lean's version of Dickens's often-filmed classic novel about the relationship of a youngster and a fugitive convict has never been bettered. Lean's film of *Oliver Twist* (1948) proved controversial, when some found the characterization of Fagin, the Jewish leader of a gang of young thieves, to be anti-Semitic. The portrayal of Fagin in the movie was carefully patterned after Dickens's depiction of him in the book, as Lean pointed out to his detractors. *Summertime* (1955) was a popular romantic comedy about a spinster falling in love with a married man, and to that extent recalled *Brief Encounter.*

But Lean did not find comedy congenial and next directed *The Bridge on the River Kwai* (1957),

filmed on location in Ceylon. It told the story of British POWs in Burma during World War II and their commanding officer, Colonel Nicholson (Alec Guinness), who is mandated to employ them in building a bridge for their Japanese captors to accommodate the Burma-Siam railway. Nicholson becomes so obsessed with the idea of making the bridge a tribute to British know-how and resourcefulness that he even tries to prevent a group of Allied commandos from blowing it up. But Nicholson and the bridge are destroyed together—ultimately, one infers, with Nicholson's complicity. The film won Academy Awards for Lean and Guinness, while the movie was named best picture of the year and encouraged Lean to continue making epic motion pictures.

Next came *Lawrence of Arabia* (1962), which focused on a British adventurer who became involved with the Arabs during World War I. Lean strove to probe deeply into the enigmatic personality of T. E. Lawrence, on whose life the film was based; it became an immediate and lasting success and again won Oscars for best director and best picture. In the film, Lawrence (Peter O'Toole) becomes the charismatic leader of the Arab hordes and leads them to victory against the Turks, with whom the British are also at war. But Lawrence unfortunately turns out to be a man defeated by his own capacity for greatness. As the Arabs begin to treat him like a god, he becomes vain, egocentric, and erratic. Lawrence's tragedy, like that of Col. Nicholson, is that of a would-be hero who is stubbornly determined to surmount staggering odds but is revealed in the process to be a self-deluded man who is as dedicated to his own self-esteem as to the principles he is championing.

Lean went on to make another king-sized film, *Dr. Zhivago* (1965), based on Boris Pasternak's novel about the Russian Revolution. Critics found the picture to be something of a disappointment when compared to its two magnificent predecessors, but *Zhivago* proved to be another box-office favorite for Lean. Lean's final film, *A*

Passage to India (1984), derived from E. M. Forster's novel of the British occupation of India, showed him working near the top of his form one last time. It centered on a young Englishwoman in India who accuses an Indian doctor of attempted rape. The film won a wide international audience.

When one considers the positive public response to many of Lean's films, it is evident that few directors have commanded such a large portion of the mass audience. Commenting on the popularity of his films, Lean, who was knighted in 1984, once remarked that if his movies have pleased a lot of people, presumably it meant that he was something of a common denominator. Like the average moviegoer, he explained, "I like to be excited and touched by a good yarn." Besides his knighthood, Lean received another singular honor posthumously when a building at Shepperton Studios outside London was dedicated to his memory. The David Lean Building stands as an enduring monument to his incalculable contribution to British cinema.

Other Films *Blithe Spirit* (1945); *Madeleine* (1950); *Ryan's Daughter* (1970).

References Brownlow, Kevin, *David Lean: A Biography* (New York: St. Martin's, 1997); Phillips, Gene D. *Major Film Directors of the American and British Cinema* (Cranbury, N.J.: Associated University Presses, 1999).

—G.D.P.

Lee, Ang (1954–) Taiwan-American filmmaker Ang Lee has distinguished himself for films that dissect the dynamics of familial relations and generational conflict. He was born in Taiwan in 1954. From 1973 to 1976 he studied theater and cinema at the Academy of Arts at Taipei, where he shot his first films in the Super-8 format. He came to America in 1978 to study dramatic art at the University of Illinois, later securing his master's in film directing at New York University. During that time he made several short films and a short feature called *Fine Line* (1985), which won him prizes for best director and best film at the New York Festival of University Films.

His first feature, *Pushing Hands* (1991), was funded by Taiwan's Central Motion Picture Corporation and marks his first Good Machine production company feature and the beginning of his longtime association with writer-producer James Schamus. It was the winner that year of the Asian Pacific Film Festival and garnered nine Chinese Golden Horse Awards nominations (winning three, including best first feature for Lee). The comfortable suburban life of Alex Chu and his American wife and son is disrupted when Alex's father, Mr. Chu, arrives from Beijing. While the grizzled but lithe old man practices his Tai-Chi (which he had adopted as a defense against the communist Red Guard persecutions in China) in the living room and watches his videotapes of Chinese opera, Linda grows increasingly distracted. She chafes at his inability to speak English, his refusal to cater to her vegetarian diet, and his influence over her little son. Aware of the tensions he is causing in the household, and resigned to his advancing age, old Chu leaves the house, determined to live on his own. Eventually, father and son are reconciled, and old Chu manages to live independently. Lee's typically clean and economical visuals and editing are reminiscent of Ozu. The central metaphor is the "pushing hands" moves of Mr. Chu. They consist of yielding to an opponent's weight during a conflict, deflecting it, and turning it back on the assailant. In other words, it is a metaphor for the dynamic of compromise and tolerance necessary for people of different ages and cultures to live together. "Identity is an issue that for us Taiwanese is central but also rather muted by our short, contradictory history," says Lee. "In [my stories] cultural, national, family and individual identities all work at cross purposes with one another."

The successful and popular Oscar-nominated *The Wedding Banquet* (1993) won many awards, including the prestigious Golden Bear Award at the 1993 Berlin Film Festival. Again, the story concerns a young Taiwanese man, Wai-Tung, who must come to terms with his more traditionally minded parents. They have come to America to attend their son's wedding and toast the prospects for grandchildren. However, not only does Wai-Tung not intend to get married, but also he is already involved in a homosexual relationship with an American, Simon. A fake marriage of convenience with a beautiful Chinese girl, Wei-Wei, is hurriedly arranged. The white lie turns into a colossal charade as Wai-Tung's father throws a lavishly traditional wedding banquet, after which Wai-Tung and Wei-Wei are literally thrown together and conceive a child. After many complications and revelations of the truth, the parents return to Taiwan, sadly reconciled to their son's sexuality and resigned to the fact that they may never see their grandchild; and Wai-Tung, in the meantime, will settle into an uneasy relationship with Wei-Wei, who will bear him a child, and with Simon, with whom he will co-adopt the child. What begins as a piquant farce about a deception wrought by a gay youth upon his traditionalist parents develops into a complex tangle of intrigues and thematic concerns. The tissue of lies and conflicts, based on sexual, generational, social, and ethnic differences is transformed into a resolution of sorts, a muddled and sad compromise where nobody wins.

Food preparation and the ritual of family dinners are the central metaphors of *Eat Drink Man Woman* (1994). Master chef Tao Chu is unhappy with the state of his world: he is a lonely widower, his three daughters are about to leave his home, and the culinary arts are declining into the tasteless fare of fast-food restaurants. Sure enough, the daughters leave, all except one, and Chu faces the prospect of a lonely future. For all of its poignant tone, there are farcical moments aplenty. And always the spirit of Ozu hovers over the picture. For example, Lee frequently will cut away from the tight-framed shots of domestic groups to montages of the city in motion—the motor scooters flitting across the intersections, the balletic gestures of the traffic cop—and the niceties of food preparation. The final moment is delicious in every sense of the word. Chu and his only remaining daughter face each other across the dinner table. He suddenly looks up from the soup he has prepared. His face lights up. Taste. He can *taste* it. He smiles in astonishment at the epiphany. "Daughter!" he whispers to her. "Father!" she replies.

Sense and Sensibility (1995) continued Ang's unbroken succession of hits. This new version of Jane Austen's 1811 novel could be subtitled, "Two Weddings and a Funeral." The two weddings are for sisters Elinor and Marianne Dashwood (Emma Thompson and Kate Winslet), who after many vicissitudes and complications will each marry the man we might least have suspected in the beginning. The funeral is a descriptive metaphor for the condition of poor John Willoughby, who discovers too late his love for Marianne. Director Lee is in complete control here, with his flair for elegant compositions, pristine-pure camera setups, and stunning rural location photography. His temperament is perfectly attuned to the sly and frequently unexpected moments of humor. The casting is well-nigh perfect: Emma Thompson's volatile emotions are carefully tucked beneath her staid exterior; Kate Winslet's moments of heartbreak are completely convincing; and (as the long-patient Col. Brandon) Alan Rickman's sturdy loyalty is buttoned up as tight as his waistcoat. Thompson won an Oscar for her performance.

By contrast to his previous pictures, *The Ice Storm* (1997) offered little to redeem a wholly nihilistic portrait of an American dysfunctional family. Two families, the Hood clan and the Carvers—intertwined by several nasty ties, like an adulterous affair—carry on their dismal Thanksgiving holiday celebrations. As the soft rains harden into ice, tree branches crack and split, and power lines fall, the myriad details and incidents of these quietly desperate lives coalesce into a treacherous sheen of deceit and disaster. All the while, the kids experiment with drugs, booze, and sex; their parents also experiment with drugs, booze,

Ang Lee on the set of *Crouching Tiger, Hidden Dragon* (Sony)

and sex. These are people who grow brittle and lurch into their own deep freeze. Like ice, they crack and split at the slightest touch.

The dynamics of family divisions continue in Lee's *Ride with the Devil,* a Civil War drama set amidst the bloody skirmishes of the Border Wars between the Kansas free-state Jayhawkers and the Missouri pro-Confederate bushwhackers. Adapted from Daniel Woodrell's 1988 novel, *Woe to Live On,* Lee immediately saw its potentials for a film. "At first I wanted to get away from a family drama and do something with more action and scope," he said in a 1998 interview. "But it turns out this story actually does both. Family values and the social system are tested by war. It's a family drama, but one where the characters represent a larger kind of 'family'—the warring factions of the Civil War

and the divisions in the national character." It is characteristic of Lee that he spends less time on the dramatic setpiece of the story, the 1863 massacre of the citizenry of Lawrence, Kansas, by the bushwhacker forces of William Clarke Quantrill, than he does on the subsequent sequences wherein the protagonist, Jake Roedel (Tobey McGuire), comes to terms with his own divided nature concerning war and politics and determines to head west to start a family of his own.

Undoubtedly his most prestigious and popular film to date is *Crouching Tiger, Hidden Dragon* (2000), which was shot in China. Assassins, thieves, and master swordsmen (and women) fly around in profusion. Life is like that in this never-land of ancient China, where magic swords, flying warriors, treachery, betrayal, and tender love mix and match in Lee's most lyric and enchanting film, a paean to romance and flight (or are they the same thing?). After a time of seclusion and meditation, master swordsman Li Mu Bai (Chow Yun-fat) has come to the Yuan Security Compound, run by his longtime friend and comrade (and would-be lover) Yu Shu Lien (Michelle Yeoh), to give up his sword, a legendary, magical weapon. When it is stolen by a dazzlingly beautiful and skilled fighter, young Jen Yu (Zhang Ziyi), a series of events lead to a mighty confrontation in the treetops. The aerial combat scenes (designed by master fight choreographer Yuen Wo Ping) pile one upon the other with increasingly dizzying effect. There's Jen's duel with Yu, as they fly across the rooftops. And Jen's dispatching of a horde of ferocious male attackers in a tavern (truly one of the most beautifully choreographed scenes of swashbuckling derring-do since the days of Douglas Fairbanks, Sr.). And the tussle between the two main female characters, Jen and Yu, a marathon squabble that utilizes every spear, sword, mace, grappling hook, and chain that comes to hand. And, of course, the treetop battle between Li and Jen, one of the most superbly staged scenes in all of the martial arts literature. Best of all, though, are the final scenes where the dying Li confesses his love to Yu, where flight and speed yield to stasis and quietude. This balance of rhythm and tone, frenetic gesture and soft embrace, reveals a master director fully in control of his medium.

"There are directors who are more surprising, more vainglorious or violent, more guaranteed to provoke," writes critic Anthony Lane, "but none of them seem to share his patience or his range of curiosity." When he speaks about his craft, the quiet, self-effacing Lee frequently utilizes culinary metaphors. "Being called a 'director' gives you a feeling of power. . . . But in truth, we don't have any real power. All we do is select ingredients during the shooting and put them together."

References Lane, Anthony, "Come Fly with Me," *New Yorker,* December 11, 2000, pp. 129–131; Tibbetts, John C., "The Hard Ride: Jayhawkers and Bushwhack-ers in the Kansas-Missouri Border Wars, *Ride with the Devil,*" *Literature/Film Quarterly* 27, no. 3 (1999): 189–195.

—J.C.T.

Lee, Spike (1957–) African-American director, screenwriter, and actor Spike Lee (Shelton Jackson) was born on March 20, 1957, in Atlanta, Georgia, the son of a jazz musician and art teacher. After graduating from Morehouse, Lee then earned a master's degree in film from New York University. Almost singlehandedly, Lee reshaped African-American cinema in the late 20th century. He was not only the best-known African-American director, but also one of the most prolific and visible American directors of the period. While still in college, he directed several shorts: *Last Hustle in Brooklyn* (1977), *The Answer* (1980), *Sarah* (1981), and his final project at NYU, *Joe's Bed-Stuy Barbershop: We Cut Heads* (1983).

Lee drew international attention with the release of *She's Gotta Have It* at the Cannes Film Festival in 1986. This film was the first directed by an African-American to be accepted for official competition. The low-budget film received wide acclaim and went on to become a box-office success. Reversing gender stereotypes regarding sexuality, the female protagonist, Nola Darling, has three male lovers kept on a leash while she enjoys her sexual fulfillment. The rape of Nola by her most reserved lover caused outcries of protest among some critics who questioned Lee's sexual politics in the film.

Lee has acted in most of his films, usually playing the best friend or sidekick of the male lead. In *She's Gotta Have It* Lee played one of the lead characters, Mars Blackmon, whose character lived on in Nike commercials. But his films created opportunities for other gifted African-American actors as well. Lee's second feature, *School Daze* (1988), was partially financed by Columbia Pictures. The film infused serious drama, comedic elements, and musical numbers within the text. Lee took on previously neglected topics that mainstream films had long ignored, including intraracial prejudice (as in the infamous "Jigaboo/Wannabee" dance sequence), and class differences between college-educated students and working-class black men. The film included actors Larry Fishburne, Giancarlo Esposito, Ossie Davis, and Samuel L. Jackson, all of whom would appear in numerous other Lee films.

Do the Right Thing (1989) remains Lee's most critiqued and controversial, groundbreaking film. Taking place on one hot summer day in Brooklyn, the film climaxes with the destruction of Sal's Pizzeria and a virtual race riot after the accidental killing of a neighborhood youth named Radio Raheem. The film received widespread attention across the political spectrum and established Lee's reputation as a provocative filmmaker of virtuosity and skill. Lee's success was such a novelty that he soon became a celebrity. The screenplays were quickly published for both *Do the Right Thing* and *School Daze,* and a 58-minute film was made by St. Clair Bourne on the making of *Do the Right Thing* in the Bedford-Stuyvesant section of New York City.

Lee moved in another direction with his next film, *Mo' Better Blues* (1990), which established the director's ongoing creative relationship with actors Denzel Washington and Wesley Snipes. This jazz-centered film, scored by Lee's father Bill, focused on a self-involved trumpeter who will not commit to any meaningful personal relationship. This film was followed by *Jungle Fever* (1991), which brought Lee once again to the center of controversy because of its strong content, involving a doomed interracial relationship between characters portrayed by Wesley Snipes and Annabella Sciorra. Lee contended that he was "not condemning interracial romance" in this film but exploring boundaries, both real and "self-imposed by man, based upon race, class, sex, [and] neighborhoods." For that reason Lee used two contrasting neighborhoods in New York City, Harlem and Bensonhurst, to define those boundaries. Snipes, Ossie Davis, Ruby Dee, and Samuel L. Jackson depicted a family torn apart by drugs, a subject

that Lee had not addressed in his previous films, to much criticism.

Lee's next film was more conventional, a sort of monument and tribute to a slain African-American leader. *Malcolm X* (1992) was Lee's sweeping, intelligent, even-handed biography of the great black leader, superbly portrayed by Denzel Washington. Although *Do the Right Thing* and *Malcolm X* are considered by most critics to be his finest works, his epic-length biopic did not live up to Lee's expectations at the box office. Lee's films since *Malcolm X* have not received the same amount of criticism that his earlier ones did, with the possible exception of his most recent film, *Bamboozled* (2000). *Crooklyn* (1994), a semi-autobiographical film, explored the dynamics within Lee's own family during the seventies. Both warmly and lovingly, Lee viewed that world through the eyes of his sister, Joie.

Clockers (1995) was a high-energy rendition of Richard Price's novel of mistaken accusation and life on the streets. *Get on the Bus* (1996), one of Lee's most underappreciated films, was a celebration of the Million Man March on Washington, D.C., and the renewed sense of black male pride and unity that transpired. Lee's foray into documentary film-making, *Four Little Girls* (1997), was a shattering film about the bombing of the black Birmingham church in 1963 and the deaths of four innocent young girls. Lee was nominated for an Academy Award for this accomplishment. *He Got Game* (1998) starred Denzel Washington as an imprisoned father who tries to renew a relationship with his son, a high-school basketball star. Lee used the film to hammer home the abuse of young athletes by colleges and universities. *Summer of Sam* (1999) was Lee's grisly tale of the summer of 1977 in a New York City victimized and terrified by a serial killer.

Lee has marketed his films with boutique items from his Forty Acres and a Mule production company headquarters in Brooklyn and with the publication of seven books. He has directed numerous music videos, which have featured Stevie Wonder, Chaka Khan, Michael Jackson, and

Spike Lee (right) directed and starred in *School Daze*
(Columbia)

Prince. His commercial work on television kept
his image before the public. Lee has always taken
chances. He made *Bamboozled* at the risk of alien-
ating his African-American following, casting
Damon Wayans as a television writer who creates,
in the words of one critic, a "painfully offensive
minstrel show—black performers shucking and
jiving in blackface—expecting to be fired," but,
surprise, the show is a hit. As a satire on minority
stereotyping and television, Troy Patterson
thought this dark farce was dead on. According to
Bamboozled costar and television veteran Tommy
Davidson, the television studios constantly
pushed him "in a certain direction—urban poor,
shuck and jive." Would anyone but Spike Lee take
on this issue?

References Lee, Spike, *Five for Five* (New York:
Stewart, Tabori and Chang, 1991); Lee, Spike, with Lisa
Jones, *Do the Right Thing: A Spike Lee Joint* (New York:
Simon and Schuster/Fireside, 1989); Lee, Spike, and
Lisa Jones, *Uplift the Race: The Construction of School
Daze* (New York: Simon & Schuster/Fireside, 1988);
Patterson, Troy, "About Face," *Entertainment Weekly*,
October 20, 2000, p. 43; Reid, Mark A., *Spike Lee's Do
the Right Thing* (Cambridge, Mass.: Cambridge Univer-
sity Press, 1997).

—G.B. and J.M.W.

Levinson, Barry (1942–) "I came to
America in 1914 by way of Philadelphia," explains
Sam Krichinsky, a newly arrived Jewish immigrant
at the beginning of Barry Levinson's *Avalon*
(1990). "That's where I got off the boat. And then
I came to Baltimore. It was the most beautiful
place you've ever seen in your life." It was the
Fourth of July. "It was a celebration of lights. I
thought they were for me!" Levinson was paying
tribute to his grandfather's discovery of the city
where he was born and grew up, a city that he
would return to in his best films, as if trying to
recover the past. As Sam says at the end of *Avalon*,
"If I had known things would no longer be, I
would have tried to remember them better." That
line is also repeated at the end of Levinson's next
Baltimore film, *Liberty Heights* (1999), and is key to
understanding Levinson's autobiographical family
films. "Baltimore is a big subject," Levinson says. "I
think the farther away I get, the bigger it gets. I
don't understand why so many movies about the
immigrant experience in America are New York
stories. Well, that was not the story of my grandfather and other relatives. They didn't come through
Ellis Island, they came through Philadelphia!"

Barry Levinson was born in Baltimore on April
6, 1942, where he grew up before moving on to
study broadcast journalism at American University
in Washington, D.C. In 1967 he migrated to Hollywood where he became a comedy writer for
Carol Burnett and, later, MEL BROOKS, as screenwriter for *Silent Movie* (1976) and *High Anxiety*
(1977). But he never forgot Baltimore, which
became the setting for his breakthrough, coming-
of-age film, *Diner* (1982), and later Baltimore pictures, such as *Tin Men* (1987) and *Liberty Heights*,
another coming-of-age picture enhanced by social
consciousness. "I came out to Hollywood looking
for something," says Levinson. "It was a dream city,
I suppose, the way Baltimore was my grandfather's
dream city."

But *Avalon* set the standard for these films. It
begins by visiting a lost era, then goes on to show
how the family is changed by a changing world.

Avalon comes to represent a nostalgic ideal of closely knit ethnic neighborhoods, fragmented by the later exodus to the suburbs and the later intrusion of television into family life at mid-century. "In the last 40 years," Levinson remarked in 1990, "television has just moved through the house—from the living room to the bedroom to the kitchen—and wherever it goes, we just talk and communicate less and less."

Tin Men and *Avalon* recreated ethnic life in the Fells Point region of central Baltimore. *Diner* and *Liberty Heights* showed family life in the Baltimore suburbs. *Liberty Heights* centered upon two brothers and was partly about teen angst, but it also confronted issues of class and racism with regard to Jews and African Americans, reflecting a developing social awareness. In his television series *Homicide: Life on the Street,* Levinson concentrated on the sometimes violent streets of downtown Baltimore during the 1990s, policed by cops who were eccentric, idealistic, and cynical by turns, trying to hold the line against violent crime in neighborhoods where family values had disintegrated.

Diner, Levinson's breakthrough picture, was another Baltimore-centered, low-budget, character-driven film that got an Academy Award nomination for best original screenplay, but it was not a large box-office success.

The Natural (1984), starring Robert Redford as baseball great Roy Hobbs and adapted from Bernard Malamud's novel, was more of a crowd-pleaser, mainly because it imposed a mythic structure upon Malamud's framework and changed the ending, making it far more upbeat than Malamud had intended. Levinson transformed the novel into a "larger-than-life, mythical, slightly old-fashioned, big-screen adult fable," as Levinson described it to David Thomson. "No baseball film had really stepped in that direction," he added, "and at the time some critics would just not accept that." But the film got Academy Award attention and was nominated for best cinematography, thanks to Caleb Deschanel's camerawork.

The Natural was followed by *Young Sherlock Holmes* (1985), a fantasy based on a Chris Columbus script, and *Good Morning, Vietnam* (1987), based on the real-life experiences of Adrian Cronauer, a disk-jockey for Saigon Armed Forces Radio, and featuring a typically manic performance by Robin Williams as Cronauer. *Good Morning, Vietnam* turned into a major hit, grossing over $200 million. *Rain Man* (1988) was even more impressive, starring Tom Cruise as Charlie Babbett and Dustin Hoffman as his mentally challenged brother, Raymond. The film was nominated for eight Academy Awards and won five, including best picture and best director, besides grossing something like $500 million. Levinson was named best director by the Directors Guild, and the film won the Golden Bear Award at the Berlin International Film Festival. The success of *Rain Man* cleared the way for Levinson to make *Avalon*.

Barry Levinson (Warner Bros.)

Levinson's popular films have enabled him to make his smaller, more personal films, such as *Liberty Heights,* which was certainly worthwhile but not a commercial success. *Bugsy* (1991) is typical of the former type, a biopic based on the lives of Benjamin "Bugsy" Siegel (Warren Beatty) and his partner in crime, Meyer Lansky (Ben Kingsley). Nominated for 10 Academy Awards, *Bugsy* won two (art direction and costume design), but it also won the Golden Globe Award as best picture. By contrast, *Toys* (1992), his next picture, starring Robin Williams and Joan Cusack, was simply too eccentric, and a commercial failure.

Nonetheless, Levinson has picked projects that have caught the public's eye, such as *Wag the Dog* (1997), coscripted with playwright David Mamet and starring Dustin Hoffman as a Hollywood producer and Robert De Niro as a Washington spin doctor, who fabricate a war with Albania as a ploy to boost the reelection prospects of an American president who needs to improve his image after involvement in a sex scandal. Interest in the film was generated because of the then-current scandals of the Clinton administration, and the film earned two Academy Award nominations, for best actor (Hoffman) and best adapted screenplay (loosely based on Larry Beinert's 1993 novel, *American Hero,* which suggested, satirically, that President George Bush had created the Persian Gulf war to boost his approval ratings). The success of *Wag the Dog* cleared the way for *Liberty Heights,* again proving Levinson's genius for working the system. Levinson has demonstrated a talent for making commercially successful blockbusters, but in general his smaller, more personal films are the ones he will be best remembered for.

Somehow, as he freely admits, no matter where his career takes him, Levinson's Baltimore roots are firm. "A lot of the old Baltimore still is there," he says. "I keep stubbing my toe on the city I knew as a kid. I guess the past is something you never really leave behind."

Other Films *Jimmy Hollywood* (1994); *Disclosure* (1994); *Sleepers* (1996); *Sphere* (1997).

References Roberts, Susan, "When Barry Met John," *Baltimore Magazine,* December 1989, 41–49; Thomson, David, *Levinson on Levinson* (London: Faber and Faber, 1992); Ward, Alex, "Barry in Baltimore," *New York Times Magazine,* March 11, 1990, pp. 47–48, 64–67, 71.

—J.M.W.

Lewis, Jerry (1926–) Funnyman-turned-director Jerry Lewis has produced a body of work that qualifies him to be regarded, as he himself puts it, as "the total filmmaker." He has been praised for contributions to comedy and for his humanitarian activities; but he has also been damned as an overrated filmmaker, a vulgar egomaniac, and an exploiter of the disabled. "More than any entertainer of his generation," writes his biographer, Shawn Levy, "he became a lightning rod for ridicule, the butt of quick laughs at the expense of charity telethons, French intellectuals, or physical comedy." However, there is no disputing the fact that his penchant for pathos and the comic gag that can exist only on celluloid, slapstick humor, and the persona of a juvenile innocent within an adult body connects him to the great traditions of the silent comedy of CHARLES CHAPLIN, Lloyd, Langdon, and BUSTER KEATON. And it is certainly true that he was the first comedian since the silent era to produce, direct, and script his films.

He was born Joseph Levitch in Newark, New Jersey, on March 16, 1926, to a vaudeville family. Before completing his education at Irvington High School, he was already developing comedy routines at Jewish resort hotels in the "borscht belt" of the Catskill Mountains. He teamed up with Dean Martin in 1946, and their legendary partnership lasted through 10 years of stage, television, and movie celebrity. While working solo in a series of features, six of which were directed by a man Lewis later credited as being his mentor, comedy veteran Frank Tashlin, and which included *Rock-a-Bye Baby* and *The Geisha Boy* (1958), *Cinderfella* (1960), and the classic *The Errand Boy* (1962), Lewis fed what was becoming his insatiable desire to craft and direct a film him-self—"licking emulsion," as he puts it. Since the early 1950s, when he made a series of 16-mm amateur movies satirizing Hollywood, he had wanted to make films. Now, assuming the position of producer of his solo features, he spent more and more time behind the camera, preparing for a career that would gain him control over the bureaucratic madness that had been his enemy for years. In Tashlin's *The Errand Boy,* in particular—about the misadventures of a "gofer" working on the Paramount lot—Lewis seems to vent his satiric displeasures at the nepotistic corporate regime that was the film industry at its worst.

The Bellboy (1960) was the first and perhaps the best of the series. Working at a frenzied pace and like what Lewis would later describe as "some kind of drugged madman," he wrote and shot the film in a matter of weeks in Miami Beach's Fontainebleau Hotel. In his autobiography, Lewis says he originally envisioned a bellboy, the entire role played in pantomime, the character a symbol of protest against people who regard bellboys, ele-vator operators and, indeed, all other uniformed workers as "faceless dummies." A virtually plotless series of gag sequences unified by the presence of Stanley, the nonspeaking bellboy, it catalogues many of the kinds of sight gags that would reap-pear throughout his subsequent work—pratfall encounters with inanimate objects, clever musical puns involving Lewis conducting an imaginary orchestra, and Lewis appearing in another persona (in a cameo as the "real" Jerry Lewis). Its spectac-ular success secured Lewis an unparalleled degree of creative autonomy that no Hollywood come-dian had enjoyed since the silent days. *The Ladies Man* (1961) also elicited much praise, especially from French critics, many of whom chose it as the best film of the year.

Significantly, as Lewis gained more control behind the camera (and in films directed by oth-ers), his personality in front of the camera split and multiplied. He plays dual roles in *The Bellboy* (1960), *The Ladies Man* (1961), *The Errand Boy* (1961), and *The Nutty Professor* (1963). In *The Patsy* (1964) he plays all three members of a female backing group; in *The Family Jewels* (1965), all seven roles; in *Three on a Couch* (1966), five roles; and in *The Big Mouth* (1967), three more. As Frank Krutnik points out, "As star, comedian, and enun-ciator, he battles to hold together the conflictual potentialities that define 'Jerry Lewis' as a subject." *The Family Jewels* is the most ambitious example. He plays six eccentric uncles—a fashion photog-rapher, a private detective, a ship's captain, a pilot, a gangster, and a clown—and a chauffeur. As for *The Nutty Professor,* Lewis's most popular film, there is an especially interesting example of this strategy, as it verges on autobiography. As Krutnik points out, "the Lewisian misfit Julius Kelp trans-forms himself into his desired alter ego, a manipu-lative and self-obsessed nightclub entertainer [Buddy Love] who, besides evoking Dean Martin, is also a monstrous incarnation of [the] 'Las Vegas Jerry.'" (For the record, Lewis debunks the alleged connection between Buddy and Dean Martin.)

Lewis ended his 17-year association with Para-mount Pictures after the disappointing box-office returns of *The Patsy* and as a result of his increas-ing bitterness about the studio's hostility to his directorial ambitions. Moving to Columbia Pic-tures, his directorial career foundered. At a time when a "new" Hollywood seemed on the hori-zon—with the release of pictures like *Bonnie and Clyde* (1967), *The Graduate* (1967), and *Easy Rider* (1969)—the viewing public seemed less interested in the pratfalls of a now-obviously middle-aged clown. Trying to adjust his screen image to older roles, the 41-year-old Lewis made *Three on a Couch* (1966), *The Big Mouth* (1967), *Don't Raise the Bridge, Lower the River* (1968), and *One More Time* (1970). The results were disappointing. "His films of the late sixties manifest a palpable embar-rassment with the comic persona upon which his fame was based," comments Krutnik. "The strangely contorted childman of Lewis' earlier work gives way to an adult who is displaced and directionless, denuded of purpose." The post-

Columbia years of the 1970s, aside from the annual muscular dystrophy telethons, were relatively unproductive. He wouldn't return to the screen again until 1980 in *Hardly Working,* in which he portrayed Bo Hooper, an out-of-work clown who gets involved in mishaps that are more labored and bitter than they are amusing. Lewis himself has said he is not proud of it.

Perhaps the most interesting film of Lewis's career has never been released. *The Day the Clown Died* has Lewis in a serious role of the aging Helmut Doork, an alcoholic German circus clown who ends up in Auschwitz, where he is ordered to entertain children as they are led into the gas chamber. Shot in 1972 in Sweden, the film's release ran aground in a welter of legal conflicts. "Here is this selfish, thoughtless man," says Lewis about the clown, in words that also could be self-descriptive, "who has lived all of his life making people laugh, but who is at heart a cold egotist. These children in the prison camp, he says to himself, who are they? Why should he descend to entertain them? But as he looks into their eyes, he sees the love they have for him, and he becomes a human being." It is perhaps tempting to compare this portrait with the persona of Lewis the telethon host; but it is more to the point that until the film is released, no can speak of it with any authority.

Frank Krutnik says the Lewis persona is a figure "who opposes the maturity and responsibility expected from 1950s corporate man," who instead lives in a "transgressive universe of irresponsibility and unruliness." Of his fabled spastic physicality, Raymond Durgnat has noted, "Like all great expressionists, he thinks with his body, and translates the soul's impulses into a semaphore of spastic acrobacy; he stutters with his feet, trips over his tongue, squints with his kneecaps and turns the simple act of crossing his legs into a bout of cat's cradle." The French critics have read his films as critiques of American capitalist society and corporate culture. He has received the French Order of Arts and Letters, been praised by JEAN-LUC GODARD and ALAIN RENAIS, and been adulated as "Le Roi de Crazy"; his American audiences and critics (with the exception of a few dedicated cinephiles) have been less than impressed since his heyday of the 1950s. A definitive reassessment has yet to take place but seems likely in view of the revival in recent years of the slapstick tradition, currently embodied in the work of Jim Carrey, Adam Sandler, and Michael Meyers.

Lewis has written two books, *The Total Film-Maker* in 1971 and his autobiography, *Jerry Lewis in Person,* in 1982. His acting roles in other films include that of a talk-show host, Jerry Langford, in MARTIN SCORSESE's *King of Comedy* (1982) and funnyman George Fawkes in Peter Chelsom's *Funnybones* (1995). Today, with the possible exception of *The Bellboy* and *The Nutty Professor,* Lewis is better known in America for his work with the Muscular Dystrophy Association of America since 1952, for which he was nominated for the Nobel Peace Prize in 1984. His most recent stage appearance was in the Broadway revival of *Damn Yankees* in 1995.

"Total film-making requires the definite point of view," Lewis wrote in *The Total Film-Maker.* "The film-maker constantly skates between himself and the audience. Which comes first? Both, hopefully, but it is such a fine line, such an intangible line, that the only way he can proceed is to first please himself."

Other Films *Which Way to the Front?* (1970); *Cracking Up* (aka *Smorgasbord* [1983]).

References Krutnik, Frank, *Inventing Jerry Lewis* (Washington, D.C.: Smithsonian Institution Press, 2000); Levy, Shawn, *King of Comedy: The Life and Art of Jerry Lewis* (New York: St. Martin's, 1996); Lewis, Jerry, *The Total Film-Maker* (New York: Random House, 1971).

—J.C.T.

Loach, Kenneth (1937–)

In his more than 40 films, television plays, and documentaries, Ken Loach has remained consistently committed to labor struggles, class politics, and to those marginalized peoples everywhere who struggle for social and economic advancement. His Marxist-based hostility to capitalism results in depictions of the ways human potentials are blunted by the economic inequalities of society. In his method and in his political persuasions, he is regarded as the standard-bearer of the British documentary movement that began in the 1930s under John Grierson.

Loach was born on June 17, 1937, in the factory town of Nuneaton, Warwickshire. Breaking out of his working-class background—although never far from it in the thematic material of his films—Loach read law at Oxford, where he also became involved in theater in the university's Experimental Theatre Club. After a stint in the Royal Air Force, he abandoned law entirely and turned to the theater. In 1960 he became a trainee director with the British Broadcasting Corporation (BBC), where he directed the famous *Z-Cars* series. Four years later he embarked on a dramatic series called *The Wednesday Play.* By now a committed socialist, Loach regarded the television medium as the perfect forum for propaganda on behalf of the working class. Plays like *Up the Junction, The End of Arthur's Marriage, The Coming Out Party,* and *Cathy Come Home* (all 1965–1966) displayed Loach's penchant for erasing the line between news documentary and fiction film. *Cathy Come Home,* particularly, which starred professional actress Carol White (who would reappear in subsequent Loach films) in a story about a homeless family hounded by a pitiless bureaucracy, depicted conditions in the then-current housing laws so graphically that some (limited) housing reform was later put in place. "Ideally, I would have liked *Cathy* to lead to the nationalization of the building industry and home ownership," Loach said at the time. "Only political action can save anything in the end."

His first three feature theatrical films in the years 1967–71—*Poor Cow, Family Life* (alternate title: *Wednesday's Child*), and *Kes*—immediately established him as one of England's most promising young filmmakers. Taking as their cue techniques and themes derived from the television plays, they were gritty, documentarylike working-class domestic dramas about characters defeated by nature and circumstance. These family units were fragile structures broken up by poverty and hardship. Shot in real locations (usually in South London) in a flat, uninflected lighting style and with minimal editing, they employed a mix of professional and nonprofessional actors working in a semi-improvisatory manner. *Poor Cow* again starred Carol White as a hapless victim of social and sexual abuse. *Kes,* his "breakthrough" film produced by his new Kestrel production company, was based on Barry Hines's novel *A Kestrel for a Knave* and was set in a Yorkshire mining town, where 14-year-old Billy Caspar struggles against abuse at home and the future laid out for him in the mines. His frustrations pour out in the loving care he devotes to his pet kestrel falcon. This glimmer of personal freedom is dashed, however, when his mean-spirited brother kills the animal and dumps it into the trash. Initially withheld from international distribution, the film went on to attract worldwide attention. Critic David Robinson pronounced it "not only one of the best and most original British films in a long time, but also one of the most directly appealing and entertaining—very funny and feeling and with vivid illumination of aspects of our society often forgotten." *Family Life,* adapted from one of Loach's television dramas, portrayed a young woman whose schizophrenia, it was argued, was a justifiable response to her blunted, conformist environment. Attempts to "cure" her prove to be unsuccessful.

Returning to more BBC productions, notably *The Rank and File* (1971), about a strike at a glassworks, Loach did not make another theatrical film until 1979 with *Black Jack,* a period drama about an 18th-century highwayman. Set in Yorkshire and crafted with Loach's characteristic semi-improvisatory style with mostly nonprofessional actors, it received the International Critics' Prize at Cannes.

In 1981 he made a kind of sequel to *Kes—Looks and Smiles*—a tale about three young people growing up in the industrial city of Sheffield, England.

After spending most of the 1980s involved in documentary proper—he claims the advent of Margaret Thatcher in 1979 necessitated his turning to the immediate venues of television documentary for his critiques of labor inequities instead of the more time-consuming theatrical film—Loach returned to features in the 1990s, directing *Hidden Agenda,* a thriller about events in Northern Ireland; a trilogy of working-class dramas, *Riff-Raff, Raining Stones,* and *Ladybird Ladybird; Land of Freedom,* about the Spanish Civil War; *Carla's Song,* a political drama; and *My Name Is Joe* (1999). The latter, set in Glasgow, won the best actor award for actor Peter Mullan as Joe Kavanaugh. It establishes a successful balance between Loach's working-class thematic priorities, crafted in a semidocumentary style, and the more frankly entertainment values of a commercial film. Joe is a likeable guy, a recovering alcoholic, who spends his time coaching the local amateur soccer team, courting pretty Sarah (Louise Goodall), the town nurse, and listening to Beethoven's music as a balm to his nerves. When one of Joe's soccer players incurs heavy debts with a local drug lord, Joe intervenes and agrees to square things by conducting a drug run. But when Sarah learns of the plan, she threatens to leave him if he goes through with it. Joe resolves to back out of the deal. In the ensuing barroom confrontation, Joe erupts in fury and goes berserk, injuring the thugs who try to block his exit. Now on the lam, Joe turns to the bottle. Eventually, he manages to save himself from the vengeful hoodlums, but not before his friend, the hapless soccer player, hangs himself. In the end, Joe walks slowly away from his friend's funeral, his girlfriend tentatively moving toward him, as if to reconcile with him. The Glasgow locations are authentic, and the mostly nonprofessional actors sport accents so thick that subtitles had to be provided. Glimpses of the working-class reality that stifles these characters are everywhere, from Joe's predicament under the welfare state (he's on the dole, and if he gets a job, he loses his income) to Sarah's visits to the houses of her patients.

Bread and Roses (2000) marks Loach's return to the subject of a labor strike. The underclass here is made of urban immigrant janitorial workers in Los Angeles—mostly Hispanics—employed by an exploitative contractor (ironically called "Angel Cleaning Services"). The disgruntled workers, not all of whom are legal and are therefore afraid to stand up for their rights, are persuaded to organize by Sam Shapiro (Adrien Brody). Caught up in the turmoil is Maya (Pilar Padilla), an illegal Mexican immigrant who lives with her older sister, Rosa (Elpidia Carillo). It is Maya who lends a sympathetic ear to Shapiro's union organization rhetoric, and soon she is cajoling her fellow workers to listen to him. The strikers are arrested but are soon released when the Angel Cleaning Services capitulates to their demands. The battle is won, but not for Maya. She, like Joe Kavenaugh in *My Name Is Joe,* suffers as a result of an act of kindness. Because she had robbed a convenience store to help a friend in trouble, she is deported back to Mexico. The film ends with her departure on a bus, leaving behind a tear-stricken Rosa. The film's title is taken from a time-honored slogan of the American labor movement. "Bread and Roses" was emblazoned on the banners of textile industry strikers in Lowell, Massachusetts, in 1912.

Despite Maya's defeat, the strikers' victory lends *Bread and Roses* an unusually upbeat tone. More often pessimistic in his films, Loach's cinema, according to commentator John Hill, "coldly details the shrunken possibilities of working-class life and the obstacles to social advancement."

Loach has borne with amazing fortitude professional setbacks and political censorship throughout his career. "It's easy to be a radical filmmaker," he says. "The people who really are on the front line aren't filmmakers. We're in a very privileged position, very free and good wages—if you can keep working."

Other Films For television: *Tap on the Shoulder* (1965); *Wear a Very Big Hat* (1965); *Three Clear Sundays* (1965); *In Two Minds* (1967); *The Golden Vision* (1968); *The Big Flame* (1969); *A Misfortune* (1973); *The Price of Coal* (1977); *The Gamekeeper* (1979); *Auditions* (1980); *A Question of Leadership* (1981); *The Red and the Blue* (1983); *Which Side Are You On?* (1984); *Diverse Reports* (1985); *Split Screen: Peace in Northern Ireland* (1989). For theatrical release: *Fatherland* (1986).

Reference Hill, John, "Every Fuckin' Choice Stinks," *Sight and Sound* 8, no. 11 (November 1998): 18–21.

—J.C.T. and J.M.W.

Losey, Joseph (1909–1984)

Losey was born in La Crosse, Wisconsin, in 1909. After attending Dartmouth and Harvard, he tried a variety of jobs; he was stage manager for several Broadway plays, until he became a stage director himself. His first big break as a director in the professional theater was *The Living Newspaper* (1936), a project of the Federal Theater that provided work for some of the thousands of unemployed actors, writers, and technicians during the depression. He directed several more plays in the legitimate theater and then was offered a contract to direct motion pictures.

After making some documentary shorts both before and immediately after World War II, Losey accepted an offer from RKO to make his first feature, *The Boy with Green Hair* (1948). The film employs the boy's green hair as a symbol of the need for peace and international understanding in the world. His first feature, although untypical of his later films, nevertheless sounded a thematic chord that would reverberate throughout his subsequent movies. "I think, basically, if I have one theme," he told this writer, "it is the question of hypocrisy; people who condemn others without looking at themselves."

It was around this time that suspicion that Losey might be a communist began to be asserted. These were the tense Cold War years that spawned Senator Joseph McCarthy's investigations of communists and the House Un-American Activities Committee hearings, which would eventually force Losey to migrate to England when he was blacklisted in Hollywood. When Losey sought to track down why he had been blacklisted, he found that he was suspect because he had openly supported Adrian Scott, the producer of *The Boy with Green Hair,* when Scott had been blacklisted before him; and because of his association with blacklisted writer Bertolt Brecht, whose play *Galileo* Losey had directed on Broadway in 1947—a play that Losey subsequently filmed in 1975. (Interestingly enough, in *Guilty by Suspicion,* a 1991 film about the Hollywood blacklist, Losey himself was portrayed as "Joseph Lesser" by film director Martin Scorsese.) Losey went to England in 1952, where he took whatever work he could find. He was initially hired to direct low-budget features, beginning with *The Sleeping Tiger* (1954). In making this film and his other early British pictures, Losey sought to depart from the established clichés of melodrama, and was willing to battle with his producers in order to improve the scripts he was handed. Losey remembered that his attitude had sometimes caused motion picture distributors to complain, "He made his film; he didn't make ours." To this Losey responded, quite characteristically, "Well, I make my film; and I don't know what their film is."

Losey filmed *The Servant* in 1963, the first of three films he made in collaboration with playwright-screenwriter Harold Pinter. The other two are *Accident* (1967) and *The Go-Between* (1971). All three films explore the moral bankruptcy of society, particularly among those of background and education. *The Servant,* moreover, reflects the class struggle in terms of a weak-willed young aristocrat who allows himself to be dominated by his manservant. The servant (Dirk Bogarde) methodically reduces the weak-willed Tony, his employer, through drugs and alcohol to a total wreck. Because Barrett resents being the servant of someone whom he considers in many ways his inferior, he not only plots to take over the household but also derives perverse pleasure from degrading Tony as a human being as well. Finally, at the film's end, when Barrett's triumph over Tony is complete, he locks the front door, sliding the bolts like a jailer. Then, as Barrett ascends the stairs on his way to sleep with his girl in the master bedroom, he passes Tony, grovelling on the stairs in a drunken stupor. Losey photographs Tony, imprisoned as he is by his addiction to alcohol and drugs as well as his emotional dependence on Barrett, through the bars of the bannister railing. The resulting movie is a chilling parable of Innocence corrupted by Evil.

The third of the three films which Losey made in creative association with Pinter, *The Go-Between,* won the Grand Prize at the Cannes Film Festival; it examines the love affair of an upper-class young woman with a working-class farmer. Accordingly, Losey told his story in the context of the British class system. The opulent look of the film belies the movie's stringent budget. "I think the degree of freedom in film making is in inverse proportion to the amount of money expended," he observed. "That's why I stay with a relatively low budget."

Losey had an even tighter budget when he made *King and Country* (1964), another of his major films that deserves attention. Losey's film is not just an antiwar movie, but also a study of the way that the class divisions of the European social system have operated during wartime between officers and enlisted men. *King and Country* centers on Hamp (Tom Courtenay), a young soldier who is court-martialed and executed during World War I for desertion. The tribunal senses that the lad was driven to desertion, not by disloyalty but by emotional fatigue and horror at the carnage of war. "I just started walking away from the guns," he explains at his trial. "I thought I was walking home." But the youth is nonetheless sacrificed to the impersonal military code that recognizes no exceptions.

Like many film directors, Losey had to face great obstacles in achieving artistic control of his films. "Working over the years," Losey reflected, "sacrificing the big, juicy jobs for the things I believe in, and doing it with no money and little encouragement, it's been exhausting." Yet, when one ponders the impressive group of films that Losey was able to make with all of the obstacles in his path, one wonders if he would have had it any other way.

Other Films *The Criminal* (1960); *Modesty Blaise* (1967).

References Caute, David, *Joseph Losey: A Biography* (New York: Oxford University Press, 1994); Phillips, Gene D., *Major Film Directors of the American and British Cinema* (Cranbury, N.J.: Associated University Presses, 1999).

—G.D.P.

Lubitsch, Ernst (1892–1947)

Acclaimed for his sly wit and mastery of the satiric comedy of manners, Ernst Lubitsch is the model example of the émigré director who made good in Hollywood. Lubitsch was born in Berlin on January 29, 1892, the son of Simon and Anna Lubitsch. His father was a tailor, for whom Ernst worked as a bookkeeper during the day, while pursuing his interest in theater by performing in cabarets and music halls at night. Lubitsch was so stagestruck as an adolescent that he quit school (Sophien Gymnasium) at the age of 16. On August 11, 1911, Lubitsch was apprenticed to the Deutsches Theater under the direction of Max Reinhardt. Lubitsch made his stage debut with the Reinhardt company in Felix Hollander's *The Fat Caesar* during the 1910–11 theatrical season. He also appeared in such plays as Shakespeare's *Henry IV, Part One,* Maeterlinck's *The Blue Bird,* and Shakespeare's *Hamlet, Romeo and Juliet,* and *A Midsummer Night's Dream.*

Around the same time that Lubitsch was honing his theatrical skills with Reinhardt's troupe he became involved with the fledgling German film industry. He became an apprentice at Berlin's Bioscope film studios and began acting in film comedies emphasizing ethnic Jewish humor. Lubitsch's first film appearance was in *The Firm Marries,* released in January 1914. This was followed by a sequel, *The Pride of the Firm,* released in January 1915. Lubitsch also began directing short films such as *Meyer on the Lam* (1913), *A Trip on the Ice* (1915), and *Miss Soapsuds* (1915). Many of these featured Lubitsch himself as a comic character known as "Meyer." According to Scott Eyman, Meyer was "something of a cross between Woody Allen (the utter helplessness in any environment but concrete) and Groucho Marx (the sexual aggressiveness, the insulting one-liners)." In 1916 Lubitsch directed his first feature-length film, *Shoe Salon Pinkus.* This was followed by more comic one- and two-reelers that emphasized ethnic humor and were quite popular to German audiences.

Ernst Lubitsch

Lubitsch made his first good impression as a director in 1918, when he directed *The Eyes of the Mummy,* an exotic film that has been described as a cross between H. Rider Haggard's *She* and du Maurier's *Svengali.* The film starred Pola Negri and Emil Jannings. That same year Lubitsch scored an international box-office hit with *Carmen* (aka *Gypsy Blood*) based on Bizet's opera and also starring Pola Negri. His greatest triumph came in 1919 with *Die Austernprinzessin* (*The Oyster Princess*). This comedy of manners, which satirized American mores, began what became known as "the Lubitsch touch." Film historian Gerald Mast described the technique as "one of omission. It is an art of 'not'—what is not shown, what is not heard, what is not said. It invests most of its screen time in objects—buttons, canes, briefcases, swords, wallets, hat, fans, corks, place cards, piano music, handbags, and so on."

Lubitsch's work during this period was divided between large-scale historical films, such as *Madame DuBarry,* aka *Passion* (1919); *Anna Boleyn,* aka *Deception* (1920); and *The Wife of Pharaoh,* aka *The Loves of Pharaoh* (1922); and comedies, such as *The Merry Husband* (1919), *Kohlhiesel's Daughter* (1920), and *The Wildcat* (1921). In December 1922 Lubitsch arrived in Hollywood at the behest of Mary Pickford. His first American film was a box-office failure, *Rosita* (1923), which starred Pickford and was based on a play, *Don Caesar de Bazan.* In 1923 Warner Bros. signed Lubitsch to a five-picture contract. Lubitsch's second film, *The Marriage Circle* (1924), was heavily influenced by CHARLES CHAPLIN's *A Woman of Paris* (1923). Lubitsch had seen it after the completion of *Rosita* and regarded it highly.

The Marriage Circle was one of Lubitsch's most successful and wittily sophisticated silent films. It began Lubitsch's long association with the comedy of manners, which had once been the special province of CECIL B[LOUNT] DEMILLE. Fraught with "Lubitsch touches," it brought a Continental sophistication to America, an attitude, in the words of critic Michael Wilmington, "at once elegant and ribald, sophisticated and earthy, urbane and bemused, frivolous, yet profound." The flowering of the "Lubitsch touch" is evident with his further films at Warners: *Three Women* (1924), *Kiss Me Again* (1925), *Lady Windermere's Fan* (1925), and *So This Is Paris* (1926).

In 1927 Lubitsch directed *The Student Prince of Old Heidelberg,* adapted from the operetta by Dorothy Donnelly and Sigmund Romberg. The film starred Norma Shearer and Ramon Novarro. Lubitsch signed a contract with Paramount studios in 1928, which was to prove both a profitable and creative relationship throughout the 1930s. In 1929 Lubitsch directed his first sound film, *The Love Parade,* with Maurice Chevalier and Jeanette MacDonald. Although it was an operetta, like so many other musicals of the day, it was truly innovative in its asynchronous union of sound and image, deserving a place alongside other contemporary "breakthrough" talkies like RENÉ CLAIR's *Under the Roofs of Paris* (1929) and ROUBEN MAMOULIAN's *Applause* (1929). Critic Theodore Huff praised it as "the first truly cinematic screen musical in America."

Much of Lubitsch's Paramount work in the early thirties is considered his best. Films such as *The Smiling Lieutenant* (1931), *One Hour With You* (1932), and *The Merry Widow* (1934) (all with Maurice Chevalier), as well as *Trouble in Paradise* (1932) and *Design for Living* (1933), are prime examples of Lubitsch's special brand of comedy and are definitive examples of "the Lubitsch touch." *Trouble in Paradise,* particularly, is one of the great Hollywood classics, a sly battle of wits between two rival jewel thieves; and its subtle eroticism throws more than a few knowing winks at the audience. In 1935 Lubitsch became production chief at Paramount, a position he held until February 1936, when he was replaced by William Le Baron. In January 1936 Ernst Lubitsch became a U.S. citizen.

Lubitsch's desire to direct Greta Garbo was fulfilled in 1939 with the classic MGM comedy, *Ninotchka,* which costarred Melvyn Douglas. The screenplay was written by Charles Brackett, BILLY WILDER, and Water Reisch. The delightful comedy was advertised with two simple words, "Garbo Laughs!" The film was Garbo's personal favorite among her American films. Lubitsch's next film, *The Shop Around the Corner* (1940), completed his two-picture stint for MGM and was based on a play written by Miklós László. The film starred James Stewart and Margaret Sullavan.

In 1942 his anti-Nazi satire, *To Be or Not to Be,* starring Jack Benny and Carole Lombard, was released by United Artists. The film received much adverse critical attention at the time, primarily due, as Scott Eyman suggests, to its black comedy, which was atypical of the period; more significant, perhaps, was the fact that Lubitsch set his film in Poland, occupied by the Nazis, and the theatrical troupe at the center of the film was comprised of Jewish actors. Jack Benny's deadpan drollery as an actor playing Hamlet, who becomes jealous of his wife during the "To Be, or Not to Be" soliloquy, now seems hilarious; but at the time the film was made, the situation apparently did not seem funny to many viewers. In 1943 Lubitsch signed a contract with 20th Century-Fox, for which he completed two films, *Heaven Can Wait* (1943) and *Cluny Brown* (1946). Two other films, *A Royal Scandal* (1945) and *That Lady in Ermine* (1948), were completed by Otto Preminger, due to Lubitsch's being stricken ill during their production. In March 1947, Ernst Lubitsch was presented with an honorary Academy Award for his contributions to the industry. Eight months later, on November 30, 1947, Lubitsch died from a heart attack. After the funeral Billy Wilder and William Wyler were walking to their cars. "Well, no more Lubitsch," Wilder sighed. "Worse than that," Wyler commented, "no more Lubitsch films."

Other Films American films: *The Patriot* (1928); *Eternal Love* (1929); *Paramount on Parade* (1930); *Monte Carlo* (1930); *The Man I Killed* (1932); *If I Had a Million* (1932), "The Clerk" sequence starring Charles Laughton; *Angel* (1937); *Bluebeard's Eighth Wife* (1938); *That Uncertain Feeling* (1941).

References Carringer, R., and B. Sabath, *Ernst Lubitsch: A Guide to References and Resources* (New York: Macmillan, 1980); Eyman, Scott, *Ernst Lubitsch: Laughter in Paradise* (Baltimore: Johns Hopkins University Press, 2000); Paul, William, *Ernst Lubitsch's American Comedy* (New York: Columbia University Press, 1983); Poague, Leland, *The Cinema of Ernst Lubitsch* (New York: A.S. Barnes, 1978); Weinberg, Herman G., *The Lubitsch Touch: A Critical Study* (New York: E. P. Dutton, 1968); Mast, Gerald, *The Comic Mind,* (New York: Bobbs-Merrill, 1973).

—R.W. and T.J.M.

Lucas, George (1944–) Even though he has personally directed only four films—*THX-1138, American Graffiti, Star Wars,* and *Star Wars: The Phantom Menace*—no director epitomizes the blockbuster era that has dominated Hollywood filmmaking since the mid-1970s like George Lucas. A member of the film-school generation that includes other luminaries like STEVEN SPIELBERG, MARTIN SCORSESE, and BRIAN DE PALMA, Lucas has played a crucial role in modern Hollywood that cannot be overestimated. While some critics lament the blockbuster mentality that has guided Hollywood since his *Star Wars* series became a fixture in popular culture, it cannot be denied that Lucas's work has agreeably enthralled two generations of moviegoers. Beyond his role as a director and creator of the most successful franchise in Hollywood history, Lucas's most enduring legacy may be in the area of technology and the special-effects techniques that have been perfected in his laboratories.

Lucas was born in Modesto, California, on May 14, 1944, and attended Modesto Junior College before transferring to the film school at the University of Southern California. A scholarship connected him with FRANCIS FORD COPPOLA, who would exert a profound influence on his career. "He encouraged me to learn how to write," remembers Lucas, "and he's the kind of director who works with actors, so I learned a whole different area, and in the process, started writing

screenplays, got a chance to direct one of them, and went off into the world of theatrical filmmaking." His breakthrough film was *THX-1138* in 1971, an expanded version of his prize-winning 15-minute futuristic fantasy, *THX 2238 4EB* (1965), about an underground totalitarian society from which the rebellious THX-1138 (Robert Duvall) strives to escape. The "look" of the film was extraordinary: A vast, white background surrounds the human characters, who are hairless and dressed in white. As commentator Vivian Sobchack notes, "The wide screen is used like a canvas on which human forms are placed at vast distances and disturbing angles from each other. One responds to these images as to modern paintings, sculpture, graphic art, a work by Mondrian or Alexander Calder; their human content becomes almost totally absorbed by abstract form."

THX-1138 afforded Lucas the opportunity to combine experimental filmmaking with more conventional narrative techniques. "Out of that came the challenge to do something really normal," he says, "—to do a regular movie that was funny and had good characters." *American Graffiti,* released in 1973, quickly became one of the biggest successes in Hollywood history and received five Academy Award nominations, including best director and best screenplay (Lucas cowrote the script with Gloria Katz and Willard Huyck). Set in 1962 and taking place on a single bittersweet night in a small town modeled after Lucas's own Modesto, *American Graffiti* is a seminal coming-of-age story steeped in nostalgia. Following a group of young people on the brink of adulthood, this is Lucas's most personal work—a poignant yet humorous look at the choices people must make on their way to maturity set against the teen car-culture that unites the disparate characters into a community. Biographer John Baxter claims that all the characters were based on Lucas's own high school acquaintances, and each had some aspect of Lucas himself—"the thoughtful Curtis, about to go to college on a scholarship, but unsure if he wants to leave; the dropout hot-rodder Milner, obsessed with cars and racing; Terry the Toad, class nerd, socially inept, especially with girls; and Steve, class president, king of the senior prom and destined for a future in business." Boasting the first significant movie roles for many actors who would go on to have amazing careers, including Richard Dreyfuss, Harrison Ford, and Ron Howard, *American Graffiti* was also innovative in featuring a virtual nonstop rock 'n' roll soundtrack, which plays as the kids go cruisin' in their cars searching for love and the answers to life. Like Fellini's *I Vitelloni,* which Lucas consciously adopted as his model, *American Graffiti* is in essence a wistful swan song to innocence, to adolescence, and to small-town simplicity and has become a modern classic. Lucas, the small-town boy who went to Hollywood to seek his fortune, seems at once nostalgic for the comforts of a bygone era while acknowledging the need to grow up and move beyond one's hometown.

The yearning to leave home and seek adventure is also at the heart of *Star Wars* (1977), the space extravaganza that changed Hollywood history. Relatively unheralded, and seen initially in only 32 theatres on opening May 25, 1977, the film went on to break box-office records and become an international phenomenon. Boasting the creative energies of Industrial Light & Magic, founded in 1975 as the special-effects division of Lucasfilm, it revived the dying art of special effects and pioneered the computerized motion-control camera and the use of fiber optics. Yet, for all its hardware, *Star Wars* was rooted in the nostalgic tradition of heroic "space operas" by pulp specialists like Edgar Rice Burroughs and E. E. "Doc" Smith and the comic strips and movie serials about Flash Gordon and Buck Rogers. *Star Wars* captured the imagination of a whole generation with the mysticism of Jedi knights and the adventures of callow young Luke Skywalker pitted against the villainous Darth Vader. It received 10 Academy Award nominations and went on to win six Oscars, although Lucas himself lost for both best director and best screenplay.

George Lucas (Lucasfilm Ltd./Twentieth Century-Fox)

The *Star Wars* saga continued with *The Empire Strikes Back* (1980) and *Return of the Jedi* (1983). While Lucas did not direct these installments—he had determined in the meantime that he never wanted to direct a film again—he was their guiding force. He has an executive producer and story credit on each and cowrote the latter. Both sequels were hugely successful and demonstrated the endurance of the characters Lucas had created.

After *Star Wars,* Lucas disappeared from directing for more than 20 years and spent a lot of time helping to produce the projects of other filmmakers. Biographer John Baxter reports that Lucas at this time envisioned joining Steven Spielberg as "architects of New Hollywood, putting their stamp on the world cinema of the twenty-first century." In the next few years ILM took on outside projects like *Dragonslayer* (1981), *Poltergeist* (1982), *Star Trek II: The Wrath of Khan* (1982), and *E.T.: The Extraterrestrial* (1982), amassing 11 Academy Award nominations, nine Oscars, and four technical achievement awards. As a producer he helmed several failures, to be sure, most notoriously *Howard the Duck* (1986), but his many successes included creating the Indiana Jones series

(*Raiders of the Lost Ark* [1981], *Indiana Jones and the Temple of Doom* [1984], and *Indiana Jones and the Last Crusade* [1989]), which earned him story and executive-producer credits and which his friend Steven Spielberg directed. Again taking inspiration from the serials and cliffhangers of his youth, Lucas chronicled the exploits of the globe-trotting archaeologist, played by Harrison Ford, as he battles the bad guys in search of magical artifacts. These old-fashioned adventure yarns, full of daring action, cliffhanging stunts, and tongue-in-cheek humor, were yet another set of box-office champs for Lucas. At the 1991 Academy Awards, Spielberg presented his friend and colleague with the Irving G. Thalberg Memorial Award for lifetime achievement.

In addition to the films he has made, Lucas's other major contribution to the world of movies lies in the area of special effects and technology. Today ILM is just one division of Lucas's diverse empire. In addition to the Skywalker Group and the THX Group there are 16 subdivisions, including the Games division, Learning Systems, LucasArts Luminaire, LucasArts Attractions, and LucasArts Licensing. Lucasfilm's THX Sound System has become synonymous with state-of-the-art sound. "The area I'm mostly focusing on," says Lucas, "which is actual production of theatrical movies, is coming more under my personal involvement; then, with the other parts of the company, because they need to grow and flourish, I'm now letting them loose, so to speak." Lucas has also recently been exploring interactive learning systems in his Learning Systems Division. Developed jointly with Apple Computer and National Geographic, the first major product is "GTV: A Geographic Perspective of American History," which consists of two videodiscs and an accompanying software system that allows manipulation of video images by users to create short shows organized along thematic lines.

In 1997 Lucas rereleased the three Star Wars films as "Special Editions," featuring some additional scenes and souped-up effects that were not possible at the time of the original releases. This rerelease was preparation for the production of a new trilogy of *Star Wars* films. Lucas originally envisioned the *Star Wars* saga as a nine-part epic, with the first three releases occupying the middle section of the story (the *Star Wars* title was amended for its original rerelease to include the subtitle, "Episode IV—A New Hope"). While it appears that Lucas has abandoned the notion of the concluding trilogy, what would have been parts seven through nine, he has gone forward with the opening three chapters.

Telling the story of the early generation of Jedi knights, of how Luke's heroic father, Anakin, turned to the dark side of the Force and became the evil Darth Vader, the new trilogy begins with *Star Wars: Episode I—The Phantom Menace* (1999), which dominated the box office but received mixed reviews. While some critics admired the look and sheer dazzle of certain sequences, the shallow characters and overly complicated plot took a beating. At times a clumsy and emotionally hollow narrative, at other times a rousing, entertaining spectacle, Lucas's first directorial effort since *Star Wars* seemed to confirm simultaneously his lack of interest in actors and his commitment to developing the latest special effects, including computer-generated characters. John Baxter asserts that the film vindicates Lucas's "belief in the supremacy of computer-generated film over that which depends on fallible human performers and artists."

Whatever the quality of Episode II (scheduled for release in 2002) in terms of plot and character, it will have the distinction of being the first major Hollywood feature shot entirely on video. Lucas believes that digital videotape is cost-effective and destined to supplant film as the standard format for filmmakers in the future. With the use of a high-definition digital camera developed by Lucasfilm, Sony, and Panavision, he contends that the image is comparable to that produced by film.

"I've continued in the independent filmmaking direction—where I started," Lucas says. "Now . . .

I'm allowing the company to expand, grow, and blossom the way it should, which gives me more time to focus on the learning system I'm developing and the movies I want to write and direct. I just want to get back to what I started doing."

References Baxter, John, *Mythmaker: The Life and Work of George Lucas* (New York: Avon Books, 1999); Curtis, James M., "From *American Graffiti* to *Star Wars*," *Journal of Popular Culture* 13, no. 4 (Spring 1980): 590–601; Eisenberg, Adam, "*Jedi's* Extra Special Effects," *American Film* 8, no. 8 (June 1983): 36–39; Gordon, Andrew, "*Star Wars*: A Myth for Our Time," *Literature/Film Quarterly* 6, no. 4 (Fall 1978): 314–26; Gordon, Andrew, "You'll Never Get Out of Bedford Falls!: The Inescapable Family in American Science Fiction and Fantasy Films," *Journal of Popular Film and Television* 20, no. 2 (Summer 1993): 2–8; Harmetz, Aljean, "Burden of Dreams—George Lucas," *American Film* 8, no. 8 (June 1983): 30–36; Kline, Sally, ed., *George Lucas: Interviews* (Jackson: University Press of Mississippi, 1999); Lancashire, Anne, "*The Phantom Menace*: Repetition, Variation, Integration," *Film Criticism* 24, no. 3 (Spring 2000), 23–44; Lev, Peter, "Whose Future? *Star Wars, Alien,* and *Blade Runner*," *Literature/Film Quarterly* 26, no. 1 (1998): 30–37; Roth, Lane, "*Vraisemblance* and the Western Setting in Contemporary Science Fiction Film," *Literature/Film Quarterly* 13, no. 3 (1985): 180–86; Salewicz, Chris, *George Lucas Close Up: The Making of His Movies* (New York: Thunder's Mouth Press, 1999); Sobchack, Vivian Carol, *The Limits of Infinity: The American Science Fiction Film* (South Brunswick, N.J.: A.S. Barnes, 1980); Sodowsky, Alice, Roland Sodowsky, and Stephen Witte, "The Epic World of *American Graffiti*," *Journal of Popular Film* 4, no. 1 (1975): 47–55; Vincenzi, Lisa, "A Short Time Ago, on a Ranch Not So Far Away . . .," *Millimeter,* April 1990, 46–56.

—P.N.C.

Lumet, Sidney (1924–) Despite the weight of his accomplishments, Sidney Lumet has been generally neglected by cinema critics, perhaps because Lumet's career and projects have been so varied and diverse that some critics have questioned his standing as an auteur, since it is difficult to discern a consistent personal style. Lumet does not consider himself an auteur, because, as critic Jay Boyer explains, Lumet considers filmmaking "a collaborative effort, not a personal statement on the part of the director." Nonetheless, Boyer finds consistencies in both the form and content of Lumet's films, to which could be added a genius for literary and dramatic adaptation. Boyer describes Lumet as "a gifted, intelligent director whose best films far outweigh the bad," though a supposedly "bad" Lumet film is usually better than the best work of other Hollywood directors.

Arguably, for example, *Equus* (1977) was a "bad" drama adaption, but Peter Shaffer's play was specifically designed for the stage, and it is doubtful that any director could have solved the challenge of translating its abstract design. Indisputably, Lumet has had a distinguished career in theater, film, and television. His films have received more than 50 Academy Award nominations, a consistent record of success.

Although he was to become known as the quintessential New York filmmaker, Sidney Lumet was actually born in Philadelphia on June 25, 1924, the son of theatrical parents, Baruch and Eugenia (Wermus) Lumet, who had immigrated to the United States from Poland. The elder Lumet was an actor, trained at the Warsaw Academy of Dramatic and Musical Arts. Making his acting debut in Poland in 1918, Lumet's father joined New York's Yiddish Art Theatre in 1926, acted on and off Broadway, and toured the country from 1939 to 1946 with a one-man show he created, "Monotheatre Varieties." He eventually acted in film and television productions, such as *Studio One, The Kraft Television Theatre,* and *Playhouse 90*.

Sidney Lumet grew up on the lower East Side of New York City and made his acting debut at the age of five with his father in 1928. His Broadway debut came at the age of 11, playing one of the "Dead End Kids" in Sidney Kingsley's *Dead End* at the Belasco Theater in 1935. His first movie experience came four years later when the play *One Third of a Nation* was filmed concurrently with its

Broadway run in 1939, followed in 1940 by Maxwell Anderson's *Journey to Jerusalem,* with a 16-year-old Sidney Lumet playing young Jesus. Though he loved acting on stage, Lumet told the *New York Times* he "hated acting in movies," adding, "I've understood all about actors ever since." The "third eye," the camera, is "going to see something you don't want seen." Lumet's long experience in theatre established his reputation as an actor's director.

Lumet enlisted in the Army Signal Corps during World War II and returned to acting after the war. At the age of 26 he became an assistant director for CBS television and within a year was directing the weekly series, *Danger,* completing 150 episodes, and also 26 episodes for the *You Are There* series, from 1951 to 1953. This soon led to his recruitment by Worthington Miner to direct teleplays for *Studio One* during television's Golden Era of live theatrical experimentation. At NBC and, later, CBS, working with *Studio One, The Kraft Television Theatre,* and *Playhouse 90,* Lumet estimates that he directed over 200 teleplays and over 2,000 actors, perhaps "more actors than almost any other director." Lumet remarked that he was "eternally grateful to television, live television, that is—which is a very different thing from what television has become—because of the opportunities it opened up."

Lumet's film directing debut resulted from his work in theatrical television, when Reginald Rose selected him to direct the film version of his teleplay *12 Angry Men,* which FRANKLIN J. SCHAFFNER had directed for television. Lumet's feature film of the Rose courtroom drama, made in 1957 with a cast led by coproducer Henry Fonda, was an auspicious beginning for Lumet. It won the Golden Bear award at the Berlin Film Festival, the best director award from the Directors Guild of America, and it was nominated for three Academy Awards, including best director and best picture.

In 1958 Lumet continued to direct teleplays for David Susskind and *The Kraft Television Theatre,*

adapting work by Tennessee Williams, Ernest Hemingway, and Robert Penn Warren's *All the King's Men.* His second feature film, also made that year, *Stage Struck,* starring Henry Fonda and Susan Strassberg, was neither a critical nor a commercial success. Later work followed: *That Kind of Woman* (1959), starring Sophia Loren; *The Fugitive Kind* (1960), starring Marlon Brando and Joanne Woodward and adapted by Tennessee Williams from his play *Orpheus Descending;* and *A View from the Bridge* (1961), adapted from Arthur Miller's play.

Lumet's next critical success came in 1962 with his adaptation of Eugene O'Neill's *Long Day's Journey into Night,* starring Katharine Hepburn, Ralph Richardson, Jason Robards, Jr., and Dean Stockwell, all of whom shared the best acting prize at the Cannes Film Festival. Lumet won his second Directors Guild award for this picture, and Hepburn was nominated for an Academy Award. This success was followed in 1964 by *Fail-Safe,* a harrowing anti-nuclear drama based on the novel by Eugene Burdick and Harvey Wheeler, with Henry Fonda playing an anguished president of the United States, pushed to the brink of nuclear war with the Soviet Union. This astonishing film was then followed by another critical success, *The Pawnbroker* (1965), with Rod Steiger's remarkable performance as Sol Nazerman, a German professor who survived the Nazi death camps, haunted by guilt because his family did not survive, and trapped in his job as a pawnbroker in Spanish Harlem. Rod Steiger was nominated for an Academy Award and won the Berlin Film Festival and British Film Academy awards for his performance.

Many films followed, in fact, too many to discuss here individually in detail. Lumet made high-concept pictures, such as *Murder on the Orient Express* (1974), adapted by Paul Dehn from Agatha Christie, and featuring an all-star cast that included Albert Finney (nominated for a best actor Oscar for his portrayal of Hercule Poirot), Ingrid Bergman (who won the Oscar for best supporting actress), Lauren Bacall, Wendy Hiller, Vanessa Redgrave, John Gielgud, and Sean Connery, among others. But most of his films could not be written off as mere "entertainments."

Lumet's police drama *Serpico* (1974), adapted from the book by Peter Maas, was serious cinema, and it earned an Academy Award nomination for Al Pacino for best actor. Pacino was again nominated for best actor for his role in *Dog Day Afternoon* (1975), another reality-based story; and Frank Pierson won an Academy Award for best original screenplay. *Prince of the City* (1981) was based on Robert Daley's journalistic biography of Robert Leuci, a New York narcotics detective who decides to become an informer for the crime commission to atone for his own misdeeds in corrupt police work.

Lumet's excursions into satire were also "serious," as was demonstrated by *Network* (1976), his most commercially successful picture. It left viewers, along with Peter Finch, "mad as hell" about television. Lumet was nominated for best director and *Network* went on to win Academy Awards for Faye Dunaway (best actress), Peter Finch (best actor), Beatrice Straight (best supporting actress), and Paddy Chayefsky (best original screenplay). The television industry was not as amused as the public.

Lumet also continued to make filmed adaptations of plays such as *The Sea Gull* (1968), starring James Mason, Vanessa Redgrave, Simone Signoret, and David Warner, and adapted from Anton Chekhov, and Peter Shaffer's *Equus* (1977), a particularly challenging adaptation of a purely theatrical vehicle, starring Peter Firth, who introduced the role of the play's disturbed protagonist, Alan Strang, in London's West End, and Richard Burton, as the burnt-out psychiatrist who treats him. *Deathtrap* (1982) was adapted from Ira Levin's play by Jay Presson Allen and featured strong performances by Michael Caine and Christopher Reeve. A convincing case has been made by Frank Cunningham for Lumet's brilliance in adapting literary material such as E. L. Doctorow's 1971 novel *The Book of Daniel* into the film *Daniel* (1983), loosely based on the lives of

Sidney Lumet (Orion/Warner Bros.)

Julius and Ethel Rosenberg and starring Timothy Hutton, Amanda Plummer, Mandy Patinkin, and Lindsay Crouse.

All of which recalls the auteur issue. Lumet himself worked out a number of thematic patterns in his films in his book *Making Movies:* "The machines are winning" (in *Fail-Safe, The Anderson Tapes,* and *Network,* for example); "Who pays for the passions and commitments of the parents? They do, but so do the children, who never chose those passions and commitments" (in *Daniel* and *Running on Empty* [1988], about radical parents who were involved in a bombing incident during the Vietnam years); "How and why we create our own prison" (*The Pawnbroker*); "When we try to control everything, everything winds up controlling us" (in *Prince of the City,* and also, arguably, in *Power* [1986]). In *Power,* Richard Gere plays a cynical power broker and image maker willing to sell his talents as political campaign manager to the highest bidder, even if that bidder is an unworthy candidate; but, as expected in a typical Lumet film, the power broker's conscience finally gets the better of him. Frank Cunningham uses *Power* and *Q & A* (1990) to define what he calls Lumet's "cinema of conscience." Lumet considers film "the last and only medium in which it is possible to tell a story of conscience, outside the printed word."

"I consider myself a director, not a writer," Lumet explained in his own book, *Making Movies,* described by critic Roger Ebert as the "one book a filmgoer could read to learn more about how movies are made and what to look for while watching them." Lumet explained, "Movie-making works very much like an orchestra: the addition of various harmonies can change, enlarge, and clarify the nature of the theme," and, "in that sense, a director is 'writing' when he makes a picture." He added, however, "Writing is about structure and words. But the process I've been describing—of the sum being greater than the parts—that's shaped by the director. They're different talents." Lumet should know.

Other Films *The Hill* (1965); *The Group* (1966); *The Deadly Affair* (1967); *Bye, Bye, Braverman* (1968); *The Appointment* (1969); *King: A Filmed Record . . . Montgomery to Memphis* (1969), co-directed with Frank Mankiewicz; *Last of the Mobile Hot-Shots* (1970); *The Anderson Tapes* (1971); *Child's Play* (1972); *The Offense* (1973); *Lovin' Molly* (1974); *The Wiz* (1978); *Just Tell Me What You Want* (1980); *Garbo Talks* (1984); *The Morning After* (1986); *Family Business* (1989); *A Stranger Among Us* (1992); *Guilty as Sin* (1993); *Night Falls on Manhattan* (1996); *Critical Care* (1997).

References Bowles, Stephen E., *Sidney Lumet: A Guide to References and Resources* (Boston: G.K. Hall, 1979); Boyer, Jay, *Sidney Lumet* (New York: Twayne, 1993); Cunningham, Frank R., *Sidney Lumet: Film and Literary Vision* (Lexington: University Press of Kentucky, 1991); Lumet, Sidney, *Making Movies* (New York: Knopf, 1995).

—J.M.W.

Lupino, Ida (1914–1995) Ida Lupino referred to herself as the "poor man's Bette Davis" and considered her Hollywood acting career as anything but stellar. Her directing career, on the other hand, was as exemplary as it was unconventional. She was born in London, England, to parents who acted on London's West End and were members of a century-long family of performers. She attended the Royal Academy of Dramatic Arts and started acting at 15. At 17 she left Britain for Hollywood on a Paramount contract. She started in small parts but in 1936 appeared opposite Bing Crosby in *Anything Goes,* a musical also starring Ethel Merman. In 1939 she had a significant role and got recognition for her performance in *The Light That Failed*. She started working for Warner Bros. and played tough, often vulgar and ambitious women. Many people consider her best part to be as Marie Garson in *High Sierra* (1941), opposite Humphrey Bogart. Lupino won the New York Film Critics award for best actress in *The Hard Way* (1942), in which she played a domineering sister.

Perhaps because she was not seen as a romantic lead, and became typecast in hardened female roles, she found her role options not coming up to her expectations or her abilities. Her powerlessness as an actress made her want to control her own career and this led her to directing. She started her own production company, originally named for her mother and later called the Filmmakers Company. Between 1949 and 1954 Lupino wrote and directed six features for her own company and starred in seven features directed by others. She directed as an independent, and so she did not have to clear the subject matter of her films with anyone. Like LOIS WEBER, who directed in Hollywood 30 years before, Lupino preferred controversial, social-problem narratives such as rape, bigamy, unwed motherhood, and the disability of polio. Her films did not pose solutions to these problems, and only rarely did her films have resolutions. As one critic wrote, her films were about "real people."

The six films she directed partake of the noir style but with a gendered twist. In her films, particularly *The Bigamist* (1953) and *The Hitch-Hiker* (1953), the male characters are reduced to the same kind of dangerous, irrational force that the femme fatale was resigned to in male-directed film noir out of Hollywood.

After the Filmmakers Company folded in 1954 Lupino turned to directing for television. She found herself in great demand as a director who excelled in dramatic action sequences. Among the many she directed were episodes of *The Fugitive* (1963), as well as *The Untouchables* (1959), *Thriller* (1960), and *Have Gun Will Travel* (1957). Later in life she maintained that she would have preferred a more conventional life, but her record of directing and the content and technical finesse she exhibited in all her productions indicate someone who was not only well suited to the job of film director but also loved doing it.

Other Films   *Not Wanted* (1949); *Outrage* (1950); *Never Fear* (1950); *Hard, Fast and Beautiful* (1951).

References   Acker, Ally, *Reel Women: Pioneers of the Cinema, 1896–Present* (New York: Continuum Press, 1991); Koszarski, Richard, *Hollywood Directors, 1914–1940* (New York: Oxford University Press, 1976); Rickey, Carrie, "Lupino Noir," *Village Voice*, October 29–November 4, 1980, p. 43; Donati, William, *Ida Lupino, A Biography* (Lexington: University Press of Kentucky: 1996).

—C.L.P.

Lynch, David (1946–   )   Much is made, even by Lynch himself, of the fact that David Lynch was born in Missoula, Montana. Perhaps the more salient fact is that Lynch grew up all over America. About two months after his January 20 birth in 1946, Lynch and his family moved to Sandpoint, Idaho. By his 14th birthday, when he moved to Alexandria, Virginia, Lynch had also lived in Spokane, Washington; Durham, North Carolina; and Boise, Idaho. Lynch's 1950s childhood was very close to the Ozzie and Harriet stereotype: photo-

graphs from the period reveal a classic nuclear family of three siblings (David was the eldest), a breadwinner father, and a housewife mom. Far from rebelling against this life, Lynch embraced it, though by his own account darker preoccupations were also present from an early age.

Such facts would be of little interest were it not for the peculiar nature of Lynch's films, which often seem to present in an almost preconscious way the materials of his upbringing as filtered through the surreal intensity of an anxious yet romantically yearning psyche. He came to moviemaking primarily through painting, which he first began doing seriously at the age of 14; Francis Bacon and Edward Hopper were strong early influences. In 1965, Lynch enrolled at the Pennsylvania Academy of Fine Arts in Philadelphia, where in addition to painting he made his first film, an animated one-minute film loop he called *Six Men Getting Sick* (1967). (Here he also met and married Peggy Reavey, his first wife; their daughter Jennifer, who would become a filmmaker herself, was born in 1968.) His next film, *The Alphabet* (1968), mixed animation with live action. At this point two pivotal events occurred: Lynch met Alan Splet, a sound engineer who would go on to design the sound for many of his best films, and he became a directing fellow at the American Film Institute in Los Angeles.

With the AFI's support, Lynch went on to make *The Grandmother* (1970), at 34 minutes his longest film to that time. More importantly, within a year of arriving at AFI Lynch had started preproduction for what may be the most unusual film he will ever make, *Eraserhead*. Shot and reshot over four years of production, *Eraserhead* is a narrative film that beggars both description and analysis. A story of urban alienation (drawing on Lynch's experiences in a crime-ridden section of Philadelphia), erotic longing and confusion, childrearing (in a manner of speaking), and the experience of the sublime, this 1976 release became a success on the midnight movie circuit; it played at one Los Angeles art house for four years.

David Lynch, the director of *Dune* (Universal)

Yet another turning point followed when, on the strength of *Eraserhead,* Mel Brooks offered Lynch the job of directing *The Elephant Man* (1980). This story of "Elephant Man" John Merrick (John Hurt) and the doctor who eventually saved him from a Victorian freak show (Anthony Hopkins) met with wide acclaim upon its release, and went on to garner eight Academy Award nominations (though it did not win any of them). Brooks's support meant almost complete creative control for Lynch, a rarity for a director's major studio debut. *The Elephant Man* is a deeply personal period film, one whose surreality closely links it with *Eraserhead,* even as Lynch also uses some very traditional narrative techniques to tell his story. This film proved to the Hollywood community that Lynch's exotic sensibilities could define his artistic vision without taking his work outside the possibility of commercial success.

In the aftermath of *The Elephant Man*'s success, Lynch was offered (but declined) the director's job for *Return of the Jedi,* and was for a time courted to direct the adaptation of Thomas Harris's novel *Red Dragon* (which Michael Mann eventually brought to the screen as *Manhunter*). Lynch chose instead to accept Dino de Laurentiis's offer to direct the troubled and much-postponed *Dune.* Released in 1984, *Dune* was a very expensive failure. Lynch himself admits that the scale and pace of production often overwhelmed him. A longer version was reedited for television, with scenes and narration added to try to flesh out the story with more expository detail; Lynch disavowed this version and had his name removed from the credits. Without question, both versions are seriously flawed, but Lynch's artistic and dramatic vision remain compelling nonetheless, and time has been kinder to this effort than one might have predicted.

The chief significance of *Dune,* however, is that in exchange for Lynch's participation, de Laurentiis agreed to finance his next project, *Blue Velvet* (1986). Arguably Lynch's best film, and certainly one of the best films of the 1980s, *Blue Velvet* maps the psycho-symbolic landscape of *Eraserhead* onto the 1950s small-town suburbia of Lynch's childhood. The movie is lyrical yet very tightly compressed. It is at once a murder mystery, a neo-noir, a coming-of-age film, a movie about families, and an exploration of oedipal rage, fetishism, and sadomasochism. At times one might even call it a bizarre variation on romantic comedy. During production Lynch met another of his essential collaborators, composer Angelo Badalamenti, whose music has come to define what many call "Lynchland" in the same way that Ennio Morricone's music defines SERGIO LEONE's films. Lynch himself wove into *Blue Velvet* several 1950s pop songs, one of which, "In Dreams," helped revive Roy Orbison's career. *Blue Velvet* also revived Dennis Hopper's career; his portrayal of Frank Booth was a perfect blend of the pitiable, the despicable, and the terrifying.

Armed with the critical and commercial success of *Blue Velvet,* Lynch entered one of the most successful phases of his career, culminating in 1990's *Wild at Heart* (winner of the Palme d'Or at Cannes) and 1989's *Twin Peaks.* In retrospect, *Wild at Heart,* adapted from a novel by Barry Gifford, may have been overpraised. Its story of the criminal Sailor (Nicholas Cage), his sweetheart Lula (Laura Dern), and the many obstacles they face on the road to true love and a nuclear family, is busily lurid and melodramatic, though often affecting and haunting as well.

Twin Peaks, by contrast, contains some of Lynch's best, most controlled, and most influential work. One might call *Twin Peaks* a TV soap opera, which it was, but like many other Lynch projects

it defies generic classification. In its two-hour pilot and the 29 episodes that followed, *Twin Peaks* portrayed an uncanny world full of uncanny characters. Lynch himself directed six episodes, most of them in the show's extraordinary first season, when the questions "Who killed Laura Palmer?" (Sheryl Lee) and then "Who shot Agent Cooper?" (Kyle MacLachlan)—along with catch phrases like "wrapped in plastic," "damn fine cherry pie," and "cup of Joe" (coffee)—were on the lips of devotees throughout America. At its zenith, *Twin Peaks* captivated fully one-third of the American TV audience each time it aired.

Unfortunately, the show's second season was a disappointment: Lynch was less involved (he had begun work on *Wild at Heart* by then), and the writing and directing suffered. But the influence and popularity of *Twin Peaks* remain. It has become a worldwide phenomenon, and it paved the way for supernatural thrillers like *The X-Files.* It also resulted in a feature film, *Twin Peaks: Fire Walk With Me* (1992), which recounted the days just before Laura Palmer's murder. Many critics thought this film so mannered as to be an unwitting self-parody, but the film has its champions and their number is growing. Still, the movie's failure was a discouraging setback for Lynch, and it was five years before his next feature film, 1997's *Lost Highway,* a movie that in many respects returns to the dreamscapes and narrative dislocation of *Eraserhead.* The movie also reunited Lynch with *Wild at Heart's* Barry Gifford, who this time collaborated with Lynch on the screenplay.

If *Lost Highway* represents a return to earlier aspects of "Lynchland," 1999's *The Straight Story,* a G-rated film made for Disney, annexes new territory. The landscape of *The Straight Story* is only sometimes that of town or city; the film's feel is much more defined by open farmland and by the character of Alvin Straight (Richard Farnsworth in his last performance, and one nominated for a best actor Academy Award), who drives many hundreds of miles on his riding lawnmower, bound on a penitential journey to reconcile with his estranged brother (Harry Dean Stanton). *The Straight Story* won many awards and was nominated for many more; it may well become a classic portrayal of the American heartland.

In 2000, Lynch planned a return to television with a series called *Mulholland Drive*. As of this writing, ABC-TV had decided not to purchase the series. It was released in 2001 as a theatrical film. The conflict is quintessential Lynch: the all-American dreamer who loves the texture of darkness, the "Jimmy Stewart from Mars" who writes avant-garde hymns to the mysteries of love.

Other Films *The Amputee* (1974); *The Cowboy and the Frenchman* (1988); *Industrial Symphony No. 1* (1990); *Lumiere and Company* (1995), one of 40 very short films; *Hotel Room* (1992), two short films in a trilogy for HBO.

References Alexander, John, *The Films of David Lynch* (London: Letts, 1993); Kaleta, Kenneth C., *David Lynch* (New York: Twayne, 1995); Nochimson, Martha P., *The Passion of David Lynch: Wild at Heart in Hollywood* (Austin: University of Texas Press, 1997); Rodley, Chris, ed., *Lynch on Lynch* (London: Faber and Faber, 1997).

—W.G.C. and J.A.

Makavejev, Dušan (1932–) This bold and inventive, "subversive" Eastern European director was born in Belgrade, Yugoslavia, on October 13, 1932, and graduated from Belgrade University in 1955 with a degree in psychology. He then learned his craft at the Academy for Theatre, Radio, Film, and Television in Belgrade. By 1957 he had established himself as an amateur filmmaker and went on to make award-winning documentaries in Zagreb (1958–64), such as *Parade* (1962), a documentary about preparations for May Day celebrations, and *New Man at the Flower Market* (1962), a political satire, according to Raymond Durgnat, "about a young couple caught making love in a park," too close to a statue celebrating "New Socialist Man."

Makavejev was a leader of a group of young radical filmmakers who sought, Durgnat claims, "not to bury, but to revitalize Socialism, to restore its humanism, in the course of Tito's 'middle way' between Leninism *pur et dur* and 'market Socialism.'" His first feature film, *Man Is Not a Bird* (1965), launched a series of perfectly outrageous pictures, marked by a wicked sense of humor and a tendency to shock audiences while thumbing his nose at conventional notions of "socialist realism" favored by the Soviet Union and its client states. Obviously talented, with a heightened sensibility

for the bizarre, the erotic, and the surreal, Makavejev became a leading figure of the so-called Yugoslav black wave, a pejorative term coined by communist officials who wanted to censor work that was intended to challenge state-sanctioned values. In fact, as Durgnat explained, these films "exposed gaps and contradictions between Marxist ideology, older cultures, and real lives," combining "social criticism, richly detailed realism, and dramatic lyricism" with "modernist constructions," especially "narrative discontinuities, genreswitches, and a montage approach" in a style that recalled Jean Vigo.

Makavejev became increasingly interested in the irrational correlations between sex and violence in his second film, *Love Affair, or the Case of the Missing Switchboard Operator* (1967), "about" a love affair between Isabela (Eva Ras), a telephone operator, and Ahmed (Slobodan Aligrudic), a rat exterminator, intercut with footage from Dziga Vertov's *Enthusiasm* and "blue" footage from the Yugoslav archives, and with interviews with an eminent criminologist and a respected sexologist. The true substance of the film, however, was to demonstrate that people, although frequently absurd and defenseless, are capable of some feeling, some compassion, and enough complexity to make the "scientific" analyses of criminologists and sexologists (and perhaps all behaviorists) suspect.

Love Affair was followed by *Innocence Unprotected,* in which Makavejev lifted footage from the first Serbian "talkie," released in 1942, a truly silly movie intercut with new footage of cinéma vérité interviews with the film's aging "hero," Comrade Aleksi, a strongman and gymnast who was also the film's actor and director, still possessed of a striking physique, still able to bend steel with his teeth, still a devotee of his Auto-Suggestive Gymnastics method. God may be dead in Tito's Yugoslavia, but this superman lived on in Serbia. The "hero" performs astonishing feats, flying over Belgrade suspended from a cable and holding on with his teeth, for example, a stunt that later "stunts" his growth, diminishing his height by two inches after a 60-foot fall that fractures legs and vertebrae—all intercut with gruesome and realistic newsreel footage shot during World War II. The "innocence" of this idiotic film-within-a-film and the simplemindedness of its maker and "star" is absolutely "unprotected" against the political situation whence it derives.

Eventually pressure was brought against Makavejev by the Veterans' League of World War II partisans, who demanded that the director be indicted on a criminal charge of derision "of the State, its agencies and representatives," claiming that Makavejev had committed "hostile acts" against the state, President Tito, and the veterans, "who, by their struggle, blood and lives, created Socialist Yugoslavia." But this indictment was not to come until after his next, even more outrageous film, *WR: Mysteries of the Organism,* which earned its director the Luis Buñuel Special Award at the Cannes Film Festival in 1971. The film was made in the United States and Yugoslavia, where it was shown only to selected audiences before being banned as "ideologically harmful" by Makavejev's own colleagues at the Neoplanta Studio in Novi Sad (no doubt responding to government pressure). Meanwhile, Makavejev faced prosecution under Article 174 of the Yugoslav criminal code,

which read: "Whoever brings into derision the Socialist Federal Republic of Yugoslavia, a Socialist Republic, their flag, coat of arms, their highest agencies or authorities or representatives thereof, the armed forces of the supreme commander, shall be punished by imprisonment for not less than three months." During the Cold War communist-bloc artists shared in common a tendency to make their statements in obscure, complicated, and frequently allegorical frames. Makavejev had apparently committed the sin of being too obvious.

The "WR" of the title of Makavejev's *WR Misterije Organizma* that so offended official Yugoslavia refers to Dr. Wilhelm Reich, an eccentric Austrian psychiatrist who immigrated to the United States and established the Orgonon Institute, dedicated to "liberating" sex research that was considered bizarre and pernicious. Makavejev had read Reich's *Dialectical Materialism and Psychoanalysis* (1929) while still a psychology student and began to believe Marxist approaches to human behavior were deficient. The film therefore contains a mini-documentary about Reich, whose ideas drive the narrative and who was finally prosecuted for his activities and died a broken man in 1957 at the Federal Penitentiary at Lewisburg, Pennsylvania. The main narrative line of the film, however, concerns a Serbian girl, Milena Dravi, and her roommate, both of whom are dedicated to the teachings of Wilhelm Reich. For Milena, Reich's name means "World Revolution," giving the "WR" of the title added significance.

The film intends to document evidence that Reich's "World Revolution" is currently in progress, while also telling the story of liberated Milena and her successful attempt to seduce a Russian ice-skating champion, Vladimir Ilich, a terribly repressed Soviet "People's Artist," here presented as a sexual maniac rather than a benevolent protector of the innocent. Whereas the ironic "message" of *Innocence Unprotected* was "Save the People's Artist," the message of *WR* is "Screw the People's Artist!" The puritanical "People's Artist" denies that there can be any difference between personal happiness and collective happiness, declaring "We have abolished the difference," yet after his defenses have been broken down and his demons released, he is seen at the end of the picture as a confused murderer, ruined by uncontrolled passion. Bloody and violent excesses would seem to be the price one pays for such extreme self-discipline and control. His body has been conditioned to serve the needs of the people, the masses, and not the needs of a single, infatuated girl.

The human distinctions made between the Serbian girl and the conditioned and regimented Soviet artist are obvious. Her natural impulses are to release passion in order to enjoy and accept life; whereas his impulses are to reject and contain such impulses. His "liberation" is therefore disastrous for Milena, whom he murders. The once self-righteous and self-assured Vladimir Ilich has been initiated to the mysterious and basic forces that govern the human organism, forces that finally prove to be quite beyond his control. *WR* was made in Yugoslavia and the United States, but thereafter Makavejev could no longer work in his native Serbia. Therefore, his next film, *Sweet Movie* (1975), was made in Canada; *Montenegro* (1981) in Sweden; *The Coca-Cola Kid* (1994) in Australia.

Critic Daniel Goulding described *Sweet Movie* as "a remake of *WR,* painted in darker and most pessimistic hues and with even wilder and more surrealistic imagistic associations," suggesting in "an ironic and satiric double critique" not only the "degeneration of communist ideals" in the East, but also the "trivialization of human values, excessive self-interest and consumer-oriented narcissism and commodity fetishism in the West." A Canadian beauty (Carole Laure) who earns the title of Miss World 1984 is degraded in ways too disgusting to enumerate, then dipped into a vat of chocolate and turned into a bon-bon, as she suffocates. The film was so pessimistic, controversial, and repulsive that its distribution was seriously impeded, and Makavejev's career as well, for seven years. His subsequent films, *Montenegro* and *The Coca-Cola Kid,* retained the director's sense for political and

social satire and his preference for surreal images and bizarre plots, but Makavejev sacrificed his experiments with discontinuous narrative structure. *Montenegro* explored the murderous and perverse impulses lurking beneath bourgeois existence; *The Coca-Cola Kid* explored, in Goulding's words, "the lunacy of market-driven psychology and product fetishism—even when the product is as effervescent, egalitarian and sensually provocative as Coca-Cola!"

Eventually Makavejev did return to Yugoslavia, in 1987, to make *Manifesto,* loosely based upon Emile Zola's short story, "For a Night of Love," involving characters drawn into an assassination plot against a middle-European king in the post-World War I Balkans. The cast featured Danish-born Camilla Söberg in the pivotal role of Svetlana, a confirmed revolutionary and would-be assassin; Alfred Molina, as a secret-police agent named Avanti; and Eric Stoltz as Christopher, a postman Svetlana is able to recruit in her conspiracy because he is infatuated with her. The film was produced by Menahem Golan and Yoram Globus for Cannon Entertainment. In *The Gorilla Bathes at Noon* (1993), made in Germany and here described by Raymond Durgnat, a Russian soldier "gets left behind during the Red Army's chaotic withdrawal from Berlin, and mounts guard on a Lenin statue due for demolition."

In Ian Cameron's *Second Wave* anthology, critic Robin Wood considered Makavejev "one of the most remarkable artists to have emerged from the post-Godard generation," though in his long analytical study he was hard-pressed to show a direct link between the New Wave and the Second Wave, other than a speculation about Brecht's "alienation effect," as applied to cinema. Amos Vogel called Makavejev a "revolutionary Cubist" and hailed *WR* as "unquestionably one of the most important subversive masterpieces of the 1970s: a hilarious, highly erotic, political comedy which quite seriously proposes sex as the ideological imperative for revolution and advances a plea for Erotic Socialism." But beneath the insane frivolity Vogel found "a more serious ideological intent: opposition to all oppressive social systems, East or West." Later dismissed by certain humorless academic critics as a mere pornographer, Makavejev was distinctively innovative and boldly satiric, though often apparently wacky. The miracle is that he could have started such work behind the Iron Curtain, in a dictatorial, semi-autonomous client state on the southern perimeter of the Soviet Empire.

References Anderson, Raymond H., "Yugoslav Acts to Indict Film Maker for Derision," *New York Times,* February 4, 1973, I, p. 2; Durgnat, Raymond, *WR—Mysteries of the Organism* (London: BFI Publishing, 1999); Goulding, Daniel J., "The Films of Dušan Makavejev: Between East and West," and Testa, Bart, "Reflections on Makavejev: The Art Film and Transgression," in *Before the Wall Came Down: Soviet and East European Filmmakers Working in the West,* ed. Graham Petrie and Ruth Dwyer (Lanham, Md.: University Press of America, 1990); MacBean, James Roy, *Film and Revolution* (Bloomington: Indiana University Press, 1975); Robinson, David, "*Joie de Vivre* at the Barricades: The Films of Dušan Makavejev," *Sight and Sound* 40, no. 4 (Autumn 1971): 180; Vogel, Amos, *Film as a Subversive Art* (New York: Random House, 1974); Wood, Robin, "Dušan Makavejev," in *Second Wave,* ed. Ian Cameron, (New York: Praeger, 1970).

—J.M.W.

Malle, Louis (1932–1995)

Louis Malle's diverse career as a filmmaker spanned nearly 40 years and many countries. He was successful both as a feature-film director as well as a documentarist, and also was one of only a few foreign directors in the 1960s to enter Hollywood, where he made several films that were critically and artistically successful. Throughout his long career, Malle often shunned convention to create a niche for himself. His films touched many viewers and he almost always received universal praise. As interviewer Philip French says, "To see a steady progress and development in his work is simply to recognize the career of a man who has been, to a degree unusual in the cinema, the master of his own fate."

Louis Malle was born on October 30, 1932, into a wealthy family in Thumeries, France, a small industrial town near the Belgian border. The family moved to Paris in 1940 at the beginning of the Occupation, where he received a strict Catholic education in the Jesuit college in Fountainebleau before studying the humanities at the Sorbonne. Malle eventually studied film at the Institut des Hautes Études Cinématographiques (IDHEC), where, after only one year, he was recruited by Jacques Cousteau to serve a three-year stint on the famed *Calypso* as a cameraman. This union proved fortuitous, for Malle shared with Cousteau both the Palme d'Or at Cannes and the documentary Oscar for the film *The Silent World* (*Le Monde du silence* [1956]). After *The Silent World,* Malle was introduced to feature films via a brief assignment with director Robert Bresson.

Malle has often been tangentially aligned with the nouvelle vague of the late 1950s, but his feature debut preceded those who formed the core group by a year. His earlier films may share some of the nontraditional characteristics of the nouvelle vague, but Malle is generally considered more of a traditionalist, and was lumped with FRANÇOIS TRUFFAUT and JEAN-LUC GODARD only by critics and columnists. Nevertheless, Malle was applauded by the nouvelle vague critics, most notably by Truffaut. Malle's first feature, *Elevator to the Gallows* (*Ascenseur pour l'échafaud* [1958], aka *Frantic*), a thriller dealing with murder and deceit, has its central character trapped in an elevator for most of the film. It starred Jeanne Moreau, who would also star in his *The Lovers* (*Les Amants* [1958]) and who would reappear, with Brigitte Bardot, in the comic western, *Viva Maria* (1965). *The Lovers* garnered Malle much critical praise, mainly for its uninhibited view of sexuality, initiating an exploration of themes that would remain in his work—relationships and human sexuality, characters trapped by fate, and moral ambiguity. His style, also established here, was not flashy or obtrusive, but rather emotional.

Zazie dans le métro (1960) is a comedy based on Raymond Queneau's novel about a precociously foul-mouthed girl visiting Paris whose one wish is to ride the Metro. *A Very Private Affair* (*Vie privée* [1961]) cast Brigitte Bardot against type as a parody of the flamboyant star. *The Fire Within* (*Le Feu follet* [1963]) is a social commentary on alcoholism and its effects, while *The Thief of Paris* (*Le Voleur* [1967]), starring Jean-Paul Belmondo, depicts the routine of a common thief, with moments of suspense, familial strife, and sexuality. After directing the "William Wilson" episode of the trilogy film *Spirits of the Dead* (aka *Histoires extraordinaires* [1967])—three tales freely adapted from Edgar Allan Poe (the other directors were Roger Vadim and FEDERICO FELLINI)—Malle returned to the form that first brought him success: the documentary. Malle said, "I've always loved documentaries. From the beginning, if I had not met Cousteau, I intended to make documentaries on my own. And after Cousteau, I made four fiction films in a row. Then I felt I needed to get back to the real world. I felt for my own sanity [I had to], grab a 16-mm camera and look at something with my own eyes, and without any preconceived ideas—just try to satisfy my curiosity."

The resulting documentaries, *Calcutta* (1968) and *Phantom India* (*L'Inde fantôme* [1969]), a seven-part television series with Malle delivering the commentary, show India in all its glory (a visit to Mother Teresa's hospital) and its squalor (beggars, overcrowded streets and homes, lack of proper plumbing and garbage collection, general filth). The films depict a unique and unusual modern India, and particular curiosities such as street performers, caste systems, religious rites, and politics. "These are possibly the most personal films I have made," Malle said. "I'm grateful to India for having forced me to start all over; I was a 15-year-old again! The narration expresses my dismay, my endless curiosity." The explicit poverty shown in the films did not please the Indian government, but it shows the country as it is, without flattery or contempt.

More controversy came with Malle's next feature film, *Murmur of the Heart* (*Le Souffle au coeur*

Louis Malle (Paramount)

[1971]), often deemed one of his very best. The film deals with incest, awakening sexuality, familial trappings, and the adult world as observed by an innocent youth, a theme that would recur in his later films. *Lacombe, Lucien* (1974), cited as one of Malle's finest works, centers upon a young man who becomes a willing Nazi collaborator, and who, through various telling incidents, meets his own fate. Malle said of this film, "I've always been interested in making a film in which the central character is somebody I find very difficult to understand. I mean, the portrait of an ordinary fascist." The film's blunt depiction is indeed harrowing, but also full of emotion.

Black Moon (1975) again explores incest and sexuality, but with a more surreal, absurdist tone. He then moved to America and spent the next decade making five features and two documentaries.

Malle's American films are perhaps his best known, certainly to audiences unfamiliar with his earlier work. *Pretty Baby* (1978) is a period piece set in early 1900s New Orleans, and is the story of a young, virginal prostitute and her life within a brothel with her mother. "I had a lot of mixed feelings about asking a child to go through these very disturbing scenes," Malle said, referring to the film's star, Brooke Shields. "I felt I had a moral responsibility." In the end, the film is disturbing only because of what it *doesn't* show. *Atlantic City* (1980) is another Malle triumph, with Burt Lancaster cast as an aging gangster. The film earned a nomination for best film, and Malle a nomination for best director.

These Oscar nominations enabled Malle to make an extraordinary film, *My Dinner with André* (1981). Shunning narrative convention, the film is an eclectic, cerebral piece in which two people have a wide-ranging conversation on art and life while enjoying a full-course meal, which takes place in real-time. "What I liked best about it was that I felt close to both characters," Malle said. "I was terribly interested." The film was meticulously shot and the set designed to specification, and it is an astonishing exercise in the film medium. Malle's two documentaries he made in America, *God's Country* (1986) and *And the Pursuit of Happiness* (1987), explore the social strata of American life, as evidenced by the titles alone.

Returning to France, Malle made his most personal and acclaimed film, *Au Revoir les enfants* (*Goodbye, Children* [1987]), a telling account of growing up under the Nazi Occupation, again showing the harshness of the world as seen through the eyes of youth. The film was universally praised and won best picture at the Venice Film Festival and earned Malle a best director award from the British Academy of Film and Television Arts. Malle was pleased by this accomplishment: "*Au Revoir Les Enfants* is austere, deprived of any sort of cinematic fireworks, but as far as my approach to filmmaking is concerned, I really think it is, so far, what I've done best, what I've been trying to achieve all these years—simplicity." Malle's description of the film and his filmmaking in general is most apt; his style does carry an air of simplicity, if only because it seems so effortless.

May Fools (*Milou en mai* [1989]) offers an intimate and comical portrait of family life. *Damage* (1992) explores more of the dark, sexual themes of his earliest work. Malle's last film, *Vanya On 42nd Street* (1994), is an interesting, original film that shows a rehearsal for Chekhov's *Uncle Vanya*. The film is a highly cinematic example of filmed theater, and shows, through excellent performances by Wallace Shawn and Julianne Moore (among others), the excitement and reward afforded through both theater and film. Malle's enthusiasm for filmmaking was cut short by his early death in 1995 from lymphoma, but his remarkable output will be looked upon as exemplary filmmaking.

Writing in 1993, interviewer Philip French said, "Malle has experienced few serious setbacks or major failures. From the beginning he has been in control of his career to an unusual degree. And while the variety of his subject matter and the absence of a consistent style have often puzzled critics, Malle's work has a rare coherence." Indeed, because Malle was eclectic in his choices and subject matter, he is remembered as a unique filmmaker who cared deeply about his subjects. From all accounts, Malle was a generous director, whose love of filmmaking clearly shows in his work and his work ethic. "If I keep being fascinated and very enthusiastic about making films, it's because I love actors, and I love nonactors even more," Malle said in a 1989 interview. "It's my way of dealing with people." His way of dealing with people is fascinating and engaging, and his films are a testament to his long engagement with the movies.

Other Films *Humain, trop humain,* documentary (1974); *Crackers* (1984); *Alamo Bay* (1985).

References French, Philip, *Malle on Malle* (London: Faber and Faber, 1993); Hickenlooper, George,

"Louis Malle: Impression Filmmaker," in *Reel Conversations: Candid Interviews with Film's Foremost Directors and Critics* (New York: Citadel Press, 1991); "Louis Malle: Dialogue on Film," *American Film* 14, no. 6 (1989): 22–28.

—W.V.

Mamoulian, Rouben (1897–1987) Rouben Mamoulian moved and worked with equal facility and success in the worlds of the Broadway theater and the Hollywood film. He was born in Tiflis (now Tbilisi), in the Caucasus Mountains of Georgia on October 8, 1897, the son of Armenian parents. At age seven he moved with his family to Paris, where he attended the Lycée Montaigne. After two years at Moscow University, where he graduated in criminal law, he studied acting, writing and directing at the Moscow Art Theatre under Eugene Vakhtangov. In 1920, determined to learn the English language via the plays of Shakespeare, he went to London and secured his first important directorial assignment in a production of Austin Page's *The Beating on the Door* at the St. James Theatre. He recalled later that this was the "first and last production" that he directed in a naturalistic manner. "In my subsequent work, my aim always was rhythm and poetic stylization."

The show's success earned him an invitation from George Eastman to come to America and organize and direct the new American Opera Company in Rochester. In a dozen productions he worked to craft a style of theater that would blend dance, music, lighting, and color. His first New York City production was DuBose Heyward's *Porgy,* followed by several more productions. Paramount Pictures duly beckoned and in 1929 Mamoulian found himself in the Astoria, Long-Island, studios studying filmmaking techniques. Undaunted by the challenges of the new synchronized technology that was revolutionizing the film industry, he embarked on a series of masterpieces in the 1929–36 period that mark the peak of his creative work.

For his first film, he adapted a novel by Beth Brown about a fading burlesque queen who sacrifices herself for her daughter. *Applause* (1929) is a landmark in the history of the American sound film. By contrast to the many static and stage-bound talkies of the day, this backstage drama liberated the camera from its shackles, shot many scenes in natural exteriors, and developed a sophisticated method of mixing multiple sound tracks to create asynchronous combinations of sound and image and imaginative "montages" of sounds and voices. *Applause* also marked the screen debut of entertainer Helen Morgan. His next film, *City Streets* (1931), was an unusually sensitive gangster saga based on a story by Dashiell Hammett. One of its technical innovations was the use of interior monologues to reveal the characters' innermost feelings.

Dr. Jekyll and Mr. Hyde (1931) further stylized the union of image and sound. The famous opening sequence adopts a "first-person" point of view as Dr. Jekyll (Fredric March) prepares himself to deliver a lecture. Everything is seen through his eyes—his hands on the keyboard of an organ, his mirror reflection, the carriage that carries him to the lecture hall, the classroom full of students, etc. The "transformation" sequence is even more startling. By means of color filters his face darkens and changes before our eyes in a continuous shot; and an innovative use of synthetic sounds and voice montages convey his distraught inner state. Moreover, the film's blunt suggestions of pathological sexuality ran it afoul of the Hollywood censors. A triumph in the history of the horror film, it earned Oscars for best actor (Fredric March) and cinematography (Karl Struss).

With *Love Me Tonight* (1933), Mamoulian delivered an authentic screen masterpiece, a musical with lyrics and score by Rodgers and Hart that paired Jeanette MacDonald and Maurice Chevalier. Part operetta, part fairy tale, part ingeniously suggestive sex comedy, it is endlessly inventive. The songs and dialogue blend in a seamless flow. The opening sequence, a duplication of a similar scene in *Porgy,* is a splendid montage of the sights and

Rouben Mamoulian (Author's collection)

sounds of Paris waking up in the morning—the tapping of shoemaker's hammer, the *swish* of a broom, the *whump* of a carpet being shaken out from a high balcony, the toot of a horn, etc.—that rises to a delirious crescendo. The rendition of the famous "Isn't It Romantic?" number displays his innovative method of using a song to bridge space and time, beginning the tune in one place and continuing it through a series of changing locations, situations, and voices—a tailor's shop, a taxicab, a locomotive, a farmer's field, a castle—in a fashion that might qualify it as a proto-"music video." Much of the dialogue is in rhymed couplets, and there is even a sequence in slow motion. "If you were to see *Love Me Tonight*," Mamoulian said in 1970, "although it is a very light, gay musical, you'd see in it most clearly what motivates me, what I like. The whole of *Love Me Tonight* is a poem, from beginning to end. Everything is

rhythm, counterpoint, stylization." Capping this extraordinarily productive period is a Greta Garbo vehicle, *Queen Christina* (1933), perhaps her finest film. The story of the 17th-century queen who sails to Spain after the death of her lover (John Gilbert) is marked by striking costume conceptions (Garbo spends much screen time dressed in men's clothes) and powerful, wordless sequences (notably, the aftermath of a loving tryst when she moves about her room, lovingly gazing upon and caressing the furniture and the draperies; and the concluding shot, wherein the camera slowly dollies in to her enigmatic face as she stands motionless in the bow of the departing ship).

Mamoulian's subsequent film career—interrupted by occasional forays back to the Broadway stage to direct *Porgy and Bess* (1935) and two Rodgers and Hammerstein musicals, *Oklahoma!* (1943) and *Carousel* (1945)—produced a number of films that have aroused considerable difference of opinion. Those like Andrew Sarris, who allege he went into decline—"Mamoulian's tragedy is that of the innovator who runs out of innovations"—cite banalities and lapses of taste in pictures like the Marlene Dietrich vehicle, *Song of Songs* (1933); the first Technicolor feature, *Becky Sharp* (1935); the "Western musicals," *The Gay Desperado* (1936) and *High, Wide and Handsome* (1937); the Clifford Odets adaptation of *Golden Boy* (1939); the swashbuckler *The Mark of Zorro* (1940); the Eugene O'Neill adaptation, *Summer Holiday* (1948); and a musical remake of *Ninotchka,* retitled *Silk Stockings* (1957). Other commentators, like Tom Milne, find in these same titles ample evidence that Mamoulian's creative powers remained unimpaired.

Mamoulian's remaining years were marked by aborted projects (*Laura* [1943] and *Cleopatra* [1961]) and the writing of plays. He died in Los Angeles on December 4, 1987. "I don't believe in naturalism on the screen or the stage," he declared. "I believe in stylization, which if properly done comes over as greater truth than reality. It's really [the] inner reality of things." To commentator Tom Milne, this stylization is best expressed in *move-*

ment: "Mamoulian films have as their real distinguishing mark their unerring sense of rhythm in exploring the sensuous pleasures of movement. . . . Movement to Mamoulian is like a brush-stroke to a painter: the delicate, infinitely variable factor which can bring life to a still life, beauty to a human face, emotion to a landscape, transforming dross into gold."

Other Films   *We Live Again* (1934); *Blood and Sand* (1941); *Rings on Her Fingers* (1942).

References   Coursodon, Jean-Pierre, *American Directors,* vol. 1 (New York: McGraw-Hill, 1983); Milne, Tom, *Mamoulian* (Bloomington: Indiana University Press, 1969).

—J.C.T.

Micheaux, Oscar (1883–1951)   Oscar Micheaux is considered the preeminent figure in early African-American independent film. He produced and directed nearly 50 films between 1918 and 1948 and was the author of seven novels. Micheaux was born in Metropolis, Illinois, in 1883, the fifth of 13 children. His father was a farmer, his mother a schoolteacher. In 1900 he moved to Chicago, where he worked as a Pullman porter for several years. He eventually saved enough money to purchase land near Gregory, South Dakota, in 1904. His first few years of homesteading were a success, and in 1910 he married Orlean McCracken. Micheaux's farming venture collapsed, though, as his marriage began to dissolve. In 1911, Orlean's father, the Reverend McCracken, brought his daughter back to Chicago. Despicable clergymen, apparently modeled after his father-in-law, appeared in countless films and novels produced by Micheaux.

In 1913 Micheaux wrote and published his novel, *The Conquest.* Two other novels, *The Forged Note* (1915) and *The Homesteader* (1917), followed. The popularity of *The Homesteader* drew the attention of the Lincoln Motion Picture Company, one of the first independent black film corporations, which wanted to film the novel. During negotiations, Micheaux was inspired to enter film pro-

duction and formed the Micheaux Film and Book Company. In 1918 he filmed the highly autobiographical *The Homesteader,* the first feature-length all-black film produced in the United States.

Micheaux's second film, *Within Our Gates* (1920), was among his most controversial because it showed a white mob lynching an African-American couple. The film was either heavily censored or banned outright throughout the United States. Micheaux dealt with themes in his motion pictures that were controversial in both the black and white community. *The Brute* (1920) dealt with "the problem of the brute in the household," in other words, domestic violence. *The Symbol of the Unconquered* (1920) illustrated the barbarism of the Ku Klux Klan. *The Gunsaulus Mystery* (1921) was based on the infamous Leo Frank case, but substituted the Jewish lynch victim with one that was African-American. Micheaux was prolific during the silent era, directing at least 28 original or reedited versions of films in the period 1919–29. Among these films is *Body and Soul* (1924), Paul Robeson's screen debut.

Because he worked outside the studio system, Micheaux often had to deliver films personally to exhibitors. In 1928 he was forced to file bankruptcy. In late 1929 he reorganized with new capital and created the Micheaux Film Corporation. His first all-talking feature film, *The Exile* (1931), was also the first black-directed sound feature produced in the United States. The added expense of sound contributed to the opinion that Micheaux's films were aesthetically inferior to white-produced films in the 1930s and 1940s. His sound films include *Temptation* (1936), *The Underworld* (1936), *God's Stepchildren* (1938), and *The Notorious Elinor Lee* (1940). By World War II, the sharp increase in production costs drove the Micheaux Film Corporation out of business. In the latter war years, Micheaux focused his attention on publishing once again, churning out four novels between 1944 and 1947. His last venture into film production was *The Betrayal* (1948), which was a financial and critical disaster. The film pioneer was lambasted in the black press for the poor aesthetic quality of the production. Micheaux died in 1951 in Charlotte, North Carolina.

References Green, J. Ronald, *Straight Lick: The Cinema of Oscar Micheaux* (Bloomington: Indiana University Press, 2000); Van Epps-Taylor, Betti Carol, *Oscar Micheaux: Dakota Homesteader, Author, Pioneer Film Maker* (Mariah Press, 1999); Young, Joseph A., *Black Novelist as White Racist* (New York: Greenwood Press, 1989).

—G.B.

Milestone, Lewis (1895–1980)

In a career that embraced an amazing variety of projects of variable quality, from the masterpieces *All Quiet on the Western Front* (1930) and *The Front Page* (1931) to the hack work of *Ocean's Eleven* (1962), Lewis Milestone remained as unpredictable as he was wildly eclectic. He was born Lev Milstein in Moldova, near Odessa, Ukraine, into an affluent Jewish family. When he was five years old his family moved to Kishinev where he showed an early predilection for theatrical matters. Rather than studying engineering in college, as his father had hoped, he impulsively left the country for America. After several years of hand-to-mouth existence in New York City and Boston, working as a janitor and salesman, he got a job as a photographer's assistant. He used his experience in the war, working for the photographic division of the Army Signal Corps, for which he made training films and edited combat footage. After his discharge in 1919, he took American citizenship, changed his name to "Lewis Milestone," and worked in Hollywood as a cutting assistant. Work with HENRY KING and THOMAS HARPER INCE soon advanced him to the position of screenwriter and assistant director; and by the mid-1920s he was cowriting pictures for Warner Bros. with another aspiring young filmmaker, Darryl F. Zanuck.

As a result of contractual and temperamental disputes with Warners and Paramount, the maverick Milestone signed a contract with Howard Hughes, just then embarking on a career as an independent producer. The rambunctious war film, *Two Arabian Knights* (1927); a sophisticated Lubitsch-style comedy, *The Garden of Eden* (1928); and a tough gangster picture, *The Racket* (1928) followed in quick succession. Now a director of some stature, he was loaned out to Universal to make what would come to be regarded as his masterpiece, *All Quiet on the Western Front* (1930), adapted from Erich Remarque's pacifistic novel of a young German idealist confronting the horrors of war. Quite apart from its deeply felt humanistic concerns, which have established it as an antiwar classic, Milestone's formidable camera mobility and sound-editing technique restored a fluidly rhythmic character to a medium that had been so recently stifled by cumbersome sound apparatus. To simulate the European settings, he shot on locations near Laguna Beach, at the Irving Ranch 50 miles outside of Hollywood, the Pathe backlot in Culver City, and at Balboa. No sooner had the film won a best picture Oscar than Milestone immediately embarked on his last film for Hughes, another instant classic that added to his growing prestige, *The Front Page* (1931). Adapted from the Ben Hecht-Charles MacArthur 1928 stage hit, it was a hard-boiled, wisecracking satiric saga of newspapermen who shamelessly sacrifice personal integrity and professional loyalty for the sake of a story. Again, Milestone's mobile camera technique and sharp editing imparted a snappy pace to what could have been a mere stagebound dramatic adaptation.

At the apex of his career in the early 1930s, Milestone acquired his own production unit. "He is the kind of director it is a pleasure to see working," opined critic Otis Ferguson, "and apparently a pleasure to work with. He knows what he wants and therefore needs no pose of weighty thought or picturesque energy . . . and he knows the theater art with its visual music and command on the emotions." However, Milestone's subsequent career never quite recaptured the unqualified success of his early pictures. For example: *Rain* (1932) seemed stagey and Joan Crawford seemed uncomfortable in the role of Sadie Thompson; *Hallelujah,*

I'm a Bum (1933) was a bizarre mixture of left-wing polemic, Rodgers and Hart songs, and grating performances by leading players Al Jolson and Harry Langdon (one of Jolson's songs, "You Are Too Beautiful," became a standard); *The General Died at Dawn* (1936) was a fascinating but flawed Clifford Odets script about an American adventurer (Gary Cooper) in contemporary China who helps peasants escape the brutal tyranny of a feudal warlord (Akim Tamiroff); and *Of Mice and Men* (1939), an adaptation of John Steinbeck's 1937 novel, which, like John Ford's contemporaneous *The Grapes of Wrath,* probed societal injustice in the manner of the documentary photographers of the day, Walker Evans and Dorothea Lange.

The war years saw Milestone shifting gears from his pacifist stance to a pro-war valorization of America and its allies. *Edge of Darkness* (1943) depicted the heroics of the Norwegian resistance. *The North Star* (1943) promoted the Russian cause in a story of the impact of the German invasion on a small Russian village. Its pro-Russian politics became an embarrassment during the HUAC hearings of the postwar years. *The Purple Heart* (1944) was concerned with the torture and trial of eight American airmen at the hands of the Japanese. *A Walk in the Sun* (1945) was undoubtedly the best of the bunch. Its chronicle of an infantry platoon's landing at Salerno and its six-mile trek inland to capture a German-held farmhouse was told in decidedly unromanticized terms in a pseudodocumentary style. Even here, Milestone incurred a measure of negative criticism. "Upon subsequent viewings," write commentators David L. Parker and Burton J. Shapiro, "*A Walk in the Sun*'s values may seem to shift: those who once found its literary stylization embarrassing may now find it sensitive and lyrical; those who once found it a poetic revelation of what the cinema could do beyond the conventional action film may now find it artificial. It remains an ambitious, touching, and distinguished attempt to show the average man's war." Historian Jeanine Basinger asserts that it is "a truly allegorical film, consciously mythologizing

the war." Moreover, "In its presentation of a long walk, from dawn until noon, made by the men in a single platoon, the film fixes the genre firmly and forever. It translates the entire experience of World War II into one representative group, one walk, one big battle with a skirmish on the way. It makes all our war combat films into one movie for us to remember more easily."

Never comfortable working within the studio system, Milestone in the immediate postwar years joined Enterprise Studios, a group of independent producers, directors, and actors. His short-lived association resulted in the ambitious but unsuccessful adaptation of Remarque's *Arch of Triumph* (1948), a portrait of Paris in the years immediately preceding the war. Political tensions arising from Milestone's avowed leftist leanings soon got him into trouble with the HUAC investigations, and although he was never officially blacklisted, his subsequent films perhaps suffered from the many personal and professional attacks he incurred, including *Kangaroo* (1952), a period film shot in the Australian outback; *Les Miserables* (1952), a disaster even according to Milestone; *Pork Chop Hill* (1959), a Korean War drama about an infantry platoon's attempts to capture a hill of minimal strategic value; and *Ocean's Eleven* (1960), a mere vehicle for the antics of Frank Sinatra's Rat Pack. Milestone's last film was a remake of *Mutiny on the Bounty* (1962), a box-office disaster marred by temperamental clashes with Marlon Brando. Milestone died on September 25, 1980.

Among the major Hollywood directors, Milestone's career is the most uneven. Ever the fiercely independent maverick, he was frequently at odds with his producers, which doubtless took its toll. Andrew Sarris, in his *The American Cinema* (1968), declares that despite Milestone's undeniable virtuosity with mobile camera and editing, his work lacks a consistent personal viewpoint. "Milestone is almost the classic example of the uncommitted director. From the beginning, his editing was mechanical rather than analytical, and his tracking synthetic rather than expressive. . . . His professionalism is as unyielding as it is meaningless." In a rejoinder to Sarris, Parker and Shapiro aver that "it is better said that he has rarely given less than the best he had to offer to even the most perfunctory of his assignments. His judicious clean storytelling is an art a great deal more difficult to achieve than its flowing, effortless unrolling would indicate. In an age obsessed with cinema auteurs, there should still be the ability to appreciate one of Hollywood's *grandes seigneurs*."

Other Films *Betrayal* (1929); *The Captain Hates the Sea* (1934); *Anything Goes* (1936); *The Night of Nights* (1939); *Lucky Partners* (1940); *The Strange Love of Martha Ivers* (1946); *The Red Pony* (1949); *Halls of Montezuma* (1950); *Melba* (1953); *They Who Dare* (1953); *La Vedova X* (1955).

References Basinger, Jeanine, *The World War II Combat Film* (New York: Columbia University Press, 1986); Ferguson, Otis, "Lewis Milestone 'Action!'" *Film Comment,* March 1974: 46–47; Parker, David L., and Burton J. Shapiro, "Lewis Milestone," in *Close Up: The Contract Director,* ed. Jon Tuska (Metuchen, N.J.: Scarecrow Press, 1976).

—J.C.T.

Minnelli, Vincente (1903–1986)

Known primarily for his 13 musical films, Vincente Minnelli was a versatile director with uncommon flair who worked in a variety of genres, including 11 melodramas and eight comedies. He was born on February 28, 1903, in Chicago into an entertainment family. His father and uncle ran the Minnelli Brothers' Dramatic Tent Show, which played one-week stands throughout the midwest. By the time he was in his mid-teens, he was designing and painting signs and drop-curtains for movie houses and designing show windows at the Marshall Fields department store. Moving on to New York he became set designer at the Paramount Theatre, where he designed Grace Moore's musical, *Du Barry.* He later worked as the stage director at Radio City Music Hall, directing several Broadway musical adaptations and the De Falla ballet, *El Amor Brujo.*

Minnelli's connections with Hollywood were tentative at first. In 1937 he took his own musical script, *Times Square,* to Paramount studios; but after eight months of inactivity he returned to Broadway. A second offer came in 1940 from producer Arthur Freed at MGM, and this time Minnelli came to Hollywood to stay. His partnership with Freed would have a significant impact on the course of the American film musical. With the exception of *I Dood It* (1943) and *On a Clear Day You Can See Forever* (1970), they would work together on all of Minnelli's musical films. With Freed's support, Minnelli was prepared to take his new post seriously, to bring to the standard musical form a new rigor and inner integrity. "I worry a great deal about the characters," he said; "—what they're thinking, what their lives are like, what their point of view is. . . . The important thing is the situation, and that is played seriously. . . . If you want to do a musical, it requires just as much plot and preparation as *Hamlet*." While spending two years learning camera and editing techniques, he staged Judy Garland's musical numbers for BUSBY BERKELEY's *Babes on Broadway* (1940). His directorial debut came with *Cabin in the Sky* (1943), featuring an all-black cast of Lena Horne, Ethel Waters, Eddie "Rochester" Anderson, and many others. Immediately, many of the distinctive Minnelli traits emerged, including the interconnections between reality and fantasy, in this case, the sleazy Paradise Café and a well-scrubbed Heaven; an elaborate dream sequence, as the Angels of Heaven and Hell contend for the soul of the protagonist, Little Joe (Anderson); an integration of music, song, and story; and a reliance on camera mobility through crane shots and tracking movements.

Minnelli's real "breakthrough," however, came a year later with the Technicolor *Meet Me in St. Louis.* As historian Joseph Andrew Casper demonstrates exhaustively in his study of Minnelli, the perfect balance of music and story, performance and décor, character and camera movement is everywhere in evidence. "I'm only interested in musical stories in which one can achieve a complete integration of dancing, singing, sound, and vision," declared Minnelli. Here, the songs arise spontaneously from their dramatic contexts rather than relying upon a "backstage" justification. For example, "Skip to My Lou" results from an impromptu party in the family home, and it in turn gives rise to the charming cakewalk number ("Under the Bamboo Tree") with Esther (Judy Garland) and her baby sister, Tootie (Margaret O'Brien). "The Trolley Song" teams Garland with a chorus of passengers during a trolley ride. "The Boy Next Door" is nothing less than a soliloquy given melodic shape as Garland gazes pensively out her window. And "Have Yourself a Merry Little Christmas" perfectly captures the bittersweet mood of the family's impending move from their lovely home to the bustle and grime of New York City. "Content or semantic value is in the form of sounds, figures, textures, shapes, colors, designs, movements, tempos, and rhythms," writes Casper. "It involves the viewer sensually, affectively, and cognitively."

Thus, *Meet Me in St. Louis* demonstrates at the outset of Minnelli's film career his ability to juggle the unreality of the musical form with the more dramatic realism of the storyline. Joel E. Siegel notes, "Minnelli's best pictures . . . are about people trying to reconcile their private dreams with the harshness and banality of the world around them." Moreover, music and dance are employed to reveal the interior, psychological states of the characters that lie beyond the flashy surfaces of the action. For example, the surrealistic *Yolanda and the Thief* (1945) featured one of the screen's first uses of an elaborately staged dance sequence to illuminate the romantic yearnings of its characters, Fred Astaire and Lucille Bremer. One of his only "backstage" musicals, *The Band Wagon* (1953) was a Fred Astaire vehicle remembered primarily for the imaginative "Girl Hunt Ballet," a veritable psychodrama modeled after the detective stories of Mickey Spillane. This theme was carried forward in his four-picture collaboration with Alan Jay

Lerner: *An American in Paris* (1951) featured GENE KELLY in an elaborate dream sequence that blended George Gershwin's music with a dream ballet of images derived from the paintings of Toulouse-Lautrec. *Brigadoon* (1954) was a more straightforward adaptation of Lerner and Loewe's Broadway hit, although it too contained dance sequences illuminating the darker conflicts of the major characters. And *On a Clear Day You Can See Forever* (1970), a Paramount picture, brought psychoanalysis to the fore when a psychologist (Yves Montand) falls in love with an earlier incarnation of one of his patients (Barbra Streisand).

Minnelli's background in literature, painting, music, and theatre led him to specialize in pictures in which artists and entertainers were the principal protagonists. Two significant examples are *An American in Paris,* which won six Academy Awards, including best picture, and *The Pirate* (1948), co-starring Kelly and Judy Garland. In the first, Kelly portrays Jerry Mulligan, an American painter who falls in love with Leslie Caron, a war orphan who is engaged to her guardian. Work and romance intertwine, as the story by Alan J. Lerner and the music of George Gershwin seek a balance. The numbers represent Minnelli at his most intimate and flamboyant, by turns. "Tra-La-La," a duet for Kelly and Oscar Levant, is a charming routine that is staged in a tiny room dominated by a grand piano. By contrast, the climactic ballet is a splashy, sometimes awkward melange of Kelly's acrobatic dance stylings, a slightly truncated version of the "American in Paris" music, and dancers who bring to life the cabaret images of Toulouse-Lautrec. (Its scale, brash energy, and lavish color—photographed by ace cinematographer John Alton—are a superb contrast to the more moderate tone of another attempt to visualize this music in a Warner Bros. picture made five years earlier, *Rhapsody in Blue.*) Yet, impressive as it is, it displays many of the problems that frequently assail Minnelli's musicals. Its effusive energy is occasionally forced and frequently borders on bad taste, charges Siegel: "Kelly poses, postures and wags his bottom with narcissistic gusto . . . [and] the male chorus, in tap shoes, joins the women, in toe shoes, for some uncomfortable-looking maneuvers involving a bent posture and steps resembling the barnyard shuffle."

Although *The Pirate* may be less prestigious than *An American in Paris* (it received some of Minnelli's worst reviews), it has emerged in the course of time as one of his most interesting musicals. Adapted from S. N. Behrman's Broadway comedy, the film has Kelly cast as "Serafin," an itinerant entertainer who masquerades as the notorious pirate Macoco ("Mack the Black") in his dalliance with the fair lady, Manuela (Judy Garland). Again, fantasy and reality sometimes stub their toes on each other, as when the *real* Macoco turns out to be gross, obese Don Pedro (Walter Slezak); and sometimes blend in a delightfully seamless whole, as when Garland daydreams Kelly into the swashbuckling freebooter of the "Pirate Ballet" (which owes not a little to the athletic exuberance of Douglas Fairbanks, Sr.). Even the tandem dancers, the Nicholas brothers, have their moment in the spotlight, as they appear near the end to join Kelly and Garland in "Be a Clown." The unlikely combination of Cole Porter music and swashbuckling romance is so outrageous it defies critical cavils. Perhaps it could only work, as it does here, in a totally romanticized, blatantly artificial Caribbean setting.

Minnelli's nonmusical films reveal a variety of subjects and moods, while retaining his unfailing sense of décor and maintaining a tension between dream and reality. In chronological order, *The Clock* (1945), adapted from a story by Paul Gallico, is a love story between a GI (Robert Walker) and a working girl (Judy Garland) that benefits more from the carefully observed soundscape of the city and the loving gestures of its protagonists than from its rather mawkish plot. *Undercurrent* (1946) was an outright melodrama in which a newly married wife (Katharine Hepburn) discovers the heretofore-hidden psychopathic tendencies of her husband (Robert Mitchum). Two comedies followed, *Father of the Bride* (1950) and *The Long, Long*

Trailer (1954). The first cast Spencer Tracy as a midwestern banker who watches in cranky bewilderment as preparations for his daughter's wedding fly out of control (perhaps not unlike Minnelli himself watching his next film go over budget and beyond deadline). *Trailer* was another kind of marital catastrophe as newlyweds Lucille Ball and Desi Arnaz embark on a disastrous vacation in the gigantic trailer of the title. *The Bad and the Beautiful* (1953) adroitly captures the ruthless opportunism and the broken dreams of life in the film industry. Kirk Douglas starred as Jonathan Shields, who never hesitates to sacrifice anyone (including himself) in the service of his art. *The Cobweb* (1955) was a noirish investigation of life inside a psychiatric clinic.

Lust for Life (1956) has been ranked by Minnelli as his favorite film, in which he indulged his passion for painting and for vivid color schemes (herein, a yellow-predominating palette) in recounting the life of Vincent Van Gogh (Kirk Douglas). *Some Came Running* (1959) was adapted from James Jones's partly autobiographical novel about a war veteran (Frank Sinatra) who returns to his small Indiana town only to encounter a viper's nest of bigotry and hypocrisy. Its riotous profusion of neon signs culminate in the deliriously mad carnival sequence, as extravagant as anything in the musicals. Among the comedies that played out Minnelli's career were *The Courtship of Eddie's Father* (1963) and *Good-bye Charlie* (1964). His last film, *A Matter of Time* (1976), was also the only one in which he directed his daughter, Liza. This portrait of a young artist (Liza) and an old dreamer (Ingrid Bergman) was a last summation of one of his favorite themes.

Vincente Minnelli died in Beverly Hills on July 25, 1986. "I have never catered to the audience," Minnelli wrote in his autobiography, *I Remember It Well* (1974). "How could I when its assessment of my work is lauded in one breath as masterly in atmosphere and dismissed as mere decoration in another? Basically, I work to please myself. But I'm the hardest person to please that

I know." Like so many of the dedicated artists in his pictures—particularly Jonathan Shields in *The Bad and the Beautiful*—Minnelli's own devotion to work left him little room for a private life. It had disastrous consequences on his three marriages, to Judy Garland, Georgette Magnani, and Denise Gigante. All three wives complained in the divorce proceedings that his work left no time for them. Ironically, as Joseph Andrew Casper notes, it is the essence of *play* and carefree pleasures that emerges from Minnelli's best work: "Minnelli's fantasy and festivity frees one from the everyday routine. More than compensation (distraction and wish fulfillment) and more than a defense mechanism (insulation), the Minnelli musical is a liberating process without which life would be intolerable."

Other Films *Madame Bovary* (1949); *Father's Little Dividend* (1951); *Kismet* (1955); *Tea and Sympathy* (1956); *Designing Woman* (1957); *The Reluctant Debutante* (1958); *Gigi* (1958); *Home from the Hill* (1960); *The Four Horsemen of the Apocalypse* (1962); *The Sandpiper* (1955).

References Altman, Rick, *The American Film Musical* (Bloomington: Indiana University Press, 1987); Casper, Joseph Andrew, *Vincente Minnelli and the Film Musical* (New York: A. S. Barnes, 1977); Minnelli, Vincente, *I Remember It Well* (New York: Doubleday, 1974); Siegel, Joel E., "'The Exception to Every Rule, Is It Not?': The Films of Vincente Minnelli & Alan Jay Lerner," *Bright Lights* 3, no. 1 (1980): 7–11, 19, 34.

—J.C.T.

Mizoguchi, Kenji (1898–1956)

One of Japan's most distinguished filmmakers, Kenji Mizoguchi's films are distinguished for their historical sweep, sensitivity to women's issues, and elaborate mise-en-scène. He was born in Tokyo on May 16, 1898. Despite his father's refusal to allow him to pursue his education beyond the level of primary school, Mizoguchi enrolled himself in the Aohashi Western Painting Research Institute. After serving an apprenticeship as a textile designer and working as a newspaper illustrator, he entered the Nikkatsu Mukojima studio as an assistant to Eizo

Tanaka and Osamu Wakayama. He directed his first film in 1923. Throughout the next two decades he worked in a wide variety of forms, including detective stories, expressionist dramas, war movies, social dramas, ghost stories, comedies, and "New School" melodramas (a form of melodrama in which male actors portrayed the roles of self-sacrificing women). It was at this time that he first worked with scriptwriter Yoshikata Yoda, with whom he would work for the rest of his career. During these formative years Mizoguchi deployed all manner of cinematic techniques, like frequent dissolves, flashbacks, rapid editing, and subjective camera. In his mature years, he fused these devices in a style that alternated static scenes with boldly sweeping action sequences.

Throughout his career, his experience in the New School surfaced in his dramas about women. In the trilogy of films adapted from the novels of Kyoka Izumi—*Nihon bashi* (1929), *The Water Magician* (*Taki no shiratto* [1933]), and *The Downfall of Osen* (*Orizuru Osen* [1935])—and in his last films, particularly *The Life of Oharu* (*Saikaku ichidai onna* [1952]) and *Music of Gion* (*Gion bayashi* [1953])— he transforms the theme of the victimized woman into depictions of female characters who are strong enough to fight for their own survival against the inequities of their socially gendered roles. *Life of Oharu* chronicles the adventures of Oharu Okui (Kinuyo Tanaka), a prostitute in late-17th-century Japan. The episodic narrative begins with her service in the Imperial Palace in Kyoto and continues through a series of persecutions at the hands of various noblemen and commoners. "Eschewing the elements of fantasy and myth that figure in his subsequent period films," writes critic Jonathan Rosenbaum, "*Oharu* combines the form of the picaresque novel with much of the social analysis common to Mizoguchi's 'contemporary' geisha films. Above all, it is a *materialist* analysis—a depiction of woman treated, traded, valued, degraded, and discarded as a material object." His last film, *Street of Shame* (*Akasen chitai* [1956]), a disturbing examination of prostitution in contemporary Japan, so aroused public outcry that a ban against prostitution was instituted.

Outside Japan, Mizoguchi's reputation rests primarily on the period dramas of the 1940s and 1950s. *The Forty-Seven Ronin* (*Genroku chuhsingura* [1941]) and *Tales of the Taira Clan* (*Shin heike monogatari* [1955]) deploy sweeping crowd scenes and elaborate mise-en-scène camera techniques (long takes, the deep-focus frame, and unobtrusive direction) against vividly realized medieval backdrops. A ghost story, *Ugetsu monogatari* (1953), ranks as one of the truly great ghost stories on film. This classic tale of the seduction of a peasant potter (Masayuki Mori) by a phantom Lady Wakasa juxtaposes action scenes of the barbarism of civil war with highly stylized ghostly scenes. The medieval fable, *Sansho the Bailiff* (*Sansho dayu* [1952]), chronicles the bitter victory of the kidnapped hero, Zushio, over the villainous slave camp overseer Sansho. In this fairy tale, however, no one lives happily ever after.

Before World War II Mizoguchi suffered a measure of critical opprobrium against a subject matter and technique alleged to be "old-fashioned." In his period films, for example, charged critic Matsuo Kishi, the preoccupation with historical authenticity and detail becomes merely a "strange devotion to meaningless trivia," which covers up a "conspicuous lack of characterization." In addition, declared critic Tadashi Ijima, Mizoguchi's undue reliance on long shots, while masterfully executed, imposed restrictions on the range of his camera technique. Contemporary critic Tadao Sato notes that Mizoguchi's postwar films, particularly *Oharu,* reveal a more subtle shading of character and emotion. Moreover, he defends Mizoguchi's mise-en-scène and compares it to the shaping gestures of Japanese dance: "[I]n moving from one [pose] to the next, the body changes its balance in a smooth, flowing manner. Similarly, Mizoguchi's one scene, one cut technique is sequential motion; motion changing from one exquisite shape to another. Short cuts cannot possibly capture this subtle, relentless flow, which

can only be caught by complex camera movements like panning and craning. Thus, far from being static, Mizoguchi's long one cut is filled with visual restlessness, interspersed with interludes of breathless anticipation for, even as we watch, the structure of any single scene is always in the process of dynamic transformation."

A powerful figure in the Japanese film industry and the director of 85 films, Mizoguchi headed the vast union that governed all production personnel in Japan. He received virtually every major Japanese film citation and award; and *The Life of Oharu* won the Grand Prize at the Venice Film Festival. Retrospectives of his 31 extant films brought him to renewed critical attention in the 1980s. He died in Kyoto of leukemia on August 24, 1956.

Other Films *City of Desire* (*Joen no chimata* [1924]); *813* (aka *The Adventures of Arsène Lupin* [1923]); *The Song of the Mountain Pass* (*Toge no uta* [1924]); *Women Are Strong* (*Josei wa tsuyoshi* [1924]); *Queen of the Circus* (*Kyokubadan no joo* [1925]); *A Paper Doll's Whisper of Spring* (*Kaminingyo haru no sasayaki* [1926]); *A Man's Life* (*Hito no issho* [1928]); *The Morning Sun Shines* (*Asahi wa kagayaku* [1929]); *And Yet They Go* (*Shikamo karera wa yuku* [1931]); *The Mountain Pass of Love and Hate* (aka *Aizo toge* [1934]); *Osaka Elegy* (*Naniwa ereji* [1936]); *Victory Song* (*Hisshoka* [1945]); *Utamaro and His Five Women* (*Utamaro o meguru gonin no onna* [1946]); *Women of the Night* (*Yoru no onnatachi* [1948]).

References Rosenbaum, Jonathan, "The Life of Oharu," in *Foreign Affairs,* ed. Kathy Schulz Huffhines, (San Francisco: Mercury House, 1991), pp. 84–87; Sato, Tadao, *Currents in Japanese Cinema* (Kodansha International Ltd., 1987).

—J.C.T.

Murnau, F. W. (1888–1931)

One of the preeminent German directors of the silent era, F. W. Murnau also achieved in his 22 films an international reputation for his flair for fantasy and allegory and his sensitivity to poetic imagery. He was born Friedrich Wilhelm Plumpe on December 28, 1888, in Bielefeld. After studying philology in Berlin and art history and literature at Heidelberg, he met the eminent stage director/producer Max Reinhardt. After service in the infantry and air corps during the Great War, he changed his name to "Murnau," a small town in Bavaria, and with Conrad Veidt and other colleagues from the Reinhardt school, formed a film company in 1919. A year later he met a man who would prove to be extremely influential to his mature films, the man who had scripted *The Cabinet of Dr. Caligari* (1919), screenwriter Carl Mayer.

After several tentative efforts with and without Mayer that would reveal little of the mature Murnau to come, he directed one of his most important films, *Nosferatu* (1922), freely adapted from Bram Stoker's *Dracula*. One of the most influential of all horror films, its initial release was limited by actions brought against it by the Stoker estate. In addition to the chilling performance by the cadaverous Max Schreck in the title role, Murnau employed a variety of cinematic skills to suggest and enhance the film's eerie mood, including the use of cast shadows (suggesting the unearthly insubstantiality of the vampiric presence), stop-action and accelerated motion (especially in the scenes when Count Orlok's coach approaches Hutter and when the vampire stacks up coffins in the castle crypt), and negatively polarized black-and-white photography (the coach scenes). Although the film grew out of the expressionistic theatrical tradition, it ventures into more naturalistic territory with an abundance of exterior location shooting, abandoning the claustrophobic distortions of a picture like *Caligari* in favor of skewed camera angles and chiaroscuro lighting schemes. Critic Robin Wood says "nature" is the real subject of *Nosferatu,* citing the many ways the vampire is associated with nature—his castle appearing to be an extension of the mountain, his appearance suggesting a nocturnal animal with fangs and claws, his movements like the sidling motions of slithering creatures. (In 1979 WERNER HERZOG

paid tribute to Murnau's achievement with his *Nosferatu: Phantom of the Night,* closely modeled after the original.)

Murnau's next three films brought his German period to its apex: *The Last Laugh* (1924), his first film for the UFA studios and another collaboration with script writer Carl Mayer, was a contemporary story that featured Emil Jannings in the role of an aging hotel doorman who falls on hard times. Entirely a studio conception, it was distinguished by a paucity of intertitles and an unprecedented visual flow, including the use by cinematographer Karl Freund of the so-called "entfesselte Kamera" (the unfettered camera) whose fluid movements became an expressive factor in the story. "The camera is the director's pencil," Murnau said. "It should have the greatest possible mobility in order to record the most fleeting harmony of atmosphere." Less overtly experimental, but cannily lyric and graceful in its photography and mise-en-scène, *Tartuffe* (1925) reunited Murnau and Jannings in an adaptation of Molière's play. *Faust* (1926), his last German film, deployed the vast resources and skills of the UFA studios in the service of a theatrically stylized and special effects–laden filmization of Goethe's play. Nowhere in all of cinema are there images more superbly baroque than the sight of Mephisto's cloak spreading over the little village like a monstrous black cloud. On the other hand, there is a tendency in Murnau to descend to *lumpen* humor, as in the heavy-footed kitsch of the romantic scenes between Faust and Marguerite (Camilla Horn), and in the ham-fisted performance of Jannings as Mephisto. It would not be the first time such regrettable lapses would mar an otherwise magnificent achievement.

Now an international celebrity, Murnau was lured to Hollywood by William Fox with a promise of carte blanche on his next film. The result was the classic *Sunrise,* scripted by Carl Mayer, an allegory about a man tortured between lust for a sensuous city girl and love for his sweet-tempered country wife. Shot entirely within the vast Fox studios, designed by Rochus Gliese (who constructed desolate marshes, a lakeside village, an amusement park, a streetcar line, and the towering spires and neon lights of the big city), it brought the studio-conceived silent film to its high-water mark (the stylized Germanesque sets were used in several Fox pictures thereafter, including John Ford's *Four Sons* [1928]). Again, however, scenes of artful sensitivity are rudely juxtaposed to those displaying a cruder sense of humor, as in the scene in the city where the reunited couple chases after an escaped pig. *Sunrise* received three Academy Awards—best actress, best cinematography (Charles Rosher and Karl Struss), and "artistic quality of production." Critic Robert Sherwood called it "the most important picture in the history of the movies." However, the film failed at the box office and, as a result of increased studio interference, Murnau lost control over his next two pictures—*Four Devils* (1928), a circus picture about tensions that threatened to destroy a trapeze act; and *City Girl* (1929), which was ultimately released as a truncated part-talkie. The latter picture is one of the tragic might-have-beens of cinema. Around the slim story of a country lad who brings home a bride from the city was envisioned a "symphony of wheat," a saga of the progress from field to finished loaf, a poem to the fecundity of Nature. It was wrested from Murnau's hands and released in altered form, while Murnau's all-silent version was put on the shelf and not seen until 40 years later.

Disillusioned with Hollywood, Murnau left for Tahiti in 1931 to collaborate with documentary filmmaker ROBERT FLAHERTY on the independently financed film *Tabu* (1931), a documentary-like story of Polynesian pearl fishers. What resulted is perhaps more Murnau than Flaherty. Its poetic vision of South Seas life and customs is staggeringly beautiful, yet far removed from reality. A few days before the film's premiere, Murnau died in an automobile accident on March 11, 1931. F. W. Murnau was a man afflicted with many contradictions, in his work and in his sexuality. Historian Lotte Eisner, who considers him "the greatest film-director the Germans have ever known," attributes his spiritual confusion to his homosexuality: "All his films bear the impress of his own inner complexity, of the struggle he waged within himself against a world in which he remained despairingly alien."

Other Films *Longing* (1920); *The Janus Head* (1920); *The Haunted Castle* (1921).

References Overbey, David L., "From Murnau to Munich," *Sight and Sound* 43, no. 2 (Spring 1974): 101–103, 115; Eisner, Lotte H., *The Haunted Screen* (Berkeley: University of California Press, 1969); Wood, Robin, "Murnau's Midnight and Sunrise," *Film Comment,* June 1976: 4–19.

—J.C.T.

Nichols, Mike (1931–) Born Michael Igor Peschkowsky on November 6, 1931, in Berlin, Germany, Mike Nichols moved to the United States at the age of seven with his parents who were fleeing Hitler's Germany. Michael's father Paul Nichols (he changed the family name upon coming to America) was a medical doctor who set up practice in Manhattan. Michael graduated from Walden High School in New York in 1949. He attended the University of Chicago between 1950 and 1953, intent on becoming a psychiatrist. However, he soon became more interested in theater and joined several theater groups. In 1955 he studied acting with Lee Strasberg at the Actor's Studio in New York and later that same year joined the newly formed Compass Players in Chicago. While with the Compass Players he renewed an association with Elaine May, whom he had known while attending the University of Chicago. When the Compass Players disbanded in 1957, Nichols and May, who had developed many comedy sketches while with the group, formed a team and soon became famous for their improvisational comedy. In 1957 the team appeared on *The Jack Paar Show* on television and Nichols himself appeared in a dramatic role on the *Playhouse 90* production of Roger O. Hirson's "Journey of the Day." On October 8, 1960, the two-person show, *An Evening with Mike Nichols and Elaine May,* opened at the John Golden Theatre on Broadway. The successful show ended July 1, 1961, and the comic team disbanded to pursue separate careers. Nichols took up play directing and, following a brief sojourn to Vancouver, Canada, where he directed *The Importance of Being Earnest* and portrayed the Dauphin in George Bernard Shaw's *Saint Joan,* he returned to New York. Between 1963 and 1966 Nichols directed seven Broadway productions and garnered Tony awards for directing. These plays include: *Barefoot in the Park* (1963), *The Knack* (1964), *Luv* (1964), *The Odd Couple* (1965), and *The Apple Tree* (1966).

His success on Broadway caused Hollywood to take notice and in 1966 he was given the offer to direct the film *The Graduate* for producer Lawrence Turman. At the special request of Richard Burton and Elizabeth Taylor, Nichols opted to first direct the film version of Edward Albee's *Who's Afraid of Virginia Woolf?* (1967). This film is credited with contributing to the demise of the Production Code with its frank use of language. Warners released the film limiting its attendance to "mature audiences only," which precipitated the MPAA ratings code under the

Mike Nichols (seated center) watching playback of a scene from *The Birdcage* (United Artists)

direction of newly appointed MPAA president Jack Valenti. The film garnered Nichols his first Academy Award nomination for best director. Nichols then directed perhaps one of the seminal films of the decade, *The Graduate* (1967), starring Dustin Hoffman and Anne Bancroft. Nichols received the Academy Award for best film director for his effort. But Mike Nichols still maintained his ties with the legitimate theater, directing a production of Lillian Hellman's *The Little Foxes* for the Repertory Theatre in Lincoln Center as well as a Broadway production of Neil Simon's *Plaza Suite,* for which he received his fourth Tony award for best director.

Joseph Heller's 1962 novel *Catch-22* was the basis for Nichols's next film project. Made in 1970 at the height of the Vietnam War, the Nichols film is unique in its European style and structure. Resembling a FEDERICO FELLINI film in many ways, the film is a worthy, if not entirely successful adaptation of Heller's novel. *Carnal Knowledge,* produced and directed by Mike Nichols from an

original screenplay by Jules Feiffer, was released by Avco Embassy in 1971. With the film Nichols again tackled frank subject matter in an area that had been a taboo subject during the days of the Production Code Administration. The year 1971 also saw the release of other films, such as PETER BOGDANOVICH's *The Last Picture Show* and STANLEY KUBRICK's *Clockwork Orange,* which tested the boundaries of the newly implemented MPAA ratings code. Nichols followed his film with an adaptation of a novel by Robert Merle. *The Day of the Dolphin* (1973) was adapted by Buck Henry, a screenwriter whose previous collaborations with Nichols included *The Graduate* and *Catch-22*. In 1975 Nichols directed *The Fortune,* with Jack Nicholson and Warren Beatty. The director then took a turn with television and coproduced the drama series *Family*. First broadcast in March 1976, the realistic series about a family of five living in Pasadena ran until 1980 on ABC. Nichols continued his theater work, directing such plays as

Comedians (1976), *The Gin Game* (1977), *The Real Thing* (1983), *Hurlyburly* (1984), and *Death and the Maiden* (1992).

Nichols's subsequent work in the 1980s and 1990s has been more realistically based than his early films. Beginning with the topical film *Silkwood* (1983), based on the true story of the events surrounding the death of Karen Silkwood, and starring Meryl Streep, Nichols entered a second, more mature phase of directing. Films in this period include: *Heartburn* (1986), *Biloxi Blues* (1988), *Working Girl* (1988), *Postcards from the Edge* (1990), *Regarding Henry* (1991), and *Wolf* (1994). Nichols's most recent work includes *The Birdcage* (1996), *Primary Colors* (1998), and *What Planet Are You From?* (2000). In 1988 Mike Nichols married the TV journalist Diane Sawyer.

Other Films   *Gilda Live* (1980); *The Gin Game* (1981), TV.

Reference   Schuth, H. Wayne, *Mike Nichols* (Boston: Twayne, 1978).

—R.W.

Olivier, Laurence (1907–1989)   Since Laurence Olivier was to become the most celebrated and respected actor in the English-speaking world during the 20th century, his accomplishments as a film director might easily be overlooked. His nearest stage competitors, John Gielgud, Ralph Richardson, and Alec Guinness, had enormous respect for "Larry," as he was known to his friends. He was born the son of an Anglican minister on May 22, 1907, in the London suburb of Dorking, in Surrey. His first acting role was in *The Taming of the Shrew,* Stratford-upon Avon, in 1922, and he was to become famous as an interpreter of Shakespeare throughout his career. Appropriately, it was through Shakespeare that he became a filmmaker.

His first assignment as director was Shakespeare's most patriotic play, *Henry V* (1945), a government-funded project intended to boost morale on the home front during World War II. But this film was far more than an exercise in propaganda. It was, as well, a profound meditation on the differences between theater and film, beginning on the stage of a reconstructed Globe Playhouse in Shakespeare's time, and then jumping back in time to 1415, the date of the Battle of Agincourt, which is the climax of the play and film, when King Henry defeats a numerically superior French army. As the action moved back in time, at the same time Olivier "opened up" the play, ever so gradually, until, finally, the camera is ready for the battle spectacle on "the vasty fields of France" (actually, Ireland, since France was under German occupation when the film was made). This film was so impressively done that no one else would attempt to adapt the play into a feature film for another 40 years.

Henry V was followed by Olivier's 1948 screen adaptation of *Hamlet,* shot in black and white, with Olivier himself in the lead. A moody interpretation of the play influenced by Freud and his critical disciple Ernst Jones, Olivier's *Hamlet* won Academy Awards for best picture, best actor, art direction, costume design, and set decoration. Years later, in 1979, the Motion Picture Academy awarded him an honorary Oscar for a lifetime contribution to the art of film.

Olivier's third Shakespeare project as director was *Richard III* (1955), in which Olivier gave an unforgettable performance as the hunchback, supported by John Gielgud as the Duke of Clarence and Ralph Richardson as the Duke of Buckingham. "I think I have managed to get it right about twice in my whole career," Olivier once said of his portrayal of Richard III, "when I felt that I had pleased the audience, that they liked what I was doing and that I had done it well."

Olivier would direct only two other films: *The Prince and the Showgirl* (1957), adapted by Terence Rattigan from his play, *The Sleeping Prince,* and starring Olivier and Marilyn Monroe, and *Three Sisters,* which Olivier adapted from Chekhov's play for the American Film Theatre in 1970, starring Olivier and his wife, Joan Plowright. All of this is to say nothing, however, of his many remarkable screen roles, including one of his personal favorites, Archie Rice, the main character of John Osborne's *The Entertainer,* on both stage and screen (directed by TONY RICHARDSON in 1960); his Shakespearean roles, including his epileptic Othello in the film directed by Stuart Burge in 1966; his sadistic dentist in JOHN SCHLESINGER's *Marathon Man* (1976); and even his Nazi hunter in *The Boys from Brazil* (1978) and his vampire-hunter Professor Abraham Van Helsing in John Badham's *Dracula* (1979).

Among his many honors, Olivier was knighted in 1947, then elevated to baron in 1970, taking the title Lord Olivier of Brighton, where he kept a townhouse. Besides his honorary Oscar, Olivier was granted the gold medallion of the Swedish Academy of Literature, the Order of the Yugoslav Flag, and the French Legion of Honor. The largest theater in the South Bank complex of the Royal National Theatre was named for Olivier, a fitting tribute for such a huge talent.

References Bragg, Melvyn, *Laurence Olivier* (New York: St. Martin's, 1984); Hirsch, Foster, *Laurence Olivier* (Boston: Twayne, 1979); Olivier, Laurence, *Confessions of an Actor: An Autobiography* (New York: Simon and Schuster, 1982).

—J.M.W.

Ophuls, Max (1902–1957) The director widely known as Max Ophuls was born Maximilian Oppenheimer on May 6, 1902, in Saarbrücken, Germany. His name can also be found spelled as Ophüls and Opus (in Hollywood credits.) His Jewish family operated a clothing business,

but he chose to attend the university in Hamburg to study journalism and acting. Between 1919 and 1922 he worked as a stage actor and a theater critic. From 1923 to 1928 he directed a number of stage productions in Germany and Austria.

By 1930 Ophuls began acting in films and eventually worked as a dialogue director for Anatole Litvak. That same year he directed his first film: *Dann Lieber Lebertram* (*I'd Rather Take Cod Liver Oil*). The state-run *Universum Film Aktiengesellschaft* (UFA) provided funding for Ophuls to direct the feature film *Lachenden Erben* (*The Merry Heirs*) of 1931–32. This was followed by a comedy titled *Die verliebte Firma* (*The Company's in Love* [1932]) and *Die verkaufte Braut* (*The Bartered Bride* [1932]), a version of Bedřich Smetana's opera.

Liebelei (1933), based on a drama by Arthur Schnitzler, recalls Ophuls's theater experience in Vienna where he had previously directed stage versions of the author's work. The plot, with a faithless military officer and young, naïve heroine, contains themes Ophuls repeatedly addressed in his later romantic dramas: opulent society and the passionate lives of men and women within. Ophuls left Germany at the time of the Nazi rise to power. In France he made a French version of *Liebelei* entitled *Une Histoire d'amour* by dubbing the German film and reshooting scenes with French actors in the principal roles. He directed *La Signora di Tutti* (*Everybody's Lady* [1934]) in Italy and *Komedie om Geld* (*Trouble with Money* [1936]) in Holland.

Ophuls became a French citizen in 1938 and was again in France to film *Sans Lendemain* (*Without Tomorrow* [1940]), the story of a former stripper who attempts to move up the social ladder to improve the life of her son. Ophuls and his family fled France in 1940; following a short stay in Switzerland, where he directed two plays and worked on an unfinished film, Ophuls arrived in Hollywood by 1941. He worked for Howard Hughes but did not complete a film project. Ophuls began as director on *Vendetta* (1946), which was completed by Mel Ferrer.

The early years in Hollywood, although not productive in terms of directorial successes, did witness the completion of his memoirs, which were published in 1946. Then, in 1947 Ophuls directed *The Exile,* a story of King Charles II, which was produced by Douglas Fairbanks, Jr. John Houseman produced his next film, *Letter from an Unknown Woman* (1948), starring Joan Fontaine and Louis Jourdan as ill-fated lovers. Although the film did not find favor with critics or audiences, it remains a classic example of Ophuls's style with its Vienna setting and tale of thwarted love. *Caught* (1949) is considered the highlight of his Hollywood years. Based on a story by Arthur Laurents, the dark drama involves a triangle of lovers: a Hughes-like millionaire (Robert Ryan), his wife (Barbara Bel Geddes), and her lover (James Mason). *The Reckless Moment* (1949) starring Joan Bennett was released prior to Ophuls leaving for France.

La Ronde (1950) marked the second phase of the director's career in France. Simone Signoret stars in the ensemble cast as a prostitute whose affair with a soldier sets in motion a number of interrelated plots that circle back to Signoret at the end of the film. The story is based on the Schnitzler play *Reigen.* The episodic structure, astonishingly mobile camera work, and frank treatment of sexual themes were credited by STANLEY KUBRICK as influences on his direction of another Schnitzler-based work: *Eyes Wide Shut.*

Le Plaisir (1951), derived from a trilogy of De Maupassant short stories, was followed by the more tragic tale of another love triangle: *Madame de . . . (Earrings of Madame De . . .)* of 1953. Ophuls's final film, *Lola Montès* (1955), is considered to be his masterpiece. The life of the famous courtesan, filmed in lavish Technicolor and CinemaScope is constructed as a series of episodic flashbacks. Made in Munich as a German-French coproduction, the film contains Ophuls's characteristically virtuosic tracking shots and elaborate mise-en-scène. Most viewers quickly recognize his distinct visual style, which although unorthodox for the 1950s, now

helps to explain why his work was so admired by the French New Wave directors. Ophuls collaborated on nearly all the scripts he filmed. He died in a Hamburg hospital on March 26, 1957.

Other Films *On a volé un homme (A Man Has Been Stolen* [1933–34]); *Divine* (1935); *Valse brillante de Chopin* (1935–36); *La Tendre ennemi (The Tender Enemy* [1936]); *Yoshiwara* (1937); *Werther* (1939); *De Mayerling à Sarajevo (From Mayerling to Sarajevo* [1940]).

References Bacher, Lutz, *Travails/Travelings: The American Career of Max Ophuls* (New Brunswick, N.J.: Rutgers University Press, 1995); Beylie, Claude, *Max Ophuls* (Paris: Lherminier, 1963; reprint 1984); Guérin, William Karl, *Max Ophuls* (Paris: Cahiers du Cinéma, 1988); Ophuls, Max, *Spiel im Desein; Eine Rückblende* (Stuttgart: Henry Goverts, 1946); White, Susan M., *The Cinema of Max Ophuls, Magisterial Vision and the Figure of Woman* (New York: Columbia University Press, 1995); Willeman, Paul, ed., *Ophuls* (London: BFI, 1978); Williams, Alan, *Max Ophuls and the Cinema of Desire: Style and Spectacle in Four Films* (New York: Arno Press, 1976).

—J.A.D.

Oshima, Nagisa (1932–) Born in Kyoto, Japan, March 31, 1932, Oshima majored in political science and graduated from the School of Law at Kyoto University in 1954. In 1951 he led a student revolt that protested the emperor's policy of not allowing his subjects freedom of speech. After taking the assistant director's entrance exam at Shochiku Ofuna Studios, he earned the top score, and his film career was launched in 1959 with his first film, *A Town of Love and Hope,* followed in 1960 by *Cruel Story of Youth, The Sun's Burial,* and *Night and Fog in Japan,* the latter pulled from circulation because of its criticism of government policies concerning student movements. As a result, Oshima founded his own production company, Sozosha.

Oshima became a leading talent of the Japanese New Wave as a result of such films as *Diary of a Shinjuku Thief* (1968) and *Boy* (aka *Shonen* [1969]), the story of an itinerant family that faked road accidents for insurance settlements, his first film released in the United States. This film told the story of a 10-year-old boy who is trained by his irresponsible parents to run into moving cars, then claim injuries so that his parents could demand money from the innocent, victimized drivers. Oshima wrote that *Boy* was based on an incident that actually took place in Japan in 1966. It made the headlines in magazines and newspapers for one week, and then was completely forgotten, "probably because of the small scale of the crime and the peculiar fact that the couple forced their own child to participate." Although Oshima generally avoids sentimentality, he described the film as "a prayer, as in the boy's tear in the final scene, for all human beings who find it necessary to live in like manner."

Violence at Noon (1966) told the story of idealistic Japanese villagers whose attempts to develop a collective farm are thwarted by a catastrophic flood. One devastated couple establishes a suicide pact, but the young woman, Shino, survives their attempt to hang themselves. She is revived and raped by Eisuke, a comrade once defined by his idealism, who later becomes a serial rapist. Although Shino does not report the crime, he is eventually apprehended. With a distinctive talent for shock cinema and rapid montage, Oshima led the Japanese New Wave and was compared to JEAN-LUC GODARD on the basis of his radical content and style, fascinated by perverse desire and sexual obsession, as seen in his most notorious feature, *In the Realm of the Senses* (1976), set in 1936, about two hedonistic lovers who, in the words of David Thomson, "abandon all sense of reason or the outer world" to explore each other's bodies erotically. As their affair becomes shockingly sadomasochistic, the woman strangles the man and cuts off his penis. In 1976 his controversial and sexually explicit *In the Realm of the Senses* brought about a sensational obscenity trial in Japan. Acquitted of all charges two years later, his next film, *Empire of Passion,* earned the best director prize at the Cannes Film Festival of 1978. Thomson speculates that this film, concerning an adulterous love affair "haunted by the ghost of the murdered husband," might

have been made "to cash in on" the spectacular success of the film that preceded it. By the time he made *Merry Christmas, Mr. Lawrence* for Universal studios in 1983, based on the Laurens Van Der Post novel *The Seed and the Sower,* Oshima was serving as president of the Director's Guild in Japan.

Merry Christmas, Mr. Lawrence, his only film released to a mass audience in America, starred David Bowie and Tom Conti as prisoners of war in Japan. It was probably too dense, cryptic, and violent for American tastes and was received as an exercise in cross-cultural mystification. Robert Redford declined the lead role because he believed "the general American audience wouldn't understand it." Oshima's response to *American Film* magazine was, "I am not interested in making films that can be understood in the first fifteen minutes." The prison camp commander, Captain Yonoi, played by Tokyo rock star Ryuichi Sakamoto, has a strong homosexual attraction for British prisoner Jack Celliers (played by British rock star David Bowie) and seeks to destroy him, for reasons that might not have been clear to American audiences.

After completing *Max, mon Amour* in 1986, scripted by Jean-Claude Carrière, Oshima stopped making films and turned to television work, as if, David Thomson speculated, he "had become weary of notoriety." In 1996 Oshima suffered a stroke at London's Heathrow Airport, but eventually recovered and returned to filmmaking to make *Taboo,* which was featured at the New York Film Festival of 2000. A samurai film set during the 1860s, the "taboo" of the title is homosexuality, brought into play when a "ravishing young man" joins a band of warriors. Though Thomson found the film "more withdrawn than Mr. Oshima's greatest work," he praised the return of the director who had "pioneered modernism in Japanese cinema."

Other Films   *The Catch* (1961); *The Rebel* (1962); *Small Adventure/A Child's First Adventure* (1964); *Pleasures of the Flesh* (1965); *Band of Ninja* (1965); *A Treatise on Japanese Bawdy Songs* (1967); *Japanese Summer: Double Suicide* (1967); *Three Resurrected Drunkards* (1968); *He*

Died after the War (1970); *The Ceremony* (1971); *Dear Summer Sister* (1972).

References Thomson, David, "A Master Returns to His Realm," *New York Times,* October 8, 2000, II, pp. 11, 18; Turim, Maureen, *The Films of Oshima Nagisa: Images of a Japanese Iconoclast* (Berkeley: University of California Press, 1998)

—J.M.W.

Ozu, Yasujiro (1903–1963) Considered Japan's finest film director, Yasujiro Ozu made films that are distinguished both for their quiet, intimate, and restrained views of family life and for their striking visual style. He was born in Tokyo on December 12, 1903. At age 10 he and his two brothers were sent with his mother to live in Matsuzaka, a large town near Nagoya, his father's birthplace, where they were educated. Because his father lived and worked in the city, Ozu grew up virtually fatherless, spoiled by his beloved mother. It is significant, therefore, that Ozu never married and that he was preoccupied throughout his career with films about familial relationships. In 1916 he entered the Uji-Yamada Middle School, where he ended his formal education. He was expelled a year later for poor grades and disruptive behavior, and he ended up spending much of his time in movie theaters in the nearby towns of Tsu and Nagoya, devouring the films of American masters like CHARLES CHAPLIN, ERNST LUBITSCH, KING VIDOR, and REX INGRAM and amassing a large collection of scripts and related memorabilia. Back in Tokyo with his family, an uncle introduced him to the manager of the Shochiku Motion Picture Company, where he began as an assistant cameraman and for whom he continued to work at various intervals for the rest of his life. There he met Kogo Noda, the writer, with whom he would frequently collaborate.

Ozu's films from the 1930s included light comedies in the American farce style, stories of contemporary life (the "gendai geki" or, more specifically, the "shomin geki" formula), and

domestic situations. His first talking picture, *The Only Son* (*Hitori musuko* [1936]), prefigured the masterpieces to come in its plot about a country woman who comes to Tokyo and finds that her son has failed in his career ambitions. After making several "home front" films early in the war years (*Brothers and Sisters of the Toda Family* (*Todake no kyodai* [1941]) and *There Was a Father* (*Chichi ariki* [1941])—films in which he carefully avoided contemporary politics in an attempt to skirt the current state government's promotion of fascist ideologies—and after a brief internment by the British as a POW in 1945, he entered his most creative phase in the 1950s and 1960s with a series of notable family films, studies of family units in times of crisis. Unlike his early films, which featured elaborate moving-camera technique and brisk editing, these later works are models of restraint and technical economy. *Tokyo Story* (*Tokyo monogatari* [1953]) is his last black-and-white film and the most famous of this cycle, described by biographer Donald Richie as "one of the greatest of all Japanese motion pictures." An elderly couple travel to Tokyo where they are treated with indifference by their career-obsessed children. Only the widowed daughter-in-law, Noriko, shows them respect and affection. Upon returning home, the grandmother dies and the grandfather resigns himself to a life alone. "This bare anecdote," writes historian David Bordwell, "becomes, in Ozu's hands, an incomparable revelation of the varied ways in which humans express love, devotion, and responsibility." Film after film reveals variations on this theme—a child leaving the family, the separation of friends, the solitude of the elderly. *Late Spring* (*Banshun* [1949]) depicts the tensions that cause a father and daughter to separate. *An Autumn Afternoon* (*Samma no aji* [1962]), Ozu's last film, one of the supreme masterpieces of international cinema, blends this theme of separation and isolation with satiric jabs at the older generation's nostalgia for the war and the rampant emergence of consumerism. "Nothing is wanting [in this picture]," writes Richie, "nothing is extraneous. At the same time there is an extraordinary intensification of mood. . . . It is autumn again, but now it is deep autumn. Winter was always near, but now it will be tomorrow. At the same time Ozu's regard was never kinder, never wiser. There is a mellowness about this picture which is stronger than nostalgia."

He won six equivalents of the Academy Award in Japan. His style and tone include the predominance of static shot/reverse shots, frontal compositions, a leisurely pacing, the use of the "tatami" camera angle (the utilization of low camera angles that approximate a vantage point from a kneeling position) and the intercutting of narrative with montage sequences depicting static views of trees, hallways, street signs, aspects of landscape, etc. "Considering the overall purpose of Ozu's cinematic style," writes Japanese critic Tadao Sato, "it can be said that he wanted to make perfect still-life paintings on film. Ozu shot each scene in its most settled wood, within the most stable frame, charged with internal tension but linked on the surface by the most tranquil of sentiments. . . . [A]lthough all large movements and dynamic sequences are suppressed in Ozu's films, they are never a collection of still photographs or cold geometric figures. Rather, as a consequence of this extreme suppression, or in spite of it, viewers concentrate more on what movement there is."

Ozu has often compared himself to a tofu salesman, who offers simple but nourishing wares. Referring to *Late Autumn* (*Akibiyori* [1960]), he summed up his credo: "People sometimes complicate the simplest things. Life, which seems complex, suddenly reveals itself as very simple—and I wanted to show that in this film. There was something else, too. It is easy to show drama on film; the actors laugh or cry, but this is only explanation. A director can really show what he wants without resorting to an appeal to the emotions. I want to make people feel without resorting to drama." At the time of his death from cancer, on December 11, 1963, his oeuvre of 53 films had established him as Japan's greatest director. On his tombstone is inscribed the single character for "mu," a term usually translated as "nothingness." But according to Zen philosophy, it is a nothing that is everything.

Other Films *Tokyo Chorus* (*Tokyo no gassho* [1932]); *Woman of Tokyo* (*Tokyo no onna* [1933]); *Dragnet Girl* (*Hijosen no onna* [1933]); *A Story of Floating Weeds* (*Ukigusa monogatari* [1934]); *An Inn in Tokyo* (*Tokyo no yado* [1935]); *Diary of a Tenement Gentleman* (*Nagaya shin-shiroku* [1947]); *The Munekata Sisters* (*Munekata shimai* [1950]); *Early Summer* (*Bakushu* [1951]); *The Flavor of Green Tea over Rice* (*Ochazuke no aji* [1952]); *Equinox Flower* (*Higanbana* [1958]); *Good Morning* (*Ohayo* [1959]); *Floating Weeds* (*Ukigusa* [1959]); *The End of Summer* (*Kohayagawa-ke no aki* [1961]).

References Anderson, Joseph, and Donald Richie, *The Japanese Film: Art and Industry* (New York: Grove Press, 1960), Richie, Donald, *Ozu: His Life and Films* (Berkeley: University of California Press, 1974); Sato, Tadao, *Currents in Japanese Cinema* (Tokyo: Kodansha International, 1987); Schrader, Paul, *Transcendental Style in Film: Ozu, Bresson, Dreyer* (Berkeley: University of California Press, 1972).

—J.C.T.

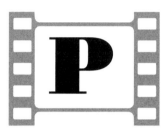

Pabst, G(eorg) Wilhelm (1885–1967)
Although his long career spanned the silent and sound years, Austrian-born G. W. Pabst's primary reputation rests upon a handful of internationally acclaimed classics he directed during the waning years of Germany's Weimar Republic. He was born on August 27, 1885, in Raudnitz, Bohemia. In 1902 he left his engineering studies to enroll at the Academy of Decorative Arts. During the next eight years he worked as an actor and director for the Deutsche Volkstheater, eventually assuming the directorship of the Neuen Wiener Buehne. He turned to the cinema in 1920 and made his directorial debut in *The Treasure* (*Der Schatz* [1924]). He came into maturity with a series of noteworthy pictures, beginning in 1925 with *The Joyless Street* (*Die freudlose Gasse*), a portrait of poverty and stifled lives that eschewed expressionist styles for a more starkly limned, blunt, and head-on approach; and continuing with *Secrets of a Soul* (*Geheimnisse einer Seele* [1926]), an early attempt to bring Freudian psychoanalytic theories to the screen (with dream sequences deploying all manner of expressionist effects and symbolism); *The Love of Jeanne Ney* (*Die Liebe der Jeanne Ney* [1927]), a melodrama featuring a splendidly photographed trial sequence; *The White Hell of Pitz-Palu* (*Die weisse Hölle vom Pitz-Palu* [1929]), a "mountain film" codirected by the founder of the genre, Dr. Arnold Fanck, and starring a young Leni Riefenstahl.

Between 1930 and 1931 Pabst directed a trio of socially conscious films that mark the summit of his reputation as a "realist." *Westfront 1918* was a bitter indictment of the recent war, seen through the disillusioned eyes of four soldiers. *Comradeship* (*Kameradschaft* [1931]) depicted in a grim, documentary style the circumstances and aftermath of a mining accident in Lorraine on the Franco-German frontier in the period around 1919. *The Threepenny Opera* (*Die Dreigroschenoper* [1931]) transformed the 1928 Bertolt Brecht/Kurt Weill stage musical's attack on repressive, bourgeois capitalism into a drama more concerned with the humanism of the characters than the polemic of the politics. For example, biographer Atwell points out, Pabst chose to emphasize the love between Mack, the leader of the underworld gang, and Polly Peachum, daughter of the King of the Beggars—a relationship treated only incidentally in the original play. It and *Westfront 1918* were banned by the Nazis in 1933.

Of particular interest at this time are the two films he made with American émigré actress

Louise Brooks, *Pandora's Box* (*Die Büchse der Pandora* [1928]) and *Diary of a Lost Girl* (*Das Tagebuch einer Verlorenen* [1929]). They are both eloquent of a suggestive eroticism that, although censored at the time, was shocking within the more conventional contexts of contemporary cinema. *Pandora* was based on the two "Lulu" plays by the modern German dramatist, Frank Wedekind: *Erdgeist* (*Earth spirit* [1895]) and *Die Büchse der Pandora* (1902). Wedekind and his contemporary, Arthur Schnitzler, were fascinated with prevailing Nietzschean theories of the primary nature of power and sex, and Freud's writing about psychoanalysis, sexual repression, and the relativity of moral truths. Thus, the character of Lulu, "the personification of primitive sexuality who inspires evil unaware," as Wedekind put it, was ruled by her passions as her various lovers fall to the wayside before her voracious appetites. Convicted of the murder of one of her lovers, she is imprisoned but escapes and flees to Paris with another lover. Later, in London, she resorts to prostitution. Unfortunately, one of her "clients" turns out to be none other than Jack the Ripper, who fatally stabs her.

In his screen adaptation Pabst cast Louise Brooks in the title role, a young American actress whom Pabst had seen in Howard Hawks's *A Girl in Every Port* (1928). Pabst condensed both Wedekind plays into a single narrative. The film begins in medias res, as we find Lulu installed in an apartment, already the plaything of several men. Subsequent scenes find her in and out of several relationships, including erotic encounters in a circus, among the gaming tables of Paris, and in the slums of London. The climactic scenes are among the finest moments in all of Pabst's oeuvre. As the prostitute Lulu and her lover Alva (Francis Lederer) settle into their sordid attic room during the Christmas season, a strange, cloaked figure is seen stalking the fog-bound streets. One night Lulu accosts the stranger. Reluctantly at first, he follows her up to her room. They embrace and he, momentarily free of the desire to kill, gives her a branch of mistletoe. But the sight of a bread knife

on the table renews his resolve, and he fatally stabs her. In the following scene, a Salvation Army band marches through the streets, singing carols, while the man passes into the night. In truth, he is Jack the Ripper. The film is masterfully constructed, photographed, and edited, moving from the flippant erotic tease of the opening scene in the luxurious apartment, to the glitter of the music hall (the entire stage performance is seen only from a backstage vantage point), the darkening tone of Lulu's murder scene, the fast-moving turmoil of the gambling den riot, to the darkling chiaroscuro of the London fogs. Above all, as biographer Atwell observes, "Pabst uses the body of Louise Brooks as the focal point of expression, employing his talent for revealing psychic states and relationships through camera angles and editing."

The second Pabst-Brooks film, *Diary of a Lost Girl,* was, like *Pandora,* ruthlessly attacked by the censors and the press as an attack on the moral and social climate of late-1920s Berlin. Brooks portrayed Thymiane Henning, a pharmacist's daughter who, after being seduced by an older man, is sent to a girl's reformatory. In an atmosphere of severely repressive discipline, Thymiane rebels and escapes. She finds herself in a brothel where she yields to her sensuous new life. After several more encounters, she marries elderly Count Osdorf and finds momentary happiness in her new wealth and social position. Although her past life is ultimately revealed, Thymiane denounces the cruelty and hypocrisy of the society around her. (Biographer Atwell reports that in Pabst's original ending, Thymiane becomes the mistress of a brothel, rejecting the comforts of society and of money.) Not as visually sumptuous as *Pandora,* the film is sharper in its realism and psychological nuances. "The fluid editing pattern in Pabst's last silent film proves," declares Atwell, "—although there are the usual explanatory and dialogue titles—the expressive eloquence of a then dying art, soon to be totally replaced by the 'talkie.'"

Pabst left Germany before the Nazi takeover. After an unsuccessful American film, *A Modern*

Hero (1934), he made a series of equally unsuccessful pictures in France, including *Don Quixote* (1934), featuring music by Jacques Ibert and a performance in the title role by the legendary Russian basso, Feodor Chaliapin. Back in Austria in 1938, he was caught up in the Anschluss, unable to obtain an exit visa. Remaining in Germany during the war years, he made *Comedians* (Komödianten [1941]), a biopic about the mid-17th-century actress Karoline Neuber, who founded the first German national theater. Aside from the fact that it praised a minor national and cultural heroine and glorified the future greatness of the German theater, it contains nothing that could be construed as overtly supportive of the Nazi regime. Similarly, *Paracelsus* (1943), another biopic of the Swiss healer of the Middle Ages who fought for the cause of natural medicine, is more interesting for its re-creation of medieval settings than for any political messages. The film is memorable primarily for a "Dance of Death" sequence wherein Paracelsus (Werner Krauss) watches horrified as the city of Basel succumbs to the infection of the Plague (the figure of Death is visible in one of the scenes). The release of the film coincided with the publishing of several books about Paracelsus, crediting him as a progenitor of Nazi ideals. Pabst's last Nazi-related film, *The Molander Trial* (Der Fall Molander [1944]), about a faux Stradivarius, was destroyed before it was released. Reviewing the two surviving films of this period, historian David Hull in his *Film in the Third Reich* writes rather patronizingly, "one gets the impression of a tired director occasionally rising to brilliance, a pale shadow of a once great talent reduced to the position of a studio hack. If Pabst willingly returned to work in Germany, he deserved the historical consequences of this deed. If this was not the case, he deserves our pity."

Pabst's reputation never recovered from his association with the Third Reich. This is unfortunate, considering that his first postwar film was *The Trial* (Der Prozess [1947]), a 19th-century drama about a lawyer famous for his defense of Jews persecuted during a wave of anti-Semitism. In 1949 he formed his own production company in Vienna, directing *Mysterious Shadows* (Geheimnisvolle Tiefen [1949]) and *The Last Act* (Der Letzte Akt [1955]), a recreation of the days before Hitler's suicide in his Berlin bunker. In 1957 Pabst developed Parkinson's disease and he was an invalid until his death 10 years later on May 29, 1967.

Biographer Atwell insists that Pabst is not a true auteur, rather, "with each new film . . . his restless sensibility sought a fresh approach; thus each work must be judged according to its merits." Regarding Pabst's influence on the British documentary school, historian Paul Rotha wrote, "I am always proud that I was once closely associated with him and gratefully record how much his films and way of working influenced me when later I came humbly to direct films myself. To have known and talked with Pabst is like saying you knew and talked with Leonardo."

Other Films *Countess Donelli* (Gräfin Donelli [1924]); *One Does Not Play with Love* (Man spielt nicht mit der Liebe [1926]); *Desire* (Abwege [1928]); *Scandalous Eva* (Skandal um Eva [1930]); *L'Atlantide* (1932); *High and Low* (Du haut en bas [1933]); *Mademoiselle Docteur* (1936); *Shanghai Drama* (Le Drame de Shanghai [1938]); *The Voice of Silence* (La Voce del silenzio [1952]); *Crazy Affairs* (Cose da pazzi [1953]); *The Confession of Ina Kahr* (Das Bekenntnis der Ina Kahr [1954]); *It Happened on July 20* (Es geschah am 20 Juli [1955]); *Roses for Bettina* (Rosen fuer Bettina [1956]); *Through the Forests, through the Fields* (Durch die Wälder, durch die Auen [1956]).

References Atwell, Lee, *G.W. Pabst* (Boston: Twayne, 1987); Hull, David Stewart, *Film in the Third Reich* (Berkeley: University of California Press, 1969); Ott, Frederick W., *The Great German Films* (Secaucus, N.J.: Citadel Press, 1986).

—J.C.T.

Paradjanov, Sergei Iosifich (1924–1990)

Sergei Paradjanov is remembered today as much as an icon of cinematic rebellion against Soviet dogma in the 1960s as for his art. He was born to

Armenian parents on January 9, 1924, in what was then Tiflis, in the Georgian Republic of the USSR—the city now known as Tblisi, Georgia. After his studies in film and music at the Moscow Institute of Cinematography, he went to work as an assistant director at Dovzhenko Studios in Kiev. His assignment to the Ukrainian studio would prove pivotal in its cultivation of his ethnic spirit, which would eventually stand him in harsh contradiction to a state apparatus officially opposed to the glorification of minority ethnic traditions in the republics.

Paradjanov made his directorial debut with 1951's *A Moldavian Tale* (*Moldovskaya skazka*), which was followed by a series of shorts and features throughout the 1950s and early 1960s, including *Andriesh* (1954), *The Golden Hands* (*Zolotye ruki* [1957]), and *Ukrainian Rhapsody* (*Ukrainskaya rapsodiya* [1961]). While these films are generally regarded as minor works, they established Paradjanov as a filmmaker with a particular interest in ethnic and folkloric themes. Moreover, Paradjanov's early films display a prophetic tendency toward open narratives and poeticism. In short, they are more like odes than straight narratives, an approach that would soon lead to his most highly regarded works.

Paradjanov's cultivation of non-Soviet (perhaps even anti-Soviet) themes and imagery was aided by Khrushchev's "de-Stalinization" period of the early 1960s, during which artists and intellectuals enjoyed greater freedoms than they had in the 1950s. Near the very end of this artistic thaw, Paradjanov created his widely acknowledged masterpiece, *Shadows of Forgotten Ancestors* (*Tini zabutykh predkiv* [1964]), a visually astonishing celebration—though an oftentimes dark celebration—of Ukrainian folk culture. Paradjanov employs a huge arsenal of stylistic experiments throughout the film, including, among others, manipulations of color, sound, handheld camera, multiple exposures, and point-of-view shots. It would not be too strong a statement to say that *Shadows of Forgotten Ancestors* is one of the most stylistically innovative films of world cinema in the 1960s.

However, the timing of the film's release proved problematic. Very soon afterward came the resignation of Khrushchev, whose departure signaled a return to strong state control over filmmaking. The Soviet hard-liner Phillip Yermash was appointed head of the USSR State Committee on Cinematography, and *Shadows* was attacked as reactionary, despite its international acclaim. Paradjanov retreated to making two modest short films in 1965 and then took a three-year hiatus from filmmaking, waiting for the political atmosphere to warm up to another film in the same vein as *Shadows*. The resulting film, released in 1968, was *The Color of Pomegranates* (*Sayat Nova*), an abstract biography of the 18th-century Armenian poet Sayat Nova. Not surprisingly, the official response to *Pomegranates* was similar to that of *Shadows*. Paradjanov's ethnic and metaphysical themes ran counter to Soviet artistic dogma, and he was officially banned from filmmaking in 1969.

Retreating to his other artistic endeavors (Paradjanov was particularly accomplished in drawing and collage), he found himself charged, in 1973, with homosexuality and trafficking in religious icons, both official state crimes. To the contemporary reader, these charges will seem persecutory by their very nature. What makes the case even more disturbing is that the charges were almost surely rigged. Paradjanov was convicted and spent the next four years in prison, where he began regular correspondence with his prestigious younger colleague ANDREI TARKOVSKY, who had himself seen his share of struggles with state censors. Paradjanov's release in 1977 was one result of that year's famous cultural workers' protests.

Upon release, still barred from filmmaking, Paradjanov returned to Tblisi, the city of his birth, where he worked as an independent artist, creating drawings, collages, and handmade dolls . . . and writing screenplays that he was not permitted to produce. He spent another 11 months in jail without trial in 1982 for governmental objections to his artworks but was redeemed under perestroika in 1984 and once again given permission to direct.

Paradjanov made three more films during the 1980s: *Legend of the Suram Fortress* (*Ambavi Suramis tsikhitsa* [1984]), *Arabesques on the Pirosmani Theme* (*Arabeski Pirosmanis temaze* [1985])—an experimental documentary on the Georgian artist Niko Pirosmani, and his final, highly celebrated film *Ashik Kerib* (*Ashugi Qaribi* [1988]). In these films, Paradjanov maintained the thematic and stylistic integrity of his famed works of the 1960s, ensuring his legacy as a director whose clarity of purpose outweighed the strength of the persecution against him. Paradjanov died from cancer in Yerevan, Armenia, in 1990 after unsuccessful treatment in a Paris hospital. He is buried in the Pantheon of Armenian Heroes in Yerevan, and the Sergei Paradjanov Museum today stands as one of the most important cultural sites in that city.

References Cahmi, Leslie, "The Steppe Father," *The Village Voice,* November 14, 1995, p. 94; Paradjanov, Sergei, *Seven Visions,* trans. Guy Bennett (Los Angeles: Green Integer, 1998); Williamson, A., "Prisoner," *Film Comment,* May–June 1989: 57–63.

—S.C.M.

Pasolini, Pier Paolo (1922–1975)

Pier Paolo Pasolini, novelist, poet, linguist, and film theorist, became the most influential Marxist filmmaker to emerge out of the cultural and political upheaval of the late 1960s. From his neorealist masterpiece, *The Gospel According to St. Matthew* (1964), to the surrealist *Teorema* (1968), and his outrageous attack on Italian fascism, *Salo, Or the 120 Days of Sodom* (1975), Pasolini's films remain as moving, often shocking, and as controversial as when they were first released.

Pasolini was born into wealth and privilege in 1922. His father was a Fascist military officer of noble birth, but Pasolini identified with the heritage of his mother, who had been born of peasant stock. This identification with the subproletariat would inform all of his artistic work. While a uni-versity student studying art history at Bologna during the early days of World War II, Pasolini was conscripted into the Italian army. In 1943, two days after Italy's capitulation, he was captured by German troops and placed in a POW camp. Pasolini escaped and made his way to the countryside of Friuli where he lived among the peasant population, learning firsthand the peasants' daily struggle for dignity against the power of the region's wealthy landowners.

The years in Friuli strengthened Pasolini's commitment to the tenets of Marxism, which would become the ideological faith that informed all his work as a poet, novelist, and filmmaker. Following World War II, Pasolini returned to the University at Bologna to study literature. He moved to Rome in 1950, where he gained success as a poet and essayist while continuing to study the neo-Marxist writings of Antonio Gramsci. In 1954 he completed his first novel, *Ragazzi di vita* (*A Violent Life*). While it proved a critical success, it was viewed by the government as obscene and led to his first, but not last, arrest for producing indecent works of art. The notoriety of the novel, and the subsequent trial, led to an invitation to work with Federico Fellini on the script of *Le Notti di Cabiria* (*Nights of Cabiria* [1957]).

In 1961, Pasolini made his first film, *Accatone* (Beggar), with Bernardo Bertolucci serving as his assistant director. The film, in the tradition of Italian neorealism, is a brutal slice-of-life depiction of a young pimp trying to earn enough money to simply survive while preserving enough human dignity to make survival worth the effort. In 1962 he wrote and directed *Mamma Rosa,* starring Anna Magnani as a former prostitute who has tried to provide her estranged teenage son with a middle-class existence. When a former pimp threatens to humiliate her son by exposing the mother's past, she is forced back into prostitution.

Pasolini's next film was an "omnibus" film, *Laviamoci il cervello* (more popularly known as *RoGoPaG* [1962]), made with a group of leftist filmmakers, including Roberto Rossellini and

Jean-Luc Godard. Pasolini's section of the film, titled "La ricotta," is a hilariously irreverent religious farce in which an American director, played by Orson Welles, is shooting a film depicting the crucifixion of Christ. The actor playing Jesus has sex with the boys in the cast before dying on the cross, not in the manner of Christ but, rather, of indigestion caused by eating too much ice cream. The film so offended the government that "La ricotta" was not only banned in Italy, but also Pasolini was arrested and given a four-month suspended sentence for "blasphemy" and "public defamation."

Ironically, his next film, *Il Vangelo Secondo Matteo* (*The Gospel According to St. Matthew* [1964]) gained Pasolini not only international fame but also accolades from the Roman Catholic Church. A simple retelling of the Gospel of St. Matthew, Pasolini employed a neorealistic style to offer a counter-image to traditional Hollywood depictions of biblical source material. In Pasolini's version of the Gospel, he chooses a nonprofessional cast, including a Marxist truck driver playing the role of Jesus, and Pasolini's own mother as the Virgin Mary. While Pasolini succeeds in bringing out the first Gospel's radical call for social justice for the poor, even politically conservative religious leaders hailed its simplicity and sincerity.

Teorema (*Theorem* [1968]) a salacious satire of conventional bourgeois society, was a marked departure from the social realism of Pasolini's earlier films. A beautiful young man, portrayed by Terence Stamp, enters the uneventful lives of a middle-class family, only to seduce each member of the family. When he leaves them as suddenly as he arrived, they are incapable of coping with the emptiness of their lives.

During the 1970s, Pasolini turned his attention to a series of politically and/or sexually subversive interpretations of classic literature, from Greek tragedy in *Edipo* (*Oedipus Rex* [1967]) and *Medea* (1970) starring opera diva Maria Callas, to scandalously erotic adaptations of Boccaccio's bawdy *The Decameron* (1971), Chaucer in *I Racconti di Can-*terbury (*Canterbury Tales* [1972]), and the anonymous *Il Fiore delle mille e una notte* (*Tales of the Arabian Nights* [1974]).

Pasolini's last film, *Salò o le 120 giornate di Sodoma* (*Salo, Or the 120 Days of Sodom* [1975]), proved to be his most controversial. A political fable based on Marquis de Sade's notorious *The 120 Days of Sodom* and Dante's *Inferno,* the film is a scathing dissection of Italian fascism, Salo being the northern lake town that was Mussolini's last capital. The film, a cinematic counterpart to Antonin Artaud's call for a "theater of cruelty," subjects the viewer to a horrific vision of political totalitarianism thinly disguised as sadomasochistic sexuality. While decidedly pornographic, Gerald Mast and Bruce Kawin have argued that "this cruel, obscene, ironic film is uncompromisingly ethical." The film's sexual perversion, "the very opposite of bourgeois society's standards and beliefs, are like fascism, itself, a product of bourgeois society. . . . By the end of the film, the distinction between the normal and the perverse has become, to say the least, problematic."

Shortly after completing *Salo,* Pasolini was murdered under suspicious circumstances in Ostia, Italy. Police authorities reported that he was bludgeoned to death by a 17-year-old boy who claimed he had been propositioned for sex by the filmmaker. Serious doubts have been cast over the accuracy of the government's scenario, and many of Pasolini's friends (including Bertolucci) continue to believe he was the victim of a political assassination. His untimely death denied the future of filmmaking by a man described by Vincent Canby as "one of the most original and perverse film poets of his generation"—adding that "it's not always necessary to understand Pasolini to be riveted by what he does."

Other Films *Hawks and Sparrows* (1966); *Porcile* (*Pigsty,* aka *Pigpen* [1969]).

References Rhodie, Sam, *The Passion of Pier Paolo Pasolini* (Bloomington: University of Indiana Press, 1996); Rumble, Patrick A., *Allegories of Contamination: Pier Paolo Pasolini's Trilogy of Life* (Toronto: University of Toronto Press, 1995); Viano, Maurizio, *A Certain Real-*

ism: Toward a Use of Pasolini's Film Theory and Practice (Berkeley: University of California Press, 1993).

—T.P.

Peckinpah, Sam (1925–1984) Sam Peckinpah was known in the American film industry of the 1970s as "Bloody Sam." Without question, the violent nature of his films was unprecedented. *The Wild Bunch* (1969) contains what one critic described as "the bloodiest massacre in screen history." No doubt, Peckinpah's *The Wild Bunch* and *Straw Dogs* (1971) brought a graphic violence to the screen that was unprecedented. Despite the controversy generated by the brutal nature of his films, Peckinpah was a superlative stylist who transformed cinematic violence into what has been compared to a "surrealistic ballet of color and motion." According to Louis Giannetti, "the mesmerizing lyricism of Peckinpah's brilliantly edited images blinds us to the fact that people are dying in all that terrible, apocalyptic beauty."

David Samuel Peckinpah was born on February 21, 1925, in Fresno, California, when the town was still part of the Wild West. As a child, he was greatly influenced by the legacy of his grandfather, Denver Church, a politically conservative judge and congressman who was known to be one of the best shots in the Sierras. Peckinpah enlisted in the Marine Corps during World War II, but to his great dismay, he never saw combat. Returning from the war, he enrolled as a theater student at the University of Southern California. Directionless after graduation, Peckinpah drifted into the job of "gofer" for director DON SIEGEL, who took a liking to the young man and made him something of a protégé. Peckinpah worked as an uncredited writer on a number of Siegel's films, including *The Invasion of the Body Snatchers* (1956).

During the late 1950s, Peckinpah moved into television at a time when westerns were at the peak of their small-screen popularity. He became a scriptwriter for a number of TV westerns, including *Gunsmoke, The Rifleman* and *The Westerner,* a series he created, produced, and directed. Peckin-

pah made his first feature film in 1961, a modest western titled *The Deadly Companions* in which a gunslinger (Brian Keith) and his sidekick (Chill Wills) accompany a dance-hall hostess (Maureen O'Hara) through hostile Indian country.

If Peckinpah's first western film was undistinguished, it paved the way for his second film, the critically acclaimed *Ride the High Country* (1962), now considered one of the greatest westerns of all time. Less a "revisionist" western than a heartfelt elegy to a western mythos that no longer existed, the film stars aging western actors Joel McCrea and Randolph Scott as old-time gunslingers who take on one last assignment to guard a gold shipment. McCrea is committed to doing a good job, if only to "enter the house justified." His companion only wants to steal the gold.

Peckinpah's 1964 western, *Major Dundee,* set in the Civil War–era West, also centers on a conflict of character between two strong men, the stoic Union major (Charlton Heston) and a flamboyant Irishman (Richard Harris) who has been fighting for the Confederacy. The two must lead a group of Confederate prisoners who have volunteered to go into Mexico to subdue a band of renegade Apaches. Following the high expectations generated by *Ride the High Country,* the film was both a critical and box-office disappointment due largely to studio interference, aided and abetted by Peckinpah's increasingly erratic behavior.

During location work in Mexico, Peckinpah was reputed to have become increasingly dependent on alcohol and drugs, leading to confrontations between the director and Heston that paralleled the conflict of character in the film. Heston later recalled that "Sam is the only person I've ever physically threatened on a set." After filming, Peckinpah's rage turned toward the film's producer and studio executives at Columbia who insisted that the film be drastically recut.

If Peckinpah developed a reputation as a director who abused his cast and crew, studio executives were more upset that he turned out films with little commercial value. They complained that he

Sam Peckinpah (right) on the set of *The Osterman Weekend* (Twentieth Century-Fox)

was self-indulgent and saw the western as a means to artistic self-expression rather than a simple Hollywood genre. In fact, Peckinpah's films are highly personal, with loosely constructed narratives given to digressions and lyrical interludes, not unlike the films of the director who most inspired his work, AKIRA KUROSAWA.

Following *Major Dundee,* Peckinpah was signed to direct Steve McQueen in *The Cincinnati Kid.* However, the highly publicized problems on the set of *Major Dundee* and his inability to work within the rules of the studio system led to his being replaced by NORMAN JEWISON. It appeared that Peckinpah's career had come to a premature end. He did not make another film for two years. Peckinpah's next film, *The Wild Bunch* (1969), would not only rejuvenate his career, but also pro-

pel him to the front ranks of Hollywood's most illustrious directors.

A revisionist western that calls into question the traditional values of the western in its classic form, *The Wild Bunch* takes place in the American West on the cusp of the 20th century, as the horse is replaced by automobile, and the six-shooter by the cold, ruthless technology of the machine-gun. In the film, a weathered William Holden, embittered by the realization that history has passed him by, leads a gang of aging gunfighters (including Hollywood veterans Ernest Borgnine, Robert Ryan, Edmond O'Brien, and Warren Oates) into one last stand. As noted by Louis Giannetti, *The Wild Bunch* pits "the bad guys against the guys who are even worse." In Peckinpah's worldview, the majestic vistas of JOHN FORD's classic westerns become a spiritual wasteland where the "romantic outlaw is cynical, opportunistic, and corrupt in many of his moral values, but he does abide by a private code of honor that sets him above the Establishment—any establishment."

Peckinpah's juxtaposition of America's pastoral past to a neurotic 20th century, portrayed as mechanistic, repressive, and emotionally sterile, led many critics to view Peckinpah's films as the work of a "romantic reactionary." *The Wild Bunch,* brilliantly photographed by cinematographer Lucien Ballard, emphasized what has come to be called "balletic violence," employing slow-motion and the freeze-frame to create a stylized orgy of violence. Not unlike one of his cinematic antiheroes, once again, Peckinpah's "private code" as a filmmaker set him at odds with the Hollywood "establishment." *The Wild Bunch* was reedited by the studio to make it a more commercially viable product. Even so, the grizzly nature of the film ignited heated controversy among critics and audiences alike. Needless to say, its influence on popular film depictions of violence has not abated.

Peckinpah continued to elicit both critical acclaim and outrage in his subsequent films, particularly *Straw Dogs* (1971). While the film is not specifically set within the American West, its themes are closely aligned with Peckinpah's revisionist westerns. Taking place in a contemporary English village, a passive American college professor (Dustin Hoffman) refuses to acknowledge how his attractive wife's flirtatious behavior excites the base and brutal animalistic nature of a group of village bullies, who set out to vent their rage against the "outsiders." When the bespectacled professor's eyeglasses are broken in an attack, he finally "sees" the reality of his situation and is forced to rely on his own animal instincts to survive. Following the success of *Straw Dogs,* Peckinpah enjoyed several years of commercial success with his popular crime thriller, *The Getaway* (1972), and a more gentle comedy, *Junior Bonner* (1972).

In 1973, MGM released Peckinpah's mutilated masterpiece, *Pat Garrett and Billy the Kid,* a highly personal rendering of the western legend. The studio had ordered Peckinpah to cut an hour from the film. While the director slaved away, removing 40 minutes without changing the picture's structure, the studio's editing department secretly produced a shortened version intended to "straighten-out" the film's original elliptical narrative. When the "ruined" studio version was released, it was greeted with dismay by critics and audiences alike. In 1988, four years after Peckinpah's death, the "director's cut" was released to critical acclaim.

Following the debacle of *Pat Garrett and Billy the Kid,* the director's subsequent films became increasingly sterile, winning little audience or critical attention. His last film, *The Osterman Weekend,* was released in 1983. Peckinpah's last directing assignments were two Julian Lennon music videos. Through good times and bad, waging ongoing battles with the Hollywood establishment, his films lavishly praised and vehemently attacked, Peckinpah continued to live hard and fast. He died of heart failure in Mexico on December 28, 1984, at the age of 59. Today, Peckinpah is acknowledged as a master of both a "lyrical" and "baroque" grand style that has been compared to Eisenstein, Visconti, and Fellini. Perhaps critic Pauline Kael said it best, "Pouring new wine into the bottle of the Western, Peckinpah explodes the bottle."

Other Films *The Ballad of Cable Hogue* (1970); *Bring Me the Head of Alfredo Garcia* (1974); *Killer Elite* (1975); *Cross of Iron* (1977); *Convoy* (1978).

References Butler, Terence, *Crucified Heroes: The Films of Sam Peckinpah* (London: Gordon Fraser, 1979); Dukore, Bernard F., *Sam Peckinpah's Feature Films* (Urbana: University of Illinois Press, 1999); Fine, Marshall, *Bloody Sam: The Life and Films of Sam Peckinpah* (New York: Donald I. Fine, 1991).

—T.P.

Penn, Arthur (1922–) Born in Philadelphia on September 27, 1922, the son of a watchmaker, Penn was drawn to the theater while attending Olney High School. During his military service in World War II he spent much of his time at the Civic Theatre in Columbia while stationed at Fort Jackson, South Carolina. His friendship with Fred Coe, who was to become a major television producer during TV's "golden age," began at this time. During the Occupation of Germany, Penn was involved with the Soldiers Show Company, which was headed by Joshua Logan and mandated by Dwight Eisenhower to entertain the Army of Occupation. Upon his return to the United States, Penn attended Black Mountain College near Asheville, North Carolina, and soon began teaching acting classes as well as staging several experimental productions. Penn finished his education in Europe where he attended the Universities of Perugia and Florence. In 1951 he was employed by NBC as a floor manager for *The Colgate Comedy Hour,* a Sunday evening variety hour that featured guest hosts such as Dean Martin and Jerry Lewis, Eddie Cantor, Bob Hope, Jimmy Durante, and Fred Allen. Penn directed a live dramatic series *Gulf Playhouse: First Person* (NBC) at the request of Fred Coe. A summer replacement for *The Life of Riley,* the television camera was the principal character, becoming the first-person singular in terms of narration in stories written by Horton Foote, Paddy Chayefsky, and Stewart Stern. From 1953 to 1955 Penn was part of a contingent of directors for *Philco Television Playhouse* (NBC), a virtual training ground for writers, directors, and actors. In 1957 and 1958 he directed several teleplays, including "The Miracle Worker" for *Playhouse 90* (CBS). Also included in his television credits are his responsibilities as an adviser to John F. Kennedy during the Kennedy-Nixon debates of 1960, for which he directed the third debate.

Paralleling his career in television was his continued work in the legitimate theater. His first major success was William Gibson's *Two for the Seesaw,* which starred Henry Fonda and Anne Bancroft and ran for 750 performances at the Booth Theatre in New York in 1958. His stage production of William Gibson's *The Miracle Worker,* starring Anne Bancroft and Patty Duke, ran for 700 performances at the Playhouse Theatre in New York and received the Tony Award for best play and best director. In 1960 he directed *An Evening with Mike Nichols and Elaine May.* And in 1976 he directed George C. Scott in a production of Larry Gelbart's adaptation of Ben Jonson's *Volpone,* titled *Sly Fox.* In addition, he has maintained a long-standing relationship with the Actor's Studio in New York and the Berkshire Playhouse in Stockbridge, Massachusetts.

Arthur Penn's initial foray into film was *The Left-Handed Gun* (1958), based on a teleplay, *The Death of Billy the Kid,* by Gore Vidal. It was first performed as "Billy" on NBC's *Philco Television Playhouse* on July 24, 1955, with Paul Newman in the title role. Newman plays the same role in Penn's film version, as a juvenile delinquent. The film was taken out of Penn's hands and cut in a fashion that made it unrecognizable by Penn when he viewed it. He did not make another film for five years. In 1962 the film version of Penn's stage success *The Miracle Worker,* starring Anne Bancroft and Patty Duke, garnered praise and awards from critics and public alike. It is with this film that Penn began to utilize the techniques of the medium, especially in his manipulation through editing. *Mickey One* (1965) is considered by many a modernist masterpiece and is the first film where Penn had absolute control. Warren Beatty portrays a nightclub comic who is hounded by unseen forces for some crime of which he is unaware. The film echoes the paranoia of modern America during the Cold War and utilizes heavy symbolism in its visual imagery. Horton Foote's *The Chase* (1966) was Penn's next film, which again was taken out of his hands by producer Sam Spiegel and reedited. The film focuses on life in a small Texas town and continues Penn's fascination with violence in America. Arthur Penn's subsequent film gained him the notoriety and critical attention he deserved and became one of the seminal films of the 1960s.

Bonnie and Clyde (1967), based on a screenplay by David Newman and Robert Benton, was originally offered to JEAN-LUC GODARD and FRANÇOIS TRUFFAUT, both of whom turned it down. Warren Beatty, who had bought the screenplay, persuaded Penn to direct the picture. The film also marked the beginning of Penn's longtime association with editor Dede Allen. Following the controversial success of *Bonnie and Clyde,* Penn made *Alice's Restaurant* (1969). This transitional film, made during a time of turmoil in American history, explores themes with which the director has been concerned since *The Left-Handed Gun:* violence, masculinity, authority figures, and marginal groups. *Little Big Man* (1970), based on Thomas Berger's novel and starring Dustin Hoffman, continued Penn's fascination with American genres and mythmaking. Penn's next film, *Night Moves* (1975), ventured into the realm of the private-detective film. Gene Hackman portrays Harry Moseby, a former Oakland football player, who is now a private eye hired to find the missing daughter of a former actress. He soon becomes enmeshed in a series of events that reflect the post-Watergate malaise in mid-seventies America. *Missouri Breaks* (1976) explored further the theme of violence within the American western genre. Thomas McGuane's screenplay centers on a distinctly unconventional hired killer (Marlon Brando) and the leader of a gang of cattle rustlers (Jack Nicholson). Penn's film output has diminished since 1976. In 1981 he coproduced and directed *Four Friends.* Based on a semi-autobiographical screenplay by Steve Tesich, it concerns a young Yugoslavian immigrant who lives through much of the violent 1960s in America. Perhaps with the passing of the sixties Penn has found less material that has relevance to him. Be that as it may, Penn's limited film output is an effective barometer of its day and age.

Other Films *Visions of Eight* (1973), an Olympics documentary for which Penn directed "The Highest" episode; *Target* (1985); *Dead of Winter* (1987); *Penn and Teller Get Killed* (1989); *Inside* (1996), for HBO.

Reference Zucker, Joel S., *Arthur Penn: A Guide to References and Resources* (Boston: G. K. Hall, 1980).

—R. W.

Petersen, Wolfgang (1941–)

Born in the north German port city of Emden near the Dutch border on March 14, 1941, Wolfgang Petersen went to work at the age of 19 as an assistant stage director for the Ernst Deutsch Theater in Hamburg and directed his first play the next year. After two years of study at private acting schools in Hamburg and Berlin (1963–65), he decided that performing was not his true vocation and studied filmmaking at the Deutsche Film und Fernsehenakademie in Berlin for four years. In 1970 he then directed a number of features for television, beginning with *Ich werde dich Töten, Wolf* (*I Will Kill You, Wolf*). In 1971 he directed "Strandgut" (Debris), the first of six 100-minute dramas for a series called *Tatort* (Scenes of the crime), followed by additional episodes in 1972—"Nachtfrost" (Night frost) and "Jagdrevier" (Hunting ground). One of Petersen's most successful early pictures was *Smog,* which won the 1975 silver Prix Futura in Berlin. Two more *Tatort* films followed—"Kurzschluss" (Short circuit [1975]) and a final episode, "Reifezeugnis" (For your love only [1976]), which not only introduced Nastassja Kinski to the screen but also won the Prix Italia 1977 and brought Petersen the best director award at the Monte Carlo Television Festival.

Petersen's other television films during the 1970s were *Van der Valk und die Reichen* (Van der Valk and the rich [1973]), an international production adapted from a thriller by Nicholas Freeling, starring Frank Finlay and Françoise Prevost. His first feature film, *Einer von uns beiden* (*One of Us Two* [1973]), won him the German national film prize for best new director. *Aufs Kreuz gelegt* (roughly translated, Pinned down) and *Stadt im Tal* (City in the valley) followed in 1974; *Stellenweise Glatteis* (Beware of slippery ice) in 1975; *Hans im Glück* (Hans in luck) and *Vier gegen die Bank* (We're going to the bank) in 1976. In 1977

Petersen directed *Planübung* (Mock exercise) and *Die Konsequenz* (The consequence), a taboo-shattering film about homosexuality starring Jürgen Prochnow. In 1978 Petersen directed *Schwarz und Weiss wie Tage und Nachte* (Black and white like day and night).

Working for producer Günther Rohrback at WDR/Bavaria, Petersen helmed one of Germany's greatest postwar commercial successes, *Das Boot* (*The Boat* [1981]), adapted from an autobiographical novel by Lothar-Günther Buchheim. The "boat" of the title is a submarine, a German U-boat forced to run seemingly impossible missions. A mood of impending doom hangs over the picture when it announces that of the 40,000 men who saw submarine service during World War II, only 12,000 survived. The odds, therefore, were against the crew, which the audience comes to know and respect, especially the captain (Jürgen Prochnow), the chief engineer (Klaus Wennemann), and his cohort in the engine room (Erwin Leder). Although no truly effective combat film can be described as "antiwar," *Das Boot* came close to achieving that goal, since its focus was not upon politics but on men caught up in a miserable and claustrophobic, dangerous kind of warfare. Produced at a cost of $12 million, *Das Boot* became the second largest moneymaker in German film history. The realistic presentation of life on a U-boat was convincing, no doubt because most of the events dramatized in the film actually happened during a dangerous 45-day mission the U-96 undertook during October 1941, when U-96 was one of 24 U-boats ordered to make a dangerous run through the Strait of Gibraltar into the Mediterranean. Although U-96 did not itself suffer the fate presented at the end of the film, what happens at the film's conclusion did actually happen to another U-boat.

Das Boot was Petersen's breakthrough film, earning Academy Award nominations for both best director and best screenplay. Petersen's following film took an unexpected but successful shift toward fantasy after the uncompromising realism of *Das Boot*. *Die Unendliche Geschichte* (*The Neverending Story* [1984]), a wonderfully made children's fable adapted from Michael Ende's novel, shot in English, was the breakthrough, crossover success that moved his career to Hollywood, where he would later become a successful commercial director of several high-concept thrillers. Petersen's next Hollywood feature was an unusual science fiction vehicle, *Enemy Mine* (1985), starring Dennis Quaid as an Earthman stranded on an alien planet and Louis Gosset, Jr., under a great deal of scaly makeup, as Quaid's enemy. The two enemy spacepilots are drawn together first by a mutual need to survive in a dangerous environment and then by the need for companionship. Once established in Hollywood, Petersen was generally defined by the projects assigned to him.

In *Shattered* (1991), for example, adapted from Richard Neely's novel *The Plastic Nightmare,* the central character, Dan Merrick (Tom Berenger), loses his memory after a terrible auto accident and must rely on his wife Judith (Greta Scacchi) and friends who may or may not be trustworthy. So disturbed is he by nightmarish memory flashbacks, he hires a private investigator (Bob Hoskins) to help him recover his past. Petersen not only directed the film but also produced it and wrote the screenplay, telling one reporter "This is my bow to ALFRED HITCHCOCK." Reviews were mixed: Hal Hinson judged *Shattered* "a startlingly satisfying, complex bit of moviemaking," for example, while Janet Maslin of the *New York Times* gave it her "hotly coveted Nuttiest Plot of 1991 citation." After completing *Shattered,* Petersen signed a two-year contract with Tri-Star Pictures and decided to settle in Los Angeles permanently.

Petersen's later Hollywood features were fairly conventional but well-made thrillers, such as *In the Line of Fire* (1993), with Clint Eastwood playing Secret Service agent Frank Horrigan, whose challenge is to protect the president of the United States from an assassination plot. A defining picture for Petersen, who was Eastwood's personal choice to direct the film, it proved to be one of the year's highest grossing films. *Outbreak* (1995), a biohazard thriller starring Dustin Hoffman and adapted from two books—Richard Preston's *The Hot Zone* (1994), a nonfiction account of an outbreak of the Ebola virus in a suburban Washington, D.C., army laboratory, and Laurie Garrett's *The Coming Plague* (1994)—was not a blockbuster hit but earned a respectable $67 million.

Air Force One (1997) starred Harrison Ford as a heroic president of the United States, battling a group of Russian terrorists led by Gary Oldman, who hijack the presidential airplane, Air Force One, shortly after it leaves Moscow for Washington, D.C. This action-adventure yarn, a summer blockbuster that earned nearly $172 million, was nominated for two Academy Awards (film editing and sound) and positioned Petersen to direct *The Perfect Storm* (1999), a reality-based disaster movie adapted from the book by Sebastian Junger, starring George Clooney as skipper Billy Tyne. With a blockbuster budget of $140 million, this sea saga recalled *Das Boot,* in a way, but was short on plot and depended rather too much on its amazing computer-enhanced technical effects, which led to its only Academy Award nomination. Critics were not especially impressed by this slow-moving fishing tale about bad judgment, hubris, and inevitable tragedy. No one doubted Petersen's competence, of course, but it was clear that he made better, more interesting films before selling his talents to Hollywood.

Other Film *Der Eine, der Andere* (The one, the other [1967]).

References Arnold, Gary, "The Darkest Voyage: U-96 Sails to War in 'Das Boot,'" *Washington Post,* March 5, 1982, p. B11; Chutkow, Paul, "Paying Homage to Hitch," *New York Times,* October 6, 1991, II, pp. 21, 28; Gleiberman, Owen, "The Wet Look," *Entertainment Weekly,* July 14, 2000, p. 51; Klawans, Stuart, "The Flounder," *Nation,* July 24/31, 2000, pp. 43–44; Lane, Anthony, "Pluck and Cluck," *New Yorker,* July 10, 2000, pp. 77–78; Lyman, Rick, "Watching Movies with Wolfgang Petersen," *New York Times,* March 30, 2001,

pp. B1, B24; Maslin, Janet, "Trying to Rebuild One's Past," *New York Times,* October 11, 1991, p. C24; O'Toole, Thomas, "Logging In on 'Das Boot's' U-96," *Washington Post,* June 29, 1982, p. B7; Pipolo, Tony, "German Filmmakers Seldom Focus on the Legacy of Nazism," *New York Times,* August 1, 1982, pp. H1, H15.

—J.M.W.

Polanski, Roman (1933–) Celebrated primarily for his penchant for the strange and macabre, Roman Polanski was born in Paris, France, on August 18, 1933. At the age of three he moved with his family to Krakow, Poland, where under Nazi occupation Polanski's parents were sent to a concentration camp. Polanski's father helped the boy escape prior to his internment. Roman managed to survive the war, often seeking sanctuary in movie houses where he became a devoted film enthusiast. After the war Polanski learned that his mother had died at Auschwitz, but his father had survived and moved back to Krakow with his son. In 1950 Polanski enrolled in the State Film College in Lodz, where he also became an actor and appeared in several films by Polish filmmaker ANDRZEJ WAJDA, including *A Generation* (1954). In 1958, Polanski directed a short film, *Two Men and a Wardrobe,* to much critical acclaim. This film and two other short films Polanski made in the early sixties, *The Fat and the Lean* (1960) and *Mammals* (1962), showed Polanski's propensity for black humor.

In 1962 Roman directed his first and last feature film in Poland, *Knife in the Water.* Although it was poorly received by Polish critics, it proved a sensation in the West. The film won the critic's prize at the Venice Film Festival and received an Academy Award nomination for best foreign film. The tense psychological drama revolves around a couple on a weekend outing and the hitchhiker that they pick up. Following the international success of this film, Polanski left Poland and made his first English-language film, *Repulsion* (1965) starring Catherine Deneuve. This classic psychological thriller concerned a young woman's descent into madness. It is one of the quietest—and most disturbing—horror films ever made. Polanski made two other films in England: *Cul-de-Sac* (1966), an offbeat, black comedy concerning gangsters, and the horror film parody, *Dance of the Vampires* (aka *The Fearless Vampire Killers Or: Pardon Me, But Your Teeth Are In My Neck* [1967]).

In the latter film Polanski costarred with the American actress Sharon Tate. Polanski married Tate in 1968, which also saw his American film debut with the horror film, *Rosemary's Baby*, based on the best-selling novel by Ira Levin. The film received an Academy Award nomination for best screenplay. In the summer of 1969 Sharon Tate, who was eight months pregnant with their first child, was brutally murdered by Charles Manson and members of his cult. Perhaps the result of Polanski's grief and anger, his next film was a bloody screen version of Shakespeare's *Macbeth* (1971).

Macbeth occupies a particularly noteworthy place among Polanski's films—and among cinematic Shakespearean adaptations in general. Ever since his student days in Krakow, recalled Polanski in his memoir, *Roman by Polanski* (1984), he had wanted to adapt a Shakespeare play to the screen. Now, writing the screenplay in collaboration with Kenneth Tynan, Polanski overturned several Elizabethan theatrical conventions, including adding more witches to the standard threesome, casting young and attractive actors as Macbeth and his Lady (Jon Finch and Francesca Annis), filming Lady Macbeth's sleepwalking scene in the nude (Polanski argued that everyone slept naked in her day), and staging Duncan's assassination on stage instead of off stage, as was the custom. Moreover, as commentator Robert F. Willson has pointed out, Polanski's obsession with graphically bloody scenes—perhaps in this instance motivated by Tate's recent murder—comes to the fore, especially in Duncan's murder, the gore-smeared daggers, and the sexually charged relationship between Macbeth and his lady. Polanski has defended himself against charges of undue violence: "*Macbeth* contained only a small fraction of the gore that

Roman Polanski on the set of *Macbeth* (Columbia)

characterizes any SAM PECKINPAH movie, but the violence was realistic. *Macbeth* is a violent play, and I've never believed in cop-outs." Although initially a box-office failure in America, it went on to enthusiastic reviews in England. Seen today, it emerges clearly as one of Polanski's most effective, and disturbing films. "The film's mise-en-scene has been described as 'claustrophobic,'" reports Willson, "creating a mood in which Macbeth and others struggle, like chained bears, to escape a certain, terrible fate." Rather than regarding Shakespeare's play as a morality fable, concludes Willson, "Polanski sees *Macbeth* as a Marxist tale about the unceasing hunger for power." Polanski moved to Europe where he eventually obtained French citizenship, and returned to the United States thereafter only to visit friends and work on film projects.

While in Europe, Polanski made *Che?* (1973), aka *What?* and *Diary of Forbidden Dreams,* a bizarre sex comedy starring Marcello Mastroianni. Polanski's next film, *Chinatown* (1974), is considered to be his masterpiece. Based on an original screenplay by Robert Towne, the film starred Jack Nicholson and Faye Dunaway in a complex drama concerning political and psychological corruption. The film is generally considered to be one of the first neo-noirs, reinventing the forties style for a modern audience. It earned Polanski an Oscar nomination for best director and a nomination by the New York Film Critics Circle for best film. Following the success of the film Polanski returned to Europe to make the dark surrealistic thriller, *The Tenant* (1976), another tale of psychological disintegration in which a man (Polanski) becomes mad after he moves into the apartment of a recent suicide.

In 1979 Polanski was convicted of the statutory rape of a 13-year-old girl. He fled the United States and resettled in Paris, where he next made *Tess* (1979), a three-hour adaptation of Thomas Hardy's *Tess of the d'Urbervilles,* starring the young Nastassja Kinski (with whom Polanski was romantically involved). At the time, *Tess* was the most expensive film made in France. Polanski received an Oscar nomination as well as a Cesar Award for both best director and best film. In 1981 Polanski returned to Poland and directed and starred in an acclaimed stage production of Peter Shaffer's *Amadeus.* Polanski's subsequent film work has proved sporadic: *Pirates* (1986) was a lackluster swashbuckler-spoof that, like his other comedies, did not totally succeed; *Frantic* (1988), with Harrison Ford, returned to thriller territory but failed both critically and commercially; *Bitter Moon* (1992) was an erotic thriller that introduced Hugh Grant; and his most recent film, *The Ninth Gate* (2000), starring Johnny Depp, returned to the genre of the psychological/supernatural thriller.

Polanski's late period has produced at least one masterpiece. *Death and the Maiden* (1994), based on a play by Ariel Dorfman, is an underrated, dark tale of political torture and rape under a Latin American dictatorship. One stormy night Paulina Escobar (Sigourney Weaver) and her husband (Stuart Wilson) receive as a guest in their seaside home, one "Dr. Miranda" (Ben Kingsley). Recognizing

him at once as the man who tortured and raped her 15 years ago, Paulina determines to enact her revenge. Polanski plays out Paulina and Miranda's game of cat-and-mouse, accusation and denial, madness and calculation, in the claustrophobic confines of a single set, the Escobar home. The film concludes with Miranda, trapped at last, confessing to his crimes. The fablelike tone of the story thus yields, in the final analysis, to stark, unrelenting terror as he chronicles with obvious relish his sadistic, horrific acts.

In 2002 Polanski won the Palme d'Or at Cannes for *The Pianist.*

Other Films As actor: *Do Widzenia, Do Jutra* (*Good Bye, til Tomorrow* [1961]); *The Magic Christian* (1969); *Cia, Federico! Fellini Directs Satyricon* (1969); *Andy Warhol's Dracula* (1973); *Back in the USSR* (1991); *A Pure Formality* (1994); *The Pianist* (2002).

References Bisplinghoff, Gretchen, *Roman Polanski: A Guide to References and Resources* (Boston: G. K. Hall, 1979); Polanski, Roman, *Roman by Polanski* (New York: Morrow, 1984); Wexman, Virginia Wright, *Roman Polanski* (Boston: Twayne, 1985); Willson, Robert F., "Macbeth," in Tibbetts, John and James M. Welsh, *The Encyclopedia of Stage Plays into Film* (New York: Facts On File, 2001), pp. 386–390.

—R.W.

Pollack, Sydney Irwin (1934–) Veteran Hollywood producer-director Sidney Pollack was born a Hoosier, in Lafayette, Indiana, on July 1, 1934, the oldest of three children of David and Rebecca Pollack. When his family moved to South Bend, Indiana, he attended South Bend Central High School (1947–52), where he became interested in drama. In 1952 he moved to New York City, where he studied under Sanford Meisner, eventually becoming Meisner's assistant at the Neighborhood Playhouse. In 1960 he moved to Hollywood to work as JOHN FRANKENHEIMER's dialogue coach on *The Young Savages.* With the encouragement of Burt Lancaster, he began directing television programs for *Playhouse 90* and *Kraft Television Theatre.* His appearance as an actor with

Robert Redford in *War Hunt* (1961) began a long association between the men that would eventually result in seven films.

Pollack's debut film as director was *The Slender Thread* (1965), starring Sidney Poitier, Anne Bancroft, Telly Savalas, and Edward Asner. It was followed by the social drama *This Property Is Condemned* (1966), starring Robert Redford and Natalie Wood; a western, *The Scalphunters* (1968), with Burt Lancaster, Shelley Winters, and Telly Savalas; and a horror film, *Castle Keep* (1969), with Burt Lancaster and Peter Falk. His breakthrough picture as director was made in 1970, *They Shoot Horses, Don't They?* adapted from a novel about a 1930s dance contest by Horace McCoy and starring Jane Fonda, Susanna York, and Gig Young. This film was both a critical and a commercial success, earning nine Academy Award nominations, including best director. Abroad it won the Special Jury Prize at the Cannes Film Festival, the Jury Prize at the Moscow, the Belgium Film Festival Award, and awards for best picture and best direction at the Yugoslavian Film Festival. At home he won the Director's Guild Award for outstanding achievement in film direction. In 1972 he directed *Jeremiah Johnson,* which premiered at the Cannes Film Festival. *Jeremiah Johnson,* praised for its realistic portrayal of life on the frontier, begins as a gritty portrait of a mountain man in the making (Robert Redford) and concludes with his transformation into mythic stature.

Pollack struck Oscar gold in 1973 with *The Way We Were,* with Barbra Streisand and Robert Redford, which garnered six Oscar nominations and won two for the film's music, composed by Marvin Hamlisch and performed by Streisand. A number of perfectly competent features would follow: *The Yakuza* (1975), an Asian thriller scripted by Paul Schrader and Robert Towne, starring Robert Mitchum and Brian Keith; *Three Days of the Condor* (1975), a spy thriller, starring Robert Redford, Faye Dunaway, Cliff Robertson, Max Von Sydow, and John Houseman; *Bobby Deerfield* (1977), a racing movie starring Al Pacino

in the title role; *The Electric Horseman* (1979), starring Robert Redford as an erstwhile rodeo champion and Jane Fonda as a woman who needs his help to liberate a prizewinning horse; and *Honeysuckle Rose* (1980), starring Willy Nelson, Dyan Cannon, and Amy Irving, with Nelson playing a country singer before the musician had himself become a celebrity.

Pollack really hit his stride as producer and director during the 1980s and on into the 1990s. *Absence of Malice* (1981) took on the important topic of journalistic ethics. A naïve reporter (Sally Field) is manipulated into publishing a story that wrongfully implicates Paul Newman in the mysterious disappearance of a labor leader in Miami, Florida. Pollack again struck Oscar gold with *Out of Africa* (1985), with Klaus Maria Brandauer, Robert Redford, and Meryl Streep, playing Karen Blixen and based on her autobiographical novel (written under the pen name of Isak Dinesen).

Sydney Pollack directed and produced *Absence of Malice* (Columbia)

Nominated for 11 Academy Awards, including Streep for best actress, the film won seven Oscars, including best picture and best director. This was followed by *Havana* (1990), set in Cuba in 1958, starring Robert Redford as a gambler caught up in the revolutionary turmoil of Fidel Castro's coup.

The Firm (1993) was flawlessly directed from a screenplay adapted by David Rabe, Robert Towne, and David Rayfiel from the 1991 best-selling novel by John Grisham, and starring Tom Cruise as a young, brilliant, and ambitious lawyer recently hired by a shady Memphis "firm" headed by Hal Holbrook and Gene Hackman as Holbrook's enforcer assigned to keep the new man in line. This well-made exercise in popular filmmaking earned two Academy Award nominations, one for Holly Hunter as best supporting actress.

Despite the apparent diversity of Pollack's films, a thematic consistency does emerge, that is, the investigation of corruption in all of its political and personal manifestations. In *Random Hearts* (1999), for example, adapted from a 1984 novel by Warren Adler, Kristen Scott Thomas plays a congress-woman from New Hampshire who discovers that her husband, killed in an airplane crash, was having an affair with the wife of a Washington, D.C., police detective (Harrison Ford). The detective, determined to prove his wife's infidelity, forces his disclosure on the congresswoman and her daughter. The two themselves become romantically involved, as the congresswoman's political enemies attempt to sniff out a scandal to spoil her political career.

Meanwhile, Pollack has also continued to take cameo roles in his own films, such as *Random Hearts* (1999), and larger roles in films directed by such colleagues as WOODY ALLEN (*Crimes and Misdemeanors* [1989]) and STANLEY KUBRICK (*Eyes Wide Shut* [2000]). He also served as producer on most of his later films. A consummate and reliable craftsman who demonstrates a facility with any genre, he belongs to a select company of filmmakers who wear the mantle of old Hollywood with elegance and assurance.

Reference Taylor, William R., *Sydney Pollack* (Boston: Twayne, 1981).

—J.M.W.

Pudovkin, Vsevelod Illarionovich

(1893–1953)   Soviet filmmaker Vsevelod Pudovkin was one of the giants of the revolutionary Soviet cinema of the 1920s and 1930s. He was born in Penza, a small town in the Volga region, on February 16, 1893. Although he was educated in chemistry at Moscow University, Pudovkin preferred to pursue film studies; but a three-year internment in a Pomeranian prisoner-of-war camp during the Great War interrupted his ambitions. Back in Moscow in 1918, he entered the State Cinema School, where he attended the celebrated "workshops" of his mentor, Lev Kuleshov.

Pudovkin's first directorial assignment was *Mechanics of the Brain* (*Mekhanika golovnovo mozga* [1925]), an educational film about Pavlov's theories of action and reaction. He then directed what is considered his masterpiece, *Mother* (*Mat* [1926]). Based on Maxim Gorky's novel, it exemplifies Pudovkin's methods of montage, which differed somewhat in theory (if not in practice) from those of his colleague SERGEI EISENSTEIN. Pudovkin argued that individual shots should be conjoined more in the manner of *linkage* rather than Eisensteinian *collision*. "The expression that a film is *shot* is entirely false," he said. "The film is not *shot,* but *built,* built up from the separate strips of celluloid that are its raw material." Among *Mother*'s more famous sequences are shots of a thawing, ice-bound river conjoined with images of an awakening army; and shots of a beetle laboring its way out of a plate of mush intercut with images of the Bolshevik struggle.

Thus, in *End of St. Petersburg* (*Konets Sankt-Peterburga* [1927]), which was made to commemorate the Bolshevik Revolution of 1917, Pudovkin chronicled the event in a fashion rather different from that of Eisenstein, who was making a film on the same subject at precisely the same time and at the same locations. Not only was his method of editing entirely his own, but he preferred using the device of the individual protagonist rather than the Eisensteinian "collective worker hero." In this way he gave a human face and character to the abstract struggles of ideology. Again, there are striking uses of shot juxtapositions for editorial effect, as when images of factory workers' faces are intercut with pieces of machinery (emphasizing the dehumanization of the worker); and when shots of the slaughter of war are intercut with scenes of buying and selling on the stock exchange (as the brokers cheer soaring stock prices, soldiers lie dying in the mud).

His last silent film, *Storm over Asia* (*Potomok Chingis-Khan*), took revolutionary fervor to the Mongolian steppes. Bair is a Mongolian hunter who, because of a trumped-up connection with Genghis Khan, is tricked by the British into becoming a puppet ruler of his people. Bair finally turns upon his enemies in the end and leads a mighty Mongol horde across Asia. Never had the details of Oriental life been portrayed so authentically on the screen.

As a theorist, Pudovkin's importance is perhaps underestimated alongside Eisenstein's. He believed that the practice of montage, of alternating long shots with closeups, cutaways, and flashbacks, was analogous to the way the human mind and the eye conspire to perceive and process information about the real world. Knowingly or not, he was extending the theories of the American psychologist, Hugo Munsterberg, and anticipating those of today's cognitive film theorists. "The film technician, in order to secure the greatest clarity, emphasis, and vividness," he wrote, "shoots the scene in separate pieces and, joining them and showing them, *directs the attention of the spectator to the separate elements, compelling him to see as the attentive observer saw. . . . The sequence of the pieces must not be uncontrolled, but must correspond to the natural transference of attention of an imaginary observer*" [italics added]. Pudovkin's theories were published in *Film Technique* (1933), which systematized his views on editing, and in *Film Acting* (1935), which contrasted performance techniques on the stage and

on the screen (advocating a more "non-theatrical," naturalistic style of performance before the camera). Originally written for his film classes, they were not published outside the USSR until 1939. His theories of asynchronous sound, written in collaboration with Eisenstein and Grigori Alexandrov in 1931, were prophetic of modern-day techniques in editing image and sound. He rejected those methods, standard at the time, of exactly coinciding the image with its sound source. Used in that way, he argued, "sound will destroy the art of montage." Rather, "only the use of sound as counterpoint to visual montage offers new possibilities of developing and perfecting montage." In sum, sound is neither more nor less important than the image, but should be considered as "a new element of montage," ensuring the artistic future of the film medium.

Of all his sound films, *Deserter* (*Dezertir* [1932]) best exemplifies these techniques. Made four years after his sound manifesto, it tells the story of a striking Hamburg dock worker, Karl Renn, who "deserts" his German colleagues to go to the Soviet Union and learn its philosophies and methods of collective labor. In the end, rather than remain in the comfortable environs of his new home, he chooses to return to Germany and carry on the fight of Soviet socialism. Throughout, images are freely conjoined with montages of sound—the blows of hammers, the hoots of ship's whistles, the pump of pistons, the chaotic babble of crowds. Sometimes Pudovkin plays out the images silently; at others, he matches them to nondiegetic background music and synthetic sounds. During the factory scenes and strike sequences, the frenetic rhythms of the cutting are confirmed and supported by the rapid-fire editing of sounds. Not as sophisticated, perhaps, as the work of RENÉ CLAIR in France or ROUBEN MAMOULIAN in America, *Deserter* is nonetheless a film of raw power and energy. Unfortunately, it was completed at a time when Pudovkin and his colleagues came under attack from the Stalinist regime for not adhering to the policy of Soviet socialist realism, i.e., for sacrificing political realities for the sake of an alleged "formalism."

Later films included a series of patriotic history films, including *Minin and Pozharsky* (1939) and *Suvorov* (1940). The first depicts Muscovite life at the beginning of the 17th century after the death of Ivan the Terrible and in the face of impending invasion by the Poles and Swedes. *Suvorov* is set in the years after the death of Catherine the Great and chronicles the exploits of the legendary Russian military hero Suvorov (portrayed by Nikolai Cherkassov), who led his armies against the French revolutionary forces. It won the Stalin Prize in 1941. In contrast to his films of the 1920s, these films valorized the past, bolstering Soviet morale against the present threat of Nazi invasion. *Admiral Nakhimov* (begun in 1941 and completed in 1946) was another portrait of a brilliant Russian military hero at the time of the Crimean War. Ironically, it ran Pudovkin afoul of the Communist Party's policies of Soviet socialist realism, and he had to make "revisions" before it was accorded Party favor. Three months after the release of his last film, *The Return of Vasily Bortnikov* (*Vozvrashcheheniye vasiliya Bortnikova* [1953]), Pudovkin died of a heart attack while vacationing on the Baltic Coast near Riga.

In his best work, Pudovkin never lost sight of the individual face and humanity behind the formal experiments and the ideologies of his stories. "For myself," he wrote, "I define montage as an all inclusive discovery and explanation of the interrelationships of the phenomena of real life."

Other Films *Chess Fever* (*Shakhamatnaya goryachka* [1925]); *Victory* (*Pobeda* [1938]); *Murderers Are on Their Way* (*Ubitzi vykhodyat na dorogu* [1942]); *Three Encounters* (*Trivstrechi* [1948]).

References Dart, Peter, *Pudovkin's Films and Film Theory* (New York: Arno Press, 1974); Pudovkin, V. I., *Film Technique and Film Acting* (New York: Crown Publishers, 1959); Leyda, Jay, *Kino: A History of the Russian and Soviet Film* (New York: Collier Books, 1973); Sargeant, Amy, *Classic Films of the Soviet Avant-Garde* (London: I.B. Tauris & Co., 2000).

—J.C.T.

Rafelson, Bob (1933–) Although he has not produced a large body of cinema, Bob Rafelson has directed at least one great film, *Five Easy Pieces* (1970), and one great adaptation, *The Postman Always Rings Twice* (1981), both films starring Jack Nicholson, a star whose reputation Rafelson helped to establish. He has, of course, made other good films as well, notably *The King of Marvin Gardens* (1972), also with Nicholson, and *Mountains of the Moon* (1990), which Rafelson considers his best film, adapted from the William Harrison novel *Burton and Speke* (1982), a chronicle of the adventures of Sir Richard Burton and John Hanning Speke, exploring the headwaters of the Nile during the 19th century.

Rafelson was born the son of middle-class Jewish parents from the West Side of New York City on February 21, 1933, and educated at Trinity School in Pawling, New York, before going on to Dartmouth University. Thereafter, he traveled the world, eventually joining the army for a tour of duty made difficult by his temper. According to his biographer Jay Boyer, he "dubbed and translated films for the Shochiku Film Company" in Japan and got experience working in radio and television.

Out of the service and back in New York, he found work as a writer with David Susskind's Tal-

ent Associates and finally became associated with Burt Schneider at Screen Gems. The two of them cashed in on the popularity of the Beatles by packaging a less talented group of Beatles imitators, called the Monkees, for a popular television series. The Monkees were then featured in Rafelson's first motion picture, *Head* (1968). Although hailed as an "American masterpiece" in France by Henri Langlois of the Paris Cinémathèque, *Head* was less than a critical success in America. In fact, Rafelson himself called it a "total disaster," but the commercial popularity of the Monkees led to Rafelson's film production company, BBS, established by Burt Schneider, Bob Rafelson, and Steve Blauner, that stood behind *Easy Rider* (1969), *The Last Picture Show* (1971), and *Hearts and Minds* (1974), as well as the two defining Rafelson films—*Five Easy Pieces* and *The King of Marvin Gardens*. All of a sudden, Rafelson was part of the so-called Hollywood New Wave.

Rafelson's early success as director was built largely upon the acting talent of his friend Jack Nicholson, who starred as the restless and troubled oil-rigger Bobby Dupea in *Five Easy Pieces,* David Staebler in *The King of Marvin Gardens,* the drifter and murderer Frank Chambers in *The Postman Always Rings Twice,* Harry Bliss in *Man Trouble*

(1992), and Alex Gates, a crooked Florida wine merchant in *Blood & Wine* (1997). In 1968 Rafelson hired Nicholson to work with him scripting *Head,* a sort of plotless wonder that featured not only the Monkees, but also a diverse cast that included Annette Funicello, Frank Zappa, and even Sonny Liston.

The screenplay for *Five Easy Pieces* was written by a friend of Nicholson's, Carole Eastman, using the pen name Adrien Joyce, who developed Rafelson's image of Nicholson playing Chopin on a piano set in the back of a pickup truck into the story of a failed concert pianist and troubled drifter, Bobby Dupea, attracted to two very different women, one a country-and-western singer, the other a trained classical musician. As finally shaped by Rafelson, the picture had the moody, existential atmosphere of a European film, and Rafelson was named best director by the New York Film Critics Circle, besides picking up four Oscar nominations, including best picture. This success was then followed by another moody Nicholson feature, *The King of Marvin Gardens,* set in Atlantic City and co-scripted by Rafelson and Jacob Brackman.

In 1981 Rafelson remade Tay Garnett's *The Postman Always Rings Twice,* casting Jack Nicholson as the drifter-protagonist of the James M. Cain novel about greed, lust, murder, and betrayal, and Jessica Lange as Cora Papadakis, with whom Frank Chambers conspires to murder her older husband, Nick, and take over the roadhouse café Nick owns. Playwright DAVID MAMET expressed some interest in writing the screenplay, so long as he could remain faithful to the Cain novel, which he respected. The result was a raw-edged presentation of animal lust, deception, and betrayal, far closer to the spirit of the novel than the "classic" treatment starring John Garfield and Lana Turner could have been in 1946 under the Production Code. The only change Rafelson made was to give Frank a stay of execution at the end, after Cora is killed in an auto accident. The film ended leaving a devastated Frank by the side of a dusty road, waiting for the police to catch up with him, for the postman to ring a second time, in other words.

Rafelson has had a hit-and-miss career during which his initial success with *Five Easy Pieces* was not to be replicated. Though he does not claim to be an auteur, Rafelson finds consistency in the way he is interested "in the effect characters have on one another in meeting these odd juxtapositions of cultures and social backgrounds," as quoted by Jay Boyer. "Confrontation is what defines a person," Rafelson added. "If you're not able to do that, then you're unable to be tender. With confrontation you are constantly discovering who you are." Rafelson's best films have been about exploration, confrontation, and self-discovery.

Other Films *Stay Hungry* (1976); *Black Widow* (1987); *Tales of Erotica* (1993); *Picture Windows* (1995).

References Boyer, Jay, *Bob Rafelson: Hollywood Maverick* (New York: Twayne, 1996); Farber, Stephen, "Rafelson's Return," *New West* (March 1981): 96–101; McGilligan, Patrick, "The Postman Rings Again," *American Film* 6 (April 1981): 50–55; Taylor, J., "Staying Vulnerable," *Sight and Sound* (Autumn 1976): 200–204.

—J.M.W.

Ray, Nicholas (1911–1979) Nicholas Ray, patron saint of the filmmaker as loner, antihero, and exile, became a cause célèbre in the critical battles of the 1960s over the auteur theory. Ray has been damned as a Hollywood hack and celebrated as one of cinema's greatest directors. An ardent admirer, JEAN-LUC GODARD, went so far as to declare, "The cinema is Nicholas Ray," adding that "if the cinema no longer existed, Nicholas Ray alone gives the impression of being capable of reinventing it." If Ray did not reinvent the cinema, his most memorable film, *Rebel Without a Cause* (1955), certainly helped "reinvent" 20th-century popular culture.

Nicholas Ray was born Raymond Nicholas Kienzle, Jr., on August 7, 1911, in the small town of Galesville, Wisconsin. Winning a college scholarship, Ray enrolled in the University of Chicago in 1931. His academic career proved short-lived. Uninspired by academic life, Ray left the Midwest in search of the Bohemian life in New York City where he joined the left-wing agitprop theater group, Theatre of Action, a company with close ties to the Group Theatre. In 1935, the company commissioned its first professional production, *The Young Go First.* The play was Ray's first professional acting job, as well as the first professional production directed by ELIA KAZAN. Ray was greatly influenced by the amount of time Kazan devoted to working with his actors, particularly through the technique of improvisation.

With the start of World War II, Ray was hired by John Houseman as a staff member of the Office of War Information. When the OWI was disbanded by anti-Roosevelt forces in Washington, Ray accepted an invitation from Kazan to come to Hollywood as an assistant on *A Tree Grows in Brooklyn* (1945). In 1947, Dore Schary, then head of production at RKO, offered Ray the chance to direct his first film, *They Live By Night* (1948). A gritty crime drama, the film is an astonishing directorial debut, a landmark study of youthful alienation, with Farley Granger as the film's anti-hero, a loner who lives outside the boundaries of conventional morality, foreshadowing by seven years Ray's treatment of youthful rebellion in *Rebel Without a Cause.*

From 1950 until early 1953, Ray proved to be one of the most productive directors for Howard Hughes at RKO. Despite Ray's leftist associations, his connection to Hughes spared him from the threat of the Blacklist. Hughes protected Ray from HUAC, and in return, Ray directed such RKO projects as *The Flying Leathernecks* (1951) with John Wayne as a tough fighter pilot.

Despite Ray's growing discontent that he was allowed to do only hack work at RKO, these films were not devoid of artistic merit. Ray's 1952 *The Lusty Men,* a gritty story about rodeo life starring Robert Mitchum and Susan Hayward, is one of his more critically acclaimed films. When Hughes sold his stock in RKO in 1953, Ray took advantage of a loophole in his contract to leave the studio. However, Ray's dream to become free of the artistic and ideological constraints of Hollywood

would prove illusive. As his wife and biographer Susan Ray has acknowledged, Ray was "brilliant but unreliable." Even so, before his "unreliability" made him an outcast in Hollywood, Ray made two films that established his name in the pantheon of American auteurs: *Johnny Guitar* (1954), perhaps the most eccentric of all Hollywood Westerns, followed a year later by one of the most celebrated works in American cinema, *Rebel Without a Cause.*

Ray referred to *Johnny Guitar* as a "baroque—very baroque" western, a gender-bending study of obsession, competition, and desire. Bar owner Joan Crawford (with six-shooters strapped to her black-leather-clad thighs) goes up against hard-as-nails landowner Mercedes McCambridge while their boyfriends, Sterling Hayden and Scott Brady, stand by their women, looking pretty.

The inversion of gender roles is likewise explored in *Rebel Without a Cause.* If the film's hero, Jim Stark (James Dean), is a rebel lacking a cause worth fighting for, the film posits a clear cause for Jim being a rebel. In keeping with the dominant cultural logics of the mid-fifties, the good-boy-gone-wrong has been raised in a middle-class family by a weak, ineffectual father and a dominating mother and grandmother. On the surface, *Rebel* is a cautionary tale addressed more to parents than to teenagers, and a rather politically conservative fable at that. Even so, from the title sequence on, the emotional intensity of the film overwhelms the conventional ideology of the script and connected in a powerful way to young audiences. In doing so, *Rebel Without a Cause* displays the excess of moral ambiguity and emotional complexity that continues to enthrall Ray's admirers and confounds his detractors.

Ray, long attracted to the theme of "wild youth," as evident in *They Live By Night, Knock on Any Door* (1949), and *Born to Be Bad* (1950), had been working on an outline for *Rebel Without a Cause* when he was introduced by Kazan to the 22-year-old James Dean. In Dean, Ray immediately knew he had found his Jim Stark. As Ray recalled, like Jim Stark, Dean was the "disappointed . . . child who skulks off to his private corner and refuses to speak. Eager and hopeful, he was the child . . . wanting more, wanting everything . . . but it was never easy for him. Between belief and action lay the obstacle of his own deep, obscure uncertainty." In working with Dean, Ray called on his own experience as a young actor being directed by Kazan. In directing Dean, Ray relied on improvisation, "without this [Dean's] powers of expression were frozen."

The film also provided Ray an opportunity to explore the new "shape" of post-television Hollywood film with its increasing reliance on CinemaScope and vivid color. As Ray noted, "the use of primary color in film is as significant as the use of a close-up." Thus, Ray asserted, Dean in a red jacket added to the actor's performance the "color value" of smoldering danger. Ray likewise used the high contrast of primary colors to bring a sense of deep focus to the otherwise flat medium of CinemaScope. Indeed, the value of the film's performances, boosted by Ray's full exploitation of CinemaScope and color, challenged the conventional "message" of the script with a cinematic virtuosity that communicated on a primal level to younger audiences. It was this "innate" cinematic vision that so impressed Godard.

No doubt the violent, unexpected death of Dean a few weeks before the film's opening also provoked an audience response unanticipated by Ray. The director learned of Dean's death while in Europe working on his next film, *Hot Blood* (1956). The two had formed a close personal relationship and the news devastated Ray. He remained in Europe, refusing to work on the post-production of his new film. Dean's death and the success of *Rebel* coincided with the beginning of Ray's decline, both professionally and emotionally, abetted by an increasing abuse of alcohol and drugs. After several financially unsuccessful studio projects, Ray determined to find a way to become an independent producer working in Europe, where he hoped to find greater artistic freedom and personal fulfillment. The forgettable *Party Girl* (1958) would be his last Hollywood film.

In 1959 Ray joined with Samuel Bronston in an ill-fated plan to "reinvent" the cinema in Spain. Instead, he found himself at the helm of the Bronston-produced biblical spectacle *King of Kings* (1961) and the equally overproduced *55 Days at Peking* (1963). While directing *55 Days,* Ray suffered a heart attack and was replaced. He would never direct another feature film. In 1959, he returned to the United States to teach at Harper College in Binghamton, New York. Ray began to shoot a student production, *We Can't Go Home Again.* A rough cut of the film was shown to acclaim at the 1973 Cannes Film Festival. However, Ray was never able to finish the project.

Acknowledging his artistic debt to Ray, German filmmaker WIM WENDERS offered Ray a small role in his *The American Friend* (1977). After Ray was diagnosed with terminal cancer, he accepted Wenders's request for the two directors, master and disciple, to make a final project to be titled *Nick's Movie,* which would explore the meaning for Wenders of Ray's impending death. Ray died on June 16, 1979. Wenders released his film as *Lightning Over Water* in 1980. As critics Robert Kohler and Peter Beichen wrote in their study of the films of Wenders, "Ray is an archetype of the unsettled filmmaker, saddled by the Hollywood system. His characters . . . are the models of the uprooted, wandering figure." Indeed, Ray chose as his personal motto a line from *Johnny Guitar,* "I'm a stranger here myself."

Other Films   *A Woman's Secret* (1949); *On Dangerous Ground* (1951); *This Man Is Mine* (1951); *Run for Cover* (1955); *Bigger than Life* (1956); *The Savage Innocents* (1959).

References   Eisenschitz, Bernard, *Nicholas Ray: An American Life,* trans. Tom Milne (Winchester, Mass.: Faber and Faber, 1993); Ray, Nicholas, *I Was Interrupted: Nicholas Ray on Making Movies,* ed. Susan Ray (Berkeley: University of California Press, 1993); "Nicholas Ray," in *Interviews with Film Directors,* ed. Andrew Sarris (New York: Avon, 1969).

—T.P.

Ray, Satyajit (1921–1992)   India's most famous film director was a true cosmopolitan who was heavily influenced by both his Bengali heritage and the cultural traditions of the West. Satyajit Ray (pronounced Shotto-jeet Rye) was born in the affluent northern section of Calcutta on May 2, 1921. After the death of his father, a publisher, he and his mother relocated to his maternal uncle's house in the middle-class southern section of the city, where he avidly devoured Hollywood movies and Western classical music. While watching the work of JOHN FORD and WILLIAM WYLER, he recalled, "I was no longer interested in just what the stars were doing, but what were the characteristics that distinguished the work of one director from another." In 1941, after college, he studied painting in Santiniketan University under the tutelage of his grandfather's friend, the Nobel Prize-winning poet, Rabindranath Tagore. Back in Calcutta during the war, he resumed his absorption in Hollywood cinema, and a few years later helped found the Calcutta Film Society.

"The raw material of the cinema is life itself," Ray said in 1948, when he was an aspiring but untrained Bengali filmmaker. "It is incredible that a country which has inspired so much painting and music and poetry should fail to move the filmmaker. He has only to keep his eyes open, and his ears. Let him do so." After viewing the Italian neorealist classic *The Bicycle Thief* two years later, he determined to put his vision into practice. He approached the widow of Bengali author Bibhutibhusan Bandyopadhyay—more widely known in the West as Bibhutibhusan Banerjee—for the rights to film Banerjee's 1929 novel *Pather Panchali,* the saga of a poverty-stricken family in the little village of Nishchindipur. Financing the bulk of the film adaptation himself, shooting on weekends away from his job as an art director in a Calcutta-based British advertising agency, Ray strove for a naturalistic manner quite distinct from the stylized melodramatic style then common to Hindi cinema. It was completed in April 1955 and had its world premiere in New York City at the invitation of the Museum of Modern Art. Ray followed its spectacular success with two more films to complete his so-called Apu Trilogy: *Aparajito,* which is based on the last third of *Pather Panchali,* and *The World of Apu,* drawn from Banerjee's *Aparajita.* The first film remains one of the most remarkable directorial debuts in film history. Not only did it revolutionize Hindi cinema's so-called parallel-cinema movement in the 1960s and 1970s with its naturalism, unobtrusive styles of lighting, subtlety of acting, but also it aroused interest abroad in Ray's work and in Indian cinema in general. When the Apu Trilogy was released in the early 1990s, critic Richard Schickel was struck anew by its "cumulative power." "In everything but physical scale [the three films] constitute an epic, as they range over two or three decades and embrace both village and city life in modern India and all the most basic human emotions in the most tender and patient way."

The Apu Trilogy underscores the humanism and technical economy that would mark all of Ray's work. Significantly, however, these were qualities he drew not from filmmakers of his native land but from European masters like VITTORIO DE SICA, JEAN RENOIR (whom he met in 1949 during a location scouting trip for the French master's *The River*), and ROBERTO ROSSELLINI. Yet, it has been argued, his films are unmistakably "Indian." To explain, one must go back to the Bengali renaissance early in the century, when high-caste (urban middle-class) Hindu families like the Tagores and the Rays—"educated natives," as the British referred to them— pursued English literature and European philosophy and politics. Ray's own grandfather, Dwarkanath, was a typical example of this class and was, reports historian Ian Buruma, "a Hindoo with an enlarged mind and a truly British spirit," a writer and composer well versed in European cultural traditions. When the British shifted the capital of the Raj to New Delhi in 1912, however, Calcutta went into decline, although vestiges of high culture stubbornly remained. As Buruma continues, "its refinement, its liberalism, its so-phisticated attempt to bridge East and West, was out of step—just as Calcutta, the old colonial capital, has been out of step for a long time with the development of India." This sense of European elegance in the midst of squalor—and the presence of characters whose intelligence and sensibility make them anomalous in their culture—are common elements in Ray's films. "I am interested in all dying traditions," Ray has said. "[The character] who believes in his future is for me a pathetic figure. But I sympathise with him. He might be absurd, but he is fascinating." One thinks of characters like the father of Apu in *Pather Panchali,* a poor literary Brahmin dreaming of writing a masterpiece while his family is on the verge of starvation; the landlord in *The Music Room,* who pretends an aristocratic lifestyle by pawning his possessions; the journalist Bhupati in *Charulata* (1964); and the landowner Nikhil, who inhabits a mansion that is divided into a section of wholly traditional rooms and a section that is distinctly Victorian English.

Other films reveal the diversity of his vision. *The Goddess* (*Devi* [1960]) examines the 19th-century cult of the Mother Goddess in Hindu philosophy. *The Big City* (*Mahanagar* [1963]) is his first examination of contemporary life in Calcutta, a story of the clashing values of an older generation that keeps women at home and a younger generation that demands changes in societal, economic, and gender roles. The so-called Calcutta Trilogy—*The Adversary* (*Pratidwandi* [1970]), *Company Limited* (*Seemabaddha* [1971]), and *The Middle Man* (*Jana Aranya* [1975])—reflects, in the opinion of biographer Andrew Robinson, "the stress of Calcutta living on young educated men at a time when this had never been more intense: the rise of revolutionary terrorism and massive government repression, followed by the Bangladesh war and refugee crisis, corruption and nationwide Emergency, leading eventually to the emergence of the Communist government that ruled Bengal in the 1980s." *Distant Thunder* (*Asani Sanket* [1973]) returns to the subject of Bengali village life during the Bengal famine of 1943–44. And *The Chess Players* (*Shantranj ke Khilari* [1977]) adopts the stars of the Bombay cinema and the stylish look of Hollywood films and was a story of chess playing and politics set in the 19th-century milieu of the pleasure-loving city of Lucknow, the "Paris of the East" in its heyday.

There are many reasons why Ray's work remains better known in the international film community than at home. Like the Japanese masters Ray reveres, KENJI MIZOGUCHI and YASUJIRO OZU, he prefers to suggest power and feeling without bursting into emotional display, as opposed to the overheated style of the popular Indian cinema out of "Bollywood." Thus, his films are criticized as being too slow, too lingering over everyday details. At the same time, because Ray made most of his films in the Bengali language—spoken by only 50 million of the country's 600 million people—his reputation at home has remained relatively obscure. In his assessment of Ray's work, biographer Robinson notes that Ray generally eschews the conventions of typical Hollywood films, rejecting glamor, gimmicks, and technical polish for its own sake. "His characters are generally of average ability and talents," explains Robinson. "Perverted or bizarre behaviour does not appear . . . and there is little violence and no explicit sex. His interest lies in characters with roots in their society rather than in those who are deracinated and drifting. . . . It is the struggle and corruption of the conscience-stricken person that fascinate him, not the machinations of the ruthless or criminal." As a result, Ray's oeuvre becomes increasingly marginalized in cultures preoccupied with showy aspects of pop culture. Although he was frequently invited to work in other countries, Ray insisted on working exclusively in India. "I feel very deeply rooted there," he said. "I know my people better than any other. It's just that I react more immediately to things Indian. I would like to narrow it down even further and say things Bengali."

Satyajit Ray died of heart failure on April 23, 1992. His autobiographical sketch was published two years later under the title *My Years with Apu.* Among his many awards were the Grand Prize at the Cannes Festival in 1956 for *Pather Panchali,* the Gold Lion of the Venice Festival in 1957 for *Aparajito,* the Selznick Award in 1960 for *The World of Apu,* the Golden Bear Award at the Berlin Film Festival in 1973 for *Distant Thunder,* the Legion of Honor in France in 1989, and an Academy Award for lifetime achievement in cinema in 1992.

Other Films *The Philosopher's Stone (Parash Pathar* [1957]); *The Music Room (Jalsaghar* [1958]); *Two Daughters (Teen Kanya* [1961]); *Nayak (The Hero* [1966]); *Days and Nights in the Forest (Aranyer Din Ratri* [1970]); *Sonar Kalla (The Golden Fortress* [1974]); *Joi Baba Felunath (The Elephant God* [1978]); *The Kingdom of Diamonds (Heerak Rajar Deshe* [1979]); *The Home and the World (Ganashatru* [1989]); *Branches of the Tree (Shakha Proshakha* [1990]); *The Visitor (Agantuk* [1991]).

References Buruma, Ian, "The Last Bengali Renaissance Man," *The New York Review,* November 19, 1987, pp. 12, 14–16; "Dialogue on Film," *American Film 3,* no. 9 (July–August 1978): 39–50; Ray, Satyajit, *My Years with Apu* (London: Faber and Faber, 1997); Robinson, Andrew, *Satyajit Ray: The Inner Eye* (Berkeley: University of California Press, 1989); Schickel, Richard, "Days and Nights in the Arthouse," *Film Comment,* May–June 1992: 32–34.

—J.C.T.

Reed, Carol (1906–1976)

The British director Carol Reed was born in London in 1906 and came to films from the theater. Reed felt that his background gave him a penchant for filming thrillers. "As a young man in the theater," he recalled, "I became an assistant to Edgar Wallace, who wrote and produced so many melodramas. It helped me to see the appealing values of thrillers."

When he moved on to a career in films he was first assigned to be a dialogue director by British producers. In this capacity he quickly demonstrated his talent for coaching actors, and he was shortly advanced to directing low-budget films.

Once he had proved his competence and dependability at this level of production, he was promoted up the ranks of studio directors and given a greater degree of freedom in the choice and handling of the subjects he filmed. The first film he directed, *Midshipman Easy* (1935), is a period picture based on Marryat's novel about a lad who grows to maturity while serving on a British vessel. Reed's early films, like *Midshipman Easy* and *Bank Holiday* (1938), are not remarkable. But he went on to direct films that—although still modestly made by Hollywood standards—demonstrated incontestably the artistry of which British filmmakers like himself were capable.

One such film is *The Stars Look Down* (1940), which brought Reed serious critical attention both in England and in America. The film's unvarnished depiction of life in a mining town has rarely been equaled. Following this Reed worked on some of the best documentaries of the World War II era, such as the Academy Award-winning *The True Glory* (1945). He also directed the documentary-like theatrical film *The Way Ahead* (1944), an uncompromising portrayal of army life during wartime. Wartime films, both documentaries and fictional features, had conditioned moviegoers in Britain and elsewhere to expect a greater degree of realism in postwar cinema; and Reed led the way in this regard in English films. The experience he had gained in making wartime documentaries was reflected in his postwar work, enabling him to develop further, in films like *Odd Man Out* (1947), the strong sense of realism that had first appeared in *The Stars Look Down.* The documentary approach Reed employed to tell the story of a group of anti-British insurgents in Northern Ireland, whose leader is relentlessly pursued by the British, found a responsive audience.

Reed's films, although wholly British in character and situation, were among the first such English pictures to win wide popularity in the United States. Among these films was, of course, *Odd Man Out*—the first Reed film to display a theme that marked many of his subsequent films. In depicting a hunted, lonely hero caught in the middle of a crisis not of his own devising, Reed suggests that one can achieve maturity and self-mastery only by accepting the challenges that life puts in one's way and by struggling with them as best one can. *The Fallen Idol* (1948) clearly exemplifies this theme; it is also the first of a trio of masterpieces that Reed made in collaboration with novelist-screenwriter Graham Greene, one of the most significant creative associations between a writer and a director in cinema history.

The team followed *The Fallen Idol* with *The Third Man* (1949), a brilliant thriller that focused on the black market in postwar Vienna. The hero of *The Third Man* is Holly Martins, an American who has come to Vienna at the invitation of an old school chum, Harry Lime (ORSON GEORGE WELLES). Martins learns that Lime is involved in the most sordid of postwar rackets: trafficking in black-market penicillin of such inferior quality that it has caused widespread sickness and death. Shaken and disillusioned, Martins agrees to help the police capture Lime, and the film reaches its climax in an exciting chase through the shadowy sewers of Vienna. There is a memorable shot near the end of the sequence taken from street level, showing Lime's fingers desperately reaching through a sewer grating, in a vain attempt to escape to the street through a manhole by dislodging its cover. Although *The Third Man* was an enormous critical and popular success, a decade passed before Reed and Greene worked together again, this time on *Our Man in Havana* (1959), a spy thriller based on Greene's own novel, centering on a diffident British vacuum cleaner salesman living in Havana, who gets enmeshed in a web of international espionage.

Because most of Reed's films in the next decade, like *The Agony and the Ecstasy* (1965), were not comparable to the films mentioned already, it was thought that he had passed his peak for good. *Oliver!* (1968) in fact proved that Reed was back in top form, for it won him the Academy Award as best director and was itself named the best picture of the year. Reed received other important awards throughout his professional life. He won British Academy Awards for *Odd Man Out, The Fallen Idol,* and *The Third Man,* which also garnered the Grand Prize at the Cannes International Film Festival. In addition, he was knighted in 1952. A genuinely self-effacing man, Reed was never impressed by the honors that he received. He told this writer that his recipe as a filmmaker was "to give the public what I like, and hope they will like it too."

Other Films *Night Train to Munich* (1940); *The Key* (1953).

References Wapshott, Nicholas, *Carol Reed: A Biography* (New York: Knopf, 1994); Phillips, Gene D., *Major Film Directors of the American and British Cinema,* rev. ed. (Cranbury, N.J.: Associated University Presses, 1999).

—G.D.P.

Reisz, Karel (1926–) Born in Ostrava, Czechoslovakia (July 21, 1926), the son of a Jewish lawyer, Karel Reisz was sent to England in 1939 to escape the Nazi occupation of his homeland. After being educated at Emmanuel College, Cambridge, he taught at the St. Marlebone Grammar School in London for two years, then turned to journalism and began writing film criticism for *Sequence* and *Sight and Sound,* in the company of Gavin Lambert, LINDSAY ANDERSON, and TONY RICHARDSON, with whom he collaborated in 1956 on his first film, *Momma Don't Allow,* a 22-minute documentary about a jazz club in London, showcased in the first "Free Cinema" program at the National Film Theatre in January of that year. By then Reisz had served as director of the National Film Theatre (1952–53) and had written *The Technique of Film Editing* (1952), commissioned by the British Film Academy. In 1957 he was coproducer of Lindsay Anderson's *Every Day Except Christmas.* His next film as director came in 1959, *We Are the Lambeth Boys,* a 52-minute film documenting a London youth club and its clientele. In order to finance this film Reisz worked for two years as full-time film officer at the Ford Motor Company, doing their advertising, and drew a dismal conclusion from his experience: "There simply is no money or audience for this kind of movie in the English Cinema."

In 1960 Reisz directed his first feature film, *Saturday Night and Sunday Morning,* adapted by Alan Sillitoe from his own novel and produced by Tony Richardson and John Osborne's Woodfall Films. The film starred Albert Finney as Arthur Seaton, an angry young man who works in a factory but wants to cut loose from the conformity others would impose upon him. Perhaps Reisz took to heart Richard Hoggart's criticism of *We Are the Lambeth Boys* for its surface approach by attempting to focus more clearly on the inner life of his character. At any rate, the film became the surprise hit of 1961 in Britain, followed by *Night Must Fall,* an MGM remake of a 1937 Robert Montgomery film that Reisz would direct, again with Finney in the lead role. Reisz was not pleased with this film, however, and considered it a "disaster." His next film, *Morgan!* (1966), was more in keeping with the times—a tribute to the Swinging Sixties—and was another popular success, featuring David Warner as the eccentric nonconformist Morgan Delt, in the words of Georg Gaston, "a romantic anarchist in conflict with conventional society." David Mercer won a British Academy Award for his screenplay, and Vanessa Redgrave won a best actress award at the Cannes Film Festival. In 1968 Reisz again directed Vanessa Redgrave in another film about a nonconformist, *The Loves of Isadora,* a biographical treatment that featured Redgrave as the celebrated and notorious dancer Isadora Duncan. Redgrave again won best actress awards for her outstanding portrayal and was nominated for an Academy Award.

Six years would pass before Reisz's next picture, *The Gambler* (1974), scripted by James Toback for Paramount and starring James Caan, Paul Sorvino, and Lauren Hutton, an intelligent study of the psychology of gambling. Turning then to United Artists, Reisz found an even more promising project, *Who'll Stop the Rain* (1978), adapted from the Vietnam novel *Dog Soldiers* by Robert Stone, the story of a disillusioned war correspondent, John Converse (Michael Moriarty), involved in smuggling heroin from Vietnam into the United States with the help of his Marine friend Ray Hicks (Nick Nolte), a warrior who will be destroyed by his involvement. The film featured one of Nolte's strongest screen performances.

Perhaps the most remarkable and inventive film of Reisz's career was his fine adaptation of the John Fowles novel *The French Lieutenant's Woman* (1981), ingeniously scripted by playwright Harold Pinter. Pinter resolved the problem of the novel's optional conclusions by setting the action in two time frames and having the 19th-century story being made into a film by 20th-century actors (Meryl Streep and Jeremy Irons) who played double roles. This adaptation won best actress awards for Streep and deservedly earned multiple Academy Award nominations. Yet another biographical picture, *Sweet Dreams* (1985), would follow, based upon the life and career of the country singer Patsy Cline and starring Jessica Lange, with Ed Harris as the singer's flawed husband. His next project, *Everybody Wins* (1990), was adapted by Arthur Miller from his one-act play *Some Kind of Love Story* about a private detective (Nick Nolte) hired by a prostitute (Debra Winger) to investigate a murder; it was dismissed by critics as a muddled disappointment. In later years Reisz directed his talents more to theater and television than to cinema. Even so, he has left a solid record of achievement behind him.

References Armes, Roy, *A Critical History of British Cinema* (New York: Oxford University Press, 1978); Gaston, Georg, *Karel Reisz* (Boston: Twayne, 1980).

—J.M.W.

Renoir, Jean (1894–1979) Jean Renoir is one of the most beloved and influential filmmakers in history. His films, while highly theatrical in manner, display many of the tenets of naturalism that would later be embraced by the Italian neorealists of the late 1940s and the New Wave directors of the late 1950s. According to André Bazin,

Renoir "is one of the masters of photographic realism, the heir of the traditions of the naturalistic novel and its contemporary, Impressionist painting." Renoir's skills as both writer and director allowed him to create indelible masterpieces, films that are as enduring as they are enjoyable. His career can be divided into four distinct periods: early experiments of the silent era of the twenties; mature French masterworks of the thirties; films as an émigré in America in the forties; and his last works after his return to Europe.

Jean Renoir was born on September 15, 1894, in Paris, son of the impressionist painter Pierre-Auguste Renoir. He was raised in Cagnes, Provence, and studied philosophy and mathematics in college. His real education, by all estimation, came from the lively artistic environment of his family home. His father's paintings were Renoir's first guide to the sights and impressions of people and life in France (and Jean's boyish face can be seen in some of those paintings). As Renoir noted, "The paintings by my father which covered the walls of our apartment were an essential part of the background of my small life." His first wife, Catherine Hessling, was a former model of his father.

At the outbreak of the war, Renoir left home to enlist in the cavalry; he fought in World War I, and sustained an injury in an aviation mishap that left him with a permanent limp. He returned home and after caring for his ailing father, took up ceramics. But he was fascinated with the cinema, and with the inheritance he received from his father's estate, Renoir set up his own production company. Although his first film, *La Fille de l'eau* (1925), was mainly an introduction (for Renoir) to the craft of the medium, it also displays his love of nature. *Nana* (1926), an adaptation of the Zola novel about a prostitute, features a naturalistic acting performance from his wife Hessling. *Charleston* (1927) also showcased Hessling in an erotic dance fantasy. Except for an adaptation of *The Little Match Girl* (*La Petite marchande d'allumettes* [1928]), which is in a fantasy mode, his other silent films continued to reveal his penchant for realism. *Tire-au-Flanc* (1928) is mainly an improvised comedy of army life. In addition to his features, Renoir also accepted commercial directing assignments to help finance his own projects. These included *Marquitta* (1927), *Le Tournoi* (1928), and *Le Bled* (1929), which all provided Renoir specific stories and sets to explore the different aspects of filmmaking.

Renoir made an easy transition to sound film and enjoyed a highly creative and successful run of movies throughout the 1930s, films that are now considered masterpieces and rank high in critics' polls as among the best films ever made. His first sound film, *Purging the Baby* (*On Purge bébé* [1931]), is a trivial domestic comedy that was very successful. By contrast, *The Bitch* (*La Chienne* [1932]) is a dark melodrama about a man who has an affair with a prostitute and later murders her. *Boudu Saved from Drowning* (*Boudu sauvé des eaux* [1932]), remade in the United States as *Down and Out in Beverly Hills* in 1986, is Renoir's first in-depth analysis of class conflict and social norms. It contrasts the stifling conventions of bourgeois life as opposed to the anarchic freedom of the tramp, Boudu, played by Renoir's frequent lead actor of this period, Michel Simon. In the film, a respectable bookseller (Simon) rescues a tramp from drowning and takes him into his home. The rescued man promptly disrupts everything, even seducing his host's wife. The tramp ultimately rejects the middle-class life and departs. The film is both humorous and unsettling; moreover, its location shooting and naturalistic sound recording lend it a refreshing, open-air quality. André Bazin said of the film, "*Boudu*'s charm lies in its glorification of vulgarity. It portrays the most blatant lubricity in a civilized and nonchalant manner. *Boudu* is a magnificently obscene film." *Toni* (1935), the story of Italian immigrant workers in southern France, uses nonactors and was shot entirely on location. Its semidocumentary feel and use of real locations and simple people later influenced the Italian neorealist films.

The Crime of Monsieur Lange (*Le Crime de Monsieur Lange* [1937]) is Renoir's most overtly personal political film and reflects his involvement with the leftist politics of the Popular Front movement in France. In shooting *The Crime of Monsieur Lange* Renoir collaborated with members of the radical October Group (including scenarist Jacques Prevert), a cooperative of artists that aimed for entertainment alternatives to the prevalent bourgeois theater that was most popular. In the film, a timid young man working in a publishing house devises the popular Wild West comic strip hero "Arizona Jim." Before the young man and his girl friend can enjoy their new success, however, they must first murder the unscrupulous boss who threatens them and their publishing collective. The story is a hymn to collective enterprise as an antidote to corrupt capitalism. Critic Elizabeth Strebel notes, "*The Crime of Monsieur Lange* is the Popular Front film *par excellence,* full of the exuberance, optimism and confidence in the ability to transform social conditions which characterized that movement."

A Day in the Country (*Une Partie de campagne* [1936]) is an adaptation of a short story by Guy de Maupassant. The film was shot on location and clearly reveals Renoir's love of nature. Indeed, its fluid camera work and sensitivity to textures is often compared to his father's landscape paintings. Renoir said, "I try to work close to nature—but nature is millions of things and there are millions of ways of understanding its propositions." In addition to its beautiful photography, the story examines a central theme in Renoir's work: relationships between different classes. The story is about a country outing, during which a young lady is seduced by a man and the two are haunted thereafter by the memory of the brief affair. It is a rustic idyll that turns dark and poignant. Alexander Sesonske said the film shows "nature lovingly perceived, and within its ambience the human antics, ridiculous, tender, sad, achieve the complexity and resonance of actions rather than remaining mere events observed."

Two films from the late 1930s, *Grand Illusion* (*La Grande illusion* [1937]) and *The Rules of the Game*

(*La Règle du jeu* [1939]), are his masterpieces. In *Grand Illusion,* the "grand illusion" is the patriotic appeal of war itself, and the film addresses how individual, personal relationships often can supplant the horrors and futility of the destructive nature of war. Three downed French pilots are captured by the Germans, sent to prison camps, and eventually to the fortress of an aristocratic German commander. The aristocrat (played by Erich von Stroheim) befriends the one French pilot who is of the same social class as he, and they have a long dialogue about the fading of class divisions in modern European society. Later, despite their friendship and sympathies, they are forced to abide by the rules of war: After one of the French prisoners attempts escape, the French aristocrat is shot by his German counterpart. Two more prisoners escape and eventually make it to Switzerland. The film protests the barriers that divide men and countries as well as being an elegy to the vanishing codes of aristocracy and art in a modern age. David Cook suggests, "Both men have been victims of a rigid code of behavior which has left them no option but mutual destruction despite their friendship; Renoir suggests that the old ruling class of Europe is doomed for precisely the same reasons." *Grand Illusion* is also known for its extensive use of protracted shots and deep-focus photography, and it received numerous awards from various film festivals.

Renoir's masterpiece, and one of the acknowledged greatest films in all of cinema, is *The Rules of the Game.* The film is a sharply observed but compassionate view of all levels of society, as aristocrats and servants, soldiers and even a poet, Octave (superbly played by Renoir himself), intermingle at a country estate for a few days of games and hunting. Misunderstandings, infidelities, and threatened class, social, and racial barriers soon split the group asunder. However, Renoir displays an openhanded compassion for all these characters because, as Octave says, "Everybody has his reasons." According to André Bazin, "The film is nothing more than a tangle of reminders, allusions, and correspondences, a carrousel of themes where reality and the moral plane reflect one another without disrupting the movie's meaning and rhythm, its tonality and melody. At the same time, it is a brilliantly constructed film in which no scene is unnecessary, no shot out of place." The film is witty and elaborate, and again demonstrates Renoir's mastery of the long take and composition in depth. For political reasons, the film was censored and not seen in its entirety until decades later.

After a brief time in Italy, Renoir spent most of the next decade in the United States. His films made in America include *Swamp Water* (1941), a semidocumentary film shot on location in Georgia, and two war propaganda films, *This Land Is Mine* (1943) and *Salute to France* (1944). *The Southerner* (1945) is another semidocumentary film about poor, southern white farmers. Because the film was shot on location, it comes closest to the poetic realism of his earlier films. Renoir also made a literary adaptation, *The Diary of a Chambermaid* (1946) (later made by Luis Buñuel), and a romantic melodrama, *The Woman on the Beach* (1947), neither of which was a success or garnered Renoir positive critical appraisal.

After leaving Hollywood, Renoir went to India to make *The River* (1951), his first film in color, which was shot by his nephew, Claude Renoir. It is a story of the tension between cultures as a British family struggles to understand Indian ways. According to André Bazin, "What interested Renoir was not the Indian religious mentality in itself, but rather its insidious attraction for Westerners." *The Golden Coach* (*Le Carrosse d'or* [1952]) is a comedy about a traveling commedia dell'arte theater troupe, made in Italy. Renoir returned to France to make several more films before retiring. *French Can-Can* (1954) is a celebration of the Moulin Rouge, photographed in an explosion of bright, flowing colors, reminiscent of the Impressionist painters. *Le Testament du Dr. Cordelier* (1959) is an adaptation of *Dr. Jekyll and Mr. Hyde*. *The Elusive Corporal* (1962) is a comedy about a French corporal who tries to escape from a German prison camp during World War II. Renoir's final film was a short piece for French television, *The Little Theatre of Jean Renoir* (*Le Petit théâtre de Jean Renoir* [1969]).

After retiring from filmmaking, Renoir settled in Beverly Hills, California, and wrote several novels, plays, stories, a biography of his father, and his own memoirs. He died in 1979. Jean Renoir's remarkable life and importance as a filmmaker is vast. His distinctive stylistic techniques—mobile camera, deep-focus mise-en-scène, and long takes—greatly influenced other directors. And there was another very important quality, more difficult to explicate. According to François Truffaut, "Renoir's work has always been guided by a philosophy of life which expresses itself with the aid of something much like a trade secret: *sympathy*. It is thanks to this sympathy that Renoir has succeeded in creating the most alive films in the history of cinema, films which still breathe forty years after they were made."

Other Films *Night at the Crossroads* (*La Nuit de carrefour* [1932]); *Chotard and Company* (*Chotard et cie* [1932]); *Madame Bovary* (1934); *Life is Ours/People of France* (*La Vie est á nous* [1936]); *The Lower Depths* (*Les Bas-fonds* [1936]); *La Marseillaise* (1937); *The Human Beast* (*La Bête humaine* [1938]); *La Tosca* (1939); *Paris Does Strange Things* (aka *Elena et les hommes* [1957]); *Picnic on the Grass* (*Le Déjeuner sur l'herbe* [1959]).

References Cook, David, *A History of Narrative Film* (New York: Norton, 1996); Bertin, Celia, *Jean Renoir: A Life in Pictures* (Baltimore: Johns Hopkins University Press, 1991); Renoir, Jean, *My Life and My Films* (New York: Atheneum, 1974); Bazin, André, *Jean Renoir* (New York: Simon and Schuster, 1973); Sesonske, Alexander, *Jean Renoir: The French Films: 1924–1939* (Cambridge: Harvard University Press, 1980); Strebel, Elizabeth, "Renoir and the Popular Front," *Sight and Sound,* Winter 1979: 36–41.

—W.V.

Resnais, Alain (1922–) Although he has been linked to the French New Wave, Alain Resnais was in fact something of a precursor, experimenting in his own distinctive ways as the

"Wave" was cresting. Historian James Monaco has called him "filmmaker's filmmaker, too cerebral for the general run of popular audiences," but who "is no more intellectually complicated" than other European filmmakers who have produced a body of cinema "that is at least as personal and thoughtful as it is entertaining and popular." His best films involve the productive interplay of history and politics, time and memory, and were created through his affiliations with avant-garde writers such as Marguerite Duras and Alain Robbe-Grillet, who were reinventing the novel in France. He also collaborated with New Wave talents Chris Marker, Claude Lelouch, and JEAN-LUC GODARD in the protest film *Far from Vietnam* (*Loin du Vietnam* [1967]).

Resnais was born in Vannes, Brittany, on June 3, 1922, the son of Jeanne Gachet and Pierre Resnais, a pharmacist. After completing high school in 1938, he moved to Paris to study acting in 1940, enrolling in an acting school, the Cours René Simon, in 1941. In 1943 he went on to attend the Institute des Hautes Études Cinématographiques, headed by director Marcel L'Herbier, but quit in 1944 before entering military service with the French army in 1945.

Resnais worked as an assistant editor for Nicole Vedrès (1911–65) on her film *Paris 1900* (1948). Also in 1948 he shot two films in 16 mm, a travel film entitled *Châteaux of the Loire* and an experimental documentary short, *Van Gogh*. In 1953 he worked with Chris Marker on *Les Statues meurent aussi* (*Statues Also Die*), banned by government censors who, Resnais claimed, "misinterpreted that the film was anti-colonialist, whereas the film was really anti-racialist," then in 1955 he helped François Truffaut edit his first film (16 mm, silent, now lost), *Une Visite*.

In 1955 he made his groundbreaking documentary short, *Night and Fog* (*Nuit et brouillard*), the title reflecting a German category for concentration camp prisoners, *Nacht und Nebel*). This astonishing meditation on the Nazi death camps had a poetic voice-over written by Jean Cayrol, a former Resistance fighter, born in Bordeaux in 1917, whose brother Pierre died in one of the camps, and who had himself been one of the *Nacht und Nebel* prisoners. The film cut back and forth between color footage of present-day Auschwitz and black-and-white documentary footage from the past that revealed the horrors of the camps. Resnais later used the same technique in *Toute la mémoire du monde* (1957), his documentary of the French National Library.

Resnais's first feature film, *Hiroshima, mon amour* (1959), also a meditation on the memory of war, written by the novelist Marguerite Duras, further established Resnais's standing as a major talent and won the International Critics Prize at the Cannes Film Festival. The film was originally intended as a documentary about Hiroshima that posed the question of how to "document" a memory. The solution was provided by Duras, who wrote the story of a 34-year-old woman whose visit to Hiroshima triggers the memory of her first love, a German soldier shot on Liberation Day, a memory she shares with the Japanese architect with whom she is now involved. The point is that forgetfulness is stronger than love, and she had repressed the memory, just as, in the words of John Kreidl, "the people of Hiroshima have subdued their memory of the atomic explosion."

While *Hiroshima, mon amour* represented an astonishing innovation in conventional film narrative, avant-garde narration would be advanced to another level in the next film Resnais would undertake, this time with the novelist Alain Robbe-Grillet, *Last Year at Marienbad* (1961), a paradigm puzzler of the European art cinema. Resnais claims that Robbe-Grillet gave him "a choice of four scripts, and I picked the one of them that was most austere." The story—such as it is—involves three characters at a mythic spa: "X," the narrator; "A," a woman; and "M," who could be the woman's husband, or guardian, or protector. "X" attempts to persuade "A" to leave with him, claiming that they had met the year before and that she had agreed to leave with him a year later. "A" rejects his memory (story? excuse?) but finally agrees to leave with him. Beyond that, the film resists explanation. Kreidl described it as a film "made up by the spectator," following what Resnais himself had said: "The film is so made that fifty percent of it is what is shown there on the screen, and the rest [comes from] the reactions and the participation of the spectator." Viewers puzzled over the film's "meaning," while Resnais offered only cryptic comments about his "dreamlike" film: "It's a musical comedy, without songs, that tries to deepen the forces of revery."

His next film was *Muriel, or a Time of Return* (*Muriel, ou le temps d'un retour* [1963]), a project Resnais had first discussed with screenwriter Jean Cayrol in 1959. *Muriel* was "named for a person, not a place," James Monaco has written, and represented an advance for Resnais: "Characters are no longer identified by pronouns and algebraic symbols; they're allowed to live. They are liberated for the first time, no longer plot- and theme-ridden but free to 'do things we don't approve of.'" The film's title is the name of a young Algerian girl tortured to death, the memory of whom becomes the personification of responsibility for Bernard, a soldier who has returned to France after serving in Algeria.

La Guerre est finie (*The War Is Over* [1966]), written by the Spanish novelist Jorge Semprum, who later scripted the film *Z* for CONSTANTIN COSTA-GAVRAS, was a bit more straightforward. The main character, Diego Mora (Yves Montand), an erstwhile Spanish militant, is still active 25 years after "the war is over." This likable protagonist, whose motto is "Patience and irony are the principal virtues of the Bolshevik," anchors two plots, one political, the other personal.

This was followed by *Je t'aime, je t'aime* (*I Love You, I Love You* [1968]), which has been called Resnais's "most practical, least theoretical film" and "masterpiece of realistic montage" that also represented, however, "a sort of cubist approach to film," in the words of James Monaco. The film, about a writer persuaded by two scientists to par-

ticipate in a time-machine experiment, was a box-office failure, unfortunately, and that failure prevented Resnais from making films for five years. Resnais rebounded, however, with the commercial success of *Stavisky . . .* (1974), a flashy historical film set in the 1930s, dramatizing the life, death, and legend of the Russian émigré Serge Stavisky (Jean-Paul Belmondo), a Gatsbyesque con man, and the "Stavisky affair," which had political implications and led to "the resignation in late January of 1934 of the entire moderate leftist Chautemps cabinet, the fascist riots of February 6, 1934," as Monaco described it, "and the ensuing downfall of the Daladier government together with the emergence of the right-wing National Union cabinet of Gaston Doumergue."

Resnais teamed up with David Mercer for his first English-language film, *Providence* (1977), which featured a remarkable performance by John Gielgud as 78-year-old Clive Langham, a blocked novelist (presumably) afflicted with rectal cancer trying to come to grips with his craft, his children, his past, and his proctological distress. Clive passes a dark night of the soul drinking to ease the pain and hallucinating about his dead wife (Elaine Stritch), his lawyer son (Dirk Bogarde), his daughter-in-law (Ellen Burstyn), and his illegitimate son (David Warner). The next morning when these relatives appear to celebrate his birthday, they seem to be calm and loving, unlike the "characters" of his creative imagination (or his paranoid delusions). Interviewed about this film, Resnais said, "I utterly agree with Cocteau when he said that the cinema is always documentary, and a documentary can equally be about what one meets in the exterior world or in the interior world."

Resnais regarded *Providence* as a comedy. When *Life Is a Bed of Roses* (*La Vie est un roman* [1982]) was released in 1983, Resnais said that "the important thing for us is that we wanted to make a comedy, but reviewers found its non-realistic style deliberately distancing and elliptical." Eventually, however, Resnais would make a comedy that mainstream audiences would be genuinely amused by.

Approaching the turn of the century at the age of 76, Resnais made an innovative romantic comedy satirizing the typical French obsessions with property and sex, entitled *Same Old Song* (*On connaît le chanson* [1998]). This was a surreal departure for Resnais, whose unusually enigmatic films had been far removed from such confections as JACQUES DEMY's *The Umbrellas of Cherbourg* (1964), even though, as reviewer Stephen Holden noted, love is still "what makes the world go round, even when that love is uncertain or duplicitous." What is most amusing is the way the characters of this film burst into song, and in this respect, the film was an homage to the British playwright DENNIS POTTER, who originated this device in his television productions *Pennies from Heaven* (1970) and *The Singing Detective* (1986). In order to avoid merely copying Potter, Resnais decided "to use only fragments of [French] songs and rarely use them to explore the protagonists' imaginations." At times, moreover, he manipulated the music by having the men singing in women's voices and the women singing in men's voices. The plot, involving love and trust and betrayal as two sisters are courted by two real-estate agents, is secondary to the technique, which carries the action forward entertainingly.

Resnais defended the film as a "realist document because in daily life when our minds wander off, we often hear fragments of popular songs in our heads. If we talked at those moments, instead of words, it would be song snippets that would emerge." The film was a surprise success for Resnais, his first box-office hit in 35 years. "My films usually sell about 300,000 tickets," the director groused. "I did not expect this film to sell 2.6 million in France alone." Hence the commercial success of this film was "a complete mystery to me—my fourteenth film and finally everybody likes it!" Perhaps by the end of the century audiences had finally caught up with his experimental innovations.

Other Films *L'An 01* (1973); *Mon oncle d'Amérique* (*My American Uncle* [1980]); *L'Amour à mort* (1984); *Mélo* (1986); *I Want to Go Home* (1989); *Smoking/No Smoking* (1993).

References Armes, Roy, *The Cinema of Alain Resnais* (New York: A. S. Barnes, 1968); Duynslaegher, Patrick, "The Accidental Tourist," *Sight and Sound* 8, no. 12 (December 1998): 14–17; Kreidl, John Francis, *Alain Resnais* (Boston: Twayne, 1977); Monaco, James, *Alain Resnais* (New York: Oxford University Press, 1979); Ward, John, *Alain Resnais, or the Cinema of Time* (New York: Doubleday, 1968).

—J.M.W.

Richardson, Tony (1928–1991) The New Wave British director Cecil Antonio Richardson was born on June 5, 1928, the son of a pharmacist in Shipley, Yorkshire, and educated at Ashville College, Harrogate, then Wadham College, Oxford, where he served as elected president of the Oxford University Experimental Theatre Club and the Oxford University Dramatic Society, while earning his B.A. in English literature in 1951. He entered the BBC director training program in 1952 and established his professional credentials in television during the next four years, including a well-received production of Shakespeare's *Othello* in 1955. Meanwhile, he completed his first short independent film, *Momma Don't Allow,* with KAREL REISZ, shown as part of the first "Free Cinema" program organized by Lindsay Anderson in 1956.

Appointed assistant artistic director of the English Stage Company in January 1956, and working with the innovative George Devine, Richardson discovered, then staged John Osborne's *Look Back in Anger* at the Royal Court Theatre, a production that revolutionized British theatre, followed by another Osborne play, *The Entertainer,* starring LAURENCE OLIVIER in 1957. Both of the Osborne plays were then adapted to cinema in 1958 and 1959, with Richardson directing his first commercial films for Woodfall Films, a production company Richardson founded with John Osborne and Harry Saltzman.

In 1960 Richardson directed his first American project, an adaptation of William Faulkner's *Sanctuary,* but he also kept active with George Devine at the Royal Court, staging Shelagh Delaney's *A Taste of Honey,* which he successfully adapted to film in 1961. In 1962 he married the actress Vanessa Redgrave and directed two films, his adaptation of Alan Sillitoe's *The Loneliness of the Long Distance Runner,* followed by his adaptation of the Henry Fielding novel *Tom Jones,* his first major Hollywood hit that brought him Academy Award attention in 1963. He followed this Hollywood success with an adaptation of Evelyn Waugh's *The Loved One* in 1964.

Keeping active in Europe as well as the United States, Richardson directed two films starring Jeanne Moreau in France—Jean Genet's *Mademoiselle* in 1966 and *The Sailor from Gibraltar* in

1967, adapted from Marguerite Duras. In 1968 he directed one of his very best pictures, *The Charge of the Light Brigade,* in England and Turkey, putting an antiwar spin on the Crimean War and showing the vanity and bureaucratic stupidity of the military establishment that resulted in a bloody massacre. In 1969 he returned to the theater and staged a groundbreaking production of Shakespeare's *Hamlet* at the Roundhouse Theatre in London, which he then adapted to film, with Nicol Williamson playing the lead as an "angry young man" with an attitude. The film was made on a shoestring budget at the Roundhouse in Camden Town while the play was still in production, and is about as fine an example of filmed theater as can be found.

Tony Richardson was one of the major shaping talents of British theater and film during the 1950s and 1960s. One of the original "angry young men" of his generation, he revolutionized traditional British theater at mid-century and carried "kitchen-sink realism" over to his work in cinema. With LINDSAY ANDERSON and Karel Reisz he was a part of the "Free Cinema" movement and arguably as important to the New Wave in Britain as FRANÇOIS TRUFFAUT was to the New Wave in France. He had a particular talent for adapting literary and dramatic works to the cinema, as evidenced by his reworking of Henry Fielding's greatest novels, *Tom Jones* and, later, *Joseph Andrews* (1977), which was even better, though some critics dismissed it, claiming that Richardson was merely attempting to repeat his earlier success. In 1984 he adapted John Irving's *The Hotel New Hampshire* to the screen successfully. His last film, *Blue Sky,* was not released until after his death in 1991 because of legal and financial problems with Orion Pictures, but it was enthusiastically received upon its release in 1994 and won a best actress Academy Award for Jessica Lange. It was an appropriate capstone to Richardson's career in cinema.

Other Films *A Subject of Scandal and Concern* (1960), for BBC television; *Red and Blue* (1967); *Laugh-*

Tony Richardson

ter in the Dark (1969); Ned Kelly (1970); A Delicate Balance (1973); A Death in Canaan (1978); The Border (1982); Penalty Phase (1986); Beryl Markham: A Shadow on the Sun (1988), U.S. television miniseries; The Phantom of the Opera (1990), television miniseries; Hills like White Elephants (1990), adapted from Ernest Hemingway, and part of the HBO trilogy film entitled Men Without Women: Stories of Seduction.

References Radovich, Don, Tony Richardson: A Bio-Bibliography (Westport, Conn.: Greenwood Press, 1995); Richardson, Tony, The Long-Distance Runner: A Memoir (New York: William Morrow, 1993); Welsh, James M., and John C. Tibbetts, The Cinema of Tony Richardson: Essays and Interviews (Albany, N.Y.: SUNY Press, 1999).

—J.M.W.

Riefenstahl, Leni (1902–) One of the most controversial film directors of the 20th century, the woman who would be known as the "Film Queen of the Third Reich" has been both admired as a documentary genius and loathed as an accessory to a murderous regime. She was born Helene Berta Amalie Riefenstahl in Berlin, Germany, August 22, 1902. Her father was a plumbing engineer and her mother was a housewife with artistic inclinations who favored her daughter's early interest in dancing and painting. In 1910 she started taking dancing lessons. She studied at the Russian Ballet School in Berlin under Jutta Klammt and Mary Wigman. She became interested in the modern dance forms introduced by Isadora Duncan and others. Mary Wigman, a Duncan disciple, influenced Riefenstahl's views on art. Throughout her life, and most clearly in her later film, Olympia (1938), Riefenstahl would allude to Grecian ideals of the body. As she would tell Andrew Sarris later in life, "I am fascinated by what is beautiful, strong, healthy, by what is living."

By 1926, Riefenstahl was a celebrated dancer with a coterie of faithful followers. But when a knee injury forced her off the stage temporarily, Dr. Arnold Fanck, a geologist and filmmaker,

approached her with a part in his film Der heilige Berg (The sacred mountain [1926]). Fanck was an exponent of the "mountain film" genre, which was becoming hugely popular in Germany at the time. These films were hymns to nature and man's indomitable courage, set in the rugged alpine wilderness and shot on location under the most difficult conditions (in sharp contrast to the artificiality of the studio-bound films that were the pride of established German studios such as UFA, Terra, and Tobis). Always curious and inquisitive, Riefenstahl posed all kinds of questions to the crew while filming proceeded, and Fanck soon adopted her as his protégée. With him she acquired the basic knowledge of his craft while she acted for his productions Der grosse Sprung (The great leap [1927]), Die weisse Hölle von Piz Palu (The white hell of Pitz Palu [1929]), codirected by G(EORG) WILHELM PABST, and others.

In 1931 Riefenstahl decided to abandon her dancing career for film and established her own film production company, Riefenstahl Films. The next year she released Das blaue Licht (The Blue Light [1932]), her first feature film as a director. It was a mystical fantasy in the style of a Mountain Film, the story of Yunta (Riefenstahl), a beautiful young girl of pure heart, who "represented idealism, love of beauty and the clean life of simple mountain people," in the words of Riefenstahl's biographer, Renata Berg-Pan. This was a far cry from the scenes of sex, greed, and sin that inundated German screens at that particular time, and it represented the conservative values that the Nazis wanted to present as their own. The Blue Light won the Silver Medal at the Venice Biennial. Adolf Hitler, on the verge of becoming chancellor of Germany and Führer of the emerging Third Reich, saw the picture and decided to appoint Riefenstahl "film expert to the National Socialist Party."

At Hitler's request, Riefenstahl shot the 1933 film Sieg des Glaubens (Victory of faith), a document of a Nazi party rally. She also published her first book, Kampf im Schnee und Eis (Struggle in snow and ice [1933]), wherein she related her adventures in the making of the Mountain Films. No copy of *Victory of Faith* is known to exist. Historians speculate that this is due to the fact that it was filmed before the massive purge within Nazi ranks that wiped out most of the upper echelons of the brown-shirt S.A. in June 1934; thus Hitler withdrew the film from distribution, not to remind the people of those who had been killed. In 1934, while arranging to film *Tiefland* (*Lowlands,* not completed and released until 20 years later), Hitler called her again to commission a film about the 1934 Nazi party rally in Nuremberg. This would become *Triumph des Willens* (*Triumph of the Will* [1935]), her most controversial film and a source of debate to this day. The opening sequence establishes the almost godlike image of Hitler that prevails throughout. From his airplane in the clouds, he descends to a crowd of adoring uniformed followers and tours streets crowded with frenzied admirers. Since the 1920s, Hitler had utilized new techniques of mass emotionalism in his propaganda to sway the German population to his agendas. The numbers of his brown-shirted political army, the Sturmabteilung, or S.A., and those of his elite protection unit, the Schutz Staffel (protection division), or S.S., were growing. Both groups, clad in military uniforms, figure prominently in the film, with all their banners, helmets, and other martial paraphernalia on conspicuous display. *Triumph of the Will* was shot by an estimated crew of 170 people, including 10 technical staff, 36 cameramen and assistants, nine aerial photographers, 17 newsreel men, 12 newsreel crews from the *Tobis* studio, 17 lighting men, two still photographers, 26 drivers, 37 watchmen and security personnel, four labor service workers, and two office assistants. They all wore S.A. uniforms so as not to be noticeable in the finished film.

Although it seems an exaggeration to say that the event was staged *only* for the sake of the cameras, it is true that Riefenstahl had ample assistance from the Nazi authorities in the making of the film. The camera crews had liberty to move around and shoot what they intuitively deemed important, since there was no means of centralized direction. However, Riefenstahl later estimated that about 50% of the finished film came from Sepp Allgeier's camera. He was the first camera operator who had worked with her and Fanck. Riefenstahl edited the miles of film from approximately 61 hours to little more than two. She has claimed that her editing technique owes much to her dancing experience. She emphasized movement and variety in every shot, and she edited to establish a unified impression of the event rather than trace its chronological order.

In 1935 Leni Riefenstahl made a documentary for the Wehrmacht, the German army, called *Tag der Freiheit, unsere Wehrmacht* (*Day of Freedom, Our Wehrmacht*), and a year later she filmed *Olympia,* in two parts entitled *Fest der Voelker* and *Fest der Schoenheit* (The people's feast and Beauty's feast). This remarkable document of the 1936 Berlin Olympic Games is stylistically very different from *Triumph of the Will.* A compromise film made under the auspices of both Hitler and the International Olympic Committee, it was, as Thomas Elsaesser points out, a project that "aimed to give the world an image of the games as supra-individual and supra-national, a celebration of youth in communal competition." For *Olympia,* Riefenstahl shot more than 400,000 meters of film (1,300,000 feet or approximately 205 hours) from every conceivable angle. She and her team used the most modern technology available, with devices such as an underwater camera to shoot the high divers, gigantic telephoto lenses, cranes and pits dug in the ground to cover the track events without obstructing the athletes. Riefenstahl then viewed, sorted, and cut the enormous mass of film material over an 18-month period, ending with a four-hour film that won the Polar Prize in Sweden, the first prize at the International Moving Picture Festival in Venice, and the Grand Prix in Paris in 1938.

After the war, Riefenstahl was imprisoned from 1945 to 1948 for her involvement with the Third

Reich. In 1952 she was acquitted of Nazism by a Berlin court. In 1954 she released her much postponed film *Tiefland,* a romantic story shot in Spain during the war and under considerable difficulties. A number of incomplete projects followed, as she was increasingly marginalized by the West German film industry and came under persecution by anti-Nazi groups in several parts of the world. Between 1961 and 1968 she made numerous trips to Africa and subsequently published her photographic work on the Nuba, an African tribe in the Sudan. In the next few years she completed a film on the Nuba (1972), published *Die Nuba von Kau* (The people of Kau [1976]), and completed *Korallengaerten* (Coral gardens), a volume of underwater photographs (she had learned scuba diving in 1975, at the age of 73).

Much has been said about the degree to which Riefenstahl compromised with the Nazi ideology. She has always claimed to be an apolitical artist pitched above loyalties to any particular ideology, and that she was only making documentaries, not propaganda. The debate on this point is far from being solved.

Other Films *Penthesilea,* script based on Kleist's play but never filmed; *Black Cargo* (1956), unrealized due to a car accident during its shooting.

References Berg-Pan, Renata, *Leni Riefenstahl* (Boston: Twayne, 1980); Infield, Glenn B., *Leni Riefenstahl, the Fallen Film Goddess* (New York: Thomas Y. Crowel, 1976); Elsaesser, Thomas, "Leni Riefenstahl: The Body Beautiful, Art Cinema and Fascist Aesthetics," in *Women in Film: A Sight and Sound Reader,* eds. Pam Cook and Phillip Dodd (Philadelphia: Temple University Press, 1993; "Tribute to Leni Riefenstahl." *Film Culture* 56–57 (Spring 1973).

—F.A.

Ritt, Martin (1914–1990) After being blacklisted from working in television during the McCarthy era, Martin Ritt built a solid directing career in Hollywood, where he lived and worked for over 30 years and established a reputation for making films committed to social issues. He was born in New York City on March 2, 1914, and educated there, first at Public School 64, then, after his parents moved to the Bronx, at Rhodes Preparatory School and DeWitt Clinton High School. His father, Morris Ritt, was a Russian immigrant. His mother, Rose Lass Ritt, became a theatrical agent for chorus girls. Morris Ritt died in 1932, leaving the mother to fend for her two children during the depression.

Determined to go to college, Martin Ritt, despite his Jewish heritage, earned a football scholarship and played for "The Fighting Christians" of Elon College in rural North Carolina, near Burlington, where he got a taste of rural life in the American South. In 1935, Ritt worked with Hallie Flanagan and the Federal Theatre Project, an operation within the Works Progress Administration, which led to his joining the Group Theatre in New York in 1937 and put him in contact with left-wing activists. Through this association he met NICHOLAS RAY and ELIA KAZAN, both of whom would eventually go on to careers in Hollywood.

The Group Theatre's goals under cofounder Harold Clurman were to address contemporary social problems and to be committed to American plays, giving Ritt experience as an actor and director, and also an agenda for his future work in film. Ritt enlisted in the Army Air Force in 1943 and was honorably discharged as a corporal in 1946. After the war Ritt resumed his directing career, then turned to television, working for CBS until 1952, when his contract was not renewed because of the Red Scare and his earlier left-wing associations.

Though Ritt was never subpoenaed by HUAC, or even "named," he was blacklisted for nearly five years, during which time he taught at the Actor's Studio in New York and took whatever theater directing assignments he could find. After he directed Arthur Miller's *A View from the Bridge* in 1955, David Susskind defied the blacklist and invited Ritt to direct a teleplay by Robert Alan Arthur, "A Boy Is Ten Feet Tall," for the *Philco Television Playhouse.* That teleplay was later developed

Martin Ritt (left) with Sally Field during the filming of
Murphy's Romance (Columbia)

into a film script that was to be Ritt's first feature,
Edge of the City, starring Sidney Poitier, JOHN CAS-
SAVETES, and Jack Warden, and released by MGM
in 1957. The film was well reviewed, and Ritt was
invited to Hollywood to work with Jerry Wald on
three pictures: *No Down Payment* (1957), and two
William Faulkner adaptations, *The Long Hot Summer* (1958), adapted from *The Hamlet,* and *The
Sound and the Fury* (1959).

Once established in Hollywood, Ritt would
direct 26 films, many of which were successful.
Hud (1963), a contemporary western starring Paul
Newman, was adapted from Larry McMurtry's
novel *Horseman Pass By,* restructured to make the
ruthless and egotistical Hud (Newman) the central
character, "a classic American heel," as Ritt
described him, "addicted to appetite." Distinguished by an Academy Award-winning cast
(Patricia Neal for best actress and Melvyn Douglas
as best supporting actor, playing Hud's father, the
ethical center of the film) and James Wong Howe's

Oscar-winning cinematography, *Hud* was a
tremendous success.

Ritt's film projects were diverse. With *The Out-
rage* (1964), the challenge was to turn AKIRA
KUROSAWA's classic *Rashomon* (1950) into a western, with Paul Newman playing the thief Toshiro
Mifune had played in the original; but since
Rashomon had no hero, only a murderous rapist at
its center, redoing it as a western made little sense.
The Spy Who Came in from the Cold (1965), adapted
from the 1963 espionage novel by John Le Carré
(David Cornwell), was based on a more adaptable
source and earned an Oscar nomination for
Richard Burton. Ritt tried his hand at social
commentary with *The Molly Maguires* (1970), a
historical drama of immigrant Irish miners in
19th-century Pennsylvania attempting to improve
their lot, starring Sean Connery and Richard Harris, and scripted by Walter Bernstein, and with *The
Front* (1976), also scripted by Bernstein, about a
blacklisted writer who asks a friend (Woody Allen)
to "front" for him. *The Front* was the first Hollywood
film to address the insanity of the McCarthy witch-
hunts. By choosing a comic approach, Gabriel Miller
explains, Ritt "was able to exorcise artistically the
ordeal of the blacklist; the act of informing, an
important motif in many of Ritt's earlier films, no
longer figures in those made after 1976."

But Ritt will probably be better remembered
for the trilogy of films he made addressing the
issues of race and racism in America: *The Great
White Hope* (1970), *Sounder* (1972), and *Conrack*
(1974). *Sounder,* the most commercially successful
of these films, was adapted from a children's novel
by William H. Armstrong, published in 1969.
Playwright Lonne Elder wrote the screenplay
about a black sharecropper's son whose coon dog
runs off after being shot by police who have
come to arrest the boy's father for stealing meat,
in order to feed his family. The film was a sentimental favorite.

The Great White Hope and *Conrack,* on the other
hand, were both based on true stories. *The Great
White Hope* told the story of the boxer Jack John-

son (James Earl Jones), as adapted for cinema by Howard Sackler from his Pulitzer Prize-winning 1968 play, a story that was more agreeable, perhaps, as agitprop theater than as cinema. *Conrack* was adapted from Pat Conroy's autobiography *The Water Is Wide* (1972), concerning his attempts to teach nearly illiterate children in a two-room schoolhouse on an island off the coast of South Carolina. The film's title reflected the way the students mispronounced Conroy's name. After a year on the job Conroy was fired because of his disregard for the school system and his unorthodox teaching methods. Although critic Pauline Kael gave the film a supportive review, African Americans criticized Ritt for making "a white exploitation film for white people" who would "feel very good about a white man who goes into the South to educate some black kids out of the kindness of his heart."

Just as *Sounder* had been about a boy, his father, and his dog, *Casey's Shadow* (1978) was about a boy, his father, and his horse, living on the edge of poverty in Cajun country. The father (Walter Matthau) is a horse trainer who wants to win the Big Race at Ruidoso Downs, not only for the money but also to get his name in the record books, a quest for fame and egotistical overreaching. The film represents one side of Martin Ritt, but another, better side is represented in 1978 by one of Ritt's best movies, *Norma Rae,* the story of a man's struggle to organize the workers in the O.P. Henley Textile Mills, filmed in Opelika, Alabama.

Norma Rae was also—and mainly—the story of one of the textile workers, in particular Norma Rae Webster (Sally Field), who grew up working for (and being exploited by) the Henley Mills. She has two children (one of them illegitimate) and has recently married Sonny Webster (Beau Bridges), who has a child from a previous marriage. Defined by her idealism, Norma Rae is arrested and jailed for her union activities, which complicates her family life. This film's strength is the way it avoids easy, sentimental attachments. At one point a romance seems to be developing between Norma

Rae and the union organizer (Ron Liebman), who is Jewish, charismatic, and from New York, but nothing finally happens, except that Norma Rae organizes a shutdown strike that puts the union in place. The characters are understated, dignified, and, over all, convincing.

Of Ritt's later films, *Cross Creek* (1983) was a reasonably good adaptation of the memoirs of the Pulitzer Prize-winning Florida novelist Marjorie Kinnan Rawlings. As Gabriel Miller notes, "excepting *The Front,* it is Ritt's most overtly personal film." *Nuts* (1987) was a reasonably good adaptation of Tom Topor's courtroom drama, but it was also a Barbra Streisand project and more her film, therefore, than Ritt's. It dramatized a sanity hearing for Claudia Faith Draper, a psychologically traumatized high-class hooker accused of murdering a john. The Streisand charisma (or vanity, perhaps) saturated nearly every frame, though the film featured a very strong supporting cast that included Richard Dreyfuss, Maureen Stapleton, Karl Malden, and Eli Wallach, in particular.

Ritt's last film, *Stanley and Iris* (1990), starred Robert De Niro, as a struggling blue-collar worker, and Jane Fonda and was adapted from Pat Barker's 1982 novel, *Union Street.* When he made the film Ritt was suffering from diabetes, and he died of heart disease a few months after its completion on December 8, 1990. Though the film was selected to open the Sundance Film Festival in Utah, reviews were tepid, and it was not a box-office success. Ritt had made better films for which he would be remembered.

Other Films *The Black Orchid* (1959); *Five Branded Women* (1960); *Hemingway's Adventures as a Young Man* (1962); *Hombre* (1967); *The Brotherhood* (1968); *Pete 'n' Tillie* (1972); *Back Roads* (1981); *Murphy's Romance* (1985).

References Adams, Michael, "How Come Everybody Down Here Has Three Names? Martin Ritt's Southern Films," in *The South and Film,* ed. Warren French (Jackson: University of Mississippi Press, 1981); MacGilligan, Pat, "Ritt Large," *Film Comment,* February 1986: 38–46; Miller, Gabriel, *The Films of Martin Ritt:*

Fanfare for the Common Man (Jackson: University of Mississippi Press, 2000).

—J.M.W.

Robbe-Grillet, Alain (1922–) Although primarily known as a celebrated French critic and novelist who revolutionized fiction with the *nouveau roman* and his experimental *ciné-romans* (film-novels), Alain Robbe-Grillet also wrote and directed several feature films. Born in Brest on August 18, 1922, Robbe-Grillet studied in Paris to become an agricultural engineer. In 1949 he earned a position in the Institut National des Statistiques given to biological research. Later work with the Institut des Fruits et Argumes Coloniaux in 1950–51 took him abroad to Morocco, Guinea, Martinique, and Guadeloupe, as well as to Eastern Europe and Latin America. His first novel, *Les Gommes* (*The Erasers*), was published in 1953. Ten years later his collection of theoretical essays, *Pour un nouveau roman* (*For a New Novel*) was published, in 1963, the year of his directing debut.

Robbe-Grillet broke into filmmaking by writing the scenario for *Last Year at Marienbad* (1961) for Alain Resnais. *L'Immortelle* (*The Immortal One* [1963]) marked his debut as director the next year, a picture he began filming in Istanbul while Resnais was still shooting *Marienbad*. Bored with the "logic" of linear time and conventional mimesis, Robbe-Grillet erased the lines between past and present and between the real and the imaginary. For both films he wrote complete shooting scripts, but soon "began to feel that this structure was not very satisfying. It was cumbersome," he told Alec Irwin, and found himself "a bit bored during the shooting. If every detail is worked out in advance, there is no creativity in the actual making of the film." So he later changed his approach. "For *Eden and After* [1971], I had practically nothing written down before we started to shoot."

"Since that time," Robbe-Grillet told Royal Brown, "I've 'written' my films less and less. By 'less and less,' I mean that the film is born in the same way as the images that take shape, immediately accompanied by montage structures. In other words, not just sequences, but structures within which the shots are arranged with absolutely no consideration of 'sequence.'" The structure is then informed by some "real setting," such as the train in *Trans-Europ-Express*. Filming *L'Homme qui ment* (*The Man Who Lies* [1968]) in Slovakia, for example, he was especially impressed by the "huge forest" that separates Slovakia from Ukraine and Poland: "The film was born *in* that forest and *of* that forest," and the main character as well. The conception of a novel "is not in any way comparable to the conception of a film, because the conception of a novel takes place within the structuring of sentences, independently of any idea of where the action takes place." In cinema, "there is almost always a generating setting (*un décor générateur*), a natural setting."

Because he knew how to work efficiently with limited budgets, Robbe-Grillet had no trouble finding producers. "Films like *La Belle captive* (*The Fair Captive* [1983]) and *Trans-Europ-Express* (1966) were shot in 18 days," he explained, "whereas Resnais might take 18 weeks!" *Trans-Europ-Express* was a departure from the Resnais style, a parody of the detective thriller that owed more to the cinema of Jean-Luc Godard. Robbe-Grillet plays a director named Jean in this film, who plans to make a film called "Trans-Europ-Express"; Jean's secretary is played by Robbe-Grillet's wife, Catherine. In 1974 he published *Glissments progressifs du plaisir* (*Accelerative Slippages of Pleasure*), his first *ciné-roman* since *L'Immortelle*, and also adapted the novel to cinema. This sexually explicit film led to a pornography trial in Italy. It was followed in 1975 by the equally explicit *Le Jeu avec le feu* (*Playing with Fire*), set in a safe house where a wealthy banker's daughter hides to protect her from kidnappers, which Manohla Dargis described as "a playpen for sexual maniacs," objecting to "the blatant stench of misogyny that permeates Robbe-Grillet's films."

Famous for making "intellectual puzzlers," Robbe-Grillet considered *L'Homme qui ment* his best film. "I detest films in which there is something to understand," he told the French journal *L'Express*: "In *The Man Who Lies* there is nothing to understand, but to see, just as in *Le Voyeur* there is nothing to understand, but to read. That is to say that the film, like the novel, deliberately rejects psychology." The film, shot in Czechoslovakia, concerns a stranger who claims to be a member of the wartime underground, though he may have been a fascist. He constantly reinvents his identity in order to gain entrance into a household of three beautiful women whose son, brother, and lover had never returned from the war. Jean-Louis Trintignant won the best actor award at the Berlin Film Festival for his performance.

In 1975 Robbe-Grillet first taught cinema at New York University and continued to do so every three years. When, in 1989, Robbe-Grillet returned to NYU to teach literature and film, at that time the Anthology Film Archives in New York mounted a retrospective that included American premieres for five of his films not yet seen in the United States. Manohla Dargis speculated that the films had been kept "under wraps" not so much because of their "overt sadomasochism" but because of "their fractured, labyrinthine structures" that stretch and distort space and time. Feminists objected to his "absurd" and "outlandish" sexual iconography and "his bias for heterosexual couplings" and "conventional fondness for softcore lesbian titillation."

In his book on Robbe-Grillet, William Van Wert noted that Robbe-Grillet "has had few champions among the critics," and that his "stature as a novelist has often been more a hindrance than a help." Critics who applauded his "stylistic innovations in the novel while ignoring or sidestepping the erotic motifs and 'pop' violence have been the same critics to cringe or shrug shoulders uncomprehendingly before the spectacle of Robbe-Grillet's cinematic innovations, before his filmic use of those same erotic motifs and that same 'pop' violence."

For this reason, perhaps, Robbe-Grillet has not been included in the major encyclopedias of filmmakers, such as Ginette Vincendeau's *Companion to French Cinema* (BFI, 1996), perhaps the most notable omission. Yet Robbe-Grillet continues to make films: *Un bruit qui rend fou* (*A Maddening Noise,* codirected with Dimitri DeClercq) was shot on the Greek island of Hydra in 1994, for example, to be followed by *La forteresse vide* (*The Empty Fortress*).

Other Films *N a pris les dés* (*N Took the Dice* [1971]); *Piège à fourrure* (*Fur Trap* [1977]); *Taxandria* (scenario only, 1990).

References Brown, Royal S., "An Interview with Alain Robbe-Grillet," *Literature/Film Quarterly* 17, no. 2 (1989): 74–83; Dargis, Manohla, "Show World," *Village Voice,* April 18, 1989, p. 66; Fragola, Anthony N. and Roch C. Smith, *The Erotic Dream Machine: Interviews with Alain Robbe-Grillet on his Films* (Carbondale: Southern Illinois University Press, 1992); Irwin, Alec, "The French Connection," *Village Voice,* April 18, 1989, p. 66; Smith, Roch C., "Open Narrative in Robbe-Grillet," *Literature/Film Quarterly* 23, no. 1 (1995): 32–38; Van Wert, William F., *The Film Career of Alain Robbe-Grillet* (Boston: G. K. Hall, 1977).

—J.M.W.

Robbins, Tim (1958–)

If any filmmaker of the 1990s could be said to exemplify liberal Hollywood values in his work, it is Tim Robbins. He was born October 16, 1958, in West Covina, California, but grew up in Greenwich Village, New York. From an early age, Robbins lived in a political environment—his parents encouraged their children to be politically aware, and his father, Gil Robbins, was a member of the folk group the Highwaymen. Robbins graduated from UCLA with a degree in drama and, as a young actor, in 1981 played a part in founding the Actors' Gang, a political theater group in Los Angeles, ultimately becoming its artistic director. As the director of just three films, he has explored the political passions close to his heart.

Robbins is better known for his acting, however, which is where he started in film. His role as the youthful, wild pitcher, Ebby Calvin "Nuke" LaLoosh, in 1988's baseball comedy *Bull Durham* was a life-changing performance, bringing him mainstream success and his partner in life, Susan Sarandon, with whom he costarred and with whom he has since had two children.

After a series of strong supporting performances, 1992 became a breakthrough year for Robbins. He starred as the murderous antihero of Robert Altman's satire of Hollywood, *The Player,* and wrote, directed, and starred in his own satire of American politics, *Bob Roberts.* Shot as a pseudo-documentary following the campaign of a conservative candidate for the Senate, folksinger Bob Roberts (Robbins), the film is a scathing look at the hypocrisies of the American right wing. In one of the film's best jokes, Roberts uses the radical folk music of the 1960s but gives it a reactionary spin in songs that Robbins himself wrote and sang for his character. While the film becomes heavy-handed in some of its more polemical speeches, it is nonetheless a smart, imaginative first feature.

In 1995, Robbins released *Dead Man Walking,* for which he received Oscar nominations for both writing and directing. Based on the memoir of Sister Helen Prejean (Sarandon in an Oscar-winning performance), a Catholic nun who counsels death-row inmates and fights tirelessly against capital punishment, *Dead Man Walking* is an emotional triumph and a complex examination of a tough issue. While the film clearly comes down against the death penalty, it takes seriously the opposing viewpoint and examines the real difficulties for a victim's family in forgiving a murderer. *Dead Man Walking* is a testament not only to Robbins's political beliefs but also to the real challenge of living out Christian value of faith and forgiveness. In addition to Sarandon's strong work, the film is anchored by a riveting performance by Sean Penn as the racist thug she counsels in his final days.

Among Robbins's most notable film performances has been the work he has done for Robert Altman. After *The Player* signaled a kind of comeback for Altman, he made two more of his trademark multicharacter collages—the often searing if uneven *Short Cuts* (1993) and the muddled *Ready to Wear* (1994)—both with Robbins in the star-studded ensembles. Altman must have been a strong influence on Robbins, since his next effort as writer-director, *Cradle Will Rock* (1999), follows the Altman tradition of examining a community of characters through several loosely connected stories. Based on true events, *Cradle Will Rock's* main focus is the arts during the Great Depression and specifically the government's attempt to shut down the radical musical from which the film takes its name. The film deals with censorship and the role of the artist in a free society and features a mixture of real-life giants like ORSON GEORGE WELLES, Nelson Rockefeller, and Diego Rivera alongside ordinary people trying to eke out a living in the theater. It is an ambitious film that sometimes attempts too much and occasionally veers into the cartoonish. While it lacks the economy and grace of *Dead Man Walking,* it nonetheless further establishes Robbins as a filmmaker willing to take chances on political subjects that others would automatically dismiss as box-office poison.

References   Bauer, Erik, and Daniel Duvall, "With a Pen of Gold: An Interview with Tim Robbins," *Creative Screenwriting* 7, no. 1 (January–February 2000): 82–85; Grundmann, Roy, and Cynthia Lucia, "Between Ethics and Politics: An Interview with Tim Robbins," *Cineaste* 22, no. 2 (1996): 4–9; Orr, David, "Script Review: *Cradle Will Rock,*" *Creative Screenwriting* 7, no. 1 (January–February 2000): 86–88.

—P.N.C.

Roeg, Nicolas (1928–) Nicolas Roeg, one of the most imaginatively visual of film directors, has specialized in his own distinctive cinema of mystification and has been characterized as a "visual trickster." He entered the industry as a cameraman, working for two decades as a cinematographer, and his second film, *Walkabout* (1971), tells its story almost entirely through its images, drawing upon the breathtaking landscape of the Australian Outback. The film was based on a second-rate, adolescent novel by James Vance Marshall that could, arguably, be considered racist in its implications. Two Anglo children are stranded in the Outback and manage to survive only because they are befriended by an aboriginal boy performing his "walkabout," a ritual survival test meant to prove his manhood. Unlike the novel, the film becomes a sensitive meditation upon the beauty of nature and the psychic advantages of living naturally, as opposed to the psychological damage that can result from living in an artificial urban-industrial setting. The children, a young boy (played by Roeg's own son) and his older sister, are unable to communicate with the boy who saves them and then misinterprets their behavior.

Nicolas Jack Roeg was born in London on August 15, 1928, and educated at Mercers School before going to work at Marylebone Studio doing odd jobs and dubbing French films. In 1950 he found work on a camera crew, and by 1958 he had become a camera operator. By 1962 he had become a lighting cameraman. Through the 1960s he worked with top directors such as FRED ZINNEMANN, JOHN SCHLESINGER, Richard Lester, and FRANÇOIS TRUFFAUT, on Truffaut's only English film, *Fahrenheit 451* (1966).

Roeg moved into directing in 1970 with the Mick Jagger feature, *Performance,* codirected with Donald Cammell, which assumed "cult" status. The ambiguous and challenging story concerns a gangster on the run (James Fox) who is taken in by a burned-out rock star (Mick Jagger) and transformed in mysterious ways. To say that this film is strange is rather like saying it is "chilly" in the Arctic Circle.

Many of Roeg's films are challenging and obscure, but a few are more accessible. In comparison to *Performance,* for example, *Walkabout* seems almost straightforward. James Vance Marshall's novel was written for children; but Roeg's treatment radically changed the means by which the children were stranded in the Wilderness and provided a coda that made his thesis, about liv-

ing in harmony with Nature, perfectly clear, transforming the novel into a story worthy of adult consideration.

Roeg's next film was entirely different, a psychological horror story set in Venice called *Don't Look Now* (1973), based on a Daphne du Maurier story and starring Donald Sutherland and Julie Christie as parents who have lost a daughter in a drowning accident in England. John, the husband, is working to restore a church in Venice, where he seems to be haunted by the ghost of his dead daughter. His wife, Laura, comes under the influence of a blind clairvoyant, whom she thinks can communicate with her daughter's spirit. John is skeptical of her powers, especially when the clairvoyant warns him that his life is in danger if he stays in Venice. ESP and spiritualism dominate the action as the plot moves toward its disturbing conclusion.

The Man Who Fell to Earth (1976), adapted from the novel by Walter Tevis, marked another seismic shift in topic and treatment. Rocker David Bowie plays Thomas Jerome Newton, a space alien who "falls to earth," landing in New Mexico, on a mission to mobilize energy conservation in order to save his drought-stricken planet, but he is sidetracked by a tart (Candy Clark) and, though he forms a corporation called World Enterprises, his plans are ultimately thwarted by the government, and he is imprisoned, tested, and released. Newton is so corrupted by the distractions of humankind that he ultimately forgets his purpose and becomes a pathetic, zoned-out media freak.

Insignificance (1985), adapted from a play by Terry Johnson, was described by *Variety* as Roeg's "most accessible film since *Walkabout.*" Set in New York City in August 1954, the plot brings together four celebrities whose paths cross. A movie star who recalls Marilyn Monroe (Theresa Russell), in New York for a shoot, seeks out a professor who resembles Albert Einstein (Michael Emil), determined to prove to him that she understands the theory of relativity. Meanwhile, a Joe McCarthy-type sleazy senator (Tony Curtis) wants to drag the scientist before his "Red Scare" senatorial hearings, while a jealous baseball player, married to the movie star, tracks her to the professor's bedroom. The professor explains to the actress that "Knowledge is nothing without understanding," and the film ends with a four-minute montage of nuclear devastation. The professor is overcome with guilt about the H-bomb and with the fear of global annihilation.

The Witches (1989), adapted from the prize-winning novel by Roald Dahl and starring Anjelica Huston as the Grand High Witch, is even more accessible, but this children's story is not exactly typical of Roeg's work. Also in 1989 Roeg directed the NBC television production of Tennessee Williams's *Sweet Bird of Youth,* starring Elizabeth Taylor. In general, however, Roeg has specialized in the dark, the supernatural, and the kinky, as evidenced, for example, by *Bad Timing: A Sensual Obsession* (1979), an X-rated movie about an affair between a woman named Milena (Theresa Russell), who abandons her husband (Denholm Elliott), and a research psychiatrist (Art Garfunkel); it was written off as "a sick film made by sick people, about sick people, for sick people."

This controversial feature was followed by another puzzler, *Eureka* (1982), adapted from the book *King's X* by Marshall Houts. The film tells the story of Jack McCann (Gene Hackman), who strikes gold in the Yukon, but the film mainly concerns his later years and his murder by a gangster (Joe Pesce), who intends to build a casino on land Jack owns. After *The Witches* and *Insignificance,* Roeg's career drifted away from mainstream cinema, achieving a kind of commercial "insignificance." *Track 29* (1988), scripted by Dennis Potter, has been called by Joseph Lanza "Roeg's craziest work to date," for example. *New York Times* reviewer Stephen Holden wrote that Roeg's *Two Deaths* (1996) "makes one of the riskiest comparisons that a serious movie could formulate between private behavior and public deportment" by "equating imperious sexual cruelty with a totalitarian mind-set." In a country that seems to resemble Romania, the action of this film "cuts

back and forth between a violent revolution in the streets and an obscenely lavish dinner party given by a successful surgeon" (Michael Gambon).

Roeg has never shied away from risky projects. In reviewing *Bad Timing* ("an oppressively bad movie") for *Newsweek,* David Ansen wrote: "In such films as *Performance, Walkabout,* and *Don't Look Now,* Nicolas Roeg established himself as one of the fancier dancers on the '70s movie scene, with a startling eye for incongruous images and a keen sense of the alienation that dogs his characters as they tumble into metaphysical rabbit holes." But with *Bad Timing* and other of his later films, "it is Roeg himself who appears to be spinning down the rabbit hole." If this director has been marginalized by the commercial cinema, the reasons are fairly obvious.

Other Films *Castaway* (1986); *Aria* (aka *King Zog Shot Back* [1987]); *Cold Heaven* (1992); *Heart of Darkness* (1993); *Full Body Massage* (1995); *Samson and Delilah* (1996).

References Ansen, David, "Nasty Habits," *Newsweek,* October 6, 1980, p. 72; Barker, S., "*Bad Timing—A Sensual Obsession,*" *Film Quarterly* 35, no. 1 (Fall 1981): 46–50; Cunningham, S., "Good Timing: Bad Timing," *Australian Journal of Screen Theory* 15–16 (1983): 102–112; Gomez, Joseph A., "*Performance* and Jorge Luis Borges," *Literature/Film Quarterly* 5, no. 2 (Spring 1977): 147–153; Gow, Gordon, "Identity," *Films & Filming* 18, no. 4 (January 1972): 18–24; Lanza, Joseph, *Fragile Geometry: The Films, Philosophy, and Misadventures of Nicolas Roeg* (New York: PAJ Publications, 1989); Milne, T., "*Eureka,*" *Sight and Sound* 51, no. 4 (Autumn 1982): 280–85; Roddick, N., "Countries of the Mind," *Cinema Papers* 53 (September 1985): 63–64.

—J.M.W.

Rohmer, Eric (1920–) Eric Rohmer is the nom de plume of Jean-Marie Maurice Schérer, born on April 4, 1920, in Tulle, France. An aspiring novelist and critic, Rohmer studied classical literature in both French and Greek, making an academic career as professor of arts and letters before turning to filmmaking. After teaching literature at the lycée in

Nancy for eight years (1942–50), Rohmer founded, with Godard and Rivette, *Le Gazette du cinéma* in 1950 and later served as editor-in-chief of *Cahiers du cinéma* from 1957 to 1963. During the 1950s Rohmer emerged with FRANÇOIS TRUFFAUT, JEAN-LUC GODARD, and CLAUDE CHABROL as one of the originating talents of the French New Wave. His first feature film, *Le Signe du lion* was completed in 1959 but was not a commercial success. The most "literary" talent of this generation of filmmakers, he wrote his own scripts, making films he later separated into two categories: the "Six Moral Tales"—including *La Boulangerie de Monceau* (*The Girl at the Monceau Bakery* [1963]), *Le Carriére de Suzanne* (1963), *La Collectionneuse* (1967), *Ma nuit chez Maud* (1969), *Le Genou de Claire* (1970), *L'Amour l'après-midi* (*Chloe in the Afternoon* [1972])—and the "Comedies et Proverbes"—*La Femme de l'aviateur* (1980); *Le Beau mariage* (1982); *Loup y es-tu?* (Wolf, are you there? [1983]); *Pauline à la plage* (*Pauline at the Beach* [1983]); *Les Nuits de la pleine lune* (*Full Moon in Paris* [1984]); *Le Rayon vert* (aka *Summer* [1986]), adapted from the Jules Verne novel, *The Green Ray;* and *L'Ami de mon amie* (*Boyfriends and Girlfriends* [1987]).

In the 1990s Rohmer undertook yet another series, "Tales of the Four Seasons," beginning with *Conte de printemps* (*A Tale of Springtime* [1989]), followed by *Conte d'hiver* (*A Tale of Winter* [1994]), *Conte d'été* (*A Summer's Tale* [1996]), and *Conte d'automne* (*Autumn Tale* [1999]). Rohmer has also made historical films, such as *Die Marquise Von O . . .,* in German in 1975, and *Perceval le Gallois* (1978), perhaps the most eccentric and unique adaptation of a literary text in the history of cinema, taken from the 12th century poem by Chrétien de Troyes. Still active at the age of 80, Rohmer shot *The Lady and the Duke* for Pathé Images in 2000, adapted from the memoirs of Grace Elliot (Lucy Russell), a British aristocrat who became the mistress of the duke of Orléans (Jean-Claude Dreyfus), the brother of Louis XVI in Revolutionary France.

Rohmer first conceived his *Six Moral Tales* in the form of fiction. The collected "tales" were published in the form of a "novel" in Paris in 1974 by Éditions de l'Herne and later translated into English and published by Viking Press in 1980. The "Moral Tales" were not "moral" in a narrow, proscriptive sense. "In my moral tales," Rohmer explained, "there is no moral message. These people—my characters—determine their own way." The contemporary filmmaker, Rohmer states in his preface to the book, "dreams of being the sole creator of his work, which implies that he assumes, among other things, the job that traditionally devolved upon the screenwriter." Rohmer contends that "it is easier to compose your images starting with a story than it is to make up a story on the basis of a series of images shot more or less at random." Always a late bloomer, at the age of 67 Rohmer wrote and produced his first play, *Trio in B Minor,* at the Renaud-Barrault Theatre.

This "academician of the New Wave" also wrote books on ALFRED HITCHCOCK (with Claude Chabrol) and on F. W. MURNAU, his favorite director. "I started late, and there was a period—from 1950 to 1970—when I didn't know if I would succeed in making films professionally," he confided in an interview with Joan Dupont in 1982. "I'm lucky to have practically complete independence, which is rare," he added. "I don't care for commercial success. If I did, I wouldn't make the films I make." Even so, his films earned awards, such as *Summer,* which got the Golden Lion award at the 43rd Venice Film Festival in 1986. *The Marquise of O . . .,* skillfully adapted from the novella by Heinrich von Kleist, won the Special Jury Prize at Cannes. Though known mainly for his "Moral Tales" and other original works, Rohmer's adaptations of Kleist and *Perceval* are absolutely distinctive and unique.

Other Films *Nadia á Paris* (1964); *Une étudiante d'aujourd'hui* (1966); *Quatre aventures de Reinette et Mirabelle* (1987); *Rendezvous in Paris* (1996).

References Dupont, Joan, "France's Eric Rohmer Adds to His Human Comedies," *New York Times,* September 26, 1982, II, pp. 1, 13; Kehr, David, "Revolutionary Production," *New York Times,* July 14, 2000, p.

B22; Monaco, James, *The New Wave: Truffaut, Godard, Chabrol, Rohmer, Rivette* (New York: Oxford University Press, 1976); Rohmer, Eric, *Six Moral Tales,* trans. Sabine d'Estrée (New York: Viking Press, 1980).

—J.M.W.

Rossellini, Roberto (1906–1977)

One of the principal architects of Italian neorealism, Roberto Rossellini enjoyed a long career that also embraced the New Wave movement in Europe and an extensive involvement in television production. He was born in Rome on May 8, 1906, the eldest of four sons (his younger brother, Renzo, would compose the music for most of his films). Because of his architect father's connections, young Roberto enjoyed contacts with many influential artists and entertainers. He saw his first films at his father's Barberini movie theater, and in 1934, after his father's death, he worked in the film industry writing screenplays and editing films.

His preoccupation with documentary realism manifested itself immediately in his first short films. When the Fascist government took over the industry as a state monopoly, the Cinecitta sound studio and the Centro Sperimentale di Cinematografia were established in the suburbs of Rome. Anxious to work, yet reluctant to declare himself a supporter of the Fascist cause, Rossellini gained his first screen credit for *Luciano Serra, pilota* (1938), about an Italian pilot fighting in the war against Ethiopia. Working with him was Tito Silvio Mursino, the nom de plume of Vittorio Mussolini. *Men of the Deep* (1940), a fascist-sponsored tribute to the Italian submarine service, became Rossellini's feature-film directorial debut.

Following the reversals in the war and the fall of fascism, Rossellini's *Rome, Open City* (1944) marked a radical departure from his early work and became the first installment of his so-called war trilogy. It marked the official start of the movement later called neorealism. Working with FEDERICO FELLINI, a former music-hall comedian and cartoonist, Rossellini shot the picture under severe hardships. Cinecitta had been obliterated by Allied bombing, and the German troops had barely left Rome. A dwindling budget and shortage of equipment and film stock forced him to use amateur actors, scavenge stray pieces of film, and shoot without sound. Because rushes were not available during the shooting, Rossellini was, in effect, shooting blind. The story was based on actual circumstances, real people—including Don Pietro Morosini, a priest who was killed by the Germans for his partisan activities, and the resistance fighter, Sergio Amidei—and shot on authentic locations. Rome itself at the time of the film's story was hardly the "open city" of the title (surely a bitterly ironic term); rather, the city was controlled by German martial law.

As a seminal document in neorealism, *Open City* demonstrated a threefold ambition: to express a sociopolitical concern for a defeated Italy, to document the living conditions of its beleaguered people, and to express a humanism that transcended mere political and national divisions. The film begins with a German patrol marching in Rome and continues with the Italian Resistance that united seemingly disparate elements of society—the sympathetic but doomed antifascist priest Don Pietro (Aldo Fabrizi) and partisan fighter Manfredi (Marcello Pagliero), communist and rightist partisans, even children and little old ladies. Significantly, few scenes actually show anti-Nazi activities, such as the children blowing up a fuel truck. Rather, every action taken by the Italian people is aimed at survival and not the destruction of the enemy. Difficult to watch, even by today's jaundiced viewer, is the torture scene of Manfredi. And Anna Magnani's performance of the music-hall actress Pina won her world acclaim and remains one of the great performances in the history of Italian cinema. The spontaneity and newsreel-like quality of the film overcome its occasional lapses into melodrama. As biographer Jose Luis Guarner writes, "The great originality of *Roma, citta aperta,* does not rest merely on the use of natural locations (essentials in any case, because the studios were destroyed during the war) but on the way they are integrated into the film, and the way the non-professional actors identify with their characters; the way characters and setting become the film itself. . . . Everything seems miraculously to have been seen for the very first time, just as it did at the birth of the cinema."

On the heels of the release of *Rome, Open City,* which was acclaimed in America with its reception of the New York Film Critics award for best foreign film of 1946, Rossellini, Fellini, and crew set out to make a film about postwar Italy, *Paisan* (1946). After six months of traveling and planning a script—which, according to neorealist dictates, was kept loosely structured to allow for change and improvisation—a story was developed in six episodes involving wartime Italy from the Allied invasion in 1943 to the liberation in 1945. In the first story, the Allies have just landed in Sicily and a soldier ("Joe from Jersey") and an Italian woman, Carmela, enjoy a brief relationship before he is killed by a German sniper. The second transpires in the rubble of bombed-out Naples as a child purchases a drunk black American soldier on the black market. The third involves a relationship between a G.I. and a prostitute. The fourth takes place in a Florence divided by strife between the Nazis and the partisans, where an American nurse and an Italian struggle to reunite with her lover and his family. The fifth involves a night-long meeting of three monks and three American chaplains. The last episode, the most celebrated of the six, depicts the massacre of partisans and American soldiers at the hands of the Germans. As the bodies are pushed into the Po River, a voice-over deadpans this message: "This happened in the winter of 1944. At the beginning of spring, the war was over."

Uniting the six episodes is the theme of contact between Italians and Americans and their difficulty in communicating with each other. The film's impact upon young Italian filmmakers was enormous. "Rossellini taught me humility in living," recalled Fellini, who shot some of the movie's

sequences. "By looking at things with the love and communion that are established from one moment to another between a person and myself, between an object and myself, I understood that the cinema could fill my life, helping me to find a meaning in existence."

The last film in the "war trilogy" was *Germany, Year Zero.* Whereas Germans were depicted as representatives of an abstract evil in *Open City,* in *Germany, Year Zero* (1947) they are sympathetically portrayed as individuals caught up in the coils of a corrupt political system. True to his neorealist principles, it was shot on location in a devastated Berlin (although the interiors were shot in a studio in Rome). The scene is viewed through the eyes of 12-year-old Edmund (Edmund Moeschke), whose family is literally starving. After a misguided attempt to save his family by poisoning his sickly father (one less mouth to feed), Edmund wanders about Berlin and finally throws himself out of a window to his death. Edmund has been corrupted by the degradation all around him, in general, and by the doctrines espoused by a teacher, a former Nazi. "When an ideology strays from the eternal laws of morality and of Christian charity," read an opening title, "which form the basis of men's lives, it must end as criminal madness. It contaminates even the natural prudence of a child."

Immediately after the release of *Germany, Year Zero* Rossellini made one of his most controversial films, at least in its time, *The Miracle* (1950). A fable of modest proportions—it clocks in at a mere 45 minutes—it derived from a story by Fellini about a goatherd, Nanni (Anna Magnani), who becomes pregnant after being seduced by a passing wanderer who she assumes is Saint Joseph. Convinced that her pregnancy is a result of "God's grace," she incurs the enmity of the church and of the villagers. Driven out to the mountains, she finds a desolate church and gives birth alone. Clearly deranged, she is nonetheless pure in spirit, and the birth of the child is a redemptive feature of her life. The subsequent controversy in America, where the film was attacked as sacrilegious by the Catholic Legion of Decency and withdrawn from theaters, created a furor that was resolved only when the United States Supreme Court declared its banning unconstitutional (clearing the way for a decision that, in effect, granted motion pictures protection as free speech under the First Amendment).

Rossellini's career underwent changes after 1948, when he began his affair with actress Ingrid Bergman while both were married to other spouses. As a result of a contractual agreement with the American studio, RKO, Rossellini directed Bergman in *Stromboli* (1949), in which she portrayed an unhappily married woman fleeing her abusive husband across the volcanic wastes of the island of Stromboli. Subsequent films embraced a wide variety of subjects, including several more vehicles for Bergman; the devout fairy tale that was *Francis, Jester of God* (1950); the wartime melodrama *General Della Rovere* (1959); and a number of television projects. His work for Italian and French television after 1960 embraced the 12-hour *Man's Struggle for Survival,* the six-hour *Acts of the Apostles,* and the five-hour *The Age of Iron.* Among the biographical historical films were *The Rise of Louis XIV* (1966), *Blaise Pascal* (1972), and *The Age of Cosimo de'Medici* (1972), in which he abandoned the conventions of the genre in favor of a new vision of history: "History, through teaching visually, can evolve on its own ground rather than evaporate into dates and names. Abandoning the usual litany of battles, it can surrender to its social, economic and political determinants. It can build, not on fantasy, but on historical knowledge, situations, costumes, atmospheres, and men who had historical significance and helped the social developments by which we live today."

To the very end, Rossellini sought to break down the artificial barriers between cinema and television. Indeed, the advent of television, he felt, assured the long life of cinema. "Modern society and modern art have been destructive of man," he said, "but television is an aid to his rediscovery."

His last film was *The Messiah* (1975), which raised anew the controversy regarding Rossellini's religious beliefs. "I'm not religious at all," he said. "I'm the product of a society that is religious among other things, and I deal with religion as a reality. We are capable of thinking in metaphysical terms—that's a reality and it has to be dealt with." For recent developments in international cinema, however—especially in what he thought was an undue preoccupation with sex and violence—he had little sympathy.

After presiding over the Cannes Film Festival in 1977, he died of a heart attack on June 3, 1977. The sheer variety and quantity of Rossellini's achievement is amazing. Yet, all his work is unified by the consciousness of the man who was at once a religious atheist and bourgeois revolutionary. "In his art or craft, as well, he was a victim of wrong expectations," writes historian Peter Brunette, "from the commercial filmmaking establishment, who wanted him to be commercial, from the political and avant-garde, who wanted him to be those things. What is perhaps most tragic and most sublime about his wonderful, failed career, is, once again, that he was neither, or both, the supreme example of the modernist artist working in a commercial medium that clung desperately to the narrative and dramatic forms it had inherited from the nineteenth century." Perhaps he is appreciated today more by critics and other filmmakers than by the general public. Indeed, his affair with Ingrid Bergman was more celebrated at the time than any of his films. In part, this lack of appreciation is due to the unavailability in the United States of many key titles—a neglect being rectified at the present time.

Other Films *Europa '51* (1952); *Journey to Italy* (1953); *Joan at the Stake* (1954); *Socrates* (1970); *Descartes* (1973).

References Brunette, Peter, *Roberto Rossellini* (New York: Oxford University Press, 1987); Guarner, Luis, *Roberto Rossellini* (New York: Praeger, 1970).

—J.C.T.

Russell, Ken (1927–) British director Ken Russell was born in Southampton, England, in 1927; he tried his hand at a career in photography before he turned to directing. He became interested in portraying historical material for contemporary audiences while making documentaries about great artists for BBC-TV. For more than a decade Russell made a succession of TV biographies of great artists like dancer Isadora Duncan (1966) and composer Frederick Delius (1968). Russell gravitated toward the past in choosing subjects for filming because, as he told this writer, he wanted to bring a fresh approach to historical subjects: "Historical films are often made as if the people living in the past thought of themselves as part of history already, living in museums. But people in every century have thought of themselves as contemporary, just as we think of ourselves as contemporary." His first TV documentaries, like that on Edward Elgar (1962), correspond to what he calls "the accepted textbook idea of what a documentary should be; you were supposed to extol the great artists and their work. Later I turned to showing how great artists transcended their personal problems and weaknesses in creating great art."

This more realistic approach, exemplified in his telefilm about Richard Strauss (1970) and his feature film about Tchaikovsky, *The Music Lovers* (1970), upset some members of the audience for both his TV and theatrical films. As Russell advanced from the small screen to the large while continuing to turn out what have come to be called his biopics, he almost singlehandedly revolutionized the whole concept of the conventional film biography—to the point where the genre will never be quite the same again. One need only recall the heavily romanticized Hollywood screen biographies of subjects like Frederic Chopin to grasp how Russell's biopics have come to grips with the problems of an artist's life in relation to his work in a way that makes for much more challenging motion pictures.

In addition to experimenting with the nature of biographical films, Russell has also endeavored by trial and error to discover in all of his films, biopics or not, to what extent a motion picture can be cut loose from the moorings of conventional storytelling; and his mind-bending science fiction thriller *Altered States* (1980) may be the best example of this experimentation. These experiments in narrative technique account for the intricate and arresting blend of past and present, fact and fantasy, that characterizes his best work, as in *Tommy* (1975) and *Valentino* (1977). Among his outstanding films must surely be numbered his screen adaptations of D. H. Lawrence's *Women in Love* (1969) and *The Rainbow* (1989), plus his TV version of Lawrence's *Lady Chatterley's Lover* as *Lady Chatterley* (1993). Lawrence's two companion novels, *Women in Love* and *The Rainbow,* focus on the personal lives of two sisters as they struggle to carve out their destinies in the modern world. Russell's TV miniseries, *Lady Chatterley,* is based on Lawrence's most controversial novel, about an upper-class Englishwoman who escapes a loveless marriage by having an affair with the gamekeeper on the Chatterley estate. Russell succeeded in being faithful to the spirit of all three Lawrence novels, and indeed, his Lawrence trilogy marks a milestone in the history of literary adaptations in the cinema.

Other films of his later career that deserve mention include *Crimes of Passion* (1984), which explores with unvarnished realism the grim life of a prostitute; also *Gothic* (1986), a film about a weird séance attended by the Romantic poets Byron and Shelley, along with Mary Godwin, Shelley's wife-to-be. The upshot of this harrowing evening is that it inspires Mary to write the classic monster tale, *Frankenstein;* Russell turned the film into a bloodcurdling horror show. Although Russell has often been called a maverick who makes films that are perhaps more subjective and personal than many directors, it is worth noting that he is the only British director

Schepisi, Fred (1939–) With PETER WEIR, BRUCE BERESFORD, and GILLIAN ARMSTRONG, Fred Schepisi was one of the architects of the so-called Australian New Wave that began in the mid-1970s. He was born on December 12, 1939, in Melbourne, the son of a greengrocer. When he was eight he entered a Catholic boarding school, later progressing to a seminary. Deciding that the celibate life of the priesthood was not for him, he dropped out to enter a career in advertising. With the advent of television, he moved into the media side of the business and formed his own production company, the Film House. His commercials and documentaries quickly established his reputation for handling a diversity of subjects and for innovative camera techniques, both trends that he would later incorporate into his theatrical features.

His first feature, *The Devil's Playground,* a coming-of-age story set in a strictly disciplined and sexually repressed Catholic boy's school, took him five years to finance, direct, and distribute (which he did himself). It won six Australian Oscars and was a hit at the 1976 Cannes Film Festival. Its success in international markets allowed him to finance more easily his next film, *The Chant of Jimmy Blacksmith* (1978), based on Thomas Keneally's novel. It became the first Australian film to be invited into the main competition at Cannes. Its story was based on fact and concerned the plight of Jimmie Governor, a New South Wales aboriginal, who in 1900 exacted a bloody revenge on the white employers who had exploited him and insulted his (white) wife. He flees to the mountains of New South Wales where he is captured and hanged. The theme of the tensions between the Australian aborigines and the encroaching white civilization—always a central issue in recent Australian films—receives an important and sympathetic examination here. As historian Brian McFarlane has noted, "[Schepisi] has made painfully clear that Jimmie—jaw half-shot away, caught asleep in a convent bed, ignominiously bundled into the back of a police van—remains to the end the victim of 'historical forces' that have, for good and bad, helped shape Australia."

Schepisi's first American film was *Barbarosa* (1981), an offbeat western starring Willie Nelson as a semi-mythic bandit. In England, *Plenty* (1985) was based on David Hare's play about a woman (Meryl Streep) whose heroic activities in the French Resistance during World War II contrast with her sense of disillusionment, waste, and futility in the sterile conformity of postwar society. *Roxanne* (1987), loosely based on Rostand's *Cyrano*

Fred Schepisi (Twentieth Century-Fox)

de Bergerac, was Schepisi's first opportunity to make a comedy. It's an enchanting update on the story of a man with the world's largest nose falling help-lessly in love with the world's loveliest woman. In this case our Cyrano is C. D. Bales (Steve Martin), a fireman who battles his foes not with a sword but with a tennis racket; and Roxanne (Daryl Hannah) is an amateur astronomer who gazes at the stars while perched on her high rooftop. She's looking for a comet, but, in a new romantic ending that displaces Rostand's downbeat original, she finds Cyrano instead.

Back in Australia, Schepisi directed *Cry in the Dark* (1988), based on a true-life Australian court case in which Lindy Chamberlain (Meryl Streep) is accused of the murder of her baby. Superficially at least, it's a variant on Peter Weir's classic *Picnic at Hanging Rock* (1975), in that a disappearance

occurs in or around a freakish geological forma-tion, in this case the fabled Ayres Rock (landscape plays an important part in both films). Part murder mystery and courtroom thriller, the film at all times is a devastating indictment of the media exploitation that attended the case. A wild depar-ture from his previous work, *Mr. Baseball* (1992) is about a bigoted and egotistical has-been baseball player (Tom Selleck) who finds himself in Japan playing an entirely more formalized—and frustrat-ing—brand of baseball.

As can be ascertained by now, Schepisi's films are difficult to categorize. They may have their roots in the cultural alienation that is a part of his Australian heritage, but they are also freewheeling investiga-tions of the manners and mores of the more inter-national scene. Perhaps all these films are related, after all—which, of course, is the theme of his 1993 film, *Six Degrees of Separation,* based on John Guare's play. As one of the characters points out, people, no matter how different by class and race, are in actuality indirectly connected. Indeed, we are, all of us, just six degrees separated from every-one else on the planet. However, the memorable scene where the Kittredge family visits the Michelangelo Sistine Ceiling and gazes upon the image of God and Adam, whose outstretched hands are separated by a narrow gap, suggests an alternative interpretation: no matter how closely we each of us may approach the other, we are still finally, definitely condemned to remain apart. Schepisi's advice to filmmakers perfectly describes his own sensibilities and ambitions: "Get out there. Walk the tightrope. Experiment. Have fun."

Other Films *The Party,* short (1970); *Iceman* (1984); *The Russia House* (1990); *I.Q.* (1994); *Fierce Creatures* (1997).

References "Fred Schepisi," *American Film,* July–August 1987, 11–13; McFarlane, Brian, *Australian Cinema, 1970–1985* (London: Secker and Warburg, 1987).

—J.C.T.

Schlesinger, John (1926–) As a youth Schlesinger, who was born in London in 1926,

wanted to become a professional magician, an avocation he feels helped lead him toward a filmmaking career. "My interest in magic may well have been the first glimmering of my ambition to translate images and illusions of life onto the screen," he told this writer. After serving in World War II, Schlesinger turned to acting and directing for the Oxford University Dramatic Society and to making experimental films. When these short films failed to arouse interest in any of the British film studios, he took up acting again, appearing in minor roles on stage and screen. Finally he began making television documentaries for BBC-TV.

Working on these documentaries, Schlesinger believes, helped him to learn the craft of filmmaking: "The speed at which you are obliged to work teaches you a sort of basic film grammar." In the late 1950s Schlesinger made several documentary segments for the BBC-TV series *Monitor*. His first major venture into commercial cinema was a documentary for British Transport entitled *Terminus*, about 24 hours at Waterloo Station; it won him an award at the Venice International Film Festival. Schlesinger's documentaries attracted the attention of producer Joseph Janni, and together they formed a creative association that lasted through several of Schlesinger's British films, including *A Kind of Loving* (1962), which won him the Grand Prize at the Berlin International Film Festival; *Darling* (1965); and *Sunday, Bloody Sunday* (1971). All three of these films reflect the principal theme of Schlesinger's work, which has continued to surface in his subsequent pictures: "My films are about the problems that people have in finding security and happiness in life, and the need for accepting what is second best when that is all that one can hope for."

Schlesinger began directing features in Britain at the point when British social realism, the cycle of low-budget, high-quality movies on social themes (called "Kitchen Sink Realism"), was in full swing. Because these films were made outside the large studio system, Schlesinger developed his own film projects. He continued to do so while directing films in Hollywood, where he has worked with increasing regularity in recent years.

His first American film, *Midnight Cowboy* (1969), won him an Academy Award as best director, while the film itself won best picture of the year. It is the tale of a Texan named Joe Buck (Jon Voight) who comes to New York with illusions of making easy money as a male companion to wealthy women. Joe is himself taken advantage of repeatedly by the assortment of tough and desperate individuals he encounters in the course of his descent into the netherworld of New York. He seems on the verge of becoming as ruthless as the rest, until he makes a friend of Ratso Rizzo, a repulsive-looking bum who needs companionship as much as Joe does. The two take refuge in each other's friendship. Their relationship is not homosexual, Schlesinger points out; but rather the story "shows how two men can have a meaningful relationship without being homosexual." Reviews of the film noted how accurately the British-born

John Schlesinger (Orion)

Schlesinger had caught the authentic atmosphere not only of New York City, but also of Miami Beach and the Texas Panhandle, as surely as he had captured the atmosphere of factory towns in his native England in films like *A Kind of Loving* and *Billy Liar* (1963).

Among the noteworthy films of his later career are *Marathon Man* (1976), a thriller about a young American who finds himself in conflict with a Nazi war criminal in New York; and *Pacific Heights* (1990), in which a hapless young landlord is victimized by a psychotic tenant. One of his most popular films of the 1990s was *Cold Comfort Farm* (1996), based on a comic novel by Stella Gibbons, about a city girl who is reduced to living on a bleak Sussex farm with her country cousins. With this British production Schlesinger returned to the realm of British social realism, a trend with which he was associated from the beginning of his career. More than one critic commented that, with this deliciously eccentric, expertly acted film, Schlesinger proved definitively that he could handle comedy as well as drama. The same can be said of a still later comedy, *The Next Best Thing* (2000), whose very title recalls Schlesinger's ongoing theme about individuals having to settle for second best in life.

Schlesinger's accomplishments as a director have not gone unrewarded, as evidenced by his Oscars and festival prizes. In addition, his contribution to British film art earned him the title of Commander of the British Empire in 1970. But he received what is perhaps his most distinguished honor in 1995, when he was awarded an Academy Fellowship by the British Academy of Film and Television Arts; this prize placed him on the same honor role with such internationally acclaimed directors as Billy Wilder and Federico Fellini. Schlesinger feels that these honors have acknowledged his efforts to make films that provide more than mere escapism. In fact, in his corpus of films he has proved as well as any director can that, in his own words, "It is possible to give people entertainment in a film that will also provoke thought, stimulate the imagination, and disturb the mind."

Other Films *Far from the Madding Crowd* (1967); *Yanks* (1979).

References McFarlane, Brian, *An Autobiography of British Cinema: As Told by the Filmmakers Who Made It* (London: Methuen, 1997); Phillips, Gene D., *Major Film Directors of the American and British Cinema* (Cranbury, N.J.: Associated University Presses, 1999).

—G.D.P.

Schlöndorff, Volker (1939–)

The movement known as the New German Cinema (Das neue Kino) begins in 1969 with a film by Volker Schlöndorff, *Der junge Törless* (*Young Torless*), made by a German who had learned filmmaking in France and worked as assistant director with ALAIN RESNAIS on *Last Year at Marienbad* (1962) and LOUIS MALLE on *Zazie dans le métro* (1960) and other talents of the French New Wave. Of course, when he returned to Germany in the mid-1960s, he would carry with him the influence of his French colleagues. As a consequence, he was to reform the moribund German cinema, which had produced very few significant films during the post–World War II era, with the exception of Bernhard Wicki's *The Bridge* (1960), concerning a group of German teenagers drafted in 1945 and left to defend a bridge against the advancing Allied army.

Volker Schlöndorff was born in Wiesbaden, Germany, on March 31, 1939. He was educated in France after his parents moved to Paris in 1956, and went on to study filmmaking at the Institut des Hautes Études Cinématographiques. After he returned to Germany, he later met and worked with Margarethe von Trotta (born in Berlin in 1942), whom he married in 1969. After collaborating with her husband on several films, von Trotta emerged as a significant feminist filmmaker herself, notable for such films as *The German Sisters* (aka *Die bleierne Zeit* [1981]) and *Rosa Luxemburg* (1986).

Schlöndorff's *Der junge Törless,* adapted from a story by Robert Musil written in 1906, was the first international success of Das neue Kino. Set in Austria-Hungary at the turn of the century, it was an exposé of boarding-school life at a military academy, where a boy named Basini becomes a scapegoat and is brutalized by his classmates. The film was an allegorical statement on the later German response to Nazism. Törless watches and understands what is happening to Basini, and, though he does not participate in the brutality, neither does he attempt to stop it by reporting what he has seen to the authorities. Although he does snatch a white rat away from a colleague who is torturing it and puts the animal out of its misery by slamming it against a wall, Törless remains detached from what is happening to Basini while musing over the nature of good and evil. When Basini is finally "given to the class" and beaten in the gym, Törless runs away. After he returns, justice is not done: Basini has apparently been expelled.

Schlöndorff was the most "literary" of the "new" German filmmakers. *Michael Kohlhass—Der Rebell* (1969) was adapted from Heinrich von Kleist, for example, and *Baal* (1969) was adapted from Brecht's semi-expressionist portrait of a sensual libertine, transformed by Schlöndorff into a hippie dropout (played by Rainer Werner Fassbinder), wrecking havoc on the bourgeois world of Munich. *Georgina's Reasons* (*Georginas Gründe* [1974]) was adapted from Henry James. *Coup de Grâce* (*Der Fangschuss* [1976]) was codirected with von Trotta and adapted from the 1936 novel by Marguerite Yourcenar. *Swann in Love* (*Un amour de Swann* [1984]) was adapted from a portion of Proust's *Remembrance of Things Past*. *Death of a Salesman* (*Tod eines Handlungsreisenden* [1985]), starring Dustin Hoffman and John Malkovich, was adapted from Arthur Miller's play. *A Gathering of Old Men* (1987) was adapted by the playwright Charles Fuller from the novel by Ernest J. Gaines. *The Handmaiden's Tale* (1990) was adapted from Margaret Atwood's anti-utopian novel, published in 1985. *Homo Faber* (*The Voyager* [1991]) was adapted from the 1957 novel by Swiss writer Max Frisch.

But merely to list such an impressive outpouring of adaptations cannot, of course, begin to reflect the intelligence that has gone into making them. One of Schlöndorff's finest adaptations was coscripted and codirected with Margarethe von Trotta, *Die verlorene Ehre der Katharina Blum* (*The Lost Honor of Katharina Blum* [1975]), brilliantly adapted from Heinrich Böll's angry and polemical novel about the invasion of a woman's privacy by government and the press. The point of the narrative is made clear by the novel's subtitle: "How Violence Can Develop and Where It Can Lead."

The story of Katharina Blum (Angela Winkler) presents an innocent, hard-working, and well-structured young woman who meets and falls in love with Ludwig Götten (Jürgen Prochnow), who is being followed by the police as a suspected terrorist. The police mount an early morning raid on her apartment, but Götten escapes. Katharina is jailed as a possible accomplice; though later released, she is constantly harassed by the police thereafter. But the most psychologically damaging consequence is the way her reputation is defiled by the press, particularly the way she is treated by an unscrupulous reporter named Werner Tötges (Dieter Laser), who invents details to make his reporting more spectacular and turns her into a notorious celebrity by making her appear to be a terrorist sympathizer and a whore. Finally, when the reporter attempts to exploit her sexually as well, she snaps, takes a gun, and shoots him.

Before the novel was published, Böll sent proofs to Schlöndorff and von Trotta, and later collaborated with them in reshaping the narrative for the film version, which took a more straightforward, chronological approach and was intended to reach a wider mass audience than the novel. The film makes the plot linear and begins with black-and-white documentary images of the terrorist suspect on a ferry, demonstrating the process of police surveillance. These shots later parallel black-and-white photographs taken by the newspaper photographer. The documentary police camera captures the suspect in the cross-hairs of a viewfinder that resemble the cross-hairs of a rifle scope and suggest that the camera can also function as a weapon of character assassination. The most striking visualization of theme comes toward the end of the story, when Katharina wrecks her tidy apartment in a fit of passionate anger and resentment, then sits in the shambles of her once well-organized life, contemplating the murder of the man who has spoiled her happiness.

The film begins by stating that "Although the names of the characters are fictitious, the story you are about to see is based on an actual occurrence," and ends with the same statement that Böll had used to begin his novel: "The characters and action in this story are purely fictitious. Should the description of certain journalistic practices result in a resemblance to the practices of the *Bild-Zeitung,* such resemblance is neither intentional nor fortuitous, but unavoidable." The Nobel Prize–winning novelist wrote the story as an angry response to the consequences of his writing an article for *Der Spiegel,* criticizing the hysterical coverage of the Baader-Meinhof gang and arguing that the terrorist Ulrike Meinhof should be given a fair trial. This was an unpopular position and was interpreted as a mark of sympathy for the terrorism Meinhof had come to symbolize. The novelist's house was searched and he was antagonized by the police, as well as by Axel Springer's widely read newspaper, *Bild-Zeitung.*

"*Katharina Blum* is not a film version of a novel in the same way that *Törless* was," the director remarked to the French film journal *Écran* (No. 46, April 1976): "What is of importance is the subject matter which Böll treated in his book. What interested us was not the literary quality, but the issues raised." In other words, the project was regarded "more as an engagement with matters of topical concern rather than the film version of a novel." Regardless, this was an effective cinematic adaptation that was utterly faithful to the spirit of its source.

Katharina Blum was the most popular literary adaptation Schlöndorff attempted before *Die Blechtrommel* (*The Tin Drum* [1979]), carefully adapted and abridged from the novel by Günter Grass, which was to become Schlöndorff's greatest international success, and the first film made by a German filmmaker to win an Academy Award. Schlöndorff had to be persuaded by Grass to undertake this adaptation. The novelist made suggestions to the director that helped him to understand how the story of the rise of Nazism in Danzig could be seen through the eyes of a child who refuses to grow physically, but whose understanding is mature and acute. Grass suggested that a child play the part of Oskar, seen over a 20-year period to create the impression that the world was changing around him. Schlöndorff wrote the screenplay with Jean-Claude Carrière, then went to Grass himself for assistance with dialogue, especially the monologue by Oskar's grandmother that closes the film. When the rough cut of the picture, which ran to three hours and 30 minutes, had to be reduced by an hour to meet contract obligations, Grass was again called in to get involved with the film's editing.

The director saw himself "as *au service* to *The Tin Drum,*" as he told the *New York Times:* "Grass said I made *The Tin Drum* because I asked the right questions and listened to his answers. But I think there's something else. If you have a piece as original as *The Tin Drum* then you can't profane yourself by making something even more original out of it," adding, "I had no need to put a personal label on this film. I think it was this approach that interested him: a professional filmmaker who did not try to make the film his own." But just as Grass was the author of the novel, Schlöndorff is the auteur of this and other author-assisted adaptations he has made so well. In this respect Schlöndorff resembles other world-class directors, such as SIDNEY LUMET and MILOŠ FORMAN, all of them outstanding, and all of them expanding the potential of the cinema in new and inventive ways.

Other Films *Mord und Totschlag* (Murder and manslaughter, aka *A Degree of Murder* [1967]); *Der plöt-*

zliche Reichtum der armen Leute von Kombach (*The Sudden Wealth of the Poor People of Kombach* [1971]); *Die Moral der Ruth Halbfass* (*The Morality of Ruth Halbfass* [1972]); *Die Ehegattin* (*A Free Woman* [1972]); *Strohfeuer* (*Summer Lightning* [1972]); *Übernachtung in Tirol* (*Overnight in the Tirol* [1974]); *Das zweite Erwachen der Crista Klages* (*The Second Awakening of Christa Klages* [1978]); *Deutschland im Herbst* (*Germany in Autumn*, codirected one episode [1978]); *Nur zum Spass—nur zum Spiel. Kaleidoskpo Valeska Gert* (Just for fun, just as a game, *Kaleidoscope Valeska Gert* [1979]); *Die Fälschung* (*Circle of deceit* [1981]); *Der Unhold* (*The Ogre* [1996]); *Palmetto* (1998).

References Elsaesser, Thomas, *New German Cinema: A History* (New Brunswick, N.J.: Rutgers University Press, 1989); Franklin, James, *New German Cinema: From Oberhausen to Hamburg* (Boston: Twayne, 1983); Sandford, John, *The New German Cinema* (Totowa, N.J.: Barnes & Noble, 1980); Vinocur, John, "After 20 Years, 'The Tin Drum' Marches to the Screen," *New York Times,* April 6, 1980, II, pp. 1, 17.

—J.M.W.

Scorsese, Martin (1942–) Martin Scorsese was born in the New York borough of Queens on November 17, 1942, to Charles and Catherine Scorsese. Strongly influenced by his parents and his Italian-American heritage (he chronicled both in a 1974 documentary entitled *Italianamerican*), the young Scorsese was shaped by two dominant forces: the church and the cinema. Although he would eventually choose the cinema as his profession, he seriously considered entering the seminary in the late 1950s. He graduated from New York University film school in 1964 and spent the next several years teaching at NYU and fitfully completing his first feature film, the independently made *Who's That Knocking at My Door?* (1969). Scorsese also became a freelance editor in the late 1960s and early 1970s, most notably helping to edit the rock documentary *Woodstock* (1970).

Like many other young filmmakers of the era, Scorsese got his first big directorial break from exploitation producer Roger Corman, and directed *Boxcar Bertha* in 1972. He followed this with his first great New York gangster saga, *Mean Streets* (1973). Besides featuring Robert De Niro and Harvey Keitel, two actors who would come to be strongly identified with Scorsese, *Mean Streets* established Scorsese's critical reputation. He followed it with a southwest story, *Alice Doesn't Live Here Anymore* (1974), which earned star Ellen Burstyn a best actress Oscar.

Returning to the New York streets, this time viewed through the window of a taxicab, Scorsese made arguably his greatest film, *Taxi Driver,* in 1976. The story of a loner cab driver named Travis Bickle (portrayed by De Niro), *Taxi Driver* cemented Scorsese's place at the forefront of American cinema and won the Palme d'Or at Cannes that year. Scorsese's follow-up, *New York, New York* (1977), was an ode to the lavish screen musicals of his youth and another film inspired by his hometown. It proved a significant artistic and financial failure. He returned to documentary film to create the cinematic portrait of the final concert by his friends in the rock group the Band, entitled *The Last Waltz* (1978). Two years later he followed with *Raging Bull* (1980), another artistic peak, chronicling the life of boxer Jake LaMotta (De Niro) in a 1950s tabloid-like black-and-white visual style. Scorsese's career faltered somewhat during the 1980s, and included *The King of Comedy* (1983) and *The Last Temptation of Christ* (1988).

The Last Temptation, based on the controversial novel about Christ's life by Nikos Kazantzakis, had a checkered production history and an even more infamous reception once it was released. Scorsese became interested in the project in the early 1970s, and began production on the film in 1983 before a nervous Paramount studio cancelled the controversial project. It was only after the financial success of *The Color of Money* (1986), starring Tom Cruise and Paul Newman, that Scorsese had the leverage to finally get *The Last Temptation* made. Upon its release, the film caused an uproar in conservative religious circles due to its unorthodox portrayal of Christ (Willem Dafoe).

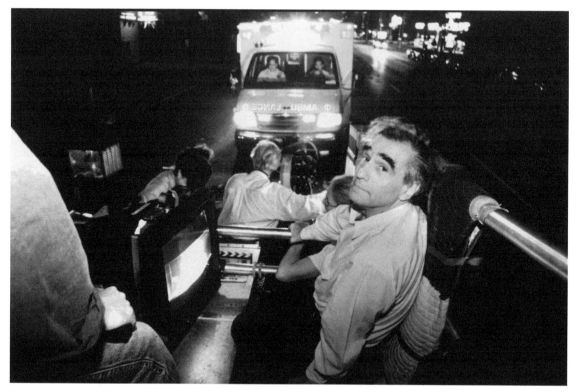

Martin Scorsese on the set of *Bringing Out the Dead* (Paramount)

Scorsese began the 1990s with *GoodFellas* (1990), a richly textured epic about modern-day gangster life starring De Niro, Joe Pesci, and Ray Liotta, which represents yet another artistic highpoint in his career. This was followed by another mainstream box-office success, *Cape Fear* (1991), which was a remake of an early-1960s psychological thriller. Much of the remainder of Scorsese's 1990s output was uncharacteristic, including the adaptation of the Edith Wharton novel *The Age of Innocence* (1993) and the Tibetan saga *Kundun* (1997). Between these two pictures, Scorsese returned to the gangster genre with *Casino* (1995), focusing this time on organized gambling. Scorsese's final 1990s film, *Bringing Out the Dead* (1999), returned him to the mean New York City streets, this time in an ambulance driven by star Nicolas Cage.

Other Films *After Hours* (1985); *New York Stories* (1989), "Life Lessons" segment.

References Ehrenstein, David, *The Scorsese Picture: The Art and Life of Martin Scorsese* (New York: Birch Lane Press, 1992); Kelly, Mary Pat, *Martin Scorsese: A Journey* (New York: Thunder's Mouth Press, 1991).

—C.M.

Sembene, Ousmane (1923–) Destined to become the first internationally respected, native African filmmaker, Ousmane Sembene was born in Ziguinchor, Senegal, on January 1, 1923, to a Muslim family of Lebou origin. He went to Dakar in 1935 to prepare for his Certificat d'É-tudes but dropped out of school after having a fistfight with his school principal. He worked as a mason until 1942, when he joined the French colonial army as an artillery technician and served in Africa and Europe until 1946. In 1948 he worked as a longshoreman in Marseilles and later studied painting and poetry in Denmark (1951–54). His first novel, *Le Docker Noir* (*The Black Dockworker*) was published in 1956. In 1957 his novel *O Pays mon beau Peuple!* (*Oh My Country, My Beautiful People!*) was published.

Thereafter, Sembene traveled extensively in the Soviet Union, China, and North Vietnam, and met W. E. B. Dubois at the First Congress of African and Asiatic Writers in Tashkent in 1958. In 1961 he returned to Africa and published *Tribal Scars,* a collection of short stories, then studied filmmaking for a year in 1962 at the Gorki Studio in Moscow. His first significant short film was *Barom Sarret* (1963), concerning the misfortunes of a cart driver in Dakar who has his cart confiscated by the police after being cheated by a client.

Sembene was already a recognized and accomplished writer when his first feature film, *Mandabi,* was released in 1968, adapted from his novel *Le Mandat* (*The Money Order*), published in 1964. He then completed *La Noire De* (*Black Girl*) in 1966, a 60-minute film in French, adapted from one of the stories in *Tribal Scars.* Most of his films that followed were in Wolof rather than French, the language of the colonial bureaucrats. At that time there were only 70 film theatres in Senegal. Since Wolof was not a written language, Sembene had to write the screenplay in French, and since the film was funded in part by the Centre National de la Cinématographie Française, two separate language versions were made of *Mandabi,* the story of an African's comic frustrations in trying to cash a money order sent by his nephew in Paris. In some significant ways, *Mandabi* shared the concerns of Italian neorealism, shooting with a largely nonprofessional cast, for example, and "exposing the uncaring face of officialdom," in the words of Roy Armes. *Emitai* (1972) was set during World War II in the Casamance region of Senegal, where Sembene had grown up as a boy, and dramatized the village peasants resisting efforts of the French to enlist villagers and to requisition the local rice harvest. For this film Sembene used the language of the Diola people. *Xala* (1974) was a satiric attack upon the black bourgeoisie in an unspecified African state. The central figure suffers from a temporary sexual impotence (*xala*) on his wedding night as he takes a third wife who is younger than his daughter.

Critic Roy Armes argues that Sembene's most important film was *Ceddo* (1977), an allegory treating Africa's response to alien intrusions in the historical past, particularly those involving a slave trader and a Catholic priest. Sembene was critical of the West but also of the "blacks themselves, their involvement in the slave trade," and their "cooperation with the colonialists on the part of tribal leaders." Sembene later insisted on making films in Wolof and Diola so as to reach his native audience, because, he believed, *"Le cinéma est l'école du soir du people,"* that "cinema is the people's night school." At the 13th Pan-African Film Festival of 1993, Ousmane Sembene was honored as "the father of African cinema," as well as an artist of international significance.

Other Films   *L'Empire sonhrai* (1963), short; *Niaye* (1964), short; *Taaw* (1970), short; *Camp de Thiaroye* (1989); *Gelwaar* (1992).

References   Armes, Roy, *Third World Filmmaking and the West* (Berkeley: University of California Press, 1987); Gadjigo, Samba, et al., ed., *Ousmane Sembene: Dialogues with Critics and Writers* (Amherst: University of Massachusetts Press, 1993); Pfaff, Françoise, *The Cinema of Ousmane Sembene: A Pioneer of African Film* (Westport, Conn.: Greenwood Press, 1984).

—J.M.W.

Spielberg, Steven (1946–)   After a 1974 screening of Steven Spielberg's feature film directorial debut, *The Sugarland Express,* BILLY WILDER was moved to declare, "The director of that movie is the greatest young talent to come along in years." Spielberg's subsequent career has fueled arguments both for and against Wilder's assertion. Born in Cincinnati, Ohio, on December 18,

1946, Spielberg is the son of Arnold (an electrical engineer and World War II Army Air Corps veteran) and Leah (a classical pianist) Spielberg. As a youth, Spielberg and his family moved often as they followed the shifting nature of Arnold's pioneering work in early computer technology. An avid technology and film buff, Arnold took his son to his first film when the boy was five. Spielberg recalls his father waking him late one night to witness a meteor shower, a memory he later depicted in his 1977 film *Close Encounters of the Third Kind*. When Spielberg was in his teens his father purchased an 8-mm home-movie camera to record family events. It was not long before young Spielberg commandeered the camera and began making short adventure/war films with titles like *Battle Squad* and *The Last Gun*. In 1964 Spielberg produced an ambitious science fiction feature entitled *Firelight,* which he would later remake as *Close Encounters.* In 1966 Spielberg's parents divorced, an event that influenced his later work.

Unlike many of the other figures in the so-called film school generation (Scorsese, Lucas, Coppola, and others), Spielberg did not graduate from film school. Though he was enrolled at the University of California at Long Beach, Spielberg spent most of his time hanging around Universal studios, where he had made several important contacts. In 1968, he directed a silent short called *Amblin',* the strength of which earned him a job directing television shows for Universal. Three years later he directed a movie-of-the-week entitled *Duel* (1971), a taut road-rage thriller that achieved some success as a theatrical release in Europe.

In 1974 Spielberg released his first theatrical feature, *The Sugarland Express,* which Pauline Kael called "one of the most phenomenal debut films in the history of the movies." Of Spielberg himself she said "[he] could be the rarity among directors, a born entertainer—perhaps a new generation's HOWARD HAWKS." *The Sugarland Express* was based on a true story about a convict couple's attempt to reunite with their toddler, who now lived with foster parents reluctant to

give him back. The film starred the young actress Goldie Hawn, a recent Oscar winner, and was filled with many dazzling scenes and humorous moments. However, it failed to appeal to a wide audience. After *Sugarland*'s lackluster performance at the box office, Spielberg released *Jaws* (1975), based on Peter Benchley's best-selling novel, and helped usher in the era of the "blockbuster." The story of the panic that sweeps a New England island community after a series of shark attacks featured Roy Scheider as the sea-hating sheriff who must confront his own fears in order to kill the beast. It helped establish Spielberg's growing reputation as a major film talent.

During the 1980s Spielberg's career expanded when he released some of his most popular films and founded his own production company, Amblin Entertainment, to begin producing films. While Amblin helped start the careers of such directors as ROBERT L. ZEMECKIS, Chris Columbus, and Kevin Reynolds, Spielberg went on to team with his friend GEORGE LUCAS (Star Wars) in 1981, and directed *Raiders of the Lost Ark*. The film, a tribute to the adventure serials Lucas and Spielberg had loved as boys, was a phenomenal success and spawned two Spielberg-directed sequels (*Indiana Jones and the Temple of Doom* [1984] and *Indiana Jones and the Last Crusade* [1989]). Spielberg's next film, 1982's *E.T.: the Extra-Terrestrial,* was another blockbuster. It was a highly personal story about the effects of divorce on children but masqueraded as a science fiction tale. In the film Elliot, a young suburban boy played by Henry Thomas, is befriended by a kindly, lost alien not long after the boy's parents have divorced. Nominated for an Academy Award for best picture, the film lost out to Richard Attenborough's *Gandhi*. Though nearly all of his films had been popular and often critical successes, Spielberg had yet to receive an Academy Award for his direction.

In 1985 he married his on-again off-again girlfriend, the actress Amy Irving, with whom he eventually had his first child, Max, also in 1985. That same year he released the film *The Color Pur-*

ple, which can be seen as his first attempt at a more "serious" work, though the film won no major prizes and caused a minor controversy among fans of the original Alice Walker novel. Afterward, Spielberg took a two-year break from directing and focused on producing films through Amblin. In 1987 he returned with *Empire of the Sun,* an underrated adaptation of J. G. Ballard's novel of the same name. The story of a young boy's experiences in a Japanese internment camp in China during World War II is the first in Spielberg's loose World War II trilogy. Spielberg and Irving, whose marriage had always been rocky, divorced in 1989, but the two remained close friends. Two years later, in 1991, he married Kate Capshaw, an actress who had played the female lead in *Indiana Jones and the Temple of Doom,* and with whom he had been closely linked in the press ever since his separation from Irving. That same year Spielberg directed *Hook,* a film that had the audacity to imagine that Peter Pan grew up to become a corporate raider, or "pirate." In fact one could argue that the film was a serious artist's attempt to address his own nature. The man-child behind *Close Encounters, Raiders,* and *E.T.* was about to grow up himself, and he would do it in Krakow, Poland.

Perhaps the most important year of Spielberg's career came in 1993, when he released both his most financially successful film and his most honored film. *Jurassic Park* (released in the summer of that year), a thriller about dinosaurs on the rampage, became one of the most successful films of all time, eventually grossing almost one billion dollars worldwide. But it was *Schindler's List* (released in December) that finally won Spielberg his Oscar. Based on the nonfiction novel by Thomas Keneally, the film is a harrowing account of the Holocaust that Spielberg claims helped him reconnect with his Jewish heritage. Shot entirely on location in Poland and Germany, *Schindler's List* is about one German businessman's unlikely, but heroic, efforts to save the lives of his Jewish factory workers. The movie was both a popular and critical success. Roger Ebert of the *Chicago Sun-Times*

called it "the best (film) he has ever made," while *New Yorker Magazine* declared it "his masterpiece . . . a work of restraint, intelligence, and unusual sensitivity, and the finest fiction feature ever made about the century's greatest evil." The same magazine also addressed the film's effect on the perception of Spielberg as merely a popular entertainer who refused to grow up: "Prince Hal has become Henry V; the dauphin has emerged a king."

After the success of the film, Spielberg founded the Shoah Foundation, an organization dedicated to raising Holocaust awareness. In 1994 Spielberg joined with Jeffrey Katzenberg and David Geffen in founding Dreamworks SKG, a new motion picture, television, and music studio. Spielberg also directed one of that studio's first major film releases, 1997's *Amistad,* based on a famous slave ship revolt and the resulting legal trials. Like *The Color Purple,* the film is a noble but ultimately flawed attempt at a profound statement on race in the United States (a subject close to Spielberg's heart, as the adoptive father of two African-American children). Still, the film does feature some stunning images and sequences.

In July 1998, only seven months after *Amistad,* Spielberg released *Saving Private Ryan,* a Dreamworks-Paramount coproduction. A massive battle epic, the film is the third in Spielberg's unofficial World War II trilogy (alongside *Empire of the Sun* and *Schindler's List*) and arguably the most successful. The opening scene, a furious depiction of the amphibious landings at Omaha Beach on D-day, has been compared in shock impact, artistry, and significance to Eisenstein's "Odessa steps" sequence from *Battleship Potemkin.* The film was considered the front-runner for best picture at 1998's Oscar telecast, but was defeated in an upset by John Madden's *Shakespeare in Love. Ryan* did, however, win Spielberg his second best-director trophy from the Academy.

Spielberg's most recent film, the science fiction allegory, *A.I.,* hovers uncertainly between the worlds of a bittersweet fairy tale, à la "Pinocchio," and a grim vision of a dehumanized world of the future, à la the late STANLEY KUBRICK. It had been Kubrick's idea in the first place. After buying the rights to Brian Aldiss's short story, "Super-Toys Last All Summer Long" (1969), Kubrick had begun planning a screen adaptation as early as 1980. Sporadically, over the course of two decades, and with the assistance of collaborators as various as Aldiss himself, Ian Watson, and personal assistant Leon Vitale (from whom he first got the idea of the "Pinocchio" allusions), Kubrick developed script ideas and commissioned thousands of artist's sketches and storyboards. In 1995, ultimately convinced that cinematic special-effects technology was not yet up to the task, he shelved the project and turned to the film that would be his last project, *Eyes Wide Shut.*

Near the end of his life, however, Kubrick's interest in *A.I.* revived, and he consulted with Spielberg about a possible coproduction with Spielberg as director and himself as producer. "Stanley thought Steven might be the right person to direct this for several reasons," says Jan Harlan, Kubrick's brother-in-law and producer. "Using a real child actor is possible for Steven who would shoot this film in twenty weeks while Stanley knew he would take years and the child might change too much. . . . [He also] saw in Steven one of the all time great filmmakers of the next generation." Another reason was Spielberg's mastery of the computer-generated imagery so necessary for the requisite effects of the film.

After Kubrick's death, Spielberg was determined to complete the film. He had not committed to a project in two years, since *Saving Private Ryan,* and he had not written a screenplay since *Poltergeist* in 1982. When Warner Bros. chairman Terry Semel gave it a green light, Spielberg called in many of his longtime colleagues, producer Kathleen Kennedy, special-effects wizards and designers, editor Michael Kahn, Dennis Muren and Stan Winston, cinematographer Janusz Kaminski, and composer John Williams.

Settling down to write his own script, armed with Kubrick's 90-page treatment and surrounded with thousands of drawings and storyboards, he was concerned with balancing his own creative priorities with Kubrick's original intentions. Available to him, but not previously to Kubrick, was computer-generated technology. "When he sent me his first treatment, I said, 'How are you going to do some of this stuff?'" recalls Spielberg. "And he said, 'I don't know if we can yet. But we will be able to, soon.' Now, he's right, anything is possible. With the computer you can do anything, you can show anything. The only limit is your own imagination." Whereas Brian Aldiss's eight-page story had merely sketched out a poetic impression of a mother's difficulty in relating to her "adoptive" three-year old robot boy, Spielberg fleshed it out with additional characters and situations. Again, he emphasized the theme of mother love—prior examples of the "mother ship" in *Close Encounters* and the searches by Jim and by Peter Pan and the Lost Boys for their mothers in *Empire of the Sun* and *Hook* immediately come to mind. And whereas Aldiss's story had concluded with David's apprehensions over the consequences of his mother's giving birth to a real child, Spielberg's script transforms the boy into a fugitive, expelled from his home, encountering many perils on the way to a reunion with his mother. It is the kind of dramatic odyssey that appears in *Empire of the Sun,* where the adventures of the innocent boy Jim's friendship and the worldly Basie parallels David's relationship with Gigolo Joe. This relationship perhaps suggests the core reality of the friendship between Spielberg and Kubrick. As critic Lisa Schwarzbaum notes, "While David yearns to pedal home to Mommy, Joe knows with inhuman sureness that he's programmed for a cold, vertiginous, Mommy-less world of violent Kubrickian sensation." In addition, the aforementioned allusions to the Pinocchio story were deeply personal for Spielberg. Not only had it been a thematic thread in *Close Encounters* (quotations from the Disney musical appeared several times), but it imparted to the basic story line the fairy-tale-like quality he desired. "It was like getting my wisdom teeth pulled all over again," Spielberg said, summing up the writing of the picture, "because Stanley was sitting on the set back behind me saying, 'No, don't do that!' I felt like I was being coached by a ghost. I finally just had to be kind of disrespectful to the extent that I needed to be able to write this, not from Stanley's experience, but from mine. Still, I was like an archaeologist, picking up the pieces of a civilization, putting Stanley's picture back together again."

Critical reactions have been mixed. "If you were wondering how Spielberg's pop exaltations would consort with Kubrick's dread and metaphysical dismay," writes David Denby in the *New Yorker*, "the answer is: strangely, confusingly." In the final analysis, Denby describes *A.I.* as "a ponderous, death-of-the-world fantasy, which leaves us with nothing but an Oedipal robot—hardly a redemption." Apart from his own quibbles, Andrew Sarris (who admits he has never had undue reverence for either Kubrick or Spielberg) applauds this Oedipal element as "a beautifully formulated meditation on the eternal intensity of filial love." He praises the "unwavering convictions" of the performances, resulting in a movie that is "an overwhelmingly haunting experience as well as an exquisite work of art." Moreover, "For myself, I regard *A.I.* as the most emotionally and existentially overwhelming Spielberg production since the ridiculously underrated and underappreciated *Empire of the Sun* (1987)." Armond White in the *New York Press* applauded it as a "breakthrough" in "raising fairytales to the level of great art."

Spielberg's career has been one of the most remarkable and successful in the history of American cinema. His popular and financial success is indisputable and perhaps unrivaled, but his reputation as an artist has always been in question. He is viewed by many as little more than a popular showman whose overly simplistic films appeal to the lowest common denominator in the American moviegoing public. Others argue that Spielberg's

films (especially those he has produced for others) are far more in love with special-effects technology than with any sense of story, theme, or art. Indeed, Spielberg, along with his friend Lucas, has often been held responsible for the perceived dumbing-down of American movies since the end of the 1970s. While it is true that Spielberg's career is dotted with unfortunate lapses into easy sentiment (*Hook* and the framing story of *Saving Private Ryan*) and occasional instances of an unfortunate racism (*Indiana Jones and the Temple of Doom*), those who devalue Spielberg's work seem to overlook (or rationalize their dislike for) the inventiveness, creativity, and power of such films as *Jaws, Close Encounters, E.T., Empire of the Sun, Schindler's List,* and *Saving Private Ryan*. Ultimately, of course, history will decide the validity of Wilder's early assessment of Spielberg, but at present there are few filmmakers in America (or anywhere else) who have had a greater impact for better or worse on the medium of motion pictures.

Other Films *1941* (1979); *Twilight Zone: The Movie* (1983), segment; *Always* (1989); *Lost World: Jurassic Park* (1997).

References Denby, David, "Face/Off," *New Yorker,* July 2, 2001, pp. 86–87; Lyman, Rick, "A Director's Journey into a Darkness of the Heart," *New York Times,* June 24, 2001, II, pp. 1, 24; Schwarzbaum, Lisa, "Sci-Fi Channel," *Entertainment Weekly,* June 29–July 6, 2001, pp. 109–110; Sarris, Andrew, "*A.I.*=(2001 + *E.T.*)2," *New York Observer,* July 4, 2001, p. 1; White, Armond, "Intelligence Quotient," *New York Press,* July 4, 2001; Kael, Pauline, "Sugarland and Badlands," *New Yorker,* March 18, 1974; McBride, Joseph, *Steven Spielberg: A Biography* (New York: Simon and Schuster, 1997); Schiff, Stephen, "Seriously Spielberg," *New Yorker,* March 12, 1994.

—F.H.

Stone, Oliver (1946–)

Oliver Stone finds his inspiration in the literature and philosophy of adventure: the tales of Greek mythology; the novels of Melville, Conrad, Hemingway, and Mailer; the works of Nietzsche, who saw the philosopher as an adventurer questing for experience beyond conventional morality, "beyond good and evil." Stone may best be understood as an adventurer in the tradition of the ancient traveler who ventured to unknown lands, or the ancient shaman (a role Stone has consciously emulated) who undertook trance-voyages to the spirit world. Ancient cultures valued these adventurers as storytellers who brought back "tales from the world beyond men," stories meant to expand human knowledge and understanding. That is the kind of storyteller that Stone has tried to be in making his films.

Born September 15, 1946, in New York City, son of a Wall Street stockbroker, Stone enjoyed a privileged upbringing, attended prep school, and in 1965 entered Yale University. That year he read Joseph Conrad's *Lord Jim,* which moved him to drop out of college and head for adventure in the Far East. He taught school in Vietnam, then sailed the Pacific with the merchant marine. After a publisher rejected Stone's novel about these experiences, Stone enlisted in the army and returned as

Oliver Stone (right) with Ron Kovic, on whose life *Born on the Fourth of July* is based (Universal)

a combat soldier to Vietnam, where he received a Purple Heart and a Bronze Star. Like many soldiers in Vietnam, Stone bought a camera and began taking pictures. He came to realize that he could tell a story with pictures as well as with words and conceived the idea of becoming a film director.

After his discharge from the army, Stone attended film school at New York University. One of his teachers was MARTIN SCORSESE, and at NYU Stone encountered the work of those directors who would influence his filmmaking style: ORSON GEORGE WELLES, JEAN-LUC GODARD, ALAIN RESNAIS, and LUIS BUÑUEL.

Stone's first attempts at directing were two horror films, *Seizure* (1973) and *The Hand* (1981). Neither was a critical or a box-office success, but both showed Stone's interest in exploring the dark side of human nature, an interest that would be on display in his later, successful films.

Stone's early success came not as director, but as screenwriter. Stone's screenplay for *Midnight Express* (1978), the story of a young American man imprisoned in Turkey on drug charges, won an Academy Award. Over the next few years, Stone participated in writing several films, including *Conan the Barbarian* (1982) as cowriter, *Scarface* (1983) as writer, *Year of the Dragon* (1985) as cowriter, and *8 Million Ways to Die* (1985) as cowriter.

Stone returned to directing in 1986. Impressed by the idealism of Warren Beatty's film *Reds* (1981), about the life of left-wing journalist John Reed, Stone decided to move away from horror films to direct movies about ideas in which he believed. The result, in 1986, was both *Salvador,* which critiqued the Reagan administration's support for repressive right-wing political groups in Central America, and *Platoon,* a fictionalized account of Stone's own combat experience in Vietnam and the first film to deal with the Vietnam war in a realistic way. *Salvador* made many lists of the top ten films of 1986, and Stone's screenplay for that film (cowritten with Richard Boyle) was nominated for an Academy Award. *Platoon* won the Academy Award for best picture and earned Stone an Oscar for best director.

Stone followed up with *Wall Street* (1987), a film that chronicled the greed and insider trading rampant in the stock market in the 1980s. *Talk Radio* in 1988 was loosely based on the killing of talk-radio host Alan Berg by members of an extremist right-wing group. Stone returned to the subject of Vietnam in *Born on the Fourth of July* (1989), based on the autobiography of Ron Kovic (played by Tom Cruise in the film), who went to Vietnam a gung-ho Marine, was shot and paralyzed from the waist down, became disillusioned with the war, and turned into an antiwar activist. The film earned Stone another Academy Award for best director. In *The Doors* (1991), Stone explored the life and work of Jim Morrison. Stone felt a powerful connection with Morrison, who, like Stone, was influenced by Nietzsche and viewed himself as a shaman.

JFK (1991) marked a turning point in Stone's career. The film attacked the Warren Commission's conclusion that Lee Harvey Oswald acted alone in assassinating President Kennedy. The film drew on the inquiry into the assassination by the New Orleans district attorney, Jim Garrison (played by Kevin Costner), and other assassination researchers to suggest that Kennedy was the victim of a coup d'etat carried out by persons in the United States government. Notable for its use of montage, which intermixed documentary footage with restaged action to build the case that there had been a conspiracy to murder Kennedy, *JFK* was also striking in its use of the Zapruder film, which gave most viewers their first look at actual footage of the Kennedy assassination. *JFK* earned eight Academy Award nominations, including best picture and best director. Pressure generated by public response to the film resulted in Congress passing the President John F. Kennedy Assassination Records Collection Act of 1992, which set up an Assassination Records Review Board to locate, review, and release to the public all records per-

taining to the assassination. But *JFK* also brought a backlash against Stone. Some professional historians accused him of distorting the past. The media began to marginalize him as an eccentric conspiracy theorist.

In 1993 Stone completed his trilogy on the Vietnam war with *Heaven and Earth*, based on the true story of Le Ly Hayslip (played by Hiep Thi Le), a Vietnamese woman who had at one time served the Viet Cong and who later had married an American soldier and had come to the United States. The movie failed at the box office, but Stone's next film, *Natural Born Killers* (1994), a satirical look at the American media's obsession with violence, was the number-one box-office draw during the movie's first week of release. Stone then directed *Nixon* (1995), a companion piece to *JFK*. The film portrayed Richard Nixon (Anthony Hopkins) as a potentially great president, done in by his own tragic flaws.

A minor part of *Nixon* dealt with the Kennedy assassination, but Stone's critics focused on that part of the film, and Stone, once again, found himself at the center of controversy. The controversy made it impossible for Stone to get financing for a movie he wanted to make about Martin Luther King, Jr. In the post-*Nixon* years, Stone moved on to directing films on less controversial topics. *U-Turn* (1997), the story of a small-time gambler (Sean Penn) caught in a series of bizarre events in an Arizona town, is notable mainly for being the only film Stone has directed that he neither wrote nor cowrote. In *Any Given Sunday* (1999) Stone examined professional football, a passionate interest of his since childhood. Stone also returned to screenwriting, cowriting the script for *Evita* (1997), and he revised the novel he had written as a young man, *A Child's Night Dream*, published by St. Martin's Press in 1997.

Oliver Stone has created a body of films that, taken collectively, serves as an account of American history in the second half of the 20th century, although it is history as told from Stone's unique and controversial point of view. And despite his critics, Stone also has his champions, who have recognized him as an artist and as someone who has made history as well as recorded it. Garry Wills has called Stone an American Dostoyevsky, and Michael L. Kurtz, writing in *Oliver Stone's USA,* has said that except for *Uncle Tom's Cabin,* "*JFK* probably had a greater direct impact on public opinion than any other work of art in American history."

References Beaver, Frank, *Oliver Stone: Wakeup Cinema* (New York: Twayne, 1994); Kunz, Don, ed., *The Films of Oliver Stone* (Lanham, Md.: Scarecrow Press, 1997); Mackey-Kallis, Susan, *Oliver Stone's America: "Dreaming the Myth Outward"* (Boulder, Colo.: Westview Press, 1996); Riordan, James, *Stone: The Controversies, Excesses, and Exploits of a Radical Filmmaker* (New York: Hyperion, 1995); Toplin, Robert Brent, ed., *Oliver Stone's USA: Film, History, and Controversy* (Lawrence: University of Kansas Press, 2000).

—D.M.W.

Stroheim, Erich Oswald (von) (1885–1957)

Although he is secure in his position as one of America's greatest, if flawed, geniuses, von Stroheim's extravagant vision, protean gifts, and mordant sensibility, were continually at odds with the conventions and restrictions of the Hollywood establishment. So successful was he in creating his own aristocratic background for the sake of the press and his public, that only recently in pioneering biographies by Richard Kozarski and Arthur Lennig has the truth about his origins come to light. He was born in Vienna on September 22, 1885, as Erich Oswald Stroheim, the son of a Jewish hat manufacturer. Restless with his middle-class upbringing, the 24-year-old young man immigrated to America, where he arrived at Ellis Island in 1909. He knew little English and had few qualifications for employment. After knocking around New York City, drifting in and out of odd jobs like waiting on tables and handling horses for the New York National Guard, he departed for San Francisco, where he began writing play scripts. In Los Angeles three years later he began

appearing as an extra and a walk-on in several DAVID WARK GRIFFITH shorts.

From those humble beginnings it was a swift trajectory to his first screen credit (a villain, of course), technical adviser to John Emerson (one of Griffith's "lieutenants"), and featured roles as the "horrible Hun" in World War I–era films. It was at this time that he began taking an active part in fashioning a screen image as "the man you love to hate," complete with the aristocratic background (he had added the "von" to his name upon his arrival in America, christening himself "Erich Oswald Hans Carl Maria von Stroheim"), monocle, shaved head, stiff postures, and sardonic manner that would remain his image for years to come. As biographer Arthur Lennig puts it, he possessed "the supreme confidence of a man who knew he would ascend the heights of his own invention." But directing was his chief ambition, and after the war he gate-crashed Universal studios, where he wrote, directed, and starred in his own script, *The Pinnacle* (the title was changed to *Blind Husbands* and released in 1918). The story of a continental adventurer's attempted seduction of an American wife (Francilia Billington) in the Tyrolean Alps was regarded as shockingly sophisticated and was promptly dubbed one of the finest films of the year. Von Stroheim's deployment of sexual symbols (the mountain peak upon which von Stroheim and his rival contend, for example), wickedly suggestive references to adulterous behavior and licentious activities, and the theme of the sexual awakening of a neglected American wife in Europe were unusual at the time—and they would only grow more daring as the 1920s wore on. After *The Devil's Passkey* (1919), another morality fable of an ingenuous American woman caught up in continental intrigues, von Stroheim's standing at Universal rose. Thus, he was in a position to begin work on his first true epic, *Foolish Wives,* a film that ultimately involved a two-year shooting schedule, a budget of almost $2 million, the construction of a costly Monte Carlo setting, an insistence on absolute realism in props and details, and the inordinate length of 30 reels. The story—by now familiar in the von Stroheim canon—of an American woman deceived by the wiles of con artist—here, "Count" Wladyslaw Sergius Karamzin (Stroheim)—was eventually cut to 10 reels and released to critical cavils and a disappointing box office.

Reined in by the "boy wonder" producer Irving Thalberg, von Stroheim was taken off his next picture, *The Merry-Go-Round* (finished by Rupert Julian in 1922). He left to join the new Goldwyn Company, where he directed his first picture with an American location, his masterpiece *Greed*. More ink has been spilled about this legendary film—its relentless realism, brilliant cinematography, extraordinary length (forcing massive cuts from 10 hours to 80 minutes for public release), and crippling impact on Stroheim's subsequent career—that an entire book by Herman Weinberg has been devoted to its reconstruction. Stroheim was determined to translate Frank Norris's 1898 novel *McTeague*—a gritty tale of a dysfunctional marriage between a lumpen dentist, McTeague, and the innocent Trina (played by Gibson Gowland and ZaSu Pitts in the film) that ends in a fatal struggle for a hoard of gold—as closely and in as much detail as possible (it is the only film Stroheim made whose source was not original). Accordingly, he took his production unit to locations in San Francisco and Death Valley, where the novel was set. However, claims that Stroheim filmed the story "page by page" are mistaken; actually, as Herman Weinberg points out, he made the novel more complex, "developing it into a work of many more layers than the author intended," like the deployment of parallel subplots and the addition of Trina's celebrated nightmare sequences. Moreover, the deep-focus mise-en-scène added to the complexities of the visual field. Cameramen William Daniels and Ben Reynolds achieved a depth of field that permitted composition in depth—allowing multiple events to transpire within the same frame—a striking departure from the soft-focus techniques common at the time.

The butchered version released to the public was a disaster at the box office and elicited damning critical attacks (one trade paper wrote it was "the filthiest, vilest, most putrid picture in the history of the motion picture business"). Recently, a four-hour reconstruction was prepared by Rick Schmidlin for broadcast on the Turner Classic Movie channel. It featured a variety of materials, including surviving footage from the initial release version, the final shooting script of March 31, 1923, and the large number of scene stills taken by the Goldwyn camera department. Most striking was the restoration by cinematographer Allen Daviau of von Stroheim's selective use of color in the otherwise black-and-white film. As reported by Richard Koszarski, von Stroheim utilized the so-called Handschiegel Process to impart a yellow hue to brass, gilded, and gold objects—a canary, gold teeth, picture frames, coins, a bedstead, etc. This contributed a certain fantastic, allegorical aspect to the film, representative of Trina's deranged mental state and the "disease" of greed in general. "A film long revered for its stark black-and-white photography must now be discussed for its use of color," declares Koszarski.

Because his contract with Goldwyn had been a multipicture deal, Stroheim was allowed to write and direct *The Merry Widow* (1925), a loose and opulent adaptation of Franz Lehár's operetta that seemed more bent on visualizing the wicked underside of Viennese life than its frothy surface. Life on the set was fraught with production cost overruns and tensions between Stroheim and temperamental actress Mae Murray. Somewhat surprisingly, however, just when Stroheim's career appeared finished, the film was a hit at the box office. His newfound clout enabled him to sign on with independent producer Pat Powers to star in and direct his most romantic film, *The Wedding March,* a nostalgic evocation of the Hapsburg era of prewar Vienna. Here, Stroheim portrays Prince Nicki, torn between his greedy opportunism to marry a rich heiress (ZaSu Pitts) and his genuine infatuation with a poor young musician (Fay

Wray). Before the ambitious picture could be completed, funds ran out, and the film was released in truncated form in 1928. (Again, Herman Weinberg has reconstructed it in a lavishly illustrated book.) Even more disastrous was another independent project, *Queen Kelly,* financed by Joseph P. Kennedy and produced by Gloria Swanson. The lurid tale of a Ruritanian convent girl who inherits a brothel in German East Africa was never completed, and it was released thereafter only in fragmentary form. It was to have been his most bizarre tale, depicting what Weinberg describes as an "incestuous universe with its solemn boredom, its degeneracies and absolute power, its complacency and unpunished complicities—a universe evolved for the creation of monsters, psychotics, victims, slaves, lackeys." Biographer Richard Kozarski has painstakingly reassembled the various scripts, notes, and fragments of film in his book, *The Man You Loved to Hate,* and in a documentary film.

Von Stroheim's Hollywood career was now virtually ended. After a few pitiful attempts at acting in pictures directed by others (*The Great Gabbo* [1930]) and a disastrous attempt to make a talking picture, *Walking Down Broadway* (it opened in 1933 under the title *Hello, Sister!*), Stroheim never would direct again until near the end of his life in 1957. Instead, during the 1930s and most of the 1940s he clung to a precarious existence, acting in a few good pictures (Renoir's *The Grand Illusion* [1937], Billy Wilder's *Five Graves to Cairo* [1944]) and more than a few bad ones (*The Mask of Dijon*). In 1950, with the part of Max von Mayerling, a chauffeur to a fading silent film actress (Gloria Swanson), in Wilder's *Sunset Boulevard,* his career revived somewhat, and he appeared occasionally in European films until his death on May 12, 1957, of cancer.

In his loving and painstaking biography, Arthur Lennig notes, "In his films, he fused art and reality, myth and naturalistic detail, love and lust, idealism and cynicism, discipline and unbelievable excess. In the process, he became the legend that he had created: Erich von Stroheim." André Bazin's assessment is particularly cogent: "[Stroheim's] reality lays itself bare like a suspect confessing under the relentless examination of the commissioner of police. Take a close look at the world, keep on doing so, and in the end it will lay bare for you all its cruelty and its ugliness."

References Koszarski, Richard, *The Man You Loved to Hate* (New York: Oxford University Press, 1983); Koszarski, Richard, "Reconstructing Greed," *Film Comment* 35, no. 6 (November–December 1999): 10–15; Lennig, Arthur, *Stroheim* (University Press of Kentucky, 2000); Weinberg, Herman, *The Complete "Greed"* (New York: Arno Press, 1972); Weinberg, Herman, *The Complete "Wedding March"* (Boston: Little, Brown and Company, 1974).

—J.C.T.

Sturges, Preston (1898–1959) Edmond Preston Biden was born on August 29, 1898, in Chicago, Illinois, the son of Edmond C. Biden and Mary Dempsey. The marriage between Preston's father and mother soon collapsed and Mary, after living in Paris, France, for several years with young Preston, returned to the United States and married the wealthy Chicago stockbroker, Solomon Sturges. In 1902 Solomon legally adopted Preston, changing his name to Preston Sturges. An arrangement allowed Mary and Preston to live six months of the year in Paris and six in Chicago. Preston attended several schools in his childhood, primarily private schools such as Lycée Janson in Paris, L'École des Roches in Normandy, and La Villa Lausanne in Switzerland. Preston served in the Army Signal Corps during World War I and was stationed in Texas, Tennessee, and Florida. After the war Preston married Estelle de Wolfe Mudge and began a career as a freelance inventor. He also composed songs for Tin Pan Alley. While hospitalized for acute appendicitis, Preston bought a book on playwriting and proceeded to write a comic operetta about surgery. His first produced play was *The Guinea Pig* at the Wharf Theatre in

Provincetown, New York, which had a one-week run starting July 13, 1928. Sturges's first major success was a three-act comedy, *Strictly Dishonorable,* which opened on Broadway on September 18, 1929. The play received good reviews and ran for 64 performances. His subsequent playwriting efforts, however, were considered financial flops. While in New York, Sturges adapted two plays for Paramount studios' New York offices, having spent the money he had received from the production of *Strictly Dishonorable.* In 1932 he moved to California and began work as a screenwriter.

The Power and the Glory (1933) was his first original screenplay for Fox studios. The film was noted for a technical device advertised as "narratage," in actuality voice-over narration. The story begins at the funeral of a suicide and is recounted in numerous flashbacks by several characters, a device that is also utilized effectively in ORSON GEORGE WELLES's *Citizen Kane* (1941). From 1934 to 1936 the writer kept busy adapting several works for various studios, among them: *Thirty-Day Princess, Imitation of Life, We Live Again* (1934), *The Good Fairy, Diamond Jim* (1935), and *Next Time We Love* (1936). In 1937 Sturges wrote *Easy Living,* a screenplay that most resembles his later efforts. Ray Cywinski notes that the film "exhibits many of Sturges's later trademarks: the theme of sudden and fortuitous wealth, mistaken identity, miraculous occurrences, the rip-snorting dialogue, the comically misspoken foreigner, and the unabashed use of slapstick." In 1938 Sturges adapted *Port of Seven Seas* (MGM), based on Marcel Pagnol's Marseilles trilogy, and Justin McCarthy's *If I Were King* (Paramount). His final screenplay as a screenwriter solely was *Remember the Night* (Paramount [1939]).

In 1940 Sturges became one of the first screenwriter/directors when he negotiated an arrangement with Paramount to direct his original screenplay *The Great McGinty* (originally titled *The Mantle of Dignity*). Sturges sold them the screenplay for $10 with the proviso that he direct the picture. The surprise hit of the season, Sturges

was hailed as a boy genius and received the Academy Award for best screenplay. More importantly, he allowed for further transitions from screenwriter to director by talents such as John Huston and Billy Wilder.

Sturges's follow-up to *The Great McGinty* was a modestly produced comedy called *Christmas in July* (1940), starring Dick Powell and Ellen Drew. This in turn gave way to two comedies that established Preston Sturges as a leading director in Hollywood in the forties. The first, *The Lady Eve* (1940), starred Barbara Stanwyck and Henry Fonda. Regarded by some as the quintessential Sturges film, it concerns the battle of the sexes and mistaken identity. The second, *Sullivan's Travels* (1941), was a satire of Hollywood that starred Joel McCrea and Veronica Lake. Although many American critics were divided over *Sullivan's Travels,* the Europeans have hailed it as one of Sturges's most important works. *The Palm Beach Story* (1942) also starred Joel McCrea along with Claudette Colbert, in one of the director's best screwball comedies. Two wartime comedies concerned homefront America and are among the director's most biting satires: *The Miracle of Morgan's Creek* (1944) and *Hail the Conquering Hero* (1944). It is a wonder that *The Miracle of Morgan's Creek* ever made it past the Hays Office since it concerns a young pregnant girl (played by Betty Hutton) and her attempts to find out who made her pregnant. All of Sturges's output had been produced and released through Paramount. But even though his films were all box-office successes and made the studio a considerable profit, especially *The Miracle of Morgan's Creek,* contract negotiations fell through and Sturges left the studio in late 1943.

He began a disastrous association with Howard Hughes in an enterprise called California Pictures Corporation in February 1944. The association ended in 1946, with the sole result being the film titled *The Sin of Harold Diddlebock,* starring silent-film comedian Harold Lloyd, and not released by Hughes until 1950 (under a new title, *Mad Wednesday*). Sturges's decline was as precipitous as his rise.

For Darryl F. Zanuck and 20th Century-Fox he made *Unfaithfully Yours* (1947), which starred Rex Harrison as a symphony conductor who believes his wife is having an affair and fantasizes about her death. And he made his only color film, a western parody with Betty Grable called *The Beautiful Blonde from Bashful Bend* (1949). Both films received mediocre reviews and did poorly at the box office. Broke and with creditors at his heels, Sturges fled to Paris and lived the life of an expatriate. Back in America he died from a heart attack on August 6, 1959, in his room at New York's Algonquin Hotel while working on his autobiography, the last entry of which read, "These ruminations, and the beer and coleslaw that I washed down while dictating them, are giving me a bad case of indigestion. Over the years though, I have suffered so many attacks of indigestion that I am well versed in the remedy: ingest a little Maalox, lie down, stretch out, and hope to God I don't croak."

Other Films As director: *The Great Moment* (1942); *Les Carnets du Major Thompson* (1955), released in the United States as *The French They Are A Funny Race* (1957).

References Cywinski, Ray, *Preston Sturges: A Guide to References and Resources* (Boston: G.K. Hall, 1984); Jacobs, Diane, *Christmas in July: The Life and Art of Preston Sturges* (Berkeley: University of California Press, 1992); Sturges, Preston, *Preston Sturges by Preston Sturges* (New York: Simon and Schuster, 1990).

—R.W.

Tarantino, Quentin (1963–) Hailed by many critics as the greatest American director since MARTIN SCORSESE, and detested with equal fervor by a number of others, Quentin Tarantino is perhaps the most audacious, controversial director of the 1990s. He is largely responsible for creating his own, mythic biography, relying on relentless self-promotion when not letting his movies speak for themselves. With the success of *Pulp Fiction* (1994), he almost single-handedly turned the so-called independent film into a valuable, money-making commodity, sending all of the major studios scrambling to align themselves with independent, art-house distributors for both the prestige and economy of the field. Tarantino has been a divisive figure throughout the decade, accused of no less than outright theft by some critics (the striking similarities of his *Reservoir Dogs* [1992] to Hong Kong director RINGO LAM's *City on Fire* [1987]), yet he has inspired many (lesser) imitators, garnered legions of fans, and won the Palme d'Or at Cannes and an Academy Award for best original screenplay (both for *Pulp Fiction*).

Born March 27, 1963, in Knoxville, Tennessee, Tarantino was soon transported with his single mother to Los Angeles. He never finished high school, preferring instead to concentrate his ener-

gies on acting. Landing small roles on television (he was an Elvis impersonator on an episode of *The Golden Girls*), he took acting classes and worked at Video Archives in Manhattan Beach, California. While he never went to film school, his time away from the video store was spent watching countless films and absorbing film techniques, dialogue riffs, and the general arcane knowledge that comes with seeing so many films. This fact has by now become myth, allowing video clerks everywhere to believe that they can make it just like Tarantino. It was during his time at Video Archives that he completed his first screenplay, *True Romance,* in 1987. Along with his coworker Roger Avary, an early friend and collaborator, he attempted to get financial backing to film the script. Unsuccessful after several years' attempts, he nonetheless completed another screenplay, *Natural Born Killers,* later optioned and made by OLIVER STONE as a violence-fueled satire on media culture (Tarantino has unsuccessfully attempted to remove his name from the credits.) Tarantino eventually sold *True Romance* to Warner Bros. for $50,000, planning to use the money to finance the filming of another screenplay he had written, called *Reservoir Dogs,* this one centered around a group of criminals who flee a botched jewelry heist.

Pulp Fiction director Quentin Tarantino (left) with producer Lawrence Bender (Miramax)

Though his first attempts at filming proved unsuccessful, the script for *Reservoir Dogs* made its way to Harvey Keitel. Keitel fell in love with the script and agreed to star in the film, which allowed for $1.5 million in financial backing from LIVE Entertainment, as well as access to quality character actors, including Lawrence Tierney, Steve Buscemi, and Tim Roth. *Dogs* was the talk of the 1992 Sundance Film Festival, causing an immediate sensation with the film's brutal violence and hip, self-conscious dialogue. While the film performed only modestly at the box office, taking in just under $2 million, it acquired cult status once released on video. Banking that they had made a major discovery, Miramax, who distributed *Dogs,* financially backed Tarantino's next project. An ambitious, sprawling rendition of three interwoven tales, *Pulp Fiction* (1994) went on to become one of the most successful films of the 1990s. The film's cultural cachet led many A-list stars to the independent cinema realm, and also sent Hollywood studios hunting for the next big independent success story. While this has been a cause for alarm to some within the independent community, it has also provided opportunities to many filmmakers who, for better or worse, would

simply not have a chance had the film not been such a major hit.

Tarantino followed up *Pulp Fiction* with a segment for the anthology film, *Four Rooms,* based on Roald Dahl's short story, "Man from the South." His next feature was a tribute to the blaxploitation pictures that he grew up watching. *Jackie Brown* (1997) is based on an Elmore Leonard novel, *Rum Punch,* and stars blaxploitation icon Pam Grier as the title character who is forced to outsmart a gun runner and federal agents if she is to stay out of jail or avoid being killed. The film is less audacious than his others, but also more mature in its pacing and characterizations. While sticking close to his themes of "deceit, trust, and cunning among small-time crooks . . . he gives the familiar material a distinctive feel through profane street lingo, soul and funk music, and other pop artifacts."

While many critics have tired of his acting performances in mediocre films, few can deny that Quentin Tarantino is a masterful manipulator of popular culture. In full command of his directorial talent, he has also used the media to mythologize himself, to create his own star, which shines as brightly as that of any Hollywood actor today.

References Woods, Paul A., *King Pulp: The Wild World of Quentin Tarantino* (London: Plexus, 1998); Clarkson, Wensley, *Quentin Tarantino: Shooting from the Hip* (Woodstock, N.Y.: Overlook Press, 1995); Dawson, Jeff, *Quentin Tarantino: The Cinema of Cool* (New York: Applause, 1995); Bernard, Jami, *Quentin Tarantino: The Man and His Movies* (New York: HarperPerennial, 1995); Barnes, Alan, and Marcus Hearn, *Tarantino A to Zed: The Films of Quentin Tarantino* (North Pomfret, Vt.: B.T. Batsford, 1996).

—J.A.

Tourneur, Maurice (1876–1961) Sadly neglected today, Maurice Tourneur was one of the most literate and pictorially gifted producers and directors of the silent cinema. He was born Maurice Thomas in Paris on February 2, 1876. His father was a jeweler and his siblings were active in the Parisian theatrical world. After completing his education at Lycée Condorcet at age 18, he served in the French artillery in the late 1890s. He worked as an assistant to sculptor Auguste Rodin and the painter Puvis de Chavannes and briefly pursued a variety of career choices, including illustrator, interior designer, stage director with the legendary realist theatrical producer André Antoine, and actor (when he adopted his pseudonym). After directing several films for the Éclair studio after 1911—where *The Lunatics* (aka *Le Système du Docteur Goudron et du Professeur Plume* [1912]) and *Waxworks* (*Figures de cire* [1912]) revealed his talent for whimsy and the bizarre—he immigrated to the United States in 1914, where he became head of a small studio Éclair had established in Fort Lee, New Jersey; and later a director for Artcraft and production head of the Paragon studio.

He quickly distinguished himself as a director of a series of visually sophisticated dramas and light comedies adapted from literary properties, including three of the most distinguished and technically adroit films of the time, *The Wishing Ring* (1914), *Alias, Jimmy Valentine* (1915), and *Trilby* (1915). The two films he did with Mary Pickford and scenarist Frances Marion, *Poor Little Rich Girl* (1916) and *The Pride of the Clan* (1917), effectively launched the peak years of Pickford's spectacular career. *Poor Little Rich Girl,* particularly, established the "little girl" image that would be repeated with minor variations in the rest of her films. The highlight of the picture was the extended dream sequence wherein Pickford's character of eight-year-old Gwendolyn travels through a Land of Dreams, populated by all manner of whimsical characters and bizarre animals. Tourneur's experience in stylized graphic and stage design, and his rich visual sense and camera savvy, came into full play in this sequence. In 1918 he formed his own production company, after which he formed Associated Producers, Inc., with THOMAS HARPER INCE. By this time Tourneur had collected a team of superior creative artists and technicians, like writers Charles El Whittaker and Charles Maigne, designer Ben

Carre, and cameramen John van den Broek and CLARENCE BROWN. From this fertile period came a careful adaptation of Henrik Ibsen's *A Doll's House* (1918); another piece of whimsy a la *Poor Little Rich Girl,* an adaptation of Maurice Maeterlinck's stage fairy tale, *The Blue Bird* (1918); and three masterful adaptations of literary classics, *Treasure Island* (1920), with Lon Chaney as Long John Silver, *Last of the Mohicans* (1921), and *Lorna Doone* (1922).

Although he became a U.S. citizen in 1921, he considered his American career finished after quitting the direction of *The Mysterious Island* in 1926. He returned to Europe where he made his last silent film, *The Ship of the Lost Men* (*Das schiff der verlorenen Menschen* [1929]), and 20 sound films, including *Volpone* (1940) and *La Main du diable* (1942). After losing a leg in a car accident in 1949, he retired into seclusion, devoting most of his time to translating detective novels from English to French. He died on August 4, 1961, survived by his talented son, Jacques, who after serving as an editor on his father's films, went on to direct many distinguished films, including *The Cat People* (1942), *Out of the Past* (1947), and *Curse of the Demon* (1957).

Whimsy and visually sophisticated fantasy were Tourneur's great gifts to the cinema. "We are not mere photographers," he said, "we are artists. At least I hope so. We must put on the screen, not literal reality, but an effect which will stimulate a mental and emotional reaction in the audience." Two of Tourneur's most enthusiastic admirers, William K. Everson and Kevin Brownlow, have continued to keep his memory and work alive in the face of contemporary neglect. Historian/preservationist/producer Brownlow declared that Tourneur was "one of the men who introduced visual beauty to the American screen."

Other Films *Monsieur Lecocq* (1914); *Le Mystère de la chambre jaune* (1914); *The Pit* (1914); *Human Driftwood* (1915); *The Pawn of Fate* (1916); *Barbary Sheep, Barbary Sheep* (1916); *The Rise of Jennie Cushing* (1916); *A Doll's House* (1918); *Prunella* (1918); *The Life Line* (1919); *Deep Waters* (1920); *The Isle of Lost Ships* (1923); *Torment*

(1924); *Aloma of the South Seas* (1926); *Le Voleur* (1934); *Königsmark* (1936); *Après l'amour* (1947).

References Brownlow, Kevin, *The Parade's Gone By* (New York: Knopf, 1968); Everson, William K., *The American Silent Cinema* (New York: Oxford University Press, 1984); Tibbetts, John C., "An Interview with Kevin Brownlow," *American Classic Screen* 5, no. 2 (1979): 24–28.

—J.C.T.

Truffaut, François (1932–1984) One of the principal architects of the French New Wave, François Truffaut effortlessly straddled the disparate domains of art and commercial cinema throughout his successful career. He was born in Paris on February 6, 1932, to Janine de Monferrand, an unwed mother, and legally adopted by Roland Truffaut the following October. He was an only child and, as biographers Antoine de Becque and Serge Toubiana have observed, an unwanted one. At age three he was taken into the home of his maternal grandparents. After the death of his beloved grandmother, he returned to his parents a shy, inordinately sensitive and introverted child. After attending the Lycée Rollin, and indulging himself on a regular diet of books and films, he organized a film club, the Cercle Cinémane (the Movie Mania Circle) in the late 1940s. The weekly screenings quickly plunged the young cineaste into debt. Forced to close the club, he was incarcerated for nonpayment of debts. To the rescue came critic and polemicist André Bazin, who took the young man under his wing and hired him as his personal secretary, a job that enabled him to live independently of his parents.

As a result of his membership in the film society, Objectif 49, he met a cherished circle of film devotees and artists, including Alexandre Astruc, ERIC ROHMER, Jacques Rivette, CLAUDE CHABROL, ROBERT BRESSON, and JEAN COCTEAU. It was an exciting but hectic time for the troubled, hypersensitive Truffaut, who, despairing of his lack of direction and funds and bored with journalism, unsuccessfully attempted suicide in 1950. Worse,

he enlisted in the army that October. Immediately, he regretted his decision, and he deserted on the eve of his departure for Saigon in what was then known as French Indochina. Despite efforts by Bazin to win his exoneration, Truffaut was incarcerated for his desertion and ordered to rejoin the army. Again he deserted, and again he was arrested and imprisoned, at which time he attempted suicide a second time. Finally, in February 1952, he was released from the service. He moved in with the Bazins and quickly resumed his relationships with the circle of young film enthusiasts, which included writing his first articles for Bazin's journal, *Cahiers du cinéma,* which had been founded in April 1951. A year later he teamed with Jacques Rivette and ALAIN RESNAIS to make short, 16-mm films. From 1956 to 1958 he assisted ROBERTO ROSSELLINI.

A short film, *Les Mistons* (1957), established at the outset of Truffaut's career most of the major themes of his life and work, that is, the fascination with women, the bittersweet maturation of the child into the adult, the obsession with memory, the gulf between observation and experience. Throughout the film, an adult narrative voice recalls the fascination of a gang of young boys with the doings of a nubile young woman (Bernadette Lafont): "Bernadette was too beautiful; we couldn't forgive her for it. She rode everywhere with her bare legs and billowing skirt. For us she was the wondrous incarnation of our secret dreams. She was our awakening to a world of luminous sensuality. . . . Too young to love Bernadette, we decided to hate her, and to torment her love." The many incidents and details of the boys' "chase" yield unforgettable moments—like the boys' sniffing of Bernadette's recently vacated bicycle seat, an erotically charged game of tennis, a "game of life and death" in an amphitheater—are nothing more or less than a series of "precious moments that enslave us all." Such arrested moments and memories, captured and rendered permanent on film (like the images of yearning immortalized in Keats's "Ode on a Grecian Urn"), clearly haunt, even obsess Truffaut and testify to his passion (I use the term advisedly) for cinema. Indeed, the clearest indication of this can be seen in one of his later films, *The Green Room* (*La Chambre verte* [1978]), wherein it is Truffaut himself who portrays a man who has memorialized his life and friends in a candlelit chapel filled with photographs of the past (including portraits of JEAN VIGO and Bazin).

His breakthrough year was 1959, when he emerged a primary force in the launching of the so-called French New Wave with his direction of *The Four Hundred Blows* (*Les Quatre cents coups*) and his conception of the story idea for JEAN-LUC GODARD's *Breathless* (aka *A Bout de souffle*). *The Four Hundred Blows* remains one of the most remarkable feature-film debuts in film history. Moreover, as historian Richard T. Jameson notes, it "did more than any other single film to focus attention on the [New Wave], and to make the way easier for dozens of cinematic confreres, talented and not-so-talented, to mount their own projects." It was not so much a definite rejection of the French cinema's traditions and practices, but a brash revisioning of those traditions and a search for a more personalized kind of cinema. Largely autobiographical, and to a degree an homage to Jean Vigo's *Zero for Conduct* (1933), it chronicled the alienation and thwarted hopes of a sensitive young man, Antoine Doinel (Jean-Pierre Léaud), who is neglected by his parents and subsequently incarcerated in a reform school for petty theft. Among its most memorable moments are a trip to an amusement park centrifuge, the boys' breaking away from their formal school outing, Antoine's direct-to-camera interview with a reform school counselor, and, of course, the heart-stopping freeze frame that concludes the film as Doinel's flight from the school is turned back by the sea's breakers. Doinel (and, by implication, Léaud and Truffaut) grew up in four more films, as the shy adolescent suitor in the "Antoine et Colette" episode of *Love at Twenty* (1962); as an older but still confused young man in *Stolen Kisses* (*Baiser volés* [1968]); as a newly married husband in *Bed*

and Board (*Domicile conjugal* [1970]); and as a divorced author whose book looks back on the entire Doinel saga (as filmed by Truffaut) in *Love on the Run* (*L'Amour en fuite* [1979]). As Gerald Mast has noted of this autobiographical cycle, "Truffaut deliberately collapses the distinction between written fiction and filmed fiction, between the real life of humans and the fictional life of characters."

The Four Hundred Blows was quickly followed by two more films—all exceptional in their utilization of the wide-screen process—that consolidated his growing international reputation. *Shoot the Piano Player* (*Tirez sur le pianiste* [1960]) was a free-wheeling evocation of the American "B" films of the 1940s, brimming with visual puns, jump cuts, allusions to genres like the detective film and the film noir, and abrupt contrasts in mood and tone. Biographer Annette Insdorf describes it as a "glorious exercise in free verse . . . jumping from comedy to tragedy, from ridiculous gangsters to real guns, comic timidity to an impotence of action that kills the two women and Charlie [the eponymous 'pianist']. The film is as unpredictable as experience itself—crazy at some moments, poignant at others; all that is certain is movement and change." With *Jules and Jim* (1961), a story of a menage à trois in the years before, during, and after World War I, Truffaut wrought his most poignant and beautiful work, superbly buoyed up by Georges Delerue's lyric score. The simple song voiced by Catherine (Jeanne Moreau)—just one of the many "Women as Other" in Truffaut's films—to the two men who share her love (Oskar Werner and Henri Serre) refers to life's "whirlpool of days"—one of the countless references, carefully enumerated by Roger Greenspun in his commentary on the film, to circles, whether they be the repetitive symmetries of experience, of camera movements, or of images themselves.

All of Truffaut's films reflect his private and public passions. His love of the arts, especially cinema, was a constant preoccupation. "When I was a critic," Truffaut wrote, "I thought that a film, to be successful, must express simultaneously an *idea of the world* and an *idea of the cinema.*" *La Nuit américaine* (*Day for Night* [1973]) is a loving tribute to the filmmaking process, in which Truffaut himself portrayed the film director. He also acted in central roles in *The Wild Child* (*L'enfant sauvage* [1969]) and *The Green Room* (*La Chambre verte* [1978]). *Fahrenheit 451* (1966) was a futuristic fantasy adapted from Ray Bradbury's nightmarish warning of the consequences of censorship and book burning. *The Bride Wore Black* (*La Mariée était en noir* [1967]) is as much about Truffaut's love of Hitchcock's films as it is a thriller adapted from the work of Cornell Woolrich. Other films continue his preoccupation with the themes of estranged children and the erotic fascination of women. *The Wild Child* (*L'Enfant sauvage* [1969]) enabled Truffaut to reverse the dynamic of his tutelage under Bazin and portray a dedicated doctor who takes charge of the education of a feral child. And *The Man Who Loved Women* (*L'Homme qui aimait les femmes* [1977]) cast actor Charles Denner as a Truffaut-like character erotically obsessed with the many women passing in and out of his life.

Rarely overtly political, like his colleague Godard (with whom he had a falling out late in life), he did direct the sublime *The Last Metro* (*Le Dernier métro* [1980]), an evocation of the French Resistance in Nazified Paris, and a testament to the value of the brittle artifice of art in relieving humanity of the burden of an otherwise unrelentingly harsh, cruel, and mortal world. Also unlike Godard, Truffaut consistently cleaved to the "old-fashioned" mode of the storytelling film in the tradition of his beloved JEAN RENOIR, who, as Truffaut noted, juxtaposed "the bitterness of the gay moments [with] the clownishness of the sad," who suffused his work with lyric style and an all-embracing compassion. Moreover, like Renoir, the narrative line itself was usually digressive, spontaneous, and unconfined. As Jameson has noted, "Truffaut came to personify the freedom of directors to detour from the strictest courses dictated by scriptoral logic, to mix moods and modes, to allow the pearly surface of illusion to be ruptured for a moment if some felicitous accident of personality or of the filmmaking process itself yielded a more engaging spectacle."

Among his critical writings is the seminal "A Tendency in the French Cinema" (1952), which introduced his ideas of the auteur theory (*the politique des auteurs*), which held that certain visionary directors—particularly Renoir, Vigo, Tati, HOWARD WINCHESTER HAWKS, JOHN FORD, and ORSON GEORGE WELLES—had demonstrated how directors could impose their "signature," or authorial stamp, onto their films. These ideas came to American and English critics in the 1960s via the writings of Andrew Sarris and Robin Wood. This theoretical position resulted in Truffaut's advocating a renewal in fresh subject matter and shooting methods, writing his own stories and scenarios, shooting rapidly and economically, and consistently using the same ensemble of actors and technicians from film to film.

After completing *Confidentially Yours,* Truffaut was diagnosed with an incurable brain tumor. "Film critics were twenty years ahead of official medicine," he joked at the time, "for, as soon as my second film opened, they declared the film couldn't possibly have been made by someone whose brain was functioning normally." After dictating a portion of a draft of an autobiography, *The Script of My Life,* François Truffaut died in Paris, October 21, 1984. Biographers de Becque and Toubiana note that a post-burial ceremony with hundreds of candles burning in the nave of Saint-Roch recalled the scene in *The Green Room* where Julien Davenne, played by Truffaut, celebrated in his chapel of candles the cult of the dead. His many awards include best director at Cannes for *The Four Hundred Blows,* the Prix Louis Delluc, and an Academy Award for best foreign language film for *Day for Night.*

Other Films *The Soft Skin* (*La Peau douce* [1964]); *Mississippi Mermaid* (*La Sirène du Mississippi* [1969]); *Two English Girls* (aka *Les Deux Anglaises et le continent* [1971]); *Such a Gorgeous Kid Like Me* (*Une belle fille* *comme moi* [1972]); *Small Change* (*L'Argent de poche* [1976]); *Finally Sunday* (*Vivement dimanche,* aka *Confidentially Yours* [1984]).

References Allen, Don, *Truffaut* (New York: Viking Press, 1974); de Becque, Antoine, *Truffaut: A Biography* (New York: Knopf, 1999); Greenspun, Roger, "Elective Affinities: Aspects of *Jules et Jim,*" *Sight and Sound* 32, no. 2 (Spring 1963): 78–82; Insdorf, Annette, *Francois Truffaut* (New York: Simon and Schuster, 1989); Jameson, Richard T., "Wild Child, Movie Master," *Film Comment* (February 1985): 34–39; Rabourdin, Dominique, comp., *Truffaut by Truffaut* (New York: Harry N. Abrams, 1987); Spielberg, Steven, "He Was the Movies," *Film Comment* (February 1985): 40–41.

—J.C.T.

Varda, Agnès (1928–) Known primarily for only a handful of films, Agnès Varda's career spans almost a half-century of sporadic activity, from the days just prior to the French New Wave up to the present. She was born on May 30, 1928, in Ixelles, Belgium, of a Greek father and a French mother. She grew up in Sète, a small seaport town on the western Mediterranean coast of France, near Montpellier. After attending the College de Sète, Varda studied literature at the Sorbonne in Paris. Unhappy with her studies, she accepted a post as official photographer to the Théâtre National Populaire in 1951, where she remained for 10 years. In between assignments she directed her first feature film in 1955, *La Pointe courte*. It juxtaposes the struggle of local fishermen against the big fishing companies with a young man's attempt to save a failing marriage. It was edited by Alain Resnais, who would soon be connected to the New Wave movement.

After making three short films for the French National Tourist Office, she directed her second feature, the classic *Cleo from Five to Seven* (*Cléo de cinq à sept* [1961]). Shot in real time, the film follows 90 minutes in the life of a pop singer (Corinne Marchand) while awaiting the results of a cancer test. The first half of the film follows Cleo home after a visit to a fortune teller; and the second half depicts Cleo interrupting a rehearsal to explore the Paris streets, where she strikes up a conversation with a soldier home on leave from the Algerian war. At the end, he accompanies her to the hospital for the test results. As biographer Alison Smith explains in her analysis of the film, the first half reveals that Cleo can construct her identity only through the eyes of others; and in the second she asserts her own identity and, instead of expecting others to look at *her,* she gazes out at the world that she now will negotiate on her own. The camera participates in this transformation: the viewer's gaze is directed *toward her* in the first half, and in the second half directed *subjectively outward* to construct the world through her eyes. *Cléo* won the Prix Méliès and became a much-admired international success.

The remainder of the 1960s saw a variety of film modes and subjects. The documentary *Salute to Cuba* (*Salut les cubains* [1964]) utilized 1,800 of Varda's own still photographs and won the Bronze Lion at the Venice Film Festival in 1964. *Le Bonheur* (*Happiness* [1965]) was a ravishingly photographed story of a happily married man who proposes that another woman live with him and his family. Among its many awards were the Prix Louis Delluc, the Silver Bear at Berlin, and the David Selznick Award in America. *Les Creatures* (1966) was a fantasy about a science fiction writer (Michel Piccoli) who goes to an island off the coast of Brittany to recover from a disabling automobile accident. He and his wife (Catherine Deneuve) meet a number of strange people on the island who become characters in the writer's next novel (or is it the other way around?). *Lion's Love* (1969) featured American avant-garde director Shirley Clarke in the role of a director who goes to Hollywood to make a movie. Reality and fantasy combine when real-life celebrities—Warhol superstar Viva and *Hair* authors Jerome Ragni and James Rado—intrude on the action; and even Varda herself appears on camera in the film-within-a-film.

In the 1970s Varda set up her own production company, Ciné-Tamaris, for which she wrote and directed *One Sings, the Other Doesn't* (*L'Une chante, autre pas* [1977]). Acclaimed by feminists, it is a species of agitprop street theater that depicts the relationship over 15 years between a feminist pop singer (Valerie Mairess) and a more conventional woman (Therese Liotard). "I wanted to create a solid friendship," said Varda, "based on real emotion, a young friendship accentuated by separation." Relocating to Hollywood for several years, Varda made two films, *Mural, Murals on the Wall* (*Mur Murs* [1980]) and *Documenteur: An Emotion Picture* (1981), a semi-autobiographical story of a female artist trying to come to terms with her young son (played by her real-life son, Mathieu).

After a series of short films in the 1980s she returned to features with *Vagabond* (*Sans toit ni loi* [1985]). Sandrine Bonnaire was cast as Mona, a homeless drifter who hitchhikes across the French countryside. The story is told in flashback after the discovery of Mona's dead body in a ditch. The bleak color palette and desultory pace accentuate the young woman's sense of alienation. Although hardly a crowd pleaser—no attempt is made to "explain" Mona's background and actions—it won a Golden Lion at the 1985 Venice Film Festival.

Jacquot de Nantes (1994) is one of three films in the 1990s concerning Varda's late husband, the French filmmaker JACQUES DEMY. It is both Varda's tribute to him and an attempt to link his formative years to his films. Demy had been one of the bright lights of the New Wave, gaining international acclaim with imaginative musicals like *The Umbrellas of Cherbourg* and *Lola*. When in middle age he learned he was dying, he agreed to allow his wife to photograph him while reminiscing about his childhood. Although they had never made a film together, *Jacquot* became their collaboration, a fairy tale wrought out of memories and fancies. The scenes of Demy's childhood in the city of Nantes—the monochrome years of World War II, the drab grays of the vocational school Jacquot attends, the scenes from his first clumsy home movies—are shot in black-and-white, intercut with images in color of Demy telling his story. Other color inserts allude to the life of the theater, a puppet show, a parade, an operetta; and still others are scenes from Demy's films. "Varda's film stands as the explicitly autobiographical film that Demy himself never made," writes biographer Smith, "and the complex transfer of memory which presided over its making is also the subject of the film." If the viewer is kept at an emotional distance from the subject, that has always been Varda's method. We are allowed to share her and Demy's memories, but ultimately we do not really *feel* them. The film is a lovely memento but, after all, it belongs to somebody else. . . .

The other two Demy-related films, *Les Demoiselles ont eu 25 ans* and *L'Univers de Jacques Demy* (1995–1996), approach their subject in a similar fashion from a variety of angles and in a mixture of memories and scenes from his films. In all, writes Alison Smith, this trilogy demonstrates that Varda "envisages memory as an active process; the past is something which has an active role in the present and which can be put to creative use as inspiration, not something to be nostalgically desired."

Varda's latest film is *Les 100 et 1 nuits* (1997), an anticommemoration, an acerbic meditation on the centenary of the cinema, that brings together allegorical figures representing figures in the cinema past. A central character, "M. Cinema," has lost his memory, but he admits that in its absence he uses his imagination. At the end, M. Cinema declares in a voice typifying Varda's typically anti-nostalgic nature, "Down with commemoration, long live anarchy; down with speeches, long live desire!"

Other Film *Daguerreotypes* (1975).

Reference Smith, Alison, *Agnes Varda* (Manchester: Manchester University Press, 1998).

—J.C.T.

Vidor, King (1894–1982) One of America's most enduring filmmakers, King Vidor's distinguished career spanned almost six decades and embraced every conceivable genre and subject. Vidor remembered Galveston, Texas, where he was born on February 8, 1894, as "a very cosmopolitan type of place, strange for Texas and strange for the United States," because of its European ethnic mix. "My grandfather was born in Budapest," Vidor told Nancy Dowd of the Directors Guild, "and came to America as the press representative and general manager of a prominent Hungarian violinist named Rimini" and stayed in New York "until the violinist returned to Hungary." His grandfather then migrated to Galveston, where he married and went into the cotton business. Vidor's father was in the lumber business, but Vidor became interested in photography and preferred not to pursue the family business. Later on, Vidor's father "sold out his interests in Galveston," moved to Hollywood, and helped his son "build the first studio I had."

Vidor attended the Peacock Military Academy in San Antonio and worked as a part-time projectionist for the first movie house in Galveston. He then wrote and directed several short films, including a two-reeler entitled *In Tow,* which was shown only in Galveston and Houston. From 1910 to 1915 he worked on "Weeklies," as newsreels were

then called, as a representative for *Mutual Weekly*. He bought a Model T Ford in 1915 and migrated to California, financing his trip by shooting footage for the Ford Motor Company, at 60 cents a foot. He then did odd jobs in California, working as an extra and writing scripts, the first of which, *When It Rains, It Pours,* sold for $30. He was learning about the industry from the ground up, working as a prop man at Universal, and finally becoming a writer in the shorts department and working as a cameraman for Judge Willis Brown on "some sort of travelogue," as he remembered it. Judge Brown gave him his first opportunity to direct.

Vidor's first Hollywood film was *The Turn in the Road* (1919), informed by his beliefs as a Christian Scientist. A year later he was hired by First National and then went to work for the Goldwyn studios in 1923. His first films for First National in 1920 were *The Jack-Knife Man,* adapted from a book by Ellis Parker Butler, and *The Family Honor.* Other journeyman work would follow: *The Sky Pilot* and *Love Never Dies* in 1921, for example; *Conquering the Woman* in 1922; *The Woman of Bronze,* with Clara Kimball Young, *Peg o' My Heart,* based on a popular play, with Laurette Taylor, and *Three Wise Fools,* also based on a play, starring Eleanor Boardman and ZaSu Pitts, in 1923; *His Hour,* an Elinor Glyn vehicle starring John Gilbert, and *Wine of Youth,* also with Eleanor Boardman and adapted from yet another play, in 1924.

Vidor's breakthrough picture, *The Big Parade,* a World War I drama written by Laurence Stallings and starring John Gilbert and Renee Adoree, was made at MGM in 1925 and was a tremendous box-office hit (in fact, the top-grossing silent film yet made). Vidor later described this film as the first part of a trilogy of American films, organized around three themes, War, Steel, and Wheat. The second film in this trilogy was *The Crowd* (1928), an urban drama concerning the rise and fall of an Everyman figure who struggles to establish and provide for his family. Vidor cast an unknown actor, James Murray, to play his Everyman "hero," and his method of filming scenes of city life with a concealed camera anticipated by over a decade the approaches and innovations of Cesare Zavattini and the Italian neorealists. The third film, *Our Daily Bread* (1934), came during the throes of the Great Depression and naively but sincerely suggested the idea of a collective farm as a means of survival for impoverished people. Its most memorable moments come in a climactic montage sequence when commune members work together to dig a ditch in order to irrigate their failing crops. Taken together, these three films represent Vidor's finest achievement as a significant American director.

In 1926 Vidor directed *La Boheme,* with Lillian Gish playing the lead. The studio was unable to buy the rights to the original opera, Vidor explained, "so we took a lot of material from a book called *La vie de la bohème* by Henri Murger," and told much of the story through flashbacks. Two Marion Davies comedies appeared in 1928, *The Patsy* and *Show People.* The latter, particularly, cast Davies as a naïve ingénue who has arrived in Hollywood in search of a movie career. It was a delightful satire on Hollywood hoopla and the star system and certainly reflected Vidor's own experiences in Hollywood.

Vidor's talking picture breakthroughs came with *Hallelujah!* (1929) and *Street Scene* (1931). The former featured an all-black cast in a story about the odyssey of a young black man, Zeke (Daniel Haynes), from humble beginnings in the cotton fields, to a career in evangelism, to the degradation of crime and punishment, to his eventual redemption as a family man. Not only was the subject matter and casting a revolutionary gesture in mainstream Hollywood, but Vidor also displayed remarkable canniness in his use of asynchronous sound. This is particularly evident in the church revival sequences where fast cutting is underpinned by frenzied choruses of singing voices; and in the penultimate swamp sequence where Zeke's pursuit of his girlfriend's murderer is accompanied by an evocative sound mix of natural sounds

and dialogue. Most reviews were ecstatic, singling out Vidor for unqualified praise. "As a creation, it is entirely his," enthused Welford Beaton in *The Film Spectator,* "as he wrote as well as directed the story. He has a place of his own among American directors. He is as fearless as are those foreign directors who give us beautiful works of screen art that enrich the screen even if they do not enrich their producers."

Street Scene was based on Elmer Rice's stage play about life in New York City tenements. Vidor's canvas was ambitious. Thirty-four characters were retained from the play, and the action is confined to the single set of a street and the front façade of a brownstone apartment built on the Goldwyn backlot. Vidor breaks up any potential monotony by photographing the action from a considerable variety of vantage points. Indeed, he and cinematographer George Barnes determined not to duplicate any of the setups from shot to shot. "I wanted to get away from that one façade," Vidor explained in an interview late in his life. "In the theater all the audience saw was a sidewalk. They didn't even see the street. I hoped I could enlarge it to include scenes in the street, and further down the block. . . . I tried to make each setup look different. I also worked out a system with the camera following anyone going out of a door, then picking up the next actor and the next extra just entering through the same door. This gave a flow to it, and it was challenging to see how much movement we could put in one static set in front of the building. I think it worked out. I think the constant change of composition makes it very interesting." The critic in *Photoplay* magazine opined that it was "an almost perfectly produced and acted picture," the "pinnacle" of Vidor's directorial career. "Here are the humor, the pathos, the gripping drama which comes to just one street of one city," the critic continued. "You've seen it again and again; you've read it as reported in your daily paper." Vidor's biographers, Raymond Durgnat and Scott Simmon, are less enthusiastic: "The film has the effect of being both direct and sidelong, deeply moving yet never quite memorable, neorealist in theme, yet profoundly anti-neorealist, almost anti-populist, in spirit. It's everything that irritates us about smart American art."

A variety of subjects followed in quick succession. *The Champ* (1931) was a crowd-pleaser about an over-the-hill prizefighter (Wallace Beery) who wins the love of a child (Jackie Cooper). *So Red the Rose* (1935) was a Civil War romance written by Laurence Stallings and Maxwell Anderson that, according to Clive Denton, anticipated "in many ways" *Gone with the Wind*. A classic tearjerker, *Stella Dallas* (1937), with Barbara Stanwyck in the lead, was adapted from the extremely popular novel by Olive Higgins Prouty about motherhood and sacrifice. Vidor would adapt other popular novels in later years, including A.J. Cronin's *The Citadel* (1938), featuring a strong cast that included Robert Donat, Rosalind Russell, Ralph Richardson, Rex Harrison, and Emlyn Williams; John P. Marquand's *H.M. Pulham, Esq.* (1941); Kenneth Roberts's *Northwest Passage* (1940); Ayn Rand's *The Fountainhead* (1949), with Rand adapting her own monumental novel for Gary Cooper, who played the heroic architect Howard Roark, and Patricia Neal as Dominique, the woman who inspires him; and the epic *War and Peace* (1956), adapted from Tolstoy, starring Audrey Hepburn as Natasha and Henry Fonda as Pierre.

Deserving its own place in the sun, as it were, is *Duel in the Sun* (1947), a huge David O. Selznick project adapted from Niven Busch's novel, a "nervous and neurotic" epic western embellished with opulent visuals and overheated, romantic excess. Selznick saw this as a Big Picture with a big stellar cast (Jennifer Jones, Joseph Cotten, Lionel Barrymore, Lillian Gish, and Walter Huston, among others) that would "top" *Gone With the Wind*. Vidor was not pleased with the script or with the interference of Selznick and his minions, William Dieterle and JOSEF VON STERNBERG, who was called in as photography consultant. The Directors Guild, of which

Vidor was first president, negotiated Vidor's credit for directing, but this overwrought western was dismissed by some satirists as "Lust in the Dust."

Vidor had earlier worked with Selznick on another big picture, *The Wizard of Oz* (1939), taking over for VICTOR FLEMING so that Fleming could begin work on *Gone With the Wind*. What survives of his directorial contributions are the scene where Judy Garland sings "Somewhere, Over the Rainbow," a number of the black-and-white Kansas sequences, and the Technicolor-hued "We're Off to See the Wizard." Vidor's last feature, *Solomon and Sheba* (1959), a Bible epic starring Yul Brynner as Solomon and Gina Lollobrigida as Sheba, was far from his best film, but one that was all too typical of the 1950s. As always, Vidor was both the product and the reflection of the times in which he worked. He died on November 1, 1982, after spending his last years teaching film production courses in several Los Angeles universities, writing a treatise on filmmaking (1972), and taking on occasional acting stints. His autobiography, *A Tree Is a Tree,* was published in 1953.

Other Films *Better Times, The Other Half* (both 1919); *Love Never Dies* (1921); *Woman, Wake Up, The Real Adventure, Dusk to Dawn* (all 1922); *Wild Oranges, Happiness* (both 1924); *Wife of the Centaur, Proud Flesh* (both 1925); *Bardelys, The Magnificent* (1926); *Not So Dumb, Billy the Kid* (both 1930); *Bird of Paradise, Cynara* (both 1932); *Stranger's Return* (1933); *Wedding Night* (1935); *The Texas Rangers* (1936); *Comrade X* (1940); *American Romance* (1944); *Beyond the Forest* (1949); *Lightning Strikes Twice* (1951); *Ruby Gentry* (1952); *Man Without a Star* (1955).

References Brownlow, Kevin, *The Parade's Gone By . . .* (New York: Knopf, 1968); Denton, Clive, et al., *The Hollywood Professionals: King Vidor, John Cromwell, Mervyn LeRoy* (New York: A. S. Barnes, 1976); Dowd, Nancy, and David Shepard, *King Vidor* (Metuchen, N.J.: Scarecrow Press, 1988); Durgnat, Raymond, and Scott Simmon, *King Vidor, American* (Berkeley: University of California Press, 1988); Vidor, King, *A Tree Is a Tree* (New York: Harcourt, Brace, 1953); Vidor, King, *King Vidor on Film Making* (New York: David McKay, 1973).

—J.M.W. and J.C.T.

Vigo, Jean (1905–1934) At the time of his untimely death in 1934, 29-year-old Jean Vigo had already established himself as one of France's leading experimental and poetic filmmakers. He was born in Paris on April 26, 1905, the son of a radical anarchist who went under the assumed name of "Miguel Almereyda." Jean was 13 when his father was killed in prison under mysterious circumstances. Farmed out to relatives and friends, Jean led a rootless existence, in and out of several schools, a lonely life he was to depict in the autobiographical *Zéro de Conduit* (*Zero for Conduct* [1933]). In 1927 his interests turned to cinema. He found a job with Franco-Film in Nice; and his first film, *À propos de Nice* (1929)—"a documented point of view," as he put it—was a satiric attack on the bourgeois vacationers in the French resort town, conveyed in a series of surreal image juxtapositions, quick cutting, and camera pyrotechnics. "In this film," said Vigo, "by showing certain basic aspects of a city, a way of life is put on trial. . . . [It is] a generalized view of the vulgar pleasures that come under the sign of the grotesque, and the flesh, and of death." Three years later, his short feature, the remarkable *Zero for Conduct,* chronicled in startlingly surreal terms the regimented educational system of a boy's boarding school. Frustrated at the bad food, the monotony, and the insensitive faculty, the boys, led by revolutionaries Colin, Caussat, and Druel (based on Vigo's boyhood friends), stage an apocalyptic pillow fight and break up a school ceremony by pelting visitors with food and old shoes. Singing lustily their war cry of freedom, they march away across a seemingly endless rooftop. *Zero* was made despite enormous difficulties in getting financing, gaining sufficient studio time, and fighting Vigo's own poor health (diagnosed as tuberculosis in 1926). The obvious shortcomings in *Zero*'s hastily arranged camera setups, the poor dialogue recording, lapses in continuity, and other deficiencies, actually impart a rough, dreamlike quality to the story. Considerably enhancing the effort is a fine score by Maurice Jaubert and photography by Boris Kaufman. Its premiere on April 7, 1933, at the Cinema Artistic on the rue de Douai was something of an event in the history of French avant-garde cinema. Among the attendees were writer André Gide and playwrights Paul Claudel and Jacques Prévert. The Catholic censoring board objected to the scenes of nudity, the subversive politics, and the mocking of the French flag. Ultimately, the film was not only censored but also suppressed entirely. It had to wait until the late 1940s before it was revived in Paris and at New York's Museum of Modern Art. (For young FRANÇOIS TRUFFAUT, its anarchic view of childhood was an inspiration for his own first feature film, *The Four Hundred Blows* [1959]; similarly, it was the model for Lindsay Anderson's *If . . .* [1968].)

Vigo's last film, *L'Atalante* (1933), his masterpiece, combined his surrealistic bent with a more natural realism. It tells the story of Jean (Michel Simon), the young captain of a motorized barge called "L'Atalante," which plies the inland waterways of France. When Jean's new bride, Juliette (Dita Parlo), runs away with a salesman, Jean despairs. But all is well when the two are eventually reunited. "Vigo's acute sense of movement is what chiefly fills in the banal outlines of the story," writes commentator Gavin Millar, "as much as the richness of invention he brings to the characters." Again, Vigo was assisted by cinematographer Boris Kaufman and composer Maurice Jaubert. Like *Zero for Conduct, L'Atalante* was "lost" for many years before being rediscovered for new generations of viewers. Exhausted by his efforts, disappointed at the mutilated version of his film that was finally released to the public, and overcome by leukemia, Vigo died on October 5, 1934. He was buried in Paris next to his father. As commentator Michael Temple notes, while Vigo's films are highly regarded (and now readily available on video), "it is probably fair to say that his extraordinary posthumous glory has transformed Jean Vigo into one of the great mythic figures of French film culture."

Other Film *Taris* (1931).

References Sallès Gomès, P. E., *Jean Vigo* (Berkeley: University of California Press, 1971); Temple, Michael, "Vigo," *Sight and Sound* 8, no. 11 (November 1998): 14–15.

—J.C.T.

Visconti, Luchino (1906–1976)   A towering figure in the history of Italian neorealist and post-neorealist cinema, Luchino Visconti's best work is a blend of richly textured surface detail and operatic flamboyance. He was born a scion of ancient nobility, Count Don Luchino Visconti di Modrone, in Milan on November 2, 1906. After attending private schools in Milan and Como, he served in the Reggimento Savoia Cavalleria in 1926–28. He began a career as a stage actor and set designer in 1928, and after moving to Paris, assisted JEAN RENOIR in his film *A Day in the Country* (*Une partie de campagne* [1937]). Renoir's influence would always remain an important part of Visconti's work, as would his association during these early years with the Italian journal, *Cinema,* in which he published his attacks on commercial Italian cinema. His first film was *Obsession* (*Ossessione* [1942]), a gritty and blunt tale of betrayal and murder, unofficially based on *The Postman Always Rings Twice,* that would have a tremendous impact on the Italian postwar neorealist style and on the film noir style in America in the late 1940s. Indeed, it is vastly superior to Tay Garnett's 1946 version and to an earlier French version by Pierre Chenal: "The novel's first-person subjective narrative is eliminated for a more omniscient and objective camera style which is, however, as obsessed with the highly formal compositions it photographs as the characters are by their passions," notes historian Peter Bondanella. Although the released film was banned by Mussolini and its negative burned (Visconti retained his own dupe negative), it was nonetheless a turning point in Italian cinema. At the same time, this free-form adaptation of James M. Cain's hard-boiled novel prefigures Visconti's tendency to take liberties with literary properties. "Whenever Visconti decided to bring to the screen a literary work," writes commentator Claretta Tonetti, "he remained only partially faithful to it, always exercising his freedom to change according to the difference of the medium and his own wish to manipulate the material."

The Earth Trembles (*La Terra Trema* [1947]), a landmark in the neorealist movement, was a saga of the lives of fisher folk filmed on location in Sicily. Adapted from Giovanni Verga's novel, *I malavoglia,* the film employed as actors the people of the locale speaking in their native dialect. The tragedy of the pressures of exploitative capitalists on the Sicilian workers' way of life was ruthlessly yet poetically examined. *Senso* (1954) was adapted from a novel by Camillo Boito, and it reveals Visconti in a far more operatic vein, blending cinematic realism with elaborate camera mise-en-scène and romantic sensibility. The story is set against the background of the risorgimento, the Italian struggle for independence from Austria and Spain, and it concerns an aristocratic Italian woman's betrayal at the hands of her lover, an Austrian lieutenant.

Rocco and His Brothers (*Rocco e suoi fratelli* [1960]) returns to the subject of the contemporary Sicilian family, this time newly arrived in Milan from the south. The episodic story centers around the efforts of Rocco to protect the solidarity of his family against the ravages of unemployment and sibling rivalry and violence. His younger brother, Luca, yearns all the while to return to his Sicilian roots. "Visconti concentrates upon the dramatic clash of differing value systems," writes Bondanella, "—that of the traditional southern peasant family and its archaic code of honor and family loyalty, on the one hand, and a more individualistic and contemporary morality reflecting industrial society, on the other." Although the locales and background details are rigorously examined in the neorealist style, Visconti again limns the action with melodramatic intensity and stylized camera mise-en-scène. His most operatic film is *The Leopard* (*Il gattopardo* [1963]), one of his most commercially successful films, adapted from the novel by Giuseppe Tomasi di Lampedusa. It is set during the time of Garibaldi's nationalist agitations and is about an aristocratic Sicilian family facing changes with the intermarriage of a family member with a nouveaux riche person. The family represents the larger context of the usurpation of the aristocracy by the bourgeoisie, which defuses the revolutionary processes at work.

Sandra (*Vaghe stelle dell'orsa* [1965]) retells the Elektra myth in terms of the ambiguously incestuous relationship between Sandra and her suicidal brother, Gianni. *The Stranger* (*L'Etranger* [1967]) adapts Camus's existentialist novel set in Algiers and about a Frenchman, Mersault (Marcello Mastroianni), who is sentenced to death for the murder of an Arab. He spends his last hours repudiating the solace of religion and affirming his belief in the futility of life. Visconti moved the action forward from 1938 to the contemporary context of the French-Algerian war; but there is the universal angst, suggests Tonetti, "the feeling of not belonging and the ambivalence of the European in a world which does not belong to him."

The so-called German trilogy marks the last and most "decadent" period of Visconti's work. *The Damned* (1967), *Death in Venice* (1971), and *Ludwig* (1973) are documents of self-indulgence, degeneration, and death. The first depicts the failing fortunes of the Von Essembeck family, steel mill owners, against the rise of Nazism in the 1930s. "After viewing *The Damned*," notes Tonetti, "one is left with the feeling of having watched a pit of vipers, reflecting through its personal battles the Nazi struggle for power on the outside." The second adapted Thomas Mann's 1911 novel about the obsessive, sexually repressed relationship between composer Gustav von Aschenbach (Dirk Bogarde) and a Polish boy, Tadzio (Björn Andrésen), set against the backdrop of cholera-ridden Venice. That Visconti found in the story a reflection of his own artistic and social concerns is evidenced by his remark, "My film describes an intellectual adventure balancing between truth and imagination in a key totally realistic and completely fantastic." *Ludwig* tells the pathetic story of the mad king of Bavaria (Helmut

Berger) from 1845 to 1886, from his assumption of the kingship to his last years of seclusion, madness, and suicide in the extravagant isolation of his castles. Despite suffering two strokes, Visconti labored mightily to complete the project. "Among the solitary souls presented by the director," notes Tonetti, "Ludwig is the most solitary and the most clearly destined to be crushed by reality." One more film remained to him, *The Innocent* (*L'Innocente* [1975]), although by now Visconti was struggling with his own infirmities. "I swear that neither old age nor illness have bent my desire to live and to work. I feel fresh for another ten films. . . . We are here for this: to burn until death, which is the last act of life, completes life's work transforming us into ashes." The story of marital infidelity and murder was based on an 1892 novel by Gabriele D'Annunzio. However, what was tragic and complex in the book was rather mawkish on screen, and the film received a mixed reception at best. Visconti died on March 17, 1976, before completing the film's editing.

In this last film, as in all of Visconti's work, a sumptuousness of décor, a virtuosity of camera mise-en-scène, and an operatic flamboyance of gesture prevail. As noted by commentator William French, Visconti was always divided personally between his professed Marxism and his sympathy for the aristocracy, torn between a sentimentalized past, which he intellectually rejected, and a future that he abhorred. As a result, Visconti's work reveals a steadily progressing preoccupation with sensuality and decadence, peaking with the languorous sumptuousness of *The Leopard* and the deterioration into madness in *Ludwig*. All the while he continued to work in plays (he directed Cocteau's *The Terrible Parents* in 1945) and on the opera stage (*La vestale* was his first Milanese production, in 1954), elements of which surface periodically in his films, as the quotation from Act Three of Verdi's *Il Trovatore* in the opening of *Senso*.

Other Films *Bellissima* (1951); *White Nights* (*Le Notti bianche* [1957]); *A Family Group* (*Gruppo di famiglia in un interno* [1974]).

References Bondanella, Peter, *Italian Cinema: From Neorealism to the Present* (New York: Frederick Ungar, 1990); Tonetti, Claretta, *Luchino Visconti* (Boston: Twayne Publishers, 1983).

—J.C.T.

von Sternberg, Josef (1894–1969) Generally regarded as one of the screen's supreme visual stylists, Josef von Sternberg exerted a tyrannical authority over his film crews and a Svengali-esque influence over his protégée and most famous actress, Marlene Dietrich. He was born Jonas Sternberg in Vienna on May 19, 1894. His family relocated to America, and he briefly attended Jamaica High School, Queens, before returning to Vienna to complete his education. As a member of the U.S. Army Signal Corps, he made training films during World War I. Between 1918 and 1924 he worked as a scenarist and assistant for several directors, and it was at this time that he tacked "von" to his name. His first directed feature film was *The Salvation Hunters* (1925), a story of lowly types in a little community on the California coast. He signed on with Paramount Pictures at this time, where he worked until 1935. These were the peak years of his career, beginning with *Underworld* (1927), an important prototype of the modern gangster film, *The Docks of New York* (1928), and *The Last Command* (1928), the strange story of a Russian general who flees the Revolution and ends up working as an extra in a Hollywood studio.

In 1930 Sternberg began his celebrated association with Marlene Dietrich with *The Blue Angel*. Six more pictures with her followed—*Morocco* (1930), *Dishonored* (1931), *Shanghai Express* (1932), *Blonde Venus* (1932), *The Scarlet Empress* (1934), and *The Devil Is a Woman* (1935). Dietrich had been a minor star on stage and screen in Germany, working for such notables as Victor Barnowski and Max Reinhardt before Sternberg approached her with an offer to star as "Lola-Lola" in *The Blue Angel,* based on Heinrich Mann's novel, *Professor Unrat.* "You have a beautiful face which lives—really lives," he said prophetically. Her performance as the

fatally attractive cabaret singer who humiliates a middle-aged college professor (Emil Jannings) helplessly in love with her—Sternberg's great theme of degradation through infatuation—is now securely a part of film legend. Unforgettable was the image of her on the smokily lit cabaret stage singing "Falling in love again," clad in high heels and black silk tights, plumes adorning her neck, a silk top hat on her head, her legs suggestively straddling a chair. Aloof, languorous, cruel—this was Dietrich's femme fatale image that Sternberg carefully, deliberately crafted through his next six pictures.

Collectively these pictures constitute one of the most remarkable series of films in Hollywood history, each a variation on the femme fatale theme. While *The Blue Angel* was being released in both German- and English-language versions, Sternberg and his protégée headed for Hollywood to make *Morocco* (1930), based on Benno Vigny's novel, *Amy Jolly.* The tale of an amoral cabaret singer who falls in love with a French Foreign Legionnaire (Gary Cooper) was something of a reversal of the dynamics of *The Blue Angel*—but not before Dietrich appeared in several memorable scenes clad in white tuxedo and top hat, a strikingly androgynous image. *Dishonored* was next, a spy story set in Vienna with Dietrich as a secret agent disguised as a prostitute. It will forever be remembered for Victor McLaglen's great line upon meeting Dietrich, "I think of death as a beautiful young woman wearing flowers." Their third film together was *Shanghai Express,* in which Dietrich is Shanghai Lily, a white prostitute aboard a train attacked by revolutionaries (the picture was dubbed a "*Grand Hotel* on rails"). In *Blonde Venus* she returns to the role of a cabaret singer, although this time she is a devoted mother who leaves her husband and lover in order to keep her child. One of the most celebrated moments in all of the Sternberg/Dietrich oeuvre is the "Hot Voodoo" number, in which the blonde-wigged Dietrich emerges from a coarse and furry gorilla suit, to the throbbing beat of voodoo drums. *The Scarlet Empress* cast Dietrich as Sophia Frederica, plucked from her homeland in Germany to go to Russia to marry the insane grand duke Peter. As Catherine the Great she uses her sexual power over men as a political weapon to overthrow Peter.

Paramount by now was uneasy about the failing box-office returns of the Sternberg/Dietrich collaborations. Moreover, tensions were developing between Sternberg's Trilby and Dietrich's Svengali. Rumors of an affair between them drove Sternberg's wife to file for divorce. At any rate, director and star were to do only one more picture together, *The Devil Is a Woman,* adapted from Pierre Louys's novel, *The Woman and the Puppet.* Seville at the turn of the century is the setting for a series of erotic encounters and betrayals, all involving Dietrich's character of "Concha Perez."

In all these films, Sternberg lavished great attention on décor, fashion, and photography (with the assistance of redoubtable cinematographer Lee Garmes). Sternberg himself was the only director of his day to earn membership in the American Society of Cinematographers. He planned his films not around a plot so much as around what he called his performers' "dramatic encounter with light." He insisted that the "dead space" between actor and camera be enlivened with a texture of some kind, through veils, smoke, candle flames. He adorned Dietrich in every conceivable kind of exotic, sometimes improbable, wardrobe from Paramount's costume designer, Travis Banton— feathers, sequins, veils, a tuxedo and slacks, even the aforementioned gorilla suit. Whether the setting was Berlin, Morocco, the Kremlin, or Seville, the results were a phantasmagoria of extravagant, even grotesque set designs and moody lighting effects. The last two films, particularly, are highwater marks in the studio-crafted film. Sternberg created a virtual aesthetic out of clutter, to the point that people are smothered and almost obscured out of existence. In *Empress,* which Sternberg himself dubbed "a relentless excursion into style," the Peterhof Palace was a nightmare of gargoyles, bell towers, twisted statuary, and enormous doors. Three sequences stand out: a banquet where human skeletons sit beside the diners; the wedding to the grand duke in a church ablaze with the tall, slim flames of thousands of candles; and Catherine's coup d'etat, wherein hundreds of mounted horsemen storm up the great staircases of the palace. In *Devil* the Carnival sequence is a tangle of veils, masks, beaded curtains, latticed partitions, falling confetti, and flaring streamers.

For the rest of his career, Sternberg was a pilgrim in search of a haven. Without Dietrich, it could be argued he was a Pygmalion without his Galatea. And without her, it was difficult for a man of his temperamental demands to secure the financing necessary for his baroque ambitions. (Late in life he declared that he stopped making films after 1935.) In England, working for ALEXANDER KORDA, he began the lavish *I, Claudius* (1937), which was ultimately abandoned and left unfinished. In only two other films did he secure any degree of independence, the noirishly stylized *The Shanghai Gesture* (1942), his only film of the 1940s, and *Anatahan* (1954), which he shot entirely on a sound stage after traveling to Japan. Sternberg himself narrated the latter film. Additional nonfilm projects included teaching a film course at the University of Southern California in 1947. He died on December 22, 1969.

Critics have taken note of Sternberg's aristocratic aloofness, a compulsive attraction to the pathological, an ambivalence toward women— worshipful on the one hand, scornful on the other—and, as commentator Jean-Pierre Coursodon has noted, "a flair for filtering erotic fantasies (predominantly of the fetishistic, masochistic variety) through the refinements of style." In his autobiography, *Fun in a Chinese Laundry,* he wrote, "I aspired to the status of an artist in a branch of the arts where it is not permitted to be one."

Other Films   *The Sea Gull* (1926); *The Case of Lena Smith* (1929); *Thunderbolt* (1929); *An American Tragedy* (1931); *The King Steps Out* (1936).

References   Coursodon, Jean-Pierre, *American Directors,* vol. I (New York: McGraw-Hill, 1983); Sternberg, Josef von, *Fun in a Chinese Laundry* (New York: Macmillan, 1965).

—J.C.T.

Wajda, Andrzej (1926–) Generally acknowledged as Poland's greatest film director, Andrzej Wajda has led a career spanning the years from the Polish renaissance of the late 1950s to the political and social films of the post-Soviet period. When he began making films, the Polish film industry produced only five to seven films a year; in his maturity, in the early 1980s when the film industry was under state control, that number had risen to 40 films, and as many made-for-television movies. "If you want to know the truth about another country," Wajda has written in his autobiography, "who is in a better position to tell it than an eyewitness?" Wajda has been such an observer and artist. Commentator Janina Falkowska divides his films into the following categories of subject matter: the period after World War II; the moral concerns of the 1950s and 1960s; the rise of Polish Solidarity; the overthrow of the socialist system; and the Jewish question. In all his films, writes biographer Boleslaw Michalek, "he keeps bandying the concepts, the common coinage, the fantasies of the Polish literary and philosophical tradition which always strike a chord in his own country but have none too clear a ring outside its borders."

He was born in Suwalki, Poland, on March 6, 1926. His father was a professional army officer and his mother a schoolteacher. He spent the years of occupation in the provinces and assisted in the restoration of paintings. After 1945 he enrolled in the Fine Arts Academy in Krakow, and four years later he left it without graduating. He transferred to the newly opened Polish Film School in Lodz and studied there from 1950 to 1952, joining the ranks of emerging young directors like Andrzej Munk and Kazimierz Kutz.

After assisting director Aleksandr Ford in 1953, he directed his first feature, *A Generation* (*Pokolenie* [1955]), the story of a group of young men and women who had fought in the Resistance during the occupation of Poland. Wajda quickly established himself in the forefront of a new generation of filmmakers in the late 1950s, who had spent their youth in the shadow of the fascist occupation and been trained in both the practical and theoretical sides of filmmaking. In their efforts to cope with the trauma of war and understand the state of political and cultural life in Poland, they forged an exciting body of work that garnered international acclaim. Wajda followed *Generation* with two other notable films, *Kanal* (1957), which chronicled the tragedy of the 1944 Warsaw uprising, and *Ashes and Diamonds* (*Popiol i diament* [1958]), which traced the actions of a young member of a small underground unit loyal to the émigré nationalist government in London during the watershed period between war and peace. The latter film was based on a novel by Jerzy Andrzejewski, one of the literary landmarks of the day. The basic themes and style of Wajda's work emerge in this trilogy—a blending of a rich, baroque visual sense with an emotionally charged view of history and a foregrounding of human relations against the chaos of politics and war. "[Wajda's] fate no longer strikes one as a search undertaken in hope," wrote Peter John Dyer, "but as a lonely, losing struggle against misanthropy and disillusion. One thing above all seems to keep him going: a burning desire to express all that is young, mortal, sentient and suffering in an absolute orgy of self-identification."

The war experience continued to be a central preoccupation of Wajda's, resulting in films like *Lotna* (1959), set in the fall of 1939 when Poland's last cavalry squadron was overrun by the Germans; *Samson* (1961), about a Jewish youth who joins the struggle against the Nazis; and *Landscape after the Battle* (*Krajobraz po bitwie* [1970]), which Wajda declared his last film about the war: "It's not I who am drawing back [from the war]," he explained. "It's the war. It and I are growing old together, and therefore it is more and more difficult for me to discover anything in it that was close to me." Since then he has tackled a variety of subjects, including an adaptation of Nikolay Leskov's "Lady Macbeth of Mtsensk," *Siberian Lady Macbeth* (*Sibirska ledi magbet* [1962]), his first film outside Poland; *Everything for Sale* (*Wszystko na sprzedaz* [1968]), a tribute to the late Polish actor Zbigniew Cybulski (who had starred in three of Wajda's earlier films); *Danton* (1982), a critique of the destructive excesses of the French Revolution; and *Czlowiek z marmuru* (*Man of Marble* [1977]). In a late-career return to the subject of war, he made *Korczak* (1990), which was based on a true story about a man who led his charges from an orphanage into the

Jewish ghetto, a deed that led to his incarceration in the concentration camp of Treblinka.

Wajda portrays those moments wherein individual lives and national destinies intersect and, briefly, intertwine. Commentator Janina Falkowska notes that his films never treat historical processes and contexts in an impersonal or abstract way; rather, "people are always presented in context, both as political subjects and as ordinary human beings." In 1986 Wajda wrote, "God blessed the film director with two eyes, one to watch the camera and one to take in everything going on around him. For the director this must become second nature, until the day he stops making films, and if you live in countries where political sensitivity is an issue in filmmaking, that day could come sooner than you expect. So don't waste any time!" His many awards include the Grand Prix at the Moscow Film Festival for *The Promised Land* (*Ziemia obiecana* [1974]), the Palme d'Or at the Cannes Film Festival for *Man of Iron* (*Czlowiek z zelaza* [1981]), and the Légion d'Honneur of France in 1982.

Other Films *Innocent Sorcerers* (*Niewinni czarodzieje* [1960]); *Gates to Paradise* (*Bramy raju* [1967]); *A Love in Germany* (*Eine liebe in Deutschland* [1983]); *Chronicle of a Love Affair* (*Kronika wypadkow milosnych* [1985]); *The Ring with the Crowned Eagle* (1993); *Natasha* (1994).

References Dyer, Peter John, "Ashes and Diamonds," *Sight and Sound* 28, no. 3 (Summer–Autumn 1959): 166–177; Falkowska, Janina, *The Political Films of Andrzej Wajda* (Providence: Burghahn Books, 1996); Michalek, Boleslaw, *The Cinema of Andrzej Wajda* (London: Tantivy Press, 1973); Toeplitz, Jerzy, "Wajda Redivivus," *Film Quarterly,* Winter 1969–1970; Wajda, Andrzej, *Double Vision: My Life in Film* (London: Faber and Faber, 1989).

—J.C.T.

Watkins, Peter (1935–) The brilliant, cantankerous British director Peter Watkins deserves more credit and attention than the critical establishment has so far given him. His career peaked early with two documentary features made for the BBC, *Culloden* (1964) and *The War Game* (1965), which won an Academy Award in 1967 as best documentary feature. Thereafter, his career began a gradual downward spiral as Watkins began to be regarded as a "difficult" talent because of his political agenda and because of his unwillingness to compromise his principles. After he expatriated himself from England and completed his biographical feature *Edvard Munch* (1976), he found it increasingly difficult to get his projects funded but continued to work independently abroad, risking obscurity thereby.

Watkins was born in Norbiton, Surrey, on October 29, 1935, and educated in Wales at the College of Christ, followed by a year at the Royal Academy of Dramatic Arts in London in 1953. After military service in 1956, he became active with an amateur theater group in Canterbury and began making films—*The Web* (1956), in 8 mm, followed by his first 16-mm film, *The Field of Red* (1958), now lost, and two award-winning films, *The Diary of an Unknown Soldier* (1959) and *The Forgotten Faces* (1961), in which he reconstructed the Hungarian Rebellion of 1956 in the streets of Canterbury so convincingly that critics thought he had somehow managed to smuggle his camera into the streets of Budapest. This pseudodocumentary short got him a job as assistant producer at BBC, which led to his first professional feature, *Culloden* (1964), in which he reconstructed the last battle fought on British soil, in Scotland, during the uprising of the Scottish pretender, Bonnie Prince Charlie, in 1745.

The success of *Culloden* enabled Watkins to direct *The War Game* for BBC, which speculated on what the effects of a nuclear strike on the south of England might be, but it was also critical of the Home Office's policy of civil defense. Watkins made his point too well, and, after a stormy two-year period of controversy, the film was banned for television, though prints were exhibited in commercial cinemas throughout Britain. The BBC television ban remained in effect until 1985, and Watkins resigned in protest.

In 1966 Watkins made his last film in Britain, *Privilege,* for Universal studios, London, the story of a pop singer (Paul Jones) whose popularity is exploited by the government. This film was effective but perhaps ahead of its time in style and technique. In 1968 Watkins left London for Sweden, where he directed *The Gladiators* (aka *The Peace Game*), a film that carried Big Brotherism into the arena of cyberspace, speculating on a future world in which warfare among nations would be controlled by computers and staged as television spectacle on the model of the Olympic Games—another film that tweaked establishment values. This was followed by his only film completed in America, *Punishment Park* (1970), which speculated about political dissidents rounded up and made to fight for their freedom through an obstacle course in the Mojave Desert. This powerfully unconventional film was scorned by critics on both the conservative right and the liberal left.

Bruised by such criticism, Watkins then moved to Oslo in 1971 to make his documentary feature *Edvard Munch* (first seen on television in Europe in 1974 and released as a feature film in New York City in 1976). The film, which concentrated only on Munch's early and turbulent career, when the artist produced his most disturbing work and was considered a madman because he painted agonizing scenes of suffering and grief, was his last critical success, though he continued to make other documentaries, such as *The 70s People* (1974) in Denmark, on the topic of teenage suicide, and *Evening Land* (1976), involving a strike at a Copenhagen shipyard and the kidnapping of a Danish minister while a summit meeting of the European Common Market is in progress. These films were hardly seen in the United States. Nor was *The Trap* (*Fällen* [1975] is the Swedish title), an excellent videodrama that Watkins directed for Sveriges Radio from a script by the journalist Bo Melander, concerning nuclear waste control in Sweden and the coming of the new millennium.

For 20 years Watkins had been contemplating a remake and updating of *The War Game* and was in a position to make the film for Channel 4 in Britain, but he wanted to increase the scope of the project at the last minute, and Channel 4 withdrew its support because of budget constraints. Frustrated by that decision, Watkins spent the next several years touring the globe to raise money for the project through local peace groups worldwide. The result was a 15-hour film called *The Journey* (1986), which critic Scott MacDonald considered "by far, the most remarkable film" Watkins has made. Indeed, the film is quite remarkable—but also quite diffuse and rather too long to be viewed at a single sitting. It contains a meditation on global problems that goes quite beyond the technology and the aftereffects of the atom bomb, but that issue alone is explored about as fully as it has ever been on film.

While researching his Munch project, Watkins became interested in the life and career of the brilliant but troubled playwright August Strindberg and finally completed another experimental and challenging biographical film, *The Freethinker* (*Fritänkaren*) in 1994, running 276 minutes and utilizing photographs, intertitles, and excerpts from Strindberg's plays to capture the complexity of the artist's life. After a long struggle to have the film financed by the Swedish Film Institute, Watkins finally completed it as a group project at the Folk Art School of the Nordic Association in Biskops-Arnö. It was exhibited as a "special presentation" of the National Film Theatre in London.

The Freethinker was followed by yet another long film, *La Commune,* filmed in France, released in 2000, and running five hours and 45 minutes, concerning the socialist Paris Commune uprising of 1871, an event usually ignored by the French education curriculum. According to Peter Lennon: "In the wake of the disastrous Franco-Prussian war, following three months of fierce defiance, of heady aspirations for justice and democracy, months of solidarity and pitiful bungling, government troops assailed the barri-cades and in one *semaine sanglante* slaughtered, street by street, more than 30,000 of their fellow countrymen and women and children over 14. It was worse than anything in the Terror of 1793, so persistently chronicled by historians." Thus Watkins returned to the sort of film he made with *Culloden,* intending to expose a shameful event in the history of a country assumed to be civilized. Calling the director an "outlawed genius," Lennon compared him to Peter Brook, "also exiled by negligence and resentment." Watkins has always been an outspoken critic who believes that there has been an "accumulation of global media power with no accountability that is not only not being challenged but is not even being debated." Watkins compared himself with the playwright director DENNIS POTTER as one who was "once able to work critically within the media" but ultimately was "marginalized." In fact, Potter accommodated himself better to the system, but for Watkins those words are dead on, and that's a pity, since, under better circumstances, Watkins could have made more and better films. He was one of the most gifted filmmakers of his generation but also, sadly, one of the most neglected.

References Gomez, Joseph A., *Peter Watkins* (Boston: Twayne, 1979); Lennon, Peter, "The Lost Hero of British TV," *The Guardian Friday Review,* February 25, 2000, pp. 1–3; Nolley, Ken, *The Journey: A Film in the Global Interest* (Salem, Oreg.: Willamette Journal of the Liberal Arts, 1991); Welsh, James M., *Peter Watkins: A Guide to References and Resources* (Boston: G. K. Hall, 1986).

—J.M.W.

Weir, Peter (1944–) One of the Australian New Wave's most distinguished directors, Peter Weir has bridged the gulf between art-house experiments and the mainstream cinema. He was born on August 8, 1944, in Sydney, where he spent a happy, active boyhood pursuing his favorite activities of sports, games, movies, and comic book collecting. At Sydney University, however, he was repelled by the dry, academic approach to literature and poetry (satirized later in *Dead Poets Society*), and he dropped out. After a restless two years in his father's firm selling real estate, he pulled up stakes and boarded a boat to several European ports. On board, he and several friends found an unused closed-circuit television camera and created shows for the other passengers. It was his first experience with theatrical events, and he was hooked. He returned to Australia determined to pursue a career in theater and television. While working as a stagehand at Channel 7 in Sydney, he began writing and performing in a variety of multimedia "off-off-Broadway" events.

His first film shorts attracted attention and won him a Young Filmmakers Award in 1969. Now a member of the Commonwealth Film Unit (now Film Australia), the following year he wrote and

Peter Weir (Warner Bros.)

directed *Michael,* which won the Grand Prix from the Australian Film Institute. A second Grand Prix came the next year with a short feature, *Homesdale.* "It was a wonderful time," Weir recalls. "We were at war in Vietnam, too. We were involved in our own student demonstrations. There was the long hair, father against son, the music, the dope, the whole upheaval. . . . Out of this whole ferment came the films we made. The camera was our AK-47. It was our truthful eye."

The mid-seventies brought him international acclaim with *The Cars That Ate Paris* (1974), a holocaust fable about a town whose citizens lure passing motorists to their deaths; *Picnic at Hanging Rock* (1975), which chronicled the mysterious disappearance of a boarding school teacher and several girls during an outing on St. Valentine's Day, 1900; *The Last Wave* (1977), a terrifying apocalyptic vision of the end of the world; and *Gallipoli* (1981), a savage indictment of the cruelty and absurdity of war during the Dardanelles campaign in World War I. Hollywood beckoned. Beginning with *Witness* in 1985, about the intrusion of murder and conspiracy into a peaceful Amish community, Weir directed a series of successful American releases, including *Mosquito Coast* (1986), adapted from Paul Theroux's novel about a fiercely individualistic man's attempt to eke out a living for himself and his family in Belize; *Dead Poets Society* (1989), the story of a maverick teacher's unsuccessful attempt to bring an anarchic vision of poetry to his students; *Fearless* (1993), an account of the aftermath of a catastrophic plane crash; and *The Truman Show* (1998), a dystopian view of a media-constructed and commodified society.

Like Puck in *A Midsummer Night's Dream* (a character he invokes literally in *Dead Poets Society*), who visits terror, trauma, and magic upon the inhabitants of Theseus's court and Oberon's fairy wood, Peter Weir enchants his characters and audiences alike, plunging them into a half-world of primordial chaos, magic, and unexplained mysteries, where terrible engines of destruction and violence are at work. As the character of Archy says in

Gallipoli, "There's a feeling we're all involved in an adventure that's somehow larger than life."

Questions of identity and alienation persist that relate directly to Weir's Australian roots. He has commented on the fact that Australia was built up by "the dispossessed of the world," who had left their past behind and came there to start over. He shares the feeling that he and his nation are always "starting from scratch" (as Allie puts it in *Mosquito Coast*), living as a race apart from others and constantly fearful of being "put out" by invasion, natural disaster, or social upheaval. At the same time—and this is made clear in *The Last Wave*—his characters suffer from the lingering, haunting guilt of having dispossessed and exploited the indigenous aborigines. His breakthrough film, the stunningly beautiful and hauntingly enigmatic *Picnic at Hanging Rock,* conveys these themes in lyric, poetic fashion, subtly conveying the brooding sense of a primal and erotic force threatening to overturn and supplant the all-too-fragile and artificially ordered gentility of the Appleyard College for Girls—a theme that commentator Gary Hentzi has described as "the persistence of primitive forces beneath the surface of a repressively rationalized modern existence." Perhaps the closest Weir has come himself to describing his method and his vision, can be found in the words of the photographer Billy Kwan in *The Year of Living Dangerously* (1982). Kwan, an elfish figure amidst the sordid world of Jakarta, subtly manipulates and photographs the lives of the people around him. Retiring to his darkroom, he surveys his images: "I'm master in the darkroom, stirring my prints in the magic developing bath," he says. "I shuffle like cards the lives that I deal with. Their faces stare out at me. People who will become other people. People who will become old, betray their dreams, become ghosts."

Characteristically, Weir views his career—now divided between Sydney and Hollywood—as something belonging to a fairy tale. "I think of myself as a character in 'Jack and the Beanstalk.' I'm Jack and I have my farm and a cow in Australia. And there's this beanstalk, which is my career, which I've climbed to the land where the Giant lives, which is Hollywood. And I go there every now and then, where I'm given the Golden Goose and where I play the Golden harp to amuse the Giant at dinner. But then it's time to go home, even though the Giant always says, 'Why don't you stay; why do you want to go home? You've got your own room here!' But no, I keep returning to my Australian farm."

Other Films *Incredible Floridas* (1972), short; *Whatever Happened to Green Valley* (1973); *The Plumber* (1978); *Green Card* (1990).

References Bliss, Michael, *Dreams Within a Dream: The Films of Peter Weir* (Carbondale: Southern Illinois University Press, 2000); Hentzi, Gary, "Peter Weir and the Cinema of New Age Humanism," *Film Quarterly* 44, no.2 (Winter 1990–91): 3–12; Shiach, Don, *The Films of Peter Weir* (London: Charles Letts, 1993); Tibbetts, John C., "Peter Weir: A View from the Apocalypse," *The World and I* 9, no. 4 (April 1994): 122–127.

—J.C.T.

Welles, Orson George (1915–1985)

A towering, gargantuan figure in international stage and screen—in reputation, achievement, personality, and size—Orson Welles was a mysterious and bewildering compound of genius and charlatan, whose career was fraught with as much failure and frustration as it was with fame and glory. He was born on May 6, 1915, in Kenosha, Wisconsin, to Richard Head Welles, a prosperous wagon manufacturer and inventor (he is credited with inventing the U.S. Army mess kit), and Beatrice Ives Welles, a gifted concert pianist. A precocious child, he was reading Shakespeare before he was five years old and staging his own little plays in a toy theater. After his parents' divorce he went to Chicago to live with his mother. When she died two years later, Orson returned to his father and enrolled at the progressive Todd School for Boys in Woodstock, Illinois. When he was not producing more than 25 theatrical productions during his five-year term, he was globetrotting with his charismatic father. It was a magical time for the youth, but it tragically ended with the suicide of his father. Now the ward of a family friend, Dr. Maurice Bernstein, Welles left the Todd School to study at the Chicago Art Institute.

These were restless years. He was just 16 when he decided to leave Chicago and journey to Ireland, where he eked out a living selling paintings. Soon, as always, he succumbed to the siren song of the theater, and he talked himself into a position with the Dublin Gate Theatre. After peregrinations across England, Spain, and Morocco, he returned to America, where he found a temporary home with Katharine Cornell's touring national repertory company during the 1935 season. While playing Tybalt in *Romeo and Juliet* he met the Romanian-born producer, John Houseman, 12 years his senior, who would play an important part in Welles's subsequent career. In his memoir, *Run-Through,* Houseman admits that he was both repelled and fascinated by Welles, and he refers to him as a "monstrous boy" possessed of "an irresistible interior violence." Their stormy association—Houseman as producer, Welles as director and actor—would last for only a few years, but it would result in some of the landmarks of American theater, radio, and film.

In the spring of 1936 Welles, 21 years of age and newly married, began working with Houseman for the Federal Theatre Project in Harlem, under the supervision of Hallie Flanagan. Designated simply as "Project 891," their theatrical unit debuted with a sensational all-black "voodoo" production of *Macbeth,* which relocated Shakespeare's story from Scotland to Haiti. The farcical *Horse Eats Hat,* after Labiche's *Italian Straw Hat,* followed, with Marlowe's *Doctor Faustus* hot on its, er, hooves. A year later the two young entrepreneurs formed the Mercury Theatre on Broadway and launched a series of notable productions, including a modern-dress *Julius Caesar,* Shaw's *Heartbreak House,* Buechner's *Danton's Death,* William Gillette's farce, *Too Much Johnson,* a Shakespearean anthology, *Five Kings,* and the controversial pro-

duction of Marc Blitzstein's socialist opera, *The Cradle Will Rock* (staged in defiance of an Equity ban). Welles's concurrent radio work—he spoke roles in *The March of Time* and was the original voice of *The Shadow*—led the Mercury Theatre to take to the airwaves on CBS in prime time on Sundays in radio adaptations of well-known dramas like *Dracula, Sherlock Holmes,* and, most memorably, the notorious broadcast on October 30, 1938, of H. G. Wells's *The War of the Worlds.*

Due in part to the notoriety of the Halloween *War of the Worlds* program, Hollywood beckoned, and in July 1939 Welles, now proclaimed a genius at the tender age of 24, arrived at the RKO studios determined to make film history with his transplanted Mercury Production. He had already dabbled in the film medium. Five years earlier he had made a short, four-minute film, *Hearts of Age,* in which he had, significantly, played the role of Death, a satire of surrealist experiments like JEAN COCTEAU's *Blood of the Poet;* and he had shot a film interlude for the Mercury production of *Too Much Johnson.* The new head of RKO, George Schaefer, gave Welles an unprecedented free rein for this picture: as long as RKO initially approved a project, it could neither influence the subsequent production nor make any alterations whatsoever without Welles's approval. Although he encountered a measure of jealous hostility in the film colony, directors JOHN FORD, Woody Van Dyke, and KING VIDOR were supportive and generous with advice. "King Vidor said to me a thing I never forgot," remembered Welles. "He said, 'A good director is a fellow who doesn't go on trying to get everything right, who knows when to walk away from something, and when to stay with something.' I think that's a wonderful definition, and I never forgot it."

Considering and rejecting a number of projects, like an adaptation of Joseph Conrad's *Heart of Darkness*—and taking a crash course in filmmaking (including numerous viewings of films by John Ford)—he settled on an idea by a young writer named Herman Mankiewicz. The story of the rise and fall of an American tycoon was fleshed out into a script entitled *American,* and subsequently changed to *Citizen Kane.* The fact that so much of the finished script reflected many aspects of the life of William Randolph Hearst—Charles Foster Kane's newspaper empire resembling the Hearst chain, the setting of Xanadu standing in for Hearst's San Simeon, the opera career of mistress Susan Alexander substituting for the film career of Marion Davies—was not accidental. Mankiewicz knew about the long-standing Hearst affair with Davies, and gossip columnist Louella Parsons was quick to detect the correlations and report them back to an outraged Hearst. He was pained not so much at what seemed a caricature of himself as a ruthless but lonely egomaniac but at the portrait of the Alexander character as an alcoholic (which Davies was) and an untalented performer (which she wasn't). Under Hearst's pressure, only a few theaters showed the film (it premiered on May 8, 1941) and the original negative barely escaped destruction. "It wasn't so much what [Hearst] did that hurt the film commercially as what others feared he might do, to them and to the movie industry," wrote critic Pauline Kael in "Raising Kane," her ground-breaking 1971 *New Yorker* essay. "They knew he was contemplating action, so they did the picture in for him; it was as if they decided whom the king might want killed and, eager to oblige, performed the murder without waiting to be asked." Its failure at the box office set the pattern for Welles's subsequent films, all of which would do only tepid business.

How much of the finished script was written by Welles and how much by Mankiewicz remains one of film history's hottest debates. It came to a head in 1971 when Pauline Kael in the aforementioned *New Yorker* essay (later the basis for her *The Citizen Kane Book*) contended that Welles's claims of authorship were exaggerated, to say the least. Kael quotes the secretary to whom Mankiewicz dictated the script to the effect that "Welles didn't write (or dictate) one line of the shooting script of *Citizen Kane.*" Kael continues that Welles could

Orson Welles

have been caught up in the frenzy of his own protean energies in insisting on his own authorship: "Because he *could* do all these things, he imagined that he *did* do them." Commentator Roger Carringer in his study of the seven script revisions insists that, at the very least, Welles was one of the *principal authors* [italics mine] of the screenplay. Certainly it is true that Mankiewicz successfully petitioned the Screen Writer's Guild to list him as "coauthor" on the screen credits.

Citizen Kane, billed as "A Mercury Production," is frequently cited by film critics as the greatest motion picture ever made. At the time of its premiere, however, critical reaction was mixed. The more negative reviews castigated Welles as too young to make a masterpiece; and others complained that the story was too political and too complicated. Writing in the *New Republic,* Otis Ferguson presented a more balanced assessment, crediting it as being, on the one hand, "the boldest freehand stroke in major screen production since Griffith and Bitzer were running wild to unshackle the camera"; and on the other, attacking its "tricks and symbols"—the business about "Rosebud"—and its talky theatricality. It was nominated for nine Oscars, winning only for best screenplay (Welles's only Oscar).

Standing aside from the hoopla, the general regard is that *Citizen Kane* undeniably is a masterpiece of structure and style. Apart from the framing device of Kane's death in the spooky, gothic mansion and the subsequent "News on the March" newsreel (a parody of *The March of Time*), the flashback-driven narrative is divided among Kane's friends, associates, and observers—recollections of mistress Susan Alexander (Dorothy Comingore), Jed Leland (Joseph Cotten), Mr. Bernstein (Everett Sloane), and the memoirs of Walter Thatcher (George Coulouris), and a final anecdote from the butler Raymond (Paul Stewart). Contributing factors include the editing of ROBERT WISE, the landmark music score by Bernard Herrmann, and the superb lensing of cinematographer Gregg Toland (embracing a panoply of chiaroscuro images, long takes, extreme deepfocus shots, ceiling shots, and skewed camera angles). Also not to be ignored is the soundtrack. Welles's radio experience influenced a richly dense soundtrack of overlapping dialogue, voice montages, and transition sound and music bites. Thematically, it prefigured much of Welles's later work in its preoccupation with death, loss of innocence, the perversions of power, and the solitude of the artist. Jorge Luis Borges has the last word here: "The subject, at the same time metaphysical and detective story-like, psychological and allegorical, is the discovery of the secret soul of a man, beyond the works he has constructed, the words he's said, the many destinies he has ruined. . . . Shapes of multiplicity and diversity abound in the film . . . [and] we understand at the end that the fragments do not have a hidden unity: the unhappy Foster Kane is a shadow, a mere chaos of appearances."

Before Welles settled on *The Magnificent Ambersons* for his next picture (another Mercury Production), he briefly considered casting W. C. Fields in an adaptation of Dickens's *The Pickwick Papers,* one of the more fascinating might-have-beens in film history. If Welles himself seems to have been partly a model for the character of Kane, he is even more present in the spoiled, self-indulgent character of George Minafer in Booth Tarkington's Pulitzer Prize–winning 1919 novel. Welles had a special regard for Tarkington and had previously adapted *Ambersons, Penrod,* and *Seventeen* for radio. George (Tim Holt) is the last of the aristocratic but doomed Amberson line, representative of the collapse of the genteel American class. His midland town likewise is fated to fall before encroaching industrialism, symbolized by the automobile manufacturer Eugene Morgan (Joseph Cotten). By the time George suffers his "comeuppance," the fairytale-like tone of the film's early sequences has yielded to a kind of soot-darkened mood. Welles intended the picture to be an elegy, as he put it, "not so much for an epoch as for the sense of moral values which are destroyed."

Again, the cinematography (this time by Stanley Cortez), editing (Wise), and music (Herrmann) are integral parts of its cumulative effect. And again, Welles's use of "radio sound" predominates. In sequences like the classic "Christmas Ball," the mise-en-scène is more complex and beautiful than anything in *Kane.* Although Welles does not appear in the film, his narrative voice is crucial. As Stephen Farber has noted, "*The Magnificent Ambersons* contains the most beautiful, pertinent use of narration I have seen in movies. The narration is not used simply to provide information; it adds to the sensuous atmosphere of the film. . . . Its literary cadences are part of the vanished courtly style that the film mourns."

As if it were falling to the same fate as the Amberson family—and as if Welles himself were receiving the same "comeuppance" that George had suffered—*The Magnificent Ambersons* received coarse treatment at the hands of RKO. Before the editing could be completed, Welles was dispatched to Brazil on February 4, 1942, to direct on behalf of the federal government's Good Neighbor Policy an episode film to be called *It's All True*. During his six-month absence (during which time miles of footage were shot of Carnival as part of a projected history of the samba), he edited *Ambersons* with Robert Wise via telephone to a two-hour length. Dissatisfied with the project, RKO ordered the picture to be shortened, and it was ultimately chopped down to 88 minutes. "They let the studio janitor cut it in my absence," Welles said. The last two reels were reshuffled and a concluding, upbeat scene not in the original script was inserted, destroying the moody tone and the narrative arc that had preceded it. As an indicator of how RKO regarded the truncated version's box-office potential, one advertising blurb proclaimed: "Scandal played no favorites when that high-and-mighty Amberson girl fell in love once too often!" Not surprisingly, the release print received a tepid critical response and was a disaster at the box-office.

No longer affiliated with RKO, Welles strove to make his next three films on time and under budget for various studios. But *The Lady from Shanghai* (1948), with second wife Rita Hayworth, angered Columbia boss Harry Cohn with its theme of greed and lust and its bizarre images and camera work (notably the celebrated "hall of mirrors" scene). *The Stranger* (1946) was a postwar film noir about the search by a detective (Edward G. Robinson) for a Nazi criminal (Welles). *Macbeth* (1948), the first of Welles's Shakespearean screen adaptations, was shot on a shoestring in just 23 days at Republic.

Branded in Hollywood as unreliable, extravagant, and unbankable, Welles did not make another Hollywood film for a decade. Instead, he continued to act in more than 60 films, indulging his penchant for sinister, flamboyant characters (Mr. Rochester in *Jane Eyre* [1943]; Cagliostro in *Black Magic* [1947]; and Harry Lime in *The Third Man* [1949]). Meanwhile, in Europe he marshaled mea-

ger resources and loyal casts and crew to eke out several notable films. *Othello* (1952) was a lavish exercise in visual stylization that at times threatened to overwhelm Shakespeare's characters and story. Regarded by commentator Jack Jorgens as "an authentic flawed masterpiece," it was a triumph over technical shortcoming, "one of the few Shakespeare films in which the images on the screen generate enough beauty, variety and graphic power to stand comparison with Shakespeare's poetic images." *Mr. Arkadin* (aka *Confidential Report* [1955]) was shot in England and its story of a legendary financial tycoon whose past life is under investigation bears striking resemblances to *Citizen Kane. The Trial* (1961), a nightmarish chaos of paranoia and hallucinatory images, was based on Kafka's novel and shot in Zagreb, Paris, and Rome. For *Chimes at Midnight* (1966), Welles returned to Shakespeare, conflating scenes from *Henry IV, Richard II, Henry V,* and *The Merry Wives of Windsor*. This somber elegy to Merrie Olde England and the death of Falstaff contains some of Welles's greatest work, particularly the amazing choreography and energy of the battle of Shrewsbury. In France he directed *The Immortal Story* (1968), an adaptation of one of Isak Dinesen's gothic tales. Welles himself appears as Mr. Clay, another in his gallery of wealthy, grotesque tyrants.

Meanwhile, the ever-peripatetic Welles frequently returned to the United States, where he embarked on his usual round of acting, commercial endorsements, and directorial efforts. For example, in addition to starring in Peter Brook's television production of *King Lear,* he appeared in an episode of *I Love Lucy* and managed to direct one of his greatest films, *Touch of Evil* (1958). Against the sleazy atmosphere of a Mexican-American border town, it was a noirish fable of the clash between good and evil, personified by a Mexican narcotics investigator (Charlton Heston) and a corrupt American cop (Welles).

Welles's last years are a wearisome grind of commercial appearances, failed attempts to fund more films (his never-completed *Don Quixote* is the classic example of such projects), and the token reception of various lifetime achievement awards (like the American Film Institute's recognition in 1975). As his massive girth and flamboyant manner and dress became a caricature of himself, he managed to complete just one more film, *F for Fake* (1973). Made in France, Iran, and West Germany, it was a labyrinthine, faux-documentary account of forgers and forgery, testifying to his own preoccupation with the hokum of stage magic and illusions.

At the time of his death at age 70, on October 10, 1985, he was contemplating making a film of the legendary first night of the WPA production of *The Cradle Will Rock* (a film project since directed in 1999 by TIM ROBBINS). His ashes were interred two years afterward in Spain in an unnamed grave.

"I started at the top," Welles once said, "and worked down." Indeed, he is the poster child of the maverick genius who can find no home in the commercial establishment. Perhaps he was its victim, perhaps he was his own worst enemy. "Undeniably, Welles was and is a mystery," writes John Russell Taylor. "If you asked the real Orson Welles to stand up and be recognized, a dozen different people would immediately spring to their feet, claiming to be the man." Whatever he was—and like Borges's analysis of Kane, that identity may remain unknowable—it was one of those inexplicable forces of nature that is its own triumph and failure. One is reminded of the story related in *Mr. Arkadin:* A scorpion asks a frog to carry him on his back across the river. The frog is reluctant, afraid that the scorpion might sting him. But when the scorpion points out that stinging him would result only in both their deaths, the frog agrees. Halfway across the river, the scorpion stings him. "There is no logic in this," protests the drowning frog. "I know," answers the scorpion, also expiring, "but it's my character."

Other Film *Journey into Fear* (1943), uncredited codirector.

References Anderegg, Michael, *Orson Welles, Shakespeare, and Popular Culture* (New York: Columbia University Press, 1999); Bazin, André, *Orson Welles: A Critical View* (New York: Harper & Row, 1978); Carringer, Robert L., *The Making of Citizen Kane,* rev. ed. (Berkeley: University of California Press, 1996); Farber, Stephen, "Magnificent Ambersons," *Film Comment* (Summer 97); Gottesman, Roland, ed., *Focus on "Citizen Kane"* (Englewood Cliffs, N.J.: Prentice-Hall, 1971); Houseman, John, *Run-Through* (New York: Simon and Schuster, 1972); Kael, Pauline, *The Citizen Kane Book* (Boston: Little, Brown, 1971); Leaming, Barbara, *Orson Welles: A Biography* (New York: Viking Press, 1985); McBride, Joseph, *Orson Welles* (New York: Jove Publications, 1977); Higham, Charles, *The Films of Orson Welles* (Berkeley: University of California Press, 1971); Naremore, James, *The Magic World of Orson Welles* (Dallas: Southern Methodist University Press, 1978); Taylor, John Russell, *Orson Welles: A Celebration* (Boston: Little Brown, 1986); Thomson, David, *Rosebud: The Story of Orson Welles* (New York: Vintage Books, 1997).

—J.C.T. and S.W.

Wellman, William Augustus (1896–1975)

Because he worked in the Hollywood mainstream throughout his entire career, accepting most of the assignments that came his way, William Wellman's 15 silent films and 62 sound pictures are of variable quality. His best work, however, was stamped with a characteristic rigor and toughness that ranks him with other action directors like HOWARD WINCHESTER HAWKS and RAOUL WALSH. Wellman's vision, notes commentator Julian Fox, "was often black, his comedy bitter, his romance based on genuine emotions, the emotions of an ordinary Joe, passionate in what he believed . . . and women who could meet men on their own terms."

He was born in Brookline, Massachusetts, on February 29, 1896, of Anglo-Irish parentage. Rough, restless, and rambunctious during his school years, he managed to graduate from Newton High School, Newton Highlands, Massachusetts, after which he joined a volunteer ambulance corps en route to France. He learned to fly planes during a stint with the French Foreign Legion.

When America entered the war, he joined the Lafayette Flying Corps, an arm of the Lafayette Escadrille, where he attained the rank of sergeant, won the Croix de Guerre, and acquired the nickname "Wild Bill." Invalided out in 1918, he went to Hollywood seeking acting jobs with his old friend, Douglas Fairbanks, Sr. After a short-lived career appearing in Fairbanks's *A Knickerbocker Buckaroo* (1919), he decided he wanted to direct, and he served an apprenticeship at the Goldwyn studio before directing his first picture, a Dustin Farnum western, *The Man Who Won* (1923).

His breakthrough came four years later with the aviation epic *Wings* (1927), which won the first Academy Award for best picture. It was the brainchild of World War I aviator John Monk Saunders, who also would write a later Wellman picture, *Legion of the Condemned* (1928). A simple story about three young people caught up in the war—Clara Bow as a vivacious nurse, Buddy Rogers as her "boy next door," and Richard Arlen as the buddy to both—is dwarfed by the spectacular aerial combat sequences, including a dazzlingly choreographed battle with a German zeppelin. Despite the gritty images of violence and carnage, never does the film stray from its central message that gallantry, courage, and ingenuity in the face of danger are man's highest attainment—a theme that constantly surfaces in Wellman's pictures. Shot in locations near San Antonio, Texas, the canvas was huge and the stuntwork authentic. The actors learned to fly their own planes and operate the cameras, and a battery of 25 cameramen employed portable cameras in the ground-combat sequences, such as the climactic battle of the Saint-Michel salient. Wellman's experiences in combat served him in good stead. "They gave me *Wings* because I was the only director who had been a flyer, in action. I was the only one who knew what the hell it was all about."

Wellman's nine subsequent aviation pictures all drew from his experiences and all contain a degree of autobiographical material, including *Men With Wings* (1938), *Island in the Sky* (1953), *The High*

and the Mighty (1954), and *Lafayette Escadrille* (1958), his last film. In rapid succession he turned out pictures demonstrating his versatility with "road pictures," gangster stories, darkly satiric comedies, westerns, and combat pictures. *Beggars of Life* (1928) was his first great road picture. Louise Brooks portrayed a young girl on the run after killing her father during a rape attempt. She teams up with a young man (Richard Arlen) as they take to the rails. Other pictures in this vein include two indisputable classics, both made for Warner Bros. in 1933, *Heroes for Sale* and *Wild Boys of the Road*. The first is quite possibly the quintessential depression-era film, depicting the misfortunes of a young ex-soldier (Richard Barthelmess) trying to cope with drug abuse, unemployment, and labor strife. It ends with a magnificent gesture of stoic acceptance as the man, after losing his job and his wife, takes to the rails and is last seen walking through a pouring rain. As the downpour slackens, he doffs his hat and announces cheerfully: "Oh, well; it's stopped raining." *Wild Boys of the Road* depicts the adventures of gangs of children who have left home in search of jobs. They had to steal and beg to survive. Their battles with railroad detectives constitute some of the most graphically violent scenes in pre-Code Hollywood.

Wellman's first great gangster film remains one of the true classics in the genre. *Public Enemy* (1931) traces the rise and fall of a Chicago mobster, Tom Powers (James Cagney in his breakthrough role). The performances, tight editing, and occasionally graphic violence made it, according to *Variety,* "the roughest, toughest, and best of the gang films to date." It was followed by the lesser-known but interesting *Star Witness* (1931), with Walter Huston as a tough, crusading district attorney. *Nothing Sacred* (1937) and *Roxie Hart* (1942), respectively, are cynical, dark comedies about tough-minded women caught up in fraud and murder. Among the westerns are *The Ox-Bow Incident* (1943), an indictment of intolerance and mob lynching adapted from a novel by Walter Van Tillburg Clark; *Buffalo Bill* (1944), which confronted the historical Bill Cody (Joel McCrea) with his "wild west" mythic image; and *Track of the Cat* (1954), another "serious" western adapted from the work of Walter Van Tillburg Clark. The combat pictures include *The Story of G.I. Joe* (1945), a humanistic view of the common infantryman, based on the writings of war correspondent Ernie Pyle; and *Battleground* (1949), an unusually gritty drama set during the Battle of the Bulge. Among his best action pictures is the classic *Beau Geste* (1939), based on the Foreign Legion novel by P. C. Wren, a gorgeously photographed remake of Herbert Brenon's 1926 silent film.

Wellman retired in 1962 and wrote his autobiography, *A Short Time for Insanity,* in 1974. Before his death from leukemia on December 9, 1975, he received many honors, including the D. W. Griffith Award in 1972 and retrospectives in Los Angeles, and in London at the British Film Institute. Because he made so many films in so many different genres, he has been the center of controversy regarding a consistency, or lack of it, in tone and method. The debate on Wellman's auteur status rages: biographer Frank Thompson contends that "his work has continuity, consistency, recurring themes, a recognizable style. The films are generally unpretentious (not always), but they are anything but anonymous, assembly-line pieces of product and their director was anything but a servile, compliant company man." However, commentator Todd McCarthy is much harsher in his estimation, declaring that, aside from "some admirably tough, strong, democratically intelligent films," the great bulk of his work "is, by turns, murky, ponderous, misfired, or actively lamentable." Wellman himself admitted that when you accept most assignments given him, as he did, the work output is bound to be uneven: "You make all kinds of things, and that, I think, is what gives you the background to eventually make some very lucky picture." By that standard, Wellman was luckier than most.

Other Films *Night Nurse* (1931); *The President Vanishes* (1934); *The Great Man's Lady* (1942); *Magic Town* (1947); *The Next Voice You Hear* (1950); *Blood Alley* (1955).

References Fox, Julian, "A Man's World," *Films and Filming,* March 1973, 32–40; McCarthy, Todd, "William A. Wellman," in *American Directors,* vol. 1, ed. Jean-Pierre Coursodon (New York: McGraw-Hill, 1983), 358–366; Thompson, Frank T., *William A. Wellman* (Metuchen, N.J.: Scarecrow Press, 1973).

—J.C.T.

Wenders, Wim (1945–) Wim Wenders belonged to a new generation of German filmmakers, known collectively as Das neue Kino, reflecting a vitality akin to the exuberance of the French New Wave. Wenders was one of the founding talents of that movement, along with his collaborator, the novelist and playwright PETER HANDKE, WERNER HERZOG, and RAINER WERNER FASSBINDER, though Wenders had little in common with the latter, other than a desire to make films.

Born in Düsseldorf on August 14, 1945, Wenders studied medicine and philosophy before turning to cinema in 1967, the year he entered the Hochschule für Film und Fernsehen in Munich. Like the filmmakers of the French New Wave, Wenders wrote film criticism for *Filmkritik* and the *Süddeutsche Zeitung.* He also wrote music criticism on rock 'n' roll, and his enthusiasm for rock music carried into his early films: "Rock'n'Roll led me to everything," Wenders stated in an interview with Jan Dawson: "It led me to filmmaking. Without Rock'n'Roll, maybe I would be a lawyer now. And a lot of people would be somebody else."

Wenders described his short film *Alabama* (1969), for example, as being "about" Dylan's song "All Along the Watchtower" and "about what happens and what changes, depending on whether the song is sung by Bob Dylan or by Jimi Hendrix." Another short, also made in 1969, entitled *3 amerikanische LPs,* was built around the music of Van Morrison, Harvey Mandel, and the Credence Clearwater Revival. His first feature film, made in 1970, was entitled *Summer in the City: Dedicated to the Kinks,* the Kinks being his favorite rock group.

In 1971 Wenders made *Der scharlachrote Buchstabe,* his adaptation of Nathaniel Hawthorne's novel *The Scarlet Letter,* starring Senta Berger as Hester Prynne and Yella Rottländer as Pearl, for WDR (Westdeutschen Rundfunk, Köln). Wenders shot the film on location in Spain because he lacked the funding to shoot it in America. In 1978 he stated that this was his least favorite project because he had little control and was forced to compromise. Senta Berger was cast contrary to the director's wishes because the producers argued that the lead had to be played by a known actress. Wenders adapted the screenplay with Bernardo Fernandez, from the scenario "Der Herr klast über sin Volk in der Wildnis Amerika," by Tankred Dorst and Ursula Enler.

Wenders really began to hit his stride with his adaptation of Peter Handke's novel, *Die Angst des Tormanns beim Elfmeter* (*The Goalie's Anxiety at the Penalty Kick* [1972]), telling the disturbing and disjointed story of Joseph Bloch (Rüdiger Vogler), an ex-soccer goalie, ex-construction worker, and murderer. Handke's novel succeeded brilliantly in creating a sense of shared psychosis while penetrating the subconscious of a protagonist antihero who was mentally disturbed. The "angst" of the soccer player becomes a metaphor for the angst of modern existence. As Bloch says in the novel, "Man gewöhnt sich daran . . . aber es ist lächerlich" ("One gets used to it . . . but it's ridiculous"). In the screenplay, which Handke also wrote, Bloch is first seen on the soccer field (in the novel he is first encountered as he is being fired from his construction job); but the story is essentially the same, following what Stanley Kauffmann called "a vaguely apprehended pattern of flight" and reflecting Bloch's sanity as in "a crazy-house mirror, exaggerating the delusions of the people around him." Wenders places us, in Kauffmann's words, "inside a man barren of the rationality that leads to and away from morality," a man "who can still make contact with society in small ritual and etiquette, but whose vacancy is, paradoxically, like a volcano that can boil up at any time." Vincent Canby of the *New York Times*

included the film in his "Ten Best" list for 1997, the year it was released in the United States.

The question for some was how much of the achievement of *Die Angst des Tormanns* was due to the director, and how much to the writer, the formidable Peter Handke? In succeeding years, however, Wenders would make a trilogy of films that would dispel all doubts: *Alice in den Städten* (*Alice in the Cities* [1974]); *Falsche Bewegung* (*The Wrong Move* [1975], scripted by Handke, updated and freely adapted from Goethe's *Wilhelm Meisters Apprenticeship*); and *Im Lauf der Zeit* (In the course of time, aka *Kings of the Road* [1976]). In Germany *Der Spiegel* praised *Falsche Bewegung* as "one of the most important German films since Lubitsch, Lang, and Murnau," while abroad Robin Wood asserted that seeing it "was like discovering Bergman with *The Seventh Seal* or Antonioni with *L'Avventura.*"

The other two films of the trilogy were "pure" Wenders, odysseys involving dislocated characters who drift through changing locales. Philip Winter (Rüdiger Vogler), the alienated "hero" of *Alice in the Cities,* having returned from a photographic assignment in the United States, finds himself wandering across Germany in the company of a lost little girl, Alice van Damn (played by Yella Rottländer), whose mother has deserted her and whose only surviving contact with her past is a grandmother who may (or may not) still be alive. No director, according to Nigel Andrews of the London *Financial Times,* "could have handled more unsentimentally the relationship between the hero and the little girl lost."

Brian Baxter's notes for the 20th London Film Festival in 1976 called *Kings of the Road* "the director's most ambitious and successful work." This film told the story of two men "on the road" in Germany—Bruno (Rüdiger Vogler, again) and Robert, the Kamikaze. "They meet casually," Baxter explained, then "move from one small town to the next in Bruno's mobile home, from which he earns his living servicing projectors in declining cinemas." In and of itself, the minimal plot was not too promising, but the voyage proves to be "one of self-discovery against a specific landscape." Wenders himself described the film as "a story about two men, but it's different from the Hollywood kind of films about men. The American films, especially those made recently," Wenders believed, "are pure repression films, in which the men's relationships to women, and between themselves, are repressed by the story, the action, and the necessity to entertain. They leave out what it's actually about!" In this regard, *Kings of the Road* clearly foreshadowed Wenders's next feature film, *Der amerikanische Freund* (*The American Friend* [1977]).

The source behind *The American Friend* was the mystery novel *Ripley's Game* by Patricia Highsmith, whose first novel, *Strangers on a Train,* was the source for one of ALFRED HITCHCOCK's finest thrillers. The pacing of the Wenders film is hardly Hitchcockian, but the film succeeds very well on its own terms. The film's merit is not to be found in the way the story is told, but in the existential portrait if offers of its sick and disturbed—and finally seduced—protagonist, a German named Jonathan Zimmerman (Bruno Ganz) and in the remarkable construction of atmosphere against which this tale of corruption and compromise is set. Zimmerman is a picture-frame maker who has also worked to restore art works, but no longer. He suffers from a rare blood disease and his living days are numbered. He is an ordinary man, a loving husband and father, and his dilemma ingratiates the viewer's sympathy. Remarkably, Wenders takes the viewer into the mind of this character without resorting to much dialogue at all. The "American friend" of the title, Tom Ripley (Dennis Hopper), suggests that Zimmerman, because he is dying and because he needs money for his surviving wife and son, may be recruited to assassinate a Jewish gangster.

In 1978 Wenders came to the United States to work out a project with FRANCIS FORD COPPOLA, a biopic based on the life of the crime-fiction writer Dashiell Hammett. Originally Wenders planned to stay in America for approximately a year and a half, but in fact his stay lasted until 1985. In a personal interview in Salisbury, Maryland, in 1978, Wenders expressed a desire to make personal films, but to do so, he knew he needed to have control over production details, which he hoped to have in working with Coppola. Wenders was disappointed, however, after he got deeply involved in the *Hammett* project, which was not completed until 1982, after a "long and contentious production history marked by interventions from executive producer Francis Coppola," as described by Peter Lev. Better working conditions for his next film would produce a better picture.

Wenders is one of the paradigm directors for what Peter Lev has called the "Euro-American cinema," involving a mix of the Hollywood style of stars, genres, and action, with the European art-film style of ambiguity, authorial commentary, and borrowings from other arts. For *Paris, Texas* (1984) Wenders worked with playwright Sam Shepard and L. M. "Kit" Carson on the screenplay to make "a film that would be recognizably American in setting, European in production methods, and a blend [Euro-American] in theme and style," according to Lev. The film starred character actor Harry Dean Stanton, along with Dean Stockwell and Germans Nastassja Kinski and Bernhard Wicki, who plays an eccentric German doctor. His German cinematographer was Robbie Müller, with whom he had worked before, and his assistant director was Claire Denis. Part-western, part-road movie, part-existential drama, and funded by Wenders's Road Movies (Berlin), Argos Films (Paris), Channel Four (London), Pro-ject Film (Munich), and Westdeutscher Rundfunk (Cologne), *Paris, Texas* won the Golden Palm at the Cannes Film Festival and was bought by 20th Century-Fox for American distribution. It also won Wenders a best director award from the British Academy Awards.

After nearly eight years in America, Wenders had "come to accept myself as a European filmmaker and come to accept myself as a German in my heart." Thus he returned to Germany for his next film, *Der Himmel über Berlin* (*Wings of Desire* [1987]), which starred Bruno Ganz as an angel who decides to become a human being, a haunting fable that became a favorite with the art-house circuit, and earned Wenders a best director award at the Cannes Festival. Wenders explained that it would be terrible to be an angel: "To live for an eternity and to be present all the time. To live with the essence of things—not to be able to raise a cup of coffee and drink it, or really touch somebody." Peter Handke wrote the screenplay with Wenders. Peter Falk played another angel who had fallen to Earth.

Wenders is a master of elliptical ambiguity, demonstrated yet again in *Lisbon Story* (1995), a "philosophical travelogue" starring Rüdiger Vogler as sound engineer Philip Winter, summoned by self-obsessed director Friedrich Monroe to Lisbon to provide sound effects for an unedited silent film he finds on the editing table, though the director is nowhere to be found. Winter does his job, befriends children in the neighborhood, falls in love with a singer, and has a run-in with some gangsters, until, finally, the director surfaces to convince Winter that the innocence of cinema still exists—Wenders's reflection on the state of cinema today. Viewers have difficulty knowing exactly where the film is going until it gets there, but the journey is worthwhile, as is Winter's journey to Lisbon.

Philip Winter was also the name of the reporter in *Alice in the Cities,* described by poet and novelist Tom Whalen as "a man who has lost his sense of self, who is without purpose, disconnected," a man who "is nearing the end of the road, but knows the road may be endless." Whalen quotes Wenders: "When you think you've got there, you haven't," then adds: "The most important lesson for his protagonists to learn is that the quest is inseparable from being." There are many journeys in the cinema of Wim Wenders, all of them worth pursuing.

Other Films *Schauplätze* (Locations [1967], short; *Same Player Shoots Again* (1967), short; *Silver City* (1968), short; *Victor I* (1968), short; *Polizeifilm* (Police film [1970]); *Aus der Familie der Panzerechsen* (The crocodile family [1974]), TV short, combined with *Der Insel* (The island [1974]), TV short for the *Ein Haus für*

Uns (A house for us) Bayerischer Rundfunk TV series; *Lightening over Water: Nick's Film* (1981); *Der Stand der Dinge* (The state of things [1982]); *Lettre d'un cinéaste; quand je m'éveille* (aka *Reverse Angle 1: NYC March '82* [1982]), for French TV Antenne II; *Room 666* (1984), documentary; *Tokyo-Ga* (1985), documentary; *Aufziechnungen zu Kleidern und Städten* (Notebook on cities and clothes [1989]); *Until the End of the World* (1991); *Far Away, So Close* (1993); *The End of Violence* (1997); *Beyond the Clouds* (1997), codirected with Michelangelo Antonioni; *Million Dollar Hotel* (2000).

References Covino, M., "Wim Wenders: A Worldwide Homesickness," *Film Quarterly* 31, no. 2 (Winter 1977–78): 131–135; Dawson, Jan, *Wim Wenders* (Toronto: Festival of Festivals, 1976); Geist, Kathe, *The Cinema of Wim Wenders: From Paris, France to Paris, Texas* (Ann Arbor, Mich.: UMI Research Press, 1988); Kauffmann, Stanley, "Wenders," *New Republic,* January 29, 1977, pp. 26–27; Lev, Peter, *The Euro-American Cinema* (Austin: University of Texas Press, 1993); Whalen, Tom, "'When You Think You've Got There, You Haven't': Wim Wenders' *Alice in the Cities,*" *New Orleans Review* 15, no. 2 (Summer 1988): 80–83.

—J.M.W.

Wilder, Billy (1906–) Commonly acknowledged as one of the screen's supreme, if idiosyncratic artists, Samuel Wilder was born on June 22, 1906, in Galicia, a province of Poland that was then still a part of the Austro-Hungarian Empire. Samuel's mother, Eugenia, had visited the United States in her youth where she had seen Buffalo Bill's Wild West Show; thus she took to calling her youngest son "Billie." The name stuck, and was eventually Americanized to "Billy." As "Billy Wilder," young Samuel would grow to be one of the most respected writer-directors of the American cinema, with a career that stretched from the end of the silent era through the highs and lows of the studios to the early 1980s.

Wilder spent most of his formative years in Vienna, Austria, eventually securing a number of reporting jobs for various Viennese papers. It was during this time, according to Wilder, that he also worked as a dime-a-dance gigolo. As many biographers point out and like most of Wilder's stories about his youth—this may be the result of more than a little elaboration and embellishment on Wilder's part. Wilder moved to Berlin in 1927, when he was 21 years old. At first he continued to scrape together a living as a reporter, but it was not long before the cinema attracted his eye.

A longtime movie buff, Wilder soon worked his way into Berlin's cinema society where he made contacts with some of Germany's finest writers, actors, directors, and executives. In 1929 he received one of his first solo screenwriting credits for the film *The Daredevil Reporter* (*Der Teufelsreporter*), based in large part on Wilder's own newspaper experiences in Vienna and Berlin. One year later Wilder teamed with other fringe-dwelling members of German cinema, such as FRED ZINNEMANN, ROBERT and Curt SIODMAK, and EDGAR

Billy Wilder

ULMER, to create and produce *People on Sunday* (*Menschen am Sonntag*), a "city symphony"–style look at Berliners relaxing after a hard week's work. Wilder is credited with cowriting the script from Curt's idea, with Robert directing, though who actually did what would remain a topic of debate among the film's makers for the rest of their lives.

When Hitler came to power in 1933, Wilder was among the many Jews in German cinema to see the writing on the wall, and he fled to Paris. It was there, also in 1933, that Wilder received his first directing credit. The film, *Bad Seed* (*Mauvaise graine*), was a car-chase thriller codirected by Alexander Essway.

Wilder was more fortunate than many of his fellow Parisian exiles in that one of his earlier screenplay ideas, *Pam-pam,* had been purchased by Fox. The studio brought Wilder over to work on the script. After a lifetime diet of American movies and his mother's stories, Billy Wilder finally arrived in what he, and many of his religion and generation, saw at that time as the promised land. When the picture fell through, however, Wilder's visa expired and he was forced to go south to Mexico to await a new visa.

It was not long before he was back in Hollywood, working on the screenplay for a film version of Kern and Hammerstein II's operetta *Music in the Air* (1934). Other writing jobs followed, and in 1938 Wilder collaborated with Charles Brackett on the screenplay for *Bluebeard's Eighth Wife.* It was the beginning of the first of two important partnerships in Wilder's career. Wilder and Brackett next collaborated on *Midnight* (1939), and on such other films as *Ball of Fire* (1941) for Howard Hawks, and, most memorably, on *Ninotchka* (1939) for Wilder's fellow German and idol, Ernst Lubitsch.

In 1942 Wilder was given the chance to direct one of his and Brackett's screenplays. The film, *The Major and the Minor,* was a light comedy starring Ginger Rogers and Ray Milland. The next year Wilder released *Five Graves to Cairo* (1943), a witty adventure set in the North African desert and featuring ERICH OSWALD (VON) STROHEIM as Field Marshal Erwin Rommel. Wilder and Stroheim would work together again on *Sunset Boulevard* (1950). In 1944 Wilder and Raymond Chandler adapted James M. Cain's novella *Double Indemnity,* creating a dark and stunning early film noir full of murder, intrigue, and double crosses. In fact, it may have been the film's gruesome nature that turned away Charles Brackett from the project. Wilder's next film, *The Lost Weekend* (1945), was a stark and at times frightening depiction of alcoholism. The film also marked Brackett's return to the fold. Named the best picture of 1945, the film also won Wilder his first Oscar as best director.

After the war, Wilder received confirmation that his mother and stepfather had both died in the Auschwitz concentration camp. Wilder's next two significant films reflected his anger at humanity for allowing such an atrocity to take place. *Sunset Boulevard* (1950), a noirish tale of a struggling screenwriter and the aged silent-movie queen who uses and is used by him, dared to lay bare the dark heart of Hollywood and, as a result, was hated within the industry. The film also marked the end of the long partnership between Wilder and Brackett. If Wilder was stung by the reception of *Sunset Boulevard,* however, he did not let it interfere with planning his next project. *Ace in the Hole* (aka *The Big Carnival* [1951]) was the bitterly funny story of a man trapped in a mine and the reporter (still more shades of Wilder's past) who exploits the situation for selfish gain. Where *Sunset Boulevard* exposed the darkness of Hollywood, *Ace in the Hole* was an angry indictment of the media and of people in general, all of whom turn a life-and-death crisis into a circus-like event. One of the rare box-office failures of Wilder's career, the film seems more prescient with each passing year.

In 1957 Wilder teamed with I. A. L. Diamond to write *Love in the Afternoon,* a Lubitsch-esque romantic comedy starring Audrey Hepburn and Gary Cooper. It was the beginning of the second important partnership in Wilder's career. Together they would write 11 more films, including such classics as *Some Like It Hot* (1959), dubbed by the American Film Institute as one of the 10 funniest films of all time; *The Apartment* (1960), another multi-Oscar winner for Wilder; and *The Fortune Cookie* (1966). In 1979 Wilder tried to recapture some of the magic of *Sunset Boulevard* with a film entitled *Fedora.* The film is another bitterly sarcastic attack on Hollywood, only this time the anger is directed at a younger director. The main character, an aged film director (played by *Boulevard's* William Holden), decries a Hollywood run rampant by "kids with beards," an obvious dig at the then-young "film school generation" of STEVEN SPIELBERG, MARTIN SCORSESE, FRANCIS FORD COPPOLA, and others. Two years later Wilder released what is, to date, his last film, a buddy comedy starring *Fortune Cookie's* Jack Lemmon and Walter Matthau called (appropriately enough) *Buddy Buddy* (1981).

Even now, nearly 20 years after his last film and well into his nineties, Billy Wilder is admired and respected by his younger peers. Filmmaker Cameron Crowe took time off from his career to conduct and publish a series of interviews with the man he calls his idol and "the greatest living writer-director," while Sam Mendes referred to Wilder as the biggest influence on his 1999 best-picture winner *American Beauty.* Though he will probably never make another film, Wilder's reputation as a creator of intelligent, entertaining studio pictures will likely last as long as the art form endures.

Other Films   *The Emperor Waltz* (1948); *A Foreign Affair* (1948); *Stalag 17* (1953); *Sabrina* (1954); *The Seven Year Itch* (1955); *The Spirit of St. Louis* (1957); *Witness for the Prosecution* (1957); *One, Two, Three* (1961); *Irma la Douce* (1963); *Kiss Me, Stupid* (1964); *The Private Life of Sherlock Holmes* (1970); *Avanti!* (1972); *The Front Page* (1974).

References   Crowe, Cameron, *Conversations with Wilder* (New York: Knopf, 1999); Lally, Kevin, *Wilder Times: The Life of Billy Wilder* (New York: Henry Holt, 1996); Sikov, Ed, *On Sunset Boulevard* (New York: Hyperion Books, 1998).

—F.H.

Wise, Robert (1914–) Coming to Hollywood from the cornfields of Indiana during the Great Depression, Robert Wise first established himself as a talented film editor at RKO, then as a journeyman director for Val Lewton during the 1940s, and finally as a genre master who made some of the most popular and memorable films of the 1950s and 1960s. He was born in Winchester, Indiana, September 10, 1914, and educated in the Hoosier state, but he was forced by the depression to drop out of Franklin College, outside of Indianapolis, and migrate to Hollywood. Only eight years after his arrival, he was nominated for an Academy Award for his editing of *Citizen Kane* in 1941, though 20 years would pass before he was destined to win an Oscar for directing *West Side Story* (sharing the credit with codirector and choreographer Jerome Robbins), a film that was honored as the best picture of 1961. Further recognition came in 1965 when *The Sound of Music* also won Academy Awards for best directing and best picture. In 1966, moreover, the Motion Picture Academy granted Wise the Irving G. Thalberg Memorial Award, its highest honor.

In 1933 his father's business was failing, and, as Wise told the National Film Society in 1978, "there was no money to go back" for his second year of college. "I couldn't get a job in my home town," Wise explained, but his older brother David "had come out to California five years before and managed to get a job at RKO," working in the accounting office. When the younger Wise arrived in Hollywood in July 1933, his brother got him "a couple of appointments with department heads at RKO." The second of these was with Jimmy Wilkerson, "who headed up the editorial department—the film editing department—at RKO, and he happened to need a kid in the film shooting room to check the prints and run the projector." This modest assignment launched Wise on a very successful Hollywood career.

Before long Wise had become a film editor, serving such talents as GEORGE STEVENS on *Alice Adams* (1935) and ORSON GEORGE WELLES, with whom he worked on both *Citizen Kane* and *The Magnificent Ambersons* in 1941 and 1942. His first assignment as director came when he was working for the Val Lewton production unit in 1943. Gunther Van Fritsch, who had begun a film entitled *Curse of the Cat People,* had committed the unforgivable "sin" of falling behind schedule in a low-budget operation where time was of the essence. Given the opportunity to complete this picture, Wise demonstrated a remarkable ability to create an effective supernatural ambience while working on a very low budget with limited resources. Later supernatural films would follow, most notably *The Haunting* (1963), with Julie Harris and Claire Bloom, based on Shirley Jackson's *The Haunting of Hill House,* and *Audrey Rose* (1977), adapted by Frank DeFellita from his novel and starring Anthony Hopkins and Marsha Mason.

Wise proved adaptable to other genre pictures as well. *The Body Snatcher* (1945) has been recognized as a classic of the horror genre, for example, and *The Set-Up* (1949), with Robert Ryan as an over-the-hill boxer who refuses to "fix" a fight under pressure from mobsters, won the Jury Prize at the Cannes Film Festival. A second fight film followed in 1956, *Somebody Up There Likes Me,* which starred Paul Newman as the boxer Rocky Graziano, a biopic scripted by Ernest Lehman that also won an Oscar for its cinematography. *I Want to Live!* (1956) was another biopic that told the story of Barbara Graham, convicted and executed in 1955 for her alleged participation in the murder of Mabel Monohan in Burbank in 1953. Wise was nominated for an Academy Award for best director, and Hayward won an Oscar as best actress for her portrayal of Graham. An immense critical success, the film was singled out by the *New York Times* as one of the "Ten Best Films of 1958."

Wise's most popular genre pictures, however, were musicals and science fiction. *The Day the Earth Stood Still* (1951), a "friendly" alien message film encouraging peace and cooperation among nations during the height of the Cold War, has since become a cult classic. It won a Golden Globe

Robert Wise (left) on the set of *Star Trek: The Motion Picture* (Paramount)

Award for "Best Film Promoting International Understanding." This was followed by *The Andromeda Strain* (1971), adapted from Michael Crichton's novel concerning the threat posed to humankind by a deadly alien virus, and *Star Trek: The Motion Picture* (1979), adapted from Gene Roddenberry's long-running cult television space opera that ran on NBC from 1966 to 1969. Nominated for Academy Awards for art direction, visual effects, and musical score, the picture later generated six sequels.

Wise had his most astonishing popular success with musicals, however, starting with *West Side Story* (1961), adapted from the play by Arthur Laurents, with music by Leonard Bernstein and lyrics by Stephen Sondheim, originally directed and choreographed for the stage by Jerome Robbins.

The play was a musical adaptation and updating of Shakespeare's *Romeo and Juliet*. "Everything about *West Side Story,*" critic Pauline Kael wrote, "is supposed to stun you with its newness, its size, the wonders of its photography, editing, cinematography, [and] music. It's nothing so simple as a musical, it's a piece of cinematic technology." Though Kael was probably damning with faint praise, the craftsmanship was quite remarkable and audiences were dazzled. A 1977 American Film Institute poll proclaimed it to be one of the 50 "Greatest American Films of All Time."

West Side Story was then followed in 1965 by *The Sound of Music,* adapted by Ernest Lehman from the play by Howard Lindsay and Russel Crouse, with lyrics by Oscar Hammerstein II and music by Richard Rodgers, which in turn had been adapted from *The Story of the Trapp Family Singers* by Maria Trapp, concerning the von Trapp family under pressure in Austria at the time of the Anschluss with the Third Reich. The film was graced by the presence of Christopher Plummer as Captain von Trapp, and, especially, by Julie Andrews as Maria, whose singing talent helped to propel the film to the AFI list of the 50 "Greatest American Films." Besides winning five Academy Awards, the film generated Golden Globe awards (best motion picture and best actress for musical/comedy), the Writers Guild Award for best-written American musical for Ernest Lehman, the Directors Guild Award for Wise's direction, and the Producers Guild David O. Selznick Award for Wise. Always a perennial favorite, *The Sound of Music* enjoyed a popular revival in London in 2000, when a cult craze saw spectators dressing up as nuns and Nazis and coming in droves to sing along with the music and interact with the screen action, following the example of *The Rocky Horror Picture Show.*

In 1966 Wise directed Steve McQueen as a sailor on a gunboat, the USS *San Pedro,* on the Yangtze River in China in 1926, the first American film made in Taiwan, with subtle echoes of America's involvement in Southeast Asia at the time the picture was filmed. *The Sand Pebbles* garnered seven Academy Award nominations and led to a Thalberg Award for Wise. The last film Wise directed, *Rooftops,* in 1989, was a musical and also intended as a tough urban drama, but it fell far short of being successful. Critic Frank Thompson notes that "although Wise did not develop a particular style that can be read throughout each of his motion pictures," he was "a master craftsman [and] a superb entertainer" who belongs, commercially, "in the *pantheon* of movie makers." Before the tremendous successes of George Lucas and Steven Spielberg, Robert Wise "was among the most profitable filmmakers in history."

Among his other accomplishments, Wise served as president of the Motion Picture Academy of Arts and Sciences from 1985 to 1987. He chaired the Directors Guild Special Projects Committee for 20 years beyond his appointment in 1976 and was elected as a trustee of the American Film Institute in 1982. In 1988 he received the D. W. Griffith Award for outstanding achievement and a lifetime contribution to film from the Directors Guild of America. In 1992 he received the National Medal of the Arts from President George Bush. He was well known in Hollywood for his kindness and cooperation as well as his quiet competence and his ability to create blockbuster hits.

Other Films *Mademoiselle Fifi* (1944); *Blood on the Moon* (1948); *The House on Telegraph Hill* (1951); *The Desert Rats* (1953); *So Big* (1953); *Executive Suite* (1954); *Run Silent, Run Deep* (1958); *Odds Against Tomorrow* (1959); *Two for the Seesaw* (1962); *Star!* (1968); *The Hindenberg* (1975).

References Thompson, Frank, *Robert Wise: A Bio-Bibliography* (Westport, Conn.: Greenwood Press, 1995); Welsh, J., "Tribute to Robert Wise," *American Classic Screen* 5, no. 5 (1980).

—J.M.W.

Wyler, William (1902–1981) One of Hollywood's most reliable and enduring directors, he was born in Mulhausen, Alsace-Lorraine, on July 1, 1902, the son of a Swiss-born haberdasher. While apprenticed in the clothing industry in Paris, Wyler was introduced to his mother's cousin, Carl Laemmle (founder and president of Universal studios), who offered him an invitation to come to the United States. Beginning as an office boy in Universal's New York shipping department, Wyler soon progressed to translating Universal's news releases into German and French prior to sending them overseas. Becoming more inquisitive about the nature of the product itself, Wyler requested a transfer to the West Coast and went through a variety of positions at Universal, including: prop boy, script clerk, extra, assistant cutter, and general errand boy. He became an assistant director in 1924, filming many of Universal's two-reel "Mustang" westerns. In 1926 Wyler directed his first feature-length film, *Lazy Lightning.* After a brief hiatus from Universal, Wyler served as an assistant director (one of many) for MGM's lavish epic *Ben Hur* (1926). His work with Universal continued into the 1930s, his most prominent feature films as a director being: *A House Divided* (1932), *Tom Brown of Culver* (1933), and *Counselor at Law* (1934). The latter film is noted primarily because it was shot on a single set and began Wyler's association with depth staging and composition.

In 1936 Wyler signed with Samuel Goldwyn and began a very lucrative relationship that brought about some of his best work. Their first production, *These Three* (1936), was an adaptation of Lillian Hellman's controversial play, *The Children's Hour* (which Wyler was to remake under that title in 1962). This was also Wyler's first association with cinematographer Gregg Toland, which was to prove fruitful over the years. *Dodsworth* (1936), adapted from Sydney Howard's stage adaptation of Sinclair Lewis's novel, starred Walter Huston, in the role he originated on Broadway, and Ruth Chatterton. The film was well received and Wyler was nominated for his first best director Academy Award. After directing the film version of the Sidney Kingsley social-realist drama, *Dead End* (1937), for Goldwyn, Wyler was loaned out to Warner Bros. to direct Bette Davis in *Jezebel* (1938). This was to be the first of three collaborations with Davis, the others being *The Letter* (1940) and *The Little Foxes* (1941). In 1939 producer Sam Goldwyn assigned Wyler the task of directing *Wuthering Heights,* with LAURENCE OLIVIER and Merle Oberon. The film, though well received, marked Wyler's first serious confrontation with producer Sam Goldwyn, who once remarked about the success of the film, "I made *Wuthering Heights;* Wyler only directed it."

During the war years Wyler directed *Mrs. Miniver* (1942), which won him his first best director Oscar. The story, based on the novel by Jan Struther, depicted the everyday life of a British family during the blitz. The film was made for MGM. Wyler received a commission as a major in the U.S. Army Air Force in 1942 and made two combat photography documentaries overseas, *Memphis Belle* (1944) and *Thunderbolt* (1944–47). While making *Memphis Belle,* Wyler sustained an ear injury that resulted in a total hearing loss in one ear and a partial loss in the other. Wyler received an honorable discharge from the U.S. Army as well as the Legion of Merit Award. His next directing project for Goldwyn was perhaps his best remembered film, *The Best Years of Our Lives* (1946), which also marked his last collaboration with both Samuel Goldwyn and cinematographer Gregg Toland (who died of a heart attack in 1948). The film received seven Academy Awards, including best picture and best director, as well as the New York Film Critics' Award.

Following the success of the film, Wyler went independent and, along with FRANK CAPRA, GEORGE STEVENS, and business manager Samuel Briskin, formed the independent production company, Liberty Films, in 1946. As part of the initial agreement, each of the directors were to make three films. The three films eventually produced by the company (Capra's *It's a Wonderful Life* and *State of the Union* and Stevens's *I Remember Mama*) were box-office disappointments. This, along with antitrust actions in the motion picture industry, resulted in the company being sold to Paramount, this arrangement including Wyler's contract. Wyler's Paramount period lasted from 1948 to 1955 and resulted in the following films: *The Heiress* (1949), based on the Henry James novel, *Washington Square; Detective Story* (1951), based on Sidney Kingsley's play and, like *Counselor at Law,* retaining a one-scene location throughout the film; *Carrie* (1952), based on Theodore Dreiser's novel *Sister Carrie; Roman Holiday* (1953); and Wyler's first foray into the widescreen process (Paramount's VistaVision), *The Desperate Hours* (1955), starring Fredric March and Humphrey Bogart. A brief venture with Allied Artists resulted in the film *Friendly Persuasion* (1956), starring Gary Cooper. In 1959 Wyler directed the widescreen epic *Ben Hur,* with

Zeffirelli, Franco (1923–)   As Franco Zeffirelli recalls in his autobiography, he was born a *bastardino,* or "little bastard," near Florence in 1923. Unable to take the name of his biological father, Ottorino Corsi, he was a *nescio nomen,* or "no name." Later he took the name "Zeffirelli," which was adapted from a reference in an aria in Mozart's *Cosi fan tutte* to the *Zefiretti,* or "little breezes." He studied architecture as a student and later fought in the Resistance in the hills around Florence during World War II. He claims that his ambitions to work in stage and cinema were confirmed by a screening of LAURENCE OLIVIER's *Henry V* and by a subsequent association in the 1940s and 1950s with mentor Luchino Visconti. He became a successful opera director, guiding the careers of such luminaries as Maria Callas and Joan Sutherland. But his theatrical films, including the Shakespearean cycle—*The Taming of the Shrew* (1967), *Romeo and Juliet* (1968), Verdi's operatic adaptation of *Othello* (1987), and *Hamlet* (1990)—have established his reputation for general audiences.

Zeffirelli has been frequently criticized for a style he describes as "lavish in scale and unashamedly theatrical." Yet, undeniably, his pictures—which also include *Brother Sun, Sister Moon* (1973), an account of the life of St. Francis of Assisi

as a sort of early "flower child"; his six-hour treatment of *Jesus of Nazareth* (1975); and the romantic idylls *Endless Love* (1984) and *Jane Eyre* (1996)—have appealed to a mass audience with their distinctive blend of flamboyant imagery and spectacle, executed with scrupulous care and craftsmanship. Arguably, more viewers have encountered grand opera and Shakespeare through his films than through the work of any other contemporary artist, though Kenneth Branagh has challenged him as an interpreter of Shakespeare.

As an interpreter of Shakespeare, Zeffirelli seemed nearly peerless, especially in his debut film, *The Taming of the Shrew,* arguably the best picture Elizabeth Taylor and Richard Burton made together. *Romeo and Juliet* was daring in its casting of two youngsters, Olivia Hussey and Leonard Whiting, but they were admirably supported by Michael York's swaggering Tybalt and John McEnery's flamboyantly melancholy Mercutio. *Hamlet* proved more of a challenge, since the text is considerably scrambled, but Zeffirelli teased wonderful performances from Ian Holm as Polonius, Helena Bonham-Carter as Ophelia, and Mel Gibson, willing to "put his career on the line" by playing Hamlet, as Zeffirelli told us: "For Gibson it was extremely risky. He was very brave." Zeffirelli

Franco Zeffirelli on location for *Jane Eyre* (Miramax)

was "madly in love" with Gibson's voice: "He speaks in a way that you understand every single word. And Mel, for all his realism, he makes 'To be or not to be' not a poetical aria, but a real suffering and a real problem that you understand. People who are not familiar at all with the speeches tell me that for the first time they understand it."

In 1964 Zeffirelli had staged *Hamlet* in Italy, brought it to the Festival des Nations in Paris, then toured Russia and Eastern Europe, yet he had always wanted "to bring it to the cinema." Zeffirelli has specialized in creating visually impressive spectacles, with gifted cinematographers such as Armando Nannuzzi and with David Watkin, with whom he worked on *Jesus of Nazareth* and *Hamlet*. "I grew up in the Tuscan countryside," Zeffirelli recalled, "which has always had for me a taste of the real Italy of the Middle Ages. I spent summers watching the traveling troupes of performers who would come and perform. They kept lamps on the floor in front of them which would throw diabolical shadows on the walls behind them—something I often do in my movies. They told stories and acted them out with shouts and blows and gestures. I have always felt these players were the true descendants of the world of Boccaccio, and I've always believed more in their fantasies than in anything else."

Though the success of *Romeo and Juliet* made him wealthy, Zeffirelli has continued working well into his 70s, though not always successfully. *Sparrows* (1993), adapted by Zeffirelli and Alain Baken from a contemporary Italian novel by Giovanni Verga, about a 19th-century nun-in-the-making, was not especially well received at the Tokyo International Film Festival, for example, but his semi-autobiographical *Tea with Mussolini* (1999), boasting an all-star cast that included Maggie Smith, Joan Plowright, Judi Dench, Cher, and Lily Tomlin, was far more successful. Set in 1935 and filmed in Tuscany and Florence, *Tea with Mussolini* was adapted by Zeffirelli and John Mortimer from the director's own memoirs. The film's elderly women, known as the *scorpioni* for their caustic wit, take in a motherless bastard, Luca Innocenti (Charlie Lucas plays Zeffirelli's fictional counterpart), who has also been cast off by his father. Done with whimsical charm, the film is a tribute to the first women in the Italian director's life.

Reference Zeffirelli, Franco, *Zeffirelli: The Autobiography of Franco Zeffirelli* (New York: Weidenfeld and Nicholson, 1986).

—J.C.T. and J.M.W.

Zemeckis, Robert L. (1952–) Robert

Zemeckis is known as much for his technical proficiency as for his string of box-office blockbusters. He was "discovered" by STEVEN SPIELBERG, who produced much of his early work, and his films share the same pop sensibilities and fascination with complex technology and simple emotions as his mentor. Another mentor, GEORGE LUCAS, said that Zemeckis "creates the kind of elegant, breakthrough effects that other directors wish they'd thought of, weaving them seamlessly into his stories." Zemeckis himself credits director FRANÇOIS TRUFFAUT with the quotation that best sums up his attitude toward the film medium: "Movies are about truth and spectacle. Movies marry them perfectly."

He was born on May 14, 1952, in Chicago, Illinois. Raised on the south side of Chicago, he began making 8-mm home movies at an early age. "I guess my passion for film came from the technical end first," he says. "I would say I was fascinated by the illusion of the movies before anything else. I was always trying to figure out how they did something, like a visual effect, or how they did an action sequence, and I became obsessed with how they synched sound up with

the picture." After graduating from high school, he attended Northern Illinois University. Later he transferred to the University of Southern California, where he majored in film. At this time he met his long-time writing collaborator, Bob Gale. After making a series of successful short films at USC, including *The Life* (1973) and *Field of Honor* (1974), he came to the attention of Spielberg and John Milius during a USC-sponsored field trip to Universal studios. Zemeckis and Gale cut their spurs writing for television series like *McCloud, Kolchak, the Night Stalker,* and *Get Christy Love!* by which time they were ready for their first script for Spielberg, *1941,* in 1979.

Zemeckis was given his first shot at feature-film directing with *I Wanna to Hold Your Hand* (1978), a fantasy about a group of teens seeking tickets to the Beatles' appearance on *The Ed Sullivan Show.* It

Robert Zemeckis (Universal)

was only a moderate success, like their next venture, *Used Cars* (1980). With *Romancing the Stone* (1984) Zemeckis scored his first major financial and critical success. The romantic adventure starring Kathleen Turner and Michael Douglas spawned a lesser sequel, *The Jewel of the Nile* (1985), which was directed by Lewis Teague. The stage was now set for several of Zemeckis's most successful films, the *Back to the Future* trilogy (1985–1990), *Who Framed Roger Rabbit?* (1988), and *Forrest Gump* (1994). *Back to the Future* was a perfect blend of popular culture and state-of-the-art special effects, with a fillip of time-travel paradoxes thrown in. "The idea of going back and seeing your roots and seeing where you came from and seeing what your parents were like when they were your age is something that everyone understands," says Zemeckis. "Everyone has a family of origin so that's a universal theme." It and its two sequels gave rise to a children's television series and an attraction at the Universal theme parks.

Roger Rabbit combined live-action actors and animation in a way never seen this side of Disney (for which it won an Oscar for its special effects). Starring Bob Hoskins and the voice of Kathleen Turner ("Jessica"), it made history by pairing Warner Bros. cartoon characters with those of the Disney studio. "I found the idea of combining Looney Tunes with film noir was just so wild," explains Zemeckis. "I had to figure out how to do it. And then Steven Spielberg was incredibly instrumental because he's the only guy on the planet that was able to get all the competing cartoon characters from all the competing studios in one movie. You'll probably never see that again. Ever!" Both it and *Back to the Future* earned more than $350 million apiece. (The Disney animators went on to produce a series of "Roger Rabbit" cartoon shorts for theatrical distribution.) *Forrest Gump* was a box-office phenomenon, his most successful film to date. The whimsical story of a simple man who not only lived through the seminal events of the previous 30 years, but who also was often personally (if accidentally) involved in

their evolution, won five Academy Awards, including best picture, best actor (Tom Hanks), and best director. The recreations of historical events, with Hanks digitally inserted into documentary footage of notables like John F. Kennedy and Richard Nixon (an effect not unlike sequences in WOODY ALLEN's *Zelig*), marked a high point for the incorporation of digital effects into mainstream filmmaking.

Less successful, but no less impressive technically, were *Death Becomes Her* (1992), a Grand Guignol comedy about the desire for beauty at any price (a theme enhanced by digital effects), starring Meryl Streep, Goldie Hawn, and Bruce Willis; and *Contact* (1997), a science fiction parable about alien contact based on the best-selling novel by Carl Sagan. Starring Jodie Foster as a female astronaut and Matthew McConaughey as her spiritual adviser, it was a more serious and thoughtful film than any of his previous work. Its digital effects culminated in a spectacular penultimate scene when Foster establishes a connection with extra-terrestrial intelligence—a scene shot completely on a digital stage. (Zemeckis's preoccupation with digital technology has led to his donation of $5 million to his alma mater, USC, for the establishment of a cutting-edge digital imaging center that bears his name. He currently sits on the board of councillors of USC's School of Cinema-Television.)

Zemeckis's latest film, *Castaway* (2000), reunites him with Tom Hanks to tell the story of a man isolated from civilization on a tropical island. Virtually wordless for much of its length, the film depends utterly upon scenic values and Hanks's pantomime with the detritus of his plane wreck (including the notorious "Wilson" volleyball) to tell its broadly human story of the basic values of life.

His leading actress in *Contact,* Jodie Foster, flatly declares that "Bob Zemeckis is probably the greatest technician director that I've ever worked with, ever. He walks onto the set every single day and invents something new and people scurry around trying to figure out how to make it. He has just one of those amazing brains that he really can translate the storytelling of the movie into a very epic, very technical, very visual sense, very visual style." As for Zemeckis, he believes the age of digital imagery is just beginning: "I believe that where we are today with digital imagery is where the car was back in the days of the Model T Ford. We can't even imagine the tremendous impact this is going to have on the world."

Other Film   *What Lies Beneath* (2000).

References   Elrick, Ted, "Gump Becomes Him: The Robert Zemeckis Interview," *DGA News* 20, no. 1 (February–March 1995): 26–31, 51; Emery, Robert J., "Robert Zemeckis," in *The Directors: Take Two,* ed. Robert J. Emery (New York: TV Books, 2000); Lavery, David, "'No Box of Chocolates': The Adaptation of *Forrest Gump," Literature/Film* Quarterly 25, no. 1 (1997): 18–22.
—M.J. and J.C.T.

Zinnemann, Fred (1907–1997)   Born in Vienna on April 29, 1907, Fred Zinnemann first turned to law as a career. "When I received my master's degree in law in 1927, I felt that I would be bored stiff working in law the rest of my life," Zinnemann told this writer. "So I decided to try a career that would be more adventurous, and decided to attend the Technical School for Cinematography in Paris." When Zinnemann finished his work at the film school he went to Germany and became an assistant cameraman. In 1929 he worked on a film called *Menschen am Sonntag* (People on Sunday), a semidocumentary about four young people spending a weekend in the country. The film was directed by ROBERT SIODMAK and written by BILLY WILDER, both of whom, like Zinnemann, would later migrate to Hollywood and become directors there.

After Zinnemann arrived in Hollywood in 1929, he met ROBERT FLAHERTY, the distinguished pioneer of documentary filmmaking, whose realistic techniques would influence Zinnemann's own films. Zinnemann was able to utilize his experience with Flaherty on his first directorial assignment, a semidocumentary entitled *The Wave* (1935), about the life of fishermen in the Gulf of Vera Cruz, where Zinnemann spent a year. On the strength of *The Wave,* Zinnemann was hired by the Short Subject Department at MGM in 1937. After making a variety of short subjects, he was at last promoted in 1941 to making features at MGM. His first notable film was *The Seventh Cross* (1944), which starred Spencer Tracy as an anti-Nazi who tries to flee Germany in 1936, after escaping from a concentration camp.

Impressed by *The Seventh Cross,* a European producer asked Zinnemann to make a film in Europe about displaced European children after World War II. The thematic note found repeatedly in his films is initially sounded in the very title of this, his first major success, *The Search* (1948). In that film the search is aimed at establishing the identity of a lad who has lost touch with his family through the cruelly impersonal events of war. This search by an individual for his self-image is the principal motif in all of Zinnemann's subsequent films. The individual achieves self-awareness by meeting a crisis; and once he or she has genuinely come to know themselves, they are capable of establishing a place for themselves in society. Thus in *High Noon* the hero is a brave marshal (Gary Cooper) standing alone against a vengeful gunman and his gang. The movie set a precedent in western films by portraying a hero who is quite capable of feeling fear while he executes his duty. Cooper won an Oscar for playing an individual overcoming his fears and achieving self-awareness by facing a challenge with courage.

Zinnemann often developed this theme by focusing on an individual who wants to achieve his self-identity while functioning within a large institution such as the army. Hence in *From Here to Eternity* (1953) Montgomery Clift played a young army private who refuses to knuckle under to his tyrannical commanding officer. *From Here to Eternity* was showered with Academy Awards, including best picture and best director. The film deserved to be honored, for Zinnemann produced a ruggedly realistic, tightly constructed version of

James Jones's sprawling novel, set at an American base in Hawaii in 1941. It is indicative of the sense of realism Zinnemann brought to the film that the newsreel footage of the Japanese bombing of Pearl Harbor, which he worked into the picture at the movie's climax, meshed perfectly with the material he had shot himself for the same sequence.

Another critical and popular success was *A Man for All Seasons* (1966), Zinnemann's screen version of Robert Bolt's play about Thomas More (Paul Scofield) and his crisis of conscience over accepting Henry VIII as head of the Church of England as well as his king. It is a disciplined film, laced with ideas applicable to our own day. As More says at one point, "When statesmen foreswear their consciences for the sake of their public duties, they are leading their country into chaos." The film won Oscars for best picture, best actor (Paul Scofield), and once again for Zinnemann as best director.

Besides the Oscars bestowed on Zinnemann and his work, he received his most prestigious prize in 1970 when the Directors Guild of America conferred on him its highest honor, the Life Achievement Award, for his entire body of work. Surveying his long career, Zinnemann mused, "The director has much more freedom today in making a film than he had during the anonymous days in Hollywood, when films were made on an assembly line." Nevertheless he was quick to point out that some of his best pictures were made under the studio system. "I will always think of myself as a Hollywood director," he added, "not only because I grew up in the American film industry, but also because I believe in making films that will please a mass audience, and not just in making films that will express my own personality or ideas. I have always tried to offer an audience something positive in a film, and to entertain them as well; and if I have managed to do that, I am satisfied."

Other Films *The Nun's Story* (1959); *Julia* (1977).

References Zinnemann, Fred, *A Life in the Movies: An Autobiography* (New York: Scribners, 1992); Phillips, Gene D., *Exiles in Hollywood: Major European Film Directors in America* (Cranbury, N.J.: Associated University Presses, 1998).

—G.D.P.

APPENDIX I
GREAT DOCUMENTARY
FILMMAKERS

Brownlow, Kevin (1938–) Although best known for his unsparing efforts on behalf of the preservation and restoration of the silent cinema, including the production of many television documentaries about early Hollywood and the European cinema, Kevin Brownlow has also directed a handful of films as an independent filmmaker. He was born on June 2, 1938, in Sussex, about 50 miles outside of London. Among his earliest memories are the V-1 bombings during the war years. He first discovered motion pictures while attending a boarding school in Crowborough, Sussex. These fragments of silent film fired his imagination and soon he was working in a photographic shop in Hampstead. In 1956 at age 18 he began work as a trainee in the cutting rooms of World Wide Pictures, a documentary film company based in Soho.

While making his first short film, *The Capture,* an adaptation of Guy de Maupassant's story, "Les Prisonniers," he began writing about films for *Amateur Cine World.* His lifelong enthusiasm for the era of the silent cinema bore fruit in 1968 when he published *The Parade's Gone By,* a semi-

nal event in silent film scholarship. It and subsequent books, including *The War, the West, and the Wilderness* (1979) and *Behind the Mask of Innocence* (1992), have established him as the world's leading authority on the subject. Since then he has spearheaded many restorations of silent film classics, most notably ABEL GANCE's 1927 epic, *Napoleon,* which played in the early 1980s at the Kennedy Center and at Radio City Music Hall, among many other venues. This in turn led to his forming Photoplay Productions, which produced several Emmy and Peabody-award-winning documentary television series with his partner, the late David Gill, including *Hollywood: The Pioneers, Buster Keaton: A Hard Act to Follow, D.W. Griffith: Father of Film, The Unknown Chaplin,* and *Cinema Europe: The Other Hollywood.* At this writing, his newest book is *Mary Pickford Rediscovered* (1999).

Meanwhile, with codirector Andrew Mollo, he directed and released two theatrical features, *It Happened Here* (1965) and *Winstanley* (1978). The first is a "counterfactual" history of what might have happened had the Nazis won the Battle of Britain and invaded England. It outraged and

Kevin Brownlow (Lisa Stevens John)

baffled many viewers with its controversial subject matter and idiosyncratic, pseudo-documentary techniques, including the simulation of newsreels and combat actuality footage. It was censored and withdrawn from circulation. *Winstanley* is a scrupulously researched and handsomely mounted chronicle of the adventures of Gerrard Winstanley and his "Diggers" in the turbulent times of 17th-century Cromwellian England. Its arcane subject matter, not to mention its catalogue of "inside" cinematic references to the films of CARL THEODOR DREYER, SERGEI EISENSTEIN, VICTOR SJÖSTROM, and others, made so few concessions to the formulas of mainstream entertainment that it

quietly faded from public view. Both films were shot on the proverbial shoestring, yet they are impressive achievements in the independent cinema movement in Great Britain in the sixties and seventies. Both are driven by distinctly "presentist" concerns, i.e., both consciously regard their subjects from the perspectives of present-day social, artistic, and autobiographical contexts; and both succeed ultimately in painting imaginative landscapes of their own devising onto the maps of history. (Both films have been recently restored and are now available from Milestone Films in Harrington Park, New Jersey.)

Brownlow attributes their commercial failure, in part, to his decision to abandon theatrical features for the sake of film preservation: "I am sure that must be one of the reasons I ended up as a film historian and not as a film director. At the time I made them I thought that I would continue in feature film making. Certainly I never expected to make my living at film preservation. However, I would not be the film historian I am without having had the experience of making *Winstanley* and *It Happened Here*." Indeed, Brownlow has devoted his life to a race against the clock to locate, preserve, and present artifacts of the film past before they deteriorate into dust. Otherwise, he warns, "posterity will judge us harshly." Fortunately, as Angela Carter has written in *The Manchester Guardian Weekly*, "His own work will evade such judgment."

References Brownlow, Kevin, *How It Happened Here: The Making of a Film* (Garden City, N.Y.: Doubleday, 1968); Tibbetts, John C., "Life to Those Shadows: Kevin Brownlow Talks about a Career in Films," *Journal of Dramatic Theory and Criticism* 14, no. 1 (Fall 1999): 79–94; Tibbetts, John C., "Kevin Brownlow's Historical Films: *It Happened Here* (1965) and *Winstanley* (1975)," *Historical Journal of Film, Radio, and Television* 20, no. 2 (2000): 227–251.

—J.C.T.

Burns, Ken (1953–) One of the most popular and celebrated documentarians in the last half of the 20th century, Ken Burns has dealt with great subjects that are the history, traditions, and diversity of the American experience. Like those "flaneur" artists and photographers in France in the middle of the 19th century who roamed the streets wresting fistfuls of images from the moving panorama of everyday life, Burns sifts through the desiderata of history with the innocent eye of the casual observer and the practiced gaze of the professional historian. "I will be a translator for people of complex subjects," he said in a 1989 interview; "be the baton in the relay race. I'm trying to take what I can from the scholars who ran the last lap and hand it on to the audience."

Kenneth Lauren Burns was born on July 29, 1953, in Brooklyn, New York. His father was a graduate student in anthropology at Columbia University. His mother died when he was 11. After graduating from high school in Ann Arbor, Michigan, Burns enrolled in Hampshire College in Amherst, Massachusetts, where he studied photography with Jerome Liebling and Elaine Mayes. At this time he met Amy Stechler, his future wife and collaborator. They worked together during his senior year directing a documentary film about Old Sturbridge Village, Massachusetts. After graduating in 1975 with a B.A. degree in film studies and design, he formed his own production company, Florentine Films.

The first Florentine release was a 60-minute documentary about the Brooklyn Bridge, based on David McCullough's book, *The Great Bridge* (1982). McCullough narrated the film, as he would several subsequent Burns projects. *Brooklyn Bridge* took four years to make; and after being entered in several film festivals, was broadcast on PBS in 1982 and nominated for an Academy Award. His second film for PBS, *The Shakers: Hands to Work, Hearts to God,* was inspired by his discovery of Hancock Shaker Village during a trip through rural Massachusetts. As placid as the Shaker film had been, *Huey Long* was charged with the grasping ambition and energetic platform manner of the fire-eating Long. It premiered in 1985 at the Louisiana State Capitol in Baton Rouge, where Long had been assassinated exactly 50 years before. *The Statue of Liberty* was released on the occasion of the centennial of its erection. Ironically, at the time, the Lady of Liberty was surrounded by the restoration scaffolding. Her "confinement," as it were, was regarded by Burns as a metaphor for the threats currently being voiced in America about curbing immigration policies.

Burns devoted the next five years to his most ambitious undertaking yet, *The Civil War.* Working 15-hour days, he shot 150 hours of film and took pictures of 16,000 still photographs acquired from dozens of archives and private collections. The project was smelted down into five parts, 11 hours of film, and 3,000 photos. When it was broadcast on PBS in September 1990, it created a sensation. In addition to garnering an Emmy, a CINE Golden Eagle, a Lincoln Prize, a People's Choice Award, and a Peabody, it spawned a book, *The Civil War: An Illustrated History,* by Geoffrey C. Ward, and a musical documentary, broadcast on PBS in August 1991, called *The Songs of the Civil War.*

Burns's next epic project surpassed even *The Civil War* in ambition and scope. *Baseball* premiered on PBS during the month of September 1994, its nine episodes clocking in at more than 18 hours. Unlike *The Civil War,* whose time-span was restricted to a five-year period, *Baseball* spanned 150 years, from the mythic origins of the game just prior to the Civil War to an open-ended gaze into the future. Indeed, Burns regarded it as a kind of sequel to *The Civil War,* inasmuch as the primary themes of racial conflict and national unity were extended and developed. His latest projects include more excursions into American history, including *Lewis and Clark: The Journey of the Corps of Discovery* (1998), *Frank Lloyd Wright* (1998), and *Not for Ourselves Alone: The Story of Susan B. Anthony and Elizabeth Cady Stanton.* His recent *Jazz* is described as the third installment of the "trilogy" begun with *The Civil War* and *Baseball.*

His best work relies almost exclusively on his selection and manipulation of still photographs, a technique he admits he learned from the classic *City of Gold* (1958), a Canadian Film Board documentary essay about the Klondike gold rush of 1898. Using a rostrum camera and a frame-by-frame exposure technique, Burns surveys and interrogates the surface of each photograph, bursting through its borders, isolating and seizing details. Exhumed, Frankenstein-like, from the morgues of photographic archives and private collections, the aggregate of images constitutes a collective metaphor, as Burns has said, for the unity-out-of-diversity dynamic of America itself—"the unum out of pluribus." As in the Brothers Grimm tale about "The Juniper Tree," where body parts yearn to conjoin again after being torn asunder, each individual photograph is like an arrow pointing to the secret meaning at the heart of their collective identity. Meanwhile, this visual flow is counterpointed with period music, quotations from letters and diary entries, and a liberal use of "talking heads" of expert historians and informed commentators. Burns's achievement is not without its critics, who regard his work as dangerously contrived, superficial glimpses of history. Burns fiercely objects: "In the last hundred years we have really murdered history. We have allowed the Germanic academic model to overtake our academy and convince historians that they need only speak to one another. History used to be the great pageant of everything that went before this moment, not some dry and stuffy subject in a curriculum. The word 'history' itself gives away its primary organization. It is mostly made up of the word 'story,' and we've forgotten to tell stories."

Other Films *Thomas Hart Benton* (1989); *The Congress* (1989); *Empire of the Air* (1992).

References Edgerton, Gary, "Ken Burns' America: Style, Authorship, and Cultural Memory," *Journal of Popular Film and Television* 21 (Summer 1993): 51–62; Tibbetts, John C., "The Incredible Stillness of Being: Motionless Pictures in the Films of Ken Burns," *American Studies* 37, no. 1 (Spring 1996): 117–133.

—J.C.T.

Flaherty, Robert Joseph (1884–1951)

Frequently described as the "father of the American documentary film," Robert Flaherty was a fiercely independent figure in the documentary movement in the first half of the 20th century. He was born in Iron Mountain, Michigan, on February 16, 1884, and educated at Upper Canada College, Toronto. During the first decade of the new century, he worked as an explorer, surveyor, and prospector for the Canadian Grand Trunk Railway. In the mid-teens he surveyed for William MacKenzie, an industrial entrepreneur, searching for iron ore deposits along Hudson Bay. It was at this time that he took a camera with him while traveling through the land of the Inuit. However, his footage was destroyed in a fire. Five years later a determined Flaherty returned to the Hudson Bay area to shoot more film of Eskimo life. Released as an experiment by Pathé Exchange, the resulting documentary feature was *Nanook of the North* (1922), a popular sensation and a landmark in the documentary film. Its success encouraged Flaherty to devote the rest of his life to making documentaries about faraway and exotic cultures whose way of life was threatened by industrialization.

He traveled to Samoa in 1923–25 and produced *Moana* for Paramount. Again, as in *Nanook,* he captured on film a "primitive" and "natural" way of life that was rapidly disappearing. Two more films about the South Seas followed in the late 1920s, *White Shadows in the South Seas* and *Tabu* (for both of which he received coproduction credit). As the box-office cachet of these films began to wane, Flaherty was forced to look elsewhere for financing. In 1931 he went to work for JOHN GRIERSON of the Empire Marketing Board in Great Britain. *Industrial Britain* was the result, although Grierson himself made the final edit. A year later Flaherty moved on to the Aran Islands, off the coast of Ireland, to begin shooting *Man of Aran* (1934). It was a gritty picture of the rugged life of the local fishermen. His next project was *Louisiana Story* (1946), a lyric and poetic tribute to Cajun life in the bayous.

For all the respect, even the veneration, accorded Flaherty in his lifetime—the term "documentary" was coined to describe his film, *Moana*—he remains a controversial figure. In his zeal to document the disappearing traditions of "primitive" ways of life, he frequently staged and even falsified the conditions he found. For example, the Eskimos he photographed in *Nanook* had long abandoned activities like igloo-building. Yet, he asked them to relearn the procedure for the camera. Some of the fishing and hunting sequences were also staged. In *Moana* he photographed an initiation ceremony wherein young males were painfully tattooed—even though that particular ritual had not been practiced by the tribe for years. For *Man of Aran* he staged a shark hunt in a lashing storm, against the better judgment of the fishermen. And in *Louisiana Story* he faked a tug-of-war between a young boy and a ferocious alligator.

While Flaherty's visual style was rather pedestrian, he had a canny sense of the medium's technological possibilities. He pioneered the use of long lenses for closeup work, utilized the new panchromatic film (for *Moana*), deployed the new 35-mm Arriflex camera (for *Louisiana Story*), initiated the practice of shooting and printing film on site, and encouraged the subjects of his films to assist in the filmmaking process. Other methods were unpredictable, even erratic. He usually worked without a plot or a script in an attitude characterized by his wife and associate, Frances, as "nonpreconception." He camped out with his subjects, and he watched and waited. He shot miles of film, seemingly without any preplanned purpose, and eventually used only a small percentage of the footage. In this way he allowed the film to assume its own shape, as it were. Only later did he begin to impose his own vision and organ-

ization onto the product. "What he seeks out among his peoples are their consistent patterns of physical behavior," writes commentator Jack C. Ellis, "rather than aberrations of human psyches and antisocial actions which are the basis for western drama from the Greeks on. Flaherty may ultimately have been most concerned with the human spirit, but what he chose to show were its basic material manifestations. . . . What it means to survive, to exist in the culture and in the environment one is born into, are the stuff of which his films are made." Flaherty's example has been followed by other American filmmakers, notably by Merian C. Cooper and Ernest B. Schoedsack in *Grass* (1925), which recorded the migration of 50,000 Bakhtiari tribesmen in central Persia (Iran) to find pasturelands for their herds; and in the popular travel-expedition pictures of the 1930s by the husband-and-wife team of MARTIN and OSA JOHNSON, *Wonders of the Congo* (1931) and *Baboona* (1935).

Other Films   *Elephant Boy* (1937); *The Land* (1942).

References   Ellis, Jack C., *The Documentary Idea* (Englewood Cliffs, N.J.: Prentice-Hall, 1989); Griffith, Richard, *The World of Robert Flaherty* (London: Victor Gollancz, 1953).

—J.C.T.

Grierson, John (1898–1972)   John Grierson is a towering figure in the development of the motion picture documentary in Britain, America, and Canada. He was born on April 18, 1898, in Deanston, Scotland, the son of a Scots schoolmaster. He studied at Glasgow University, where he took a degree in philosophy in 1923. After military service in the Royal Navy during World War I, he came to Chicago in 1924 on a research grant in social sciences. Dismayed at the apathy he saw all around him, disturbed at what he regarded as the failure of the American "melting pot," yet encouraged by the role the American popular press was playing in the education and assimilation of foreign immigrants, he formulated a mission in life—nothing less than the moral and political education of the citizenry by means of the motion picture. "I look on cinema as a pulpit," he declared.

His meeting with documentary pioneer ROBERT JOSEPH FLAHERTY was a turning point in his life. Hailing his films—he coined the term "documentary" in reaction to Flaherty's *Moana*—he developed a love-hate relationship with the man. He acknowledged Flaherty's position as the "father of the documentary," yet he deplored his seeming obsession with filming the remote and the primitive to the exclusion of contemporary life, what Grierson described as "the drama of the doorstep." Another major influence came Grierson's way while in New York, when he helped prepare SERGEI EISENSTEIN's *Potemkin* (1926) for its New York debut. The editing techniques by the visionary Russian would quickly become a part of Grierson's cinematic vocabulary.

In 1927 he was back in England and associated with the Empire Marketing Board, whose mission was to promote trade and unity among the various parts of the British Empire. Convinced that the motion picture could play a key role in this mission, he made his first film, *Drifters* (1929), a gritty depiction of life among the herring fishermen of the North Sea. Apart from the Flaherty model, *Drifters* had no interest in picturesque traditions and quaint fishing villages. Rather, it declared that the modern fishing industry had become "an epic of steam and steel," and its final scenes depicted the quayside auctioning of the catch and its injection into international trade.

After the success of *Drifters,* Grierson increasingly assumed the role of creative organizer of his pictures, rather than of hands-on director. Entering into his most fertile and productive period, he formed his own EMB Film Unit. His organizational skills and sympathy for the working class enabled him to find finances for his projects while, at the same time, shield his workers from bureaucratic interference. By the mid-1930s the Film Unit had collected an outstanding team of talented young filmmakers, including Stuart Legg, Paul Rotha, ALBERTO CAVALCANTI,

and Basil Wright. Even Robert Flaherty worked at the unit for a short time (on *Industrial Britain*).

A committed leftist, Grierson avoided pretentious aestheticism in favor of working-class propaganda and exposés of inadequate educational systems and poor slum conditions. Art is a hammer, not a mirror, he insisted. Films like *Housing Problems* and *Coal Face* (1935–36) urged reform of working and living conditions. The British government, on the other hand, grew suspicious of these "communist" leanings, preferring that EMB deliver a more supportive picture of working-class conditions.

The EMB Unit was dissolved in 1934, and Grierson moved on with his team to the General Post Office. This bureau was not just a post office, but a kind of communication ministry trying to develop the mediums of wireless, radio, and television. Important GPO productions (released through the Gaumont-British studio) included *Song of Ceylon* (1935), a poetic examination of the impact of the tea trade on the country of Ceylon, and *Night Mail* (1936), director Harry Watt's classic chronicle of the mail-train routes between Edinburgh and London. *Housing Problems* and *Workers and Jobs* (1935) were innovative in that they took microphones to the workers so that they could talk directly into the camera about the problems of their daily lives and rat-infested environment.

After resigning from the GPO in 1937, Grierson set up the Film Centre, which did not produce films but developed nontheatrical distribution outlets for documentary movies. A year later he went to Canada to help coordinate legislative support for that country's film production. Accordingly, the National Film Act was passed in 1939, and Grierson was elected as Canada's film commissioner. The result of his activities was the National Film Board of Canada, which was fully operating by the end of World War II. Grierson's ambition was to use films to reach the scattered population of Canada, particularly the territories to the west. At one time, 30 mobile film units took to the road and screened films for local citizens. Friends and colleagues were called in to support the mission, including Stuart Legg, Joris Ivens, Boris Kaufman, and NORMAN MCLAREN. The NFB stands as the most impressive and active monument to Grierson's vision of the use of film by governments in communicating with their citizens.

After the war, Grierson left the board and went to New York City. He was increasingly assailed by attacks from the right against films that allegedly favored communist-dominated unions. In 1947 he went to Paris as director of mass communications and public information for UNESCO. In the years after 1955, he returned to Scotland, where he worked for television and the Films of Scotland Committee. He died on February 19, 1972.

In the assessment of historian Jack C. Ellis, Grierson's great value lies in his "multi-faceted, innovative leadership in film and in education." Moreover, "As a theoretician he articulated the basis of the documentary film, its form and function, its aesthetic and its ethic. As a teacher he trained and, through his writing and speaking, influenced many documentary filmmakers, not only in Britain and Canada, but throughout the world."

Other Films As producer: *The New Generation* (1932); *Cargo from Jamaica* (1933); *Granton Trawler* (1934); *Children at School* (1937); *The Face of Scotland* (1938); *Judgment Deferred* (1951); *Man of Africa* (1953).

References Ellis, Jack C., *The Documentary Idea* (Englewood Cliffs, N.J.: Prentice-Hall, 1989); Hardy, Forsyth, ed., *Grierson on Documentary* (New York: Harcourt, Brace, 1947); MacCann, Richard Dyer, *The People's Films* (New York: Hastings House, 1973).

—J.C.T.

Jennings, Humphrey Sinkler (1907–1950)

Humphrey Jennings will always be remembered as the poetic voice of the wartime English documentary film. He was born in 1907 in Walberswick, on the Suffolk coast. He was educated at Perse School and Pembroke College, Cambridge, where he took his degree in 1934. Immediately upon leaving university he took a job at the General Post Office Film Unit as scenic designer and editor. The coming war brought Jennings the urgency and drama he needed to come into full flower as a filmmaker. He never felt the urge to use his films to harangue or educate his viewers. Rather, he preferred to illuminate human behavior through vignettes and representative anecdotes. For these reasons, perhaps, he never won the wholehearted support of his chief, JOHN GRIERSON, who preached that films should support leftist political ideals.

Listen to Britain (1942) eschews the expected melodrama and shrill propaganda of wartime combat and delivers instead an impressionistic mosaic of a London citizenry quietly going about its business—until the viewer realizes that unsettling implications of a country at war are intruding subtly into the imagery. A second look at the offices and buildings reveals thousands of protective sandbags. The shadows under the trees conceal tanks. The picture frames in the National Gallery are empty. The audience for a lunchtime piano recital by Dame Myra Hess is comprised mostly of uniformed soldiers. An acoustic weave of fragments of narration, snatches of dialogue, items from a news broadcast, songs (ranging from ditties sung by women at the factory lathes to music-hall tunes and a choral rendition of "Rule Britannia") coalesces into a collective "voice of a nation."

Jennings's feature-length masterpiece, *Fires Were Started* (1943), documented one day in the life of the Auxiliary Fire Service during the air raids on London. The action is seen through the eyes of a new recruit, Barrett. Dialogue consists mostly of the small talk of firemen while waiting for the alarm call. In the climactic fire scene, a man is killed in a scene as graphically dramatic as anything by FRITZ LANG or ALFRED HITCHCOCK. Yet, as historian David Thomson points out, there are no phony histrionics or plot contrivances to mar the drama: "This fire is arbitrary, inevitable, and in its way radiant. . . . There is equally little reason to recollect it as the work of wicked Germans. The fire is, rather, the life these men expect. It needs to be extinguished, but the men would not have purpose or fellowship without fire. This is the kind of crisis, or 'disaster,' that gave people the best years of their lives." Jennings provides no commentary, just a tapestry weave of actions, conversations, phone calls, maps, and chalkboards.

A Diary for Timothy (1945) is Jennings's most ambitious and poetically complex film. More than any other film it relies on narration (written by E. M. Forster and voiced by Michael Redgrave). In this case the "voice" is a "diary" written for and addressed to one "Timothy James Jenkins," a baby born late in the war. It is a voice of assurance, and it is a voice of warning. The war is almost over, yet a potential Armageddon lies ahead for the next generation. A symbolic dissolve shows the baby emerging from the flames of war. Jennings was only 38 years old when the war ended. Yet, he never recovered his purity and intensity of vision. "Good films could only be made in times of disaster," he confessed.

In 1950, while preparing a film for a series called *The Changing Face of Europe,* he died as a result of a fall from a cliff on the Greek island of Paros. In the opinion of historian Jack C. Ellis, Jennings's great gift was to provide a note of self-reflection in times of crisis. His films brought quiet reassurance to a country surrounded by the chaos of war. "In rising to this particular occasion," notes Ellis, "Jennings became one of the few British filmmakers whose work might be called poetic. He is also one of a small international company of film artists whose propaganda for the state resulted in lasting works of art."

Other Films *London Can Take It* (1940); *Heart of Britain* (1941); *A Defeated People* (1946); *Dim Little Island* (1949); *Family Portrait* (1950).

References Thomson, David, "A Sight for Sore Eyes," *Film Comment,* March–April 1993: 54–59; Ellis, Jack C., *The Documentary Idea* (Englewood Cliffs, N.J.: Prentice-Hall, 1989).

—J.C.T.

Leacock, Richard (1921–) Acclaimed as one of America's foremost practitioners of the so-called *cinéma-verité,* or "direct cinema," Richard Leacock specializes in documentaries that were photographed on the wing. He was born in the Canary Islands on July 18, 1921, where his family owned a banana plantation. Aptly enough, the 13-year-old Leacock's first film was entitled *Canary Island Bananas* (1935). He received his secondary education in England and in 1938 went to the United States to study physics at Harvard. During World War II Leacock served as a combat photographer in the American army.

In 1946 he garnered his first important assignment when he went to work photographing ROBERT JOSEPH FLAHERTY's *Louisiana Story,* a documentary commissioned by Standard Oil to show the initial steps taken in searching and drilling for oil in the Louisiana bayous. According to historian Richard Barsam, "Out of materials that might otherwise have become a prosaic industrial film, Flaherty made a dramatic film showing the difficulty and danger involved in the discovery of oil." Leacock's images of the swamplands are staggeringly beautiful, and he soon gained the attention of other filmmakers who utilized his services, Louis de Rochemont, John Ferno, and Willard Van Dyke.

In the 1950s Leacock directed several episodes of the landmark television show *Omnibus.* He also was responsible for two performance films, *Bernstein in Israel* (1958) and *Bernstein in Moscow* (1959). Both documentaries record concert tours by Leonard Benstein and the New York Philharmonic. It was at this time that he joined a group of fellow documentarians at Time, Inc., headed by Robert Drew. Other associates included D. A. Pennebaker, ALBERT MAYSLES, James Lipscomb, and Gregory Shuker. In 1961 the group left Time, Inc., and organized as Robert Drew Associates. Barsam notes the group's significance, stating, "Their belief in the spontaneous, uncontrolled cinematic recording of important events, issues, and personalities established an approach so strong that it dominated the further development of the form."

Indeed, Drew Associates's work was characterized by its use of sync-sound location shooting and the absence of a narrator to present its subjects as objectively and immediately as possible. Perhaps the most famous film from this period was *Primary* (1960), in which Leacock served as codirector, cophotographer, and editor. *Primary* follows the Democratic Party campaign in the 1960 Wisconsin primary through the eyes of the candidates Hubert H. Humphrey and John F. Kennedy. Utilizing shoulder-mounted cameras, the documentarists record the "endless handshaking, speeches, and street-corner electioneering that are the essence of American political campaigns." Leacock's other films at Drew Associates, loosely grouped under the label "the Living Camera series," include *On the Pole* (1960), *Yanqui No* (1960), *The Children Were Watching* (1961), *The Chair* (1962–64), and *On the Road to Button Bay* (1962). Although it is difficult to assess precisely just how much of the shooting and editing was Leacock's alone, as opposed to collaborations with other members, historian Stephen Mamber asserts, "[Leacock's] profound influence on all Drew Associates work as well as his own remarkable shooting deserves substantial recognition. The term 'Drew-Leacock' seems most appropriate because it was the initial collaboration of the two that appears to have sparked the whole movement."

After leaving Drew Associates, Leacock made several notable documentaries with another prominent figure in the television documentary field, D. A. Pennebaker. *Crisis* (1963) concerned the court-ordered integration of black students at the University of Alabama and was filmed partly from the offices of President Kennedy and Attorney General Robert Kennedy. *Happy Mother's Day* (1963), codirected by Joyce Chopra, records the reactions of a small South Dakota town to the birth of quintuplets by a local woman. According to Balsam, the film "focuses on many delightful details: the solemn discussion by the town's businessmen as they suggest ways to satisfy tourists and to protect the Fisher's privacy, the planning of a parade, commemorative souvenirs, and a testimonial luncheon, the refusal by the doctor who delivered the quints to join the parade." The next two years saw two celebrated documentaries about music and musicians. *A Stravinsky Portrait* provides a glimpse into the working life of the distinguished composer Igor Stravinsky, capturing intimate moments with the composer at lunch with his wife and friends and planning a ballet scenario with George Balanchine. And *Don't Look Back* is a portrait of the 1965 London tour of Bob Dylan and Joan Baez.

In 1969 Leacock became the founder and head of the film department at the Massachusetts Institute of Technology in Cambridge. One of the primary exponents of "direct cinema," his later films include *Portrait of Van Cliburn* (1966), *Monterey Pop* (1967), *Lulu* (1967), *Chiefs* (1969), and *Queen of Apollo* (1970).

Other Films *Galapagos Islands* (1938); *The Lonely Boat* (1951); *How the F-100 Got Its Tail* (1955); *Petey and Johnny* (1961); *Kenya, South Africa* (1962); *Portrait of Geza Anda* (1964); *Portrait of Paul Burkhard* (1964); *Republicans—The New Breed* (1964); *Ku Klux Klan—The Invisible Empire* (1965); *Hickory Hill* (1968); *Keep on Rockin'* (1973); *Lulu in Berlin* (1984); *Impressions de l'Ile des Morts* (1986).

References Barsam, Richard M., *Non-Fiction Film: A Critical History* (Bloomington: Indiana University Press, 1992); Blue, James, "One Man's Truth: An Interview with Richard Leacock," *Film Comment* 3, no. 2 (Spring 1965); Mamber, Stephen, *Cinema Verite in America: Studies in Uncontrolled Documentary* (Cambridge, Mass.: The MIT Press, 1974); Marcorelles, Louis, "Leacock at M.I.T.," *Sight and Sound* 43, no. 2 (Spring 1974).

—J.C.T.

Moore, Michael (1954–) Michael Moore is the self-proclaimed champion of lost causes, defender of the working class, and enemy of right-wing corporate America. He was born in Davison, Michigan, in 1954 and grew up in the city of Flint, where his father and most of his relatives worked in General Motors factories. Moore had other ideas, and he quit the day he was to begin working at Buick. In 1972, shortly after the ratification of the 26th Amendment to the U.S. Constitution, giving 18-year-olds the right to vote, Moore ran for the local School Board. He won, becoming one of the youngest persons in the country ever elected to public office. At age 22 he founded and for 10 years edited *The Flint Voice* (later the *Michigan Voice*). Then he turned to independent filmmaking, although he has confessed that at the time he "didn't know the difference between an f-stop and 'F-Troop.'"

His breakthrough film was the celebrated *Roger and Me* (1989), an agitprop documentary seeking to expose an elusive subject, the eponymous Roger Smith, chairman of General Motors. When Smith announced that he was closing down three factories and eliminating 30,000 jobs in Flint, Michigan, Moore organized his company, Dog Eat Dog, and, armed with a small film crew, launched a two-and-a-half-year quest to locate and confront

Michael Moore (Miramax)

Smith with the consequences of his actions. Despite its humorous gallery of characters—the "pet or meat" rabbit seller, the sad-sack eviction officer named "Deputy Fred," the Amway saleswoman, game show host Bob Eubanks—Moore insists it was always a serious-minded project. The scenes of a family's eviction at Christmas time, the debacle of Flint's attempt to build an arts center, the humiliation of the automotive workers forced to hawk fast food at the local McDonald's or work as prison guards are heartbreaking. "I wanted to show people what happened to my hometown," he says, "but as a larger issue I wanted also to show what is happening to the whole country. There's a growing gap between the rich and poor, and there's a lot more poor people these days than at the beginning of the 1980s." The problem, says Moore, is not specifically Smith, or even General Motors, "but an economic system that is unjust and unfair. This is a problem that is coming to *your* town. I don't want to see the country go that direction." The film was financed by Moore himself, with the help of the citizenry of Flint (who held weekly bingo game fundraisers to the tune of $50,000). Moore's one successful attempt to confront Smith at a General Motors stockholders' meeting is defeated ultimately when someone literally pulls the microphone plug. Profits from *Roger and Me* were used to establish the Center for Alternative Media, a foundation dedicated to supporting independent filmmakers and social action groups. In 1992, Moore filmed a "sequel" to *Roger and Me*, provocatively titled *Pets or Meat: The Return to Flint*.

In 1998 Moore released *The Big One*, which was partly financed by Britain's BBC. "It's about what Wall Street is doing to Main Streets's working families," he declares. Again, Moore tackles the conflicts between labor and big business. He travels across the country launching assaults on Nike shoes, Pillsbury, Pay-Day candy bars, and Borders bookstores. Each encounter yields the same results: yes, the corporation is raking in heavy profits; yes, to remain competitive, the company must either downsize or relocate to a foreign country; and no, Moore and his people must get the hell out of there. Meanwhile, Moore pays clandestine visits to union organizers. The highlight of the film is his confrontation with Nike chief Phil Knight. Moore's pleas for corporate mercy—including some blatant extortion to persuade Knight to open a shoe plant in Flint—are dismissed. We squirm while watching this scene, not just at Knight's insensitivity to the human quotient, but perhaps also at Moore's own willingness to shamelessly cut a deal. *The Big One* has a larger scope than *Roger and Me*. Who knew, for example, that the American government spends three times more money on *corporate* welfare than on social welfare?

The formula of "ambush journalism" and satiric attacks on corporate America has been packaged into several television series, including several seasons of *TV Nation* (1994–96) and *The Awful Truth* (1999). Moore continues to work through his Dog Eat Dog company, which in actuality consists of just five people—Moore, his wife, and three staff members. As he becomes a media celebrity, however, he is in danger of jeopardizing the purity of his causes, relegating them to a secondary position. His on-camera presence, his comic stand-up routines, his self-promotion threaten to become the real story. From under the brim of his clunky baseball hat, standing in his trademark dirty tennis shoes, and swaying slightly with his rotund girth, he's no longer the "Joe Six-Pack" of old but a media image every bit as recognizable and saleable as Nike's corporate logo.

Other Film *Canadian Bacon* (1995).

References Corner, John, *The Art of Record: A Critical Introduction to Documentary* (Manchester University Press, 1996); Moore, Michael, *Downsize This!* (New York: Random House, 1989); interviews by author, December 5, 1989 and March 12, 1998.

—J.C.T.

Morris, Errol (1948–) Literary critic Elizabeth Phillips once described Emily Dickinson as a "biographer of souls"; the same description could be applied to Errol Morris, who documents and arranges external realities as a way of suggesting and exploring internal realities. Morris was born in Hewlett, Long Island, New York, on February 5, 1948. His father, a physician, died when Morris was two years old; that early loss helped inform Morris's abiding concern with mortality. Another of his abiding concerns is epistemology—how do we know what we know, and just what knowledge can we be sure of, especially when we're trying to know ourselves? Like his mother an accomplished musician (Werner Herzog calls him a cello "prodigy"), Morris studied at the Julliard School of Music; eventually he majored in history at the University of Wisconsin at Madison. Morris then did graduate work in philosophy at Princeton, Oxford, Harvard, and the University of California at Berkeley. For various reasons, he dropped out of all four programs.

Before leaving Berkeley, however, Morris discovered the Pacific Film Archive, an art cinema where, by his own account, he went to the "University of Film" by watching two to four movies a day for almost a year. Shortly thereafter, Morris moved to Plainfield, Wisconsin, to conduct many hours of interviews (taped on audio cassette) with serial killer Ed Gein, the model for Norman Bates in *Psycho*.

Morris's growing interest in film and in long-form, nondirective interviews led to his first feature-length film, *Gates of Heaven* (1978). Inspired by a newspaper headline about 400 animals to be exhumed from a failed pet cemetery, Morris made a documentary film that recorded this event and explored the lives, ethics, and psychodynamics of everyone connected with it: the owner of the failed pet cemetery and the owner of the successful one where many of the pets were reburied, the business associates (in the case of the successful cemetery, members of the owner's family), many of the pet owners involved, even a comically cynical renderer. Morris made the film almost entirely out of "talking head" interviews in which the camera does not move and people speak freely and at length. Roger Ebert has called the result one of the 10 best films of all time. Morris's next effort, *Vernon, Florida* (1981), is an hour-long film featuring what Morris calls the "metaphysicians" of the title town as they discuss life, death, God, and folk neurology, among numerous other topics. With mosquito spray at the beginning, a sermon on the word "therefore" in the middle, and a concluding lament over the fact that there are more buzzards than turkeys in the world, *Vernon, Florida* is a darkly funny philosophical essay moving from bemused hope to pessimism, if not despair. *The Thin Blue Line* (1988) moves in the opposite direction. Begun as a study of "Dr. Death," a court-appointed psychiatrist who routinely testified that accused killers ought to be put to death because they would surely kill again, *The Thin Blue Line* quickly became another story altogether when Morris interviewed Randall Adams, a man who had spent many years on Death Row, wrongly convicted of murdering a Dallas police officer. As a direct result of Morris's interviews and detective work (Morris had actually worked as a private investigator during the hiatus between *Vernon, Florida* and this film), the real killer confessed to the crime and Adams was eventually freed from prison.

While *The Thin Blue Line* maintained Morris's emphasis on long takes of people talking, it also introduced three new elements into his documentary style: a musical score (by Phillip Glass), more-overt manipulation of mise-en-scène (including reenactments of various eyewitness accounts), and interpolated clips from other movies. Morris's techniques were controversial, and he has admitted feeling some tension between his desire to make the documentary that would free Adams and his desire to make a movie answering to his own artistic ends. He justifies the most controversial element of the film, the reenactments, by pointing out that he never portrays what really happened; each hyperstylized reenactment is a vivid portrait of false or mistaken eyewitness accounts. *The Thin*

Blue Line remains Morris's most famous film, and it brought some measure of financial security to Morris's career; after it, he was able to get enough work shooting commercials (which he continues to do) to keep his primary career as a filmmaker viable. Indeed, shortly after *The Thin Blue Line* Morris was hired to direct a Hollywood feature film, *The Dark Wind* (1991), a film that Morris quickly lost control over and now disavows.

Returning to independent filmmaking, Morris continued to push at the limits of documentary film language in *A Brief History of Time* (1992), an adaptation of physicist Stephen J. Hawking's best-seller. Instead of conducting interviews on location, Morris built elaborately furnished sets and shot the interviews there. And instead of merely dramatizing Hawking's theoretical arguments, Morris wove Hawking's thought and biography together into a movie that dramatizes Hawking's ideas and at the same time explores ways in which they reflect Hawking's personal experiences and obsessions.

For the next few years Morris worked on a film he would eventually call *Fast, Cheap & Out of Control* (1997). During this time he developed yet another innovative tool, the Interrotron. This invention uses two Teleprompters: one displays an image of Morris's face over the interview camera, and the other displays an image of the interviewee's face over the camera trained on Morris. In this way Morris's subjects would look directly into the camera while making eye contact with him. Convinced that this was at last a truly "first person" camera, Morris used the Interrotron to interview four subjects about their careers: a lion tamer, a robotics expert, a topiary gardener, and an expert on mole rats. Into this footage Morris cut location shots, some of them heavily altered by means of multiple film formats, variable film speeds, and other techniques, as well as film clips from old "B" movies. The result is very difficult to describe or summarize, but at the very least *Fast, Cheap & Out of Control* is a movie about art, love, mortality, community, and the imagination, subjects that appear throughout Morris's work but in this film take on a new and often breathtaking metaphorical and lyrical intensity, aided by a wonderfully evocative score written by Caleb Sampson. Morris has called the film a kind of "crazy elegy" for his mother and stepfather, both of whom died during the film's production. The film was a critical success, winning best documentary awards from the National Society of Film Critics, the National Board of Review, and the Boston Society of Film Critics, among others.

In 1999 Morris's next film appeared, *Mr. Death,* the story of electric-chair repairman and Holocaust denier Fred Leuchter. *Mr. Death,* like *The Thin Blue Line,* explores the nature of self-deception; like *A Brief History of Time,* it analyzes the connections between biography and vocation; like *Fast, Cheap & Out of Control,* it documents personal obsessions with an often hyperstylized mise-en-scène and cinematography. Morris walks a tightrope in this film between a detailed, sometimes quite sympathetic portrait of the colossally self-deluded Leuchter and the need to rebut Leuchter's Holocaust denial clearly and decisively. Morris does not leave his judgment of Leuchter in doubt, but he does successfully complicate that judgment for the viewer, to the extent that we cannot easily ignore our own self-deceptive tendencies or the hubris that often fuels them. Morris has said that his films document "an interior world, a mental landscape, how people see themselves as revealed through how they use language."

In Morris's films, we are allowed to know our fellow human beings in their acts of not quite knowing themselves. Because the gap between self and articulation of self is a universal condition, Morris's work is compassionate, not condescending. And because we can genuinely come to know others in this way, to find community with them as they speak to Morris's camera, his work is hopeful.

Other Films *Stairway to Heaven* (short documentary of Temple Grandin [1998]); *First Person* (short documentaries using the Interrotron, initially planned for Fox as *Interrotron Stories* and then developed for the Bravo cable channel [2000]).

References Rothenberg, David, "Outside the Cage Is the Cage," interview in *The New Earth Reader: The Best of Terra Nova* (Cambridge, Mass.: MIT Press, 1999); "Interrotroning History: Errol Morris and the Documentary of the Future," in *The Persistence of History: Cinema, Television, and the Modern Event,* ed. Vivian Sobchack (New York: Routledge, 1996).

—W.G.C.

Ophuls, Marcel (1927–) Marcel Oppenheimer was born November 1, 1927, in Frankfurt am Main, Germany. Retaining the pseudonym "Ophuls" from his famous father, Max, he is known primarily as a writer and director of documentary films. With his family he fled Nazi Germany and lived in France, Switzerland, and the United States. He graduated from Hollywood High School in 1945 and then attended Occidental College and the University of California at Berkeley. He also studied at the Sorbonne in Paris. He completed military service in Japan during the Occupation period. He holds both French and U.S. citizenship. He worked as an assistant director to JOHN HUSTON on *Moulin Rouge* (1953) and to his father on *Lola Montès* (1955). He also worked as reporter, producer, and editor for print, radio, and television news companies. He married Regina Ackermann in 1956.

His first film was *Matisse, ou le Talent de bonheur* (Matisse, or the talent for happiness [1960]). His first feature film: *Peau de banane* (*Banana Skin*) of 1963 starred Jeanne Moreau and Jean-Paul Belmondo. Critics indicate that the disappointment of his second feature, *Feu à volenté* (*Fire at Will* [1964]), may have prompted Ophuls's move to TV journalism, where he enjoyed much success. He directed his first major documentary, titled *Munich/Peace in Our Time,* in 1967.

The film about occupied France that brought him critical acclaim was *Le Chagrin et la pitié* (*The Sorrow and the Pity* [1969–71]). Some critics labeled the film as "anti-French," as it debunked the myth of widespread participation in the French Resistance. Originally intended for television broadcast, the film was refused by its backers and released to theaters. French TV would not air the film until 1981. Ophuls focused on events in the town of Clermont-Ferrand, which was part of Vichy France until the nominally free area was also occupied. His style of interviews cut with newsreel footage would be used in later projects.

Other major documentaries followed: *Hotel Terminus: The Life and Times of Klaus Barbie* (1988), *November Days* (1991), and *Veillées d'armes* (*The Troubles We've Seen: A History of Journalism in Wartime* [1994]). *Hôtel Terminus* won the Critic's Prize at Cannes and the Academy Award for best documentary of 1988. It recounts the career of Klaus Barbie, former Gestapo chief, known as the "Butcher of Lyon." The film describes his military career, his extradition from Bolivia, and the trial in France. Ophuls conducted interviews with 80 witnesses and worked with 120 hours of rushes as he edited the final film.

Veillées d'armes began as a history of war correspondents, from Capa in Spain to Hemingway at D-day, but soon focused on the fighting in Sarajevo and the international journalists who operated from their base at the Holiday Inn. As a documentarian, Ophuls never uses voice-over narration and often includes himself directly in the interview process. The director has claimed that his films lack a cohesive style and, in fact, may appear dry and careless. Critics, however, consistently note the power of his interview techniques and the masterful editing that create memorable visual, as well as emotional experiences for audiences.

Other Films   *Love at Twenty* (1962); *The Harvest of My Lai* (1970); *A Sense of Loss* (1972); *The Memory of Justice* (1976).

References   Barta, Tony, "November Days," in *Screening the Past; Film and the Representation of History,* (Westport, Conn.: Praeger, 1998); Jeancolas, Jean-Pierre, "Marcel Ophuls on Hôtel Terminus," *Projections 99,*

French Film-makers on Film-making (New York: Faber and Faber, 1999), pp. 111–122; Ophuls, Marcel, "Interview with F. Strauss," *Cahiers du cinéma,* September 1988.

—J.A.D.

Wiseman, Frederick (1930–)   "In an age of inane sitcoms," Frederick Wiseman declared to Paul Wilkes of the *New York Times* (June 18, 1988), "shouldn't there be an alternative so you can actually think about what you are seeing?" Wiseman, who began his career as a lawyer in Boston, went on to become an extraordinary, award-winning documentary filmmaker in the so-called cinema-verité style who has formed his own production and distribution company, Zipporah Films. His work is generally focused on institutions, such as mental hospitals (*Titicut Follies* [1967]), health care (*Hospital* [1970], *Blind* [1986], *Deaf* [1986], *Near Death* [1989]), education (*High School* [1968]), the military (*Basic Training* [1971], *Manoeuvre* [1979], *Missile* [1987]), criminal justice (*Law and Order* [1969], *Juvenile Court* [1973]), and colonialism (*Canal Zone* [1977]). Additionally, Wiseman has made two fiction films: *The Cool World,* which he produced in 1963, adapted from Warren Miller's novel about gang life in Harlem, and directed by Shirley Clarke; and *Seraphita's Diary* (1982), written, adapted, produced, edited, and directed by Wiseman himself.

Wiseman was born in Boston on January 1, 1930, and educated at a local preparatory school. After receiving a B.A. in 1951 from Williams College, Massachusetts, and a LL.B. in 1954 from Yale Law School, he served in the army from 1955 to 1956. Upon his discharge from the service, he went to Paris, where he studied law under the G.I. Bill. It was there, however, that his interests radically shifted from the study of law to the screening of films at the Cinémathèque Française and the making of his own first 8-mm experiments. In 1963, back in America and after teaching stints at Boston University's Institute of Law and Medicine and at the Harvard Graduate School, he began his professional filmmaking career with *The Cool*

World, which received a generally favorable critical and popular reception.

Beginning with *Titicut Follies,* Wiseman and his cameraman William Brayne created and developed a distinctive documentary approach that critic Barry Grant has called the "observational" documentary. As opposed to documentaries like ALBERT and DAVID MAYSLES's *Salesman* (1969) and Pennebaker's *Don't Look Now* (1965), which follow the activities of a few individuals, Wiseman's films have no leading characters in the conventional sense. "What interested me was to try and apply [my] documentary technique to ordinary experience as represented in institutions important to the functioning of society," Wiseman explains. "I would try to make the institution the star, rather than any one person." All his films display the following structural formula: A rapid flow of brief images and sequences plunges the viewer, without comment or explanation, into a complex, sometimes confusing milieu. As the film proceeds, the viewer must make his or her own sense and meaning of events. The editing process, usually conducted at Wiseman's headquarters in a Boston harbor warehouse, strives, in the words of commentator Thomas R. Atkins, "to create a film reflecting the complicated and ambiguous actuality that [Wiseman] encountered during the filming in order to make it a true 'discovery' experience for the audience."

The idea for his controversial first documentary, *Titicut Follies,* came as a result of visiting the Massachusetts State Prison for the Criminally Insane at Bridgewater, Massachusetts. The film opens with scenes from a variety show performed by the staff and inmates (from which the film takes its title) and continues in a succession of scenes depicting encounters between employees and inmates—a psychiatrist's interrogation of a man committed for sexual offenses against children, a humiliating strip search of inmates, methods of force-feeding with rubber tubes, etc. It is obvious that both staff and inmates are caught in an institutional trap where there are no "answers" to problems and no place to assign the blame. In this, as in all of Wiseman's subsequent work, contends historian Stephen Mamber, "It is the first where the point comes through that the problems are too large, sensitive, and complex to be handled by an institutional bureaucracy, that the institution itself is a friction point." Portions of *Titicut Follies* were so brutally frank that it was barred from general public showing by United States court order. Nonetheless, it received critical praise and was chosen as best film at the Mannheim International Filmweek in 1967 and best film at the Italian Festival dei Popoli.

Titicut Follies led to Wiseman's idea of developing a series of "institutional" films, a policy he has pursued ever since. Wiseman's procedure was first "to find somebody within the system who wants the film made. I go to that person and I make what's known as a complete disclosure: I tell them how I'm going to work, that is, there'll be a crew of three; a hand-held camera, hand-held tape recorder, no lights; nothing is staged; nobody is photographed who doesn't want to be photographed." The process will be consensual, but Wiseman "will not get written releases," because, "in the case of public institutions, I do not believe I need tape recorded consents, but I will always respect a person's wish not to be photographed or to have their voice recorded."

Apart from *Titicut Follies,* where Wiseman admits to reformist intentions, he claims not to have any preconceived notions about the material. Rather, he is interested "in having the film be a report on what I've learned as a consequence of the experience of making the film, rather than going out and looking for things that may fit a particular ideological bent which I may have started with." In the case of *High School,* for example, Wiseman selected Northeast High in the Philadelphia area because he believed it to be "typical," neither especially good nor especially bad. On the first day of filming, an administrator who called himself "the Dean of Discipline" introduced himself to Wiseman and said, "You ought to come to my office at 9:15 in the morning, and you'll see the culprits lined up outside the door." Wiseman was fascinated because, "first, what he said was very funny, in a very sad way; and, second, in giving out the punishments, he felt compelled to rationalize to the student the reason for the punishment." Wiseman added that such rationalizations "are very hard to get in this kind of film-making, because it's rare that the people who run the institution are sitting back and reflecting about what they're doing in a real situation."

Wiseman's method is simply to observe and record, not to editorialize. His documentaries avoid voice-over commentaries that cue a viewer's reactions. The films always "speak" for themselves. In *Meat* (1976), for example, filmed at the Montfort packing plant in Greeley, Colorado, Wiseman intended to "follow cattle from the range to the hamburger patty," so "in the first seventeen or eighteen minutes, there's practically no dialogue." In *Zoo* (1993), about the Miami Metro Zoo, Wiseman pointed out "there's hardly any dialogue at all. I think the whole transcript of the film is about thirty pages. Whereas in a movie like *Near Death* [1989], which is very dependent on dialogue, and is also much longer, the transcript is a couple of hundred pages." As Barry Grant noted, "If Wiseman's previous films have documented 'a natural history of how we live,' in *Near Death* he examines aspects of the way we die," as the film follows "the developments of four patients in intensive care, all of whom are kept alive by life-support technology." As in his other work, the grim process here is observed and analyzed and viewers are left to draw their own conclusions.

Law and Order, an examination of the daily lives of the Kansas City police force over a six-week period, perfectly exemplifies Wiseman's insistence on avoiding simple judgments and instead presenting multiple points of view. Much of the film is occupied with daily police routines, the hunt for a stolen purse, finding a lost child, settling a taxi fare dispute, breaking up a family altercation, etc. "What makes most of these scenes so effective,"

writes Atkins, "is the attention to small details, sudden intimate gestures that may reveal more than larger, more dramatic actions." Although there are examples of what might appear to be police insensitivity and brutality—particularly in a night raid by the vice squad during which a policeman nearly strangles a black prostitute—Wiseman is careful not to editorialize. "He does not see police behaviour as the root of the difficulty but as a manifestation of a far deeper and more malignant sickness," continues Atkins. "The community that pays the police and prescribes the laws that they must enforce is infected with racism and blighted with poverty. At his best the policeman can temporarily ease the problems; at his worst he contributes to them."

Remembering the reception of *Titicut Follies,* Wiseman said: "It was all so simple then—make a film, show a situation and produce instant change. But then I continued through life and began to realize the complexity of people and the places they work and live in." That purpose is certainly achieved in his long documentary *Canal Zone,* which takes its time to "document" the life and work of Americans transplanted to Panama. By 1988 his goals were "much more modest," as he explained: "I look at each of my films as one tiny bit of information that people can draw upon, that I hope they want to draw upon. If there's any evolution in my work over the years, I guess it's that."

In February 2000, Wiseman's 30th film, *Belfast, Maine,* opened a Wiseman retrospective at New York's Lincoln Center's Walter Reade Theatre. This four-hour film, anatomizing a "typical" blue-collar New England town of 6,000, could be considered Wiseman's capstone masterpiece. In his *New York Times* review, Stephen Holden found Wiseman's treatment both "romantic" and "spellbinding" in the way Belfast represents the director's elegiac vision of an American community that works. In his *Nation* review, Stuart Klawans called it "the grand synthesis" and a "fitting summary of Fred Wiseman's work, and of his life as well."

Other Films *Essene* (1972); *Primate* (1974); *Welfare* (1975); *Sinai Field Mission* (1978); *Model* (1980); *The Store* (1983); *Racetrack* (1985); *Adjustment and Work* (1986); *Multi-Handicapped* (1986); *Central Park* (1990); *High School II* (1994); *Ballet* (1995); *Public Housing* (1997).

References Atkins, Thomas R., ed., *Frederick Wiseman* (New York: Simon and Schuster, 1976); Atkins, Thomas R., "American Institutions: The Films of Frederick Wiseman," *Sight and Sound,* 43, no. 4 (Autumn 1974): 232–235; Grant, Barry Keith, *Voyages of Discovery: The Cinema of Frederick Wiseman* (Urbana: University of Illinois Press, 1992); Holden, Stephen, "Seaside Town under the Microscope," *New York Times,* January 28, 2000, p. B17; Klawans, Stuart, "As Maine Goes," *The Nation,* February 14, 2000, pp. 34–37; Mamber, Stephen, *Cinema Verité in America: Studies in Uncontrolled Documentary* (Cambridge, Mass.: Massachusetts Institute of Technology, 1974); Wilkes, Paul, "Documentarian Offers Viewers a Challenge," *New York Times,* June 19, 1988, p. 31; Wiseman, Frederick, "Documentaries Ask Viewers to Participate," *Media & Culture* 1, no. 2 (August 1993): 5–7.

—J.M.W. and J.C.T.

APPENDIX II
GREAT ANIMATION AND
EXPERIMENTAL FILMMAKERS

Brakhage, Stan (1933–) Stan Brakhage has been called the "foremost living experimental filmmaker" and is credited with radically impacting other filmmakers' perspectives. Working at the margins of avant-garde filmmaking for more than 45 years, he has produced films—*Reflections on Black* (1955); *Anticipation of the Night* (1958); *Dog Star Man* (1961–64); *The Art of Vision* (1965), derived from *Dog Star Man; Mothlight* (1963); and *The Text of Light* (1974)—that are relatively unknown to the general public but are acknowledged as avant-garde classics.

Stan Brakhage was born in Kansas City, Missouri, on January 14, 1933. He began working at age four and trained as a singer and pianist until 1946. Brakhage performed as a boy soprano on live radio and for recordings. In 1951 he began studies at Dartmouth College, but dropped out the next year, still a freshman. Then, at age 19, he began to make films. *Interim* (1952) was his first film. It has narrative elements and is a love story with a very personal expression involving the woman with whom he was in love at the time. He ran a small theater in Central City, Colorado,

where he made films and staged theatrical works by Wedekind and Strindberg.

In 1953 he went to San Francisco, to the Institute of Fine Arts, where he met "beat" poets and other artists such as Kenneth Rexroth, Kenneth Patchen, Michael McClure, Robert Duncan, Robert Creeley, and Louis Zukofsky. These were some of the members of the avant-garde who influenced him in the next few years. In 1954 he relocated to New York, met composer John Cage, and studied with Edgard Varese. He became acquainted with avant-garde filmmakers MAYA DEREN, Marie Menken, Willard Maas, Jonas Mekas, and Kenneth Anger. Brakhage's early works include *The Way to Shadow Garden* (1954) and *Reflections on Black* (1955), winner of the Creative Film Foundation Award in 1957. Also in 1955 he shot *Tower House* for Joseph Cornell and another film with Larry Jordan (an untitled film of Geoffrey Holder's wedding). From 1956 to 1964 he lectured on film, and he worked on many commercial film projects, such as television commercials and industrial films. In 1957 he and Jane Collum were married. They eventually had five children before they divorced in

1986. Jane was the inspiration for a shift toward domestic family life in the subject matter of his films. In 1958 Brakhage went to the Brussels film festival and viewed films of Peter Kubelka and Robert Breer. In 1960 he began presenting his own films in public and lecturing. He moved his family to Colorado and made films in the most meager of circumstances while living in the Rockies at Lump Gulch (elevation 9,000 feet.) There he gained an "esthetic distance" from other filmmakers.

After his 16-mm equipment was stolen, Brakhage concentrated on 8-mm filmmaking and completed major works like *Art of Vision* and *Dog Star Man* (1964). He also released *Dog Star Man* with a lengthy manifesto on his theories of vision (published in full by *Film Culture* in 1963) and *Metaphors on Vision*. This film demonstrated his idea of "hypnagogic" (closed-eye) vision. This film and its accompanying text radically influenced the course of avant-garde film. In 1969 Brakhage lectured in film history and esthetics at the University of Colorado, and in 1970 began teaching at the School of the Art Institute in Chicago. In 1974 he completed *The Text of Light,* a major abstract film. In 1981 he left Chicago for a teaching position at the University of Colorado, in Boulder. Brakhage currently resides near Boulder with his second wife Marilyn and their two children.

His early films display narrative elements. Later he moved to abstraction, finding ways to use film as a medium for artistic expression without resorting to narrative elements. Brakhage has concerned himself with the formal elements of cinema as a light-activated, moving medium for artistic expression. Although he has worked virtually alone, many of his techniques, radical esthetics, and philosophy have been absorbed into mainstream cinema (ranging from MTV and Nike commercials to films by OLIVER STONE). He has explored film for its inherent rhythm and movement, and he has preferred the esthetic of soundless film. For example, Brakhage has scratched and painted on the film itself to best represent the colors and shapes of the body's sensations that he saw when he viewed images behind his closed eyelids. While viewing one of these films, the shapes and colors that race across the screen at dizzying speed are enough to trigger a seizure in someone prone to them and to set off headaches in the rest of us. The result is actual physical pain as if one were rubbing one's eyes hard enough to "see stars."

Brakhage's honors and awards include the U.S. Library of Congress selecting his monumental film *Dog Star Man* (1961–64) for inclusion in the National Film Registry; the James Ryan Morris Award (1979); the Telluride Film Festival Medallion (1981); the MacDowell Medal (a prestigious award honoring the most influential American artists in many fields); and the American Film Institute award (the first) for independent film and video artists (the "Maya Deren Award").

References Barrett, Gerald R., *Stan Brakhage: References and Resources* (Boston: G. K. Hall, 1982); Brakhage, Stan, *Film at Wit's End: Eight Avant-garde Filmmakers* (Kingston, N.Y.: McPherson & Company, 1989); Camper, Fred, "Material and Immaterial Light: Brakhage and Anger," in *First Light,* New York Anthology Film Archives, 1998 [an exhibition catalogue edited by Robert Haller]; Dorsky, Nathaniel, "In-situ will present Stan Brakhage. . . .," *In★situ,* Austin, Texas, September 1997 [promotional material for In★situ, a local film society]; Ganguly, Suranjan, "All that is light: Brakhage at 60," interview, *Sight & Sound* 3 (1993): 20–23; Johnson, Jerry, with John Ausbrook, "Film at Wit's End," telephone interview with Stan Brakhage for *The Austin Chronicle,* September 15, 1997; Sitney, P. Adams, *Visionary Film: The American Avant-garde 1943–1978,* 2nd ed. (New York: Oxford University Press, 1979). Note: Connecticut State University's Brakhage information site features a biography and an extensive list of films.

—S.K.W.

Burton, Tim (1958–) Tim Burton's taste for fantasy and the bizarre has established him as one of America's most successful and imaginative directors. He was born August 25, 1958, and grew up a fan of horror and science fiction. At the California Institute of the Arts he studied animation. Although he is now regarded as an outsider and artistic loner, he began his Hollywood career in the midst of the establishment, when he was hired by Disney studios as an animator in 1980. Burton worked on mainstream films, such as *The Fox and the Hound* (1981), and he also served as animation director on Disney's experiment with science fiction, *Tron* (1982). More important to his artistic development were a pair of short films he made while working at Disney—*Vincent* (1982), a stop-motion animated short in tribute to (and narrated by) his hero, Vincent Price, and *Frankenweenie* (1984), a satiric homage to Frankenstein films, about a boy resurrecting his dead dog. Disney refused to release the latter film nationally, but Paul Reubens saw it, and asked Burton to direct the big-screen debut of his Pee-Wee Herman character in *Pee-Wee's Big Adventure* (1985).

The resulting surrealistic fantasy (and box-office smash) revealed Burton's distinct talent for visual storytelling. After creating the animated "Family Dog" episode of STEVEN SPIELBERG's *Amazing Stories* anthology series (followed eight years later by a one-season spinoff cartoon that he produced), Burton created his next hit, the over-the-top ghost story *Beetlejuice* (1988), a vibrant excursion into exotic Grand Guignol. (The following year, Burton developed the film into a Saturday-morning cartoon.) The film also marked the beginning of his collaborations with actors Jeffrey Jones and Michael Keaton and composer Danny Elfman.

In 1989, the back-to-back success of his first two features prompted Warner Bros. to tap the 31-year-old director to helm their big-budget *Batman,* and his Gothic depiction of the comic book character became one of the highest-grossing movies of all time. After turning out three blockbuster hits, in 1990 Burton directed one of his most personal films, the fairy-tale-like *Edward Scissorhands,* starring frequent Burton actors Johnny Depp and Winona Rider, as well as featuring the

last live-action feature film performance of Vincent Price, playing the creator of the title character. The film, a fable about acceptance of outsiders, revealed an intimate, personal aspect to his storytelling, all too often overshadowed by blockbusters like *Batman Returns* (1992), his twisted sequel to the original mega-hit, and *Batman Forever* (1995), the Burton-produced third film in the series.

In 1993, he returned to his animation roots when he produced the dazzling stop-motion feature *Nightmare Before Christmas,* directed by Henry Selick from Burton's story and storyboard layouts. The same team created a live-action/stop-motion blend in 1996 with their adaptation of Roald Dahl's *James and the Giant Peach.* Burton's own most recent directorial efforts have focused on tributes to the types of film that first inspired his creative genius. Although a commercial failure, *Ed Wood* (1994) was possibly his greatest critical success to date. This black-and-white biopic of the "worst director of all time" is an affectionate tribute to a man who loved to make movies but who never found true happiness in Hollywood—much like Burton himself, whose desire is to make films that inspire the imagination. *Mars Attacks!* (1996), an attempted parody/homage to "Space Invader" films of the 1950s, suffers from its own excesses; despite its visual punch and quick humor, it attempts too often to be more a true blockbuster than a tongue-in-cheek pastiche of low-budget science fiction films. Burton clearly regained his footing, however, with the release in 1999 of *Sleepy Hollow,* an atmospheric spin on the Washington Irving story, inspired by, and paying reverence to, the ROGER CORMAN/Vincent Price/ Edgar Allan Poe films of the 1960s. This American Romantic adaptation (which plays as freely with Irving's text as Corman always did with the works of Poe or Hawthorne) tells its story using the typically proto-Gothic chiaroscuro and *sfumato* of a Burton film. Burton's most recent project is the big-budget remake of *Planet of the Apes* (2001).

Burton's other non-filmic projects include a book of short stories, *Oyster Boy & Other Stories,* released by William Morrow in 1997, which continues his fascination with the macabre.

Other Films *Hansel and Gretel* (1982); *Aladdin and His Wonderful Lamp* (1984); *The Black Cauldron* (1985); *Cabin Boy* (1994).

Reference Hanke, Ken, *Tim Burton: An Unauthorized Biography of the Filmmaker* (New York: Renaissance Books, 2000).

—H.H.D.

Deren, Maya (1917–1961) Maya Deren is known, perhaps primarily, for her surreal film *Meshes of the Afternoon* (1943), but she also deserves credit for her role in organizing and promoting the avant-garde cinema community in New York City. She was born Elenora Derenowsky to a Jewish family in Kiev, Russia. Shortly after they emigrated in 1922, her father shortened the name to Deren. She received an excellent and advanced education in Geneva, Switzerland, returned home, married, finished college at NYU, and, after separating from her first husband, she got a master's degree in English literature from Smith College in Massachusetts. Her thesis was on the symbolist poets but she also studied perception and gestalt psychology. She wrote furiously and it was a habit she continued throughout her life. One film scholar has noted that in Deren's hands, language and language systems became weapons as they enabled her to rebel against a society that "denied women a voice of power."

In 1941 she took a job as a secretary to the modern dance choreographer Katherine Dunham. It was during this time that she began taking daily amphetamines and sleeping pills prescribed by Dr. Max Jacobson, drug physician to celebrities and politicians from the mid-1940s to the 1970s. It was this addiction that most likely caused the cerebral hemorrhages she died from at age 44. Deren traveled with Dunham to Los Angeles where she met her second husband, Alexander Hamid. They made *Meshes of the Afternoon* together in 1943. This film has been interpreted as significant because it has been constructed as a distinctly

woman's discourse. It revises Hollywood's objectification of women by focusing on a female subject who must struggle with her own objectification.

At Land (1944), their second film together, does not critique the Hollywood representation of women and does not divide the action between waking and dreamlike episodes. But it again organizes the narrative action around a female protagonist whose identity is tested by her adventures with the constantly changing objects, people, and various environments surrounding her. The use of multiple selves in her films is a way of interrogating multiple identities as a means toward self-discovery. This theme in her films had been interpreted by some early male critics as an examination of schizophrenia. Deren also disagreed with the majority of (male) critics at the time who consistently tied her films to surrealism and the European avant-garde of the 1920s. She maintained in all her discussion and writing about her films that they were ultimately and rationally ordered and structured. Another film, *Ritual in Transfigured Time* (1946), explores a woman's desire for self-fulfillment through her sociosexual role, albeit in a very abstract manner, and finally concludes that the fulfillment of that role and also fulfilling oneself as a woman are incompatible.

Deren tried always to provide a discursive context within which people viewed her films. She most often traveled with her films to show them at festivals and later to colleges and art museums around the country, and she would very carefully provide an interpretation for them so people would have an understanding of the film as she intended it to be understood. She wanted to make sure that her films were viewed as oppositional to Hollywood's forms and language. In the 1940s and 1950s she lectured on film theory and independent cinema at NYU, Yale University, Smith, Vassar, the Universities of Wisconsin, Chicago and Oregon, Syracuse, Pittsburgh State, Colorado State, Ball State Teacher's College, and the University of Havana. She, more than any other practicing independent filmmaker, brought these new aesthetic ideas and concerns—percolating but focused in New York City—out to the Midwest and the West. She was an accomplished and charismatic speaker and developed a following of young filmmakers such as STAN BRAKHAGE, Kenneth Anger, and Curtis Harrington. In the late 1940s she made the transition from filmmaking to organizing the discourse surrounding films and organizing other independent filmmakers into an art community. She helped organize the Film Artist's Society in 1953, which became the Independent Filmmaker's Association in 1955. And she created the first grant-lending organization for independent filmmakers, the Creative Film Foundation, in 1955. By the time she died in 1961 she, together with others, had created a self-sustaining organizational network for independent filmmaking that ensured the continuation of a vibrant avant-garde cinema in the United States.

Other Film   *A Study in Choreography for the Camera* (1945).

References   Rabinovitz, Lauren, *Points of Resistance: Women, Power and Politics in the New York Avant-garde Cinema, 1943–1971* (Urbana: Illinois University Press, 1991); Acker, Ally, *Reel Women: Pioneers of the Cinema, 1896–Present* (New York: Continuum Press, 1991); Clark, VèVè A., Millicent Hodson, and Catrina Neiman, *The Legend of Maya Deren, A Documentary Biography and Collected Works,* 2 vols. (New York: Anthology Film Archives/Film Culture, 1984).

—C.L.P.

Disney, Walter Elias (1901–1966)   Motion picture mogul and amusement park entrepreneur, creative artist, and business visionary, Walt Disney has become synonymous with "family entertainment." Born in Chicago on December 5, 1901, to a midwestern farmer, Elias Disney, he moved with his parents, brothers, and sister to a farm in nearby Marceline, Missouri, five years later. In 1910 the family relocated to Kansas City, Missouri, where the boy Walt went to work delivering newspapers and studying art at the Kansas City Art Institute. After service as an ambulance driver in World War

I, he returned to Kansas City and by 1922 was experimenting with cartooning and animation. He served his apprenticeship with the Pesmen-Rubin Commercial Art Studio and the Kansas City Slide Company (later renamed the Kansas City Film Ad Company), where he met another Kansas Citian, the brilliant UBBE ("UB") ERT IWERKS. The two men established their own business that year, Laugh-O-Gram, and made short film advertisements and a handful of fairy tales that were shown in local theaters.

In 1923, bankrupted and seeking new horizons, young Walt took a train westward to Los Angeles, determined to become a movie director. While living with his older brother, Roy, and after failing in his attempts to secure work at the studios, Walt again turned to animation at his own studio on Hyperion Avenue in 1926—a risky move, considering that most animation production at that time was centered on the East Coast. With Iwerks, who in the meantime had followed Walt to Los Angeles—initiating a pattern that would soon be followed by other Kansas Citians, including ISADORE ("FRIZ") FRELENG, Hugh Harmon, Rudolph Ising, and composer Carl Stalling—and who assumed most of the drawing chores, Walt produced a series of "Alice in Cartoonland" shorts that combined a live-action little girl with animated backgrounds and situations. The moderate success of these films led to a contract with M. J. Winkler to make "Oswald the Lucky Rabbit" shorts. In 1928 Walt faced disaster when the Winklers and Universal Pictures wrested the character away from him, along with most of his staff. But Iwerks loyally remained, and the two quickly devised a new character, Mickey Mouse.

From his very first released theatrical short, a synchronized-sound cartoon called *Steamboat Willie* (1928), Mickey was a public sensation. By 1932 he was a full-fledged movie star, whose name frequently appeared on theater-house marquees above the rest of the bill. Mickey may rightly be considered the alter-ego, or childlike personification, of Walt himself. Indeed, not only did Walt provide Mickey's falsetto voice until 1947, but also his animators studied Walt's manner and gestures as a model for Mickey. Soon Walt relocated his studio to Burbank.

The 1930s were years of great experimentation and development, closely supervised and guided by Walt. The "Nine Old Men," as they came to be called—including Ollie Johnston, Frank Thomas, Arthur Babbitt, Les Clark, Wolfgang Reitherman, and Fred Moore—were Walt's top staff of young animation directors who revolutionized animation techniques and established standards of quality that were the envy of the rest of the industry. The series of "Silly Symphonies" pioneered technological innovations, like Technicolor (*Flowers and Trees* [1932]) and the three-dimensionality of the multiplane camera (*The Old Mill* [1937]), whose artistic success was consolidated in the features *Fantasia* (1940) and *Pinocchio* (1941). Other characters joined Mickey in the Disney stable of luminaries, including Donald Duck, whose screen debut was in 1934 with *The Wise Little Hen.* Feature-length animation was launched by the celebrated *Snow White and the Seven Dwarfs* (1938), the riskiest—its expense and its scope caused it to be dubbed "Disney's Folly"—yet the most successful of the Disney product so far.

All the while, Disney was instituting merchandising schemes that expanded his empire into ever-widening enterprises. Newer, larger facilities were demanded, and in 1938 a new studio, located on Buena Vista Street in Burbank, was opened. The war years were times of boom and bust for Walt. On the one hand, the studio threw its energies behind the war effort, producing many training and propaganda films, including Disney's only feature, the animated *Victory Through Air Power* (1944), and the notorious short cartoon *Der Fuehrer's Face* (1943), whose "politically incorrect" rampant stereotyping of the Nazis has occasioned its withdrawal from circulation today. On the other hand, the studio was riven by labor unrest. Walt was outraged when many of his animation staff walked out in 1941. He regarded it not only

as a personal betrayal but also as the result of communist conspiracy in Hollywood. He would be bitter about this experience for the rest of his life. That may be a reason why, as the 1950s dawned, he increasingly directed his efforts away from animation to live action features, theme parks, television, and new robotics technologies.

The television series, beginning with *Disneyland* in 1955 and *The Mickey Mouse Club* a year later, cleverly were used not only to recycle existing Disney materials, but also to promote new films like *20,000 Leagues Under the Sea* and *Mary Poppins* and, most especially, the Disneyland theme park. (The television show had several later incarnations, *Walt Disney Presents* in 1959, and *Wonderful World of Color* a year later.) Convinced from his childhood experiences that most amusement parks were sleazy and unsanitary, he was determined to establish a "destination resort"— call it a tidy utopia—that would be more of a family living experience rather than a mere succession of thrill rides. To help build Disneyland, Walt created a separate entity from the studio and called it WED Enterprises (named from his initials), his personal organization for activities outside of filmmaking. Dedicated on July 17, 1955, Disneyland was divided into four regions— Adventureland, Frontierland, Fantasy Land, Tomorrowland—all revolving around the central hub of Main Street U.S.A., through which everyone entering the park must pass (purportedly patterned after the main street of his boyhood home, Marceline, Missouri).

Refusing to rest on his laurels, Walt next turned to an even more ambitious project, Walt Disney World, in Orlando, Florida. Opening in 1971, it was originally intended to include Walt's dream for an "experimental prototype Community of Tomorrow," or EPCOT. Intended as an experiment in urban living, community development, and ecological study, EPCOT was to be a place where the cleanliness and order of Disneyland could be extended to real life. "In its way it is an astonishingly prescient proposal," writes commentator J. Tevere MacFadye, "anticipating the demand for an urban model less dependent on and less dominated by the automobile. At the same time, the plan is as Orwellian as it is utopian, achieving its theoretical perfection only through manipulation of residents and their environment." However, the vision remained unrealized at Walt's death of a circulatory ailment on December 15, 1966.

Since then, under the aegis of Michael Eisner and Roy Disney, Jr., EPCOT has taken a different direction toward a series of international pavilions and, in the case of Spaceship Earth, exhibition spaces devoted to the sciences and transportation, and to man's future on the planet and in outer space. It would no longer have residents; it would have only visitors. Other theme parks include Tokyo Disneyland, which opened in 1983, and Euro Disney in Marne-la-Valle, about 20 miles east of Paris.

In his lifetime Walt Disney won more than 700 awards, including 29 Oscars, four television Emmys, the French Legion of Honor, and Mexico's Order of the Aztec Eagle. Paradoxically, the key to his enormous achievement, and the secret of his universal popularity, was rooted in the humble soil of the Midwest. "It is possible to say that the operative instinct was like the farmer's, which is ever and ever to cut away the underbrush, clear the forest and thus drive out the untamed," writes Richard Schickel. "The drive . . . was . . . a sort of multiple reductionism: wild things and wild behavior were often made comprehensible by converting them into cutenesses, mystery was explained with a joke, and terror was resolved by a musical cue or a discreet averting of the camera's eye from the natural processes."

Walt Disney, more than any other filmmaker in history, embodied what French commentator André Bazin called "The Myth of Total Cinema." From his earliest short films to his later features there is a steady trajectory from crude, two-dimensional, silent cartoons, to works that display an increasing degree of reality: successively, color, wide-screen formats, stereophonic sound, three-dimensionality, and live-action footage; from then on, his live-action films are soon superseded by theme parks, new technologies (ranging from audio-animatronic robotics to digital technologies), and experiments in community living. In sum, he moves from simulated reality to reality itself. Only this "reality" is what Richard Schickel has called "the Disney version," i.e., a view of life and society and art that is packaged and commodified by the cultural manipulations of global corporate capitalism.

Behind it all, the figure of Walt remains rather elusive. The precise nature of his authorship is forever in question. He neither drew, designed, wrote, nor directed; yet he remained at the center of his enterprises, moving like a bee, he said, from flower to flower, from artist to artist and from enterprise to enterprise, pollinating and cross-pollinating them all. Paradoxically, his very omniscience guaranteed his invisibility. "In some respects," writes Jonathan Rosenbaum, "there may be no cultural figure in the West who is as potentially controversial as Walt Disney, even though love and hatred for what he represents are frequently felt by the same people. At the same time, there is certainly no other filmmaker whose aesthetical and ideological preoccupations have permeated so much of modern life."

Other Films   As producer or executive producer: *Dumbo* (1941); *Bambi* (1942); *The Three Caballeros* (1945); *Treasure Island* (1950); *Peter Pan* (1952); *Old Yeller* (1957); *Sleeping Beauty* (1959); *Pollyanna* (1960); *The Absent-Minded Professor* (1961); *Mary Poppins* (1964); *The Jungle Book* (1967).

References   Care, Ross, "Cinesymphony: Music and Animation at the Disney Studio, 1928–1942," *Sight and Sound,* Winter 1976–77: 40–44; MacFadyen, J. Tevere, "The Future: A Walt Disney Production," *Next,* July–August 1980: 5–32; Rosenbaum, Jonathan, "Walt Disney," *Film Comment,* January–February 1975: 64–69; Schickel, Richard, *The Disney Version* (New York: Avon, 1969); Thomas, Frank, and Ollie Johnston, *Disney Animation: The Illusion of Life* (New York: Abbeville Press, 1981).

—J.C.T.

Freleng, Isadore ("Friz")   (1906–1995)

During a career in the commercial animation business spanning almost 60 years, "Friz" Freleng became, with TEX AVERY and CHARLES MARTIN ("CHUCK") JONES, the top cartoon director-producer at Warner Bros., responsible for developing the characters of Porky Pig, Bugs Bunny, Elmer Fudd, Yosemite Sam, and many others. His nickname "Friz" was derived from a fictional politician named "Frisby." Freleng was born in Kansas City, Missouri, on August 21, 1906. He knew WALTER ELIAS DISNEY, a fellow Kansas City resident, during Walt's apprentice years in the early 1920s, but he didn't work for him until 1927, when he left Kansas City to join Walt's Los Angeles operation to work on the "Alice in Cartoonland" and "Oswald the Lucky Rabbit" shorts. Soon after, he went over to the Winkler Picture Corporation in New York to work on the popular "Krazy Kat" cartoon series.

He found his true niche at Warner Bros. in 1930, where he remained as a mainstay director/producer for three decades (excepting a brief period in 1937–38 when he worked at MGM), directing more cartoons than anyone else (about 266). The Warner animation unit on Sunset Boulevard (housed in a rickety building affectionately dubbed "termite terrace" for obvious reasons), under the supervision of Disney's former Kansas City animators Hugh Harmon and Rudolph Ising, was developing a mouselike character called "Bosco," and to Freleng went the assignment of animating him in his first "Looney Tunes" adventure, *Sinkin' in the Bathtub* (1930). In many more "Looney Tunes" and "Merrie Melodies" cartoons Freleng either created, supervised, or directed with fellow animators Bob Clampett, CHARLES MARTIN (CHUCK) JONES, Tex Avery, and Robert McKimson a new group of zany, iconoclastic characters, including the stuttering Porky Pig (who debuted in Freleng's *I Haven't Got a Hat* [1935]), the manic Daffy Duck (who first appeared in *Porky's Duck Hunt* [1937]), the befuddled Elmer Fudd (*Elmer's Candid Camera* [1940]), and wiseacre Bugs Bunny (*A Wild Hare* [1940]), the

tussling Sylvester the Cat and Tweetie Bird (the Oscar-winning *Tweetie Pie* [1947]), and Speedy Gonzales (the Oscar-winning *Speedy Gonzales* [1955]). Another character, Yosemite Sam, remained one of Freleng's favorites. The gun-totin' blowhard debuted in Freleng's *Hare Trigger* (1945). "I was looking for a character strong enough to work against Bugs Bunny," recalled Freleng. "For me, Elmer Fudd wasn't it—he was so dumb a chicken could outsmart him. So I thought to use the smallest guy I could think of along with the biggest voice [Warner's voice ace, Mel Blanc] I could get." Yosemite reached his pinnacle with the Oscar-winning *Knighty-Night Bugs* (1958). Freleng's special passion and sensitivity for music led to many happy associations with Warner composer, Carl Stalling (another of Disney's former Kansas City colleagues), including a special favorite, *Rhapsody Rabbit* (1947), in which a tuxedo-attired Bugs Bunny performs Franz Liszt's "Second Hungarian Rhapsody" to a boogie-woogie beat.

In 1960 he turned to television and worked with Chuck Jones on the *Bugs Bunny Show*, aired on the ABC network. By means of transitional moments and new animation, Freleng and Jones assembled existing six-minute cartoons into half-hour formats for the two-season series of weekly shows. In 1963 he launched his last major creative venture with former Warner Bros. executive David H. DePatie. Still working from within the Warner plant, the independent DePatie-Freleng Enterprises created several successful television cartoon projects, including more Warner Bros. "Road Runner" and "Speedy Gonzales" cartoons and the popular "Pink Panther" series (both the celebrated pre-title sequences for Blake Edwards's "Panther" movies and the short cartoons). The first Pink Panther short, *The Pink Phink* (1964), won an Oscar (the only one of his five Oscars that Freleng accepted personally). A feature-length compilation of his work appeared in 1981, *Friz Freleng's Looney Looney Looney Bugs Bunny Movie*.

Freleng was modest about his work and always credited his associations with other gifted directors as a mutually creative enterprise: "We didn't actually steal from each other, but everybody did learn things from each other, little nuances that one director does, like Chuck Jones. Chuck would see things in my cartoons that he applied to his. And I saw things in his that would apply to me. I took some from him, he took some from Tex Avery, and so on. We all learned from the other person. That's the way it went."

In his history of Warner Bros. animation, *That's All, Folks!*, Steve Schneider praises Freleng's accomplishments: "Freleng made crucial contributions to every phase of Warner Bros.' development. . . . As a director, his impeccable timing and ability to fashion fully rounded, credible characters gave his cartoons a kind of classicism—a wholeness and balance through which humor and beauty became one. . . . Freleng was alone in animation in his ability to make cartoons that were both charming and rowdily funny."

References Beck, Jerry, and Will Friedwald, *Looney Tunes and Merrie Melodies: A Complete Guide to the Warner Bros. Cartoons* (New York: Henry Holt, 1989); Catsos, Gregory J. M., "An Animated Conversation with Friz Freleng: Hare-Raising Tales from a Life in 'Toons,'" *Outre* 19: 54–61, 78, 80–81; Merritt, Russell, and J. B. Kaufman, *Walt in Wonderland: The Silent Films of Walt Disney* (Baltimore: Johns Hopkins University Press, 1993); Schneider, Steve, *The Art of Warner Bros. Animation* (New York: Henry Holt, 1988).

—J.C.T.

Jones, Charles Martin ("Chuck")

(1912–2002) With his wry grin, tousled hair, and trim bow tie, Chuck Jones personified the sophisticated wit and childlike energy of the American cartoon. During his peak years with Warner Bros., he directed more than 200 cartoons, many of which are regarded as masterpieces of the form. He was born in Spokane, Washington, on September 21, 1912. He received his art training at age 15 at Chouinard Art Institute in Los Angeles and his training as an animator with Ub Iwerks and Walter Lantz. In the mid-1930s he came to the home of "Looney Tunes" and "Merrie Melodies," the Leon Schlesinger Studio (dubbed "Termite Terrace" in honor of the nonhuman critters who inhabited the place), to work as an assistant for Tex Avery. After two years with Avery, Jones took over his own unit. "When I first started animating, it never occurred to me that I'd be a director," recalls Jones. "I was so delighted to animate. . . . But once I got the feeling of direction and being a director, I never wanted to do anything else and I still don't want to do anything else."

As a director, it was his responsibility to supervise six-minute cartoons under severe budgetary and time restrictions. He oversaw the conceptualizing, the writing, the key drawings, the storyboards, and the timing of a picture before it was sent to the animators. He tended to choose subjects that were less weird and abrasive than those of, say, Tex Avery. Many featured small, quiet char-

Chuck Jones (Author's collection)

acters negotiating a rather forbidding environment. For example, his very first cartoon was *The Night Watchman* (1938), which was about a kitten who took his father's place as night watchman in a kitchen. Other examples include *Dog Gone Modern,* where two puppies are trapped in a "House of the Future"; and *Curious Puppy,* about a dog that accidentally throws a switch that activates an amusement park. Jones's first original character, Sniffles the Mouse, likewise struggles to survive in an oversized world of humans. *Old Glory* was a real departure for Jones and for the studio: Porky Pig learns the true meaning of the Pledge of Allegiance from Uncle Sam in the studio's first completely serious cartoon. Jones inherited the established Warners characters, of course, and in 1940 his *Elmer's Candid Camera* teamed up Bugs Bunny with Elmer Fudd. Meanwhile, he began experimenting with the assistance of layout/background artists John McGrew, Bernyce Polifka, and Eugene Fleury. In the surreal *Inki and the Lion* (1943), a youthful cannibal named Inki is confronted at unlikely moments by an exasperating mynah-bird character who hops through the scenes to the strains of Mendelssohn's "Fingal's Cave Overture."

The period from 1946 to 1956, when Warner Bros. bought out the Schlesinger Studio, saw Jones in full stride. His chief collaborators were writer Michael Maltese, animators Ken Harris and Ben Washam, layout artist Maurice Noble, voiceman Mel Blanc, composer Carl Stalling, and background artist Philip De Guard. As historian Leonard Maltin notes, Jones loved to explore his characters. "He refined his grasp of comic nuance to the point where he could get a laugh just by having a character wriggle his eyebrow." He loved to pit Bugs Bunny against Daffy Duck in the early 1950s in cartoons like *Rabbit Fire* and *Duck! Rabbit! Duck!* Jones quickly made Bugs over into his own conception. "A wild hare was not for me," he says; "what I needed was a character with the spicy, somewhat erudite introspection of a Professor Higgins, who, when nettled or threatened,

would respond with the swagger of D'Artagnan as played by Errol Flynn, with the articulate quick-wittedness of Dorothy Parker—in other words, the Rabbit of My Dreams."

In 1953 he and Michael Maltese created one of the true masterpieces of the field, *Duck Amuck,* a tasty piece of meta-cinema, in which Daffy battles an unseen animator who arbitrarily changes the background scenery, alters Daffy's form and voice, and with a pencil eraser threatens to annihilate him altogether. When the defeated and baffled Daffy finally begs to know who is responsible for these outrages, the camera pulls back to reveal Bugs Bunny at the drawing board. "The cartoon stands as an almost clinical study of the deconstruction of a text," notes commentator Louis Black, "in the way it presents a whole at the beginning and then dismembers every facet of the cartoon, only to put them together at the end." Meanwhile, other classics included the Jones "deconstruction" of Wagnerian opera in *What's Opera Doc?,* his spoof of science fiction serials in *Duck Dodgers in the $24^1/_2$ Century* (1953), and the immortal *One Froggy Evening* (1955), with Michigan J. Frog's reiterated refrains of "Hello, My Baby." New characters leaped from Jones's drawing board: "Pepe LePew" was an aggressively amorous French skunk; Road Runner (*Accelerati Incredibus*) and Wile E. Coyote (*Carnivorous Vulgaris*) debuted in *Fast and Furry-ous* (1948). Speed and gravity were the major forces on display here, and most of the gags grow out of them.

After Warner Bros. closed down the animation unit in 1962, Jones moved to MGM, where he directed more than 30 "Tom and Jerry" cartoons. He also continued to keep the Warner Bros. cartoon stars alive with a series of television specials, including a feature, *The Bugs Bunny-Road Runner Movie* (1979), which blended new footage with old cartoons. Other television specials included *How the Grinch Stole Christmas* (1967) and *Rikki-Tikki-Tavi* (1975). His one feature-length venture was *The Phantom Tollbooth* in 1971. He won three Academy Awards, for *So Much, So Little* (1949), *For*

Scentimental Reasons (1949), and *The Dot and the Line* (1965).

Other Films *Good Night Elmer* (1940); *The Scarlet Pumpernickel* (1950); *The Rabbit of Seville* (1950); *Lumber Jack Rabbit* (1955), in 3-D; *To Hare Is Human* (1957).

References Jones, Chuck, *Chuck Amuck: The Life and Times of an Animated Cartoonist* (New York: Avon, 1989); Kenner, Hugh, *Chuck Jones: A Flurry of Drawings* (Berkeley: University of California Press, 1994); Maltin, Leonard, *Of Mice and Magic: A History of American Animated Cartoons* (New York: New American Library, 1980).

—J.C.T.

McCay, Winsor (1867–1934)

By no means the first filmmaker to make animated cartoons, Winsor McCay nonetheless was an important pioneer in the field. As biographer John Canemaker writes, "McCay's work set a high standard for character animation, not to be surpassed until the Golden Era of the Walt Disney studio in the mid-1930s." He was born Zenas W. McKay on September 26, 1867, in Canada. His father Robert worked in the lumber business, and Zenas—he dropped the name in favor of his middle name, Winsor, and adopted the spelling of "McCay"—grew up in the Michigan lumber camps a shy and introverted boy. A precocious artist, Winsor found his first jobs as an illustrator in Chicago and Cincinnati before moving on to New York in 1903 to execute his celebrated comic strips for the *New York Herald*.

McCay's interest in the animated film was a logical extension of his work for the *World,* including his "Little Nemo" and "Dreams of a Rarebit Fiend" series, in which he displayed a fantastic imagination and a natural affinity for depicting motion and sequential actions; moreover, he was inspired by viewing early works by two of his contemporaries, J. Stuart Blackton ("Humorous Phases of Funny Faces" [1906]) and the French animation pioneer Emile Cohl. McCay's first film, *Little Nemo in Slumberland* (1910–11), adapted from his comic strip, utilized approximately 4,000 drawings on rice paper, animated frame-by-frame in conjunction with a bracketing live-action story in which he presented the cartoon to his newspaper cronies (played by actors, including John Bunny). Upon each of the 4,000 images he drew the entire picture, including the foreground and background elements, a staggering achievement. Released by Vitagraph, the short film displayed pure black lines and tints against a blank white background, metamorphosing its characters of Nemo, Impie, and Flip into a seamless succession of fantastic distortions. It received ecstatic reviews. The writer in the *Moving Picture World* noted, "Little Nemo and his friends are made to do amusing and surprising stunts. Indeed, after watching these pictures for a while one is almost ready to believe that he has been transported to Dreamland along with Nemo and is sharing his remarkable adventures." McCay utilized the film, as he did his subsequent films, in a vaudeville act in which he quickly drew images on a large drawing pad and interacted from the stage with the projection of his cartoons. In this wise, he began the tradition in which the comic-strip artist and movie cartoon engage in a symbiotic relationship, later more fully exploited in the work of Bud Fisher (*Mutt and Jeff*), Rudolph Dirks (*The Katzenjammer Kids*), and Charles M. Schulz (*Peanuts*).

McCay's next animated short, *How a Mosquito Operates* (1912), was derived from another of his newspaper strips, *Dreams of a Rarebit Fiend.* Again, a live-action story (now lost) bracketed the animated narrative, the adventures of a singularly hungry mosquito that displays anthropomorphic tendencies (and a human wardrobe to boot). And again, McCay toured the vaudeville circuit with the picture. Two years later, McCay released his most famous film, *Gertie the Dinosaur,* a landmark in character animation. McCay's industry, with the help of a young assistant, John A. Fitzsimmons, was awesome, tediously retracing the drawings—detailed background and all—onto each of the thousands of rice-paper images before the camera.

"I animated even the 'still' figures," he explained in justification, "which some movie cartoonists don't do. Unless all the live [sic] figures vibrate, the picture really isn't animated." The narrative was divided into what McCay called a "split system," where the action was broken into primary (or extreme) poses, between which the transitional movements were drawn. This technique was later termed "in-betweening" at cartoon studios like Disney and the Fleischer brothers. The story is simple: Gertie appears from behind some rocks and dutifully obeys the dictates of a live-action McCay to perform various actions, like bowing to the audience and drinking up the lake and tossing a rock at a mastodon. At the end, a cartoon McCay is lifted up and positioned between Gertie's jaws as the amiable dinosaur saunters away. Again, McCay toured with the film on the vaudeville stage, in effect interacting with the images.

By far McCay's most ambitious film, *The Sinking of the Lusitania* (1918), was inspired by the real-life tragedy of May 7, 1915. Whereas before McCay had worked essentially alone in his first films, painstakingly animating his rice-paper drawings, one by one, without the benefit of the time-saving cell or the "slash" techniques, he now turned to more elaborate methods, drawing on acetate cells and utilizing wash and crayon in addition to pen and ink. It was an amazing feat, requiring over 25,000 drawings and 22 months of work. A live-action prologue explained how McCay came to make the film. This was followed by the extended animated sequences, displaying striking visual angles and subjective shots of the *Lusitania* and the pursuing German submarine, dramatizing the action, contends biographer John Canemaker, in a way no live-action documentary could. The series of explosions and the listing and sinking of the ship are strikingly beautiful in an art-nouveauish way. The last image depicts a mother and her baby sinking beneath the waves. "*The Sinking of the Lusitania* is a monumental work in the history of the animated film," writes Canemaker. "While it did not revolutionize the film cartoons

of its time, the film was a milestone in the demonstration of the alternatives available to the creative animation filmmaker. The dark somber mood, the superb realistic draftsmanship, the timing of the actions, the excellent dramatic choices of 'camera' angles and editing—all these qualities would reappear only with Disney's mature work."

Of McCay's remaining six films, three survive as fragments—*The Centaurs,* about a family of mythical beasts; *Gertie on Tour,* a reprise of the famous dinosaur; and *Flip's Circus,* a vaudeville pastiche—and three others allude to his *Rarebit Fiend* comic strip: *Bug Vaudeville,* a parody of circus performers; *The Pet,* a nightmare about a dog that grows to monstrous proportions; and *The Flying House,* about a trip to the moon.

During the last 13 years of his life McCay found himself an outsider in the industry he helped create. "As far as he could see in 1921, his beautiful dream of animation as moving art had not been realized," writes Canemaker. "He always felt his own films were mere beacons shining light on a path leading to something never seen before. He was distressed that he had not achieved his impossible dream, and he was afraid that from the look of things no one else was even attempting it." Beyond his disappointment at the state of contemporary animation, McCay had other laments. Beginning in 1914 he had fallen victim to the machinations of his newspaper boss, William Randolph Hearst, who blackballed notices regarding McCay's films and performances in his papers out of pique that McCay was taking time away from his day job. Hearst eventually prohibited McCay from appearing in vaudeville altogether. Chained to his job while frantically trying to maintain his independent filmmaking, McCay left the Hearst papers under pressure and failed to maintain elsewhere his comic-strip career. Instead, he returned to editorial art, complaining all the while of the vulgar condition of the industry he helped found. He died on July 26, 1934, from a massive cerebral hemorrhage.

Never one to minimize his contributions to the animation industry, McCay proclaimed: "I believe the public is becoming a little weary of going to art museums where they can only see some unanimated object, at the most, and I can safely predict that these so-called revolutions in art that I have originated will within the next generation achieve great popularity."

References Canemaker, John, *Winsor McCay: His Life and Art* (New York: Abbeville Press, 1987); Crafton, Donald, *Before Mickey: The Animated Film, 1898–1928* (Cambridge, Mass.: MIT Press, 1982); Hoffer, Thomas W., *Animation: A Reference Guide* (Westport, Conn.: Greenwood Press, 1981).

—J.C.T.

McLaren, Norman (1914–1987)

A film *maker* in the most literal sense of the word, Norman McLaren's experimental animation techniques and films have won worldwide recognition. He was born in Stirling, Scotland, in 1914, and while a student at the Glasgow School of Art began experimenting with the film medium. In 1936, after seeing some of his work, documentary guru JOHN GRIERSON invited him to join the General Post Office (GPO) Film Unit. McLaren made films about every conceivable subject, from the London telephone directory to the airmail service. Three years later he moved to New York where as the recipient of Guggenheim Foundation grants he began making hand-drawn films, some of which featured synthetic sound tracks. In 1941 McLaren and Grierson reunited at the National Film Board of Canada, where McLaren remained for the rest of his life. Taking advantage of an unparalleled freedom of creative work, McLaren established an animation department that drew upon many of the finest young talents in the world—including Grant Munro, Jim McKay, René Jodoin, George Dunning, Wolf Koenig, and Colin Low—and offered residencies to artists like Alexander Alexeieff, Claire Parker, and Lotte Reiniger.

McLaren's more than 50 short films won him numerous international awards. Among the formative influences on his work, McLaren acknowledges that Len Lye, his predecessor at the Film Board, was particularly important. Above all, he applauds the Film Board's allowing him creative latitude: "It's very rare for a creative film person to have the kind of freedom I have had. Yet for an artist it's an absolute must. It doesn't ensure he'll make good art, but it's the only way he'll have a chance."

McLaren has always been interested in small-budget films. "Limited means (whether budgetary or technical) stimulate the imagination to new directions of thinking and filmmaking," he says. When the film medium is stripped of its secondary characteristics, such as lighting, settings, backgrounds, properties, costuming, and sound, the bare skeleton that remains "can hold firmly the attention of an audience; all that is really essential is that the action be clear, and artfully planned." Examples of this are the "hand-drawn film method," as explicated by McLaren in his booklet, *Cameraless Animation* (1958)—a technique by which inks and other marking materials are applied to the individual frames or the continuous strip of acetate film; the "paper method" of replacing costly celluloid cells with semi-transparent paper; the "flat puppet method" of utilizing flat-jointed silhouette puppets; and the "pixillation," or frame-by-frame photography of real human beings. "Cameraless animation" includes contributions to the War Savings Campaign: *Dollar Dance, Five for Four, V for Victory,* and *Hen Hop;* and two of his most celebrated shorts, *Begone Dull Care* and *Fiddle-De-Dee* (1947–1949), are abstractions consisting of a happy tumble of colors and forms. McLaren was probably the first to inscribe sound tracks directly onto the film without the technology of sound recording.

Several of McLaren's most celebrated classics, *Neighbours* (1952), his favorite film; *Pas de Deux* (1968); and *Little Phantasy on a Nineteenth Century Painting* (1946) demonstrate the expressive possibilities of these and other techniques. In the first, two people act out a simple parable of greed, violence, and brutality as they fight over the possession of a dainty little flower that sprouts in the grass between their houses. Their quarrel leads the men to build a fence between them, to destroy each other's respective houses, then to a vicious fight that leaves their dead bodies bruised and hideously contorted. Finally, their freshly laid-out graves are surrounded by a white picket fence, and on either grave a flower grows identical to the original object of dispute. The words "Love Your Neighbour" appear on screen in a dozen different languages. Many of the shots that appear to move in fairly normal tempo were shot with both camera and actors moving slower than normal; conversely, the speeded-up human action was the result of pictures taken eight times slower than the rate of human locomotion. *Pas de Deux* is perhaps McLaren's best-known short. To the ravishing musical performance by the United Folk Orchestra of Romania, two backlit dancers, dressed in white and photographed against a completely black background and floor, move at a shooting speed of 48 frames per second, which gives its projection at the standard projection speed of 24 frames per second a slight slow-motion effect. As the dancers interact, their bodies fragment and split into a fan of multiple trace images. This was done in the optical printer, wherein the original negative was exposed many times successively, each time delayed, or staggered, by a few frames. "Thus," explains McLaren, "when the dancers were completely at rest, these successive out-of-step exposures would all be on top of each other, creating the effect of *one* normal image; but when the dancers started to move, each exposure would start moving a little later than the preceding one, thus creating the effect of multiplicity." *Phantasy* embellishes a painting by Arnold Boecklin with animated shapes and eerie lights suggestive of a horror film. These and other techniques are demonstrated and discussed by McLaren himself in the documentary film produced by the BBC in 1970, *The Eye Hears, the Ear Sees.*

McLaren put to use his expertise in making much of little during his two United Nations Edu-

cational Scientific and Cultural Organization–sponsored stints in China and India in the early 1950s. He taught local Chinese and Indian artists how to make simple animated films as part of social and health education in the villages. "Such films were intended to implant new ideas in the minds of the villagers," he continues, "such as the need to boil drinking water, the value of children taking physical training, how to make compost from cow dung, the dangers of letting flies tramp around with their dirty feet on your food, etc."

Norman McLaren died on January 26, 1987. As a tribute, the National Film Board dedicated its corporate headquarters building in his name.

References Collins, Maynard, *Norman McLaren* (Ottawa: Canadian Film Institute, 1976); Starr, Cecile, "Norman McLaren and the National Film Board of Canada," in *Experimental Animation: Origins of a New Art,* Robert Russett and Cecile Starr (New York: Da Capo Press, 1976), pp. 116–128.

—J.C.T.

Méliès, Georges (1861–1938)

A filmmaker of protean talents, Georges Méliès was a stage illusionist and pioneering fantasy film designer, director, and producer who made an estimated 500 films between 1896 and 1912. He was born in Paris on December 8, 1861, the son of a wealthy bootmaker, and educated at the Lycée Imperial and the Lycée Louis-le-Grand. At the age of 23 he was introduced to stage illusions by the English conjuror John Maskelyne. After purchasing the Théâtre Robert-Houdin, he began a successful career as an illusionist. So impressed was he with the possibilities of the cinema as a tool for his stage acts—he attended Louis and Auguste Lumière's program of projected films on December 28, 1895—that he bought an Animatographe projector in London from Robert Paul, developed a camera, built his first studio at Montreuil, and began making trick films under the imprimatur of "Star Films."

Early films, notably *The Magician* (1898), *The Astronomer's Dream* (1898), and *A Trip to the Moon*

(1902), exemplify his formula of blending stage tricks and illusions with the editing resources of the film medium for his hundreds of pantomimes, burlesques, fairy tales, dream pictures, historical subjects, literary adaptations, and magic acts. It made no difference if the subject at hand was a *faerie* drama (*The Palace of a Thousand-and-One Delights* [1905]) or a reflection of contemporary headlines (*The Coronation of King Edward VII* [1903]); it always was clothed in a fantastic set conception, a wholly artificial world replete with magical effects. Possibly the most famous stage illusion in the theater's magic repertory, the "vanishing lady" (wherein a woman was made to disappear from under a draped chair) was utilized by Méliès both in his stage acts and in his films. To effect the disappearance, Méliès simply stopped and restarted the camera, a technique that, in the opinion of historian John Frazer, "became a landmark in the development of the art of the motion picture, when for the first time Méliès created a magical effect by stopping the camera and rearranging the objects within a scene." Indeed, the theatrical magic show, as historian Katherine Singer Kovacs reports, was to remain his primary inspiration: "It was only natural for him to use the [magic show] as a source of techniques, plots, and themes. It was also an important force in shaping Méliès' film aesthetic. For even when he substituted photographic illusions for the flaps, traps, scrims, and mirrors of the stage, Méliès's point of view remained essentially theatrical."

His Montreuil studio was one of the most elaborate facilities of its kind. Its design bespoke his thorough knowledge of and experience with traditional staging methods. It was a shed constructed entirely of glass, containing a stage with a below-stage area and a rigging loft—just like the stage he had formerly operated for his "live" productions. The shooting was done with a stationary camera set up in a special recess at the far end of the stage. The foot of the camera was connected with the lateral edges of the set with cords to establish the parameters of a proscenium-like platform. The scenic flats were painted in trompe-l'oeil perspective, and the floor was covered with a canvas painted to simulate parquet flooring, carpet, tiles, etc.

His influence on other filmmakers was marked. Pathé and Gaumont in France and England, Edison and the Mutoscope Company in America, all took note of his success and duly incorporated more elaborate scenic designs and trick effects into their films. The American, EDWIN S. PORTER, for example, had an opportunity to study closely these films in his position as a theater projectionist; and he immediately imitated their effects in his own films by the turn of the century. Méliès's growing status as a filmmaker and entrepreneur is evidenced by his election to the presidency of the International Convention of Cinematograph Editors in 1900 and leadership of the Chambre Syndicale de la Prestidigitation. His Star Films opened distribution offices in Berlin, Barcelona, London, and New York. By the time he retired from directing and producing in 1912, he had expanded his vision of short films lasting a mere two or three minutes to multireel movies like *The Conquest of the Pole* (1912).

Georges Méliès was the complete filmmaker and a man of extravagant imagination. He drew and designed his sets, painted the scenery, and directed and acted in the films. However, the advent of feature-length films and the arrival of a tougher mode of realism bypassed Méliès, and he spent the rest of his life as an outsider, neglected by the industry he helped found. He gave his last performance as a stage illusionist at the Théâtre Robert-Houdin in 1920, by which time he was deeply in debt, many of his films sold as scrap. He died in Paris on January 21, 1938.

Other Films *Cleopatra* (1899); *The Treasures of Satan* (1902); *The Kingdom of the Fairies* (1903); *The Clockmaker's Dream* (1904); *Faust and Marguerite* (1904); *The Palace of the Arabian Nights* (1905); *The Doctor's Secret* (1910); *Cinderella, or the Glass Slipper* (1912).

References Frazer, John, *Artificially Arranged Scenes* (Boston: G. K. Hall, 1979); Kovacs, Katherine Singer,

"Georges Méliès and the 'Faerie,'" *Cinema Journal* 16, no. 1 (Fall 1976): 1–13.

—J.C.T.

Vertov, Dziga (1896–1954) Pioneering Soviet newsreel filmmaker Dziga Vertov is best known for his experimental techniques and his theories of the "Kino Eye." Denis Arkadievitch Kaufman was born in Bialystok in Russian-controlled Poland, the son of Jewish intellectuals, on January 2, 1896. Denis studied music at the Bialystok Conservatory, interrupting his studies when obliged to flee with his parents from the onset of war and the German invasion of the czar's share of Poland. Settling in Moscow, he began to study medicine and to write verse and science fiction. Around 1916 he adopted the pseudonym "Dziga Vertov," which means "spinning top" (as Vertov explained, the onomatopoeia of the first name reproduced the repetitive sound of a camera crank turning). In 1918 he was appointed head of Moscow's All-Russian Central Executive Committee and became editor of the first newsreel programs produced by the Soviet government. In 1920 he toured the battlefronts of southwest Russia on a propaganda train known as "The October Revolution," from which came a series of documentary films. These led to his celebrated "Kinopravda" (Film-Truth) films of 1922–25, produced by the State Film School, Goskino, and named in honor of *Pravda* (the Soviet daily newspaper founded by Lenin). These newsreel magazines reported on a wide variety of subjects concerning the issues and problems confronting the young Soviet regime during this period of rapid industrialization. Working as his cameraman was Vertov's brother, Mikhail. A year later, Vertov completed his theoretical manifesto, *Kinoks: A Revolution,* from which came his theories of the "Kino-Glaz" or "Camera Eye." The Kino Eye concept "unshackled" the camera from the function of mere copying, allowing its "eye" its own autonomy to "catch life unawares," as he put it. "I am eye," he proclaimed, "I am mechanical eye. I,

a machine, am showing you a world, the likes of which only I can see. I free myself from today and forever from human immobility. I am in constant movement . . . maneuvering in the chaos of movements, recording one movement after another in the most complex combinations. . . . My road is towards the creation of a fresh perception of the world. Thus I decipher in a new way the world unknown to you." Vertov worked with juxtapositions of shots of unstudied subject matter in an attempt to form a kind of cinematic alphabet that would synthesize elements that to the human eye heretofore appeared merely chaotic and disordered. These attempts to "decipher reality" with the camera lens resulted in such early newsreels as the *Kino-Nedlia* (Weekly reels) and *The Discovery of Sergei Radonezhsky's Remains.* After breaking from the Goskino studios, Vertov aligned himself with VUFKU, a Pan-Ukrainian production unit. Here, he produced his most significant films, *The Eleventh Year* (1928), *Man with a Movie Camera* (1929), and *Enthusiasm* (1930).

The rest of his career was clouded by political interference from those Stalinists who objected to his "formalist" tendencies. His last film assignments were newsreels. He died in Moscow on February 12, 1954, of cancer. His most famous feature film, *Man with a Movie Camera,* was made in 1928–29, and its view of people's lives and activities from morning to night constitutes a virtual lexicon of his film theories and techniques. The intricate use of stop motion, slow motion, split screen, unusual camera positions, crazy superimpositions, and bizarre image juxtapositions fragments the surfaces of reality and reconfigures them in ways that are both startling and insightful. The theme of the anthropomorphism of the camera underlies and unifies the film. Indeed, at the very end, the camera loads itself and walks about on its tripod, quite apart from its human operator (Mikhail Kaufman). The concluding shot superimposes a huge closeup of the camera lens with a closeup of the human eye. Vertov's concepts of the Kino-Eye anticipated many of the theories and work of the cinema-verité movement of the 1960s and 1970s. His dedicated, if single-minded approach to filmmaking—his exhaustive efforts to record and decipher the details of everyday life and his rigid adherence to the principles of montage, and the insistence on the autonomy of the camera eye, have earned him a secure place as one of Soviet Russia's foremost visionary artists. "Vertov's disdain of the mimetic, his concern with technique and process stamp him as a member of the constructivist generation," writes biographer Annette Michelson. "He shares with them an ideological concern with the role of art as an agent of human perfectibility, a belief in social transformation as the means for producing a transformation of consciousness and a certainty of accession to a 'world of naked truth.'"

Other Films *Stride, Soviet!* (1926); *Three Songs of Lenin* (1934); *Famous Soviet Heroes* (1938); *For You at the Front: The Kazakhstan Front* (1943).

References Feldman, Seth R., *Dziga Vertov: A Guide to References and Resources* (Boston: G. K. Hall, 1979); Michelson, Annette, *Kino-Eye: The Writings of Dziga Vertov* (Berkeley: University of California Press, 1984).

—J.C.T.

Warhol, Andy (1928–1987) Andy Warhol's date and place of birth have long been in dispute among scholars of his life and work. In a 1967 interview, the artist indicated that he made up a different account every time he was asked about his background. Most sources agree he was born Andrew Warhola, son of Ondrej, a miner and construction worker, and Julia Zavacky. A birth certificate filed at Pittsburgh in 1945 states that Warhol was born August 6, 1928. The place of his birth has been suggested as either Forest City or McKeesport, Pennsylvania. Warhol attended Carnegie Institute of Technology, graduating with a BFA degree in 1949. He moved to New York City that same year and worked as a designer of advertisements for fashion magazines and window displays for department stores. His first solo exhibit was held in 1952. He went on to become a pop-culture icon himself while using objects from popular culture as subject matter for his art.

The filmmaker and actor Jack Smith may have directly influenced the artist's entry into the medium. Warhol made a three-minute silent film titled *Andy Warhol Films Jack Smith Filming "Normal Love"* in 1963. In the same year, while in Los Angeles to attend an exhibit of his Elvis Presley and Elizabeth Taylor paintings at the Ferus Gallery, Warhol made the two-hour-long *Tarzan and Jane Regained . . . Sort of.* Warhol's style of filming, using a stationary camera, presented a striking contrast to contemporary films that exploited the effects of handheld cameras. In 1964 he won the Independent Film Award presented by *Film Culture* magazine. He was praised for his abandonment of the forms and subjects of traditional cinema. That year he had excerpts from four films of 1963 (*Sleep, Kiss, Haircut, Eat*) screened at Lincoln Center.

Warhol began to work with Ronald Tavel, and the two scripted a number of films, including *Screen Test #2* (1965) and *The Life of Juanita Castro* (1965). In 1965 Warhol met Paul Morrissey and began a long collaboration. Many of the Morrissey-directed films bear Warhol's name, including *Trash, Heat, Bad, Dracula,* and *Frankenstein.* In fact, all "Warhol" films made after 1967 were directed by Morrissey.

Andy Warhol experimented with what has been termed the "objective camera." He rarely edited his films, at times doing nothing more than splicing together the ends of reels. He would seem to both exemplify and defy the auteur definition. He specifically selected subjects and wrote scenarios, yet filmed unscripted improvisations by actors and incorporated accidents, including the camera falling off the tripod, into the finished film. He directed films of extreme length that tested the endurance of audiences. *Empire* (1964), with the Empire State Building as subject, is eight hours of the static skyscraper filmed in near darkness. *Sleep* (1963) runs six hours, and ★★★★ (aka *Four Stars* [1966]) runs 25 hours and contains 30 reels of film, each with its own title, such as "Gerard Has His Hair Removed with Nair."

Chelsea Girls (1966) was the first experimental film to be screened in a commercial theatre. Its 12 reels, each 35 minutes in length, describe activities in the different rooms of the New York City hotel. The projectionist could choose the order in which to present the reels, with at least two being shown simultaneously. Warhol's studio space, known as the "Factory," functioned as a kind of production facility in support of his film projects. A sofa, salvaged from the sidewalk, became a regular fixture of the studio and was the subject of *Couch* (1964).

Various celebrities as well as groupies who frequented the "Factory" appeared in his films, including *The Thirteen Most Beautiful Boys* of 1965, in which each person was filmed for the length of one film roll (three minutes). Certain individuals, such as Nico, Edie Sedgwick, and Joe Dallesandro, rose to celebrity status because of their connection to Warhol's films. Warhol was long obsessed with Hollywood and aspired to be noticed by the major studios, but any hope of studio backing for his films was unfounded, due to their noncommercial nature.

Following gall bladder surgery, Warhol died in New York on February 22, 1987. Considering the confusion regarding the circumstances of his birth, it is only fitting that rumors regarding a life-after-death should flourish. As late as 1989 he was supposedly sighted in places as varied as Germany, Russia, and upstate New York. The majority of the films plus his entire video collection are housed in the Andy Warhol Museum in Pittsburgh.

Other Films *Dance Movie/Roller Skates* (1963); *Harlot* (1964); *Vinyl* (1965); *Lupe* (1965); *Restaurant* (1965); *The Velvet Underground and Nico* (1966); *Lonesome Cowboys* (1967).

References Bourdon, David, *Warhol* (New York: Harry N. Abrams, 1989); Gidal, Peter, *Andy Warhol, Films and Paintings* (New York: E. P. Dutton, 1971); Koch, Stephen, *Stargazer: Andy Warhol's World and His Films* (New York: Praeger, 1973); Smith, Patrick, *Andy Warhol's Art and Films* (Ann Arbor, Mich.: UMI Research Press, 1986).

—J.A.D.

LIST OF CONTRIBUTORS

B.M.—Ben Meade, an assistant professor of film at Avila College in Kansas City, Missouri, is also an independent filmmaker who most recently organized the Halfway to Hollywood Film Festival in Kansas City, April 2001.

C.L.P.—Catherine Preston is associate professor of film studies at the University of Kansas in Lawrence.

C.M.—Chris Meissner is currently completing his Ph.D. in film studies at the University of Kansas, researching the history of the AMC (American Multi-Cinema) theater chains in the Midwest.

D.K.—Derek Kilgore is a graduate of Avila College in Kansas City, Missouri, who works professionally in video and film production.

D.M.W.—Donald M. Whaley teaches history and American studies at Salisbury University in Maryland. He edited the first Vietnam special issue of *Literature/Film Quarterly* and has also published works on Oliver Stone.

F.A.—Fernando Arenas is currently completing his Ph.D. in film studies at the University of Kansas. His special interests include the films of Atom Egoyan.

F.H.—Fred Holliday is currently completing his Ph.D. in film studies at the University of Kansas. His special interests include Asian cinema.

G.B.—Gerald Butters has a specialized interest in African-American cinema and teaches at Aurora University in Illinois.

G.D.P.—Rev. Gene D. Phillips, S.J., is a professor of English at Loyola University, Chicago, a pioneer in the field of literature and film, and contributing editor of *Literature/Film Quarterly* for more than 30 years. He has authored several books on film directors—*Stanley Kubrick: A Film Odyssey* (1975), *Ken Russell* (1979), *John Schlesinger* (1981), *George Cukor* (1982), and *Alfred Hitchcock* (1984)—and other books treating Graham Greene, Joseph Conrad, F. Scott Fitzgerald, William Faulkner, and other writers, including *The Films of Tennessee Williams* (1980). He contributed to *The Encyclopedia of Novels into Films* (1998) and is primary editor of the forthcoming *Encyclopedia of Stanley Kubrick* (Facts On File, 2002).

G.M.—Georgia Mueller is a member of the art/communications faculty at Avila College in Kansas City, Missouri.

H.H.D.—Hugh H. Davis, a graduate of the University of Tennessee, is an instructor of English literature at Hertford County High School in Ahoskie, North Carolina, and has also taught at Chowan College in Murfreesboro, North Carolina. He has been active in the Popular Culture Association of the South and won the Ray and Pat Brown Award given by PCAS at the 1998 conference held in Augusta, Georgia.

J.A.—John Ahearn is currently completing his Ph.D. in film studies at the University of Kansas and has specialized in American independent cinema.

J.A.D.—Jean Ann Dabb is an associate professor of art history and department chair in the Department of Art History at Mary Washington College, Fredericksburg, Virginia. Her specialized areas of research and publication include 12th-century French architecture and sculpture.

J.B.—Joseph Benson, a professor of English at North Carolina A&T State University in Greensboro, North Carolina, has been active in the Literature/Film Association.

J.C.T.—John C. Tibbetts is an associate professor of film studies at the University of Kansas. He has written eight books, including *Dvořák in America, 1892–1895* (1993) and *The American Theatrical Film* (1985) and is the coeditor (with James M. Welsh) of this volume as well as *The Encyclopedia of Novels into Film* (1998). He has served as president of the Literature/Film Association.

J.M.W.—James M. Welsh, professor of English and film at Salisbury University, has edited the journal *Literature/Film Quarterly* for 30 years and was founding president of the Literature/Film Association. Included among his 10 published books are *Abel Gance* (1978, with Steven Philip Kramer), *Peter Watkins: A Guide to References and Resources* (1986), and *The Cinema of Tony Richardson: Essays and Interviews* (1999, coedited with John C. Tibbetts for SUNY Press). He is coeditor with John Tibbetts of *The Encyclopedia of Novels into Film* (1998) and also of the present volume.

K.L.R.—Kasey Riley is an assistant professor of communication at Avila College in Kansas City, Missouri.

L.H.—Lynette Hudseth is a graduate student in English at Avila College in Kansas City, Missouri.

M.J.—Matt Jacobson is an assistant professor in film and video production at the University of Kansas in Lawrence. His films and videos have won many awards.

P.N.C.—Peter N. Chumo II graduated from the University of California at Berkeley with an M.A. in English and has since been a regular contributor to *Magill's Cinema Annual*. His articles have appeared in numerous journals, including *Film Quarterly, Cinema Journal, Literature/Film Quarterly,* and *The Journal of Popular Film and Television.*

R.W.—Ron Wilson has completed his Ph.D. in film studies at the University of Kansas. He is currently researching the southwestern theater chains of Karl Hoblitzelle.

S.C.M.—Stu Minnis recently completed his Ph.D. in film studies at the University of Kansas and wrote his dissertation on the cinema of Andreiy Tarkovsky.

S.K.W.—Sharyl Keller Wright is an assistant professor of art at Avila College in Kansas City, Missouri.

S.W.—Sarah Miles Watts teaches English at SUNY Geneseo in New York and has been nominated for a Pulitzer Prize. Her essay on Stanley Kubrick's *Lolita* was recently published in *Literature/Film Quarterly* 29, no. 4 (2001).

T.J.M.—Toni J. Morris is an associate professor of English at the University of Indianapolis.

T.P.—Tom Poe is an assistant professor of communications at the University of Missouri-Kansas City, where he teaches film studies.

T.Prasch—Tom Prasch is a professor of history at Washburn University in Topeka, Kansas. He is an editor of the *American Historical Review.*

T.W.—Tony Williams, a professor of cinema studies at Southern Illinois University at Carbondale, is the author of several books, including *Jack London: The Movies* (1992), *Hearths of Darkness: The Family in the American Horror Film* (1996), and *Larry Cohen: The Radical Allegories of an Independent Filmmaker* (1997). He recently coedited *Jack London's The Sea Wolf: A Screenplay* (1998).

W.G.C.—W. Gardner Campbell is associate professor of English at Mary Washington College in Fredericksburg, Virginia. He is currently at work on a monograph entitled *John Milton and the Poetics of Provocation.*

W.M.D.—William M. Drew is a freelance writer and researcher based in Santa Clara, California, intensely involved with all aspects of American and foreign silent cinema. He is the author of *D. W. Griffith's Intolerance: Its Genesis and Its Vision* (1986) and *Speaking of Silents: First Ladies of the Screen* (1990), the first of two interview books with actresses of the silent era. He holds degrees in English and history from Santa Clara University.

W.V.—William Verrone is a Ph.D. candidate in film studies at the University of Kansas, Lawrence, Kansas.

A SELECTED REFERENCE BIBLIOGRAPHY

Compiled by James M. Welsh

Acker, Ally. *Reel Women: Pioneers of the Cinema, 1896 to the Present.* New York: Continuum, 1993.

Allon, Yoram, et al. *The Wallflower Guide to Contemporary North American Directors.* London: Wallflower Press, 2000.

Armes, Roy. *French Cinema Since 1946,* 2 vols. London: A. Zwemmer, 1966.

Astruc, Alexandre, "The Birth of a New Avant-Garde: La Camera-stylo." In *The New Wave,* ed. Peter Graham, 17–23. Garden City, N.Y.: Doubleday, 1968; originally appeared in the weekly *L'Écran français* in 1948.

Barnard, Timothy, and Peter Rist. *South American Cinema: A Critical Filmography, 1915–1994.* Austin: University of Texas Press, 1998.

Barthes, Roland, "The Death of the Author." In *Image Music Text,* by Roland Barthes, 142–148. New York: Hill and Wang, 1977.

Bazin, André, "On the *politique des auteurs.*" In *Cahiers du cinéma: The 1950s: Neo-Realism, Hollywood, New Wave,* Jim Hillers, 248–258. Cambridge, Mass.: Harvard University Press, 1985; originally appeared in *Cahiers du cinéma* 70 (April 1957).

Belton, John, ed. *Cinema Stylists.* Metuchen, N.J.: Scarecrow Press, 1983.

Björkman, Stig. *Film in Sweden: The New Directors,* trans. Barrie Selman. London: Tantivy Press, 1977.

Bordwell, David. *Making Meaning.* Cambridge: Harvard University Press, 1991.

Bordwell, David, and Kristin Thompson. *Film History: An Introduction.* New York: McGraw-Hill, 1994.

Bordwell, David, Janet Staiger and Kristin Thompson. *The Classical Hollywood Cinema: Film Style & Mode of Production to 1960.* New York: Columbia University Press, 1985.

Braudy, Leo, and Morris Dickstein, eds. *Great Film Directors: A Critical Anthology.* New York: Oxford University Press, 1978.

Bucher, Felix. *Screen Series Germany: An Illustrated Guide.* London: A. Zwemmer, 1970.

Caputo, Raffaele, and Geoff Burton. *Second Take: Australian Film-Makers Talk.* Australia: Allen and Unwin, 1999.

Caughie, John. *The Companion to British and Irish Cinema.* London: Cassell/BFI, 1996.

———. *Theories of Authorship.* London: Routledge and Kegan Paul, 1981.

Connors, Martin, Beth A. Fhaner, and Kelly M. Cross, eds. *The VideoHound & AMG All-Movie Guide Stargazer.* Detroit: Visible Ink, 1996.

Coursodon, Jean-Pierre, ed. *American Directors,* 2 vols. New York: McGraw-Hill, 1983.

Cowie, Peter. *Finnish Cinema.* London: Tantivy Press, 1976.

———. *Screen Series Sweden: An Illustrated Guide,* 2 vols. London: A. Zwemmer, 1970.

Crowdus, Gary, ed. *A Political Companion to American Film.* Chicago: Lake View Press, 1994.

Desser, David, and Lester D. Friedman. *American-Jewish Filmmakers: Traditions and Trends.* Urbana and Chicago: University of Illinois Press, 1993.

Dixon, Wheeler W., ed. *The "B" Directors: A Biographical Directory.* Metuchen, N.J.: Scarecrow Press, 1985.

Elsaesser, Thomas, ed. *The BFI Companion to German Cinema.* London: BFI Publishing, 2000.

Emery, Robert J. *The Directors: Take One.* New York: TV Books, 1999.

———. *The Directors: Take Two.* New York: TV Books, 2000.

Foucault, Michel, "What Is an Author?" In *Language, Counter-Memory, Practice: Selected Essays and Interviews,* ed. Donald F. Bouchard. Ithaca, N.Y.: Cornell University Press, 1977.

Gelmis, Joseph. *The Film Director as Superstar.* New York: Doubleday & Company, 1970.

Gifford, Denis. *British Cinema: An Illustrated Guide.* London: A. Zwemmer, 1968.

Graham, Peter. *A Dictionary of the Cinema.* London: A. Zwemmer, 1964.

Gunton, Sharon R., ed. *Contemporary Literary Criticism,* vol. 16. Detroit: Gale Research, 1981; vol. 20 is also devoted to film directors.

Halliwell, Leslie. *The Filmgoer's Companion,* 3rd ed., rev. New York: Hill & Wang, 1970.

Hibbin, Nina. *Screen Series Eastern Europe: An Illustrated Guide.* London: A. Zwemmer, 1969.

Higham, Charles, and Joel Greenberg. *The Celluloid Muse: Directors Speak.* Chicago: Henry Regnery, 1969.

Hillstrom, Laurie Collier, ed. *International Dictionary of Films and Filmmakers, Directors.* Detroit: St. James Press, 1997.

Hochman, Stanley, ed. *A Library of Film Criticism: American Film Directors.* New York: Frederick Ungar, 1974.

Jacobs, Diane. *Hollywood Renaissance.* New York: A. S. Barnes, 1977.

Johnson, Randal. *Cinema Novo x 5: Masters of Contemporary Brazilian Film.* Austin: University of Texas Press, 1984.

Kael, Pauline. "Circles and Squares: Joys and Sarris." In *I Lost It at the Movies,* 264–288. New York: Bantam Books, 1964; originally in *Film Quarterly* 16, no. 3 (Spring 1963):

Katz, Ephraim. *The Film Encyclopedia.* New York: G. P. Putnam/Perigee, 1982.

———. *The Macmillan International Film Encyclopedia,* new ed. New York: Macmillan/HarperCollins, 1994.

Krautz, Alfred, ed. *Encyclopedia of Film Directors in the United States of America and Europe.* München: K. G. Saur, 1993.

Kuhn, Annette, ed. *The Women's Companion to International Film.* Berkeley: University of California Press, 1994.

LaBeau, Dennis. *Theatre, Film and Television Biographies Master Index.* Detroit: Gale Research, 1979.

McCarthy, Todd, and Charles Flynn, eds. *Kings of the Bs: Working within the Hollywood System.* New York: E. P. Dutton, 1975.

McFarlane, Brian, ed. *An Autobiography of British Cinema.* London: Methuen, 1997.

McFarlane, Brian, Geoff Mayer, and Ina Bertrand, eds. *The Oxford Companion to Australian Film.* South Melbourne: Oxford University Press, 1999.

Merrit, Greg. *Celluloid Mavericks: A History of Independent Film.* New York: Thunder's Mouth Press, 2000.

Narwehar, Sanjit. *Directory of Indian Filmmakers and Films.* Westport, Conn.: Greenwood Press, 1994.

Nowell-Smith, Geoffrey. *The Companion to Italian Cinema.* London: Cassell/BFI, 1996.

Pfaff, Francoise. *25 Black African Filmmakers.* Westport, Conn.: Greenwood, 1988.

Phillips, Gene D. *Exiles in Hollywood: Major European Directors in America.* Bethlehem, Pa.: Lehigh University Press, 1998.

————. *Major Film Directors of American and British Cinema.* Bethlehem, Pa.: Lehigh University Press, 1999.

Roud, Richard, ed. *Cinema: A Critical Dictionary: The Major Film-Makers,* 2 vols. London: Secker & Warburg, 1980.

Sadoul, Georges. *Dictionary of Film Makers,* trans. Peter Morris. Berkeley: University of California Press, 1972.

Sampson, Henry T., *Blacks in Black and White: A Source Book on Black Films.* Metuchen, N.J.: Scarecrow Press, 1977.

Sarris, Andrew. *Interviews with Film Directors.* New York: Avon Books, 1967.

————. *The American Cinema: Directors and Directions, 1929–1968.* New York: E. P. Dutton, 1968.

————. *Confessions of a Cultist: On the Cinema, 1955–1969.* New York: Simon and Schuster, 1970.

————. "Notes on the Auteur Theory in 1962." In *Film and/as Literature,* ed. John Harrington, 240–253. Englewood Cliffs, N.J.: 1977; originally in *Film Culture* 27 (Winter 1962–63): 1–8.

————, "The Auteur Theory Revisited," *American Film* (July–August 1977: 49–53.

Sarris, Andrew, ed. *The St. James Film Directors Encyclopedia.* Detroit: Visible Ink, 1998.

Schuster, Mel, ed. *Motion Picture Directors: A Bibliography of Magazine and Periodical Articles, 1900–1972.* Metuchen, N.J.: Scarecrow Press, 1973.

Singer, Michael, ed. *A Cut Above: 50 Film Directors Talk about Their Craft.* Los Angeles: Lone Eagle, 1998.

Svensson, Arne. *Screen Series Japan: An Illustrated Guide.* London: A. Zwemmer, 1971.

Taylor, John Russell. *Cinema Eye, Cinema Ear: Some Key Film-Makers of the Sixties.* New York: Hill and Wang, 1964.

Thomas, Bob, ed. *Directors in ACTION.* New York: Bobbs-Merrill, 1973.

Thomas, Nicholas, ed. *International Dictionary of Films and Filmmakers,* 2nd ed., 4 vols. Chicago: St. James Press, 1991.

Thompson, Frank. *Between Action and Cut: Five American Directors.* Metuchen, N.J.: Scarecrow Press, 1985.

Thomson, David. *A Biographical Dictionary of Film,* 3rd ed. New York: Knopf, 1994.

Truffaut, François, "A Certain Tendency of the French Cinema," *Cahiers du cinéma* 31 (January 1954).

Tuska, Jon, ed. *Close Up: The Contract Director.* Metuchen, N.J.: Scarecrow Press, 1976.

————. *Close Up: The Contemporary Director.* Metuchen, N.J.: Scarecrow Press, 1981.

————. *Close Up: The Hollywood Director.* Metuchen, N.J.: Scarecrow Press, 1978.

Vincendeau, Ginette. *The Companion to French Cinema.* London: Cassell/BFI, 1996.

Vincendeau, Ginette, ed. *Encyclopedia of European Cinema.* New York: Facts On File, 1995.

Wakeman, John. *World Film Directors,* 2 vols. New York: H. H. Wilson, 1988.

Whittemore, Don, and Philip Alan Cecchettini. *Passport to Hollywood: Film Immigrants Anthology.* New York: McGraw-Hill, 1976.

INDEX